CHINA REVIEW OF
MARITIME AND COMMERCIAL ARBITRATION(2021)

(中英文)

中国海事商事仲裁评论

(2021)

新时代中国海事商事仲裁的创新发展

李虎　主编

The Innovative Development

of China Maritime and Commercial Arbitration

in the New Era

图书在版编目(CIP)数据

中国海事商事仲裁评论. 2021 / 李虎主编. —北京：北京大学出版社，2022.12
ISBN 978-7-301-33680-9

Ⅰ.①中… Ⅱ.①李… Ⅲ.①海事仲裁—中国—文集—2021 ②商事仲裁—中国—文集—2021 Ⅳ.①D925.7-53

中国国家版本馆CIP数据核字(2023)第004726号

书　　名	中国海事商事仲裁评论（2021）：新时代中国海事商事仲裁的创新发展 ZHONGGUO HAISHI SHANGSHI ZHONGCAI PINGLUN(2021): XINSHIDAI ZHONGGUO HAISHI SHANGSHI ZHONGCAI DE CHUANGXIN FAZHAN
著作责任者	李　虎　主编
责任编辑	周子琳　王建君
标准书号	ISBN 978-7-301-33680-9
出版发行	北京大学出版社
地　　址	北京市海淀区成府路205号　100871
网　　址	http://www.pup.cn　http://www.yandayuanzhao.com
电子信箱	yandayuanzhao@163.com
新浪微博	@北京大学出版社　@北大出版社燕大元照法律图书
电　　话	邮购部 010-62752015　发行部 010-62750672 编辑部 010-62117788
印　刷　者	三河市北燕印装有限公司
经　销　者	新华书店
	650毫米×980毫米　16开本　30.25印张　478千字 2022年12月第1版　2022年12月第1次印刷
定　　价	88.00元

未经许可，不得以任何方式复制或抄袭本书之部分或全部内容。
版权所有，侵权必究
举报电话：010-62752024　电子信箱：fd@pup.pku.edu.cn
图书如有印装质量问题，请与出版部联系，电话：010-62756370

编委会成员名单

主　任　柯良栋
副主任　张月姣　沈四宝　张永坚　刘晓红　李　虎
委　员　(按姓氏笔画排序)
　　　　王承杰　王彦君　王雪华　牛　磊　刘　超
　　　　刘亚军　刘敬东　关正义　杜焕芳　杨国华
　　　　肖永平　宋迪煌　张文广　张晓君　陈　波
　　　　陈云东　郑　蕾　赵　云　郭　雳　黄　巍
　　　　蒋　弘　韩立新　覃华平　喻　敏　蔡晨风
　　　　谭　剑　薛　虹　薛　源

编辑部成员名单

主　编　李　虎
副主编　陈　波　黄　巍　王成栋　齐　骥
编　辑　刘　颖　徐　飞　黄晨亮　洪慧敏　郑秋钰
　　　　贾云鹏　周　昕　黄智含　莫之颖　耿　迪
　　　　张傲霜　唐嘉玮　肖　鹏　陈　迅　王　辰
　　　　陈末末

前　言

时光如白驹过隙,转瞬之间,中国仲裁事业的发展已经迈入第66个年头。为更好地满足国内外仲裁专家、学者、从业人士交流学习的需求,推动中国海事商事仲裁事业的高质量发展,在业内同仁的大力支持下,中国海事仲裁委员会(以下简称"中国海仲")经过一年多的筹备,正式推出《中国海事商事仲裁评论》(以下简称《评论》)系列丛书。

出版专业文集,以承载业务宣传、理念交流、文化培育等功能,是国际领先仲裁机构的通行做法。2021年以来,中国海仲贯彻中共中央办公厅、国务院办公厅《关于完善仲裁制度提高仲裁公信力的若干意见》,围绕"服务航运贸易实务,促进仲裁研讨交流"这一宗旨,精心筹划,聚焦理论研究、热点追踪、案例分析、法律解读等内容,依托行业资源,向具有权威性、代表性的国内外专家主动约稿,通过"海仲杯"中国海事商事仲裁征文大赛向青年仲裁从业者征集文章,力求《评论》在体现前瞻性强、参考价值高、影响力大的权威专家观点的同时,为新时期的涉外法治人才培养交流提供平台。总体而言,《评论》呈现出以下亮点:

一是立足中国仲裁发展实际,充分展现中国仲裁的实践优势和理论特色。自中国国际贸易促进委员会的涉外仲裁肇始,历经半个多世纪的风风雨雨,仲裁早已深深植根于社会主义市场经济的土壤,在改革开放的春风中绽放出无数绚烂的花朵。《评论》所辑录之作着眼于中国仲裁的特有实践,深度剖析中国仲裁变革发展所回应的现实关切,精心提炼、传播、弘扬中国仲裁在服务大局、普惠民生、传播法治文化等方面所形成的"东方经验",同时亦体现反思意识,倡导不忘初心、正本清源、去芜存菁,以批判的眼光直面当前仲裁实践中存在的问题,以坚定的立场毫不动摇地推进中国仲裁在曲折中前进。

二是探讨国际仲裁的发展趋势和创新成果,为中国仲裁的进步提供参考思路。"以我为主,为我所用"是涉外法律工作者需要一贯坚持的原则,对于我们前方道路的选择至关重要。《评论》鼓励国际视野,努力汇集各方声音,及时追踪、观察、评析国际仲裁中的最新实践,力求以域外经验推动中国仲裁顶层设计、理论和实操层面的不断完善;同时注重兼顾当下国情,强调从当前中国仲裁的实际需求出发,辩证地看待各类解决方案。

《评论》将认真贯彻习近平法治思想,在借鉴国际先进经验的基础上,力争为探索适合中国国情的仲裁发展道路贡献力量。希望理论界、实务界同仁积极支持本书、踊跃投稿,同时也希望读者为本书多多提出宝贵的意见和建议。未来,我们将全力把《评论》办好、办精,努力将其打造为中国仲裁法律领域的代表性文集,切实服务于中国仲裁事业的发展。

《中国海事商事仲裁评论》编委会
2022年9月1日

目 录

从一起伦敦仲裁案看同步仲裁与合并仲裁在实务中的应用及
若干法律问题 …………………………………………………… 001
 一、案情简介 ………………………………………………… 002
 二、案件处理 ………………………………………………… 003
 三、同步仲裁与合并仲裁 …………………………………… 004
 四、当前英美法系对合并仲裁或同步仲裁的态度 ………… 009
 五、合并仲裁或同步仲裁可能面临的问题 ………………… 010
 结　语 ………………………………………………………… 011

航空地服合同争议的仲裁关注点 …………………………………… 013
 一、航空地服合同是否属于委托合同，当事人是否有法定的
   单方任意合同解除权 …………………………………… 015
 二、如何理解航空地服合同中的免责条款 ………………… 016
 三、航空地服合同纠纷中服务费及代垫费用的事实认定 … 020
 四、航空地服合同的仲裁条款 ……………………………… 021

临时仲裁制度及司法审查相关问题研究 ………………………… 024
 前　言 ………………………………………………………… 024
 一、我国临时仲裁制度的晚近探索与实践 ………………… 026
 二、《仲裁法》纳入临时仲裁制度的重要意义 ……………… 028
 三、建立临时仲裁司法审查制度的若干建议 ……………… 032
 结　论 ………………………………………………………… 043

论"合并仲裁"规则
 ——兼评《中国海事仲裁委员会仲裁规则》第19条的理解、
   适用及完善 ……………………………………………… 044

一、合并仲裁制度的产生背景与制度价值 …………………… 044
　　二、比较法上的合并仲裁——以美国的合并仲裁实践为例 …… 048
　　三、强制合并仲裁的逻辑——默示合并合意的解释 …………… 051
　　四、合并仲裁的构成要件——在不同仲裁规则视角下 ………… 052
　　五、我国司法实践对合并仲裁的回应 …………………………… 057
　　六、《中国海事仲裁委员会仲裁规则》第19条的理解与适用 …… 061
　　七、《中国海事仲裁委员会仲裁规则》第19条的完善建议 ……… 067
　　结　　语 …………………………………………………………… 070
数字贸易知识产权风险分析与管理 ………………………………… 072
　　一、数字贸易的范围与特点 ……………………………………… 073
　　二、数字贸易知识产权风险分析 ………………………………… 075
　　三、数字平台内经营者知识产权风险管理 ……………………… 076
　　四、数字贸易知识产权保证 ……………………………………… 088
　　结　　论 …………………………………………………………… 100
后疫情时代世界海事仲裁发展概况 ………………………………… 101
　　中国篇 ……………………………………………………………… 101
　　内　　地 …………………………………………………………… 101
　　一、海事仲裁相关法律的发展 …………………………………… 102
　　二、海事仲裁的发展 ……………………………………………… 105
　　三、海事仲裁相关司法实践的发展 ……………………………… 110
　　结　　语 …………………………………………………………… 122
　　香港特区 …………………………………………………………… 123
　　引　　言 …………………………………………………………… 123
　　一、专业知识 ……………………………………………………… 124
　　二、独立和公正的法律体系 ……………………………………… 125
　　三、《仲裁条例》(第609章) ……………………………………… 126
　　四、关于内地与香港特别行政区法院就仲裁程序相互
　　　　协助保全的安排 ……………………………………………… 130
　　五、裁决书的执行 ………………………………………………… 131
　　六、实体法 ………………………………………………………… 132
　　七、香港特区海事仲裁的惯常做法、HKMAG仲裁规则及

机构仲裁程序 …………………………………………… 132
　八、建议使用的仲裁条款 ……………………………………… 134
新加坡篇 …………………………………………………………… 135
　一、技术的使用 ………………………………………………… 136
　二、仲裁庭组成 ………………………………………………… 138
　三、开庭审理 …………………………………………………… 138
　四、裁决作出的期限 …………………………………………… 138
　五、提高适用简易程序的限额 ………………………………… 139
　六、任命仲裁员的标准条款 …………………………………… 139
　七、变更代理人须经仲裁庭批准 ……………………………… 139
　结　论 …………………………………………………………… 139
英国篇 ……………………………………………………………… 140
　引　言 …………………………………………………………… 140
　一、英国法律下的仲裁程序 …………………………………… 141
　二、重要更新 …………………………………………………… 143
　三、伦敦海事仲裁规则和发展情况 …………………………… 143
　四、近期的案例法 ……………………………………………… 146
　结　语 …………………………………………………………… 148

国际海洋法法庭迅速释放案件中主体特点及对中国的启示 …… 149
　引　言 …………………………………………………………… 149
　一、迅速释放程序中的船旗国 ………………………………… 150
　二、迅速释放程序中的专属经济区所属国 …………………… 158
　三、迅速释放案件对我国的启示 ……………………………… 163
　结　论 …………………………………………………………… 168

完善司法支持监督仲裁机制　促进中国仲裁事业高质量发展 … 170
　一、依法履行司法审查职能，引导仲裁行业健康发展 ……… 171
　二、发布司法解释和规范性文件，营造支持仲裁友善监督的
　　　司法环境 …………………………………………………… 174
　三、参与仲裁法修订，积极推动仲裁法律制度完善 ………… 177
　四、建设国际商事纠纷多元化解决机制，支持中国仲裁国际
　　　化发展 ……………………………………………………… 177

国际仲裁中心是形成的 ………………………………………… **179**
 一、国际仲裁中心是仲裁服务软实力动态竞争后形成的
  市场格局 ……………………………………………… 180
 二、现代国际商事仲裁发源于专业人士的自发性创造 ………… 181
 三、现代国际商事仲裁中心地位的确立是仲裁软实力培育
  发展的结果 …………………………………………… 183
 四、中国特色国际仲裁中心形成之时代机遇 ………………… 191
 五、中国特色国际仲裁中心形成之策略方向 ………………… 193
 结 语 ……………………………………………………… 196

CONTENT

The Practice and Legal Issues of Concurrent Arbitration and Consolidated
Arbitration from a London Arbitration ·· 199
   Ⅰ. Brief Introduction of the Case ·· 201
   Ⅱ. Handling of the Case ·· 202
   Ⅲ. Concurrent Arbitration and Consolidated Arbitration ·············· 203
   Ⅳ. Consolidated/Concurrent Arbitration Under Common Law ······ 209
   Ⅴ. Potential Problems of Consolidated/Concurrent Arbitration ······ 210
   Conclusion ·· 212
Focuses in Arbitration of Disputes in the Standard Ground Handling
Agreement ·· 214
   Ⅰ. Is SGHA a Commission Contract and Whether the Parties Have
      the Statutory Right to Unilaterally and Arbitrarily Rescind the
      Agreement ·· 217
   Ⅱ. How to Interpret the Exemption Clause in the SGHA ············· 220
   Ⅲ. Factual Determination of Service Fees and Disbursement Fees
      in SGHA Disputes ··· 225
   Ⅳ. The Arbitration Clause of the SGHA ···································· 228
Research on Ad Hoc Arbitration Regime and Its Judicial Review ·········· 231
   Foreword ··· 232
   Ⅰ. Recent Exploration and Practice of China's Ad Hoc Arbitration
      Regime ·· 234
   Ⅱ. The Importance of Incorporating the Ad Hoc Arbitration Regime
      into the PRC Arbitration Law ··· 238

Ⅲ. Some Suggestions on Establishing the Judicial Review System
of Ad Hoc Arbitration ································· 243
Conclusion ··· 261
Consolidation Provision in Arbitration Rules: Interpretation and Application
of Article 19 (Consolidation of Arbitrations) of the CMAC Arbitration
Rules and Proposal for Amendments ································ 263
Ⅰ. Background and Values of Consolidation of Arbitration ········ 264
Ⅱ. A Comparative Perspective: Consolidation of Arbitrations
in the United States ······································ 268
Ⅲ. The Logic Behind Compulsory Consolidation: Interpretation of
Implicit Consent ·· 272
Ⅳ. Criteria for Consolidation of Arbitrations: Consolidation
Provisions in Major Institutional Arbitration Rules ············· 273
Ⅴ. Latest Practice for Judicial Review of Consolidated Arbitration
in China ··· 280
Ⅵ. CMAC's Consolidation Provision (Article 19): Scope of
Application and Interpretation ······························ 286
Ⅶ. Amendment Proposals for Article 19 (Consolidation
of Arbitrations) of the CMAC Arbitration Rules ················ 295
Conclusion ··· 299
Intellectual Property Risk Management in Digital Trade ················ 301
Ⅰ. Digital Trade: Scope and Characteristics ···················· 302
Ⅱ. Analysis of Intellectual Property Risks in Digital Trade ········ 304
Ⅲ. Intellectual Property Risk Management for Businesses Operating
on Digital Platforms ······································ 305
Ⅳ. Intellectual Property Warranty in Digital Trade ················ 316
Conclusion ··· 327
Review of Maritime Arbitration in Post-Covid-19 Era ················ 329
Report on Development of Maritime Arbitration in
China's Mainland (2020-2021) ····························· 330
Ⅰ. Developments in the Law and Legislation Relating to Maritime

  Arbitration ··· 330
 Ⅱ. The Development of Maritime Arbitration in China's Mainland
  ·· 335
 Ⅲ. Development of Judicial Practice Relating to Maritime
  Arbitration in China ··· 343
 Concluding Remarks ·· 361
Maritime Arbitration in Hong Kong ·· 363
 Introduction ·· 363
 Ⅰ. Expertise ·· 363
 Ⅱ. An Independent and Impartial Legal System ······················· 365
 Ⅲ. The Arbitration Ordinance (Cap. 609) ······························· 366
 Ⅳ. Arrangement Concerning Mutual Assistance in Court-ordered
  Interim Measures in Aid of Arbitral Proceedings by the Courts of
  the Mainland and of the HKSAR ·· 371
 Ⅴ. Enforcement of the Award ··· 372
 Ⅵ. Substantive Law ·· 373
 Ⅶ. The Practice of Hong Kong Maritime Arbitration, the HKMAG
  Terms and the Procedures for the Administration of Arbitration ··· 374
 Ⅷ. Recommended Arbitration Clauses ······································· 376
Singapore Maritime Industry Users in a New Era the SCMA Arbitration Rules
(4th Edition) ·· 377
 Ⅰ. The Use of Technology ··· 380
 Ⅱ. Constitution of the Tribunal ·· 381
 Ⅲ. Oral Hearings-optional ··· 382
 Ⅳ. Time Frame for Issuance of an Arbitral Award ····················· 382
 Ⅴ. Increased Claim Threshold for Expedited Proceedings ············ 383
 Ⅵ. Standard Terms of Appointment ·· 383
 Ⅶ. Power to Prevent Change of Counsel ·································· 384
 Conclusion ·· 384
Maritime Arbitration in the UK ··· 384
 Introduction ·· 384

Ⅰ. The Arbitration Process Under English Law …………………… 385
Ⅱ. Important Update ……………………………………………… 388
Ⅲ. London Maritime Arbitration Rules and Developments ………… 389
Ⅳ. Recent Case Law ……………………………………………… 393
Summary ………………………………………………………… 396

Characteristics of Applicants in Prompt Release Cases of the ITLOS
and Enlightenment for China ……………………………………… 397
Introduction ……………………………………………………… 398
Ⅰ. The Flag State in the Prompt Release Procedure ……………… 399
Ⅱ. The Coastal State with the Exclusive Economic Zone in Prompt
Release Procedure ……………………………………………… 409
Ⅲ. The Enlightenment for China in Prompt Release Cases ……… 416
Conclusion ……………………………………………………… 425

Improve Judicial Supervision and Support for Arbitration and Promote
the High-quality Development of Arbitration in China …………… 427
Ⅰ. The People's Courts Conduct Judicial Review in a Manner Consistent
with the Rule of Law and Provide Guidance on the Healthy
Development of Arbitration …………………………………… 428
Ⅱ. The Supreme People's Court Publishes Judicial Interpretations
and Normative Documents and Create an Arbitration-friendly
Environment with Judicial Support and Supervision …………… 434
Ⅲ. The Supreme People's Court Participates in the Revision of
the Arbitration Law and Actively Promoting the Improvement of
the Arbitration Legal System …………………………………… 439
Ⅳ. The Supreme People's Court Builds a Diversified Mechanism for the
Settlement of International Commercial Disputes and Supporting the
International Development of Chinese Arbitration ……………… 440

A Review on the Formation of International Arbitration Hub …… 443
Ⅰ. The International Arbitration Hub is a Market Pattern
Formed by Dynamic Competition in the Soft Power of
Arbitration Services …………………………………………… 445

II. Modern International Commercial Arbitration Originated
    from the Spontaneous Creation of Professionals ·················· 447
III. Cultivation of Soft Power is the Core Factor Affecting
    the Formation of International Commercial Arbitration Hubs ··· 449
IV. Opportunities for Establishing an International Arbitration
    Hub with Chinese Characteristics ································· 459
V. Strategic Directions for Forming an International Arbitration
    Hub with Chinese Characteristics ································· 462
Epilogue ··· 467

从一起伦敦仲裁案看同步仲裁与合并仲裁在实务中的应用及若干法律问题[*]

宋 斌[**] 杨运涛[***]

摘要：本文以笔者亲历的一起伦敦仲裁案为例，介绍了同步仲裁规则在实务中的应用，同时根据同步仲裁与合并仲裁各自不同的特点、仲裁规则或法律规定分析了两者的区别，研究了当前英美法律下对同步仲裁与合并仲裁的基本态度及两者在法律实践中可能面临的一些问题，同时对于完善中国海事仲裁规则在此两种制度方面的规定提出了一些建议。

关键词：同步仲裁；合并仲裁；多方当事人争议

众所周知，仲裁因其私密性、可执行性等优点，相较于选择法院诉讼这种争议处理方式，在国际商事领域，无论是事前订立合同或是事后处理争议，更容易为当事人所接受。

因历史形成的原因，伦敦海事仲裁员协会（London Maritime Arbitrators Association，LMAA）仍是国际贸易及航运人士解决国际海事海商争议的首选机构。LMAA 2020年的统计数据表明，在这一年中，尽管受到了新冠肺炎疫情的影响，LMAA 仍接受并指派了3010名仲裁员处理争议案件，登记的新仲裁案件有1775件，总共下达了523份仲裁裁决。这一年成为自2015年以来LMAA受理案件数量最多的年份，在全球各大仲裁机构中处于领先地位。

---

[*] 本文完成于2021年8月。
[**] 香港明华船务有限公司商务部副总经理。
[***] 招商局集团有限公司风险管理部/法律合规部/审计部部长。

中国海事仲裁委员会成立60多年来,已审理裁决各类案件数千件,涉外案件占比高达60%,案件涉及英国、丹麦、美国、新加坡、巴拿马等40多个国家和地区,案件类型主要包括货运代理、提单运输、租船、船舶碰撞、船舶建造、船员劳务、船舶修理、保险等,仲裁国际化程度不断提升,中国海事仲裁的国际公信力和影响力日益增强。

在当前信息技术革新的全球背景下,国际商事交易逐步呈扩大化趋势,由此促使很多交易模式的改变,很多商事交往已逐渐突破了传统的双方合同交易,多方当事人的合同越来越频繁地出现,从而导致争议的类型中无论是链式争议(chain dispute)或是并列式争议(也叫伞状争议,parallel dispute)也逐渐增多,这一点在国际贸易、国际航运、建设工程领域愈发明显,因此实务中同步仲裁(concurrent arbitration)或合并仲裁(consolidated arbitration)的情形也越来越多。

笔者以自己亲身经历的一起伦敦仲裁案为例,谈谈实践中如何根据案件的具体情况和实际需要,通过采用同步仲裁的技巧,灵活地运用仲裁规则,以期达到更好地维护己方法律利益的目的。

一、案情简介

2007年,原船东A公司将某轮期租给B公司,B公司又期租给C公司,C公司程租给D公司,D公司又转程租给E公司,承运一载巴西至中国的15万吨铁矿石,租约链上共有五方当事人。E公司同时也是该票铁矿石的国内买方,X公司是国外卖方,Y公司为X公司下属的码头公司。(如图1)

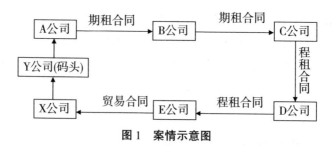

图1 案情示意图

该轮在巴西装港伊塔瓜伊(Itaguai)靠泊过程中碰撞码头,码头 Y 公司向原船东 A 公司索赔约 3000 万美元,原船东在巴西提供完担保后,遂根据租船合同以不安全泊位为由沿租约链条向下索赔。这是航运业务中一起十分典型和常见的租约链条纠纷,涉案相关方所涉及的法律或事实问题基本是一样的。

笔者当时所代表的公司为 D 公司,案件进行过程中,C 公司为获取 D 公司的担保,当时不仅在美国申请 RULE B 扣押了 D 公司的美元往来款项,还扣押了 D 公司所属的一条自有船舶,给 D 公司的正常经营造成了巨大的影响。

对于 D 公司而言,这本是一起相对简单的背靠背案件,但由于存在几个方面的问题,导致这起案件扑朔迷离、错综复杂。本案中,D 公司虽然上下合同都为程租合同,但在至关重要的管辖权和法律适用方面却存在严重的不一致:其与船东 C 公司之间是伦敦仲裁,适用英国法;与租家 E 公司之间是北京仲裁,适用中国法。这种上下合同管辖权和法律适用的不一致导致了巨大的不确定性。此外,E 公司为 D 公司战略合作客户,因此 D 公司不太可能对 E 公司采取过分激烈的法律措施,导致大量的取证、抗辩工作都将依赖于 D 公司自身的努力,而 D 公司作为租约链中一个程租租家,这些工作无疑是一个巨大的挑战。

二、案件处理

本案中由于 D 公司直接面临 C 公司的索赔,考虑到 C 公司在租约关系中对上是期租,对下是程租,难保两个合同下的义务和责任能完全背靠背。同时鉴于 D 公司资产被扣押,不得已向 C 公司提供了金额巨大的银行担保,为能充分利用 C 公司担心其法律地位可能非背靠背的心理,从而实现利用其作为抗辩原船东不安全泊位索赔的屏障,同时达到用 D 公司信誉担保替换银行担保以减轻担保成本的目的,在案件处理过程中,D 公司巧妙地利用了伦敦仲裁的程序规则,以仲裁私密性为由,拒绝了 C 公司的同步审理(concurrent hearing)请求,最大限度地给 C 公司施加了压力,迫使其尽可能向己方阵线靠拢,一起对抗原船东的索赔。

后因案情发展,在另案诉讼中,该港口泊位被英国高等法院认定为不安全泊位,导致D公司诉讼地位急转直下,败诉风险陡然增加。为保证D公司证据能在租约链上下的仲裁中直接使用,从而最大限度地提高己方抗辩的力度以及降低中间各方放弃抗辩的可能性,尽可能控制己方败诉的法律风险,D公司改变了原本不同意同步审理的态度,同意了C公司同步审理的请求。

2012年,各方在伦敦召开调解会,最终成功达成和解,D公司以较小的代价与其他各方共同分摊了码头的损失,成功地解决了这起金额巨大的码头损失索赔案件。

三、同步仲裁与合并仲裁

在本案前期处理过程中,D公司成功地利用了有关同步仲裁的一些技术性规定,为案件处理朝着对己方有利的方向发展奠定了基础,但在实践中,不少人较容易把同步仲裁(concurrent arbitration)与合并仲裁(consolidated arbitration)混为一谈。虽然两者可能都涉及多个关联合同或者多方当事人,在仲裁程序中存在共同的事实或法律问题,仲裁请求可能是基于同一个交易或连续交易,但两者还是有着较大的区别。纵观中国或是英国仲裁法,其实并未对上述两种仲裁的概念有过明文规定,更多是学界或是实务界针对业务过程中产生的多个关联合同或多方当事人的仲裁所赋予的一个称谓。

根据通常理解,合并仲裁是指把多个法律或事实相关的仲裁合并或变为一个单独的仲裁。仲裁庭有权针对所有的仲裁作出一个仲裁裁决。同步仲裁是指仲裁庭针对几个法律或事实相关的不同仲裁下的申请、证据同时进行审理,之后针对不同的仲裁作出相应的多个裁决。[①] 这一点在两者的英文表述"consolidate"和"concurrent"上也能看出有着不小的区别。

根据《牛津词典》的解释,"consolidate"通常是指"to join things together into one",翻译过来是指把几个事物变成一个,"concurrent"通常是指

[①] The Chartered Institute of Arbitrators Practice Guideline 15: Guidelines for Arbitrators on How to Approach Issues Relating to Multi-Party Arbittations, 27 March 2019, para. 2.2.

"existing or happening at the same time",即在同一时间同时存在或发生。虽然"concurrent"一定程度上也有"合并"的意味,但更多强调的是同时进行的概念,在一些文献中经常看到把"concurrent arbitration"或"concurrent hearing"直接翻译成"合并仲裁"或"合并审理",严格地说并非完全准确。

笔者梳理了国际上主要的一些仲裁协会或机构在这两者的描述和具体规定上的一些区别。

以LMAA仲裁规则历年的若干版本为例,其并未提及有关"consolidation"或"consolidated arbitration"(合并仲裁)的概念,而仅在其条款中提到了"concurrently"(即同步仲裁或同步审理)的程序问题。① 如最新的LMAA Terms 2021版本第17条(b)款是这么描述的:

> (b) Where two or more arbitrations appear to raise common issues of fact or law, the tribunals may direct that they shall be conducted and, where an oral hearing is directed, heard concurrently. Where such an order is made, the tribunals may give such directions as the interests of fairness, economy and expedition require including:
>
> (i) that time limits for service of submissions may be abbreviated or modified in the interests of saving costs or minimizing delay, or otherwise enhancing efficiency;
>
> (ii) that the documents disclosed by the parties in one arbitration shall be made available to the parties to the other arbitration upon such conditions as the tribunals may determine;
>
> (iii) that the evidence given in one arbitration shall be received and admitted in the other arbitration, subject to all parties being given a reasonable opportunity to comment upon it and subject to such other conditions as the tribunals may determine.

简要而言,大意为当两个或多个仲裁涉及共同的法律或事实问题时,仲裁庭可以指示进行仲裁,如果需要开庭的话,也可以同时审理。仲裁庭作出此类决定后,为实现仲裁的公平、经济和快捷,还可以作出如下

---

① The London Maritime Arbitrators Association(LMAA) Terms 2002, 2006, 2012, Article 14(b); The LMAA Terms 2017, Article 16(b); The LMAA Terms 2021, Article 17(b).

指令:(i)为节省成本或避免延误,提交陈述或抗辩的时限可以缩短,或采取其他更有效的方式;(ii)根据仲裁庭确定的条件,一个仲裁中当事人披露的文件应当披露给另一个仲裁中的当事人;(iii)根据仲裁庭确定的条件,在给所有当事人陈述意见的合理机会后,一个仲裁中提交的证据应该在另一个仲裁中被接受和采纳。由此显而易见,concurrent hearing 或者 concurrent arbitration 更多针对的是两个或几个仲裁同时进行审理的情形,典型的例子如上文中提到的船舶租赁业务中较常出现的链式争议,但并非把几个仲裁合并为一个仲裁的概念。

而新加坡国际仲裁中心(Singapore International Arbitration Centre, SIAC)2016 版的仲裁规则却恰恰相反,未提及同步仲裁(concurrent arbitration),更多强调的是多份合同仲裁(multiple contracts)和合并仲裁(consolidation of arbitration)的程序问题。

如第 6 条标题为"Multiple Contracts",6.1 条具体内容为:

6.1 如果案件的争议事项由多份合同引起或者与多份合同有关,申请人可以:

    a. 就援引的每一份仲裁协议分别提交一份"仲裁通知书",并同时按照第 8.1 条的规定申请合并该些仲裁案件;或者

    b. 就援引的所有仲裁协议仅提交一份"仲裁通知书",但"仲裁通知书"中应包括对每份合同和其分别援引的仲裁协议的陈述以及对是否已经满足了第 8.1 条所规定适用条件的说明。如果这样做,则申请应被视为开始了多个仲裁程序(每个仲裁协议对应一份仲裁程序),根据本第 6.1(b)条提交的"仲裁通知书"应被视为是根据第 8.1 条提出的将所有该些仲裁程序进行合并审理的申请。

第 8 条标题为"Consolidation",8.1 条的具体内容如下:

8.1 在拟合并的各仲裁案件的仲裁庭均未组成之前,拟合并的各仲裁案件符合下列条件之一的,一方当事人可以向主簿提出申请,要求将两个以上根据本规则正在进行的待决仲裁案件合并为一个仲裁案:

    a. 所有当事人同意合并仲裁;

b. 各仲裁案件的所有请求是依据同一份仲裁协议提出;或者

c. 各仲裁协议相容,并且:(i)争议由相同法律关系产生;(ii)产生争议的多个合同系主从合同的关系;或者(iii)争议由同一交易或同一系列交易产生。

香港国际仲裁中心(Hong Kong International Arbitration Centre, HKIAC)2018版的仲裁规则,却与以上两个机构仲裁规则的规定又有所不同,HKIAC的仲裁规则同时规定了合并仲裁与同步仲裁的相关程序,如第28条是有关合并仲裁(consolidation of arbitration)的规定,"经当事人申请,并与当事人和已被确认或指定的仲裁员商议后,HKIAC有权在以下条件满足时,决定将依本规则正在进行的两个或多个仲裁合并:(a)各方当事人同意合并;或(b)各仲裁中的所有请求均依据同一仲裁协议提出;或(c)请求依据多于一个仲裁协议提出,而所有仲裁中存在相同的法律或事实问题,请求救济的权利均涉及或源于同一交易或同一系列相关联的交易,且各仲裁协议彼此兼容"。第30条是有关同步仲裁(concurrent proceeding,中文版名称也叫做"平行程序")的规定,"经征求当事人意见后,仲裁庭可在以下条件满足时,依本规则同时进行两个或两个以上仲裁,或一个紧接另一个地进行仲裁,或暂停任何仲裁直至任何其他仲裁作出决定:(a)各仲裁中的仲裁庭组成相同;且(b)所有仲裁均涉及共同的法律或事实问题"。可见在香港国际仲裁中心的仲裁程序中,对于合并仲裁与同步仲裁有着不同的规定,前者是将多个仲裁合并或变为一个,后者则是指多个仲裁同时进行。

回到1996年《英国仲裁法》,该法第35条对于"合并仲裁"和"同步仲裁"程序并没有混为一谈,该条是这样描述的:

Section 35 Consolidation of proceedings and concurrent hearings:

(1) the parties are free to agree——

 (a) that the arbitral proceedings shall be consolidated with other arbitral proceedings, or

 (b) that concurrent hearings shall be held, on such terms as may be agreed.

(2) Unless the parties agree to confer such power on the tribunal, the

tribunal has no power to order consolidation of proceedings or concurrent hearings.

从上述法律条文的表述来看,《英国仲裁法》也是将"consolidation"与"concurrent"进行了区分,作为不同的程序来看待。

随着中国对外贸易、商事交流的扩大与深入,我国仲裁机构如中国国际经济贸易仲裁委员会(以下简称"贸仲")、中国海事仲裁委员会(以下简称"海仲")在合并仲裁、同步审理方面也是与时俱进的。《中国国际经济贸易仲裁委员会仲裁规则(2015版)》(以下简称"贸仲规则")第14条为"多份合同的仲裁"①,第19条为"合并仲裁"②。《中国海事仲裁委员会仲裁规则(2021版)》(以下简称"海仲规则")第14条为"多份合同的仲裁",第19条为"合并仲裁",此两条与贸仲规则的规定完全相同。与贸仲规则相比,海仲规则多了第53条的"合并开庭"条款,英文版翻译为"consolidation of hearings",具体内容如下:

> 为公平、经济和快捷地进行仲裁程序,如果两个或多个仲裁案件涉及相同的事实或法律问题,在征求各方当事人意见后,仲裁庭经征求仲裁委员会仲裁院意见可以决定对两个或多个仲裁案件合并开庭,并可决定:
> (一)一个案件当事人提交的文件可以提交给另一个案件当事人;
> (二)一个案件中提交的证据可以在另一个案件中被接受和采纳,但是应当给予所有当事人就该等证据发表意见的机会。

从以上规定可以看出,海仲规则第53条名称虽然是"合并开庭",英

---

① 《中国国际经济贸易仲裁委员会仲裁规则(2015版)》第14条规定:"申请人就多份合同项下的争议可在同一仲裁案件中合并提出仲裁申请,但应同时符合下列条件:1.多份合同系主从合同关系;或多份合同所涉当事人相同且法律关系性质相同;2.争议源于同一交易或同一系列交易;3.多份合同中的仲裁协议内容相同或相容。"

② 《中国国际经济贸易仲裁委员会仲裁规则(2015版)》第19条规定:"(一)符合下列条件之一的,经一方当事人请求,仲裁委员会可以决定将根据本规则进行的两个或两个以上的仲裁案件合并为一个仲裁案件,进行审理。1.各案仲裁请求依据同一仲裁协议提出;2.各案仲裁请求依据多份仲裁协议提出,该多份仲裁协议内容相同或相容,且各案当事人相同、各争议所涉及的法律关系性质相同;3.各案仲裁请求依据多份仲裁协议提出,该多份仲裁协议内容相同或相容,且涉及的多份合同为主从合同关系;4.所有案件的当事人均同意合并仲裁。"

文翻译为"consolidation of hearings",但其本质反而更类似于 LMAA 或 HKIAC 仲裁规则下的同步仲裁或同步审理的内容。鉴于法律语言的严谨性以及与国际通行表述的一致性,建议海仲考虑将此处的"合并开庭"调整为"同步仲裁"或"同步审理",将英文表述调整为"concurrent arbitration"或"concurrent hearing",避免与"合并仲裁"概念混淆,也更为符合实际情况,更加准确严谨。

四、当前英美法系对合并仲裁或同步仲裁的态度

英国对于合并仲裁或同步仲裁秉持的通常原则是尊重当事人的意思自治,认为只有在当事人一致同意的情况下,才可以进行合并或同步仲裁,这一点从《英国仲裁法》的条文可见一斑。根据上述《英国仲裁法》第 35 条的规定,只有在当事人同意或者同意赋予仲裁庭合并或同步仲裁的权利后,仲裁庭才能启动合并或同步仲裁程序。

英国法院对于这个问题的态度曾在 1984 年的"The Eastern Saga 案"[①]中得到充分体现。该案中,船东把船舶出租给了租家,租家又背靠背转租给了分租家。争议出现后,上下两个仲裁同时启动,仲裁庭的组成也完全相同。之后仲裁庭鉴于上下两个仲裁涉及的争议和法律问题相同,遂对两个仲裁进行了同步审理(concurrent hearing)。船东向法院提出异议,认为仲裁庭没有权利强行将上下两个仲裁进行同步审理。法院经审理后最终认为:"在没有当事人同意的情况下,仲裁员无权决定同步审理或类似程序;无论是仲裁庭或是当事人都无权坚持要求对所有争议进行同步审理,无论该类争议彼此联系多么密切,或者多么一致,或者进行同步审理在程序上有多么方便;仲裁员唯一所享有的权力就是在他所委任的仲裁中行使的,不能因争议与其他争议有多么类似就可以将该等权力延伸至另一个仲裁中。"由此可见,在缺少约定授权或法定授权的情况下,英国法院并不愿意支持强制同步仲裁或合并仲裁。

---

① Oxford Shipping Co. LTD. v. Nippon Yusen Kaisha(The Eastem Saga), 2 *Lloyd's Law Report* 373(1984).

美国在1993年的United Kingdom v. Boeing Co.案[①]中明确了除非当事人一致同意合并仲裁,否则仲裁庭或法院均无权命令进行合并仲裁。该案中英国政府在一次直升机试飞中遭受损失,该飞机由Boeing公司和Textron公司分工建造。两公司分别与英国签订了建造合同。发生事故后,英国政府对两公司在纽约提起仲裁,当事人对是否能进行合并仲裁产生争议。最终美国最高法院认为,在《美国联邦仲裁法》下,仲裁协议应当被视为当事人之间所订立的合同,因此如果当事人没有在仲裁协议中约定合并仲裁,则仲裁庭或法院均无权根据当时的法律强制进行合并仲裁。

由此可见,当前英美法律下对于合并仲裁或同步仲裁更倾向于当事人的意思一致才予以认可。这也是本案中笔者代表D公司能够底气较足地向仲裁庭表示拒绝同步仲裁的理由所在。

五、合并仲裁或同步仲裁可能面临的问题

合并仲裁或同步仲裁是解决多方当事人仲裁的一种新方式,虽然从未来发展趋势上看可能符合仲裁的实践需求,但由于很多国家或地区法律以及国际公约在此问题上的模糊不清,可能会面临复杂的承认和执行问题。

获得具有可执行力的仲裁裁决是当事人选择仲裁的初衷。作为国际商事领域最重要的国际公约之一,截至2021年7月,《承认及执行外国仲裁裁决公约》(又称《纽约公约》)已有168个国家和地区加入。该公约第5条第1款载明了缔约方法院可不予承认和执行仲裁裁决的情形,即"……(c)裁决处理的争议不属于提交仲裁的标的或不在仲裁条款之列,或包含超出提交仲裁范围事项的决定的;(d)仲裁庭组成或仲裁程序与当事人合意不符,或无仲裁协议而与仲裁地所在国法律不符;……"故对于合并仲裁而言,如果仲裁庭最终仅作出一份仲裁裁决,对被合并的单一仲裁案件而言,该裁决可能会被认为违背第(c)项;通过强制合并仲裁作出的仲裁裁决,则可能因违反第(d)项而得不到承认与执行。

以当前英美法律对待合并仲裁或同步仲裁的态度而言,倘若欠缺当

---

① Government of United Kingdom v. Boeing Co. , 998 F. 2nd 68(1993).

事人明示的意思表示一致,而由仲裁庭单独决定合并仲裁或同步仲裁的程序,事后则有可能会被当事人借口违反《纽约公约》而拒绝承认和执行。

我国贸仲、海仲最新的仲裁规则虽对合并仲裁或同步仲裁(此处将海仲规则中的"合并开庭"本质上视为"同步仲裁")作了较多前瞻性的规定,有些仲裁规则甚至赋予了仲裁庭或仲裁委员会强制合并仲裁的权利,但就我国当前的仲裁立法而言,我国《仲裁法》和《民事诉讼法》并无针对合并仲裁或同步仲裁的相关规定,合并仲裁或同步仲裁有可能无法适用。我国《仲裁法》第 4 条明确规定:"当事人采用仲裁方式解决纠纷,应当双方自愿,达成仲裁协议。没有仲裁协议,一方申请仲裁的,仲裁委员会不予受理。"根据该条规定,仲裁程序的启动需要满足当事人之间存在仲裁协议,即以意思一致为前提条件。实践中,一旦发生纠纷,当事人往往更多从己方利益考虑,达成合意的合并仲裁或同步仲裁的可能性较低。但如果仲裁庭或仲裁委员会强制适用合并仲裁或同步仲裁的程序,若是国内仲裁,则可能会与我国《仲裁法》第 4 条相冲突;若是国际仲裁,则可能会因违反《纽约公约》而被国外法院拒绝承认和执行。因此,建议今后在修改《仲裁法》时能考虑到合并仲裁或同步仲裁的实践需求,设立相关规定以规定这两种新的仲裁方式,肯定二者的合法性并为二者的适用提供法理基础。

除立法上予以完善外,对于合并仲裁和同步仲裁这两种相互区别又有联系的仲裁方式,各仲裁委员会的仲裁规则亦需对二者的仲裁前提、仲裁程序、适用范围及仲裁裁决等作出更详细、更严谨的规定。通过区别规定、具体规定合并仲裁和同步仲裁以提高各自的机制和制度功能,若一味以"合并仲裁"一个概念笼而统之,不加区分,可能更容易造成法律实践中的混乱。

结　　语

本案中笔者一方通过利用同步仲裁程序的规则取得了较好的效果。从近年来国际商事仲裁发展的趋势来看,多方当事人争议随着商事经济的发展已愈发增多,合并仲裁或同步仲裁在解决多方当事人争议方面的必要性和优势日益显著。合并仲裁或同步仲裁能避免互相矛盾的裁决、促进公平正义及提高仲裁效率,但也可能存在与当事人意思自治、仲裁保密性原则冲突的情形,甚至违背《纽约公约》而导致仲裁裁决无法得到承认和执行的问题。因此,在处理合并仲裁、同步仲裁方面的问题时,无论是立法层面或是仲裁规则修订完善,以及法律实践,需要尽可能寻求程序正义、实体正义和当事人意思自治、效率和公平方面的平衡。

合并仲裁、同步仲裁对传统仲裁原则的冲击可谓不小,但紧紧跟随国际商事仲裁领域的发展潮流,建立并不断完善我们自己合并仲裁或同步仲裁方面的制度,不仅有助于切实解决多方当事人之间的纠纷,而且对于推动中国仲裁事业的进步,尤其是我国海事仲裁事业的国际化无疑将具有重要作用。

航空地服合同争议的仲裁关注点*

聂 颖** 高 峰***

摘要:航空地服合同是机场公司就其在机场区域为航空公司正常运营提供的各类专业服务(包括值机、货运、旅客运输、航线维护、牵引拖车、廊桥、摆渡车等服务)而与航空公司签署的合同或协议。笔者以国际航空运输协会标准航空地面服务代理合同为例,解读该类合同纠纷的主要关注点,包括合同性质、合同解除权、免责条款、仲裁条款以及服务费与代垫费用的事实认定问题。航空类争议具有很强的专业性和国际性,适合通过仲裁方式予以解决。目前中国内地的仲裁机构已基本具备提供高质量国际化航空仲裁服务的条件,仲裁机构在为中国民航提供专业、高效的争议解决服务的同时,也会进一步影响和促进现有航空业法律体系的建立和完善,不断提升中国在国际民航界的话语权。

关键词:民航;航空地服合同;国际航空运输协会;仲裁;争议解决

2017年12月16日,中国海事仲裁委员会(以下简称"中国海仲")航空争议仲裁中心在北京正式成立,该中心致力于为我国民航业内争议提供更加专业、高效的仲裁解决途径。自2018年10月1日起施行的《中国海事仲裁委员会仲裁规则》第3条规定:"(一)仲裁委员会根据当事人的约定受理下列争议案件:……2.航空、铁路、公路等相关争议案件;……(二)前述案件包括:1.国际或涉外争议案件;2.涉及香港特别行政区、澳

---

* 本文完成于2021年7月。
** 北京恒礼管理咨询有限公司董事长。
*** 国浩律师事务所合伙人。

门特别行政区及台湾地区的案件;3.国内案件。"由此可见,中国海仲亦将航空相关争议案件明确列入主要的受案范围。根据笔者多年的民航业工作经验,航空类争议的专业性和国际性很强,非常适合通过仲裁解决。笔者拟以国际航空运输协会(以下简称"国际航协")航空地面服务代理合同(以下简称"航空地服合同")为例,解读该类合同纠纷案件的主要关注点。

航空地服合同是机场公司就其在机场区域为航空公司正常运营提供的各类专业服务(包括值机、货运、旅客运输、航线维护、牵引拖车、廊桥、摆渡车等服务)而与航空公司签署的合同或协议。航空公司一般会与机场公司签订一个全面的航空地服合同,也可能分别与相关机场公司、航空地服专业公司就不同的服务代理工作签署不同的合同。随着航空业的发展以及航空地服合同的推广使用,与航空公司运营相关的其他专业公司也逐步使用航空地服合同或者参照该合同条款与航空公司签署相关服务合同,比如航空配餐或者食品公司与航空公司签署的《航空配餐合同》,航油公司与航空公司签署的《注油服务合同》或《航空油料保障协议》,飞机维修公司与航空公司签署的《飞机维修合同》,航空信息服务公司与航空公司签署的《信息系统服务合同》等。虽然服务内容有所不同,但是合同双方当事人的权利义务,尤其是赔偿与责任条款基本一致,故本文中的航空地服合同讨论亦包括上述相关航空服务合同。

为了提高航空运营效率,明确责任划分和便于保险安排,国际航协为此制定了标准的航空地服合同文本并不断更新,根据更新时间分别为航空地服合同1998版、2004版、2008版、2013版、2018版等。截至目前,上述合同版本均是有效文件,供签约各方选用。因为目前我国境内使用较为广泛的还是航空地服合同1998版,笔者以下的分析亦是依据该版本的航空地服合同。航空地服合同一般包括主协议和两个附件,主协议主要是列明双方主要权利义务;附件A是地面服务项目,一般列明各类地服内容(比如值机、货运、旅客运输、航线维护、牵引拖车、廊桥、航食、注油等服务,供当事人选择适用);附件B是地点、服务项目和收费标准,一般列明提供地面服务的地点、双方约定的服务项目、收费标准以及双方需要约定的其他事项(比如对主协议中责任限额、管辖法院或者争议解决方式等条款进行补充或修改)。

一、航空地服合同是否属于委托合同，当事人是否有法定的单方任意合同解除权

我国《民法典》第919条规定："委托合同是委托人和受托人约定，由受托人处理委托人事务的合同。"第920条规定："委托人可以特别委托受托人处理一项或者数项事务，也可以概括委托受托人处理一切事务。"第933条规定："委托人或者受托人可以随时解除委托合同。因解除合同造成对方损失的，除不可归责于该当事人的事由外，无偿委托合同的解除方应当赔偿因解除时间不当造成的直接损失，有偿委托合同的解除方应当赔偿对方的直接损失和合同履行后可以获得的利益。"这与我国已经失效的《合同法》第410条规定的"委托人或者受托人可以随时解除委托合同。因解除合同给对方造成损失的，除不可归责于该当事人的事由以外，应当赔偿损失"一脉相承。

由于航空地服合同的服务内容一般是机场公司或者地服专业公司受航空公司委托为其提供航空地面代理服务，基本符合委托合同的特征，但是笔者经检索相关法院判例发现，法院一般均将航空地服合同认定为服务合同而非委托合同，而将与航空地服合同类似的飞机委托运营协议或者航空器托管合同认定为委托合同。如上诉人中一太客商务航空有限公司（以下简称"中一公司"）与被上诉人北京亿度投资有限公司（以下简称"亿度公司"）委托合同纠纷一案[①]，法院认为，亿度公司根据公务机运营管理规定与中一公司签订的《飞机委托运营协议》系双方真实意思表示，合法有效，该协议为有偿委托合同。该协议所约定的委托事务包括公务机引进阶段服务和飞机引进后的运营管理业务服务，该案只涉及飞机委托引进服务纠纷。而在泰国暹罗航空有限公司（以下简称"暹罗航空"）与广州白云国际机场股份有限公司（以下简称"白云机场"）服务合同纠纷一案[②]中，法院认为，暹罗航空与白云机场签订的《广州白云国际机场地面代理服务协议》《广州白云国际机场综合保障服务协议》是双方

---

① 参见辽宁省沈阳市中级人民法院(2017)辽01民终4433号民事判决书。
② 参见广东省高级人民法院(2018)粤民终765号民事判决书。

当事人的真实意思表示,内容不违反我国法律、行政法规的强制性规定,应为合法有效。在广州白云国际机场股份有限公司与俄罗斯威姆航空公司服务合同纠纷一案①中亦是如此认定。在北京仲裁委员会/北京国际仲裁中心(以下简称"北仲")裁决过的航空地服合同纠纷案件中,包括某航油公司与某航空公司的《航空燃料保障协议》争议案,某航信香港公司与泰国某航空公司的《系统服务协议》争议案,北京某航空服务公司与某公务机公司的《公务机地面服务协议》争议案,仲裁庭的分析意见一般是,上述合同是双方的真实意思表示,属于一般的服务合同,考虑到合同内容不违反中国现行有效的法律和行政法规的强制性规定,亦未发现其他可能导致合同无效的情形,仲裁庭对其效力予以认可。当然,仲裁庭对于上述合同未认定为委托合同,除从合同内容考虑外,更主要的是关注到民航的特殊情况和相关规定。比如《民用机场管理条例》(2019年修订)第21条规定:"机场管理机构应当按照运输机场使用许可证规定的范围开放使用运输机场,不得擅自关闭……机场管理机构拟关闭运输机场的,应当提前45日报颁发运输机场使用许可证的机关,经批准后方可关闭,并向社会公告。"第45条规定:"运输机场航空燃油供应企业停止运输机场航空燃油供应业务的,应当提前90日告知运输机场所在地区民用航空管理机构、机场管理机构和相关航空运输企业。"基于此,笔者认为,航空地服合同不应直接认定为委托合同,合同双方当事人也不享有法定的单方任意合同解除权,而是应根据合同的具体条款和约定确定双方的权利义务。当然,笔者认为,还要考虑到航空公司的服务标准和行业标准的要求,如果机场服务达不到相关服务标准,航空公司应有权单方面解除合同。

二、如何理解航空地服合同中的免责条款

航空地服合同中的责任与赔偿条款(以航空公司与机场公司的合同为例)一般约定:除本合同另有约定外,由于机场公司履行本协议的作为或不作为导致以下情况时,航空公司不应向机场公司提出任何索赔,并补

---

① 参见广州市白云区人民法院(2017)粤0111民初14470号民事判决书。

偿机场公司因履行协议产生的索赔或诉讼而承担的任何法律责任,包括由此产生的任何费用和开支,除非机场公司是故意引起损失、死亡、迟延、伤害或毁损,或者明知可能导致损失、死亡、迟延、伤害或毁损的发生而轻率地作为或不作为:(a)对航空公司承运和将要承运的人员造成的延迟、人身伤害及死亡;(b)航空公司雇员的伤害及死亡;(c)航空公司承运和将要承运的行李、货物或邮件的损失、延迟或丢失;(d)航空公司拥有、使用或在其名义下的财产的毁损、丢失及由此引发的间接的损失或损坏。同时,合同中还约定:上述"航空公司"或"机场公司"的表述,应当包括它们的正式雇员、辅助工作人员、代理人及分包者;而"作为或不作为"包括疏忽大意。

根据上述合同约定,就航空地面代理服务而言,除非索赔或诉讼的法律责任是由于机场公司故意或明知可能造成损失而轻率地作为或不作为造成的,否则航空公司无权要求机场公司承担赔偿责任,给予机场公司全面的免责。笔者认为,由于航空业的高风险、高投入以及高波动等特点,其法定责任均需要通过购买高额保险的方式转移,而相应地,为保障航空运输正常运营的机场、航油、维修等航空服务专业公司则无须为此再重复购买相关保险,仅是收取相对较低的服务代理费用并要求航空公司给予相应免责。航空公司的所有赔偿责任通过航空公司法定责任险予以补偿,这是航空业的内在运行逻辑,也是航空地服合同上述免责的商务基础和约定缘由。即在一般情况下,航空公司均应无条件给予机场公司免责,除非机场公司有合同明确约定的除外情形,即故意或明知可能造成损失而轻率地作为或不作为。那什么是"明知"？什么是"轻率"呢？笔者认为,应根据合同可适用的法律予以解释。不同的国家或地区,不同的法域,对此亦有不同的理解和法律规定,国际社会对此并无统一的适用标准。笔者在此尝试适用中国法律予以解读。我国《民用航空法》第132条规定:"经证明,航空运输中的损失是由于承运人或者其受雇人、代理人的故意或者明知可能造成损失而轻率地作为或者不作为造成的,承运人无权援用本法第一百二十八条、第一百二十九条有关赔偿责任限制的规定……"《海商法》第118条规定:"经证明,旅客的人身伤亡或者行李的灭失、损坏,是由于承运人的故意或者明知可能造成损害而轻率地作为或者不作为造成的,承运人不得援用本法第一百一十六条和第一百一十七条限制赔偿责任的规定……"从我国的司法实践来看,亦有相应的理解或判定。比如《最高人民法院公报》案例(毛雪波诉陈伟、嵊泗县江山海运有限公司船舶碰撞损害责任纠纷案①)载明:"判断海事赔偿责任限制权利是否丧失,应综合考量船舶所有人等责任人本人是否对损害结果的发生具有故意,或者明知可能造成损失而轻率地作为或者不作为。但诸多严重违法航行行为(如无证航行、超航区航行、不办理签证航行、肇事后擅自驶离现场等)的集合和长期、屡次或反复实施,可能足以推定船舶所有人等责任人本身具有重大主观过错。因此,对于严重违法航行的,应当综合行为的内容、性质及违法的严重程度等因素,综合认定责任人是否丧失海事赔偿责任限制权利。"由此可见,法院通过认定"重大主观过错"明确了何为"明知可能造成损失而轻率地作为或者不作为"。又如在某航空公司与机场公司的航空地服合同纠纷一案②中,法院认为:机场公司忽视安全防范,在平台车反复发生的故障未彻底解决,不能保障运行安全和正常使用时,未立即停止使用,违反了《民用机场专用设备使用管理办法》第24条和《民用机场运行安全管理规定》第5条的规定,足以认定机场公司就此事故存在重大过失。由此可见,法院认为"重大过失"属于"明知可能造成损失而轻率地作为或者不作为"情形。再如最高人民法院在某飞机工程公司与某货运航空公司的航空地服合同纠纷终审判决中认为:从飞机维修工程师的上述陈述来看,其对起落架手柄处于收起位置,地面安全锁销被拔除、开启液压按钮,飞机可能会触地是知道的,只不过由于其在操作时没有注意到起落架手柄处于收起位置,而轻率地下令拔除了地面锁销,又接通了液压按钮,从而导致飞机触地,其行为特征符合主协议(即航空地服合同的主协议——笔者注)约定的第二种除外情况,即知道其行为可能造成损坏后果而轻率行事。其作为飞机工程公司的工程师,受飞机工程公司委派对涉案飞机进行维修,飞机工程公司应对其职务行为承担责任,故飞机工程公司不能享有免责的权利。当然,现实情况总是错综复杂的,需要具体问题具体分析。比如2015年12月10日08:03,福州机场运行指挥中心接到福建空管塔台电话通知,在03号跑

---

① 参见上海市高级人民法院(2016)沪民终24号民事判决书。
② 参见海口市中级人民法院(2019)琼01民终2507号民事判决书。

道端头的 CA1822 航班右发动机冒火。08：07 机场消防分部 8 辆消防车赶到现场时发现 03 号跑道端头附近有两架同为波音 737-800 机型的飞机，其中，国航飞机处于关车状态，无异常情况，而旁边的同型号福州航空飞机，其发动机尾喷口有尾气冒出。事发紧急，在当时应急救援的情况下，为确保万无一失，现场消防指挥官即决定对该福州航空飞机进行降温处置。08：09 运行指挥中心发现此情况后，当即通知更正，消防队接到指令后，转向国航飞机进行施救，08：15 现场得到控制①，但是该事件给国航和福州航空均造成了重大损失。依笔者之见，本次事件就是一起典型的涉及多方主体的航空地服合同纠纷，国航以及福州航空的损失是否应由福州机场承担，或者福州机场是否可以免责，需要根据相关事实来分析判断福州机场是否存在"明知可能造成损失而轻率地作为或者不作为"的情形而定。从多起航空地面服务合同案件看，依据中国法律，"故意或者明知可能造成损失而轻率地作为或者不作为"比较接近于《民法典》规定的"故意或者重大过失"。

在北仲审理的上述仲裁案件中，案涉航空地服合同对于上述免责条款还存在一些不同约定，比如约定"因机场公司提供本协议项下的服务造成的一切损失由机场公司承担"。我国《民法典》第 506 条规定："合同中的下列免责条款无效：（一）造成对方人身伤害的；（二）因故意或者重大过失造成对方财产损失的。"故笔者理解，上述赔偿责任一边倒的合同约定可能因违反法律的强制性规定而部分无效。还比如约定"因机场公司故意或重大过失造成的一切损失由机场公司承担；因航空公司故意或重大过失造成的一切损失由航空公司承担"，或者约定"除非机场公司故意或重大过失，一切损失由航空公司承担；除非航空公司故意或重大过失，一切损失由机场公司承担"。根据上述合同约定，笔者认为，对于非航空公司（或者机场公司）一方故意或重大过失造成的损失不能免责，应视为航空公司与机场公司未约定。

航空公司与机场公司之间的责任承担要看其与保险公司之间的保险合同安排，一般情况下，航空公司的保单是覆盖航空服务产业链的，服务

---

① 参见《福州飞北京航班发动机冒火　各方回应处置经过》，载民航资源网（http://news.carnoc.com/list/331/331044.html），访问日期：2022 年 3 月 1 日。

商可以有一定的免责,航空公司和保险公司必须明确免责范围,航空公司和机场公司也需要明确责任范围。

三、航空地服合同纠纷中服务费及代垫费用的事实认定

某航信香港公司与泰国某航空公司的《系统服务协议》争议案以及北京某航空服务公司与某公务机公司的《公务机地面服务协议》争议案均遇到了同样的一个问题。在航空服务过程中,服务方一般会按照合同约定的时间(一般是每个月或者每季度)定期向航空公司发送服务费以及代垫费用(包括代航空公司向其他第三方专业服务公司支付的服务费)账单,有时是通过邮件发送,有时是通过快递寄送。合同一般也会约定航空公司有权在收到费用账单之日起几个工作日内提出异议,服务方如未收到航空公司的异议,则会开具发票向航空公司收取相关费用。前述案件中的双方当事人在合同履行过程中发生争议,其中就包括对于上述费用数额的异议。仲裁庭在审理过程中发现,存在上述问题的原因是多方面的,有的是服务方未按合同约定的方式(比如邮件)将账单按期发送到联系人(合同约定的指定联系人)的指定邮箱或者指定地址;有的是服务方代垫费用支出超出合同约定的范围或者标准,亦未事先取得航空公司的同意,导致航空公司事后不予认可并拒绝支付;有的是航空公司并未在合同约定的异议期间及时向服务方就相关费用的数额或收取标准提出异议,直至仲裁过程中当庭才提出异议,并以未经双方确认为由拒绝支付。比如在北京某航空服务公司与某公务机公司的《公务机地面服务协议》争议案中,合同第7.1条约定:双方结账采用月结的方式,每月15日之前,服务方将账单发给公务机公司,公务机公司在收到账单后5个工作日内予以答复,无回复视为确认账单金额。公务机公司认可服务方与第三方的结算方式,对于账单中公务机公司提出异议的部分,服务方应向公务机公司提供第三方的收费账单、收据、发票,或其他收费记录予以说明,公务机公司不应不合理地拒绝给予确认。双方确认金额后,服务方向公务机公司开具发票,公务机公司将款项以转账方式支付给服务方。第7.6条约定:代垫费用。公务机公司应补偿服务方代垫的其他应由公务机公司支付的费用,包括但不限于政府收费、税费、飞机及客舱清洁费用、飞

机卫星通信费用、数据链费用……以及本协议及其附件规定的除服务费以外的代垫费用。服务方将提供相关单据或其他证明文件证明账单中的实际支出费用。根据上述合同约定,在审理过程中,服务方(航空服务公司)作为申请人向仲裁庭提交证据,用以证明其已经按照合同约定向被申请人(即公务机公司)寄送了代垫费用账单及票据并发送了催款函。公务机公司对账单的送达情况未提出异议,也未向仲裁庭提交其曾经对账单提出过异议的相关证据。根据合同约定,公务机公司应在收到服务方账单后5个工作日内予以答复,无回复视为确认账单金额。最终仲裁庭认为公务机公司未举证证明其在合同履行期间曾经对服务方账单的具体数额以及收取标准提出过异议,故仲裁庭支持了服务方的仲裁请求。当然,鉴于民航业的很多收费标准均系政府指导性价格,比如航油、客桥费、旅客服务费、安检费等专业服务的收费标准,如有民航主管机关不时发布的规范性文件(比如《民用机场收费标准调整方案》等),仲裁庭亦会予以考虑。

航空业的结算系统还不是非常完善,有的业主与服务商之间的结算还停留在手工阶段。国际航协有机票结算系统,希望中国航协尽快完善中国航空业的商业结算系统。

四、航空地服合同的仲裁条款

众所周知,仲裁有很多优点,比如专业、保密、管辖确定、程序灵活、一裁终局、域外执行、允许双方当事人选定仲裁员等,但其前提是合同双方当事人要通过仲裁协议或者合同中的争议解决条款选择仲裁解决方式,并且该仲裁约定必须有效。许多民航企业对商事仲裁了解不够,对仲裁的好处了解不足,甚至连仲裁是什么都不清楚。

在某航空地服合同纠纷仲裁案中,涉案合同第9.1条约定:如双方对协议的内容、表述或履行产生分歧或争议时,双方应尽量采取所有合理的行动争取在双方内部解决。如果未能达成解决方案,协议双方可选择仲裁的方式以解决问题(可以选择一个仲裁员也可选择一个仲裁庭)。如果协议双方不同意采用仲裁方式,则应按照附件B中所指明的所在国家的法律和关于管辖范围之规定,通过诉讼程序解决争议。而双方签署的附件 B 中约定:根据主协议第 9.1 条的规定,本协议的适用法律为中华人民共和国法律,诉争的管辖法院处为空白,双方并未约定。机场公司作为该案的被申请人向受理案件的仲裁委员会提出管辖权异议,认为航空地服合同约定的仲裁条款属于"或裁或审"条款,应无效。最后仲裁委员会授权仲裁庭就此作出决定。仲裁庭审阅上述合同约定后认为,我国《仲裁法》第 16 条规定:"仲裁协议包括合同中订立的仲裁条款和以其他书面方式在纠纷发生前或者纠纷发生后达成的请求仲裁的协议。仲裁协议应当具有下列内容:(一)请求仲裁的意思表示;(二)仲裁事项;(三)选定的仲裁委员会。"第 18 条规定:"仲裁协议对仲裁事项或者仲裁委员会没有约定或者约定不明确的,当事人可以补充协议;达不成补充协议的,仲裁协议无效。"第 20 条规定:"当事人对仲裁协议的效力有异议的,可以请求仲裁委员会作出决定或者请求人民法院作出裁定。一方请求仲裁委员会作出决定,另一方请求人民法院作出裁定的,由人民法院裁定。当事人对仲裁协议的效力有异议,应当在仲裁庭首次开庭前提出。"根据上述法律规定,有效的仲裁协议或者仲裁条款应当具有请求仲裁的意思表示、仲裁事项和选定明确的仲裁机构三项内容。如不具有明确仲裁机构的约定,或者约定不明确,双方又无补充协议给予约定,则该仲裁协议或仲裁条款无效。该案中,航空地服合同(即主协议)中的仲裁条款并未指明仲裁机构,双方在附件 B 中亦未就此达成补充协议,故仲裁条款无效。同时,由于该案涉及的航空地服合同与附件 B 具有同等法律效力,而仲裁条款中包含有"或裁或审"的约定,故其仲裁的约定亦属无效。最终仲裁庭认为受理该案的仲裁委员会对于该案没有管辖权。

此外,在某航空地服合同仲裁案中,涉案合同中约定:适用法国法律,约定的是临时仲裁,双方各选一名仲裁员,首席仲裁员由双方选定的仲裁员共同选定,适用国际航协仲裁委员会仲裁规则。笔者代表的中方航空公司是被申请人,而申请人是法国的一家货运代理公司。在案件审理初期,因申请人未能按期预付全部的仲裁费(主要是三名仲裁员的预估费用),被申请人提出异议,仲裁庭最终以视为申请人撤回仲裁请求为由撤销该案。因为根据国际航协仲裁委员会仲裁规则的规定,仲裁费应由申请人和被申请人各自预付二分之一,如被申请人拒绝预付,则需要由申请人全额预付,否则视为撤回仲裁请求。笔者以此举例是想说明,上述合同约定的临时仲裁因适用法国法律而有效。如果合同约定适用中国法律,目前来看应属于无效。根据我国《涉外民事关系法律适用法》第 18 条的规定,当事人可以协议选择仲裁协议适用的法律。若该案合同当事人约定适用中国法律,则需要根据中国法律确认所涉仲裁条款的效力,即仲裁条款中应具有选定的仲裁委员会,如果对仲裁委员会没有约定的(比如临时仲裁),则仲裁条款无效。

通过分析上述航空地服合同纠纷的仲裁解决,可以看出,中国内地仲裁机构已经基本具备提供高质量国际化航空仲裁服务的条件,而仲裁机构在为中国民航提供专业、高效争议解决服务的同时,也会进一步影响和促进现有航空业规则的设立和完善,进一步提升中国在国际民航界的话语权。民航强国,仲裁助航。

临时仲裁制度及司法审查相关问题研究[*]

刘敬东[**] 刘 艳[***]

摘要：临时仲裁制度是现代国际商事争端解决的重要方式之一，也是各国仲裁法律制度中的重要组成部分。虽然最高人民法院在相关司法意见中规定了在自贸区内先行先试"三特定"的仲裁规则，但鉴于现行《仲裁法》对于临时仲裁制度未予规定，导致临时仲裁在中国落地尚不能得到充分的法律保障，也导致临时仲裁的司法审查与中国现有司法审查制度的衔接、法律救济等方面存在诸多问题。而此次《仲裁法》修改将临时仲裁制度融入我国仲裁法律体系之中必将对我国现有仲裁制度产生积极而深远的影响，也会成为中国的商事仲裁制度接轨世界、日渐成熟的重要标志。笔者以此为背景，从临时仲裁在中国落地的角度出发，分析我国《仲裁法》纳入临时仲裁的必要性和可行性，再结合临时仲裁的特点，研究并探讨与临时仲裁有关的司法审查制度构建问题，为《仲裁法》纳入临时仲裁司法审查制度的路径提出对策和建议。

关键词：临时仲裁；司法审查；仲裁法修改

前 言

根据现行《仲裁法》第16条和第18条的规定，当事人在订立仲裁协

---

[*] 本文完成于2021年8月。
[**] 中国社科院国际法研究所国际经济法室主任、研究员，博士生导师。中国仲裁法学研究会副会长，中国海事仲裁委员会仲裁员。
[***] 中国社科院研究生院国际法专业硕士研究生。

议时,必须有选定的仲裁机构,如果没有选定仲裁机构或者无法达成补充协议的,仲裁协议无效。① 可见,我国《仲裁法》在立法层面只承认机构仲裁,并未规定临时仲裁在我国法域内的适用。对于我国《仲裁法》中未确立临时仲裁制度的原因,全国人大常委会法工委曾作出如下解释:"主要有两个原因:一是在仲裁制度的发展史上是先有临时仲裁,后有机构仲裁,从今后的发展趋势看,临时仲裁已趋于衰落。二是中国设立仲裁的历史较短,只有机构仲裁而没有临时仲裁。"② 对于这样的理由,从一开始就有学者提出反驳:并不能依据临时仲裁的出现早于机构仲裁就认定临时仲裁已经衰落,也不能认为当时不存在临时仲裁,我们以后就不需要临时仲裁。③ 有学者认为,我国的《仲裁法》没有纳入临时仲裁制度,是因为当时中国的客观条件还不成熟;再加上临时仲裁的随意性和私密性等特点,使得我们研究临时仲裁没有可供考察的具体数据,贸然引入临时仲裁会使得该制度在纠纷解决中变得不可控制,大概率会影响司法的公信力。④ 还有学者认为,中国经历了长期的计划经济,经济活动受到政府的严格控制,以当事人自治为基础的临时仲裁与计划经济不相适应,如果允许争端各方由自己选择一名或多名个人来履行准司法职能,并作出一项有待法院执行的决定,那就违背了当时的经济和社会规范。⑤

笔者认为,这些考量都带有时代的印记。在当初我国商事仲裁市场发展尚不成熟、社会诚信制度尚未建立的历史阶段,贸然引进临时仲裁制度确实不利于我国仲裁市场的规制以及商事仲裁制度的发展,但是随着我国仲裁市场的不断健全、当事人主体对仲裁需求的不断增加,特别是在我国法治社会建设取得巨大成就、社会诚信制度日趋完善的今天,引入临时仲裁这一国际流行的仲裁制度,对我国商事仲裁事业的发展有着特殊

---

① 《仲裁法》第 16 条规定:"仲裁协议包括合同中订立的仲裁条款和以其他书面方式在纠纷发生前或者纠纷发生后达成的请求仲裁的协议。仲裁协议应当具有下列内容:(一)请求仲裁的意思表示;(二)仲裁事项;(三)选定的仲裁委员会。"
《仲裁法》第 18 条规定:"仲裁协议对仲裁事项或者仲裁委员会没有约定或者约定不明确的,当事人可以补充协议;达不成补充协议的,仲裁协议无效。"
② 江伟、肖建国主编:《仲裁法》,中国人民大学出版社 2016 年版,第 22 页。
③ 参见江伟、肖建国主编:《仲裁法》,中国人民大学出版社 2016 年版,第 22 页。
④ 参见高菲、徐国建:《中国临时仲裁实务指南》,法律出版社 2017 年版,自序,第 1 页。
⑤ Judy Li Zhu, "Time to Loosen up on Ad Hoc Arbitration in China," *Asian International Arbitration Journal* 15, No. 1(2019): 44.

的重要的意义。因此,应当摒弃过去全然保守的态度,积极推动临时仲裁制度与我国现有仲裁法律制度的融合与衔接。

一、我国临时仲裁制度的晚近探索与实践

2017年《最高人民法院关于为自由贸易试验区建设提供司法保障的意见》(以下简称《意见》)第9条规定了一定范围内的临时仲裁制度(以下简称"三特定")①,这是我国对临时仲裁制度的一次有益尝试。《意见》对临时仲裁作出的重要尝试无疑体现了中央关于自由贸易试验区"先行先试"这一原则精神。

上述意见公布后,据笔者掌握的资料,截至目前,2017年9月上海银行业调解中心完成了首例自贸区临时仲裁案件,2018年4月3日上海银行业调解中心首例跨自贸区临时仲裁案落地。其他一些地方的仲裁机构也作出了相关探索。但实践中,一些仲裁机构对于依据《意见》就临时仲裁制定的仲裁规则是否会被人民法院确认、依据仲裁规则作出的临时仲裁裁决是否会被法院执行等尚存在不小的顾虑,未来需要通过法院受理的具体案例和司法裁决来加以消除。

2017年3月23日,横琴新区管委会和珠海仲裁委员会在横琴自贸片区举行发布会,正式发布《横琴自由贸易试验区临时仲裁规则》(以下简称《横琴规则》)。这是中国首部具体的临时仲裁规则,是对现行商事仲裁规则的重要创新,在中国仲裁发展历史中具有里程碑意义。② 从结构和

---

① 2017年《最高人民法院关于为自由贸易试验区建设提供司法保障的意见》第9条规定:"在自贸试验区内注册的外商独资企业相互之间约定商事争议提交域外仲裁的,不应仅以其争议不具有涉外因素为由认定相关仲裁协议无效。一方或者双方均为在自贸试验区内注册的外商投资企业,约定将商事争议提交域外仲裁,发生纠纷后,当事人将争议提交域外仲裁,相关裁决做出后,其又以仲裁协议无效为由主张拒绝承认、认可或执行的,人民法院不予支持;另一方当事人在仲裁程序中未对仲裁协议效力提出异议,相关裁决作出后,又以有关争议不具有涉外因素为由主张仲裁协议无效,并以此主张拒绝承认、认可或执行的,人民法院不予支持。在自贸试验区内注册的企业相互之间约定在内地特定地点、按照特定仲裁规则、由特定人员对有关争议进行仲裁的,可以认定该仲裁协议有效。人民法院认为该仲裁协议无效的,应报请上一级法院进行审查。上级法院同意下级法院意见的,应将其审查意见层报最高人民法院,待最高人民法院答复后作出裁定。"

② 参见《横琴自贸片区发布实施中国首部临时仲裁规则》,载金投网(http://kuaixun.cngold.org/c/2017-03-23/c530706.html),访问日期:2020年4月30日。

内容上来说,该规则采用机构仲裁与临时仲裁的双轨制模式,一方面强调仲裁机构对临时仲裁的服务功能,另一方面则是在最高人民法院意见的基础上对临时仲裁进行规制,谨慎适用临时仲裁制度,并没有突破《意见》的范围。① 并且,根据该规则第3条第4款的规定,要想选用临时仲裁制度,还必须有明确的选择临时仲裁的意思表示,如果仲裁协议中约定选择适用《珠海仲裁委员会仲裁规则》的,仍旧视为选择机构仲裁。② 这是该规则的一大特色。

2017年9月19日,中国互联网仲裁联盟在广州举行的第七届大中华仲裁论坛上发布了《中国互联网仲裁联盟临时仲裁与机构仲裁对接规则》(以下简称《互联网对接规则》)。③ 在该规则的指导下,联盟负责运营机构仲裁与临时仲裁对接的网络平台(又称"易简网")。④ 该平台的建立是该规则的突出特点,它比起普通的仲裁机构来说覆盖的仲裁员更多,不仅包括联盟仲裁机构的仲裁员,还包括非联盟仲裁机构的仲裁员以及根据我国《仲裁法》或仲裁地法规定的有资格成为仲裁员的人员。⑤ 此外,该规则在制定时就有较强的前瞻性,因为它没有忽视非自贸区注册企业申请临时仲裁的需求以及该类企业向境外申请临时仲裁的现实可能性,也

---

① 参见杨俊:《论"互联网+"时代临时仲裁与机构仲裁的对接路径——以〈横琴自贸区临时仲裁规则〉为切入点》,载《黑龙江省政法管理干部学院学报》2018年第5期。
② 《横琴规则》第3条第4款规定:"当事人协议选定珠海临时仲裁规则、横琴新区临时仲裁规则、珠海仲裁委员会仲裁规则的表述,或者其他可以推断为唯一选定本临时仲裁规则的表述,均视为对本规则的有效选定。当事人约定适用《珠海仲裁委员会仲裁规则》《珠海国际仲裁院仲裁规则》的,不属于临时仲裁,案件应由珠海仲裁委员会或珠海国际仲裁院管辖。"
③ 参见蔡敏捷:《中国互联网仲裁联盟发布临时仲裁规则》,载中国新闻网(http://www.chinanews.com/gn/2017/09-20/8335406.shtml),访问日期:2020年4月30日。
④ 《中国互联网仲裁联盟临时仲裁与机构仲裁对接规则》第3条规定:"中国互联网仲裁联盟(以下简称"联盟")是由仲裁机构、高等院校、律师协会、仲裁员协会以及互联网技术企业等共同组成,旨在实现仲裁机构及相关各界之间交流合作、互联互通、共商共建共享,推动仲裁创新发展的民间组织。联盟设总协调人。互联网仲裁云平台(又称"易简网")由联盟负责运营,是临时仲裁与机构仲裁对接的网络平台,由广州易简在线争端法律服务有限公司提供服务和技术支持。仲裁机构是指根据《中华人民共和国仲裁法》规定由市人民政府组织有关部门和商会统一组建或者由中国国际商会组织设立的中国内地仲裁机构,或者在其他国家、地区依当地法律设立的仲裁机构。"
⑤ 《中国互联网仲裁联盟临时仲裁与机构仲裁对接规则》第7条规定:"易简网设开放且方便当事人选择仲裁员的仲裁员库,仲裁员库由以下人员组成:(一)联盟所有仲裁机构仲裁员名册上的仲裁员;(二)非联盟仲裁机构仲裁员名册上的仲裁员;(三)其他具有《中华人民共和国仲裁法》或者仲裁地法规定的仲裁员资格的人员。"

敏锐地意识到临时仲裁在我国落地的必要性,这是为了方便仲裁裁决的承认与执行。业内普遍认为,该规则是对高科技时代仲裁规则发展的有力推动,但是未来临时仲裁在我国可以独立进行时,该规则就不再有存在的必要,如果在临时仲裁的执行方面,我们仍旧选择需要与仲裁机构对接并获得仲裁机构的确认,则该规则可以被立法者借鉴。①

尽管最高人民法院对临时仲裁作出了有益的尝试,从长远来看,临时仲裁真正能被广泛运用于日常的商事纠纷解决之中,尚需从《仲裁法》层面确立临时仲裁制度,这是解决临时仲裁在我国仲裁法体系中正当地位问题的根本之道。

二、《仲裁法》纳入临时仲裁制度的重要意义

由于长期以来,我国仲裁立法中缺失临时仲裁制度,这种情形对于我国的商事仲裁事业乃至涉外商事争端解决制度构建均产生了不利影响,主要体现在以下三个方面:

1. 事实上造成对外国申请人的超国民待遇

从对临时仲裁裁决相互认可和执行的角度来说,《承认及执行外国仲裁裁决公约》(又称《纽约公约》)中规定的承认与执行外国仲裁裁决的义务包括承认与执行机构仲裁裁决和临时仲裁裁决的内容。② 我国是《纽约公约》的缔约国,对于外国临时仲裁庭作出的仲裁裁决,我国法院有义务承认和执行。我国法院也确实履行了承认和执行外国临时仲裁裁决的义务,例如,2019 年 3 月 23 日,新加坡满升航运有限公司向天津海事法院申请承认和执行仲裁员大卫·法林顿(David Farrington)在伦敦作出的临

---

① 《中国互联网仲裁联盟临时仲裁与机构仲裁对接规则》第 21 条规定:"临时仲裁程序的当事人或仲裁庭可以根据争议解决的需要,按照本规则选择与机构仲裁进行程序或裁决文书的对接。自由贸易试验区内注册企业之间约定按特定规则、特定地点以及特定人员进行的临时仲裁,可以选择与机构仲裁对接,也可以选择不对接。非自由贸易试验区内注册企业的临时仲裁可以通过联盟与机构仲裁进行对接。境外根据临时仲裁程序作出的裁决文书,为便于在国内的承认与执行,可以通过联盟与国内机构仲裁进行对接。"

② 《纽约公约》第 1 条第 2 款规定:"仲裁裁决"不仅包括每一案件中指定的仲裁员所作的裁决,也包括当事人提请常设仲裁机构所作的裁决。

时仲裁裁决①,以及 2018 年 11 月 22 日,瑞典斯万斯克蜂蜜加工公司向江苏省南京市中级人民法院申请承认和执行在瑞典斯德哥尔摩由彼得·索普(Peter Thorp)、斯图雷·拉尔森(Sture Larsson)和尼尔斯·埃利亚松(Nils Eliasson)仲裁员作出的临时仲裁裁决②。对于这两项临时仲裁裁决,我国相关法院根据《纽约公约》第 5 条以及我国《民事诉讼法》和司法解释的相关规定,经司法审查后均支持了申请人的申请,对这两个临时仲裁裁决予以承认和执行。③ 而现实中,我国境内的临时仲裁裁决却长期不被法律认可,更不可能被执行,这就造成了事实上的对外国人的"超国民待遇",也造成了我国享有的条约权利和承担的条约义务不对等的现象。

2.很大程度上妨碍了商事主体自主选择救济方式的权利

当下临时仲裁在我国的存在不是以法律的形式确定下来的,而是体现在《最高人民法院关于为自由贸易试验区建设提供司法保障的意见》和几个仲裁机构颁发的仲裁规则中,而且仅规定了在特定条件下当事人才可以选择临时仲裁解决争端的权利,没有具体规定临时仲裁在实施过程中遇到仲裁协议效力不明、能否采取临时措施以及怎样采取临时措施、裁决作出后遇到执行问题如何解决等具体内容,这就可能导致以《意见》和仲裁规则为依据的临时仲裁在实际操作中的巨大困难。例如,因缺乏法律依据而无法继续进行、仲裁庭因有效的仲裁协议有管辖权而无法操作、法院因仲裁协议有效却无权管辖的双重困境,导致权利人的利益无法得到救济。④ 这无形中减少了当事人可选择的争端解决方式的范围,也给需

---

① 参见天津海事法院(2019)津 72 协外认 1 号民事裁定书。
② 参见江苏省南京市中级人民法院(2018)苏 01 协外认 8 号民事裁定书。
③ 2015 年《最高人民法院关于适用〈中华人民共和国民事诉讼法〉的解释》第 545 条规定:"对临时仲裁庭在中华人民共和国领域外作出的仲裁裁决,一方当事人向人民法院申请承认和执行的,人民法院应当依照民事诉讼法第二百八十三条规定处理。"
2017 年修正的《民事诉讼法》第 283 条规定:"国外仲裁机构的裁决,需要中华人民共和国人民法院承认和执行的,应当由当事人直接向被执行人住所地或者其财产所在地的中级人民法院申请,人民法院应当依照中华人民共和国缔结或者参加的国际条约,或者按照互惠原则办理。"
④ 参见孙巍:《中国临时仲裁的最新发展及制度完善建议——〈最高人民法院关于为自由贸易试验区建设提供司法保障的意见〉与〈横琴自由贸易试验区临时仲裁规则〉解读》,载北京仲裁委员会、北京国际仲裁中心组编:《北京仲裁》(第 101 辑),中国法制出版社2017 年版。

要临时仲裁的当事人增加了解决争端的成本——被迫转为诉讼或者到境外进行临时仲裁①,这并不利于我国仲裁事业的发展。

3. 对"一带一路"商事争端解决机制的完整性产生影响

为推进"一带一路"法治化体系构建,中国应推动建立完善的"一带一路"商事争端解决机制,临时仲裁作为一种非常重要的争端解决方式,是国际商事领域中商事主体的一个重要选择,是"一带一路"商事争端解决中不可或缺的重要制度内涵。纵观"一带一路"沿线主要伙伴国家,我国《仲裁法》正处于《联合国国际贸易法委员会国际商事仲裁示范法》(以下简称《示范法》)法域的"包围圈"内。其中,颇具影响力的新加坡等,更是有基于《示范法》而又超越《示范法》的态势,这体现在它们的立法正不断触及《示范法》所未涉及的领域。相比之下,我国《仲裁法》已然滞后,其中尚有诸多有待"升级"之处。② 临时仲裁制度的缺失,正是我国《仲裁法》相对滞后的一个重要因素。

如果未来长时间内不从立法上确立临时仲裁制度,我国将会丧失与临时仲裁相关的法律服务市场,失去维护我国公民和企业合法权利的一种重要途径,对于构建"一带一路"商事争端解决机制显然不利。为了更好地打造辐射全球的亚太仲裁中心和维护我国当事人的合法利益,"升级"我国的《仲裁法》,纳入临时仲裁的内容是非常重要的第一步。

鉴于以上考虑,目前正在修订的我国《仲裁法》应当将临时仲裁制度纳入其中,将其作为与机构仲裁并行的一种仲裁方式,为商事主体提供更多的商事纠纷解决方案和途径。此外,纳入这一制度,对于我国仲裁事业的国际化、现代化并提升中国在国际仲裁领域的话语权具有重要意义,主要体现为:

第一,有利于推动《中共中央办公厅、国务院办公厅关于完善仲裁制度提高仲裁公信力的若干意见》(以下简称《两办意见》)和"中国仲裁2022方案"的贯彻落实。2018年9月10日,我国《仲裁法》的修改已经列

---

① 参见李广辉、王瀚:《仲裁法》,对外经济贸易大学出版社2011年版,第19页。
② 参见王徽:《〈国际商事仲裁示范法〉的创设、影响及启示》,载《武大国际法评论》2019年第3期。

入第十三届全国人大常委会立法规划第二类项目中。① 借此次《仲裁法》修改之际将临时仲裁制度纳入我国仲裁法律体系,有利于积极推动《两办意见》②的贯彻落实和"中国仲裁 2022 方案"的快速实施,健全完善仲裁工作体制机制,不断丰富仲裁服务方式,加快建成具有区域乃至全球影响力的仲裁中心。

第二,有利于推动我国的民商事纠纷解决体系与国际接轨,提升商事纠纷解决制度的国际化程度。将临时仲裁制度纳入我国的仲裁法律体系,有利于推动我国的纠纷解决方式与国际纠纷解决方式的接轨,提高我国处理商事纠纷的国际化程度,推动中国商事仲裁制度的国际化,在"一带一路"建设过程中更好地发出中国声音③,加快打造面向全球的亚太仲裁中心,进而有助于吸引更多的外国投资者和资本进入中国市场。④

第三,有利于更好地履行国际条约义务,展现我国积极履行国际法义务的大国形象,充分维护我国商事主体的合法权益。在《纽约公约》中,临时仲裁是一项重要的国际仲裁形式,将临时仲裁制度及时纳入我国《仲裁法》也是我国全方位履行《纽约公约》的重要体现。同时,也能打破外国公民和企业在中国临时仲裁领域的超国民待遇,更好地维护我国当事人的合法权益,从法律依据上彻底改变当下我国法院只能承认和执行国外的临时仲裁裁决而无法执行国内临时仲裁裁决的尴尬局面。

第四,有利于完善我国国内现有民商事司法体系,化解法院在民商事领域面临的巨大案件压力,减轻法院负担,及时解决民商事纠纷。对

---

① 第十三届全国人大常委会立法规划第二类项目是指需要抓紧工作、条件成熟时提请审议的法律草案,《仲裁法》修改在此类列表中排在第 46 位,由国务院牵头。参见《十三届全国人大常委会立法规划》,载全国人大网(http://www.npc.gov.cn/npc/c30834/201809/f9bff485a57f498e8d5e22e0b56740f6.shtml),访问日期:2020 年 3 月 27 日。

② 2018 年 12 月 31 日,《中共中央办公厅、国务院办公厅关于完善仲裁制度提高仲裁公信力的若干意见》提出完善司法支持监督机制的要求:人民法院要积极支持仲裁事业发展,建立与仲裁委员会之间的工作协调机制,及时沟通有关情况,提高审理有关仲裁司法审查案件的效率。改革完善司法监督机制,完善仲裁法相关司法解释,规范仲裁协议效力的认定、仲裁保全、裁决撤销和不予执行程序,依法支持和监督仲裁。

③ 参见王徽:《〈国际商事仲裁示范法〉的创设、影响及启示》,载《武大国际法评论》2019 年第 3 期。

④ See Song Lianbin, Zhao Jian and Li Hong, "Approaches to the Revision of the 1994 Arbitration Act of the People's Republic of China," *Journal of International Arbitration* 20, No. 2 (2003): 186.

国内司法环境来说,将临时仲裁制度纳入我国的纠纷解决法律体系,一方面有利于缓解司法资源紧张的压力,拓宽解决纠纷的方式,加快构建完善的民商事纠纷解决体系;另一方面也有利于促进我国当事人在国内以临时仲裁的方式解决纠纷,节约纠纷解决的时间和宝贵的司法资源。

三、建立临时仲裁司法审查制度的若干建议

仲裁之所以能够有效地发挥司法解决纠纷的替代作用,就在于仲裁裁决的执行力,而这种执行力是以国家强制力为保障的,构建一套完整的仲裁司法审查体制对于临时仲裁而言十分必要。[①] 司法审查就是司法对仲裁的监督和保障,监督主要体现在司法对仲裁的合法性审查,保障主要体现在司法对仲裁程序的协助和对当事人权利的救济。这一原理同样适用于临时仲裁制度。

为了实现临时仲裁与机构仲裁的有机融合,践行"友好仲裁"的理念,笔者研究了临时仲裁制度中关于司法审查制度的若干重要问题,并提出相关建议。

(一)临时仲裁协议效力审查方面

仲裁协议效力是仲裁合法性的前提,这对于临时仲裁制度而言更显重要和突出,根据我国现行《仲裁法》理论及实践,结合临时仲裁的特点,笔者认为,应当在审查临时仲裁协议效力方面作出以下完善和努力:

1. 取消仲裁机构所在地作为管辖连接点

我国现行《仲裁法》是以仲裁机构所在地为司法管辖连接点的,具体而言,2006年《最高人民法院关于适用〈中华人民共和国仲裁法〉若干问题的解释》第12条对确认仲裁协议效力案件的管辖权分配采取了"内外

---

① 参见张卫平:《现行仲裁执行司法监督制度结构的反思与调整——兼论仲裁裁决不予执行制度》,载《现代法学》2020年第1期。

有别"的做法。① 换言之,对于国内的仲裁裁决优先由仲裁机构所在地的中级人民法院管辖,仲裁机构不明确的才选择仲裁协议签订地或者被申请人住所地的中级人民法院管辖;对于涉外仲裁裁决,则是三个连接点选其一即可。② 之后,2017年《最高人民法院关于审理仲裁司法审查案件若干问题的规定》第2条对有管辖权的法院作了趋同化的处理,但是仍旧将仲裁机构所在地作为一个连接点。③

笔者认为,仲裁机构所在地是在特殊时期专门针对机构仲裁设立的连接点,在建立临时仲裁制度之后,应将仲裁地作为机构仲裁与临时仲裁的连接点,这既有利于降低当事人的维权成本,也有利于加快中国与国际接轨的进程。

2.充分赋予仲裁庭自裁管辖权

中国在国际法层面对自裁管辖权原则采取了肯定的态度,这一点主要体现在中国所加入的国际条约中。④ 例如,中国在加入《关于解决国家和他国国民之间投资争端公约》时并未对该公约中的自裁管辖权提出保留。⑤ 但是,根据《仲裁法》第20条的规定,有权确定仲裁协议效力的是仲裁委员会和人民法院,即该法并未赋予仲裁庭自裁管辖权。虽然在实

---

① 2006年《最高人民法院关于适用〈中华人民共和国仲裁法〉若干问题的解释》第12条规定:"当事人向人民法院申请确认仲裁协议效力的案件,由仲裁协议约定的仲裁机构所在地的中级人民法院管辖;仲裁协议约定的仲裁机构不明确的,由仲裁协议签订地或者被申请人住所地的中级人民法院管辖。申请确认涉外仲裁协议效力的案件,由仲裁协议约定的仲裁机构所在地、仲裁协议签订地、申请人或者被申请人住所地的中级人民法院管辖。涉及海事海商纠纷仲裁协议效力的案件,由仲裁协议约定的仲裁机构所在地、仲裁协议签订地、申请人或者被申请人住所地的海事法院管辖;上述地点没有海事法院的,由就近的海事法院管辖。"

② 参见朱华芳:《2019年度仲裁司法审查实践观察报告——主题一:确认仲裁协议效力制度实践观察》,载微信公众号天同诉讼圈2020年3月23日(https://mp.weixin.qq.com/s/bSjOUG7L45htll BDDGPDA),访问日期:2020年5月7日。

③ 2017年《最高人民法院关于审理仲裁司法审查案件若干问题的规定》第2条规定:"申请确认仲裁协议效力的案件,由仲裁协议约定的仲裁机构所在地、仲裁协议签订地、申请人住所地、被申请人住所地的中级人民法院或者专门人民法院管辖。涉及海事海商纠纷仲裁协议效力的案件,由仲裁协议约定的仲裁机构所在地、仲裁协议签订地、申请人住所地、被申请人住所地的海事法院管辖;上述地点没有海事法院的,由就近的海事法院管辖。"

④ 《关于解决国家和他国国民之间投资争端公约》第41条第2款规定:"争端一方提出的反对意见,认为该争端不属于中心的管辖范围,或因其他原因不属于仲裁庭的权限范围,仲裁庭应加以考虑,并决定是否将其作为先决问题处理,或与该争端的是非曲直一并处理。"

⑤ 参见霍伟:《论仲裁自裁管辖权原则》,中国仲裁与司法论坛暨2010年年会会议论文,重庆,2010,第191页。

践中,仲裁委员会更多的是以仲裁规则为媒介,将该权限转授权给仲裁庭,但仲裁庭确定仲裁协议效力仍缺乏直接的法律依据。① 从实践角度来说,如果直接赋予仲裁庭自裁管辖权还有诸多方面隐忧的话,可以在赋予仲裁庭自裁管辖权之后给予一定程度的司法监督,有些国家或地区在确立仲裁庭的自裁管辖权方面也采取了类似的路径。

例如,新加坡法律对自裁管辖权增加了一次到法院起诉的机会。若当事人不服仲裁庭的自裁管辖权结果,可先向新加坡高等法院提起诉讼。若不服新加坡高等法院的裁判,当事人还可以向新加坡上诉法院提起二审。② 此外,《示范法》第 16 条第 3 款规定:"……仲裁庭作为一个初步问题裁定其拥有管辖权的,任何一方当事人可在收到裁定通知后三十天内请求第 6 条规定的法院对此事项作出决定,该决定不得上诉;在对该请求未决期间,仲裁庭可以继续进行仲裁程序和作出裁决。"

我国可以根据仲裁实践发展的需要以及实际情况,参考以上成功经验,综合考量仲裁员的素质以及仲裁的效率问题,在法律中确立仲裁庭的自裁管辖权,同时对自裁管辖权司法监督的程序作出法律规定。

3. 明确有效临时仲裁协议的构成要件

仲裁协议包括合同中订立的仲裁条款和以其他书面方式在纠纷发生前或者纠纷发生后达成的请求仲裁的协议。《仲裁法》第 16—18 条从正反两个方面规定了有效仲裁协议的构成要件和排除要件,这也是《仲裁法》确立机构仲裁的重要基础。为了引入临时仲裁的内容,同样可以从这里入手,删除法条中关于必须选定仲裁机构的强制性规定,不再严格区分机构仲裁和临时仲裁,将目前适用于机构仲裁的制度直接适用于临时仲裁。

事实上,《新加坡国际仲裁法》、2001 年我国台湾地区"仲裁法"、1923 年《仲裁条款议定书》及《示范法》等法律文件都是以同一方式确立机构仲裁和临时仲裁协议效力的,不同之处就在于,我国台湾地区"仲裁法"要求书面仲裁协议的存在且要求约定仲裁员或者仲裁庭;《新加坡国际仲裁法》强调只要一方声称存在仲裁协议而另一方未作出相反的意思表示,则

---

① 参见王徽:《〈国际商事仲裁示范法〉的创设、影响及启示》,载《武大国际法评论》2019 年第 3 期。

② 参见王徽:《〈国际商事仲裁示范法〉的创设、影响及启示》,载《武大国际法评论》2019 年第 3 期。

可证明存在有效的仲裁协议且不要求仲裁协议在固定的文件中①;《示范法》对仲裁协议的要求更为宽松,即便是以口头形式订立也有机会获得认可。根据国际惯例,如果当事人表现出仲裁意愿,则协议有效。② 并且,当事人之间的仲裁协议,只要不违反有关法律的强制性规定,不损害第三方或公共政策,就应受到尊重。③

为了进一步营造仲裁友好型司法环境,《仲裁法》的修改可以以此为导向——不再严格区分机构仲裁和临时仲裁,并且规定,当事人之间的仲裁协议不论以何种形式存在,只要不违反有关法律的强制性规定,不损害第三方或公共政策均应予以司法认可。

(二) 撤销和不予执行临时仲裁裁决案件审查方面

目前国内仲裁法律体系中对仲裁的救济途径是从撤销或者不予执行仲裁裁决的角度出发的,并且,根据我国《仲裁法》第9条的规定,撤销仲裁裁决与不予执行仲裁裁决效果一致,即当事人可以起诉,也可以重新达成仲裁协议去申请仲裁。

根据国际上的普遍观点,仲裁裁决被撤销的效果是仲裁裁决自始无效,无论是国内还是国外,裁决都没有被执行的可能性,除非申请执行法院认为被撤销的仲裁裁决仍旧可以被执行。当然,被撤销的仲裁裁决与不予执行的仲裁裁决二者之间在法律后果上还是有区别的。一般而言,不予执行仲裁裁决的效果是裁决只是在申请执行地法院不被执行,如果申请到其他国家或者地区法院执行,只要有可供执行的财产且财产所在地法院同意执行,被申请人的财产就会被执行。因此,不予执行的效力只发生在一国境内,而被撤销仲裁裁决的效力发生在本国境内以及不承

---

① 《新加坡国际仲裁法》中规定:"在仲裁或法律程序中,如当事一方在诉讼文书、申诉书或任何其他文件中声称仲裁协议存在,在该声称必须回应而当事他方未予否认的情况下,将被视为当事各方之间存有有效仲裁协议。"

② 《联合国国际贸易法委员会国际商事仲裁示范法》第7条第2款和第3款规定:"仲裁协议应为书面形式。仲裁协议的内容以任何形式记录下来的,即为书面形式,无论该仲裁协议或合同是以口头方式、行为方式还是其他方式订立的。"

③ See Song Lianbin, Zhao Jian and Li Hong, "Approaches to the Revision of the 1994 Arbitration Act of the People's Republic of China," *Journal of International Arbitration* 20, No. 2 (2003): 174.

认被撤销仲裁裁决效力的国家。

很明显,我国的情况是,二者之间没有效果上的明显不同,被撤销和不予执行的仲裁裁决均自始无效,都可以申请重新仲裁或者起诉。有学者认为,不予执行制度对国外仲裁裁决才有意义,因为国外仲裁员或者仲裁庭作出的裁决有可能违反我国法律或社会公共利益,从维护我国法律和社会公共利益的角度,我国有权拒绝执行该国外仲裁裁决。但对于国内仲裁裁决,不予执行制度就没有意义了,完全可以通过撤销仲裁裁决制度来防止不合法仲裁裁决的存在,也就实现了不予执行制度所要达到的救济目的。[1] 从这个角度来说,应将撤销与不予执行作为两种不同的制度区分开,对于国内仲裁裁决仅设立撤销制度,而对国外裁决和涉外裁决设立承认与不予执行两项制度。

但是,我国仲裁法律体系通过《最高人民法院关于人民法院办理仲裁裁决执行案件若干问题的规定》第18条赋予了案外人申请不予执行仲裁裁决的权利救济机制,并且《仲裁法》第58条以"穷尽式"列举的方式否认了案外人申请撤销仲裁裁决的权利,如果在执行程序中取消案外人申请不予执行的权利,则必然导致一些案外人失去维护自身合法权益的救济机制。[2] 因此,能否仅用撤销的方式取代不予执行国内仲裁裁决仍旧是一个需要认真考虑的问题。

2006年《最高人民法院关于适用〈中华人民共和国仲裁法〉若干问题的解释》第21条规定,在当事人伪造证据或者隐瞒重要证据的情况下,法院有权决定是否让仲裁机构重新仲裁,这在一定程度上是司法对当事人仲裁权利的保护。[3] 但对于临时仲裁裁决来说,法院能否以这种理由要求

---

[1] 参见张卫平:《现行仲裁执行司法监督制度结构的反思与调整——兼论仲裁裁决不予执行制度》,载《现代法学》2020年第1期。

[2] 《最高人民法院关于人民法院办理仲裁裁决执行案件若干问题的规定》第18条规定:"案外人根据本规定第九条申请不予执行仲裁裁决或者仲裁调解书,符合下列条件的,人民法院应当支持:(一)案外人系权利或者利益的主体;(二)案外人主张的权利或者利益合法、真实;(三)仲裁案件当事人之间存在虚构法律关系,捏造案例事实的情形;(四)仲裁裁决主文或者仲裁调解书处理当事人民事权利义务的结果部分或者全部错误,损害案外人合法权益。"

[3] 2006年《最高人民法院关于适用〈中华人民共和国仲裁法〉若干问题的解释》第21条规定:"当事人申请撤销国内仲裁裁决的案件属于下列情形之一的,人民法院可以依照仲裁法第六十一条的规定通知仲裁庭在一定期限内重新仲裁:(一)仲裁裁决所根据的证据是伪造的;(二)对方当事人隐瞒了足以影响公正裁决的证据的。人民法院应当在通知中说明要求重新仲裁的具体理由。"

仲裁员或者仲裁庭重新仲裁是有待考量的。就临时仲裁来说,是没有仲裁机构的,仲裁员的选择可能是随机和瞬时的,仲裁庭在仲裁裁决作出之后即解散。如果法院以当事人伪造证据或者隐瞒重要证据为由决定让仲裁庭重新仲裁,一方面会增加当事人的维权成本,另一方面也会违背当事人选择临时仲裁的初衷。因此,上述关于"重新仲裁"的规定能否适用于临时仲裁是值得商榷的。

在司法审查问题上,《仲裁法》设定的审查标准对临时仲裁和机构仲裁应当是一致的。此前已有先例,例如,裁定不予执行涉港澳台仲裁裁决的理由分布在 2000 年《最高人民法院关于内地与香港特别行政区相互执行仲裁裁决的安排》第 7 条①、2007 年《最高人民法院关于内地与澳门特别行政区相互认可和执行仲裁裁决的安排》第 7 条和 2015 年《最高人民法院关于认可和执行台湾地区仲裁裁决的规定》第 14 条中,这些规定基本上都是对《示范法》的转述,并没有严格区分机构仲裁和临时仲裁。

对于外国临时仲裁裁决,我国履行了《纽约公约》的义务,在《最高人民法院关于适用〈中华人民共和国民事诉讼法〉的解释》第 543 条②中规定了对外国临时仲裁裁决的处理参照《民事诉讼法》第 290 条,即对外国临时仲裁裁决和外国机构仲裁裁决均按照国际条约或者互惠原则办

---

① 2000 年《最高人民法院关于内地与香港特别行政区相互执行仲裁裁决的安排》第 7 条规定:"在内地或者香港特区申请执行的仲裁裁决,被申请人接到通知后,提出证据证明有下列情形之一的,经审查核实,有关法院可裁定不予执行:(一)仲裁协议当事人依对其适用的法律属于某种无行为能力的情形;或者该项仲裁协议依约定的准据法无效;或者未指明以何种法律为准时,依仲裁裁决地的法律是无效的;(二)被申请人未接到指派仲裁员的适当通知,或者因他故未能陈述意见的;(三)裁决所处理的争议不是交付仲裁的标的或者不在仲裁协议条款之内,或者裁决载有关于交付仲裁范围以外事项的决定;但交付仲裁事项的决定可与未交付仲裁的事项划分时,裁决中关于交付仲裁事项的决定部分应当予以执行;(四)仲裁庭的组成或者仲裁庭程序与当事人之间的协议不符,或者在有关当事人没有这种协议时与仲裁地的法律不符的;(五)裁决对当事人尚无约束力,或者业经仲裁地的法院或者按仲裁地的法律撤销或者停止执行的。有关法院认定依执行地法律,争议事项不能以仲裁解决的,则可不予执行该裁决。内地法院认定在内地执行该仲裁裁决违反内地社会公共利益,或者香港特区法院决定在香港特区执行该仲裁裁决违反香港特区的公共政策,则可不予执行该裁决。"

② 《最高人民法院关于适用〈中华人民共和国民事诉讼法〉的解释》第 543 条规定:"对临时仲裁庭在中华人民共和国领域外作出的仲裁裁决,一方当事人向人民法院申请承认和执行的,人民法院应当依照民事诉讼法第二百九十条规定处理。"

理,符合国际上的通行做法,继续沿用即可。①

(三)临时仲裁制度中的临时措施方面

我国法律体系中并没有引入临时措施这一术语,而是将类似于"临时措施"的保全措施分散规定于《仲裁法》《民事诉讼法》等法律和相关司法解释中。目前,其他各国对此也没有统一的称谓,或称中间裁决,或称临时性的保护措施、临时裁决、强制性命令等。② 但是无论何种称谓,"临时措施"的目的和性质是一样的,都是为了临时救济当事人的利益。

1976年《联合国国际贸易法委员会仲裁规则》第26条规定的临时措施仅仅涉及对标的物的保全。③ 1985年《示范法》对临时措施作出了更为具体全面的规定:从程序上来说包括仲裁庭下令采取临时措施的权力、准予采取临时措施的条件、初步命令的申请和下达初步命令的条件、担保、披露、费用与损害赔偿、临时措施的承认与执行、拒绝承认或执行临时措施的理由、法院下令采取的临时措施等④;从内容上来说,包括财产保全、行为保全、证据保全等⑤。《香港仲裁条例》中规定的临时措施基本采用

---

① 《民事诉讼法》第290条规定:"国外仲裁机构的裁决,需要中华人民共和国人民法院承认和执行的,应当由当事人直接向被执行人住所地或者其财产所在地的中级人民法院申请,人民法院应当依照中华人民共和国缔结或者参加的国际条约,或者按照互惠原则办理。"

② 参见杜玉琼、林福辰:《"一带一路"背景下我国国际商事仲裁临时措施制度的立法及完善》,载《西南民族大学学报(人文社科版)》2018年第10期。

③ 1976年《联合国国际贸易法委员会仲裁规则》第26条规定:"应当事人任何一方的要求,仲裁庭认为有必要时,得对争议标的采取任何临时措施,包括成为争议标的货物的保存在内,诸如将货物交由第三者保存或出售易损的货品。这些临时性的措施得以临时性裁决的方式为之。仲裁庭有权要求为这些措施的费用提供保证。"

④ 《联合国国际贸易法委员会国际商事仲裁示范法》第17J条规定了法院下令采取的临时措施:法院发布与仲裁程序有关的临时措施的权力应当与法院在诉讼程序方面的权力相同,不论仲裁程序的进行地是否在本国境内。法院应当根据自己的程序,在考虑到国际仲裁的具体特征的情况下行使这一权力。

⑤ 《联合国国际贸易法委员会国际商事仲裁示范法》第17条规定:"(1)除非当事人另有约定,仲裁庭经一方当事人请求,可以准予采取临时措施。(2)临时措施是以裁决书为形式的或另一种形式的任何短期措施,仲裁庭在发出最后裁定争议的裁决书之前任何时候,以这种措施责令一方当事人实施以下任何行为:(a)在争议得以裁定之前维持现状或恢复原状;(b)采取行动防止目前或即将对仲裁程序发生的危害或损害,或不采取可能造成这种危害或损害的行动;(c)提供一种保全资产以执行后继裁决的手段;(d)保全对解决争议可能具有相关性和重要性的证据。"

了《示范法》的规定,但排除了对第 17I 条(拒绝和承认临时措施的理由)和第 17J 条的适用(法院下令采取的临时措施)。

此外,若根据有权作出临时措施决定的主体进行划分,可以把实施"临时措施"的国家或地区分为三类,第一类是只有法院有权作出临时措施决定的,第二类是法院和仲裁庭均可以决定的,第三类是只有仲裁庭有作出采取临时措施的权力,必要时可以辅以法院的审查。根据我国《仲裁法》的规定,在我国,有权作出此类措施决定的主体只能是人民法院。

1. 临时仲裁财产保全的启动

根据我国法律规定,仲裁前申请财产保全,不需要通过仲裁机构向法院申请;如果仲裁中申请财产保全,则需要通过仲裁机构向法院申请。① 但是对于临时仲裁来说,没有仲裁机构,只有仲裁庭或者仲裁员,所以,目前在我国法院申请临时仲裁中的财产保全是没有法律依据的。②《最高人民法院关于人民法院办理财产保全案件若干问题的规定》(以下简称《财产保全规定》)第 3 条规定,仲裁当事人不能直接向人民法院递交财产保全申请书,必须通过仲裁机构向人民法院提交申请,仲裁委员会应将当事人的申请按照民事诉讼法的有关规定提交人民法院。仲裁委员会在当事人和人民法院之间充当了"申请资料传递者"的角色,没有实质审查权,更无权决定是否准许。③

如果《仲裁法》纳入临时仲裁制度,则必须考虑改变仲裁机构"申请资料传递者"的角色,规定只要仲裁庭作出决定,人民法院就应当裁定执行,或者改变这种"申请资料传递者"为仲裁财产保全服务者,例如《横琴规则》第 13 条第 4 款规定:"当事人申请保全的,可以直接或通过仲裁庭向有管辖权的法院提出,当事人申请保全需要仲裁机构配合的,可向指定仲裁员机构提出请求,指定仲裁员机构不是仲裁机构或者不履行职责

---

① 参见陈彤彤:《如何申请仲裁财产保全》,载微信公众号朝律青声说 2019 年 7 月 15 日(https://mp.weixin.qq.com/s/vG7Mxab5pmxLlc8z0tZdoQ),访问日期:2020 年 5 月 7 日。

② 参见孙巍:《中国临时仲裁的最新发展及制度完善建议——〈最高人民法院关于为自由贸易试验区建设提供司法保障的意见〉与〈横琴自由贸易试验区临时仲裁规则〉解读》,载北京仲裁委员会、北京国际仲裁中心组编:《北京仲裁》(第 101 辑),中国法制出版社 2017 年版。

③ 参见赵奇、詹晖、王瑞华:《商事仲裁财产保全机制之完善》,载北京仲裁委员会、北京国际仲裁中心组编:《北京仲裁》(第 107 辑),中国法制出版社 2019 年版。

的,由珠海仲裁委员会承担该项职责。"在这里,仲裁机构成为财产保全的服务者。

2. 申请临时仲裁财产保全要提交的材料

《民事诉讼法》及其司法解释虽然规定了当事人可以申请财产保全,但是并未规定当事人申请财产保全需要递交何种材料。《仲裁法》也规定了当事人可以申请财产保全,但也没有明确要提交的具体材料。较为明确的是《财产保全规定》第 1 条:"当事人、利害关系人申请财产保全,应当向人民法院提交申请书,并提供相关证据材料。申请书应当载明下列事项:(一)申请保全人与被保全人的身份、送达地址、联系方式;(二)请求事项和所根据的事实与理由;(三)请求保全数额或者争议标的;(四)明确的被保全财产信息或者具体的被保全财产线索;(五)为财产保全提供担保的财产信息或资信证明,或者不需要提供担保的理由;(六)其他需要载明的事项。"该规定对申请财产保全应当提交的材料采取了未穷尽列举的方式,在实际操作中,人民法院有诸多可自由裁量空间,因此,就出现了实践中各地法院对相关材料的要求多有不同,审查标准不尽统一且无法通过公开渠道获取各地法院的审查标准的现象,导致当事人递交的材料难以一次性满足要求,退回材料、不予立案的情形时有发生,严重影响纠纷解决的效率。[1] 更重要的是,该规定并非专门针对仲裁财产保全,我们可以借《仲裁法》修改之时机,明确包括临时仲裁财产保全在内的仲裁财产保全应提交的材料,降低实际操作的难度。

近年来,一些仲裁机构的仲裁规则中列明了需要提交的相关材料,比如《中国(上海)自由贸易试验区仲裁规则》第 19 条第 2 款规定了临时仲裁申请人向仲裁委员会申请协助时要提交的材料:"1. 仲裁协议;2. 符合本规则第二十条第(一)款规定的临时措施申请书。仲裁委员会经审查后认为可以协助的,应在收到前述文件之日起 3 日内将该文件转交具有管辖权的法院,并通知临时措施申请人。"第 20 条第 1 款规定了申请书应当包括的内容:"1. 当事人的名称和住所;2. 申请临时措施的理由;3. 申请的具体临时措施;4. 临时措施执行地及具有管辖权的法院;5. 临时措施执行

---

[1] 参见赵奇:《商事仲裁财产保全的流程、问题与完善》,载《人民法院报》2019 年 10 月 10 日,第 8 版。

地有关法律规定。"这些对申请材料的规定,可以为我们在今后立法时提供借鉴。

3.确立仲裁庭对财产保全的决定权

《示范法》第17H条第1款规定:"仲裁庭发出的临时措施应当被确认为具有约束力,并且除非仲裁庭另有规定,应当在遵从第17I条各项规定的前提下,经向有管辖权的法院提出申请后加以执行,不论该措施是在哪一国发出的。"我国法律规定,只能由人民法院作出保全的决定并据此执行,而仲裁庭则无此项权力。

虽然《示范法》不具有强制执行力,但是很多国家的仲裁法都是在《示范法》的基础上变通而来的,这造成了我国国内法和国际通行规则的冲突,外国仲裁庭作出的采取临时措施的决定在我国法院该如何执行就成为一个亟待解决的法律难题。如果全然否定外国仲裁庭作出的临时措施决定,不予承认与执行,则不利于友好仲裁环境的构建,增加当事人的维权成本。但是如果承认与执行外国仲裁庭作出的临时措施决定而不执行我国临时仲裁庭的临时措施决定,势必会失去一定的仲裁服务市场。因此,在一定程度上赋予仲裁庭财产保全的决定权是必要的。

此外,将仲裁程序的保全决定权全部或部分前移至仲裁庭,一方面,可以更准确地判断是否确有必要作出保全措施,也可以减少当事人申请仲裁保全在仲裁机构和法院之间的流转成本,减轻法院审查仲裁保全的工作压力,分流法院的执行工作。① 另一方面,也可以更好地满足当事人对保密性和效率的要求,在国际商事仲裁中以更中立的角度作出决定。② 在近年来的仲裁实践中,一些仲裁机构的仲裁规则为了对接国际,已经将该权力部分"分给"了"紧急仲裁庭(员)",比如《中国(上海)自由贸易试验区仲裁规则》第三章规定的临时措施,包括临时措施的范围、仲裁前的临时措施、仲裁程序中的临时措施、紧急仲裁庭、临时措施决定的作出、临时措施决定的变更和临时措施决定的遵守。《中国海事仲

---

① 参见赵奇、詹晖、王瑞华:《商事仲裁财产保全机制之完善》,载北京仲裁委员会、北京国际仲裁中心组编:《北京仲裁》(第107辑),中国法制出版社2019年版。
② 参见桑远棵:《国际仲裁中紧急仲裁员程序研究》,载朱文浩主编:《中财法律评论》(第10卷),中国法制出版社2018年版,第125页。

裁委员会仲裁规则》也作出了类似的规定,将临时措施的决定权一部分赋予仲裁庭或者仲裁员,但这种紧急仲裁员制度只是针对在仲裁庭组成之前发生的特殊情况,在仲裁程序中如果发生特殊情况,仲裁庭或者仲裁员有没有决定权,该规则并没有作出规定。

4. 商事仲裁证据保全和行为保全

对于商事仲裁的证据保全和行为保全,我国《仲裁法》和《民事诉讼法》及其相关司法解释中规定的是比较少的,只是在《仲裁法》第68条规定了涉外仲裁证据保全的管辖法院①,在《民事诉讼法》第84条规定了可以申请仲裁前证据保全的情形,在《民事诉讼法》第103条规定了当事人可以申请行为保全的情形和条件②,在《著作权法》第50条规定了可以申请行为保全的情形③。但《民事诉讼法》和《著作权法》规定的行为保全能否适用于仲裁领域,相关法律并没有明确的规定。

鉴于此,当务之急就是要整合现有的规定,将涉及商事仲裁证据保全和行为保全的相关程序性规则具体化,在《仲裁法》中可以专门章节列示临时措施的内容、申请临时措施要提交的材料、与启动临时措施相关的程序内容、有权决定机关和执行机关、审查标准等,在方便仲裁申请人采取临时措施的基础上,实现机构仲裁与临时仲裁的有效融合。

除以上商事仲裁证据保全的程序性规定外,为了解决内地当事人在特殊情况下取证困难的问题,协助当事人顺利完成仲裁程序,高效解决纠纷,我们也可以在《仲裁法》中纳入"法院协助取证"的具体规定。《香港仲裁条例》除《示范法》第17条规定的临时措施包括证据保全以外转化适用了《示范法》第27条关于"法院协助取证"的规定,并根据香港特区法律的实际情况,作出了更为具体的规定。内地也可以在这方面作出努

---

① 《仲裁法》第68条规定:"涉外仲裁的当事人申请证据保全的,涉外仲裁委员会应当将当事人的申请提交证据所在地的中级人民法院。"
② 《民事诉讼法》第103条规定:"人民法院对于可能因当事人一方的行为或者其他原因,使判决难以执行或者造成当事人其他损害的案件,根据对方当事人的申请,可以裁定对其财产进行保全、责令其作出一定行为或者禁止其作出一定行为;当事人没有提出申请的,人民法院在必要时也可以裁定采取保全措施。人民法院采取保全措施,可以责令申请人提供担保,申请人不提供担保的,裁定驳回申请。人民法院接受申请后,对情况紧急的,必须在四十八小时内作出裁定;裁定采取保全措施的,应当立即开始执行。"
③ 参见李晶:《国际商事仲裁中临时措施在中国的新发展——以民诉法修改和仲裁规则修订为视角》,载《西北大学学报(哲学社会科学版)》2014年第6期。

力,对法院协助商事仲裁当事人取证作出规定,以支持仲裁友好环境的建设。

结　　论

临时仲裁制度是现代国际商事争端解决的重要方式之一,也是各国或地区仲裁法律制度中的重要组成部分。虽然最高人民法院在相关司法意见中规定了在自贸区内先行先试"三特定"的仲裁规则,但鉴于现行《仲裁法》对于临时仲裁制度未予规定,导致临时仲裁在中国落地尚不能得到充分的法律保障,也导致临时仲裁的司法审查与中国现有司法审查制度的衔接、法律救济等方面存在诸多问题。

在《仲裁法》制定之初,我国商事仲裁市场处于发展尚不成熟、社会诚信制度尚未建立的历史阶段,贸然引进临时仲裁制度确实不利于我国仲裁市场的规制以及商事仲裁制度的发展。但随着我国仲裁市场的不断健全、当事人主体对仲裁需求的不断增加,特别是在我国法治社会建设取得巨大成就、社会诚信制度日趋完善的今天,引入临时仲裁这一国际流行的仲裁制度,对我国商事仲裁事业的发展有着特殊的重要意义。因此,应当摒弃过去全然保守的态度,积极推动临时仲裁制度与我国现有仲裁法律制度的融合与衔接。而此次《仲裁法》修改若将临时仲裁制度融入我国仲裁法律体系之中,必将对我国现有仲裁制度产生积极而深远的影响,也会成为中国的商事仲裁制度接轨世界、日渐成熟的重要标志。

构建一套完整的仲裁司法审查体制对于临时仲裁而言十分必要,司法审查就是司法对仲裁的监督和保障。监督主要体现在司法对仲裁的合法性审查,保障主要体现在司法对仲裁程序的协助和对当事人权利的救济。这一原理同样适用于临时仲裁制度。因此,应当在临时仲裁协议效力审查、撤销与不予执行临时仲裁裁决案件审查、临时仲裁制度中的临时措施等主要方面开展深入研究,结合自身特点,吸纳《示范法》以及临时仲裁发达国家或地区的成功经验,制定既符合国际通行做法又具有中国特色的临时仲裁司法审查制度,确保临时仲裁在我国落地生根、发展壮大。

论"合并仲裁"规则

——兼评《中国海事仲裁委员会仲裁规则》第 19 条的理解、适用及完善[*]

刘凯湘[**]

摘要：合并仲裁规则在解决复杂商事纠纷案件中发挥着重要的作用，本文从合并仲裁的概念、价值评判、制度比较等方面出发，通过研究国内外合并仲裁的相关实践并结合世界其他主要仲裁机构的有关规则，探析并指明合并仲裁特别是强制合并仲裁的本质特征。在此基础上，笔者对《中国海事仲裁委员会仲裁规则》第 19 条的理解、适用进行了分析，并就其完善提出建议。

关键词：合并仲裁；强制合并仲裁；默示合意合并仲裁；理解与适用

一、合并仲裁制度的产生背景与制度价值

（一）合并仲裁制度的形成与发展

不少业界同仁早已经关注到这样的事实：在国际经贸法律关系中，为实现特定商事交易目的，许多重大项目的实施中存在大量相互关

---

[*] 本文完成于 2021 年 7 月。
[**] 北京大学法学院教授，博士生导师，中国国际经济贸易仲裁委员会仲裁员，中国海事仲裁委员会仲裁员。在写作过程中，笔者的研究生吕佳臻在资料收集与整理、观点讨论等方面对本文贡献殊多，在此致谢！当然，文章的观点由本人负责。

联的协议。① 例如,在建筑工程合同、海上货物运输合同,以及某些贸易部门的连锁合同中,这种现象尤为突出。② 这些协议构成并列式交易结构或者连锁式交易结构等形式。受前述影响,近年来在商事仲裁领域涌现出一些涉及多方当事人和数份协议的复杂案例。在这些案例中,根据一份合同作出的仲裁裁决可能影响到通过另一份合同参与同一项目的其他当事方的权利或利益。③ 根据国外学者的研究,30 多年前在国际商会(International Chamber of Commerce,ICC)国际仲裁院受理的案件中,仅有五分之一的案例涉及三方及以上的当事人④,而近年来这一比例提升至三分之一⑤。为了此类纠纷的高效、公平解决,一些仲裁机构的仲裁规则中规定了合并仲裁。

合并仲裁是指将由同一仲裁机构受理的两个及以上彼此独立且相互关联的仲裁案件进行合并审理的制度。⑥ 在类型方面,按照是否出于各方当事人一致的意思表示,合并仲裁可以分为合意合并仲裁与强制合并仲裁两类。合意合并仲裁是指各方当事人均同意进行合并仲裁;而强制合并仲裁是指在缺乏一方或多方当事人同意,或者当事人未就合并仲裁问题达成协议的情况下进行的合并仲裁。⑦ 按照各案当事人是否相同,合并仲裁可以分为当事人相同的合并仲裁与当事人不同的合并仲裁。其中,当事人不同的合并仲裁需要满足更为严格的构成要件。按照享有决定权主体的不同,合并仲裁可以分为仲裁机构决定的合并仲裁、仲裁庭决

---

① See Richard Bamforth & Katerina Maidment, "'All Join In' or Not? How Well Does International Arbitration Cater for Disputes Involving Multiple Parties or Related Claims?" 3 *ASA Bulletin* (2009).
② See Vladimir Filipovic, *Multiparty Arbitration and Consolidation of Arbitral Proceedings*, 39 ZBORNIK PFZ 506 (1989).
③ See Sandeep Bhalothia, *Joinder and Consolidation of Parties in Arbitration*, 5 CT. UNCOURT2 (2018).
④ See Martin Platte, *When Should an Arbitrator Join Cases?*, 67 Arbitration International (2002).
⑤ See Ioannis Giakoumelos, *The Need for Implementation of a Consolidation Provision in Institutional Arbitration Rules*, 17 PEPP. Disp. Resol. L. J. 23 (2017).
⑥ 参见〔意〕莫鲁·鲁比诺-萨马塔诺:《国际仲裁法律与实践》,中信出版社 2003 年版,第 297 页。
⑦ See T. Evan Schaeffer, *Compulsory Consolidation of Commercial Arbitration Disputes*, 33 St. Louis U. L. J. 495 (1989).

定的合并仲裁与法院决定的合并仲裁等模式。具体采用哪一种模式,依不同国家或地区的相关法律制度而有所差异。最后,按照所处程序阶段的不同,合并仲裁可以分为仲裁庭组成前的合并仲裁与仲裁庭组成后的合并仲裁。

(二)合并仲裁的价值评判

在合并仲裁规则的评价方面,相关支持与反对的观点莫衷一是。支持者认为,合并仲裁在时间和费用上的效益是显而易见的。[①] 例如,就相关事实争议无须在两个关联的案件中反复举证,也可以减少中间商的证据搜寻成本,同时解决中间商面临的时效问题。[②] 并且,合并仲裁有利于防止裁决冲突,即避免或者减少类案作出不一致甚至完全不同的裁决。反对者则认为,由于仲裁本身具有契约性,其核心是充分尊重当事人的意思自治[③],而合并仲裁可能与当事人意思自治相冲突。并且,合并仲裁有违仲裁保密性原则,不同案件的当事人参与其他案件的审理过程将挑战仲裁的保密性,尤其是强制合并仲裁。[④] 此外,合并仲裁可能违反正当程序。由于《承认及执行外国仲裁裁决公约》(又称《纽约公约》)和我国法律并没有对合并仲裁予以规定,仲裁结果可能得不到承认和执行,这将使得仲裁丧失解决纠纷的意义。[⑤] 对于合并后仲裁员的人数及遴选方式、如何组庭、涉外案件法律适用、简易或普通程序选择等实际操作问题,究竟如何进行程序运作就会成为困扰仲裁的难题,且相关问题还不局限于此,各种期限的截止和计算也并非易事。[⑥]

就支持者与反对者的前述观点,笔者认为基于程序效率和实体正义

---

① 参见易扬:《仲裁程序的合并与现代国际商事仲裁》,载《法学评论》1991年第6期。
② 在连锁式交易安排中,中间商可能要等待前一个仲裁裁决结果确定才能决定是否对其前手提起仲裁,在等待的过程中就存在时效期间届满的风险。
③ 参见陈治东:《国际商事仲裁法》,法律出版社1998年版,第6—9页。
④ 参见马骁潇:《合并仲裁问题比较研究》,载北京仲裁委员会、北京国际仲裁中心组编:《北京仲裁》(第107辑),中国法制出版社2019年版。
⑤ 参见范瑞:《合并仲裁现有理论之若干反思——兼论合并仲裁制度之程序构建》,载北京仲裁委员会、北京国际仲裁中心组编:《北京仲裁》(第102辑),中国法制出版社2018年版。
⑥ 参见张建:《合并仲裁的实践困境与制度引入——兼论北仲〈新规则〉第29条之操作可行性》,载北京仲裁委员会组编:《北京仲裁》(第91辑),中国法制出版社2015年版。

的双重考量,面对日益复杂且频繁的商业活动,构建并应用合并仲裁制度具有必要性与合理性;至于其弊端,则可以通过具体的规则设计来克服。

(三)合并仲裁与其他类似规则之异同

1. 合并仲裁与多份合同仲裁

多份合同仲裁是指在符合规定条件的前提下,申请人就多份合同项下的争议合并提出仲裁申请的制度。多份合同仲裁在构成要件方面,与强制合并仲裁具有很大的相似性。例如,要求仲裁协议相同或相容,争议源于同一或同一系列交易,所涉法律关系性质相同等。但是与合并仲裁不同的是,多份合同仲裁仅涉及两方当事人①,而且从立案时始至裁决作出时终,存在且仅存在一个仲裁案件。与此不同的是,合并仲裁被认为是多方参与的,因为有超过两方当事人参与到程序之中,同时存在数个彼此独立的案件被合并为同一个案件的过程。

2. 合并仲裁与合并开庭

合并开庭是指如果两个及以上仲裁案件涉及相同的事实或法律问题,在征得各方当事人意见后,有权机关决定对两个或多个仲裁案件合并开庭的制度。与合并仲裁的目的价值类似,合并开庭也是出于对仲裁经济性、快捷性的考虑;同时在效果上也能达到数个案件"共享"证据、文件的目的。但不同之处在于,合并开庭仅是对开庭程序的合并,所涉及的数个案件本质上仍然彼此独立,在其他仲裁程序的运行包括裁决的作出方面仍具有绝对的独立性。

3. 合并仲裁与同步开庭

同步开庭在香港国际仲裁中心(Hong Kong International Arbitration Centre, HKIAC)规则中又称"平行程序",是指在满足规定条件时,有权机关决定同时进行两个或两个以上仲裁,或一个紧接着另一个进行仲裁,或暂停任何仲裁直至任何其他仲裁作出决定。② 同步开庭与合并仲裁有着相似的制度目的,即都是为了解决多方当事人仲裁的问题。不同之处在

---

① See Martin Platte, *When Should an Arbitrator Join Cases?*, 67 Arbitration International (2002).
② 《香港国际仲裁中心机构仲裁规则(2018)》第30条。

于采取的进路有所不同,合并仲裁采用直接将不同案件合并为同一个案件的方式;而同步开庭在保持各个案件彼此独立的前提下,通过时间安排上的同步,解决复杂仲裁案件面临的事实认定困难、可能产生裁决冲突等问题。

4.合并仲裁与仲裁第三人

合并仲裁适用于两个已经开始的仲裁程序之间;而仲裁第三人是仲裁程序之外的第三人主动或者被动加入已经存在的仲裁程序,即在程序数量上不会产生变化。① 此外,合并仲裁的当事人一定存在仲裁的意思表示,而仲裁第三人可能会抵牾当事人的意思自治。

二、比较法上的合并仲裁——以美国的合并仲裁实践为例

美国合并仲裁的主要模式为法院命令合并。有关仲裁的法律规则体系包括1925年美国国会通过的《联邦仲裁法》(Federal Arbitration Act, FAA)、1955年统一州法律全国委员会通过的《统一仲裁法》(Uniform Arbitration Act, UAA)及其2000年修正案(Revised Uniform Arbitration Act, RUAA)、《美国仲裁协会商事仲裁规则》②。此外,也存在一些法院适用《联邦民事诉讼法》的相关规则③来作为合并仲裁依据的情况。④ 其中,FAA与UAA并未就合并仲裁问题作出规定,而RUAA第10条允许法院可以在以下情况中命令进行合并:(1)索赔源于相同(或相关系列)的交易;(2)共同的法律或事实问题造成(在单独的仲裁程序中)裁决冲突的可能性;(3)不合并所造成的损害并没有被不适当的延迟风险或对反对合并的各方的权利的损害或困难所抵消。由于大多数州并没有采纳RU-

---

① 参见林一飞:《论仲裁与第三人》,载《法学评论》2000年第1期。
② 有关合并仲裁问题,规定在《美国仲裁协会商事仲裁规则》的初步审理程序中。
③ 美国《联邦民事诉讼法》第42(a)条规定:当涉及共同的法律或事实问题的诉讼在法院待审时,法院可以命令对诉讼中的任何或所有问题进行联合听证或审判;可以命令合并所有的诉讼;并且可以就其中的程序作出可能有助于避免不必要的费用或延误的命令。
④ Andrew A. Davenport, *Consolidation of Separate Arbitration Proceedings: The Effect of the United States Arbitration Act on the District Court's Power under Federal Rules of Civil Procedure* 42 (a) and 81(a)(3), 42 MERCER L. REV. 1675 (1991).

AA规则①,所以"遵循先例"在美国合并仲裁司法实践中发挥着极大的作用。

美国各巡回法院就合并仲裁问题有着不同的态度与处理方式。根据相关司法判例,总体而言绝大多数联邦巡回法院现在的立场是,如果当事人没有在其仲裁协议中明确允许合并,联邦法院无权合并仲裁案件。②具体的情况可以分为三类:纯粹的强制合并、无明确合意不合并及基于解释的强制合并。

首先,"纯粹的强制合并"体现于美国第二巡回法院的"Nereus案"中。在该案中,第二巡回法院适用《联邦民事诉讼规则》作为依据判令合并仲裁,其认为"在这两起仲裁中,不仅存在共同的法律和事实问题,而且有可能出现相互冲突的结论……"③西班牙石油公司作为保证人实际上与船舶所有人的代理人和租船人履行的是同一个合同。所有人、租船人、保证人签订一个备忘录及援引带有仲裁条款的租船合同的行为,被视为同意进行一个仲裁程序。④而在纽约南部地区采用"Nereus测试法"的其他裁决(如"Elmarina案")表明,存在明示或默示的合并协议并不是命令合并的必要条件,因此第二巡回法院的做法被称为"纯粹的强制合并"。⑤即只要符合特定的条件,不需要当事人同意,法院即可命令合并仲裁。在"Nereus案"中,第二巡回法院考虑的因素包括:(1)程序是否涉及共同的法律和事实问题;(2)是否有可能出现相互冲突的裁决或不一致的结果;(3)如果单独进行仲裁程序,是否可能损害实质性权利;(4)如果进行合并程序,是否会损害实质性权利。

其次,第五和第九巡回法院采取了"无明确合意不合并"的做法。在"Weyerhaeuser案"中,存在两个互相关联的船务纠纷。第一起纠纷涉及

---

① Jonathan R. Waldron, *Resolving a Split: May Courts Order Consolidation of Arbitration Proceedings Absent Express Agreement by the Parties*, 2005 J. Disp. Resol. 177 (2005).

② See Okuma Kazutake, *Party Autonomy in International Commercial Arbitration: Consolidation of Multiparty and Classwide Arbitration*, 9 ANN. Surv. INT'l & COMP. L. 189 (2003).

③ See Compania Espanola de Petroleos, S. A. v. Nereus Shipping, 527 F. 2d 966 (2d Cir. 1975), cert. denied, 426 U. S. 936 (1976).

④ 参见乔欣、赵玲:《浅议强制合并仲裁》,载北京仲裁委员会组编:《北京仲裁》(第64辑),中国法制出版社2008年版。

⑤ See T. Evan Schaeffer, *Compulsory Consolidation of Commercial Arbitration Disputes*, 33 St. Louis U. L. J. 495 (1989).

一个船东和租船人。第二起纠纷涉及同一租船人和一个分租商。租船人请求法院将两个仲裁程序合并。尽管在两份合同中都包含了相同的仲裁条款,但是法院仍以各方不存在明示的合并合意为由,拒绝了租船人的合并请求。法院的上述做法系出于对 FAA 规则的严格遵守,其强调仲裁是合同的产物,无合同则无仲裁。FAA 规则赋予法院确认并执行有效仲裁协议的职权①,但法院并没有权力为当事人创造合同内容。

再次,第四巡回法院的实践强调在 FAA 规则的框架下对当事人默示合意进行解释,即"基于解释的强制合并"。在"Maxum 案"中,法院在缺乏当事人明确合意的情况下,对两个仲裁程序进行了合并。其中,一个案件发生于业主和承包商之间,而另一个案件发生于承包商和分包商之间。法院认为,两份合同间的结构安排和条款具体使用的字句暗示了双方的合并仲裁合意。② 如此为之,法院成功绕过了"FAA 规则是否赋予法院强制合并仲裁的权力"这一问题,为强制合并仲裁提供了第三种进路。

最后,就"拒绝合并仲裁条款"(non-consolidation clause),即各方当事人在仲裁条款中明确表示不接受合并仲裁,第九、第五巡回法院及第四巡回法院均采用了严格遵循当事人合同约定的做法,不予进行合并仲裁。

总而言之,美国各巡回法院就合并仲裁问题的不同态度,源于法院在

---

① 美国《联邦仲裁法》第 4 条规定:根据协议未能仲裁;请求享有管辖权的美国法院作出强制仲裁之命令;请求通知与送达;审理与裁定。双方当事人签订了书面仲裁协议,对于对方不履行、拖延或者拒绝仲裁而受侵害的一方可以请求依照法律、衡平法或者海事法庭的法典的规定对争执引起的诉讼有管辖权的任何美国法院,命令依照协议规定进行仲裁。上述请求应当用书面通知违约方,并给予 5 日的期限。通知书应当依照法定送达传票的办法送达。法院应当审问双方当事人,如果关于仲裁协议的签订或者违背一点没有异议,法院应当命令双方当事人依照协议规定进行仲裁,但是审问和其他程序必须在提出请求的地区进行。如果关于仲裁协议的签订或者违背一点有异议,法院应当进行审判。如果被认为违约的一方不要求用陪审制审判,或者争执属于海事法庭管辖权之内,即由法院审问并作出决定。如果争执不是海事案件,被认为违约的一方可以在通知书应当缴回之日或者以前提出用陪审制审判的要求。法院接到要求,应当命令按照法律规定,用陪审制审判衡平法诉讼案件的办法交给陪审团审问,或者特别召集陪审团。如果陪审团查明,确实没有书面仲裁协议并且有违约情形,法院应当命令双方当事人依照协议规定进行仲裁。

② 在该案中,第四巡回法院认为:分包商对业主负有一定的责任,而业主对分包商也负有一定的责任。虽然承包商与业主和分包商都签订了合同,但它们都没有直接与对方签订合同,这种形式不应该掩盖所有三个参与者之间的动态互动。该建筑项目的相互关联性、合同的相互关联性以及共同的法律和事实问题导致法院认定,协议中相同的仲裁条款包括在一个诉讼中进行仲裁的义务。仲裁条款本身暗示了这一结论,因为它规定了涉及共同的法律和事实问题的合并。

解释 FAA 规则的目的和具体条文时,于严格的"契约主义"原则和宽松的"自由构建"原则间的不同选择。①

三、强制合并仲裁的逻辑——默示合并合意的解释

承前所述,美国第四巡回法院强制合并仲裁的实践强调对当事人默示合意的解释。其法律逻辑在于,合并仲裁条款是仲裁协议的必要组成部分。但由于并非所有的仲裁协议都对合并仲裁进行了安排,所以在明示约定缺位的情况下,法院有权进行补充解释,也可以理解为合同漏洞填补的作业。而进行补充解释时通常考虑以下三个方面的因素:(1)仲裁协议使用的字句;(2)交易所涉系列合同的关系及结构;(3)仲裁协议的目的。

具体而言,首先,仲裁协议中对有关仲裁程序的安排越详尽充分,越可能表示当事人不希望进行合并仲裁,相对而言,一个仅仅表述仲裁基本要素的仲裁协议反而暗示着当事人合并仲裁的意愿。另外,出现在不同合同中的同一或者近似的仲裁条款,也会被认为当事人具有合并仲裁的意思表示。其次,当事人的潜在意图也体现在他们之间的合同安排与法律关系方面。例如,在一般协议中(general agreement)出现仲裁条款,并附有不同的附属协议(ancillary agreement),可能表明当事人有意将不同附属协议所产生的争端在一个法庭上解决。② 最后,合并仲裁的主要目的是有效解决纠纷,避免裁决冲突。因此,如果当事人选择仲裁是出于效率的考虑,则可以解释为当事人有意允许合并。

基于上述不难发现,默示合意解释所面临的最大问题在于没有明确可供参考的标准,这会导致就同一问题不同解释主体所得出的结论会有所不同。从该逻辑出发,为了明确解释的标准,同时对有权主体的决定权进行一定程度的限制,有必要规定强制合并仲裁的构成要件。

---

① See Michael L. DeCamp, *Consolidation of Separate Arbitration Proceedings: Liberal Construction versus Contractarian Approaches-United Kingdom of Great Britain v. Boeing Co.*, 1994 J. Disp. Resol. 113 (1994).

② Ioannis Giakoumelos, *The Need for Implementation of a Consolidation Provision in Institutional Arbitration Rules*, 17 PEPP. Disp. Resol. L. J. 23 (2017).

四、合并仲裁的构成要件——在不同仲裁规则视角下

按照内容要素的不同,合并仲裁的构成要件可以分为程序要件和实体要件。其中,程序要件侧重考察合并仲裁在发生阶段、申请权(启动)主体、决定权主体等方面的要素;而实体要件则关注不同案件的实体法律关系、事实关系等具体情况。需要注意的是,不同类型的合并仲裁对具体程序要件和实体要件的要求也不同。例如,就合意合并仲裁的构成要件而言,在程序方面要求一方或者多方当事人申请,在实体方面要求且仅要求各方当事人一致同意进行合并仲裁。而强制合并仲裁则在实体要件方面有更多的关注。例如,要求不同案件系源自同一或者同一系列交易,有相同的法律或事实问题,并同时要求基于同一、相同或者相容的仲裁协议等。就当事人相同的合并仲裁与当事人不同的合并仲裁而言,相较于前者,当事人不同的合并仲裁对实体法律关系的关联性与交易的关联性之要求更为严格。就仲裁庭组成前的合并仲裁与仲裁庭组庭后的合并仲裁而言,后者要考虑的因素也更多。

需要强调的是,合并仲裁构成要件在合并仲裁制度中的地位和作用并非唯一和绝对的,即满足合并仲裁的程序要件和实体要件,并不意味着一定会产生合并的结果。是否进行合并仲裁,根本上还是有权机关行使职权的结果。纵观不同仲裁规则下的合并仲裁制度,可以发现将数个原本彼此独立的案件进行合并仲裁,是以构成要件的适当性与决定权行使的合理性两者同时满足为前提的。

为了进一步了解全球各主要仲裁机构的仲裁规则中相关合并仲裁的内容,并进行制度比较,笔者挑选了国内外不同机构的仲裁规则,共计10例进行分析。具体内容将从程序启动、程序阶段、当事人情况、仲裁协议、实体关系五个构成要件方面与决定权归属及行权要素两个方面,共计七个[①]方面进行分析。具体情况如表1。

具体而言,各机构仲裁规则就合并仲裁的规定呈现出如下特点:第一,在仲裁程序的启动方面以当事人申请为主,而且形式上往往没有特别

---

① 出于后文对相关问题讨论的便利,特将"合并后仲裁庭组成"也纳入表1。

表 1 全球各主要仲裁机构合并仲裁规则制度比较①

序号	仲裁规则	程序启动要件	程序阶段要件	当事人情况要件	仲裁协议要件	实体关系要件	决定权	考虑的其他因素	合并后仲裁庭组成
1	ICC规则②	当事人申请	案件尚未作出裁决	各方当事人相同	仲裁协议同一、相同或者相容	同一法律关系	仲裁院	仲裁庭的组成情况	—
2	HKIAC规则③	当事人申请	案件正在进行	—	仲裁协议同一	相同法律或事实问题;同一或一系列交易	仲裁机构	其他当事人和已确定仲裁员的意见	仲裁机构指定
3	SIAC规则④	当事人申请	仲裁庭组成前或者仲裁庭组成后	—	仲裁协议同一或相容	相同法律关系;同一或一系列交易;争议的多个合同系主从合同关系	组庭前由仲裁院决定,组庭后由仲裁庭决定	必须满足均未组庭或者部分未组庭或者各仲裁庭组成相同	仲裁院和当事人共同确定

① 由于合意合并仲裁的内容与适用具有普遍性,该表格研究的重点就集中在强制合并仲裁规则的构建方面。
② ICC Arbitration Rule, §10(2021).
③ 《香港国际仲裁中心仲裁规则(2018)》第28条。
④ 《新加坡国际仲裁中心仲裁规则(第六版)》第8条。

（续表）

序号	仲裁规则	程序启动要件	程序阶段要件	当事人情况要件	仲裁协议要件	实体关系要件	决定权	考虑的其他因素	合并后仲裁庭组成
4	LCIA规则①	仲裁院决定启动，或者仲裁庭根据一方当事人的申请启动	仲裁庭组成前或者相同的仲裁庭组成后	各方当事人相同	仲裁协议同一或相容	—	仲裁院或仲裁庭（需要经仲裁院同意）	各方当事人意见	—
5	CEPANI规则②	当事人或者仲裁申请	案件正在进行	—	仲裁协议同一或相容	同一或者同一系列法律关系	任命委员会或者仲裁机构主席	是否事先约定排除合并仲裁；各仲裁程序的进展情况及仲裁庭的组成情况；仲裁地的选定情况；已经作出初步裁决、受理决定或实体裁决的不能合并；若当事人一致要求合并且就合并方式达成合意则应当合并	任命委员会或者仲裁机构主席任命

① LCIA Rules, § 22 (2014).
② RULES of CEPANI, § 13, § 15. 8 (2020).

(续表)

序号	仲裁规则	程序启动要件	程序阶段要件	当事人情况要件	仲裁协议要件	实体关系要件	决定权	考虑的其他因素	合并后仲裁庭组成
6	JCAA规则[1]	当事人书面申请	仲裁庭组成前	各方当事人相同,或者在当事人不同时征得被合并案件的当事人书面同意	仲裁协议同一或相容	相同法律或事实问题	仲裁庭	是否适用JCAA规则或者由JCAA仲裁;待合并案件在仲裁地,仲裁员数量,语言等仲裁程序方面的相容性	—
7	SCC规则[2]	当事人申请	新开始的案件与案件在审案件	—	仲裁协议同一或相容	同一或同一系列交易	理事会	当事人和仲裁庭意见;案件进展阶段,程序的高效性	理事会可以决定解除
8	北仲规则[3]	当事人申请	案件正在进行	—	—	—	仲裁机构	仲裁协议情况;案件关联情况,阶段;仲裁庭的组成,案件的程序,仲裁员选任和指定情况	—

① JCAA 2015 Rules, § 53.
② 《斯德哥尔摩商会仲裁院商会仲裁规则(2017)》第15条。
③ 《北京仲裁委员会仲裁规则(2019)》第30条。

(续表)

序号	仲裁规则	程序启动要件	程序阶段要件	当事人情况要件	仲裁协议要件	实体关系要件	决定权	考虑的其他因素	合并后仲裁庭组成
9	贸仲规则①	当事人申请	案件正在进行	—	仲裁协议同一、相同或者相容	法律关系性质相同,所涉合同为主从合同关系	仲裁机构	各方当事人意见;案件之间的关联性;仲裁员选任、指定情况	—
10	深国仲规则②	—	案件已经进入仲裁程序	—	—	—	仲裁机构	仅在当事人书面同意时才可以决定合并	—

---

① 《中国国际经济贸易仲裁委员会仲裁规则(2015)》第19条。
② 《深圳国际仲裁院仲裁规则(2020)》第18条。

要求,仲裁机构或者仲裁庭基本上处于消极、被动的地位。第二,在程序阶段方面,除少数仲裁规则要求只有在组庭前才能合并外,大多数仲裁规则下的合并仲裁可以发生在裁决作出前的任意阶段。第三,大多数仲裁规则允许对当事人不同的数个案件进行合并。第四,仲裁协议同一、相同或者相容是强制合并仲裁的普遍要求。第五,实体关系考察要素设置的底层逻辑是对当事人默示合并合意的解释。第六,有权机构在决定合并与否时,通常要考虑当事人的意见及案件程序安排情况。

在制度评价方面,合并仲裁制度的优劣及其效果的合目的性离不开对构成要件的设计。而就构成要件需要考虑的要素及其具体内容而言,需要合理平衡程序效率与当事人意思自治之间的关系。具体而言,既不能仅关注效率而不顾当事人的内心真意,否则就违背了商事仲裁的本质;但同时又不能机械地拘泥于形式证据而不通过考察系列交易、法律关系和不同案件之间的彼此关联,探析当事人潜在的真实意思。总而言之,一个好的合并仲裁决定,既要尊重当事人的利益,同时要为解决复杂仲裁案件提供高效的方案。①

五、我国司法实践对合并仲裁的回应

由于我国《仲裁法》并未就合并仲裁规则作出明确的规定,故而各仲裁机构的仲裁规则中有关合并仲裁的规定,实际上缺少上位法的明确依据,所以其在合法性方面是否存在问题有必要进一步研究。而由于人民法院是仲裁裁决效力的审查机关和仲裁裁决的执行机关,相关司法案例中法院对合并仲裁的认定和回应,就直接反映了仲裁裁决的效力和执行力情况。

经检索,相关案件所涉案由主要包括"撤销仲裁裁决"与"执行异议"(不予执行仲裁裁决)两大类,共计94例。考虑到研究目的,在对上述案件范围进一步限缩后,本文研究的案例均同时满足以下三个方面的要求:第一,在原仲裁程序中进行合并仲裁;第二,就合并仲裁当事人提起撤销

---

① See Ioannis Giakoumelos, *The Need for Implementation of a Consolidation Provision in Institutional Arbitration Rules*, 17 PEPP. Disp. Resol. L. J. 23 (2017).

仲裁决议或者不予执行仲裁决议之诉;第三,人民法院将合并仲裁的合法性问题归纳为争议焦点并作出认定。按照上述条件筛选后,共有相关案件9例。同时,根据申请理由、申请是否得到法院支持、合并仲裁的类型(合意合并或者强制合并)、裁决支持合并仲裁的理由及是否进行实质审查①和所涉及的仲裁机构等几个方面的内容进行了分类汇总,具体情况如表2。

经过对上述案件的初步检视,可以发现大部分案件为中国国际经济贸易仲裁委员会(以下简称"贸仲")受理的仲裁案件。这反映出相较于国内其他仲裁机构,合并仲裁在贸仲的应用较多。而就这些案件而言,所涉及的合并仲裁的类型均为合意合并,这从一个侧面说明相比强制合并,合意合并在贸仲的适用更为普遍。此外,申请人申请撤裁或者申请不予执行的理由普遍为仲裁程序违法。② 所谓仲裁程序违法,是指违反仲裁法规定的仲裁程序和当事人选择的仲裁规则可能影响案件正确裁决的情形,应当以违反法定程序达到严重影响当事人程序权利且实质性影响案件正确裁决为标准。③ 而相关案件中所有的申请均被裁定驳回,恰恰可以证明就合并仲裁本身而言,其并不构成程序违法的事由。再者,法院在审

---

① 此处所指的实质审查,即法院在审理过程中就纠纷所涉及的实体法律关系、交易情况、仲裁协议等进行的审查。

② 《仲裁法》第58条规定:"当事人提出证据证明裁决有下列情形之一的,可以向仲裁委员会所在地的中级人民法院申请撤销裁决:(一)没有仲裁协议的;(二)裁决的事项不属于仲裁协议的范围或者仲裁委员会无权仲裁的;(三)仲裁庭的组成或者仲裁的程序违反法定程序的;(四)裁决所根据的证据是伪造的;(五)对方当事人隐瞒了足以影响公正裁决的证据的;(六)仲裁员在仲裁该案时有索贿受贿,徇私舞弊,枉法裁决行为的。人民法院经组成合议庭审查核实裁决有前款规定情形之一的,应当裁定撤销。人民法院认定该裁决违背社会公共利益的,应当裁定撤销。"

《民事诉讼法》第237条规定:"对依法设立的仲裁机构的裁决,一方当事人不履行的,对方当事人可以向有管辖权的人民法院申请执行。受申请的人民法院应当执行。被申请人提出证据证明仲裁裁决有下列情形之一的,经人民法院组成合议庭审查核实,裁定不予执行:(一)当事人在合同中没有订有仲裁条款或者事后没有达成书面仲裁协议的;(二)裁决的事项不属于仲裁协议的范围或者仲裁机构无权仲裁的;(三)仲裁庭的组成或者仲裁的程序违反法定程序的;(四)裁决所根据的证据是伪造的;(五)对方当事人向仲裁机构隐瞒了足以影响公正裁决的证据的;(六)仲裁员在仲裁该案时有贪污受贿,徇私舞弊,枉法裁决行为的。人民法院认定执行该裁决违背社会公共利益的,裁定不予执行裁定书应当送达双方当事人和仲裁机构。仲裁裁决被人民法院裁定不予执行的,当事人可以根据双方达成的书面仲裁协议重新申请仲裁,也可以向人民法院起诉。"

③ 参见银隆新能源股份有限公司与中信证券股份有限公司申请撤销仲裁裁决案,北京市第四中级人民法院(2019)京04民特656号民事裁定书。

表 2 相关案件分类汇总[1]

序号	案号	审理法院	申请理由	是否支持申请	合并类型	裁决支持合并仲裁的理由	是否进行实质审查	仲裁机构
1	(2018)京04民特172号	北京市第四中级人民法院	程序违法	否	合意	申请人同意合并仲裁,合并仲裁不违反法定程序	否	贸仲
2	(2018)京04民特461号	北京市第四中级人民法院	程序违法	否	合意	申请人同意合并仲裁,合并仲裁不违反法定程序	否	贸仲
3	(2020)京04民特662号	北京市第四中级人民法院	程序违法	否	合意	当事人均同意且当事人相同,所涉法律关系性质均相同	是	贸仲
4	(2019)京04民特2号	北京市第四中级人民法院	程序违法	否	合意	当事人均同意合并仲裁协议	是	贸仲
5	(2021)京04民特37号	北京市第四中级人民法院	程序违法	否	合意	当事人均同意合并仲裁且基于同一份仲裁协议	否	贸仲

[1] 表 2 中的贸仲特指"中国国际经济贸易仲裁委员会"。

（续表）

序号	案号	审理法院	申请理由	是否支持申请	合并类型	裁决支持合并仲裁的理由	是否进行实质审查	仲裁机构
6	（2017）粤06民特31号	广东省佛山市中级人民法院	程序违法	否	强制	案涉担保合同法律关系或抵押物监管合同法律关系，以借贷合同法律关系为基础，且为便于仲裁庭正确认定各方当事人之间的权利和义务，依法认定各自的责任顺位，避免重复受偿，仲裁申请人与各仲裁被申请人亦应有权互相知晓对方的仲裁权利主张，有义务协助仲裁庭查清案件事实	是	佛山仲裁委员会
7	（2019）湘04民特17号	湖南省衡阳市中级人民法院	程序违法	否	强制	案涉债权债务关系类似，仲裁法律未规定合并仲裁必须经当事人同意，合并仲裁未违反法律规定，反而更经济。合并仲裁不影响事实的认定	是	衡阳仲裁委员会
8	（2017）黔01民特130号	贵州省贵阳市中级人民法院	程序违法	否	合意	相关案件诉争事项和依据事实一致，被申请人为同一主体，仲裁庭合并审理，并未违反双方当事人同意将案件合并至贵阳仲裁委员会《仲裁法》及贵阳仲裁委员会仲裁规则》规定的相关法定程序	是	贵阳仲裁委员会
9	（2016）皖01执异60号	安徽省合肥市中级人民法院	程序违法	否	强制	诉讼标的为同一种类，申请人的申请，仲裁庭依据仲裁，合并仲裁更符合经济、便捷原则，并无不当	是	淮北仲裁委员会

理的过程中是否进行实质审查,与合并仲裁的种类系属合意合并抑或强制合并存在着相当的关联。在仲裁程序中,若各方当事人就合并仲裁达成一致,则法院往往不会进行实质审查;反之,法院则会审查仲裁协议的情况、案件相互关联的情况等。最后,对强制合并仲裁的态度,一些地方法院较为包容,并认为合并仲裁属于依法行使仲裁权的范畴。①

综上所述,可以得出下述结论:(1)合并仲裁本身不构成仲裁程序瑕疵的事由;(2)我国合并仲裁的实践尚不活跃,目前存在的合并仲裁类型以合意合并为主;(3)司法实践对合并仲裁的审查并不十分严苛;(4)未来合并仲裁制度在我国的实践还有广阔的空间。

六、《中国海事仲裁委员会仲裁规则》第 19 条的理解与适用

中国海事仲裁委员会(以下简称"海仲")是中国较早引入和应用合并仲裁制度的机构,在 1996 年审理的平安星轮Ⅰ运费、滞期费争议案与平安星轮Ⅱ运费、滞期费争议案中,就进行了合并仲裁。② 但在该案中,即便合并仲裁取得了各方当事人的同意,天津海事法院仍以仲裁规则未规定合并仲裁为由,要求重新仲裁。据此,两案重新开庭并作出裁决,而结果均维持了原裁决且得到了当事人的自动履行。就在该案之后,海仲于 2000 年将合并仲裁写进仲裁规则,并在 2015 年版、2018 年版及于 2020 年 11 月 6 日最新一次修正中予以保留。

最新修正的《中国海事仲裁委员会仲裁规则》(以下简称《仲裁规

---

① 参见衡阳崇业建设开发集团有限公司、王崇顺与被申请人傅小年、傅巧云、李晓钊申请撤销仲裁裁决案,湖南省衡阳市中级人民法院(2019)湘 04 民特 17 号一审民事裁定书。
② 船方 K 公司与租方 D 公司签订了航次租船合同确认书,约定自中国张家港的一个安全泊位装运夹板到美国温哥华港。后租方 D 公司又与下家租方 I 公司签订了同一轮的航次租船合同,约定内容大致相同,也是该批货物的运输问题。由于 D 公司与 I 公司就合同项下运费计算方式发生争议,D 公司要求 I 公司支付按毛体积计算的运费差额和本航次的滞期费,并向中国海事仲裁委员会(以下简称"海仲")提起仲裁。K 公司也要求 D 公司赔偿此次航运运费、滞期费损失,并于同日向海仲提起仲裁。两个仲裁庭考虑到这两个仲裁案件许多事实相同,建议合并开庭审理,三方当事人也均同意并签署书面协议。开庭审理后,两个仲裁庭于同日分别作出两个裁决。由于裁决书均裁决 D 公司承担主要责任,D 公司向天津海事法院申请撤销裁决。参见蔡鸿达:《关于重新仲裁问题的探讨》,载《仲裁与法律》2000 年第 2 期。

则》)第19条①中的合并仲裁,在类型方面既包括合意合并又涵盖了强制合并,既调整当事人相同的合并亦规范当事人不同的合并;在具体内容上,不仅规定了合并仲裁的实体要件和程序要件,也明确了决定权行使需要考虑的因素;就其他内容方面,确定了有权决定合并的主体为仲裁机构,强调了具体合并的方式和合并后的程序安排。而承本文第四部分所述,一个完善的合并仲裁条文需要包含以下四方面要素:第一,决定合并仲裁的主体;第二,合并仲裁的启动方式;第三,合并仲裁的构成要件和决定合并时考虑的要素;第四,合并仲裁的时间限制。由此可见《仲裁规则》第19条就合并仲裁规定的内容方面而言,还是比较全面的。

而就该条具体内容中需要关注的重点和理解与适用中的难点而言,主要包括以下几个问题:一是该条第1款所规定的四种不同条件的具体内容应如何理解,彼此之间又存在何种联系;二是如何理解仲裁协议内容"相容";三是如何理解多份合同为"主从合同关系";四是就该条第2款规定的各个因素具体应该如何进行考量;五是该条第2款与第1款之间关系如何;六是该条第3款、第4款应该如何理解。

第一,就"问题一"的理解。第1款除就合并仲裁的定义、启动条件和决定主体进行规定外,其余部分实质上是关于合并仲裁构成要件的规范。具体而言,前三项属于强制合并的构成要件,而第4项则属于合意合并的构成要件。合意合并的要件不言自明,即需要各方当事人一致同意,而该项表述性质上属于注意规定。但需要强调的是,在形式上,与比较法上绝大部分仲裁规则相同②,当事人同意既可以采用口头方式又可以采用书面

---

① 《中国海事仲裁委员会仲裁规则》第19条规定:"(一)符合下列条件之一的,经一方当事人请求,仲裁委员会可以决定将根据本规则进行的两个或两个以上的仲裁案件合并为一个仲裁案件,进行审理。1.各案仲裁请求依据同一个仲裁协议提出;2.各案仲裁请求依据多份仲裁协议提出,该多份仲裁协议内容相同或相容,且各案当事人相同、各争议所涉及的法律关系性质相同;3.各案仲裁请求依据多份仲裁协议提出,该多份仲裁协议内容相同或相容,且涉及的多份合同为主从合同关系;4.所有案件的当事人均同意合并仲裁。(二)根据上述第(一)款决定合并仲裁时,仲裁委员会应考虑各方当事人的意见及相关仲裁案件之间的关联性等因素,包括不同案件的仲裁员的选定或指定情况。(三)除非各方当事人另有约定,合并的仲裁案件应合并至最先开始仲裁程序的仲裁案件。(四)仲裁案件合并后,在仲裁庭组成之前,由仲裁委员会仲裁院就程序的进行作出决定;仲裁庭组成后,由仲裁庭就程序的进行作出决定。"

② 在本文所研究的仲裁规制中,仅日本商事仲裁协会(Japan Commercial Arbitration Association,JCAA)规则要求当事人书面申请合并仲裁。

方式作出。就强制合并的构成要件而言,前三项的规定既彼此独立又有所关联。彼此独立,是指满足其中的一项要求即该当于强制合并仲裁的构成要件,而不需要同时满足两项或以上。有所关联,是指此三项分别规定了不同层面和情况下的强制合并仲裁之构成要件,同时又有所交叉。具言之,在仲裁请求所依据的仲裁协议情况方面,第 1 项要求仲裁请求基于同一个仲裁协议,而第 2、3 项要求出自多个相同或者相容的仲裁协议;在不同案件所涉及的当事人情况方面,第 2 项是关于当事人相同的强制合并仲裁之规定,第 3 项则调整当事人不同的合并仲裁,而第 1 项对当事人情况没有特别要求。

理解各个构成要件的含义,要从规则制定时所考虑的要素方面着手进行目的解释。由于合意合并仲裁几乎不存在争议,故并非检讨之重点问题。而在强制合并仲裁方面,承前所述,有必要按照尊重当事人意思自治的尺度来进行解释。即第 1 款前三项就强制合并仲裁三种要件的规定,其实质是"当事人默示合并合意"的解释标准①,而不仅是字面意思所表达之强制合并仲裁的适用条件。亦即并非"纯粹的强制合并仲裁",而是属于"默示合意合并仲裁"。②

第二,关于"问题二"的理解。该条第 1 款第 2 项就当事人相同的强制合并仲裁,要求仲裁请求所依据的仲裁协议内容相同或相容。而就何为仲裁协议的内容"相容",在理解与适用的过程中可能存在问题。就"相容"一词,英文版本的《仲裁规则》所对应的表述为"compatible"。对相同问题,英文版 HKIAC 规则使用的词汇同为"compatible",而其对应的中文翻译版本为"兼容"一词。另外,ICC 规则、伦敦国际仲裁院(London Court of International Abitration, LCIA)规则等使用的对应词汇亦均为"compatible"。考虑到我们目前的合并仲裁规则一定程度上是法律移植

---

① 满足(1)各案仲裁请求依据同一个仲裁协议提出;(2)各案仲裁请求依据多份仲裁协议提出,该多份仲裁协议内容相同或相容,且各案当事人相同、各争议所涉及的法律关系性质相同;(3)各案仲裁请求依据多份仲裁协议提出,该多份仲裁协议内容相同或相容,且涉及的多份合同为主从合同关系该三项之一,就可以解释并推定当事人具有默示合并仲裁的意思表示。

② 这两者的差别主要体现在当事人事先约定了"拒绝合并仲裁条款"(non-consolidation clause)的情况下,若按照纯粹的强制合并仲裁的逻辑,该种情况下仍可以决定合并,但是若按照默示合意合并仲裁来理解,则不能进行合并。

的产物,故而有必要从"相容"一词对应的英文词汇"compatible"出发去理解其真实含义。一方面,根据《牛津词典》,compatible具有三种含义,包括"可以共同使用且不会产生问题的""可以共存的"以及"关系好且相处和睦的"。其中,最后一种含义仅在人际关系方面适用。此外,《元照英美法词典》中compatibility①的含义特指夫妻间的和谐关系及不同工作内容之间互不冲突且彼此协调。综上,就字面意思而言,该词汇有两层意思:一是不同事物之间互不冲突,二是不同事物彼此协调共同发挥作用。由此可见,相较于"相容"一词,采用"兼容"的表述更为贴切。另一方面,要理解compatible一词在合并仲裁中的含义,还需要结合合并仲裁制度的具体内容来理解。具体而言,即在个案中结合具体多个仲裁协议的内容。根据中国海事仲裁委员会示范仲裁条款②及《仲裁法》第16条,并参酌香港国际仲裁中心示范条款③及斯德哥尔摩商会仲裁院示范仲裁条款④等,一份仲裁协议可以包括以下内容:①仲裁的意思表示;②仲裁事项;③选定的仲裁委员会;④仲裁适用的仲裁规则;⑤仲裁条款适用的法律;⑥选定的仲裁地;⑦仲裁员的人数;⑧仲裁适用的语言。其中,前三项为有效仲裁协议的必备要素。

据此采用"compatible"的标准逐一检讨,可以得出如下结论:其一,各仲裁协议均需要具有请求仲裁的意思表示。其二,有关仲裁事项的约定

---

① 为compatible的名词。参见薛波:《元照英美法词典》,法律出版社2003年版,第268页。

② 中国海事仲裁委员会示范仲裁条款:凡因本合同引起的或与本合同有关的任何争议,均应提交中国海事仲裁委员会,按照申请仲裁时该会现行有效的仲裁规则进行仲裁。仲裁裁决是终局的,对双方均有约束力。

③ 香港国际仲裁中心示范条款:凡因本合同所引起的或与之相关的任何争议、纠纷、分歧或索赔,包括合同的存在、效力、解释、履行、违反或终止,或因本合同引起的或与之相关的任何非合同性争议,均应提交由香港国际仲裁中心管理的机构仲裁,并按照提交仲裁通知时有效的《香港国际仲裁中心机构仲裁规则》最终解决。本仲裁条款适用的法律为……(香港法),仲裁地应为……(香港),仲裁员人数为……名(一名或三名)。仲裁程序应按照(选择语言)来进行。仲裁条款的适用法在一般情况下管辖仲裁条款的存在、范围、效力、解释、履行、违反、终止及可执行性。其不得取代主合同的适用法律。

④ 斯德哥尔摩商会仲裁院示范仲裁条款:任何因本合同产生或与本合同有关的争议、纠纷或索赔,或者有关违约、终止合同或合同无效的争议,均应当根据《斯德哥尔摩商会仲裁院仲裁规则》通过仲裁的方式最终予以解决。建议附加如下:仲裁庭应当由三名仲裁员(一名独任仲裁员)组成。仲裁地应为……仲裁语言应为……本合同应当受……实体法所管辖。

可以不同但不能互相冲突①,即仅就重合的事项可以合并仲裁。其三,选定的仲裁委员会必须相同。其四,选定的仲裁规则必须相同。其五,仲裁员的人数必须相同。其六,仲裁适用的语言必须相同。而关于仲裁条款适用的法律是否可以不同、选定的仲裁地是否可以不同,则要结合不同的案件情况具体判断。例如在"Elmarina案"中②,法院就将仲裁地分别选定在伦敦和纽约的两个案件进行了合并。

第三,对于"问题三"而言,在解释路径上与"问题二"类似,即综合运用文义解释与目的解释的方法。2015年版《仲裁规则》所规定的合并仲裁要件,首次要求案件涉及的多份合同为主从合同关系。在中国法语境下,主合同与从合同的分类侧重于法律效果上的主从关系,即从合同的从属性。表现为从合同在产生、变更、消灭、内容、效力与范围等各个方面的从属性,例如主合同无效则从合同也当然无效。主债权债务合同与为其提供担保的担保合同,是最为典型的主从合同。由此不难发现,按照字面意思理解,第1款第3项可以适用的范围是十分有限的。此外,由于实践中大量存在担保人于主合同文件中一并作出担保意思表示的情况,这会导致主从合同共用同一个仲裁条款;所以,此时直接适用第1款第1项的规定决定合并仲裁即可。这样一来,第3项的规范功能也就大大减弱了。

SIAC规则第8.1条c项同样规定,在存在多份仲裁协议的情况下,合并仲裁需要案涉多个合同为主从合同关系。③ 其对应标准的英文表述,与《仲裁规则》(英文版)也相一致,即"principal contract"与"ancillary contract

---

① 例如,就同一纠纷,部分仲裁协议约定可以仲裁,部分仲裁协议约定不得仲裁或没有约定是否可以就此提交仲裁,此即构成互相冲突。

② 该案中,船东和租船人之间的仲裁协议要求在伦敦进行仲裁,而租船人和货主之间的协议则要求在纽约进行仲裁。最后,法院引用了"Nereus案"作为具有约束力的先例,将这两个案件合并。See T. Evan Schaeffer, *Compulsory Consolidation of Commercial Arbitration Disputes*, 33 St. Louis U. L. J. 495 (1989).

③ 《新加坡国际仲裁中心仲裁规则(第六版)》第8条规定:"在拟合并的各仲裁案件的仲裁庭均未组成之前,拟合并的各仲裁案件符合下列条件之一的,一方当事人可以向主簿提出申请,要求将两个或以上根据本规则正在进行的待决仲裁案件合并为一个仲裁案:……c.各仲裁协议相容,并且:(1)争议由相同法律关系产生;(2)产生争议的多个合同系主从合同的关系;或者(3)争议由同一交易或同一系列交易产生。"

(s)"。结合相应词语之含义①,在英美法系中,"principal contract"与"ancillary contract(s)"之间的关系,除包括类似担保合同与所担保的主合同之间的关系外,亦强调不同合同在系列交易安排中地位的主从性。在该种理解下,典型的主从合同关系,也包括工程承包合同与分包合同。

所以,结合合并仲裁的规范目的,从在交易中所处地位的角度看待"主从合同关系",有必要对《仲裁规则》第19条第1款第3项之规定做一定程度的扩大解释,即将"涉及的多份合同为主从合同关系",解释为案件所涉及的多份合同系出自同一或同一系列交易。

第四,就"问题四"而言,第19条第2款是对仲裁委员会行使决定权时需要考量的因素所作出的不完全列举。一方面,该款明确了仲裁委员会应当考虑当事人意见和案件关联性等因素;另一方面,就该款没有明确的其他因素,仲裁委员会也应当进行考虑。例如,已确定的仲裁员就合并仲裁的意见等。此外,"不同案件的仲裁员的选定或指定情况",具体包括仲裁庭是否已经组成、仲裁员是否相同、仲裁员人数是否相同等因素。一般而言,在尚未组成仲裁庭,或者已经组成的仲裁庭在人数、人员方面均相同,又不存在"拒绝合并仲裁条款"的情况下,仲裁委员会将极可能决定合并仲裁。

第五,关于"问题五"的理解。承前所述,第19条第1款系规定合并仲裁的构成要件,而第2款是行使仲裁委员会的决定权并列举行使决定权须考量的要素。就该两款的关系,在逻辑方面,满足合并仲裁的构成要件是仲裁委员会行使决定权的前提条件;在效力方面,是否进行合并取决于仲裁委员会的决定,亦即仲裁委员会有权在构成要件已经成就的情况下,决定不予合并仲裁。在SESDERMA, S.L.申请撤销仲裁裁决案中,北京市第四中级人民法院就以是否决定合并仲裁为行使仲裁权的范畴为由,驳回了申请人的撤裁请求。②

第六,就"问题六"的理解,该条第3款、第4款分别是对合并方式与

---

① "principal contract"的含义为引起附属合同的合同;"ancillary"含义为补充的、次要的、隶属的。See Bryan A. Garner (ed.), *Block's Law Dictionary (Ninth Edition)*, West Press, 2009, p.372.

② 参见SESDERMA, S.L.申请撤销仲裁裁决案,北京市第四中级人民法院(2021)京04民特144号民事裁定书。

程序安排所作的规定。在合并方式上,与大多数其他机构的做法相同,即出于效率的考量,将其他案件合并至最先开始的案件当中。在程序安排上,第 4 款实质上为一种注意规定:合并后仲裁程序的决定权,于组庭前后分别由仲裁委员会和仲裁庭行使是当然之义。

七、《中国海事仲裁委员会仲裁规则》第 19 条的完善建议

综合本文前述所及之内容,海仲合并仲裁规则(集中规定于第 19 条)可以从以下几个方面加以完善:其一,肯定当事人之间"拒绝合并仲裁条款"的效力,坚守遵循当事人意思自治的底线;其二,在强制合并仲裁的情况下,赋予当事人抗辩权;其三,增加就产生自同一或者同一系列交易的案件进行强制合并仲裁的构成要件;其四,就合并后仲裁庭的组成作出明确规定;其五,尝试对合并仲裁案件的仲裁费用进行适当调整。

第一,强制合并仲裁并非没有边界,亦不是有权机关单纯行使决定权的结果。其本质根源于对当事人默示合并合意所作出的意思表示解释。所以,若当事人事先明确表示了拒绝合并的意思,就客观上排除了解释出合并意思的可能性。故而,在该种情况下,有权机关无论如何不能决定合并。第 19 条并未就此作出规定,所以理论上存在仲裁委员会不顾"拒绝合并仲裁条款"而决定合并的可能。同时从规范的指引功能出发,对此加以明确有利于提示当事人在事先就是否接受合并仲裁作出合理安排,从而减少适用强制合并仲裁规则时可能面临的矛盾和阻碍。出于上述几方面的考量,有必要对第 19 条进行相关修正。

第二,在强制合并仲裁的情况下,赋予当事人抗辩权。首先,这是私权处分原则的题中之义,强制合并仲裁实质上等于处分了本应由非主动合并方当事人享有的权利,其当然可以就此进行抗辩。其次,当事人为行使抗辩权而进行举证,有利于充实仲裁委员会的解释资料,从而对构成要件的该当性作出正确判断。最后,赋予被合并方当事人抗辩权,体现了合并仲裁的正当性。虽然,第 19 条第 2 款已经明确规定了仲裁委员会需要征求各方当事人的意见,但这尚属于行使权力的范畴,而没有赋予当事人权利和仲裁委员会相应的职责。故而,有必要完善相关规定。

第三,承前所述,第 19 条第 2 款第 3 项关于"主从合同关系"的要件

规定,适用范围较窄且功能有限。而作为解决多方当事人复杂仲裁的制度,合并仲裁应用的典型情境之一,即为适用于由同一或同一系列交易引发的纠纷当中。而现有规则不能明确地体现此规范目的,也不能完善地发挥合并仲裁的制度功能,故有必要就此进行补充规定,在构成要件中增加"纠纷产生自同一或者同一系列交易"。

第四,在合并仲裁前,若各案件均未组成仲裁庭或者均已组成仲裁庭但是仲裁庭的组成相同,那么这种情况下仲裁庭的组成当不存在困难。而针对在合并仲裁前,各案件组成了存在差异的仲裁庭或者部分组成了仲裁庭部分没有组成仲裁庭等情况,有必要对组成仲裁庭的规则进行明确。就相关问题,在"Nereus 案"中,仲裁员的组成方式是由三方各选择一名仲裁员,再由这三名选定的仲裁员选择两名仲裁员组成仲裁庭。[①] 但这种较复杂的组庭方式笔者并不认可。此外,HKIAC 规则、SCC 规则、SIAC 规则、比利时仲裁和调解中心(Belgian Centre for Arbitration and Mediation,CEPANI)规则均不同程度地将合并后组庭的权力交给了作为第三方的机构或其职能部门。对此有国外学者研究认为,如果合并案件中的仲裁庭存在差异,但当事人仍坚持合并,应给予当事人在一定时间内更换不匹配的仲裁员的机会;只有在各方当事人未能就新的候选人达成一致的情况下,才应由仲裁机构的主管部门进行指定。[②] 这一观点,既考虑到当事人在组庭中的参与权又兼顾了仲裁程序的效率,对此笔者亦持相同意见。还需要注意的是,对当事人重新协商的时间期限需要进行合理设计。

第五,关于合并仲裁后的仲裁费用调整。将不同案件合并仲裁后,对共同的事实争议,即可通过一个仲裁程序中一次举证,而不需要在多个程序中频繁进行,从而有利于节省费用。[③] 这种费用的减少主要体现在两个方面,一是使仲裁机构、仲裁庭获益的成本减少,例如仲裁员工作时间的减少;二是使当事人直接获益的费用减少,体现在证据搜集成本等方面。但是,并不是每一次合并都会同时产生以上两方面获益或者两者间

---

① See Okuma Kazutake, *Party Autonomy in International Commercial Arbitration: Consolidation of Multiparty and Classwide Arbitration*, 9 ANN. Surv. INT'l & COMP. L. 189 (2003).
② See K. S. Stepanova, Consolidation of Cases in International Commercial Arbitration, 2016 HERALD CIV. PROC. 210 (2016).
③ 参见易扬:《仲裁程序的合并与现代国际商事仲裁》,载北京仲裁委员会组编:《法学评论》(第64辑),中国法制出版社2008年版。

一成不变的获益比例,具体情况需要结合案情进行具体分析。但肯定的是,对仲裁机构、仲裁庭获益的部分,当事人也可以分享其利益。此外,如本文第四部分所述,合并仲裁的实践在我国还并不活跃。故而,在仲裁费用方面,给予合并仲裁的案件减少仲裁费用的优惠,有利于鼓励当事人就合并仲裁达成一致。① 当然,考虑到不同案件的情况不同,参照 HKIAC 规则②,可以赋予仲裁机构酌情调整仲裁费用的权力。

综上所述,第19条可能的修改方案如下:

(一)符合下列条件之一的,经一方当事人请求,仲裁委员会可以决定将根据本规则进行的两个或两个以上的仲裁案件合并为一个仲裁案件进行审理,但是当事人之间的仲裁协议明确约定拒绝合并仲裁的除外。

1. 各案仲裁请求依据同一个仲裁协议提出;

2. 各案仲裁请求依据多份仲裁协议提出,该多份仲裁协议内容相同或相容,且各案当事人相同、各争议所涉及的法律关系性质相同;

3. 各案仲裁请求依据多份仲裁协议提出,该多份仲裁协议内容相同或相容,且涉及的多份合同为主从合同关系,或各争议涉及同一交易或同一系列相关的交易;

4. 所有案件的当事人均同意合并仲裁。

(二)根据上述第(一)款决定合并仲裁时,仲裁委员会应考虑各方当事人的意见、已经组成的仲裁庭的意见及相关仲裁案件之间的关联性等因素,包括不同案件的仲裁员的选定或指定情况。

(三)除非各方当事人另有约定,合并的仲裁案件应合并至最先开始仲裁程序的仲裁案件。

(四)仲裁案件合并前各案件均未组成仲裁庭的,仲裁庭的组成应当依照本规则第三节的规定进行;仲裁案件合并前各案件均已经组成相同仲裁庭的,合并后不再另行组成仲裁庭;仲裁案件合并前部

---

① 参见乔欣、赵玲:《浅议强制合并仲裁》,载北京仲裁委员会组编:《北京仲裁》(第64辑),中国法制出版社2008年版。

② 参见《香港国际仲裁中心机构仲裁规则(2018)》第28条第10款规定:在合并申请提交后,HKIAC 可调整其管理费和(如适当)仲裁庭的收费。

分案件已经组成仲裁庭,部分案件尚未组成仲裁庭的或者组成的仲裁庭不相同的,参照本规则第三十三条①的规定,由各方当事人就合并后仲裁庭的组成进行协商,如果各方当事人未能在接到合并通知后15天内达成一致意见,则由仲裁委员会主任指定仲裁庭三名仲裁员,并从中确定一人担任首席仲裁员。

（五）仲裁案件合并后,在仲裁庭组成之前,由仲裁委员会仲裁院就程序的进行作出决定;仲裁庭组成后,由仲裁庭就程序的进行作出决定。

（六）仲裁委员会可以就合并仲裁后的仲裁费用进行调整。

结　　语

合并仲裁包括合意合并仲裁与强制合并仲裁两类。其中,与合意合并仲裁大相径庭的是,强制合并仲裁面临着理论与实践等方面的诸多争议。将两个及以上彼此独立但存在关联的案件合并仲裁,不仅有利于提高仲裁效率,而且有利于避免出现裁决冲突,实现实体公正。但是合并仲裁的确存在违背当事人意思自治的可能,特别是在强制合并仲裁情况下。

为了克服合并仲裁的上述弊端,就要杜绝纯粹的强制合并仲裁,进而通过意思表示解释的方法,将强制合并仲裁导向默示合意合并仲裁的轨道。就此,结合美国相关合并仲裁的实践经验与世界其他主要仲裁机构的有关规则,一方面要通过设置一定的构成要件来明确解释的标准,另一方面要肯定当事人达成的"拒绝合并仲裁条款"的效力。此外,笔者还主张赋予被合并方当事人抗辩权,以此维护合并仲裁的正当性。

在理解与适用海仲仲裁规则中的合并仲裁制度时,需要重点关注

---

① 《中国海事仲裁委员会仲裁规则》第33条规定:"（一）仲裁案件有两个或两个以上申请人及/或被申请人时,申请人方及/或被申请人方应各自协商,各方共同选定或共同委托仲裁委员会主任指定一名仲裁员。（二）首席仲裁员或独任仲裁员应按照本规则第三十一条第（二）、（三）、（四）款规定的程序选定或指定。申请人方及/或被申请人方按照本规则第三十一条第（三）款的规定选定首席仲裁员或独任仲裁员时,应各方共同协商,提交各方共同选定的候选人名单。（三）如果申请人方及/或被申请人方未能在收到仲裁通知后15天内各方共同选定或各方共同委托仲裁委员会主任指定一名仲裁员,则由仲裁委员会主任指定仲裁庭三名仲裁员,并从中确定一人担任首席仲裁员。"

六方面的问题。其中对"仲裁协议相容"的理解,必须结合仲裁协议的具体内容进行判断。同时基于合并仲裁的制度目的,有必要针对"多份合同为主从合同关系"进行一定程度的扩大解释。进行合并仲裁,需要同时满足构成要件的该当性与决定权行使的合理性两方面要求。仲裁委员会在行使决定权时需要综合考虑多方面要素,包括已经组成的仲裁庭的意见。在上述基础上,海仲合并仲裁规则的完善可以从五个方面来进行。

我国的相关司法实践表明,合并仲裁在我国尚不活跃,而司法对合并仲裁在很大程度上持包容的态度。故而,未来合并仲裁在我国还有广阔的发展空间。

数字贸易知识产权风险分析与管理*

薛 虹**

摘要:数字贸易为国际贸易发展带来新的机遇,也增加了经营者的知识产权风险,数字贸易的经营者对于控制与管理知识产权风险有着强烈的需求。一方面,数字平台为经营者提供了知识产权风险管理的规则与设施,另一方面,国际贸易法中的知识产权保证制度正在焕发生机,重构进出口方风险与利益的分配模式。在数字贸易的新环境下,经营者增强管理与控制相关知识产权风险的能力,对于避免与减少损失、保护自身的贸易利益具有重大意义。

关键词:数字贸易;风险管理;数字平台;争议解决;知识产权保证

数字化与互联网深刻地改变了国际贸易的环境、形式与价值链构成,使全球化的市场成为更为有效的信息系统。由此,国际货物贸易、服务贸易、知识产权贸易进入了深度全球化的新阶段,得到了前所未有的发展。数字网络技术所支撑的数字贸易已经在国际贸易总量中占据很大的比重,并正在逐渐成为国际贸易的主流形式。

世界贸易组织正在进行关于数字贸易市场准入与公平竞争方面的谈判,亚太经济合作组织建立了跨境数据流动的项目,联合国国际贸易法委员会、亚太经社理事会等在进行关于无纸化贸易、电子签名、电子身份认证的国际谈判与立法,联合国贸易和发展会议正在开展援助发展中国家、弥合数字鸿沟的项目,其他国际组织在进行关于网络安全、网络税收等议

---

* 本文完成于 2021 年 11 月。
** 北京师范大学教授,国家贸易数字化专家委员会委员。

题的讨论……凡此种种,都从不同侧面、在不同程度上为数字贸易构建国际法律体系。但是数字贸易有其自身的特点,适应数字贸易需要的国际贸易法律规则尚待完善。

中共中央、国务院于 2021 年 9 月 22 日印发的《知识产权强国建设纲要(2021—2035 年)》强调,要打通知识产权创造、运用、保护、管理和服务全链条,更大力度加强知识产权保护国际合作。数字贸易增大了贸易活动中的知识产权风险,指引经营者重新评估与构建风险管控路径、措施与策略,是值得专门研究与探索的问题。

一、数字贸易的范围与特点

数字贸易一词虽然广为人知,但是尚无全球统一的定义,故对其范围的理解多有不同。可以肯定的是,数字贸易不能等同于使用数字、网络技术的国际贸易活动,否则数字贸易将几乎成为国际贸易的代名词。

一种观点认为,数字贸易约等于跨境电子商务。但是,跨境电子商务是通过网络跨境销售商品或服务的活动[1],其侧重点在于通过数字网络订立交易,未通过数字网络订立交易但是通过数字网络交付或履行的贸易活动被排除在外。[2] 例如,跨境网络银行服务合同的签署需要国外客户在银行柜台完成身份认证、信息核验等线下步骤,但合同订立后,银行完全通过网络提供服务。事实上,跨国企业间(B2B)订立的重大合同,为慎重起见,仍然可能在线下订立,但其履行可以通过数字网络进行。还有数量很大的存量合同,包括交易时因技术条件等原因并非通过网络订立的国际服务贸易合同(例如企业间的软件服务、产品设计等),在现有条件下已经通过互联网提供或履行。所以,数字贸易不能局限于跨境电子商务的范围。

同样,数字贸易也不能局限于通过数字网络交付或履行的贸易活

---

[1] 根据我国《电子商务法》的规定,电子商务是指通过互联网等信息网络销售商品或者提供服务的经营活动;电子商务平台的定义,更能反映电子商务侧重交易的特征,即在电子商务中为交易双方或者多方提供网络经营场所、交易撮合、信息发布等服务,供交易双方或者多方独立开展交易活动。

[2] 世界贸易组织于 1998 年建立的部长级电子商务项目将电子商务的范围扩展到电子形式的生产、发行、推广、销售或交付商品或服务。但是,该广义的电子商务概念并未得到大多数国家或地区的普遍认可,多数国家或地区仍将电子商务限于交易活动的范围内。

动,否则通过网络达成但在线下交付或履行的国际货物买卖或服务贸易就将被排除在外(例如线上订立的境外租车合同)。①

因此,将数字网络交易与数字网络交付或履行两个方面结合起来,才能反映数字贸易的全貌,即数字贸易是通过数字网络订立交易和/或通过数字网络交付或者履行的国际贸易形式。② 数字化交易与数字化交付两者存在交叉、重叠,并非彼此排斥,也非并列条件。既数字化交易又数字化交付的贸易活动(例如电子书等数字产品贸易),当然属于数字贸易。两者仅具其一,例如数字化交易但线下交付/履行的货物贸易或服务贸易,或者线下交易但数字化交付/履行的服务贸易、知识产权贸易,也属于数字贸易的范围。

数字贸易涉及的范围非常广泛,横跨货物贸易、服务贸易、知识产权贸易(包括数字产品贸易),贸易主体包括企业、个人、消费者、政府主管部门及其他公共或私营机构等,贸易形式包括企业之间(B2B)贸易、企业面向消费者(B2C)贸易③以及个人之间(C2C)贸易。

在数字贸易中,数字平台发挥着十分重要的作用。数字贸易因此具有平台经济的鲜明特色。数字贸易的迅猛发展在很大程度上得益于数字平台的支持。数字平台,又称互联网平台,是通过网络信息技术,使多个卖方与多个买方在特定载体提供的规则下直接交互以创造价值的商业组织形态。数字平台最为突出的特点是不享有平台内交易的货物或服务的所有权,不是平台内交易的主体,因此对于平台内卖方与买方而言,平台提供的是第三方服务或"中介服务"。亚马逊等企业兼顾自营与第三方业务,实质上其自营业务属于B2C贸易,第三方业务才是平台服务。④ 数字平台有的收取平台内经营者费用(例如苹果应用商店 App Store 收取佣

---

① 中国信息通信研究院于2020年发布《数字贸易发展白皮书——驱动变革的数字服务贸易》将数字贸易界定于数字服务贸易,不仅贸易方式数字化,而且贸易对象也要数字化,即关于数据、数字内容与数字服务的贸易才属于数字贸易。

② 经济合作与发展组织、世界贸易组织、国际货币基金组织于2020年发布《数字贸易测度手册》(Handbook on Measuring Digital Trade)第一版,将数字贸易定义为数字网络订立交易和/或通过数字网络交付或者履行的贸易。

③ 例如,我国企业建立的快时尚出口跨境电子商务公司希音(Shein),业务主要面向美国、欧洲、中东、印度等海外市场,覆盖全球100多个国家和地区。

④ 据亚马逊2019年报披露,其第三方服务的经营额在总营收中的占比不断增大,从1999年开始在20年中增长到58%。

金),有的则对经营者免费但通过广告推广等服务获取收益(例如阿里巴巴跨境电子商务平台 AliExpress)。不论盈利模式如何,数字平台承载数量众多的经营者,为交易及交付、履行活动提供自动信息系统,制定实施贸易活动规则,维持平台内经营活动的秩序,已经发展成为数字贸易的基础设施,深刻地改变了国际贸易的广度与深度。①

借助全球性的数字平台,大量中小微企业甚至个人得以进入国际贸易领域,与境外主体直接进行贸易活动。传统国际贸易以 B2B 大宗货物买卖为主,但在数字贸易中,B2B 贸易与 B2C、C2C 贸易并重,除大型企业外,中小微企业、个人及其他组织均为活跃的贸易主体;货物贸易、服务贸易并驾齐驱,新兴的结合了数字产品、数字内容与数据服务的知识产权贸易异军突起。由于数字平台面向全球市场,国内企业之间可以根据需要建立全球化的供应链,通过外国平台进行贸易活动,从而进入数字贸易的范围。数字贸易呈现出的新特点,极大地拓宽了国际贸易的维度。

二、数字贸易知识产权风险分析

数字贸易蓬勃发展,经营者的知识产权风险不容小觑。除了假冒、盗版等黑灰产,数字贸易的经营者对于控制与管理知识产权风险有着强烈的需求。知识产权风险管理通过预估、识别、判断经营活动可能面临的知识产权纠纷风险采取尽量避免或者减少损失的策略与措施。即所谓未思进先思退,知进退,明得失,料成败。知识产权风险可以从频率与烈度两个维度予以分析,有些风险发生概率小,但一旦发生造成的损失却可能很大,而另一些风险相对频发,但成本较低。因此,经营者管理知识产权风险的策略要综合考虑两个维度的互动,灵活采取避免与减少损失的措施。总之,控制成本与风险,保障经营活动,是经营者知识产权风险管理的总体策略。

国际知识产权法律体系由国际公约、条约、协定所组成,虽然在很大程度上协调了世界主要经济体的知识产权法律制度,但是国家/地区间知识产权法律体系仍存在差异,且差异随着法律制度的发展还在扩大。与 21 世纪初期贸易全球化的迅猛势头相比,现今数字贸易面对的是更为复

---

① 参见 2021 年 2 月 7 日《国务院反垄断委员会关于平台经济领域的反垄断指南》。

杂多变的知识产权法律制度,更为严厉与广泛的知识产权执法措施以及前所未见的知识产权新问题。然而,与从事传统国际贸易的大型、跨国企业不同,大量中小微企业、个人涌入数字贸易的洪流,因明显缺乏国际法律经验、资源与能力,更可能暴露于知识产权风险之中,给经营活动造成重大损失,甚至因此遭遇灭顶之灾。

由于数字贸易与平台经济高度耦合,很多经营者误以为知识产权风险主要来自平台展示的商品或服务因权利人的通知而被从平台删除、屏蔽等。这种理解是非常片面的,数字贸易的知识产权风险遍及商品或服务展示、推销、交易、支付、交付或履行等全过程,并不限于数字平台在交易达成之前的阶段采取的所谓"通知—删除"措施,而且即便不使用数字平台的经营者也同样面临知识产权风险。何况,数字贸易的新手们还可能因缺乏对于知识产权保证等法律制度的了解,错失规避风险的机会,增大暴露风险的可能性。

在更为严峻的知识产权环境中,数字贸易的经营者还要面对不同国家或地区法律适用与司法管辖冲突等问题,整体上知识产权风险在增大。固守旧的风险管理策略与措施,无法适应新的形势,难以抵御不断增大的风险。笔者选取数字贸易经营者知识产权风险最为突出的场景进行分析,研究有关的风险管控策略与措施。

三、数字平台内经营者知识产权风险管理

跨境电商、社交媒体、应用商店等数字平台通过建立与实施平台规则(或称"政策")进行平台治理。数字平台治理既出于维护平台自身利益的目的,也符合规避有关法律责任的需求。数字平台依据平台规则,基于与平台内经营者的契约关系,设定知识产权保护的要求,在必要时对经营者采取限制或制止贸易活动等处罚措施。数字平台的知识产权治理早已不是自发行为,而是被纳入法律规范与监督的范畴。法律一方面以责任机制激励数字平台对经营者采取知识产权治理措施[1],另一方面又对数字平台知识产权治理的正

---

[1] 数字平台对于平台内发生的知识产权侵权是否及如何承担责任,不是本文所要讨论的问题。简而言之,虽然有的国家或地区法律规定数字平台承担直接侵权责任,有的则规定承担中介责任,但是无一例外地要求数字平台尽到合理的注意义务,不允许对平台内的侵权行为装聋作哑、听之任之。

当性与适当性进行监督。平台内经营者只有深入理解数字平台知识产权规则与措施,才能构建有效充分的知识产权风险控制策略与措施。

(一)数字平台知识产权规则

数字平台内经营者的知识产权风险主要来自平台采取的限制或终止经营者交易能力或者履行/交付能力的措施。数字平台基本上是私营企业,虽然不具有政府机关的公权力,但却可以通过建立与实施平台规则并将之纳入与经营者之间的合同关系,对平台内的经营者等主体加以约束。数字平台的知识产权规则不断发展、日趋复杂,一部分是对经营者提出知识产权要求,预防知识产权风险的发生,另一部分则是在认定经营者涉嫌知识产权侵权时采取的限制或制止贸易活动的处罚措施。

1. 经营者监督平台规则的合法性

数字平台建立的预防性规则,可以帮助经营者管理有关的知识产权风险,基本上对经营者有利。但是也可能出现数字平台的知识产权要求过高,经营者难以达到或者疲于应付的情况。[①] 例如,亚马逊平台建立了卖家品牌注册机制,拥有品牌注册的卖家享有免费地编辑所售商品的名称与描述、添加广告推销的商品资料、使用推广工具、自动识别与删除假冒商品等品牌保护特权。以往,拥有任何国家商标注册的经营者都可以申请品牌注册,但自2019年起亚马逊修改了规则,在某个国家销售商品的经营者必须在该国拥有商标注册,才能进入平台的品牌注册机制。如中国卖家向美国出售商品,必须事先获得美国专利商标局的文字或图形商标注册。虽然此举可使经营者避免与美国在先注册或使用的商标发生冲突而卷入法律纠纷或者丧失原有品牌,但是美国商标注册申请程序长达1年,而且必须雇用美国当地的律师提交注册申请[②],费时费力,明显增加了经营者的负担。

一旦经营者被认定为违反有关的平台规则,数字平台采取的处罚对经营

[①] 平台规则不得降低法定的知识产权保护标准或为知识产权保护设置不合理的条件,但是也不应随意扩大权利保护的范围,不合理地缩小权利的限制与例外,导致其他公众使用知识产权自由受到妨碍。参见薛虹:《国际电子商务法通论》,中国法制出版社2019年版,第96—101页。

[②] 自2019年8月起,所有住所地不在美国的经营者必须通过美国律师向美国专利商标局递交商标注册申请。

者杀伤力巨大。2021年4月底至6月,亚马逊平台将我国多个跨境卖家的商品下架,一些有自主品牌的规模较大的卖家遭受重大打击。从亚马逊垂直类目上的销售情况来看,这些卖家每暂停一分钟,其损失数以万元计。亚马逊平台下架商品的处罚措施让跨境卖家噤若寒蝉。从亚马逊的公开声明看,该数字平台"暂停部分卖家的销售权限"是因为这些卖家"刷单炒信"违反了亚马逊"规则和政策"。① 其中也不乏卖家是因销售涉嫌假冒的商品而受到波及。

数字平台与经营者之间虽然是契约关系,但是双方的缔约地位与能力明显不对等。数字平台(特别是大型全球性平台)处于数字市场"守门人"的关键位置,经营者则在很大程度上依附于平台。② 数字平台不是无法之地,大平台势力庞大可能走到公共利益的反面。平台经济正在逐渐进入深水区,世界主要经济体正在尝试不同的法律规范与机制,对于日趋强大的平台治理权力进行认真的审视。数字平台滥用其治理权力,制定与实施不合法、不适当的规则损害经营者合法权益的,经营者应当有获得法律救济的渠道。

2021年5月,美国法院审理的英佩游戏公司(Epic Games)诉苹果公司垄断一案(以下简称"Epic案")表明,数字平台的规则及其治理行为的合法性正在受到更加严厉的司法审查。③ 苹果应用商店是苹果公司经营

---

① 2021年5月,亚马逊发布公开信,称:"近期,我们暂停了部分卖家的销售权限。""亚马逊的政策明确要求卖家不可以滥用评论。""无论卖家的业务规模大小、所在何地,亚马逊商城的规则和政策对所有卖家都是公平的、一视同仁的。我们也秉持严格的执行标准,确保政策实施的准确性、一贯性。""未来,我们也将持续履行这一职责,严谨地监督商城的运营环境并慎重地采取行动。"

② 2020年欧盟《数字市场法案》将规模大、用户多、存续时间长的大型在线平台称为市场的"数字守门人",并规定了相应的法律义务。

③ 2020年8月,在苹果应用商店下架堡垒之夜游戏之后,英佩游戏公司以苹果公司妨害竞争为由,向美国加利福尼亚州北区联邦地区法院提起诉讼。该案于2021年9月由审理法官作出判决。英佩游戏公司还同时在澳大利亚、英国对苹果公司以基本相同的理由起诉。[英佩游戏公司随后起诉苹果公司,指控苹果公司对苹果应用商店内的开发商滥用权力,施加限制性条款,强迫开发商使用苹果支付技术,以保障苹果公司对应用商店内开发商的销售额抽取15%至30%的佣金。苹果公司辩称,要求开发商使用苹果支付系统是为了确保应用商店的安全性和隐私性,并且其收费标准与其他游戏平台(例如微软公司的Xbox)相近。2021年8月26日,苹果公司发布应用商店自2022年起生效的一系列新政策,其中包括允许App开发者通过邮件订阅等方式向用户提供苹果iOS支付系统以外的购买方式,以此绕开苹果公司的抽成。这意味着,苹果公司感受到了美国App开发者的反垄断官司的压力。2021年9月10日,"Epic案"的法官判决,责令苹果公司修改其应用商店的规则,允许应用程序的开发者在程序中设置链接或按钮向用户提供非苹果支付方式的选项。此判决将使开发者有机会免于被苹果公司征收高达30%的佣金。]

的在数以十亿计的苹果手机 iOS 系统内运行的数字平台,英佩游戏公司等开发商就是该平台内的卖家。英佩游戏公司的堡垒之夜游戏于2020年被苹果应用商店强行下架,理由是该公司推出自己的应用程序内置付款系统,规避苹果公司征收的高达30%的佣金。如英佩游戏公司名称所示,该案确有划时代的意义。该案争议的焦点在于苹果公司在其经营的平台上实施向开发商收取30%佣金等政策是否合法。苹果应用商店向来被苹果公司视为自己"有围墙的花园"。英佩游戏公司要证明的就是苹果公司没有"我的花园我做主"的权力,一旦平台规则和平台治理行为破坏正常的市场竞争秩序,违反法律规定,就应经司法审查被认定为无效。

"Epic 案"不仅为平台经济反垄断执法提供了非常重要的判例,而且为法律监督数字平台规则及治理的合法性开辟了新的路径。数字平台虽然势力庞大,但经营者并非只能逆来顺受,为了维护自身的合法权益,可以起诉数字平台,请求否定平台规则的效力、终止有关规则的实施。数字平台及其规则必须遵守企业所在地/注册地的法律,并接受合法性审查。在有些国家和地区的竞争法中,主管部门有权对数字平台妨碍市场竞争的行为予以行政处罚。① 经营者如能证明数字平台的知识产权规则与措施损害市场竞争、涉嫌垄断,可以依法提起诉讼或者向主管部门投诉,请求终止平台有关规则和政策的执行。在上文提到的亚马逊平台下架事件中,经营者如能证明亚马逊平台的规则及实施行为涉嫌垄断,也可依据美国的反垄断法律提起诉讼,请求终止平台有关规则和政策的执行。

2.经营者参与平台治理

推翻数字平台的规则毕竟是经营者迫不得已采取的极端手段。经营

---

① 例如,我国《电子商务法》规定,电子商务平台经营者利用服务协议、交易规则以及技术等手段,对平台内经营者在平台内的交易、交易价格以及与其他经营者的交易等进行不合理限制或者附加不合理条件,或者向平台内经营者收取不合理费用,由市场监督管理部门责令限期改正,可以处 5 万元以上 50 万元以下的罚款;情节严重的,处 50 万元以上 200 万元以下的罚款。又如,欧盟明显加强其关于平台经济的反垄断执法措施,将电子商务平台经营者视为数字守门人,对其妨碍或者破坏市场竞争的行为予以坚决的制裁与打击。欧盟《数字市场法案》规定,数字平台对经营者实施歧视性商业规则的,主管部门对其处以的罚款最高达该公司全球市场年收入的 10%。再如,美国联邦贸易委员会于 2021 年向联邦法院起诉 Facebook 涉嫌滥用社交媒体市场支配地位的行为。

者以此为风险控制的手段,成本与代价太高。经营者如能在日常经营活动中参与平台规则的制定、监督平台规则的实施,既能避免与数字平台对簿公堂的窘境,又能达到事半功倍的效果。

与美国及欧盟的法律相比,我国不仅在大力加强平台经济反垄断执法的力度,而且在监管平台规则、平台治理方面走在世界前列,为数字经济的法治建设开创了新的局面。我国 2019 年开始实施的《电子商务法》深刻揭示了平台经济的基本事实,即电子商务平台通过制定与执行平台规则及其衍生的服务协议,以实现对平台的治理。平台规则是平台制定与实施的规章制度,通过服务协议成为对所有平台内经营者与消费者具有约束力的合同条款。《电子商务法》不仅将平台规则纳入法律规范的体系,认可平台的治理权力,而且明确规定平台进行治理的法定义务。

我国《电子商务法》对于平台制定与实施规则提出一系列要求,包括:平台规则的制定应当遵循公开、公平、公正的原则;平台规则的修改应当公开征求意见并不得强行适用于用户;平台规则应当充分有效地公开;平台规则应具有合法性;平台规则一旦实施对于平台用户具有强制性;平台有权依照服务协议与平台规则的约定,对违约用户实施警示、暂停或者终止服务等措施,但应及时公示;平台内经营者受到平台规则和服务协议处罚的,有权投诉、举报。[①] 平台治理违反有关的法定义务,将依法受到主管机关的行政处罚。

我国《电子商务法》最为突出的创新在于,确立了利益有关各方共同参与制定实施平台规则的法律原则。根据其规定,平台应当遵循公开、公平、公正的原则制定平台服务协议和平台规则,明确平台与其用户(经营者与消费者)的权利和义务。如要修改制定后付诸实施的平台规则,平台应当在其首页显著位置公开征求意见,采取合理措施确保有关各方能够及时充分表达意见。其中,"有关各方"当然包括平台内经营者(卖家)与消费者,而且还可以包括平台外的公众。由此,电子商务平台规则制定与修改中的开放性被上升到法定义务的高度。平台内经营者依法有权参与

---

① 详见我国《电子商务法》第 32—36 条、第 59 条。

到平台规则制定与平台治理的过程之中。①

依据我国《电子商务法》的规定,平台内经营者不再是平台规则与平台治理的被动接受者,而是享有法定权利的平台治理参与者,不仅有权对平台实施的不当治理行为提出投诉举报,寻求法律救济,而且可以直接参与平台规则的修改过程,充分表达意见。平台规则的修改内容应当在实施前予以公示,接受法律与社会公众的监督。

假如亚马逊平台适用我国《电子商务法》,品牌注册机制等知识产权规则的修改就应当经平台内经营者事先评议。经营者通过反对于其不利的规则修改,管理有关的知识产权风险。虽然外国数字平台适用我国法律的可能性不大,但是平台规则与治理行为日益受到各国、各地区法律的规范与监督,却是不争的事实。

即便其他国家或地区尚未吸纳我国《电子商务法》的先进经验,亚马逊这样的超大型数字平台为了行稳致远,也在自觉完善其平台治理体系,争取经营者对平台规则的支持与认同。这为数字平台上的千百万中小微经营者强化自身的知识产权风险控制提供了极好的契机。随着平台经济发展成熟,数字平台早已不再是"独唱团",必须融进有关各方协商、配合的合唱之中。

(二)版权通知

从1998年美国《数字千年版权法》开始,主要经济体与贸易区域相继作出法律规定,不约而同地要求提供信息存储(web hosting)与定位(information location)的网络服务提供者尽到合理的注意义务,制止用户的版权侵权行为,并且在收到版权通知时及时删除被通知的内容与信息,作为享受责任限制(避风港规则)的条件。此类法律机制尽管在不同国家或地区的适用范围有异(例如我国《电子商务法》规定的知识产权通知不限于版

---

① 我国电子商务平台治理的法律规定深受互联网治理的影响。根据2005年联合国信息社会世界峰会互联网治理工作组对于互联网治理的定义,互联网治理是指利益相关的各方各司其职,共同发展和应用塑造互联网演进与使用有关的原则、规范、规则、决策程序及项目的活动。互联网治理的基本原则是开放透明,有关各方共同参与。法律对于数字平台治理的规范也主要由此入手,要求平台规则必须充分有效地公开、透明,保障经营者等利益相关方在一定程度上可以参与平台规则的制定与平台的决策过程。

权领域)①,但逐渐发展成为网络版权责任体系中最广为人知的部分。

美国通过与其贸易伙伴国签订的双边或者多边自由贸易协定,将《数字千年版权法》中版权通知的法律机制"输出"到国际贸易法律体系中。近年来比较突出的例证是 11 个国家于 2018 年签订《全面与进步跨太平洋伙伴关系协定》,其中的知识产权章节比较完整地吸收了美式的版权通知机制。②

1. 版权通知机制的演进

以美国为代表的版权通知机制的主要构成为:网络服务提供者收到版权通知后立即对被通知网络内容采取终止访问的措施,并尽快通知被采取措施的用户,将用户提交的不侵权声明(反通知)转发通知人,如通知人未能在收到转发的反通知后一定期限(10—15 日)内向法院起诉,则终止所采取的措施。

在此类通知机制中,网络服务提供者只需按照权利人通知与用户的反通知行事,不必对其内容加以判断。但是因通知仅是网络服务提供者责任体系的一个组成部分,并不能免除其所承担的善良管理人义务,即便没有收到通知,如被证明知道或应当知道用户的侵权行为却不采取措施的,网络服务提供者仍然要承担相应的侵权责任。此类案例已经屡见不鲜。③

网络服务提供者发展成为数字平台之后,呈几何级数增长的用户规模、不断扩张的服务范围与日益强大的治理能力,促使其不再对权利人的通知作出被动反应,而是寻求在通知机制中扮演更为主动积极的角色。目前有一定规模的数字平台(例如 Facebook、Amazon、App Store)无不建立

---

① 我国《电子商务法》第 42 条第 1 款规定,知识产权权利人认为其知识产权受到侵害的,有权通知电子商务平台经营者采取删除、屏蔽、断开链接、终止交易和服务等必要措施。通知应当包括构成侵权的初步证据。因此,该通知机制适用于包括版权在内的各类知识产权。

② 具有讽刺意味的是,美国虽是始作俑者,但在《全面与进步跨太平洋伙伴关系协定》签署之前,当时的特朗普政府于 2017 年 1 月退出了协定的谈判。该协定最终由日本、加拿大、澳大利亚、智利、新西兰、新加坡、文莱、马来西亚、越南、墨西哥和秘鲁签署。该协定虽然于 2018 年 12 月 30 日生效,但是其中部分条款(包括关于网络服务的条款)被暂时搁置。我国于 2021 年 9 月正式申请加入该协定。

③ 参见薛虹:《国际电子商务法通论》,中国法制出版社 2019 年版,第 110—114 页。

了知识产权规则与治理机制,并将法律规定的版权通知纳入其中。①

数字平台治理推动版权通知机制从原来的1.0版本升级到2.0版本。欧盟2019年颁布与实施的《数字单一市场版权指令》,对升级后的版权通知机制作出规定,即在线内容分享服务提供者在收到版权人的证据充分确凿的通知后,应当尽快对被通知的内容实施终止访问或删除网站的措施,并尽最大努力防止这些内容被再次上传;版权人在请求服务提供者采取有关措施时,应当提供适当与正当的理由;同时,服务提供者与版权人合作,不应导致用户上传的非侵权性内容被无辜屏蔽或波及。

与1.0版本相比,服务提供者在2.0版本的版权通知机制中的地位与作用发生了明显的变化,依法获得评判与认定版权通知是否"证据充分确凿"及理由是否适当与正当的权力。服务提供者不再听凭版权人的一面之词就采取行动,还要考虑被通知的内容是否属于非侵权性的内容,例如用户是否享有合理使用该内容的权利。

在1.0版本中,网络服务提供者的用户(即经营者)管理知识产权风险主要是及时提交不侵权声明(反通知),寄希望于服务提供者采取的措施能尽快终止;并在能证明权利人恶意(错误)通知的情况下,请求权利人赔偿因网络服务提供者采取措施而遭受的损失。② 在2.0版本中,经营者风险管理的空间明显增大了,可以在平台调查判断权利人的通知是否证据充分、理由正当的过程中,及时举证证明自身有使用被通知内容的合法权益,阻止平台采取有关措施;还可以在平台采取终止访问或删除网站等措施后,积极向平台投诉,请求尽快终止有关的措施。

2. 通知机制适用范围的扩展

在数字贸易中,版权通知不可避免地涉及国际版权法律问题。例如,中国版权人通知欧盟国家的数字平台删除涉嫌侵权的信息,平台须依据所在国法律识别版权通知及采取措施是否有相应的法律依据。由于数

---

① 将版权通知纳入数字平台治理机制,有其历史渊源。美国《数字千年版权法》在原初设计的版权通知机制中规定,网络服务提供者对多次侵权行为人实施终止网络服务的政策或规则,是其享受避风港待遇的法定前提条件之一。

② 与美国《数字千年版权法》不同,我国《电子商务法》加重了发出通知的知识产权人的责任,即:只要通知错误造成平台内经营者损害的,不论有无过错,均应依法承担民事责任;恶意发出错误通知,造成平台内经营者损失的,加倍承担赔偿责任。

字平台基本上建立在世界主体经济体内,依据《国际版权法》规定的原则,只要版权内容已在世界上任何一个主要国家出版(或同时出版)就能够在平台所在国获得版权法律保护,数字平台根据版权通知采取措施就有本国法律的根据。[1] 数字平台上的经营者出于版权风险管理的需求,应当充分了解平台所在国的相应法律,并依据所适用的法律针对版权通知提供自身享有合法权益的抗辩理由,例如,专为盲人或视力障碍者改编作品的国际转让,不需版权人许可。[2]

根据欧盟《数字单一市场版权指令》的规定,仅规模较大、营利性的在线内容分享服务提供者可以接受版权通知。该通知机制适用对象与范围均较狭窄。2020年年底欧盟《数字服务法案》(目前尚未生效)对通知机制加以发展,要求所有数字平台均须接收关于任何违法内容、产品、服务或行为的通知;销售假冒商品、擅自使用版权材料等行为均在通知范围之内。[3] 提供网络存储的数字平台必须建立便于访问、界面友好、电子形式的通知接收机制,并以"清晰与毫不含糊的语言以易于访问的形式公布"平台实施的任何限制平台内经营者的条款或者条件;而且平台在依据上述条款或条件限制或处分平台内经营者的,应当以审慎、客观与适度的方式行事,并将相关各方的权利与合法利益考虑在内。平台如决定将某一平台内经营者商品下架,必须给出清楚与明确的理由,其中包括下架所适用的地域范围、所依据的法律规范或者平台规则、经营者可以寻求的救济途径。欧盟法律特别强调,平台必须给予被下架商品的经营者通过平台内机制进行投诉、寻求处理的机会,经营者对于平台处理决定仍然不服的,应有权选择欧盟内的非讼争议解决程序寻求进一步的救济。总之,数

---

[1] 世界贸易组织《与贸易有关的知识产权协定》吸收了《保护文学艺术作品伯尔尼公约》(简称《伯尔尼公约》)规定的版权保护原则,即作者在成员国中享受和行使《伯尔尼公约》规定的权利不需要履行任何手续,但各国依据本国法律对外国作品予以保护,不受作品来源国版权保护的影响。

[2] 2016年生效的《关于为盲人、视力障碍者或其他印刷品阅读障碍者获得已出版作品提供便利的马拉喀什条约》建立了便利盲人、视力障碍者或其他印刷品阅读障碍者获取已出版作品的国际版权法律规范,允许不经版权人允许复制、发行、提供及国际转让特定格式的作品。该条约由世界知识产权组织管理,中国、美国、欧盟国家等主要国家均已加入该条约,并在本国法中承认该条约建立的法律规则。

[3] 此外,涉嫌儿童色情信息、非法仇恨信息、歧视性信息、恐怖主义信息、侵犯隐私的信息、非法追踪等违法信息也在被通知的范围内。

字平台对实施下架经营者商品的规则与治理行为,要承担相应的法律义务,并受到欧盟内发达的争议解决程序的监督。

在数字贸易中,通知机制适用范围扩大到商标、专利、植物新品种权等工业产权,难免涉及不同国家的法律冲突与选择等复杂问题。有的数字平台仅承认以所在国的权利为基础的通知。例如,权利人在欧盟获得的注册商标与专利权并不当然在我国得到承认与保护,只有在我国获得同等的商标注册或专利批准,我国平台才承认基于该权利发出的通知。也有的平台面向全球市场,对通知的权利基础作广义解释。例如,在亚马逊平台上主张商标权或专利权受到侵犯的通知,必须证明在所主张遭受侵权的国家享有相应的权利,在其他国家享有的权利则不足为据。因此,数字平台内的经营者在面对知识产权通知时,应先分清权利主张的地域范围与法律依据,再提出相应的抗辩理由。

（三）争议解决

数字平台收到知识产权人关于平台内经营者涉嫌侵权的通知或投诉后,由于自身资源与能力所限,难以对复杂的事实与法律问题作出判断的,可以借助专家机制解决此类问题。在专家机制中,知识产权人在自愿的基础上,将有关的投诉提交数字平台建立的争议解决系统,该系统就知识产权人与平台内经营者之间的纠纷进行分析判断,所作认定（判定）由数字平台直接执行,或者作为平台采取相关措施的依据。

1. 数字平台争议解决的特点

数字平台的专家争议解决机制具有合法性、专业性、网络化、快速性等特点。依据我国《电子商务法》的规定,平台如果选择建立此类机制则应符合有关的法定要求,制定并公示有关的争议解决规则。平台内经营者基于契约关系,受平台制定并公示的争议解决规则的约束,只要不退出平台,就必须受争议解决程序的管辖。知识产权人只要选择使用平台提供的机制进行投诉,也必须明示接受平台争议解决规则的约束。因此,平台争议解决规则是争议解决机制运行的基础,类似于依托于域名注册管理体制而运行的域名争议解决机制。①

域名注册管理机构一般授权专业性的争议解决机构,依据其所制定与公示的争议解决规则,独立裁决投诉的商标权人与域名持有人之间的争议。② 域名争议解决机制在运行机构上的独立性是该程序得以公平与公正解决当事人争议的客观保障。

欧盟建立的消费者在线纠纷解决机制也可供参考。依据欧盟《消费者在线纠纷解决机制条例》,自2016年2月起,在欧盟数字化单一市场框架内,所有面向消费者的电子商务经营者(包括数字平台)都必须实施跨境消费者纠纷网上解决机制。在欧盟27个成员国区域内,消费者可以向在线争议解决平台提交有关跨境电子商务纠纷的投诉,通过平台上注册的争议解决服务提供者解决争议。欧盟内所有电子商务经营者都必须在其网站上以醒目方式设置通向在线争议解决平台的链接,向消费者提供其在线联系方式及指定的在线争议解决机构,并告知消费者在线争议解决平台的信息与使用方法。欧盟在线纠纷解决机制为电子商务经营者与消费者提供了跨国界、多语种、简单快捷、费用低廉的非诉讼的在线争议解决途径,保障了交易安全与消费信心。从欧盟上述法律规定看,消费者在线争议解决是通过专业性的争议解决服务提供者运行的,并未由经营者自行运行。

因此,数字平台建立争议解决机制可以授权独立的第三方知识产权或者争议解决专业机构,依据争议解决平台规则,通过在线系统,以当事人谈判、专家调解、专家裁决等各种方式解决知识产权争议。独立运行的平台争议解决机制可以满足程序正义的要求。

数字平台争议解决机制利用数字技术、采用网络化的方式,突出快速程序的特点。在线的案件管理与程序运行可以大幅提高审理效率、节省

---

① 域名争议解决机制由域名注册管理机构建立,以域名注册人与注册机构签署的域名注册协议作为程序管辖的基础。域名注册人必须在注册协议中承诺接受域名争议解决机构的管辖。商标权人认为注册域名损害其商标权益的,即可向域名争议解决机构投诉。域名争议解决机制已经成功地裁决了数万起域名与商标发生冲突的纠纷案件,有效地在全球域名系统内制止了恶意抢注他人商标为域名的行为,保护商标权人的正当权益,使其免于为了投诉域名而在不同国家的法院间疲于奔命,在很大程度上制止与遏制了域名抢注造成的流量劫持和恶意使用商标等问题。

② 例如,我国国家域名".cn"的争议解决机构为中国国际经济贸易仲裁委员会、香港国际仲裁中心与世界知识产权组织。

时间成本。数字平台争议解决还可以参考域名争议解决的经验,将从案件受理到审结的全过程限定在60日内完成,避免程序拖延,且便于与其他争议解决方式进行衔接。很多数字平台已经尝试建立网上自动信息系统,接受投诉,并衔接争议解决程序。例如,阿里巴巴集团的大众评审机制自2012年上线以来,已经由近500万名志愿者累计完成了1亿次买卖方之间纠纷的判定。

2. 数字平台知识产权争议解决

2019年起亚马逊平台为解决专利权纠纷建立了专门的争议解决专家机制。首先,享有美国外观设计专利的权利人向亚马逊平台发出侵权通知,指明平台上的侵权商品及构成专利侵权的理由。其后,亚马逊平台告知被指控侵权的平台内经营者,与权利人联系协商解决争议。如被控侵权的经营者置之不理,权利人可以再次通知亚马逊平台,进入专家争议解决程序。之后,亚马逊平台将争议解决的协议发给双方当事人,双方有21日考虑是否签署协议,并向亚马逊平台支付4000美元的费用。如经营者在此期间拒不签署协议,平台则根据专利权人的通知下架经营者的商品或服务。如争议双方均同意进入争议解决程序,并各自支付4000美元作为指定裁决争议的专利律师的费用,双方均应提交指出其主张的理由。亚马逊平台选定的专利律师将基于双方的主张在2个月内审理争议案件并作出裁决。亚马逊平台根据裁决结果决定所采取的措施(下架或者维持经营者的商品或服务)。"败诉"一方缴纳的4000美元作为争议解决的费用,"胜诉"一方缴纳的4000美元予以返还。

数字平台争议解决机制不排斥司法管辖。当事人对于争议解决结果不满的,仍然可以向有管辖权的法院起诉。[①] 但是知识产权纠纷如能快速高效、公平公正地解决,当事人诉诸法院的比例并不会很高。域名争议解决程序已经证明这一点。

---

① 亚马逊平台将其专利争议解决机制称为"仲裁"。在国际贸易中,当事人双方可以协议明确约定采取不依托于任何仲裁机构的临时仲裁解决纠纷,仲裁结果是终局性,排除司法管辖。我国《仲裁法》的修订稿中参考了《联合国国际贸易法委员会国际商事仲裁示范法》关于临时仲裁的规定,允许涉外商事纠纷的当事人自愿采用临时仲裁。但在数字贸易中,除非当事人之间特别明示约定,数字平台争议解决机制不等同于临时仲裁,不能排除司法管辖。

数字平台的争议解决机制对于数字贸易中的跨境纠纷尤为重要。不论是知识产权人还是平台内经营者,都借此避免面对域外的司法管辖与法律适用问题,得以通过快速高效的在线程序解决纠纷。① 经营者通过此机制获得与知识产权人直接沟通的渠道,应根据争议解决程序的性质与特点,采取相应的策略。如争议解决程序为谈判或调解机制,经营者应积极与知识产权人进行谈判,争取协商和解或者调解达成协议,从而化解纠纷;如争议解决程序为专家裁决机制,经营者应利用相对平等的地位进行有效的举证与抗辩。总之,数字平台的争议解决机制为经营者知识产权风险管理提供了重要契机。

四、数字贸易知识产权保证

在数字贸易中,知识产权人直接起诉外国经营者侵权的情况并不多见。这是因为知识产权人到经营者所在国跨境起诉,成本高、耗时长、效率低;在本国起诉,法院作出的裁判须经经营者所在国法院承认才能执行,执行成本也很高。② 故此,精于成本收益分析的知识产权人一般不会选择起诉外国经营者。但是,经营者绝不可因此松懈知识产权风险管理。

数字贸易不仅包括 B2C、C2C 等贸易形式,也包括 B2B 贸易。在 B2B 数字贸易中,经营者出口商品或服务,买方进口后从事分销、转售、商业性使用等经营活动。基于法律规定或当事人之间的合同约定,经营者(出口方/卖方)对买方(进口方)承担知识产权保证的义务。知识产权人可以在商品或服务进口到本国之后,对买方(进口方)提起知识产权侵权诉讼,请求本国法院依据本国法律追究买方的侵权责任,或追加外国卖方作为共同的侵权被告。在此情况下,除非经营者能在进口国法院胜诉(或者

---

① 我国《电子商务法》规定,要推动建立与不同国家、地区之间的跨境电子商务争议解决机制,其中也包括跨境平台的争议解决机制。

② 例如,我国《民事诉讼法》第 282 条规定了承认和执行外国法院裁判的条件与程序,即人民法院对申请或者请求承认和执行的外国法院作出的发生法律效力的判决、裁定,依照中华人民共和国缔结或者参加的国际条约,或者按照互惠原则进行审查后,认为不违反中华人民共和国法律的基本原则或者国家主权、安全、社会公共利益的,裁定承认其效力,需要执行的,发出执行令,依照该法的有关规定执行。违反中华人民共和国法律的基本原则或者国家主权、安全、社会公共利益的,不予承认和执行。

支持买方胜诉),否则不仅将承担知识产权侵权责任,而且基于对买方的知识产权保证义务将承担相应的违约责任(包括免除价款或/和赔偿买方损失)。由于知识产权保证义务"反射"给数字贸易经营者的知识产权风险,并不亚于被知识产权人直接起诉,所以从事 B2B 贸易的经营者如果对此缺乏准备与对策,难免遭受重大的损失。

数字贸易经营者的知识产权保证(intellectual property warranty)主要包括两部分,即保证与贸易有关的知识产权的合法性与有效性,以及保证买方不会因与贸易有关的知识产权遭受第三方侵权指控。经营者的知识产权保证义务既可来源于有关的法律规定,也可来源于当事人之间的合同约定。

很多从事数字贸易的中小微企业缺乏对于知识产权保证的理解,误以为只要不在贸易合同中约定有关的条款,就不必承担有关的保证义务与责任。实质上,即便合同没有约定知识产权保证,经营者(卖方/出口方)也需依据贸易活动所适用的法律承担有关的保证义务。

(一)我国法律规定的知识产权保证

因适用的法律不同,法定知识产权保证的对象、保证义务的方式、承担责任的范围也有所不同。当事人在数字贸易合同中选择适用或根据冲突法规则适用我国法律的,如合同未约定知识产权保证,应适用我国《民法典》的有关规定。我国《民法典》虽然没有专门规定知识产权保证的条款,但是规定买卖合同的出卖人就交付的标的物①,负有保证第三方对该标的物不享有任何权利的义务,但是法律另有规定的除外②。第三方对标的物不享有的"任何权利",其中应当包括知识产权。《民法典》第 612 条可以视为我国对于卖方知识产权保证义务的规定。其他类型的合同可以参照此规定。例如,《民法典》规定,只有合法拥有技术的权利人,才能订

---

① 根据《民法典》第 646 条的规定,法律对其他有偿合同有规定的,依照其规定;没有规定的,参照适用买卖合同的有关规定。因此,买卖合同关于权利保证的规定,亦可适用于其他类型的合同。
② 《民法典》第 612 条规定:"出卖人就交付的标的物,负有保证第三方对该标的物不享有任何权利的义务,但是法律另有规定的除外。"

立技术转让、技术许可合同。① 因此,技术转让人、许可人必须向对方当事人保证与技术有关的知识产权合法有效。

依据我国《民法典》的规定,除非法律另有规定,数字贸易的卖方(出口方)必须对买方(进口方)承担知识产权保证义务。买方有确切证据证明第三方对标的物享有知识产权的,可以中止支付相应的价款,除非卖方提供适当担保。② 据此,买方只要证明第三方对标的物享有知识产权,就可以请求卖方承担知识产权保证义务,既不必证明卖方缔约时的主观心理状态(知情与否),也不必证明第三方是否对标的物实际提出了权利主张。

为了避免卖方的知识产权保证义务过于沉重,平衡买卖双方的利益关系,我国《民法典》还规定,卖方如能证明买方订立合同时知道或者应当知道第三方对买卖的标的物享有权利的,则不承担上述保证义务。③ 鉴于买方"实际知道"或"应当知道"第三方的权利均可构成卖方保证义务免除的条件,卖方的保证义务与举证责任得到一定程度的减轻。买方的关联公司、股权结构、交易记录及所涉知识产权状态都可成为推定买方是否"应当知道"第三方权利的证据。其中,所涉知识产权是否经公示,尤甚可观。专利、商标、企业名称(含商号)④、植物新品种、集成电路布图设计等工业产权,其权利状态必须依法公示,理论上买方在缔约时尽合理的查询、检索义务,应知道第三方权利的存在。但是,对于商业秘密等不公开的知识产权,则难以推定买方应当知道第三方是否就标的物享有权利。就版权、表演者权、录音制品制作者权等而言,买方是否应当知道第三方就标的物享有权利,情况则更加复杂。与作品普遍进行版权登记的美国等国不同,我国版权人可以自愿向主管机关登记,作为权利的证明,不登

---

① 《民法典》第862条规定:"技术转让合同是合法拥有技术的权利人,将现有特定的专利、专利申请、技术秘密的相关权利让与他人所订立的合同。技术许可合同是合法拥有技术的权利人,将现有特定的专利、技术秘密的相关权利许可他人实施、使用所订立的合同……"

② 《民法典》第614条规定:"买受人有确切证据证明第三方对标的物享有权利的,可以中止支付相应的价款,但是出卖人提供适当担保的除外。"

③ 《民法典》第613条规定:"买受人订立合同时知道或者应当知道第三方对买卖的标的物享有权利的,出卖人不承担权利保证的义务。"

④ 我国建立了国家企业信用信息公示系统,可以查询企业名称等信息。

记一般情况下不妨碍权利的存续与行使。① 因此,卖方一般难以推定买方在缔约时应当知道第三方就标的物享有版权等权利。

总之,依据我国《民法典》的规定,买方有确切证据证明第三方对标的物享有知识产权,卖方却无法证明买方缔约时知道或者应当知道此事的,卖方应承担违反权利保证义务的违约责任。买方有权要求卖方免除相应的标的物价款,并赔偿由此造成的损失,但赔偿范围不应超过卖方缔约时预见到或者应当预见到的因违约可能造成的损失。② 由此可见,数字贸易合同在适用我国《民法典》的情况下,虽然卖方(出口方)承担知识产权保证义务不以其缔约时知道或者应当知道第三方对标的物的权利为前提,导致保证义务成立的风险较大,但是卖方赔偿买方损失的责任仍以其缔约时可以预见的范围为准,一定程度上避免卖方违约责任过于沉重。而且,卖方如能证明买方在缔约时知道或应当知道第三方享有与合同标的有关的知识产权的,其保证义务可被免除。

(二)《联合国国际货物销售合同公约》规定的知识产权保证

联合国国际贸易法委员会于 1980 年通过的《联合国国际货物销售合同公约》(以下简称《合同公约》),为国际货物销售提供了现代化的、统一的法律制度,谨慎地平衡了买方和卖方的利益,并启发了各国的合同法改革。迄今,包括我国在内的 94 个国家或地区成为该公约的成员。

1.《合同公约》的适用范围

《合同公约》适用于营业地位于不同缔约国的当事方之间的货物销售合同,或者适用于国际私法规则指定适用于缔约国法律的情形,或者因当事方的选择而适用公约。《合同公约》仅适用于国际交易,不适用于单纯

---

① 《著作权法》第 12 条第 2 款规定:"作者等著作权人可以向国家著作权主管部门认定的登记机构办理作品登记。"第 28 条规定:"以著作权中的财产权出质的,由出质人和质权人依法办理出质登记。"

② 《民法典》第 584 条规定:"当事人一方不履行合同义务或者履行合同义务不符合约定,造成对方损失的,损失赔偿额应当相当于因违约所造成的损失,包括合同履行后可以获得的利益;但是,不得超过违约一方订立合同时预见到或者应当预见到的因违约可能造成的损失。"

的国内销售①,也不适用于面向消费者的销售合同及某些特定类型的货物销售合同。

《合同公约》不适用于服务贸易合同已有定论,但是否适用于知识产权贸易合同则有争议。在联合国国际贸易法委员会公布的适用公约代表性案例中,有成员方法院认为,《合同公约》第 7 条规定,公约解释应考虑国际特征、促进公约统一适用的需求、尊重国际贸易中建立的善意原则。鉴于《合同公约》第 1 条对货物销售并无定义,为实现该公约法律统一化与消除国际贸易法律障碍的目的,"货物"应作广义的解释,将无形财产包括在内。故而,《合同公约》适用于计算机软件,即便并未记录于 DVD、CD、U 盘等物理介质之上,软件许可协议亦可被视为《合同公约》项下的销售合同。② 因此,至少在判例法中,《合同公约》可以适用于关于知识产权许可或转让等贸易合同。

近年来,软件(特别是移动互联网应用程序 APP)、网络游戏、音乐、视频等数字产品的跨境贸易发展迅猛,元宇宙、非同质化代币等概念甚嚣尘上③,但是相关的得到国际公认的贸易法律规则极度缺乏。数字产品贸易的经营者们尚在暗中摸索的阶段,承担着极大的贸易不确定性与知识产权风险。如果《合同公约》能够适用于数字产品贸易,关于知识产权保证的规定也适用于数字产品交易,则不仅能为新型贸易提供现有国际贸易

---

① 国内企业之间通过外国数字平台进行的货物贸易活动,虽然属于数字贸易的范围,但不能适用《联合国国际货物销售合同公约》。

② See United Nations Commission on International Trade Law Case Law on UNCITRAL Texts, Case 1586. 荷兰法院 2015 年判决。该案争议焦点在于加拿大软件公司(卖方)与荷兰公司(买方)之间的在线软件许可协议。买方下载了卖方提供的软件程序,并将程序转移给第三方公司。卖方指责买方违反软件许可协议将软件转移给第三方。因荷兰与加拿大均系《合同公约》成员方,法院认定《合同公约》适用于当事人之间的协议。根据《合同公约》第 8 条的规定,对于合同约定的文字不应作绝对的理解,而应考虑到当事人的意图与合理的人在合同场景下的理解。买方使用软件并无时间限制,向第三方转移软件发生于一次性付清价款而非分期支付的情况下。法院认为,许可协议与《合同公约》项下销售合同特征相同,根据《合同公约》第 42 条保证第三方对交付的"货物"不享有权利与主张。虽然协议名称不同,当事人的目的是订立销售合同。在销售合同中,完全禁止权利转让的约定是无效的。因此,法院判决,买方将软件转移给第三方不违反许可协议的约定。

③ 非同质化代币(non-fungible token,NFT),简单地说,是指基于区块链技术对艺术作品等知识产权客体进行加密所形成的独一无二的、不可分割与替代的安全交易对象。元宇宙来自构建了平行于现实世界的虚拟世界的科幻作品,理论上说,NFT 等虚拟财产未来适合在元宇宙的虚拟世界中交易与使用。

法律的支撑,而且为经营者知识产权风险管理提供了新的路径。

2.《合同公约》的知识产权保证条款

数字贸易中的 B2B 销售合同适用《合同公约》的情况是比较多的。《合同公约》规定的知识产权保证条款,对买卖双方的权利义务均有较大的影响。

《合同公约》第 42 条第 1 款规定:

> 卖方所交付的货物,必须是第三方不能根据工业产权或其他知识产权主张任何权利或要求的货物,但以卖方在订立合同时已知道或不可能不知道的权利或要求为限,而且这种权利或要求根据以下国家的法律规定是以工业产权或其他知识产权为基础的:
>
> (a)如果双方当事人在订立合同时预期货物将在某一国境内转售或做其他使用,则根据货物将在其境内转售或做其他使用的国家的法律;或者
>
> (b)在任何其他情况下,根据买方营业地所在国家的法律。

《合同公约》第 42 条第 2 款规定:

> 卖方在上一款中的义务不适用于以下情况:
>
> (a)买方在订立合同时已知道或不可能不知道此项权利或要求;或者
>
> (b)此项权利或要求的发生,是由于卖方要遵照买方所提供的技术图样、图案、程式或其他规格。

《合同公约》的上述条款,结构复杂、表达晦涩、令人费解。历经 40 年的实践,适用《合同公约》裁判的案件数不胜数,有关的著述成果浩如烟海,但是适用其中知识产权保证条款的案例及关于该条款的专门研究却较为罕见,侧面说明该条款的复杂性妨碍其在实践中发挥作用。联合国国际贸易法委员会开发的案例系统,收录了成员方提交的适用《合同公约》第 42 条的代表性案例,提供了某些深入理解该条款的经验与线索。

对于卖方的知识产权保证义务,《合同公约》第 42 条第 1 款从卖方是否知情、有关的时间节点、特定地域三个方面加以限定。在案例中,这些限定因素如何具体适用得到了检验。

在奥地利最高法院判决的一起案件①中,德国公司(卖方)向奥地利公司(买方)出售空白 CD。此批货物系德国公司从中国母公司购买,该母公司享有制造与销售 CD 的许可。权利人许可母公司在德国境内出售空白 CD,但许可协议并无在奥地利境内出售该货物的约定。其后,母公司与权利人之间的协议因许可费纠纷被解除,两方处于法院争讼程序中。奥地利公司得知有关诉讼的消息后,向德国公司询问无果。出于对所购货物被第三方提出权利主张及可能被追索许可费的担忧,决定停止向德国公司支付许可协议终止后购买与交付货物的价款。德国公司称,其母公司并未违反许可协议,故买方不可能承担支付许可费的风险,而且交付给买方的 CD 系许可协议终止前所生产,买方当然免于被权利人追索;而且买方未在合理期限内就所指控的货物瑕疵通知卖方。

一审法院未接受德国公司的辩解,认为根据《合同公约》第 42 条的规定,买卖双方既然默示同意买方不应为任何许可费负责,买方就无义务调查许可协议是否仍然有效或是否正被合法解除。在现有情况下,买方已经在合理期限内通知卖方停止付款的意图,有权终止合同。上诉法院也认为买方有权终止合同,并请求赔偿,但不认为买方有权停止付款。

奥地利最高法院认为,在卖方违约的情况下,买方有权停止付款直至卖方履行合同义务。卖方对被许可货物的保证义务是指双方当事人缔约时预期货物将在转售或做其他使用国家内所承担的义务,或者在任何其他情况下,在买方营业国内所承担的义务。为维护自身利益,依赖公约条款的一方当事人应承担相应的举证责任,除非基于衡平原因另作安排。一审法院未能认定双方当事人缔约时预期货物将被转售或使用的国家。因此,奥地利最高法院无法认定卖方是否违约,案件被发回一审法院重审。

上述判决说明,买方主张卖方承担知识产权保证义务,系维护自身利益的行为,应承担相应的举证责任,特别应依据《合同公约》第 42 条第 1 款的规定证明卖方承担知识产权保证义务的特定国家,即在双方当事人缔约时预期货物将在某一国境内转售或做其他使用的情况下,卖方的义

---

① See United Nations Commission on International Trade Law Case Law on UNCITRAL Texts, Case 753, Austria Oberster Gerichtshof (Supreme Court of Justice), 12 September 2006.

务限于该转售国或使用国之内;或者在其他情况下,限于在买方营业地所在国之内。由于《合同公约》第 42 条第 1 款规定中"国家"(State)一词系单数表达,因此,买方必须举证证明卖方义务具体指向的特定国家。

在一份韩国首尔高等法院作出的判决①中,买方是美国公司,卖方是韩国公司。卖方制造销售汽车用 LED 灯。根据买卖合同,卖方制造销售灯具提供给买方,买方享有该灯具在美国的独家销售权。根据买方的订单,卖方交付货物。在合同履行过程中,一家美国第三方公司向买方发出停止侵权的律师函,指控卖方提供给买方的灯具侵犯该美国第三方公司的专利权。买方主张卖方有义务提供依据美国法律第三方无知识产权与主张的货物,然而卖方提供的货物有可能侵犯美国第三方公司的专利权,应赔偿因违约给买方造成的损失。

审理法院认为,卖方应当根据《合同公约》第 42 条第 1 款承担知识产权保证义务,不论第三方的权利主张是否依法成立,均系卖方应承担的风险。法院确认该案属于《合同公约》第 42 条第 1 款规定的货物被第三方以侵犯专利权为由提出主张的情形,但是卖方承担违反知识产权保证义务的责任,以其缔约时知道或不可能不知道第三方的专利权或主张为条件;所谓"知道或不可能不知道"是指故意无视该权利主张或者因重大过失导致不知该主张。由于美国第三方公司的专利权是在买卖合同订立及货物交付之后所获得,在买方通知第三方公司提出专利权侵权主张之前,卖方难以知道或者难以被认定为不可能不知道第三方公司专利权的存在。因此,法院认定,卖方并未违反知识产权保证义务。

上述判决说明,卖方依据《合同公约》第 42 条第 1 款承担知识产权保证义务,以符合规定的时间节点为条件,即在销售合同成立时卖方即知道或不可能不知道第三方的权利或主张,因此第三方在缔约(履行)之后获得的知识产权及其主张,不能作为卖方承担违约责任的依据。法院判断卖方是否知情的标准也具有启发性,即卖方在缔约时故意无视第三方的权利或主张或者因重大过失而不知该权利或主张的,才属于《合同公约》

---

① See United Nations Commission on International Trade Law Case Law on UNCITRAL Texts, Case 1803, Republic of Korea: Seoul High Court, 24 December 2015.

规定的"知道或不可能不知道"的情形。① 法院还认定,第三方的权利或主张不论是否依法成立,均不妨碍卖方承担知识产权保证义务。

根据《合同公约》第42条第2款的规定,即便卖方的知识产权保证义务依该条第1款成立,也可在符合本款规定的条件下被免除。除了买方向卖方提供技术图样、图案、程式或其他规格以定制货物等特殊情况,该款焦点在于卖方能否证明买方在订立合同时已知道或不可能不知道第三方的权利或主张。法院在审理相关案件中对此进行了解释与认定。

在法国科尔马上诉法院2002年作出的一份判决②中,从德国某公司进口一批衬衫并在法国东部拥有六家服装店的法国某公司,被第三方公司起诉,原因是所进口衬衫纤维涉嫌侵犯第三方公司的专有权。

一审法院判决,买方对第三方公司的专利侵权责任成立,卖方应就买方承担的侵权责任承担权利保证义务。二审法院同样认定买方的侵权责任成立,但减少了侵权赔偿金,并重启了知识产权保证程序,要求买卖双方确认是否适用《合同公约》第42条的规定。在双方均确认适用《合同公约》知识产权保证条款的情况下,二审法院判决,买方基于其专业能力不可能不知道对第三方构成侵权,因此,根据第42条第2款的规定,买方在缔约时对所涉及的第三方权利知情,卖方为此不再承担知识产权保证义务,故此,推翻一审判决,驳回买方的请求。

在法国最高法院2002年作出的一份判决③中,卖方西班牙公司向买方法国公司出售的鞋子上有假冒的丝带。丝带的知识产权人从买方获得了侵权赔偿。买方起诉,要求卖方支付假冒货物赔偿金并赔偿买方的损失。

里昂上诉法院驳回了买方的请求。买方不服,上诉到法国最高法院。法国最高法院驳回了买方的上诉,认定买方作为专业公司,不可能不知道假冒商品的存在,因此买方在缔约时对于第三方的权利是知情的。法国

---

① 《联合国国际货物销售合同公约》第42条第2款规定了买方"知道或不可能不知道"的情形,其表述与卖方相同,其判断的标准也应与卖方相同。

② See United Nations Commission on International Trade Law Case Law on UNCITRAL Texts, Case 491, France: Court of Appeal of Colmar, 13 November 2002.

③ See United Nations Commission on International Trade Law Case Law on UNCITRAL Texts, Case 479, France: Court of Cassation, 19 March 2002.

最高法院判定,里昂上诉法院适用《合同公约》第42条第2款正确,免除卖方知识产权保证义务的结论正当。

在上述两个法国案例中,法院均强调,买方作为专业的公司,理应具有专业能力在缔约时得知所购货物涉及第三方的专有权。如果买方在其专业领域故意无视或者有重大过失致使不知第三方的权利,则应被认定为缔约时知情,卖方为此不承担相应的知识产权保证义务。虽然法国法院对于《合同公约》第42条第2款中关于买方"不可能不知道"作出的相对宽松解释不一定得到其他国家法院的完全认同,但是适当增加买方在缔约时的注意义务,适当减轻卖方知识产权保证的压力,不失为一种促进贸易诚信、合理分配风险的解决方案。

总之,《合同公约》第42条的规定虽然复杂,但是总体上比较倾向于保护卖方及均衡买卖双方的权益。在各国司法实践中,适用《合同公约》该条文也没有造成卖方知识产权保证义务过重的后果。但是,由于该条文表述文辞繁复、晦涩难懂,某些中文翻译表达不确切造成含义扭曲,所以数字贸易中的很多中小微企业对此望而却步,或者不作抗辩就缴械投降,导致自身利益遭受不应有的损害。实际上,即便买方指责卖方违反知识产权保证义务,根据《合同公约》第42条第1款的规定,买方的主张也不一定能够成立;即便成立,卖方仍可根据《合同公约》第42条第2款的规定,举证免除自身的知识产权保证义务。数字贸易中的中小微企业只要增强知识产权风险管理能力,有效保护自己权益的可能性是很大的。

(三)约定的知识产权保证

知识产权风险在很大程度上来源于不确定性与不可知性。数字贸易的经营者与其被动等待发生纠纷时适用法律规定的知识产权保证,承受因法律规定与法律解释的不同而带来的风险,不如通过谈判在合同中明确约定买卖双方均可接受的卖方知识产权保证义务的范围、条件及方式,并借此合理安排双方在合同中的权利与义务。约定的知识产权保证以法律规定为依据,可以将法定保证明确化、具体化、精细化,避免语义模糊与多重解释的问题。约定保证还可以超出法定保证的范围,卖方向买方提供高于法律规定的知识产权保证水平,也可以获得更高价款等合同利益。但是,合同约定不能排除法定的知识产权保证义务或者降低法定保证的水平,否则当事人就有经营/进出口假冒、盗版商品的嫌疑,导致该约定因违法而无效。

依赖于数字网络的全球大市场中的贸易活动空前活跃,贸易伙伴空前广泛。经营者的保证义务如果仍覆盖所有类型的知识产权,则在数字贸易的大环境下可能遭遇前所未有的风险。约定保证可以明确保证的知识产权类型与范围,从而有效地降低卖方的知识产权风险。1994年世界贸易组织《与贸易有关的知识产权协定》(TRIPS协定)在《保护工业产权巴黎公约》《保护文学和艺术作品伯尔尼公约》等国际法律文件的基础上,奠定了国际贸易中知识产权法律的基础,确立了世界主要经济体共同认可的知识产权法律原则与制度。① 近三十年过去,国际贸易中的知识产权法律制度已经发展演变、更加复杂。在国际法律体系外,不同国家的知识产权法律制度有了不同的发展,一些新的权利、义务与法律要求不断涌现。某些国家建立了保护传统知识(traditional knowledge)、生物基因资源等的专门性知识产权法律制度。即便TRIPS协定并无相关规定,但是与这些国家从事数字贸易的经营者却可能受到影响。一个例证是从保加利亚向新西兰出口的一批木雕纪念品,由于未经许可使用了新西兰法律保护的原住民传统纹饰,受到原住民社区抗议,被进口海关查扣。

约定的知识产权保证可以将适用范围限定为国际知识产权法公认的版权、商标、专利、外观设计、地理标志等权利,避免买卖双方因第三方新权利的出现而发生争议。买卖双方还可以灵活约定卖方为公认的权利类型承担保证责任的条件。

约定保证还可以明确卖方保证义务的期限。在法定保证的情况下,买方主张卖方违反知识产权保证义务的,须在合理期限通知卖方后才能追究卖方的违约责任(例如停止付款或减低价款等)。② 但是,何为买方通知的"合理期限",买卖双方往往各执一词,发生争议。约定保证则可以发挥其优势,事先约定卖方承担保证义务的期限,或者买方通知卖方承

---

① 《与贸易有关的知识产权协定》确立了成员之间保护版权、商标、专利、外观设计、地理标志、秘密信息等知识产权国际法律标准。
② See United Nations Commission on International Trade Law Case Law on UNCITRAL Texts, Case 1644, Republic of Korea: Seoul High Court, 15 November 2012. 该案中,韩国首尔高等法院判决,买方如要依据《合同公约》第42条主张卖方交付的货物不符合约定,必须通知卖方后才能行使减低货物价款的权利。

担保证义务的期限。约定的期限可以公平合理地反映买卖双方的利益诉求,既不因过短而使买方缺乏利益保障,也不因过长而使卖方承担过重的风险。

在法定保证中,卖方知识产权保证的地域范围一直是争议很大的问题。约定保证则可以明确买卖双方的权利与义务,避免争议,较好地解决这一问题。买卖双方可以明确约定卖方承担保证义务的国家。与《合同公约》中仅限一个国家的法定保证不同,合同可以约定卖方在多个相关国家承担担保义务,这对于数字贸易的买方可能具有重大的意义。进入 21 世纪以来,大量涌现的双边或区域性自由贸易协定在很大程度上推高了 TRIPS 协定确定的知识产权执法水平。比如,TRIPS 协定规定,成员方法律应当规定海关中止放行疑似假冒、盗版的进口货物,并可以规定海关中止放行疑似侵权的出口货物。[①] 但是,欧盟法律在修订后,已经允许商标权人在疑似侵权的货物经欧盟转运时申请由海关中止放行,即便该货物并不在欧盟进口或者出口。[②] 在新的知识产权执法环境中,买卖双方如约定卖方的保证义务不仅覆盖货物转售国或买方营业地所在国,而且扩展到货物转运国,显然更有利于保障合同目的的实现。当然,合同约定卖方承担更大保证义务的同时,一般给予卖方更多的权利或利益来平衡。由于当事人之间合约安排出于自愿,争议的可能性会大为降低。

约定保证还有助于解决知识产权法中复杂的平行进口问题。简而言之,平行进口(又称"权利用尽"或"灰色市场")是指商品在一国经合法授权生产后,能否进口至另一国且不经该国知识产权人许可。平行进口的商品并非假冒侵权的商品,但是本应在特定国家或地区销售,却被进口到另外的国家或地区。平行进口导致卖方知识产权保证义务复杂化。在适

---

① 《与贸易有关的知识产权协定》第 51 条规定:"各成员应在符合以下规定的情况下,采取程序使在有正当理由怀疑假冒商标或盗版货物的进口有可能发生的权利持有人,能够向行政或司法主管机关提出书面申请,要求海关中止放行此类货物进入自由流通。各成员可针对涉及其他知识产权侵权行为的货物提出此种申请,只要符合本节的要求。各成员还可制定关于海关中止放行自其领土出口的侵权货物的相应程序。"

② 《欧洲共同体商标条例》于 2016 年生效后,欧盟的商标权人可以禁止任何第三方将使用相同或者近似商标的货物(包括转运的货物)运进欧盟,除非货主或报关人能够证明商标权人无权在货物目的地主张权利。2008—2009 年间,印度出口巴西的 19 个集装箱仿制药曾在荷兰转运时被海关以专利权侵权为由扣押。世界卫生组织批评此类措施可能危及患者的生命健康权。

用法定保证的情况下,卖方知晓货物在进口国会遇到平行进口的问题(例如卖方仅有在出口国国内销售的授权,或者卖方作为权利人已经在进口国许可了独家经销商),仍向买方出口该货物的,应承担知识产权保证义务。但是,卖方在何种情况下"不可能不知道"平行进口问题,则很难判断。更何况各国法律针对版权、商标、专利的平行进口所作规定很不相同,国际知识产权法对此也没有统一的法律规范。[①] 故此,由当事人明确约定知识产权保证是否包含平行进口,可事半功倍,避免争议并化解风险。

在数字贸易中,经营者普遍使用自动信息系统进行交易、履行等贸易活动。此数字贸易独特性,既带来了新的知识产权风险与问题,也提供了新的风险管理可能。如自动信息交易系统基本参数设置大致相同,不根据贸易活动的具体情况进行调整,千人一面,当然导致知识产权风险增大。但是,如果自动信息交易系统引入了人工智能的因素,则能够根据进出口国或地区知识产权法律状况,灵活设置不同的交易条件,适当调整权利保证的范围、条件与方式,实现千人千面,则卖方的知识产权风险将比在传统贸易中得到更为有效的管理与控制。

结　　论

数字贸易的特点增大了经营者知识产权风险,同时也带来了风险管理的新渠道、模式与机遇。依托数字平台的各种机制,数字贸易的经营者可以建立相应的知识产权风险管控策略,尽量降低侵权风险并减少相关的损失。知识产权保证等传统法律制度也在数字贸易中焕发出新的生机,使经营者借助技术手段增强了管理知识产权风险的能力。总之,数字贸易的经营者只要积极应对知识产权风险,审时度势,管控风险,定能在贸易活动中避免与减少损失,使自身的合法权益获得保障。

---

① 《与贸易有关的知识产权协定》第6条规定:"就本协定项下的争端解决而言,在遵守知识产权公约和最惠国原则的前提下,本协定的任何规定不得用于处理知识产权的权利用尽问题。"

后疫情时代世界海事仲裁发展概况[*]

彭先伟　莫世杰　林健良　彭　德

摘要： 当新冠肺炎疫情成为人类社会"新常态",世界海事仲裁的发展也呈现出了诸多新特色、新亮点。网上开庭、电子送达等新技术手段在促进仲裁便利化、数字化、信息化的同时,也打破了仲裁法律服务的时间、地域限制;海事仲裁机构、海事仲裁员协会纷纷修订规则,进一步提升仲裁程序质效,加强裁决过程及结果的公正性;仲裁法律体系及仲裁司法审查制度的不断完善,对于规范海事仲裁实践、营造仲裁友好型的司法监督环境具有积极意义。有鉴于此,本文特别邀请来自中国、新加坡、英国的资深海事律师、仲裁员,围绕各法域海事仲裁相关的立法动向、规则修改、司法审查进行系统阐述,以飨读者。

关键词： 海事仲裁;立法动向;规则修改;司法审查

中国篇

内　地[**]

2020年年初的新冠肺炎疫情以来,所有法律行业,包括海事仲裁也经历了

---

[*] 本文完成于2022年1月。

[**] 本篇作者为彭先伟,大连海事大学法学院博士研究生,中国海事仲裁委员会仲裁员,北京德恒律师事务所合伙人。兼任最高人民检察院民事行政案件咨询专家,司法部"千名涉外律师人才库"入库律师,国际商会ICC商法与惯例委员会专家,北京律师协会海商海事专业委员会副主任,美国律师协会国际运输法律专业委员会副主任,以及上海、南京、海南、包头等20余家仲裁委员会仲裁员。

很多新的发展和变化。就此期间的中国内地海事仲裁发展情况,详述如下。

一、海事仲裁相关法律的发展

(一)海事仲裁相关立法进展

中国内地民商合一,并没有专门的海事仲裁法律,而是适用相关的民商事程序和实体法律。从立法的角度来看,中国内地最近几年民商事立法变化很快,新法频繁出台。但海事海商立法相对还处于一个较为稳定的状态,近期新的海事海商立法不多。就其中与仲裁相关的而言,值得关注的如下:

2020年1月,交通运输部提交了《海商法(修改送审稿)》提请国务院进行审议。《海商法》的修订引起了包括海事仲裁在内各界的广泛关注。而且,据新闻报道,《海事诉讼特别程序法》也正在进行修订的前期调研。[①]

2021年4月,第十三届全国人民代表大会常务委员会第二十八次会议通过了新的《海上交通安全法》,该法自2021年9月1日起施行。其中,该法第115条规定:"因海上交通事故引发民事纠纷的,当事人可以依法申请仲裁或者向人民法院提起诉讼。"

实务之中,海上交通事故引发民事纠纷,当事人往往考虑的救济渠道是政府主导的行政或者诉讼模式,很少有去仲裁的。但是,行政或者诉讼模式各有各的不足之处。例如,2011年6月4日,康菲石油公司位于渤海湾的"蓬莱19-3"油田溢油事故发生后,经过协商形成了政府主导的赔偿模式。有观点认为,在政府主导的赔偿模式下,因行政机关人员专业素质参差不齐,实践中很难执行统一的赔付规则和标准,容易出现该赔未赔、同损不同赔情形,引起受害人的不满,引发新的矛盾和纷争。针对政府主导的赔偿模式不足问题,当时就有仲裁机构研究过如何以调解、仲裁去解决"蓬莱19-3"漏油事故索赔纠纷的可能。[②]

---

① 参见《国际法学院曲涛副教授应邀参加〈海事诉讼特别程序法〉修改南部片区调研座谈》,载华东政法大学国际法学院官网(https://gjf. ecupl. edu. cn/2020/0102/c8985a153195/page. htm),访问日期:2021年9月2日。
② 参见王红松:《从漏油事故处理看第三方主导赔偿模式的优势》,载北京仲裁委员会北京国际仲裁中心网站(https://www. bjac. org. cn/news/view. asp? id = 2109),访问日期:2021年9月2日。

对比之下,1983年《海上交通安全法》第46条规定:"因海上交通事故引起的民事纠纷,可以由主管机关调解处理,不愿意调解或调解不成的,当事人可以向人民法院起诉;涉外案件的当事人,还可以根据书面协议提交仲裁机构仲裁。"2016年《海上交通安全法》第46条也是如此规定。从字面意思来看,由于之前的措辞是涉外案件的当事人可以就海上交通事故引起的民事纠纷提交仲裁机构仲裁,似乎非涉外当事人并不享有这一权利。此次修订,使得海上交通事故引起的民事纠纷,例如因海上交通事故引起的人身损害和环境污染等非涉外案件也可以通过仲裁来解决。对于海事仲裁机构而言,在发生大型的海上事故(例如船舶油污事故)时,可以与政府机构联系一起推动仲裁解决相关争议。例如,由污染方设立专门的赔偿基金,政府机关则依据海事仲裁机构出具的裁决书或者调解书从相关基金中对污染受害者进行赔偿。如果采用这种模式,政府机关依据第三方的仲裁或者调解结果去赔偿,可以在很大程度上避免这种争议。

(二)海事仲裁相关司法解释发展

随着最高人民法院陆续发布了关于海上保险、海事赔偿责任限制、船舶油污损害等司法解释,近几年来最高人民法院发布海事相关司法解释的速度逐渐放缓。2020年以来,最高人民法院出台的海事海商司法解释只有《最高人民法院关于审理涉船员纠纷案件若干问题的规定》(以下简称《船员劳动纠纷司法解释》),该司法解释于2020年6月8日由最高人民法院审判委员会第1803次会议通过,自2020年9月29日起施行。

在起草该司法解释时,其草案曾规定:

第一条 【依据诉讼请求涉及的事项是否与在船期间相关,按照不同的途径确定争端解决方式】

船员与船舶所有人因确认劳动关系,或订立、履行、变更和终止劳动合同或劳务合同发生争议,依据诉讼请求是否与在船期间相关,按如下不同情形处理。

(一)诉讼请求与在船期间有关的,当事人可以直接向海事法院提起诉讼。当事人之间存在仲裁协议的除外……

但是,这一规定受到了一些质疑,例如湖北省船员服务协会认为,该条中的"仲裁协议"是否为有效的协议存在疑问,因为劳动争议仲裁委员会是劳动争议的法定仲裁机构。①

目前来看,《船员劳动纠纷司法解释》删除了草案第1条关于"当事人之间存在仲裁协议"这一规定。从某种意义上讲,船员劳动纠纷②是否可以约定仲裁,可能还会存在一定的争议。但从最近的司法实践来看,法院对此采取的是支持的态度。例如,在郑祥摄与青岛凯瑞特船舶管理有限公司、深圳联达拖轮有限公司船员劳务合同纠纷案中,法院内部也有一种观点认为船员服务协议约定由中国海事仲裁委员会仲裁的仲裁条款无效,理由是针对船员劳务纠纷,相关劳动争议仲裁委员会才有权受理。最终,广州海事法院(2020)粤72民初565号民事裁定书认为,该仲裁条款有效,理由是:应秉承支持海事仲裁的态度,根据《仲裁法》等法律规定判断当事人是否有提交仲裁的意思表示。③ 在林某恩与某船务公司船员劳务纠纷案中,双方签订的《船员上船协议》约定发生纠纷由中国海事仲裁委员会仲裁。原告林某恩工作中受伤,劳动仲裁后对裁决不服,继而将被告某船务公司诉至泉州市泉港区人民法院。其后,泉州市中级人民法院以该案属海事法院专属管辖为由,作出(2020)闽05民终848号民事裁定,将该案移送厦门海事法院审理。厦门海事法院审理期间,被告提出管辖权异议,认为应提交中国海事仲裁委员会仲裁。原告则认为双方之间属于劳动合同关系,协议约定的仲裁条款违反了劳动合同纠纷应当劳动仲裁前置而不应由其他仲裁机构仲裁的强制性法律规定,应属无效。最

---

① 参见《本会回复对〈最高人民法院关于审理船员纠纷案件若干问题的规定(一)〉(征求意见稿)的意见》,载湖北省船员服务协会官网(http://www.hbcsa.org/show.aspx?id=1570),访问日期:2021年9月2日。

② 传统上,我国民事审判领域存在劳动合同和劳务合同的区分,《最高人民法院民事案件案由规定》也分别对劳动合同纠纷、劳务合同纠纷作了规定。在海事司法领域,《海事诉讼特别程序法》只使用了"船员劳务合同"这一表述,但此处所指"船员劳务合同"涵盖了船员劳务(即狭义的雇佣)合同、船员劳动合同等。参见王淑梅、郭载宇:《〈关于审理涉船员纠纷案件若干问题的规定〉的理解与适用》,载澎湃网(https://m.thepaper.cn/baijiahao_11720287),访问日期:2021年9月2日。

③ 参见《郑祥摄与青岛凯瑞特船舶管理有限公司、深圳联达拖轮有限公司船员劳务合同纠纷案》,载中华人民共和国广州海事法院官网(https://www.gzhsfy.gov.cn/hsmh/web/content?gid=92739),访问日期:2021年9月2日。

终,厦门海事法院认为①,中国内地法律没有明文排除海商事仲裁的强制性或禁止性法律规定,该案《船员上船协议》中的仲裁条款约定应属有效。

此外,2020年8月南京海事法院发布了《南京海事法院海事仲裁司法审查案件审理指南》,其中比较值得注意的规定有②:当事人就原合同欠款另行达成还款协议的,还款协议仍受原合同仲裁条款的约束;在违约与侵权竞合的情况下,当事人提起侵权之诉的,该纠纷仍受合同仲裁条款约束;当事人约定在我国境内进行临时仲裁的,仲裁协议无效;对没有涉外因素的海事争议,当事人约定外国仲裁机构仲裁或到外国仲裁的,应认定仲裁协议无效。2021年2月,厦门海事法院通过了《厦门海事法院仲裁司法审查案件审理工作指南》。③ 值得注意的是,该指南特别规定:经审查拟撤销仲裁裁决的,在报福建省高级人民法院核准之前,可听取仲裁机构的意见;仲裁司法审查案件审结后,应当向相关仲裁机构送达裁定副本。

二、海事仲裁的发展

2020—2021年是中国内地海事仲裁事业大发展的两年。其中,2020年11月6日,在司法部的大力支持下,经中国国际贸易促进委员会和上海市人民政府同意、上海市司法局核准,中国海事仲裁委员会上海分会升级更名为"中国海事仲裁委员会上海总部",并正式举行了揭牌仪式。④ 2021年5月1日,经过精心的换届准备,中国海事仲裁委员会新一届仲裁员名册启用,任期5年。中国海事仲裁委员会新一届仲裁员共计826名,来自36个国家和地区。其中,内地仲裁员704名,覆盖全国35个城市,地域分布更加合理,我国港澳台籍及外籍仲裁员122名,外籍仲

---

① 参见《船员劳务合同约定商事仲裁的效力问题评析》,载网易新闻网(https://www.163.com/dy/article/FKQ2SB5J0518JG8L.html? spss=adap_pc),访问日期:2021年4月12日。
② 参见《南京海事法院海事仲裁司法审查案件审理指南》,载南京海事法院官网(http://njhsfy.gov.cn/zh/judical/detail/id/1418.html),访问日期:2021年4月12日。
③ 参见《厦门海事法院仲裁司法审查案件审理工作指南》,载厦门海事法院官网(http://www.xmhsfy.gov.cn/swxx/gfxwj/202102/t20210218_175377.htm),访问日期:2021年4月12日。
④ 参见《中国海事仲裁委员会上海总部揭牌仪式在沪隆重举行》,载中国海事仲裁委员会官网(http://www.cmac.org.cn/index.php? id=105),访问日期:2021年9月2日。

裁员国别分布更为广泛。本届仲裁员专业领域更加齐全,构成比例更为科学,能够更好地满足中国内地海事仲裁业务发展需要。①

2021年10月9日,中国海事仲裁委员会在北京召开新闻发布会,发布《中国海事仲裁委员会仲裁规则(2021年版)》(以下简称《仲裁规则》),该规则于2021年10月1日起施行。相比上一版,《仲裁规则》考虑到新冠肺炎疫情带来的问题,系统性地规定了电子送达、视频开庭、视频作证、电子签名以及网络安全和隐私及数据保护等。《仲裁规则》还有值得关注的诸多创新之处,例如:

(1)关于仲裁庭秘书。由于国际仲裁的发展日趋复杂化及与日俱增的案件量、工作量,仲裁界逐渐出现了辅助仲裁庭的秘书。实践中使用仲裁庭秘书已经是普遍的现象,甚至已成为一种惯例。但由于缺乏必要的透明度,仲裁庭秘书的身份、背景和角色未能披露给当事人,也没有审核利益冲突情况,甚至有的秘书参与分析证据和准据法,参与讨论和准备起草仲裁裁决,实质上变为第四仲裁员。② 因此,在正当程序的背景下,有必要对仲裁庭的秘书进行规范。对此,《仲裁规则》第40条专门规定了仲裁庭秘书相关问题,其中首次区分机构案件经办人和仲裁庭秘书,规定仲裁委员会仲裁院工作人员可以担任仲裁庭秘书,但不得担任同一仲裁案件的经办人。第40条还规定,仲裁庭秘书在接受指定前应签署声明书,披露可能引起对其公正性和独立性产生合理怀疑的任何事实或情况,当事人也可要求仲裁庭秘书回避。第40条的这些规定有力地保障了当事人的知情权,防止了利益冲突。

(2)关于专家咨询制度。仲裁实践中,为了处理重大疑难案件,很多仲裁机构都有专家咨询相关制度。2018年12月31日,《中共中央办公厅、国务院办公厅关于完善仲裁制度提高仲裁公信力的若干意见》(以下简称《两办意见》)发布,其中第6条也特别提出要建立重大疑难案件的专家咨询制度。为了在实践中行之有效以及《两办意见》确认的专家咨询委

---

① 《加强仲裁公信力建设,优化仲裁员队伍——中国海仲新一届仲裁员名册启用》,载中国海事仲裁委员会官网(http://cmac.org.cn/index.php? id=77),访问日期:2021年9月2日。

② 桑远棵:《国际仲裁中仲裁庭秘书之研究》,载北京仲裁委员会、北京国际仲裁中心组编:《北京仲裁》(第102辑),中国法制出版社2008年版。亦可参见 J. Ole Jensen, *Tribunal Secretaries in International Arbitration*, Oxford University Press, 2019。

员会制度进一步落实,《仲裁规则》第61条特别规定:"仲裁庭或仲裁委员会可以就仲裁案件的程序和实体等重大疑难问题提请仲裁委员会专家咨询委员会研究讨论,并提供咨询意见。专家咨询意见由仲裁庭决定是否接受。"

中国海事仲裁委员会李虎副主任接受记者访问时特别指出,经办人制度和专家咨询委员会制度是这一次修订中最重要的内容。① 经办人制度区分了案件经办人和仲裁庭秘书。案件经办人代表机构为仲裁案件提供管理服务,仲裁庭秘书为仲裁庭提供秘书服务;仲裁庭秘书不得参与案件表决,不得参与撰写裁决书的实质内容。这样能够进一步厘清机构和仲裁庭之间的职责范围,防范利益冲突,切实提高仲裁透明度。

(3)关于裁决书的发布。传统上,当事人选择仲裁的重要原因之一是其可以保密,以保护当事人的隐私、商业秘密等。但与此同时,商事仲裁的保密性特征要求案件文书不得对外公布,进而使得案外人对于了解仲裁技术、仲裁庭对案件法律适用的看法等变得困难,反过来这种保密机制又使得当事人对商事仲裁的可预期性产生疑惑。为此,很多外国仲裁机构都规定,在采取脱密措施后可以发布裁决书。例如,2021年6月国际商会(International Chamber of Commerce, ICC)宣布将携手全球最具广泛性的国际法与仲裁搜索引擎——Jus Mundi,为公众提供截至2019年1月1日的所有可公开的国际商会仲裁裁决及相关文件。② 2021年12月22日,我国司法部经过脱密处理发布了3个"仲裁工作指导案例",主要集中在旅游合同纠纷、建设工程合同纠纷和投资合同纠纷领域。③ 因此,仲裁裁决需要一定程度的公开基本上是各界的共识。此次《仲裁规则》借鉴了美国仲裁协会、国际商会国际仲裁院的做法,在第58条规定经征得当事人同意,机构在对裁决进行脱密处理后可以公开发布裁决书,以提高仲裁透

---

① 参见黄玉玲:《中国海仲委:〈中国海事仲裁委员会仲裁规则(2021年版)〉正式施行八个"首次"实现新突破》,载央广网(https://baijiahao.baidu.com/s? id = 1713135843355367606&ufr),访问日期:2022年1月22日。

② 参见《国际商会携手Jus Mundi免费提供可公开的国际商会仲裁裁决》,载山东仲裁网(http://www.sdad.org.cn/cms/cms_ContentPage.do? ARTICLE_ID = c0e97f29 - ab01 - 4952 - 87c3 - df39418a7975),访问日期:2022年1月22日。

③ 参见张维:《司法部发布仲裁工作指导案例》,载法治日报(http://www.moj.gov.cn/pub/sfbgw/gwxw/xwyw/202112/t20211222_444268.html),访问日期:2022年1月22日。

明度。

(4)关于仲裁文书的送达。《仲裁规则》第 8 条第 2 款规定,仲裁文书可以向当事船舶船长送达。关于向船长送达司法文书,《海事诉讼特别程序法》第 80 条第 2 款规定了"有关扣押船舶的法律文书也可以向当事船舶的船长送达"。《仲裁规则》第 8 条第 2 款借鉴了《海事诉讼特别程序法》第 80 条第 2 款的规定,首次规定可以向当事船舶船长送达仲裁文书。这一规定非常具有创新性,也符合海事仲裁的特点和海事纠纷解决的传统。

(5)关于仲裁中因更换代理人而导致的利益冲突问题。一般来说,仲裁组庭之前,仲裁员会考虑案件当事人和代理律师情况,以决定是否能接受指定。但是,如果仲裁组庭后当事人更换代理律师,当事人新任命的律师和已经组成的仲裁庭有利益冲突,此时就可能构成对仲裁程序的公正性的威胁。为解决这一问题,国际律师协会(International Bar Association,IBA)发布的《国际律师协会关于国际仲裁中当事人代理的准则(2013)》(IBA Guidelines on Party Representation in International Arbitration)第 5 条规定:仲裁庭组成后,如果某人与仲裁员之间存在会造成利益冲突的关系,则该人不应接受代表一方参加仲裁,除非在适当披露后没有任何一方反对。第 6 条则规定:仲裁庭可以采取适当措施保障仲裁的完整性,包括禁止当事人新的代理人参加全部或部分仲裁程序。司法实务中,Hrvatska Elektroprivreda d. d. v. Slovenia 和 Rompetrol v. Romania① 均出现了当事人以仲裁代理人与仲裁员之间存在利益冲突为由而要求更换代理人的情形。在 Hrvatska Elektroprivreda d. d. v. Slovenia 中,仲裁庭从"经正当程序组成的仲裁庭应具有稳定性"(immutability of properly-constituted tribunals)这一原则出发,推定仲裁庭有权就挑战仲裁代理人事宜进行决定,并有权要求当事人更换被挑战的代理人。《仲裁规则》借鉴了《国际律师协会关于国际仲裁中当事人代理的准则(2013)》的规定,首次明确仲裁庭可以采取必要措施避免因当事人代理人变化而产生的利益冲突。

---

① 参见《国际仲裁中的代理人职业道德建设:路漫漫其修远兮》,载搜狐网(https://www.sohu.com/na/496142915_120677543),访问日期:2022 年 1 月 22 日。

(6)关于仲裁员的民事赔偿责任以及责任限制问题。如足球运动的裁判一样,仲裁员也是人,也可能因为故意或者过失而犯错误,导致当事人权益受到侵害。《仲裁法》第 38 条规定:"仲裁员有本法第三十四条第四项规定的情形,情节严重的,或者有本法第五十八条第六项规定的情形的,应当依法承担法律责任……"但是,对于这里的法律责任是否包括民事赔偿责任,一直争议很大。早在 2008 年 10 月举办的中国国际私法学会年会上,中国国际经济贸易仲裁委员会秘书长就透露,我国已经有数起针对仲裁员或仲裁机构的民事诉讼案件,但案件细节并未见到公开报道①,近期相关的公开报道是李某某与某仲裁委员会不当得利纠纷一案。在该案中,李某某请求法院判令某仲裁委员会返还仲裁费 224998 元,理由是该仲裁委员会所作出的裁决被法院撤销了。最终,十堰市中级人民法院(2017) 鄂 03 民终 2210 号民事裁定书维持了一审驳回起诉的裁定,理由是:民法调整平等主体的自然人、法人和非法人组织之间的人身关系和财产关系。但仲裁委员会在仲裁过程中,与双方当事人并非平等主体之间的民事法律关系;仲裁委员会依照双方当事人的仲裁协议处理民事争议,与双方当事人不产生财产关系和人身关系。且仲裁委员会在仲裁期间依照相关规定收取费用,其费用收取是否合理不具有可诉性,不属人民法院民事案件的受案范围。此案裁定出来后,仲裁员和仲裁机构的民事责任问题一度成为热点话题。近期国外也有类似的案例,例如在 Texas Brine Co. v. Am. Arbitration Assc., No. 18-CV-31184② 中,2018 年 7 月 6 日,得克萨斯布赖恩公司(Texas Brine)对美国仲裁协会及两名仲裁员提起诉讼,指控三名被告在仲裁程序中有故意和不正当的欺诈行为,并请求支付 1200 万美元的损害赔偿和衡平救济。为了回应这一问题,借鉴伦敦国际仲裁院(London Court of International Arbitration,LCIA)及中国香港国际仲裁中心(Hong Kong International Arbitration Centre,HKIAC)规则的规定,《仲裁规则》首次引入了责任限制条款。

(7)此外,其他比较重要的变化还有:《仲裁规则》增加了由机构管理

---

① 参见张圣翠:《仲裁民事责任制度探析》,载《上海财经大学学报》2009 年第 1 期。
② 参见《法院驳回当事人基于仲裁员未披露潜在利益冲突要求仲裁机构及涉案仲裁员赔偿仲裁费用的请求》,载知乎(https://zhuanlan.zhihu.com/p/345170820),访问日期:2022 年 1 月 22 日。

费和仲裁员报酬组成的仲裁费用表,允许当事人通过特别约定选择适用,以更好地满足当事人需求,激发仲裁活力。《仲裁规则》还规定当事人可以在中国海事仲裁委员会仲裁员名册外选定仲裁员,同时规定首席仲裁员和独任仲裁员应从仲裁员名册中产生;规定当事人无法共同指定首席仲裁员的,由双方当事人所选定的两位仲裁员共同指定,在期限内无法指定的,由仲裁委员会主任指定。①

就案件受理情况而言,根据中国国际贸易促进委员会会长高燕2021年7月16日在2021中国海事商事仲裁高级别研讨会上的介绍②,2020年中国海事仲裁委员会审理裁决海事商事案件数量居世界仲裁机构前列,涉外案件占全部受案量的35%,当事人来自22个国家和地区,仲裁国际化程度不断提升。就仲裁调解而言,2021年11月11日上海海事法院发布的《上海海事法院与中国海事仲裁委员会海事案件委托调解白皮书(2011—2021)》指出③:①自2011年至2020年,委托调解机制保持平稳运行,上海海事法院委托中国海事仲裁委员会上海总部调解处理案件共200余件,案件数量呈现逐年稳步上升趋势。②案件涉及42个国家和地区,标的总额超过5亿元,全部案件中有141件具有涉外因素。③全部案件标的总额达到了人民币5.68亿元,案件平均标的额达人民币269.22万元。其中标的额最高为人民币5671.82万元。④在全部案件中,调解成功的共有102件,调解成功率为48.34%。而且,近年来,调解成功率有显著提高,特别是2020年度,委托调解成功率为75%,达到10年来的最高值。

三、海事仲裁相关司法实践的发展

关于2020—2021年海事仲裁司法审查的发展,结合2020年11月人民法院出版社出版的《涉外商事海事审判指导2018年第1辑(总第36

---

① 参见《中国海事仲裁委员会发布2021年版仲裁规则》,载中国海事仲裁委员会官网(http://www.cmac.org.cn/index.php?id=542),访问日期:2022年1月21日。

② 参见高燕:《锚定方向、奋楫前行:推动中国海事仲裁事业行稳致远》,载中国国际贸易促进委员会官网(http://www.ccpit.org/Contents/Channel_3434/2021/0804/1358085/content_1358085.htm),访问日期:2022年1月21日。

③ 《上海海事法院与中国海事仲裁委员会海事案件委托调解白皮书(2011—2021)》,载中华人民共和国上海海事法院官网(http://shhsfy.gov.cn/hsfyytwx/hsfyytwx/spdy1358/hsspbps1434/web/viewer.html?file=2011-2021.pdf),访问日期:2022年1月21日。

辑)》、2021 年 9 月人民法院出版社出版的《最高人民法院商事仲裁司法审查年度报告(2019)》、各个海事法院发布的海事审判白皮书,以及网上检索的裁判文书情况,笔者归纳如下:

1. 关于仲裁协议的效力

(1)在中国外运股份有限公司工程设备运输分公司与上海招商明华船务有限公司航次租船合同纠纷案中,双方的租船确认书约定"如若仲裁应交由中国海事仲裁委员会于北京进行,适用中国法"(G/A arbitration if any to be settled in Beijing with China Maritime Arbitration Commission, Chinese law to apply)。上海海事法院在(2020)沪 72 民初 1588 号民事裁定书中认为该条款无效,理由为:这是双方当事人对涉案纠纷提起仲裁时的仲裁地点和所适用法律作出的特别约定,不构成双方之间唯一的纠纷解决方式,并未排除诉讼管辖。①

(2)在苏黎世财产保险(中国)有限公司(以下简称"苏黎世保险")与东京海上日动火灾保险(中国)有限公司(以下简称"东京海上保险")申请确认仲裁协议效力案中,苏黎世保险请求确认其与东京海上日动火灾保险(中国)有限公司上海分公司(以下简称"东京海上上海分公司")签订的分保条(reinsurance slip)中无仲裁条款。最终,上海金融法院在(2019)沪 74 民特 27 号民事裁定书中驳回了苏黎世保险的申请,理由是:再保险合同约定,包括管辖在内的事项均参照原保单,此即合同条款

---

① 在最高人民法院(2009)民四他字第 36 号、(2016)最高法民他 3 号复函之中,案涉仲裁条款约定:Arbitration if any to be settled in Hong Kong with English law to apply。最高人民法院并未认定其无效,而只是认定其不构成双方之间唯一的纠纷解决方式,并未排除诉讼管辖。但是,在最高人民法院(2015)民四他字第 21 号复函中,案涉仲裁条款约定:Arbitration if any in Benxi and Chinese law to be applied。对此,最高人民法院除了认定其不构成双方之间唯一的纠纷解决方式,并未排除诉讼管辖,而且认为根据《仲裁法》第 16 条第 2 款第(一)项的规定,该仲裁条款当属无效。此外,除了"if any",与之类似的问题还有如果仲裁条款使用了"may""可以"等措辞时,其效力如何。在最高人民法院(2003)民四他字第 7 号复函中,最高人民法院认为:英文仲裁条款中的"may"主要作用于主语,其含义是指"任何一方"(any party)都可以提起仲裁,而不应理解为"既可以提起仲裁,也可以提起诉讼",该案纠纷应通过仲裁方式解决。在福建省高级人民法院(2011)闽民终字第 819 号民事裁定书中,案涉分包合同第 25 条约定"履行合同发生争议,可自行和解或要求有关部门调解,任何一方不愿和解、调解或和解、调解不成的,可由青岛仲裁机构裁决"。对此,福建省高级人民法院则表示:该条款仅约定发生争议可由仲裁机构裁决,而非必须由仲裁机构裁决,现原告选择诉讼作为争议解决方式,说明其放弃了仲裁的意愿,可予准许。

的并入。再保险合同将管辖(jurisdiction)与保险利益、保险期限等事项单独列出,明确约定这些事项参照原保险单。申请人认为,jurisdiction 仅指司法管辖,由于原保单仅约定仲裁条款而并无司法管辖的约定,因此再保险合同无参照内容,也不可能适用仲裁条款。法院则认为,该案双方均为外资保险公司,涉案合同也均以英文起草并签署,在双方就 jurisdiction 的含义产生争议的情况下,应按照该词语通常的含义予以界定。在英文中,jurisdiction 并非特指司法管辖,也可在指代诉讼、仲裁等纠纷解决方式的层面上适用。该案原保单中没有司法管辖的约定,双方约定参照原保单中的中国海事仲裁委员会上海分会仲裁条款,该约定有效。

2. 关于租约仲裁条款并入提单问题

在《对湖北省高级人民法院就厦门国贸集团股份有限公司诉国王航运公司(King Navigation Co.)海上货物运输合同纠纷一案仲裁条款效力请示的答复》[(2018)最高法民他 52 号]之中,最高人民法院指出:从提单记载内容看,其未明确租约的当事人名称、租约编号等可以确定租约的准确信息,不能据此确定并入的是哪一份具体的租约,租约仲裁条款对提单持有人收货人不具有约束力。而且,最高人民法院特别指出,英国法院对仲裁条款效力的认定以及签发的禁诉令,亦不影响收货人在中国提起诉讼。① 在山东省高级人民法院(2020)鲁民辖终 201 号民事裁定书中,法院也认为涉案提单正面仅有关于"运费支付依照 2019 年 5 月 24 日的租船合同"的记载,没有关于租船合同当事人名称的具体信息,没有关于将特定化的租船合同及其仲裁条款并入提单的内容,不产生仲裁条款并入提单并约束提单持有人的法律效力。

3. 关于保险代位和仲裁条款的关系

在珠海杰腾造船有限公司、英大泰和财产保险股份有限公司珠海中心支公司船舶建造合同纠纷案[广东省高级人民法院(2020)粤民辖终 258 号民事裁定书]中,法院认为,保险人代位求偿时,船舶建造合同中约定的新加坡海事仲裁院仲裁条款并不约束保险人。在中国人民财产保险股份有限公司南昌市分公司、江西中远海运集装箱运输有限公司保险人

---

① 参见杨万明主编、最高人民法院民事审判第四庭编:《涉外商事海事审判指导 2018 年第 1 辑(总第 36 辑)》,人民法院出版社 2020 年版,第 32 页。

代位求偿权纠纷案[江西省南昌市中级人民法院(2020)赣01民终1950号民事裁定书]中,法院则认为,运输合同中约定的中国海事仲裁委员会仲裁条款可以约束提起代位追偿的保险人。对此,需要注意的是《全国法院民商事审判工作会议纪要》(以下称《九民纪要》)第98条对此区分了国内和涉外两种情形,即非涉外案件的,被保险人和第三者在保险事故发生前达成的仲裁协议对保险人具有约束力。就涉外案件而言,《九民纪要》未作规定,但主流的观点基本上是认为此种仲裁协议不约束提起代位追偿的保险人。

4.关于当事人以缔约过失或者侵权为由起诉时,仲裁条款是否适用的问题

(1)在上海海事法院审理的一起还款保函纠纷案中,恒顺船务公司在伦敦提起仲裁,要求浦发银行支付1422万美元及相应利息。仲裁庭判令恒顺船务公司败诉后,恒顺船务公司又在上海海事法院对浦发银行提起诉讼,理由是浦发银行出具保函时有缔约过失。最终,上海海事法院认为恒顺船务公司依据保函中的仲裁条款申请仲裁,其在仲裁请求被驳回后又主张浦发银行出具保函时存在过错致其损失,该诉请内容属于与保函相关的争议,涉案争议已由伦敦仲裁解决,法院对此没有管辖权。①

(2)在天津海事法院审理的中国服装集团有限公司(以下简称"中服公司")诉扬州远扬国际码头有限公司、扬州远扬国际码头有限公司江都分公司(以下简称"远扬公司")申请诉讼财产保全损害责任纠纷案中,远扬公司在仲裁败诉后,向法院申请撤销该仲裁裁决,并在执行裁决程序中提出执行异议,均被法院裁定驳回。其后,远扬公司对中服公司提起海事侵权诉讼,并对中服公司提出财产保全申请,后中服公司胜诉,并就财产保全错误要求远扬公司赔偿。对此,天津海事法院认为,远扬公司提起的侵权诉讼,实质上仍是对仲裁裁决持有异议,其在提出执行异议的程序终结后再次提起侵权诉讼并采取财产保全措施,存在主观过错,申请保全错

---

① 参见《上海海事法院与中国海事仲裁委员会海事案件委托调解白皮书(2011—2021)》第43—44页。

误,应承担因此导致的相应损失。①

5. 关于境外海事仲裁境内财产保全问题

(1)在天际国际集团公司(Skyline International Corp.)申请扣押"尼莉莎"轮(M/V NERISSA)案中,申请人于伦敦仲裁前向青岛海事法院申请扣押约30万吨的马绍尔群岛籍油轮"尼莉莎"轮,青岛海事法院对此予以准许。而且,考虑到该轮原计划于青岛港卸下13万多吨原油后,继续前往天津港卸剩余的15万多吨,若无法如期前往天津港卸货,将产生滞期费3万美元/天,且将导致交付迟延、工厂停产等损失,青岛海事法院作出(2019)鲁72财保108号之一号民事裁定,准许"尼莉莎"轮继续营运,完成自青岛港经天津港至秦皇岛港的航次。最终,该案经青岛海事法院组织各方当事人调解成功。该案得到了最高人民法院的高度赞扬,并入选最高人民法院2020年9月发布的"2019年全国海事审判典型案例"。

(2)在中资租船有限公司诉福清市添翼建材有限公司(以下称"福清添翼公司")航次租船合同纠纷案中,申请人中资租船有限公司因租约纠纷,在中国香港特区对承租人马来西亚某沙业公司及担保人福清添翼公司启动了仲裁程序,然后在厦门海事法院申请保全被申请人福清添翼公司264000美元的银行存款或其他财产,厦门海事法院作出(2020)闽72财保17号民事裁定予以准许。值得注意的是,有观点认为②,对于境外仲裁当事人是否可以向内地法院申请财产保全,《海事诉讼特别程序法》对此有所突破。但突破的范围仅限于海事请求保全,不能扩大至其他非海事请求保全。无论仲裁前还是仲裁中,保全对象也仅限于船舶、船载货物、船用燃油和船用物料,不能扩大至其他财产。因此,对于境外仲裁之前或者之中是否能保全被申请人的银行账户,可能还会有争议。

(3)上海海事法院2021年5月25日发布的《上海海事法院服务保障船舶产业发展审判情况通报》显示,2020年上海海事法院根据《最高人民法院关于内地与香港特别行政区法院就仲裁程序相互协助保全的安排》

---

① 该案例入选《2020年天津海事法院审判工作白皮书》典型案例,载天津海事法院官网(https://tjhsfy.chinacourt.gov.cn/article/detail/2021/03/id/5927724.shtml),访问日期:2022年1月21日。

② 参见吴胜顺:《论境外仲裁非海事请求保全之限制》,载《中国海商法研究》2015年第3期。

审查了首例准许香港特区仲裁程序中财产保全申请的案件。①

6. 关于境外仲裁裁决的承认与执行情况

(1) 在中原租船有限公司申请认可和执行香港特区仲裁裁决案中,上海海事法院在(2019)沪72认港1号民事裁定书中裁定认可和执行莫世杰(Mok Sai Kit)和杨良宜(Philip Yang)作出的关于"Silvia Glory"轮租船合同纠纷的五份仲裁裁决。

(2) 在申请人中远海运特种运输股份有限公司与被申请人恒冠船务有限公司租船合同纠纷案中,厦门海事法院在(2020)闽72认港1号民事裁定书中裁定认可和执行香港国际仲裁中心作出的仲裁裁决书。而且,2020年2月18日,厦门海事法院还承认了新加坡国际仲裁中心编号为2019年第023号的部分终局仲裁裁决和编号为2019年第059号的终局仲裁裁决的效力。据悉,这是厦门海事法院第一例承认新加坡仲裁裁决的案件。②

(3) 在上海佳船机械设备进出口有限公司、美克斯海洋工程设备股份有限公司申请承认与执行外国仲裁裁决案之中,嘉兴市中级人民法院在(2019)浙04协外认1号民事裁定书中裁定承认了伦敦海事仲裁员协会(London Maritime Arbitrators Association,LMAA)独任仲裁员克莱夫·阿斯顿(Clive Aston)作出的船舶建造合同仲裁裁决。

(4) 在安富尔自由贸易区公司(以下简称"安富尔公司")、广东粤新海洋工程装备股份有限公司(以下简称"粤新公司")申请承认和执行外国仲裁裁决案中,广州海事法院在(2020)粤72协外认1号民事裁定书中裁定承认和执行新加坡海事仲裁院独任仲裁员加雅·普拉喀什(Jaya Prakash)作出的一份船舶建造合同纠纷仲裁裁决。值得注意的是,在该案中,被申请人粤新公司辩称:安富尔公司仅提出要求粤新公司支付中山船厂视察费用7262美元的仲裁请求,但仲裁庭除裁决粤新公司承担该中山船厂视察费用外,还裁决粤新公司需按照年利率6%支付该费用利

---

① 参见《上海海事法院服务保障船舶产业发展审判情况通报》,第25页。
② 参见《厦门海事法院首度裁定承认新加坡海事仲裁裁决》,载厦门海事法院官网(http://www.xmhsfy.gov.cn/xwzx/fydt/202002/t20200220_166987.htm),访问日期:2022年1月21日。

息,超出了仲裁请求范围,构成超裁。对此,广州海事法院不予认可,理由是:根据《新加坡海事仲裁院仲裁规则(第三版)》第37.2条的规定,仲裁庭可以对裁决的任何金额按其认为公正的利率裁定单利或复利,该案仲裁裁决8.1条对此也作出了"仲裁庭在利息裁定方面拥有极大的自由裁量权"的说明。故在安富尔公司已向仲裁庭请求中山船厂视察费用的情况下,仲裁庭对中山船厂视察费用利息的裁决不属于超裁。

(5)在沃泰思航运有限公司(Vertex Shipping CO.,LTD.)申请执行LMAA仲裁员蒂莫西·马歇尔(Timothy Marshall)和伊恩·冈特(Ian Guant)关于"IZUMI"轮租船合同纠纷仲裁裁决案中,上海海事法院在(2019)沪72协外认3号民事裁定书中对其予以承认和执行。值得注意的是,在该案中,就被申请人提出其已针对最终裁决向英国法院提起诉讼的抗辩,上海海事法院没有认可,理由是该提起诉讼的行为并不等同于仲裁庭作出的仲裁裁决已失去拘束力。①

(6)在海龙游艇项目(中国)有限公司(以下简称"海龙公司")申请承认执行英国仲裁裁决案②中,海龙公司与青岛造船厂因游艇建造合同发生纠纷,经LMAA仲裁员作出裁决后,海龙公司申请承认执行。青岛海事法院经审查认为存在仲裁程序与当事人约定不符的情形,拟拒绝承认执行,并上报山东省高级人民法院。山东省高级人民法院多数意见拟同意青岛海事法院的意见,主要理由是:双方签订的《造船合同》第13条对于裁决的通知(notice of award)约定应通过传真或者电子邮件方式发送给双方当事人;第17条"通知"部分还约定,有发送回执的电子邮件自收到阅读回执起视为送达。2014年1月9日和2014年1月21日仲裁员发送邮件,通知裁决已经作出并将未签名的裁决书发送给双方,但海龙公司未举证证明仲裁员发出上述两邮件后收到了阅读回执。因此,仲裁员发送上述邮件并不产生将裁决通知青岛造船厂的效果。在不能确认上述电子邮件被收件人打开时,仲裁员可以按照《造船合同》第13条的约定,尽快通

---

① 参见《外国仲裁裁决拘束力的审查》,载上海海事法院官网(http://m.shhsfy.gov.cn/hsfyytwx/hsfyytwx/spdy1358/jpal1435/2020/09/10/09b080ba744e77de017476c4671d3387.html),访问日期:2022年1月21日。

② 参见杨万明主编、最高人民法院民事审判第四庭编:《涉外商事海事审判指导2018年第1辑(总第36辑)》,人民法院出版社2020年版,第52—66页。

过传真方式通知青岛造船厂,而仲裁员并未通过传真方式发出裁决的通知。仲裁员未按照双方当事人的约定向青岛造船厂发送裁决的通知,仲裁程序与当事人的约定不符。但最终,最高人民法院没有认可山东省高级人民法院的多数意见,理由是:《造船合同》第17条是对当事人双方之间发送通知的约定,而非对仲裁程序的约定,该条关于通知的约定不适用于仲裁程序中发送裁决的通知。

(7)在满升航运有限公司、卓联海运有限公司申请承认和执行外国仲裁裁决民事案中,天津海事法院在(2019)津72协外认1号之一民事裁定书中裁定承认和执行 LMAA 仲裁员大卫·法灵顿(David Farrington)于2017年10月26日作出的关于定期租船合同纠纷的仲裁裁决及于2018年8月23日作出的关于仲裁费用的裁决。

7. 关于内地法院拒绝承认执行境外仲裁裁决的情况

总体来看,内地法院对境外的海事仲裁裁决都采取了相对支持的态度。但值得注意的是,也有少数裁决被拒绝承认执行,或者被部分拒绝承认执行。

(1)在《最高人民法院关于天津市高级人民法院就申请人帕尔默海运公司与被申请人中牧实业股份有限公司申请承认和执行外国仲裁裁决一案请示的复函》中①,最高人民法院答复同意拒绝执行一份伦敦仲裁裁决,理由是:中牧实业股份有限公司于2016年5月20日就该案纠纷向广州海事法院起诉,要求帕尔默海运公司承担货损责任,帕尔默海运公司以双方存在仲裁协议为由提出管辖权异议。本院以(2017)最高法民他83号复函答复广东省高级人民法院,认为租约中的仲裁条款并未并入提单且提单背面仲裁条款无效。在中国法院已对当事人之间仲裁条款的存在及效力作出否定性判断的前提下,承认及执行基于上述仲裁条款作出的仲裁裁决,其结果是在同一法域针对相同的事实作出了截然相反的司法判断,这种在司法判断结论方面自相矛盾的情形有违国家法律价值观念的统一和一致。无论对《纽约公约》中规定的"公共政策"作怎样的限制性解释,国家法律观念与司法判断结论之统一和一致都不应当被排除在

---

① 参见杨万明主编、最高人民法院民事审判第四庭编:《涉外商事海事审判指导2018年第1辑(总第36辑)》,人民法院出版社2020年版,第74—75页。

"公共政策"范围之外。

实务中,最高人民法院以公共政策为由拒绝承认执行境外仲裁裁决的不多,但仲裁裁决和内地法院的管辖权冲突的,最高人民法院一般会拒绝承认执行。例如,在"永宁公司案"和"浩普公司案"中,最高人民法院(2008)民四他字第11号复函及(2016)最高法民他8号复函均以此为由拒绝承认执行境外裁决。但是,值得注意的是,最高人民法院在(2013)民四他字第46号复函中指出:"涉案仲裁裁决系于2010年12月23日和2011年1月27日作出,而我国法院关于仲裁条款无效的裁定系于2011年12月20日作出,仲裁裁决的作出时间显然早于我国法院裁定的生效时间……外国仲裁裁决和我国法院生效裁定对同一仲裁条款效力的认定虽然存在冲突,但尚不足以构成违反我国公共政策的情形。"因此,如果境外仲裁庭就仲裁条款效力的认定早于境内法院,其仲裁裁决依然可能得到承认及执行。

(2)在特莱顿国际集装箱有限公司申请承认美国仲裁协会国际争议解决中心(International Centre for Dispute Resolution, ICDR)仲裁裁决案中,海南泛洋航运有限公司(以下简称"泛洋公司")、海南泛洋航运有限(中国香港)公司(以下简称"泛洋中国香港公司")与特莱顿国际集装箱有限公司(注册于百慕大群岛)于2010年至2011年间签订了六份集装箱租赁协议。洋浦经济开发区建设投资开发有限公司(以下简称"建投公司")在其中一份协议——HPO42号协议中以共同承租人的身份签字,并授权泛洋公司、泛洋中国香港公司代表其行使与该协议有关的权利,承诺对该协议相关的费用及产生的损失与两公司承担连带责任;但对其他协议,建投公司未签字或作出类似承诺。因泛洋公司、泛洋中国香港公司拖欠租金,特莱顿公司依据前述六份协议向ICDR提交了仲裁申请。在仲裁过程中,泛洋公司、泛洋中国香港公司与特莱顿公司签订了一份《违约处理协议函》,该协议函是对六份协议的合并处理,泛洋公司代理人代表建投公司参与了该协议函的签署。依据该协议函,ICDR遂裁决泛洋公司及建投公司就涉案六份协议向特莱顿公司连带赔偿65817973.41美元。最终,海口海事法院认为,泛洋公司无权代表建投公司在《违约处理协议函》中对全部六份协议的处理进行签字;建投公司仅为HPO42号协议的当事人,而并非其他五份协议的当事人,故HPO42号协议之外其他五份协议中的仲裁条款对建投公司不具有约束力。最终,经报请最高人民法院审核,海口海事法院对该 ICDR 仲裁裁决部分进行了承认与执行。①

8. 关于境外裁决执行所涉及的管辖权问题

在航运实务之中,很多被执行人可能是离岸公司,而其实际营业地在境内,此时中国内地法院对其是否有管辖权就会存在争议。从如下案例可以看出,就实际营业地在境内的离岸公司而言,若其主要办事机构所在地在境内的,中国内地法院可能会享有仲裁裁决执行的管辖权。

(1)在上海海事法院(2020)沪 72 协外认 1 号民事裁定书中,LMAA 仲裁员就申请人东盛航运有限公司(ORIENTAL PRIME SHIPPING CO., LIMITED)与被申请人商行荣耀国际航运有限公司(HONG GLORY INTERNATIONAL SHIPPING COMPANY LIMITED)的租船合同纠纷作出终局裁决后,申请人向上海海事法院申请执行。被申请人对管辖权提出异议,理由是其登记注册地为马绍尔群岛,在中国内地未设立主要办事机构,也没有任何财产。最终,上海海事法院驳回了这一异议,理由是:申请人与被申请人签订的租船确认书载明被申请人的地址为中国上海。涉案仲裁裁决书载明,被申请人的经营地在中国上海,履行涉案航次期间相关业务的往来邮件内容显示,被申请人确认其与 HONG GLORY SHIPPING CO., LIMITED 是同一家公司,而 HONG GLORY SHIPPING CO., LIMITED 的办公地址与租船确认书载明的被申请人地址一致。据此,法院综合认定被申请人的主要办事机构所在地为中国上海。值得指出的是,上海海事法院特别认为:涉案被申请人为注册在境外的离岸公司,在司法实践中对该类公司的主要办事机构所在地的认定标准可以适当降低,只要有证据证明被申请人与法院地存在一定程度的联系即可。②

(2)类似地,在天津海事法院(2019)津 72 协外认 1 号民事裁定书中,申请人申请执行 LMAA 裁决,被申请人也提出了类似的抗辩。最终,天津海事法院及天津市高级人民法院根据其出具放货保函、沟通使用的电子邮箱与北京某公司企业电子邮箱一致,支付租金使用的地址与该

---

① 参见海口海事法院(2015)琼海法他字第 1 号民事裁定书。
② 参见《纽约公约项下涉离岸公司案件的法院管辖权确定》,载上海海事法院官网(http://shhsfy.gov.cn/hsfyytwx/hsfyytwx/spdy1358/jpal1435/2021/12/10/09b080ba7d9ee309017da314737a06d5.html),访问日期:2022 年 1 月 21 日。

公司企业通信地址一致,被执行人唯一股东及董事与该公司法定代表人一致等因素,认为该 BVI 公司主要办事机构所在地为北京,天津海事法院有权管辖。此案入选了 2020 年天津海事法院十大案例,而且天津海事法院特别强调:审查法人或者其他组织的住所地,应当首先确定其主要办事机构所在地。尤其对于类似该案被申请人为在境外注册的离岸公司,更应当通过确定其主要经营活动、办公场所等所在地来确定其住所地,以防止这些在中国境内经营的离岸公司通过其境外公司地位,逃避责任,规避法律监管,破坏市场公平交易环境。①

9. 关于内地海事仲裁裁决的承认与执行

(1)2020 年 3 月,南京海事法院承认了中国海事仲裁委员会就舟山某船舶修造公司与南京某船业公司因船舶修造合同纠纷作出的仲裁裁决。值得注意的是,这是南京海事法院执结仲裁裁决的首案。②

(2)厦门海事法院 2020 年 7 月发布的《2019 年厦门海事法院审判工作白皮书》披露,在申请执行人 CHILIN KANGIN 与被执行人何文朝申请执行仲裁裁决异议案中,厦门海事法院执行了中国海事仲裁委员会上海分会的裁决。③ 值得注意的是,在该案中,被执行人认为仲裁未裁决其支付迟延履行利息,申请人要求执行该项内容缺乏依据。对此,厦门海事法院没有认可,理由是迟延履行利息的计算和收取是以 2017 年《民事诉讼法》第 253 条而非仲裁裁决为依据。

(3)在张欣、张科富执行审查案中,张科富的"海纳 5188"散货船因驾驶过失触礁沉没。该轮沉货被打捞出水后,张科富与其船舶保险人阳光财产保险股份有限公司重庆市万州中心支公司(以下简称"阳光财险")找到张欣并与其磋商达成了沉货买卖事宜,并在买卖合同中约定由中国海事仲裁委员会上海分会仲裁。其后,沉船货主的保险人赔偿了货主,然后对张科富和阳光财险提起追偿诉讼,该案经调解解决。由于张欣

---

① 参见《2020 年天津海事法院审判工作白皮书》,载天津海事法院官网(https://tjhsfy.chinacourt.gov.cn/article/detail/2021/03/id/5927724.shtml),访问日期:2022 年 1 月 21 日。
② 参见《200 余万修船款到账!南京海事法院执结仲裁裁决执行首案》,载北青网(http://news.ynet.com/2020/06/16/2666344t70.html),访问日期:2022 年 1 月 22 日。
③ 参见《2019 年厦门海事法院审判工作白皮书》,载厦门海事法院官网(http://www.xmhsfy.gov.cn/sjbg/bps/202007/t20200716_168900.htm),访问日期:2022 年 1 月 21 日。

未依约付款,张科富与阳光财险签订了《债权转让协议》将买卖合同下的债权转让给阳光财险,并对张欣发出了债权转让《通知函》。此后,张科富、阳光财险向中国海事仲裁委员会上海分会提起了仲裁申请,仲裁庭裁决张欣向阳光财险支付货款480938元及其利息。在执行程序中,张欣提出异议认为:《债权转让协议》不具备转让基础,该协议和债权转让通知不产生法律效力;张欣与阳光财险之间没有订立仲裁协议,阳光财险也无权通过债权转让行为直接适用仲裁条款。对此,武汉海事法院在(2020)鄂72执异44号执行裁定书中没有认可,理由是:作为涉案部分债权的受让人,阳光财险接受《买卖合同》中的争议解决条款,自愿受其约束,与张科富共同向仲裁委员会提起针对张欣的仲裁,没有损害张欣的合法权益,符合法律规定。从该案可以看出,保险公司也可以通过约定的债权转让而获得被保险人对第三者的赔偿请求权。

(4)在中电电建建设有限公司、中国外运股份有限公司申请撤销仲裁裁决案中,天津海事法院在(2021)津72民特6号民事裁定书中裁定驳回了申请人提出的撤销中国海事仲裁委员会(2020)中国海仲京裁字第0010号裁决书(以下简称"20-10号裁决书")的申请。值得注意的是,在该案中,撤裁申请人认为仲裁违反法定程序,理由是20-10号裁决书认定内容与中国海事仲裁委员会(2017)海仲京裁字第0015号裁决书(以下简称"17-15号裁决书")认定内容构成实质性冲突,裁判标准明显不统一,违反了类案及关联案件强制检索的法定程序。最终法院没有认可撤裁申请,理由是:《仲裁法》第58条规定的"违反法定程序",是指违反《仲裁法》规定的仲裁程序和当事人选择的仲裁规则可能影响案件正确裁决的情形。撤裁申请人主张违反法定程序的理由是,20-10号裁决书与17-15号裁决书对于合同条款的理解适用标准不统一,不符合《最高人民法院关于落实司法责任制完善审判监督管理机制的意见(试行)》的规定。但该意见是最高人民法院发布的就完善人民法院审判监督管理机制对各级人民法院相关工作提出的意见要求,不属于《仲裁法》规定的仲裁程序或当事人选择的仲裁规则。而且,20-10号裁决书与17-15号裁决书系针对不同的请求事项与合同条款依据分别作出认定,并不存在实质性冲突。

(5)在郑贤忠申请撤销仲裁裁决案中,申请人申请撤销中国海事仲裁委员会(2019)中国海仲沪裁字第042号裁决书,理由是中国海事仲裁委员会无权认定当事人合同的效力,无权就此作出仲裁。上海海事法院在(2020)沪72民特27号民事裁定书中驳回了申请人的撤销申请,并指出:仲裁庭对合同效力的解释或认定,实际上属于对合同解释的一个方面,而对合同的解释及对合同效力的认定,又是决定合同的履行及其法律后果的先决条件。该案申请人要求被申请人支付船舶价款39万元及利息,仲裁庭就此作出裁决,此为合同的履行问题。上述事项均未超出合同双方当事人仲裁协议的范围,申请人申请撤裁的理由不成立。

(6)在上海中船重工万邦航运有限公司(以下简称"中船公司")、南京中港船业有限公司(以下简称"中港公司")民事执行异议案中,中国海事仲裁委员会对中港公司与中船公司光船租赁合同纠纷作出(2020)中国海仲沪裁字第002号裁决书,中港公司申请执行,中船公司对法院的执行行为不服,理由是:案涉仲裁裁决是关于双方对购船选择权的争议,根据裁决书,在中港公司选择购买船舶的情况下,双方还应协商船舶买卖条款、签署船舶买卖合同,然后才涉及船舶变更登记手续,中港公司无权在不履行船舶买卖合同付款义务的情况下直接要求中船公司配合办理船舶登记手续。对此,南京海事法院在(2021)苏72执异10号执行裁定书中予以驳回,理由是:案涉仲裁裁决第一项裁定《"双龙海"轮光船租赁合同》第四部分选择权条款有效,中船公司应配合中港公司办理船舶买卖及变更船舶登记手续相关事宜。根据该项裁决内容,中船公司同时负有两项义务,一是配合办理船舶买卖,二是配合办理船舶变更登记,其任何一项义务不履行,中港公司均可向法院申请强制执行。仲裁裁决作出后,由于双方经磋商未能自行达成船舶买卖合同,也未能共同办理船舶变更登记手续,中港公司遂向法院申请强制执行,并将《"双龙海"轮光船租赁合同》约定的1780万元购船尾款全部交至法院账户用于保障中船公司合同利益的实现。在此情况下,南京海事法院作出(2020)苏72执139号之一执行裁定,要求将登记在中船公司名下的"双龙海"轮过户至中港公司名下,符合法律规定。

结　　语

总体来看,虽有疫情的影响,2020—2021年中国内地海事仲裁相关的法律和司法实践依然在稳步发展,中国内地海事仲裁事业的国际影响力也在不断扩大。如青岛海事法院审理的"尼莉莎"轮案所体现出来的中国内地法院一贯对境外海事仲裁在境内的扣船等财产保全持支持态度。就仲裁司法审查而言,中国内地法院承认和执行了来自中国香港、新加坡、伦敦等地区的裁决,只有少数被不予承认执行或者部分不予承认执行。而且,中国海事仲裁委员会的诸多裁决也都得到了承认执行,这显示了中国内地法院一贯对海事仲裁的支持和友好态度。

此外,值得提及的是,在 BOA BARGES AS 与南京奕淳船舶制造有限公司船舶建造合同纠纷案中,挪威籍船东 BOA BARGES AS 与南京奕淳船舶制造有限公司就三份总价款近5000万美元的《半潜重型甲板货驳造船合同》发生争议。案涉合同原本约定的争议解决方式为向伦敦国际仲裁院申请仲裁并适用英国法,但双方于2020年5月16日签订《补充协议》,将争议解决方式变更为由南京海事法院管辖并适用中国法。然后,南京海事法院通过互联网办案方式组织调解,仅用时27天促成双方当事人达成调解协议。该案成功入选了2020年全国海事审判典型案例,而且最高人民法院特别指出:外国当事人在纠纷发生后,协议变更争议解决方式和适用法律的约定,主动选择向南京海事法院起诉并适用中国法律,既是基于对中国建设国际海事司法优选地的信任,也是对中国海事法院专业司法能力的充分认可。[①] 从该案来看,笔者也认为,随着中国内地海事司法和仲裁不断地为境内外当事人认可,中国内地海事司法和仲裁事业必将随之迎来更大的发展。

香港特区[*]

引　言

中国香港特别行政区(以下简称"香港特区")作为一个自由港,从小渔村发展成今天繁荣的国际城市,航运和贸易一直植根于此。这些业务

[①] 参见《2020年全国海事审判典型案例》,载中华人民共和国最高人民法院官网(http://www.court.gov.cn/zixun-xiangqing-317811.html),访问日期:2021年3月21日。

[*] 本篇作者为莫世杰,独立商业及海事仲裁员。

深受地缘政治和全球经济影响,故易于产生大量争议,由于其国际性,遇上争议或分歧通常以仲裁来解决。

香港特区作为世界领先的金融和商业中心之一,凭借其公正独立、享誉国际的法律体系,是进行各种国际仲裁的当然选择。自20世纪90年代中后期以来,越来越多的商业人士在海事合约中选择以香港特区作为仲裁地。这主要受益于亚洲经济的快速增长及中国作为世界航运和商品贸易发动机的快速崛起。

一、专业知识

香港特区在海事及贸易各领域均有不同专长。作为传统的航运中心,香港特区现在是航运和海事服务的枢纽,提供例如船舶管理、船舶经纪、船舶金融、海上保险等服务。大部分船舶互保协会都在香港特区设立了办事处,服务来自世界各地的会员的需要。这里有为数不少的法律知识渊博且经验丰富的航运和国际贸易律师,为客户提供称职的法律服务;也有一些掌握商业和技术知识的专家,能高效地提供协助及在仲裁开庭时提供专家证据。

香港海事仲裁协会(Hong Kong Maritime Arbitration Group, HKMAG)是香港特区一个专门提供海事争议仲裁服务的本土仲裁机构。HKMAG由一群具有不同背景、专业知识和行业经验的海事专业人员于2000年成立,原为香港国际仲裁中心(Hong Kong International Arbitration Centre, HKIAC)的一个分支,成立的目的是促进使用香港特区海事仲裁和调解服务。为了应付瞬息万变的市场需求,HKMAG于2019年3月成为正式的独立机构。现时HKMAG的业务通过HKMAG委员会进行。HKMAG委员会成员都是协会的全职会员。其他会员类别包括会员和支持性会员。HKMAG的全职会员和会员都是香港特区居民。

强调与航运业的联系是HKMAG的一个独特且重要的特点。HKMAG的多数会员对海事争议解决深感兴趣,在航运和相关专业拥有商业或法律经验,并在国际仲裁程序方面具有广泛的知识和经验。扎根于香港特区的HKMAG会员有着多元的背景,来自不同的种族,使我们更能体会并理解东西方的文化差异。文化差异的影响在国际仲裁中普遍地被视为一个值得关注的问题。

部分 HKMAG 的会员能读写中文和英文。虽然拥有双语能力对以英语作为工作语言的海事仲裁来说未必十分重要,但在书面和口头证据中使用中文并不少见的情况下,翻译费用会十分昂贵,而在翻译时证据的意思更有可能被遗漏,特别是口头证据。若仲裁庭中有双语背景的仲裁员,可以减少甚至避免这种费用及风险。

二、独立和公正的法律体系

香港特区的法律建基于法治和审判独立。在"一国两制"的大原则下,中国在 1997 年恢复对香港行使主权后,香港特区仍保留英国的普通法制度,是中国唯一行使普通法的管辖区,其法律是全球唯一的双语普通法。

每一个仲裁地点都极为强调"自然公正"这一神圣不可侵犯原则的重要性。在香港特区,这些原则体现在《仲裁条例》(第 609 章)中。该条例适用于香港特区所有的仲裁。①

《仲裁条例》第 46 条第(2)款规定,仲裁庭必须平等对待各当事方。《仲裁条例》第 46 条第(3)款进一步要求仲裁庭必须独立,在各当事方之间公平和公正地行事,并采取公平及适当的程序,协助双方有效地解决争端,降低成本。这些规定奠定了香港特区仲裁的基础,而这基础深受香港特区令人信赖的法律制度、诚信可靠的专业人士以及低贪污率所支持。②

最近,英国高等法院汉布伦(Hamblen)大法官③在 Shagang South Asia (Hong Kong) Trading Co. Ltd. v. Daewoo Logistics (The Nikolaos A) [2015] EWHC 194 (Comm)④中称赞中国香港特区为:

---

① 参见电子版香港法例网(https://www.elegislation.gov.hk/hk/cap609),访问日期:2022 年 1 月 5 日。
② 贪污对争议解决服务的发展带来重大不利的影响。请参考以下案例:Michael Cherney and Oleg Vladimirovich Deripaska [2008] EWHC 1530 (Comm),载 http://www.bailii.org/ew/cases/EWHC/Comm/2008/1530.html,访问日期:2022 年 1 月 5 日。
③ Hamblen 大法官原为大律师,处理海事争议,现为英国最高法院大法官。
④ 参见 http://www.bailii.org/cgi-bin/format.cgi?doc=/ew/cases/EWHC/Comm/2015/194.html,访问日期:2022 年 1 月 5 日。

一个知名和受尊重的仲裁地点,拥有中立的声誉,尤其是因为它的监督法院。

中立、公正和独立是香港特区仲裁的特色。这些特色也得到了全球当事方和仲裁从业人员的广泛认可。① 美国伟凯律师事务所与伦敦大学玛丽皇后学院2021年国际仲裁调查报告②显示,中国香港特区被评为全球最受欢迎的第三个仲裁地点。

三、《仲裁条例》(第609章)

以香港特区作为仲裁地点的仲裁受《仲裁条例》的支持及监督。《仲裁条例》以《联合国国际贸易法委员会国际商事仲裁示范法》为基础,并辅以与1996年《英国仲裁法》相类似的规定为依据。它尊重仲裁当事方的自治,以最大限度扩大仲裁员的权力,并尽量减少法庭的干预为目的。《仲裁条例》具有现代、全面、结构清晰及良好实用性等特征,并不时作出增修,与时并进。③ 以下是《仲裁条例》的一些特点。

1. HKIAC 为法定机构

HKIAC④是一个在香港特区注册的非营利组织机构。它肩负不同的角色和职能,其中包括作为《仲裁条例》中所指定的法定机构,行使其所赋予的权力。⑤

《仲裁条例》第23条赋予HKIAC在双方就仲裁员人数没有协议的情况下代为决定仲裁员人数的权力。HKIAC亦可根据《仲裁条例》第24条的授权,代仲裁当事方任命独任仲裁员,或在缺席的情况下代为委任仲裁员,或在没有协议的情况下代为委任第三名仲裁员。

---

① 参见美国伟凯律师事务所(White & Case)与伦敦大学玛丽皇后学院联合进行的2015年国际仲裁调查,载 http://www.arbitration.qmul.ac.uk/media/arbitration/docs/2015_International_Arbitration_Survey.pdf,访问日期:2022年1月5日。
② 参见 http://www.arbitration.qmul.ac.uk/media/arbitration/docs/LON0320037-QMUL-International-Arbitration-Survey-2021_19_WEB.pdf,访问日期:2022年1月5日。
③ 《仲裁条例》近期作出修订,容许知识产权争议可透过仲裁解决及第三方资助适用于仲裁。
④ 参见香港国际仲裁中心官网(www.hkiac.org),访问日期:2022年1月5日。
⑤ 参见《仲裁条例》第13条。

2. 仲裁庭可以决定自身的管辖权

根据《仲裁条例》第 34 条的规定,仲裁庭可以决定其管辖权,包括对仲裁协议的存在或有效性的任何异议。当事方可以在仲裁开始时(但不迟于提交答辩书时)向仲裁庭提出申请,以确定仲裁庭是否具有审理争议的管辖权。仲裁庭可以对有关挑战以初步问题形式或在对实体争议作出的裁决书中作出裁决。如果仲裁庭以初步问题形式作出裁决,任何一方均可在收到仲裁庭对其具有管辖权的决定的通知后 30 天内请求香港特区法院对挑战作出裁决。

3. 临时措施

此外,《仲裁条例》第 35 条授权仲裁庭以裁决书的形式给予临时措施。该条为各当事方提供以下有力措施。

(1)维持现状或恢复原状,例如以裁决书形式禁止一方把一艘特种船撤出集体经营,有关例子可见 Lauritzen Cool AB v. Lady Navigation Inc. (2004) EWHC 2607 (Comm)。①

(2)取得仲裁庭的止诉令,限制在香港特区外的司法管辖区进行诉讼从而违反仲裁条款的行为。这种情况通常发生在提单下的货物索赔中,其管辖权条款规定了在香港特区进行仲裁,但货方在卸货港的法院展开诉讼,例如 Ever Judger Holding Co. Ltd. v. Kroman Celik Sanayii Anonim Sirketi [2015] 3 HKC 246。②

(3)保护资产以满足将来的仲裁裁决。该临时措施可以冻结令的形式下达。冻结令用于禁止一方,通常是仲裁的答辩方,转移、耗散或处置其资产,以使索赔方在之后的仲裁中胜诉后,其索赔不会变得毫无价值。③

(4)保全证据。使用此临时措施可促进对争议的公平解决。

---

① 参见 https://www.bailii.org/ew/cases/EWHC/Comm/2004/2607.html,访问日期:2022 年 1 月 5 日。

② 参见香港法律资讯中心官网(http://www.hklii.org/eng/hk/cases/hkcfi/2015/602.html),访问日期:2022 年 1 月 5 日。

③ 但要注意,仲裁庭的指令对仲裁协议的当事方以外的第三方不具有约束力。有关申请应向法院提出,例如根据《仲裁条例》第 45 条向中国香港法院申请。参见 Top Gains Mineral Macao Commercial Offshore Limited and TL Resources Pte Ltd. [2015] HKCFI 2101,载 https://www.hklii.org/cgi-bin/sinodisp/eng/hk/cases/hkcfi/2015/2101.html,访问日期:2022 年 1 月 5 日。

《仲裁条例》明白当事方对采取临时措施的需要,特别是在仲裁尚未启动或仲裁庭尚未正式组成的情况下。因此,《仲裁条例》第 45 条规定,法院可就已在或将会在香港特区或香港特区以外地方展开的任何仲裁程序提供临时措施协助。

4. 仲裁庭的一般权力和命令讼费担保的权力

除被授予临时措施权力外,仲裁庭还有权根据《仲裁条例》第 56 条在仲裁程序中作出各种命令。这些权力主要与证据有关。例如,仲裁庭可以命令文件披露,要求通过誓章的形式提供证据,对相关财产进行抽样、检查或者保存。

《仲裁条例》第 56 条第(1)(d)(i)款明确地容许仲裁庭可下令出售相关财产。例如,在处理易损货物或船东在面对欠租而对货物行使留置权的情况下,这出售财产的权力将派上用场,例如 Dainford Navigation Inc. v. PDVSA Petroleo SA(The "Moscow Star")[2017] EWHC 2150。① 在该案中,船东根据 1996 年《英国仲裁法》第 44 条第(2)(d)款向英国高等法院提出申请,要求出售因承租人欠租而被船东留置的货物。1996 年《英国仲裁法》第 44 条第(2)(d)款与《仲裁条例》第 56 条第(1)(d)(i)款及第 60 条第(1)(a)款类似。值得注意的是,该权力仅予英国法院行使。而《仲裁条例》赋予该权力给以中国香港特区为仲裁地的仲裁庭[第 56 条第(1)(d)(i)款]和香港特区法院[第 60 条第(1)(a)款]。

《仲裁条例》的第 56 条第(1)(a)款赋予仲裁庭权力去指令提出索赔或反索赔的一方,为其索赔或反索赔可能败诉,并且可能出现不支付胜诉方的费用的情况时,指示索赔或反索赔的一方向另一方就其费用提供担保。一般而言,有关指令的决定,视乎是否存在真实风险,索赔人将不会支付成功抗辩该索赔或反索赔的答辩人的费用。

若未按指令提供讼费担保,将导致索赔(或反索赔)被搁置或撤销的情况出现,详细规定参见《仲裁条例》的第 56 条第(4)款。

5. 延长期限

《仲裁条例》第 58 条规定,仲裁庭可以下达命令延长仲裁协议中规定

---

① 参见 http://www.bailii.org/ew/cases/EWHC/Comm/2017/2150.html,访问日期:2022 年 1 月 5 日。

的索赔时效。有关例子可见 Korbetis v. Transgrain Shipping BV［2005］EWHC 1345（QB）。① 在英国的判例 Perca Shipping Ltd. v. Cargill Inc.［2012］3759(QD)12D② 中,英国高等法院参考了1996年《英国仲裁法》第12条的适用范围,当中的措辞与《仲裁条例》第58条相类似。

6. 索赔因怠于推进程序而被撤销

《仲裁条例》第59条容许仲裁庭当一方在仲裁的过程中无故推迟其索赔,可作出裁决书将有关索赔撤销,并指令禁止该方就此项索赔开展任何仲裁程序。有关例子可见 Dera Commercial Estate v. Derya Inc.［2018］EWHC 1673（Comm）。③

7. 裁决的终局性

根据《仲裁条例》第73条的规定,仲裁庭颁发的裁决书为终局裁决,对当事方具有约束力,不能对其裁决进行审查。仲裁裁决书只会在特定的情况下被撤销④,且这些情况与裁决的事实和法律问题无关⑤。

如果当事方希望拥有如1996年《英国仲裁法》中有限的上诉权利,则可以选择加入《仲裁条例》附表二中的条款,其作为仲裁协议的一部分,允许双方就法律问题提出上诉。有关例子可见 Maeda Kensetsu Kogyo Kabushiki Kaisha and others v. Bauer Hong Kong Limited［2017］HKCFI 1582;HCMP 1342/2017。⑥

附表二同时包括与1996年《英国仲裁法》类似的条文,可让当事方以"严重不正常"为由,就裁决书提出上诉。

---

① 参见 https://www.bailii.org/cgi-bin/format.cgi?doc=/ew/cases/EWHC/QB/2005/1345.html,访问日期:2022年1月5日。
② 另参见 Haven Insurance Company Limited v. Eui Limited（T/A Elephant Insurance）［2018］EWCA Civ 294,载 https://www.bailii.org/ew/cases/EWCA/Civ/2018/2494.html,访问日期:2022年1月5日。
③ 该案涉及仲裁庭根据1996年《英国仲裁法》第41条第(3)款对撤销申请的裁决。按照第41条第(3)款的规定,如果仲裁出现"过分且不可原谅"的延误,则仲裁庭可以撤销索赔。《仲裁条例》第59条与其有所不同,它要求延误须为"不合理的"。
④ 参见《仲裁条例》第81条。
⑤ 参见《仲裁条例》第81条第(3)款。
⑥ 参见香港法律资讯中心官网(http://www.hklii.org/eng/hk/cases/hkcfi/2017/1582.html),访问日期:2022年1月5日。

四、关于内地与香港特别行政区法院就仲裁程序相互协助保全的安排

根据《仲裁条例》第61条第(1)款的规定,仲裁庭就仲裁程序而作出的命令或指示,不论是在香港特区或是在香港特区以外地方作出的,均可犹如具有同等效力的原诉讼法庭命令或指示般,以同样的方式强制执行。然而,其他司法管辖区的仲裁法未必有类似的规定。

当事人可能希望向法院寻求临时措施,尤其是考虑到将来裁决书执行的问题或所需的临时措施涉及第三方的情况下。但是,能否向法院申请临时措施来协助境外仲裁程序,很大程度上取决于该法院的程序法。

在中国内地,法院一般不会为境外的仲裁程序作出临时措施指令,并且不会执行由境外的仲裁庭作出的临时措施指令。值得一提的是,海事请求在内地得到特殊的待遇。内地海事法院根据《海事诉讼特别程序法》①及《最高人民法院关于适用〈海事诉讼特别程序法〉若干问题的解释》②,可以作出临时措施指令以协助境外的仲裁程序。不过,根据解释,申请范围只限于"船舶、船载货物、船用燃油以及船用物料"③。

2019年,中华人民共和国最高人民法院和中国香港特别行政区律政司签订《关于内地与香港特别行政区法院就仲裁程序相互协助保全的安排》。根据该安排,以香港特区作为仲裁地,并由被指定的合资格的仲裁机构所管理的仲裁的当事方,可向内地法院申请临时措施。④ 有关的临时措施的种类包括"财产保全、证据保全和行为保全"。HKMAG 是该安排下的合资格机构之一。

五、裁决书的执行

仲裁是在各方同意下以文明手段解决争端的方法。但如果裁决书中

---

① 参见《海事诉讼特别程序法》第14条。
② 参见《最高人民法院关于适用〈海事诉讼特别程序法〉若干问题的解释》第21条。
③ 参见《最高人民法院关于适用〈海事诉讼特别程序法〉若干问题的解释》第18条。
④ 此安排不适用于临时仲裁。

判定的权利无法得到有效的执行,则当事各方投入时间和金钱进行仲裁可说是徒然。尤其是在租船合约、提单和国际贸易合约层面上,因为参与其中的公司大多位于不同地方。

联合国国际贸易法委员会《承认及执行外国仲裁裁决公约》(又称《纽约公约》)①减轻了这方面的忧虑。《纽约公约》在缔约国家和地区承认和执行外国或地区仲裁裁决书方面提供了一种简单的方法。全世界已有160多个国家及地区加入了该公约。

香港特区是《纽约公约》的缔约成员,在香港特区作出的仲裁裁决书可以在所有缔约国家及地区执行。

内地与香港特区之间有相关的安排,以方便香港特区的仲裁裁决书在内地执行。② 2021年5月19日起,当事方可以在内地和香港特区同时启动执行程序,但在两地法院执行裁决所收回的总金额不可超过裁决金额。

香港特区与澳门特区也有类似的相互执行仲裁裁决书的安排:《关于香港特别行政区与澳门特别行政区相互认可和执行仲裁裁决的安排》。

就香港特区执行仲裁裁决而言,在近期香港特区法院的 KB v. S and Others [HCCT 13/2015]③中,法官在判词中强调执行应该"几乎是行政程序的事情"且法院应该"尽可能机械化"。这个案例说明了香港特区法院对仲裁和裁决书的执行抱有支持的态度。

六、实体法

合约中的实体法是指当事双方在合约中约定选择用于解决争议的实体法律。在海运合约中,适用法通常为英国法律,这主要是因为英国法律的高透明度、可预测性、利商性及拥有大量的法律先例可援引。

如前所述,英国普通法制度适用于中国香港特区。中国香港特区紧

---

① 参见联合国国际贸易法委员会官网(http://www.uncitral.org/uncitral/zh/uncitral_texts/arbitration/NYConvention.html),访问日期:2022年1月5日。
② 参见《关于内地与香港特别行政区相互执行仲裁裁决的安排》。
③ 参见香港法律资讯中心官网(http://www.hklii.org/eng/hk/cases/hkcfi/2015/1787.html),访问日期:2022年1月5日。

随并依照英国商业法解决商业纠纷。对于习惯于以英国法律管理业务的商人来说,以香港法在香港特区仲裁纠纷应不会感到陌生。

七、香港特区海事仲裁的惯常做法、HKMAG 仲裁规则及机构仲裁程序

1. 惯常做法

大多数在香港特区进行的海事仲裁都是临时仲裁,有关做法与伦敦类似。在香港特区根据《仲裁条例》的规定进行的临时仲裁,仲裁程序灵活,不拘形式。仲裁庭可以与当事方就争议度身订造一套简化特定的仲裁程序;海事仲裁通常由一名独任仲裁员或两名仲裁员进行,无须指定第三名仲裁员;当中大多数的仲裁都是在"文件审理"的基础上进行。

2. HKMAG 仲裁规则及小额索赔程序

HKMAG 得到伦敦海事仲裁员协会(London Maritime Arbitrators Association,LMAA)的许可,全面采用了 LMAA 仲裁规则和 LMAA 小额索赔程序,并就纳入香港特区程序法进行了修改,使其成为《HKMAG 仲裁规则(2021)》和《HKMAG 小额索赔程序(2021)》,旨在应用于在香港特区进行的海事仲裁。这使得中国香港特区海事仲裁与国际做法一致。

HKMAG 仲裁规则与 LMAA 仲裁规则基本相同。除有关仲裁程序的一般规定外,HKMAG 仲裁规则允许仲裁庭决定争议是否以"文件"解决,是否同步进行两个或多个仲裁。针对 COVID-19,HKMAG 仲裁规则明确指出庭审包括通过使用科技的虚拟或混合庭审,并为虚拟庭审提供指引。HKMAG 仲裁规则拥抱数字化理念,允许以电子签名签署仲裁裁决书,除非在作出裁决书前收到通知,否则不会签署打印的副本。这加快了裁决书颁布的速度,节省仲裁员的时间和成本,并减少碳足迹。

关于 HKMAG 仲裁规则的使用,有两点值得一提。

首先是仲裁条款起草草率,没有规定仲裁员人数的问题。根据《仲裁条例》,希望将争议提交仲裁的当事方可能需要向 HKIAC 提出申请,以决

定应由独任仲裁员还是三名仲裁员来审理争议。① 这将带来延误并产生不必要的费用。《HKMAG仲裁规则》第9段(a)明确指出,仲裁员默认为3人,从而解决了这一问题。第9段(b)(i)提供了一种任命机制(即14天的默认程序),以确保仲裁庭能迅速成立。根据默认程序,如果一方在收到另一方的通知后14日内未能任命其仲裁员,则可以将已被任命的仲裁员指定为独任仲裁员。第9段(b)(ii)规定,已委任的两名仲裁员可以不必任命第三名仲裁员,直到进行实质聆讯或者他们无法就与仲裁有关的任何事项达成协议为止。

《HKMAG仲裁规则》第26段允许当事方根据《仲裁条例》附表二第4—7条的规定,以严重不正常为由对裁决提出异议,亦可就法律问题对裁决提出上诉。有关异议和上诉可以作为维持海事仲裁员质素和水平的额外措施,并允许中国香港特区法院发展和解释法律。

当事方若希望保留根据《HKMAG仲裁规则》就法律问题对裁决提出上诉,应确保选择中国香港特区法律而非英国法律作为其海事合同的适用法。个中原因是,对香港特区法院而言,香港特区外法律是事实问题。由英国法律作为合同的实体法而引起的任何法律问题可能会被视为事实问题,而不是法律问题。② 换句话说,如果选择英国法律为适用法,则当事方会被视为选择退出《仲裁条例》附表二第5—6条。

3. HKMAG机构仲裁管理程序

HKMAG还根据《HKMAG仲裁规则》制定了仲裁管理程序。制定仲裁管理程序的目的,是希望让当事方能够利用《关于内地与香港特别行政区法院就仲裁程序相互协助保全的安排》所带来的好处。该程序采用非常宽松的方式,由HKMAG管理或监督进行仲裁。HKMAG将根据该程序收取注册费和管理费。这些费用由HKMAG委员会检讨决定。目前,HKMAG不收取任何注册费,而管理费仅固定为港币5000元。

无论是临时仲裁还是管理仲裁,使用《HKMAG仲裁规则》可确保仲

---

① 若是三名仲裁员,根据《仲裁条例》第23条第(3)(a)款的规定,说明一方在收到另一方的仲裁通知后,需要在30天内委任其仲裁员,其后双方仲裁员需在30天内对第三名仲裁员作出委任。

② See Reliance Industries Ltd. v. Enron Oil and Gas India Ltd. And Oil & National Gas Corporation(2002)1 Lloyd's Rep 645.

裁程序以高效、迅速和节约成本的方式进行。

八、建议使用的仲裁条款

仲裁是基于双方同意的解决争议的程序。一条如下述的简单仲裁条款就已足够把争议提交香港特区仲裁：

Arbitration in Hong Kong. English law to apply.

这种仲裁条款通常在由亚洲当事方订立的租船合约、订租确认书及货物买卖合约中出现。然而，由于过于简单，在实际操作上往往带来延迟，妨碍仲裁的顺利进行，甚至带来不必要的枝节诉讼。[①]

HKMAG制定了标准仲裁条款，可用于所有海事合同。拟定这些条款的目的是解决一些已知的问题，并确保海事仲裁以有序和有效的方式进行。建议使用的两种仲裁条款，一种是临时仲裁条款，具有长短格式；另一种是机构仲裁条款，建议希望获得在内地申请临时措施的途径以协助在香港特区进行仲裁的当事方使用。

在2020年，波罗的海国际航运公会（Baltic and International Maritime Council, BIMCO）在《BIMCO法律和仲裁条款2020》中将中国香港特区指定为四个仲裁地之一。该条款的统一措辞经四个仲裁地的同意后颁布。BIMCO的指定反映了香港特区长期以来被市场认可为享有盛誉的海事争议解决中心。

上述推荐使用的HKMAG仲裁条款和《BIMCO法律和仲裁条款2020》可在HKMAG网站（www.hkmag.org.hk）上找到。所有条款都适用HKMAG仲裁规则。

[①] 详见Shagang South Asia (Hong Kong) Trading Co. Ltd. v. Daewoo Logistics (The Nikolaos A) [2015] EWHC 194 (Comm)，载http://www.bailii.org/cgi-bin/format.cgi?doc=/ew/cases/EWHC/Comm/2015/194.html，访问日期：2022年1月5日。

新加坡篇[*]

自1819年新加坡成立以来,海上贸易一直是新加坡经济的命脉。现如今,新加坡已发展成为一个全球性港口,连接着120多个国家和地区的600个港口,被普遍认为是世界上最繁忙和最重要的港口之一。下述统计数字也能够印证这一点:

(1) 2020年新加坡港口的货物吞吐量高达5.903亿吨;

(2) 2020年新加坡港口的船舶到达总吨位为29亿总吨(GT);

(3) 2020年新加坡是世界上最大的加油港,销售量达4980万吨;

(4) 新加坡船舶登记处是世界上十大船舶登记处之一,反映了新加坡作为国际船东首选的优质船旗国的优良声誉。[①]

新加坡作为世界上最大的贸易中心之一,与海运贸易密切相关。它是从金属到石油贸易等所有主要大宗商品贸易的领导者,也是许多重要国际贸易商建立基地的首选区域。

考虑到海事和贸易领域对新加坡的重要性,建立一个能够确保争议得到有效和及时解决的框架是十分重要的。

新加坡海事仲裁院(Singapore Chamber of Maritime Arbitration, SCMA)最初成立于2004年,并于2009年重组。其旨在根据行业反馈采取相应措施,以满足该地区海事和贸易相关纠纷解决的需求。

尽管面临新冠病毒的挑战,但SCMA在2020年处理的案件数量仍然有所增加,其中有43起案件涉及的索赔总额超过4900万美元,其中一半以上的争议来自亚洲。

SCMA专注于商业且具有成本效益的临时仲裁框架,无疑为各方提供了灵活的仲裁方式。同时,当事人可以接触来自普通法和大陆法司法

---

[*] 本篇作者为林健良,其礼律师事务所驻上海代表处(Clyde & Co)合伙人及其礼律师事务所的关联新加坡律所(Clasis LLC)总监,同时作为SCMA程序委员会和促进委员会的成员,积极参与了《SCMA仲裁规则2022》的起草和制定。其礼律师事务所新加坡办公室李子璇对本篇亦有贡献。

[①] 参见2021年1月13日新加坡海事港务局新闻稿,载新加坡政府官网(https://www.sgpc.gov.sg/media_releases/mpa/press_release/P-20210113-1),访问日期:2022年1月5日。

管辖区的多样化仲裁员。SCMA还设有一个专门的秘书处,必要时向当事人提供协助。

尽管如此,海事仲裁领域仍在不断发展。为了与实践保持紧密的契合度,SCMA于2020年中期开始修订其第三版规则中的部分事项,例如仲裁庭组成人员的任命程序、拟任命仲裁员的默认人数、提交案件陈述书的时间以及开庭的必要性等,并向公众征求意见。经过一年多的磋商和审议,SCMA现已发布《新加坡海事仲裁院仲裁规则(第四版)》(以下简称《SCMA规则2022》),该规则于2022年1月1日生效,并将适用于此后提交的所有SCMA仲裁。至此,SCMA规则得到了进一步简化,以反映现代仲裁实践,并旨在促进以用户友好、高成本效益和高效率的方式解决亚洲海事和贸易纠纷。

笔者旨在介绍《SCMA规则2022》中较为重要的修订。正如前文所述,本次修订主要集中在三个关键领域:

(1)成本效益;

(2)促进技术的使用,特别是在新冠肺炎后疫情时代;

(3)加强信息共享。

众所周知,在新冠肺炎疫情期间,仲裁程序和开庭是以线上或者混合(部分线上部分现场)的方式进行的。《SCMA规则2022》对仲裁程序中技术的使用提供了更清晰的说明,从而显著地节约了成本,并整体提高了仲裁程序的效率。

一、技术的使用

(一)电子送达

根据《SCMA规则2015》,虽然书面通信可以通过电子邮件进行,但任何实质性通知的送达仅在纸质送达[1]后才会被视为已收到。《SCMA规则2022》第3.1条规定,除纸质送达外,任何通知和/或通信均可通过电子邮件以电子方式送达。《SCMA规则2022》第3.2条规定,通过电子邮件发

---

[1] 参见《SCMA规则2015》第3条。

送收据将构成有效送达的证明。有鉴于此,笔者建议各方在仲裁程序中送达电子通知和/或发送电子通信时利用"送达收据"功能。

(二)通过电子手段实现仲裁现代化

《SCMA 规则 2022》在第 34.4 条规定允许以电子方式签署仲裁裁决。

此外,《SCMA 规则 2022》在第 17.3 条和第 25.3 条明确规定,庭审和案件管理会议可以线上方式进行。

(三)加强信息共享

《SCMA 规则 2022》第 6 条(之前的《SCMA 规则 2015》第 4 条)涉及启动仲裁程序的问题。新增加的第 6.1 条对仲裁通知的内容提出了更多要求。其要求申请人对索赔性质进行说明,而这一点在 2015 年版规则中并无强制性要求。它还要求申请人尽可能明确相关的适用法条款和索赔金额。

《SCMA 规则 2022》第 6 条的目的是促进双方和仲裁庭之间事先分享信息。这意味着双方将从一开始就更加清楚申请人的索赔请求是什么,而被申请人将反过来详细了解需要面对的案件和需要准备的答复。从案件管理的角度来看,仲裁庭也会受益,因为它现在已经在早期阶段就知道了问题的确切内容。

在这方面,笔者必须提醒申请人,应严格遵守这些关于仲裁通知内容的要求,因为不遵守这些要求可能会使被申请人就仲裁通知的有效性提出异议,从而导致仲裁是否正式启动的争议。

笔者认为增加对仲裁通知的要求会得到使用者的认可,因为这将使各方变得更有效率,能够减少消极被申请人的持续延迟,从而更有利于节约成本。

值得一提的是,《SCMA 规则 2022》第 6.2 条要求申请人在向被申请人提交仲裁通知的同时向 SCMA 秘书处发送仲裁通知副本,这无疑有利于 SCMA 充分了解在其规则下进行的所有仲裁程序。鉴于 SCMA 仲裁的特殊性(临时仲裁),可能有许多仲裁根据 SCMA 规则进行,但从未通知 SCMA。这项修正将使 SCMA 更好地注意到正在进行的仲裁的实际数量,并在适当时候提供更准确的统计数据。然而,需要注意的是,仲裁通知不会因申请人不遵守这一规定而失效。

二、仲裁庭组成

《SCMA 规则 2022》中组成仲裁庭的仲裁员人数的默认情况与 2015 年版规则保持一致,即三名仲裁员。

然而,相比《SCMA 规则 2015》中"如果任命三名仲裁员,则两名任命的仲裁员将任命第三名仲裁员"而言,《SCMA 规则 2022》第 8.4 条有了一个重要的改变,即仲裁可以仅由两名仲裁员进行,不需要指定第三名仲裁员,除非需要进行实质性审理或两名仲裁员无法达成一致意见。虽然《SCMA 规则 2022》第 8.4(c)条确实要求在任何实质性审理之前指定第三名仲裁员,但如果仲裁程序没有导致实质性审理,两名仲裁员即有权作出裁定、命令和裁决。这是简化程序的结果,反映了海事仲裁领域的变化。

三、开庭审理

根据《SCMA 规则 2015》,除非双方另有约定,否则必须开庭审理。《SCMA 规则 2022》第 25.1 条不再强制要求仲裁庭开庭审理,仲裁庭有权决定是否开庭,或只进行书面审理。但是,如果任何一方当事人要求开庭,则仲裁庭必须开庭。

四、裁决作出的期限

《SCMA 规则 2022》第 27.1 条规定,除非双方同意或仲裁庭另有指示,否则仲裁程序应在任何最终书面陈述或庭审之日起 3 个月后作出裁决。第 34.1 条规定,仲裁庭必须在审理终结的 3 个月内作出最终裁决。

当然,双方当事人可以同意延长仲裁庭作出最终裁决的期限。但是,需要注意的是,如果仲裁庭的费用仍未支付,仲裁庭将有权拒绝交付最终的裁决书(《SCMA 规则 2022》第 34.5 条)。

五、提高适用简易程序的限额

根据《SCMA 规则 2015》,小额索赔程序将适用于索赔和/或反索赔总额低于 150000 美元的索赔。小额索赔程序规定由一名独任仲裁员担任,缩短了送达案件陈述书的时限①,且除非仲裁庭要求,否则不会进行开庭审理②。

《SCMA 规则 2022》现在将适用简易程序的限额提高为 300000 美元。这一规定取代了原先的限额 150000 美元。如果仅进行书面审理,仲裁庭必须在收到各方陈述后的 21 天内作出裁决。

六、任命仲裁员的标准条款

《SCMA 规则 2022》第 40.2 条规定,如果双方及其各自的仲裁员尚未就仲裁员的任命条款达成一致,则适用一套标准的任命条款。这些标准条款的目的是确保仲裁员任命的更大确定性和透明度,除非另有约定,这一标准将默认适用于所有 SCMA 的仲裁。

七、变更代理人须经仲裁庭批准

实务中,不愿参与仲裁程序的一方经常采取拖延战术,如变更代理人。《SCMA 规则 2022》第 4.4 条规定,如果仲裁庭确信变更代理人存在妨碍仲裁的正常进行或损害裁决的可执行性的重大风险,则仲裁庭有权拒绝批准变更代理人。

结 论

新制定的《SCMA 规则 2022》将受到不断发展的、快节奏的海运业的

---

① 参见《SCMA 规则 2015》第 46.4 条。
② 参见《SCMA 规则 2015》第 46.6 条。

欢迎。SCMA已经听取了业界要求更好、更完善的规则版本的呼声,并作出了回应。对《SCMA规则2015》的修订反映了SCMA有意识、谨慎地努力实现其规则的现代化,其最终目标是通过提高效率和降低成本来造福各方当事人。预计更新后的SCMA规则将大大有助于SCMA成为当事人解决海事和贸易纠纷的一个更有吸引力的选择。

英国篇[*]

引　言

英国,特别是伦敦,曾经被誉为航运业的中心,但全球货运趋势和中国在世界贸易中的主导地位日益增强,使得该行业向东转移——按集装箱吞吐量计算,世界上最繁忙的10个港口中有7个在中国。然而,时至今日,伦敦仍然是世界海事仲裁的中心。在伦敦、中国香港特区或新加坡举行的国际航运仲裁,伦敦占比约90%。

伦敦海事仲裁通常被理解为有别于在伦敦进行的"国际商事仲裁"。然而,两者虽然有一些区别,但是在一些机构与伦敦作为仲裁地之间的高度联系下,这些区别不应被过分夸大。这两种类型的仲裁都有共同的特点:它们都与国际商业纠纷有关,都受1996年《英国仲裁法》的约束。参与这两种仲裁的人员,包括仲裁员和从业人员本身,到作为仲裁使用者的当事人,也有很大的重叠。在伦敦,绝大多数的仲裁是根据伦敦海事仲裁员协会(London Maritime Arbitrators Association, LMAA)的规则开展的,案件数量多于机构仲裁,许多就法律问题向商事法院提出的上诉都来自航运案件。

本篇将探讨1996年《英国仲裁法》的最新更新,《伦敦海事仲裁员协会仲裁规则》(以下简称《LMAA规则》)、《劳合社打捞仲裁处规则》和《伦敦国际仲裁院仲裁规则》的一些主要发展。最后将简要介绍英国最近的两项判决,这两项判决反映了一些有趣的仲裁发展。

---

[*] 本篇作者为尼古拉斯·彭德(Nicholas Poynder),夏礼文律师事务所上海代表处合伙人。

一、英国法律下的仲裁程序

任何在伦敦进行的仲裁,无论是海事仲裁还是其他仲裁,都要遵守1996年《英国仲裁法》的规定。一般来说,根据1996年《英国仲裁法》第1条的原则,伦敦仲裁的上诉程序或挑战伦敦仲裁裁决都受到第67—69条的约束。

1. 一般原则

本编之规定基于下述原则,并以其作为解释依据:

(a)仲裁之目的在于由公平的仲裁庭,在没有不必要的拖延和开支的情况下,使争议得以公正解决;

(b)当事人应当自由约定争议解决方式,仅受制于充分保障公共利益之必须;

(c)除本编另有规定外,法院不得干预本编规定之事项。

1996年《英国仲裁法》权衡了两个方面的考虑:第一是终局性。许多法院系统面临着无休止的上诉。第二是需要有司法审查的权利,以接受法律不是一成不变的,而是持续发展的。航运仲裁案件的上诉为英国普通法提供了许多重要案例。

在1996年《英国仲裁法》中,上诉/挑战的理由只有3个:(1)第67条,仲裁庭没有实质性的管辖权;(2)第68条,存在影响仲裁庭、程序或裁决的严重违规行为;(3)第69条,关于法律问题的上诉。第67条和第68条是强制性条款,与第69条不同,其不能被排除。

另一个重要的区别是,根据第69条提出的上诉需要得到法院的许可,而根据第67条或第68条提出的挑战则不需要。根据第67条提出的管辖权异议甚至会导致在法院进行强制性的全面重新听证,并向法院提供证据。

2021年,尽管COVID-19大流行造成了业务中断,但公布的仲裁统计数据表明,挑战的成功率与往年类似,依旧很低。英国商业法院公布,在2020—2021年,有25个在第68条下提出的挑战仲裁裁决的申请,尽管在撰写报告时,由于一些等待听证的案件需要送达,导致需要更长的听证时间①,所以这一数字尚未最终确定,但这只比2019—2020年的28个略有减少。

法院的统计数据显示,平均每年只有大约30%的申请根据第69条的要求获得了上诉许可。② 此外,在实质性听证会上,申请人必须克服更具挑战性的障碍,即证明仲裁庭在法律问题上有错误。在2019—2020法律年度的最新统计中,37次挑战中只有4次成功,其比例约为11%。③

尽管最近出现了一系列对仲裁裁决的成功挑战,但英国法院一般不采取干预措施,最终成功挑战仲裁裁决的概率很低。

第67条的挑战通常被视为最后的手段,只有在关于管辖权的最终裁决下达后才能提出挑战,因为仲裁员有权对其管辖权作出第一裁决。最近的案件进一步澄清了第67条的适用④,例如,确认不遵守先决条件(通过所谓的waterfall条款在仲裁开始前进行谈判的要求)属于仲裁的可受理性,而不是实体管辖权问题。

关于第68条,英国上议院认为第68条"实际上是最后的办法,只有在极端的情况下才能使用,即仲裁庭在其行为中出错……而正义要求纠正仲裁庭的行为"⑤。

一方若想根据第69条规定获得许可,除其他因素外,仲裁庭的决定需是"明显错误的",或者是"具有公共重要性的",并且"至少可以引起严重怀疑"。关于第69条挑战成功的例子,请参见下文近期的案例法部分。

---

① 参见伦敦国际仲裁院官网(https://lcia.org/lcia-rules-update-2020.aspx),访问日期:2022年1月12日。
② 参见英格兰和威尔士法院官网(https://www.judiciary.uk/wp-content/uploads/2020/12/CCUG-Minutes-November-2020-0112.pdf),访问日期:2022年1月12日。
③ 参见英格兰和威尔士法院官网(https://www.judiciary.uk/wp-content/uploads/2021/12/Commercial-Court-User-Committee-Meeting-Minutes-24Nov21.pdf),访问日期:2022年1月12日。
④ 参见英格兰和威尔士法院官网(https://www.judiciary.uk/wp-content/uploads/2021/12/Commercial-Court-User-Committee-Meeting-Minutes-24Nov21.pdf),访问日期:2022年1月11日。
⑤ 参见英国议会官网(https://publications.parliament.uk/pa/ld200506/ldjudgmt/jd050630/leso-1.htm,访问日期:2022年1月12日。

二、重要更新①

2021年11月30日,英格兰和威尔士法律委员会宣布将对1996年《英国仲裁法》的审查纳入其第14个法律改革计划。法律委员会认为该法案成立25周年是确保其继续有效的好契机,尤其是在许多其他司法管辖区最近进行改革的情况下。

据悉,该审查的总体目标是"保持英格兰和威尔士作为争端解决的"目的地"的吸引力,以及英国法律作为适用法的卓越地位"。该审查于2022年第一季度启动,目标是在2022年年底发布一份咨询文件。审查的范围将在未来几个月内确定,可能要考虑的问题包括:

(1)在仲裁程序中概略地驳回无理的索赔或抗辩的权力;
(2)法院为支持仲裁程序可行使的权力;
(3)挑战管辖权裁决的程序;
(4)就法律问题提出上诉的可能性;
(5)关于仲裁程序中的保密性和隐私的法律;
(6)文件的电子送达、电子仲裁裁决和虚拟听证。

该审查还将研究引入信托法仲裁,以及更广泛的信托法现代化工作。

三、伦敦海事仲裁规则和发展情况

在英国,有许多不同的仲裁规则可供当事人选择。大部分的伦敦海事仲裁都受LMAA规定的条款和程序管辖。LMAA仲裁往往用于处理商业纠纷,如根据提单和租船合同提出的索赔、租船合同纠纷、船舶销售和造船案件、海事保险纠纷以及近海、石油和天然气行业的其他商业纠纷。救助事宜和碰撞事故则由专业规则处理。例如,劳合社理事会的救助仲裁分会建立了一个两级的仲裁程序,称为伦敦救助仲裁。一些海事纠纷也会根据伦敦国际仲裁院(London Court of International Arbitration,

---

① 参见英国法律委员会官网(https://www.lawcom.gov.uk/law-commission-to-review-the-arbitration-act-1996/),访问日期:2022年1月12日。

LCIA)的规则提交仲裁。这些纠纷往往是与造船、船舶融资和能源相关的合同纠纷。

以下内容强调了2021年引入的常用仲裁规则的主要更新。

1.《LMAA规则(2021)》

在诸多可供选择且适用于英国的海事仲裁规则中,最受欢迎的是《LMAA规则》。这一规则最初是在1997年起草的,此后经过多次的修订,最近又进行了更新。目前的《LMAA规则(2021)》适用于2021年5月1日或之后发生的所有任命。2020年,LMAA收到约1775起案件,其成员收到3010份新的仲裁任命,并下达523项裁决。

负责修订《LMAA规则》的委员会表示,他们在更新规则时采取了"轻触"的方式,并牢记不断提高时间和成本效率的需要。该委员会将他们对《LMAA规则(2021)》的处理方式描述为"务实和实用"。从新版规则中可以看出,更新是为了反映时代的变化和应对2017年以来出现的具体问题。例如,由于虚拟听证的使用越来越多,LMAA的虚拟和半虚拟听证指南作为新的第六个附表,被纳入修订后的规则中。关于新规则的更详细评论可在LMAA网站上找到,笔者将在下文中概述。

《LMAA规则(2021)》条款的关键更新:

第10段:独任仲裁员的指定程序现在采用了《LMAA标准仲裁条款》中的程序,该程序比1996年《英国仲裁法》中规定的程序更简单、更快捷。

第12段:如果原仲裁员显然无法主持程序或出席庭审,主席现在有权指定一名替代仲裁员。这是为了解决用户对仲裁员和指定替代仲裁员的疑虑。

第15段第(c)(d)款:本规则现在明确承认,听证会可以以虚拟方式进行。

第24段:规则现在明确规定,裁决书可以用电子方式签署,也可以在对应本上签署,还可以用电子方式通知各方当事人。这为裁决书的编制和公布提供了更大的灵活性,特别是在可能难以获得仲裁员手写签名的情况下。[①]

---

① 参见伦敦海事仲裁员协会官网(https://lmaa.london/wp-content/uploads/2021/05/COMMENTARY-ON-THE-LMAA-TERMS-2021.pdf),访问日期:2022年1月12日。

2. LMAA 小额索赔程序

LMAA 小额索赔程序适用于简单的索赔,并有一个固定的费用。2012 年版规则建议,如果任何索赔或任何反诉的总金额不超过 50000 美元,应使用小额索赔程序。在 2017 年和 2021 年版的规则中,这一数额被提高到 100000 美元。

LMAA 小额索赔程序的关键更新:

第 7 段:引入了一项明确的要求,即除非各方当事人另有约定,否则仲裁员应作出理由充分的裁决,这与 1996 年《英国仲裁法》的立场相同。

第 8 段:只要有可能,就应该根据小额索赔程序作出单份裁决,其中包含涉及任何有关费用的裁决,而不是另作一份单独的费用裁决。①

3. LMAA 中等金额索赔程序

LMAA 中等金额索赔程序于 2009 年引入,并在 2021 年更新。中等金额索赔程序适用于 100000 至 400000 美元的索赔,并将限制仲裁费用作为其目的之一。因此,中等金额索赔程序的一个主要特点是对当事人和仲裁庭的费用引入了费用上限。

中等金额索赔程序的关键更新:

第 5 段:与《LMAA 规则(2021)》第 10 段类似,指定独任仲裁员的程序采用了《LMAA 标准仲裁条款》中的程序,因为它比 1996 年《英国仲裁法》规定的程序更简单、更快捷。

第 13 段:对措辞进行了澄清,以表明在一方迟延的情况下,仲裁庭可酌情允许或要求非迟延方向仲裁庭出示进一步的材料。

第 16 段:现在的措辞明确了适用于当事人可获得费用的数额上限(通常为索赔人货币索赔金额的 30%)应不包括利息和费用。②

4. 劳合社打捞仲裁处

2021 年年中,劳合社宣布其正在考虑是否关闭救助仲裁处。这将对劳合社标准格式救助协议的未来管理和继续使用劳氏保单(Lloyd's Open

---

① 参见伦敦海事仲裁员协会官网(https://lmaa.london/wp-content/uploads/2021/05/COMMENTARY-ON-THE-LMAA-TERMS-2021.pdf),访问日期:2022 年 1 月 12 日。

② 参见 https://www.bailii.org/cgi-bin/format.cgi?doc=/ew/cases/EWCA/Civ/2021/1712.html&query=(K)+AND+(Line)+AND+(Pte)+AND+(Ltd),访问日期:2022 年 1 月 12 日。

Form)产生深远的影响。然而,在2021年7月,劳合社宣布,在国际海事界的强烈要求下,经过对其代理服务的审查,劳合社将继续运营救助仲裁处和劳氏保单。一个关键的更新是修订后的使用劳氏保单的收费结构,于2021年10月1日生效,并正在考虑进一步发展。

5. 伦敦国际仲裁院仲裁规则

如前所述,《伦敦国际仲裁院仲裁规则》有时被用来管辖伦敦的海事仲裁。这些规则由前任主席朱迪斯·吉尔(Judith Gill QC)更新,并从2020年10月1日起生效。此次更新旨在使仲裁和调解程序对仲裁员、调解员和当事人来说更加简化和清晰。由于COVID-19,更新考虑到开展业务的新方式,包括使用虚拟听证和使用电子通信。

《LCIA评注》对《伦敦国际仲裁院仲裁规则》所强调的重大修正如下:

(1)允许仲裁员加快程序的额外工具,并明确提到了早期驳回裁决的可能性;

(2)完善和扩大适应使用虚拟听证的规定,也支持在新常态下进行的仲裁;

(3)确认与伦敦国际仲裁院和仲裁中的电子通信的首要地位,以及确认为电子签名的裁决提供便利;

(4)纳入涉及法庭秘书作用的明确规定;

(5)扩大LCIA法院和仲裁庭的权力,以命令合并和仲裁的同时进行;

(6)明确考虑数据保护和监管问题。

仲裁员和调解员的最高小时费率,由450英镑提高到500英镑,以反映复杂纠纷的要求。①

四、近期的案例法

2021年,伦敦发生了多起重要的海事仲裁案件。本节探讨了2021年度最重要的两项判决。

---

① 更新后的规则请参见伦敦国际仲裁院官网(https://www.lcia.org/Dispute_Resolution_Services/lcia-arbitration-rules-2020.aspx),访问日期:2022年1月12日。

1. K Line PTE Ltd. v. Priminds Shipping (HK) Co. Ltd. [2021] EWCA Civ 1712

本案澄清了正在进行的仲裁中的一方也可以根据1996年《英国仲裁法》第45条向法院提出申请,确定一个初步的法律问题。应该指出的是,这一程序在实践中很少使用。法院必须确定一个初步的法律观点,关于当承租人未能在约定的装卸时间内装船或卸船时,根据航次租约应支付的滞期费的性质。法院赞扬了双方根据1996年《英国仲裁法》第45条将此案提交给法院的决定和共同协议,以便为后续事项提供法律澄清。本案的法律问题涉及滞期费是承租人未能在指定的装卸时间内装货或卸货的所有后果的违约赔偿金,还是只是关于其中的一些后果的违约赔偿金。法院接受了这一法律问题对双方的权利产生了实质性的影响,从而将其纳入第45条的范围。上诉法院推翻了关于这个问题的一审判决。① 马莱斯·L. J. (Males L. J.)在作出上诉法院判决时,确定滞期费(在双方没有相反协议的情况下)清偿船东因承租人未能在装卸时间内完成货物操作而造成的所有损失,而不是像一审时认为的那样,仅仅是延误造成的收入损失。船东需要证明有单独的违约行为,才能在延误造成的滞期费之外获得赔偿。②

2. CVLC Three Carrier Corp v. Arab Maritime Petroleum Transport Company [2021] EWHC 551 (Comm)

如上所述,挑战1996年《英国仲裁法》第69条的成功案例非常罕见。第69条允许就仲裁裁决中产生的法律问题向英国法院提出挑战。这种挑战的权利不是强制性的,因此可以排除。诸如LCIA和国际商会(International Chamber of Commerce, ICC)等仲裁机构在其规则中排除了1996年《英国仲裁法》第69条。本案详细讨论了怎样才能成功申请第69条下的挑战,并强调了法院审查申请的高标准。

简要介绍一下背景,本案源于CVLC Three Carrier Corp和CVLC Four

---

① 参见 https://www.bailii.org/cgi-bin/format.cgi?doc=/ew/cases/EWCA/Civ/2021/1712.html&query=(K)+AND+(Line)+AND+(Pte)+AND+(Ltd),访问日期:2022年1月12日。
② 参见英国夏礼文律师事务所官网(https://www.hfw.com/Bliss-for-charterers-Court-of-Appeal-rules-in-next-round-of-The-Eternal-Bliss-Nov-2021),访问日期:2022年1月12日。

Carrier Corp(船东)与 Al-Iraqia Shipping Services and Oil Trading(租家)之间的两份几乎相同的租约所引起的仲裁。船东们得到了阿拉伯海上石油运输公司(Arab Maritime Petroleum Transport Company,AMPTC)的担保函,作为该担保函的第一债务人保证了租船人准时履行付款义务。船东们声称,租船人违反了租船合同,因此,他们对 AMPTC 提起了仲裁程序。船东们还试图扣押 AMPTC 拥有的一艘船,以便为他们在租约下的索赔提供担保。AMPTC 接着向独任仲裁员提出了紧急申请。AMPTC 要求声明,该协议包括一个默示条款,即当涉及该协议所涵盖的事项时,船东不会寻求"额外的担保"。AMPTC 辩称,该默示条款因此阻止了船东根据协议扣押 AMPTC 的船只。仲裁员作出了有利于租船人的裁决。船东向英国商业法院申请允许根据 1996 年《英国仲裁法》第 69 条对裁决提出上诉。[1]

该判决的一个有趣的结果是,科克里尔(Cockerill)法官澄清说,根据 1996 年《英国仲裁法》第 69 条提出的申请不必限于纯法律问题。合同解释的问题也有可以挑战的可能,尽管它与事实紧密相连。科克里尔法官继续补充说,"法官在考虑许可申请时,对法律问题的重塑绝非前所未闻"。这突出了法院在许可阶段重新表述问题的权力,将问题缩减到需仲裁庭决定的真正的法律问题。科克里尔法官讨论了 1996 年《英国仲裁法》第 69 条申请成功的后果,表明在某些情况下,如果情况允许,法院有可能不把问题发回给仲裁员,法院有可能完全推翻仲裁裁决,而不需要仲裁庭进一步审议。

结　　语

展望未来,伦敦海事仲裁将积极应对仲裁实践中的挑战和全球发展。从目前的情况来看,伦敦显然仍是海事仲裁的首选目的地。英国法院会一如既往地支持仲裁程序,并对成功率不高的对仲裁裁决的挑战采取谨慎的态度。伦敦也有可能进一步利用其作为海事仲裁领先中心的地位,长期向虚拟听证和混合听证转变,使仲裁从业人员、律师和客户不再需要为参与伦敦海事仲裁而长途旅行。

---

[1] 参见 https://www.bailii.org/cgi-bin/format.cgi?doc=/ew/cases/EWCA/Civ/2021/1712.html&query=(K)+AND+(Line)+AND+(Pte)+AND+(Ltd),访问日期:2022 年 1 月 12 日。

国际海洋法法庭迅速释放案件中主体特点及对中国的启示*

陈 恒** 白 艳***

摘要:近年来,国际海洋法法庭处理了多起沿海国家或地区之间的迅速释放争议案件,在这类案件中,法庭对于船旗国身份的审查和认定、专属经济区所属国权利的确认等是影响案件走向的关键。我国是海洋大国,在远洋捕捞业中,作为船旗国会面临需要迅速释放船只和船员的情形,作为专属经济区所属国也会遇到扣留外国违法船舶和船员的问题。国际海洋法法庭迅速释放船舶和船员的实践值得我们研究,以便从其审判实践中得到启发,探寻中国在船旗国、方便旗国或是专属经济区所属国等不同身份下,面对涉及海洋的争议的处理方案,更好地维护我国海洋权益。

关键词:迅速释放;船旗国;管辖权

引 言

自1996年成立以来,国际海洋法法庭一共审理了29起案件,其中10起属于迅速释放案件,分别是1997年"塞加号"案(The M/V SAIGA Case)、1999年"塞加号"案[The M/V SAIGA (No.2) Case]、2000年"卡莫

---

* 本文完成于2021年11月。
** 西北政法大学法律硕士研究生。
*** 西北政法大学副教授。

科号"案(The Camouco Case)和"蒙特·卡夫卡号"案(The Monte Confurco Case)、2001年"大王子号"案(The Grand Prince Case)和"柴斯利礁号"案(The Chaisiri Reefer 2 Case)、2002年"伏尔加河号"案(The Volga Case)、2004年"朱诺商人号"案(The Juno Trader Case)、2007年"丰进丸号"案(The Hoshinmaru Case)和"富丸号"案(The Tomimaru Case)。

除国际海洋法法庭第9号案——"柴斯利礁号"案撤诉外,"塞加号"案、"卡莫科号"案、"蒙特·卡夫卡号"案、"伏尔加河号"案、"朱诺商人号"案以及"丰进丸号"案这6起案件已被国际海洋法法庭判决扣押国迅速释放被扣押船只和船员。①

依据《联合国海洋法公约》(以下简称《海洋法公约》)、《国际海洋法法庭规约》(以下简称《法庭规约》)和《国际海洋法法庭规则》(以下简称《法庭规则》),国际海洋法法庭有效地解决了海洋争端中的船只和船员释放问题,体现出其在处理此类案件中的重要国际地位,充分发挥了和平解决国际海洋权益争端的作用。迅速释放案件中涉及的争端当事国分别是船旗国与专属经济区所属国,一般由船旗国作为申请方向法庭提出迅速释放的申请,专属经济区所属国作为被申请方为维护自身的海洋权益作出相应的举措。

一、迅速释放程序中的船旗国

《海洋法公约》赋予国际海洋法法庭在迅速释放案件中的强制管辖权,但是能够向法庭申请迅速释放的主体只能是船旗国或者是经授权以船旗国名义提出申请的代理人。因此,当争端当事国对国际海洋法法庭能否管辖迅速释放案件存在异议时,法庭应当首先审查和认定船旗国的身份。

---

① 另外3起案件:
1999年"塞加号"案[The M/V SAIGA (No. 2) Case]:扣留国几内亚并非未立即释放船只和船员,但违反了《海洋法公约》关于行使紧追权的规定;
2001年"大王子号"案(The Grand Prince Case):伯利兹无证据证明其为船旗国,法庭对该案无管辖权;
2007年"富丸号"案(The Tomimaru Case):扣留国俄罗斯先行提起国内诉讼并已没收船只。

根据《海洋法公约》第 287 条和第 292 条的规定,有权管辖迅速释放案件的法律机构有国际法院、国际仲裁法庭、国际特别仲裁法庭,以及国际海洋法法庭。① 若当事国双方(即船旗国与沿海国)均为《海洋法公约》的缔约国,则任一方可以自主选择前三个机构处理迅速释放案件。如果缔约国双方自扣留发生之日起 10 日内未能达成将迅速释放申请提交其他法院或法庭的协议,则争端双方协商一致可将申请交由国际海洋法法庭处理,这时法庭拥有对迅速释放案件的管辖权。具体而言,当争端当事国根据《海洋法公约》第 287 条的规定以声明方式都接受国际海洋法法庭作为解决争端的程序时,法庭对所有关于《海洋法公约》解释与适用的争端拥有强制管辖权。即使没有根据《海洋法公约》第 287 条作出声明,但如果争端当事国未能在一定时间内就将争端提交其他法院或法庭达成协议,国际海洋法法庭对于《海洋法公约》第 292 条规定的迅速释放船只和船员的申请仍拥有强制管辖权。② 自国际海洋法法庭于 1996 年开始运作以来,向其提交的大部分案件都是依据《海洋法公约》的这两条规定启动迅速释放程序。《海洋法公约》任一缔约国可以单方申请立案。

就目前已发生的迅速释放案件来看,有关争端当事国选择向国际海洋法法庭提出申请,请求其作出迅速释放船只和船员的裁判,法庭在受理案件之后都会首先审查和认定申请主体资格。

(一)申请主体

沿海国扣留船只的行为不仅会影响船主的财产利益,也会危及船长、船员的人身权益。在多数情况下,被扣留船只的国籍与船员的国籍并不相同,这就导致迅速释放的申请主体可能多方并存。《海洋法公约》第 292 条第 2 款规定,有关船只和船员迅速释放的申请,仅可由船旗国或以

---

① 1982 年《联合国海洋法公约》第 287 条第 1 款规定:"一国在签署、批准或加入本公约时,或在其后任何时间,应有自由用书面声明的方式选择下列一个或一个以上方法,以解决有关本公约的解释或适用的争端;(a)按照附件六设立的国际海洋法法庭;(b)国际法院;(c)按照附件七组成的仲裁法庭;(d)按照附件八组成的处理其中所列的一类或一类以上争端的特别仲裁法庭。"

1982 年《联合国海洋法公约》第 292 条第 1 款规定:"……释放问题可向争端各方协议的任何法院或法庭提出,如从扣留时起 10 日内不能达成这种协议,则除争端各方另有协议外,可向扣留国根据第二百八十七条接受的法院或法庭,或向国际海洋法法庭提出。"

② 参见《国际海洋法法庭审判程序指南》第 6 页"强制管辖权"部分。

该国的名义提出。这表明有权向国际海洋法法庭提起迅速释放案件的申请主体有且只有两个:一是船旗国,即只有船只的国籍国享有迅速释放请求权,而船员的国籍国无权申请迅速释放程序;二是经授权以船旗国名义提出申请的代理人,即代理人以船旗国名义提出申请之前必须经过船旗国主管机关的授权,并且该授权书应由主管的国家机关工作人员出具,比如一国的外交部部长、司法部部长或总检察长。①

1. 船旗国申请

如上所述,被扣留船只的船旗国是《海洋法公约》第 292 条明确规定的迅速释放案件的申请主体,因此船只的国籍是法庭审查提出迅速释放程序申请主体的唯一考虑因素。1982 年《海洋法公约》第 91 条制定了有关船只国籍的规定,其中对于船只与船旗国之间的关系问题,要求船只必须在一国领土内登记并且登记国与船只之间有真正的联系,否则船旗国无权申请迅速释放。② 1986 年《联合国船舶登记条件公约》第 1 条就明确了该公约的宗旨,即"确保或加强一国与悬挂其国旗的船舶之间的真正联系"③。这表明只要船只具有一国国籍,即使船主或船员不具有船旗国国籍,也不会影响船旗国作为申请主体向法庭提起迅速释放程序。船旗国主管机关在向符合船舶登记条件的船舶依法予以登记并发放船舶法定证书后,船旗国有义务对悬挂其旗帜的船只实行有效的各项管理和控制。因此,在船只和其船员被扣留后,船旗国是最能代表利益受损者提出迅速释放程序的适格申请方。

迄今为止,国际海洋法法庭一共审理了 10 起迅速释放案件,其中有 3 起案件是直接由船旗国政府提起的。例如,2002 年"伏尔加河号"案是俄罗斯作为船旗国根据《海洋法公约》第 292 条规定向法庭提起了迅速释放

---

① 参见《国际海洋法法庭审判程序指南》第 23 页"诉讼程序"部分。
② 1982 年《联合国海洋法公约》第 91 条规定:"1. 每个国家应确定对船舶给予国籍、船舶在其领土内登记及船舶悬挂该国旗帜的权利的条件。船舶具有其有权悬挂的旗帜所属国家的国籍。国家和船舶之间必须有真正联系。2. 每个国家应向其给予悬挂该国旗帜权利的船舶颁发给予该权利的文件。"
③ 1986 年《联合国船舶登记条件公约》第 1 条规定:"为了确保或加强一国与悬挂其国旗的船舶之间的真正联系,并为了在船舶所有人和经营人身份的查明和承担责任方面以及在行政、技术、经济和社会事务方面对这些船舶切实施行管辖和监督,船旗国须适用本公约所载的条款。"

申请。在该案中,由于俄罗斯籍长线渔船"伏尔加河号"在澳大利亚南部海域内非法捕鱼被澳方扣押,俄方和澳方自渔船和船员被扣留发生时起10日内未能达成将迅速释放申请提交其他法院或法庭的协议,因此船旗国俄罗斯直接向法庭提请迅速释放本国渔船和船员。再如,2007年"丰进丸号"案和"富丸号"案是由于两艘日本籍渔船"丰进丸号"和"富丸号"在俄罗斯专属经济区内违法捕鱼,被俄罗斯海岸防卫队逮捕扣押,日本政府根据《海洋法公约》第292条规定向法庭提起申请,要求俄罗斯分别释放被其扣押的两艘船只及其船员。这些案件由船旗国政府直接提出申请,由该国政府官员作为案件代理人参与其中。这类直接由船旗国作为申请主体提起的迅速释放案件相对较少。

2. 以船旗国名义申请

迅速释放案件中的涉案船只大部分悬挂的是方便旗国旗帜①,与船旗国之间没有真正联系,即船只的实际控制人大部分并非船旗国国民,且目前大多数船员是劳务输出的非船旗国国民,在此情况下,非国际法主体的个人无权自行向法庭申请迅速释放程序。

在国际社会中,出于人道主义对个人的生命与安全权利的保护,也为了避免船只和船员不能及时获得救济,《海洋法公约》第292条规定船只和船员的迅速释放申请可以船旗国名义提出,即船长或船东等个人可以聘请相关代理人以船旗国名义向法庭申请迅速释放。② 但为避免代理人滥用释放被扣留船只的法律程序及防止代理人申请过于私人化,《海洋法公约》第292条要求代理人代表船旗国提出的申请应当以该国的名义作出,即代理人必须在提起迅速释放申请前获得船旗国主管机关的授权,否则法庭不会受理未经国家机关授权的代理人提出的申请。《法庭规则》第110条第2款规定,船旗国可以随时将有权授权代理人提起迅速释放请求的主管机关及经授权代表该国提起请求的代理人的姓名和住址通知法庭。即船旗国政府应当履行已完成授权的通知程序,并且释放申请书必须依据《法庭规则》第110条第3款的规定附有提出申请的授权书、授权

---

① 注:方便旗是指一国的船只不在本国而在船舶登记宽松的国家进行登记,从而悬挂登记国家的国旗。
② 1982年《联合国海洋法公约》第292条第2款规定:"(船只与船员的迅速释放——笔者注)这种释放的申请,仅可由船旗国或以该国名义提出。"

说明、证明文件等相关文件。①

在法庭的实践中,经船旗国授权的代理人有权以船旗国名义提出申请时,他们大多数是由船主聘请的律师并主要代表船方的利益,船旗国只是名义上参加诉讼,案件审理结果的效力直接作用于船方,此时经国家授权的代理人会积极配合案件的审理,被扣押的船只和船员也会及时获得救济。由于大多数国家是在发生争议后临时指定授权机关,其指定依据为各国国内法,因此各国做法各不相同,如表1所示。

表1 迅速释放案件的申请主体及相关信息

案件	船旗国	代理人	授权机关	船长和船员国籍
"塞加号"案 (The M/V SAIGA Case)	圣文森特和格林纳丁斯	英国律师	司法部	乌克兰籍
	"塞加号"油轮在几内亚专属经济区内向当地渔船供应汽油涉嫌走私行为,被几内亚依其国内法扣押。			
"卡莫科号"案 (The Camouco Case)	巴拿马	比利时律师	外交部	西班牙籍
	扣押国法国认为"卡莫科号"渔船进入其专属经济区内非法捕鱼而扣押了该船只及其船长。			
"蒙特·卡夫卡号"案 (The Monte Confurco Case)	塞舌尔	比利时律师	农业和海洋资源部	船长为西班牙籍;船员为西班牙、秘鲁、智利等多国国籍
	"蒙特·卡夫卡号"渔船在法属凯尔盖朗群岛捕鱼被法国军舰以在其专属经济区内非法捕鱼为由扣押,其船长也被羁押。			
"大王子号"案 (The Grand Prince Case)	伯利兹	西班牙律师	司法部	船长为西班牙籍;船员为西班牙籍和智利籍
	"大王子号"渔船在法国专属经济区内非法捕鱼被法国当局扣押,其船长被控诉。			

---

① 《国际海洋法法庭规则》第110条第3款规定:"代表船旗国的申请应附有第2款所指的授权书以及相关文件,以说明提交该申请的人是授权书中指定的人。它还应包含一份证明,证明申请书和所有支持文件的副本已交付船旗国。"

(续表)

案件	船旗国	代理人	授权机关	船长和船员国籍
"朱诺商人号"案（The Juno Trader Case）	圣文森特和格林纳丁斯	法国律师	司法部	一名船员为乌克兰籍,船长和其余船员为俄罗斯籍
	"朱诺商人号"冷藏箱船在几内亚比绍专属经济区内非法捕鱼时被几内亚比绍当局逮捕,并对其处以罚款且没收了船上的鱼。			

由此可见,国际海洋法法庭已经审理的以船旗国名义申请迅速释放的这些案件都是由非船旗国公民的外籍律师作为代理人,经过各国指定的授权机关的授权以船旗国的名义向法庭申请迅速释放程序,以保障和救济船只和船员的权益。这些授权机关主要可分为两类:一类是主管司法或外交事务的机关,在此情况下的迅速释放案件虽然是由代理人——代表国家的非利害关系人以船旗国名义提请,但由于通常归属于一国司法或外交部门负责,因此对于船旗国来说,仍然是国家间诉讼;另一类是渔业主管部门,迅速释放案件的申请主要是由于渔船在沿海国所管辖海域内非法捕鱼而被扣押,因此与之联系最为密切的就是渔业主管部门,此类授权便于船旗国与方便旗国之间的交往与合作。

（二）船旗国身份的认定

由于提起迅速释放程序的申请只能由被扣船只的船旗国或代理人经授权以船旗国名义提出,并且在既往判例中,国际海洋法法庭必须始终确信其对已经申请提交的案件有管辖权。因此,在法庭立案后,当船旗国身份的认定成为争端当事国的争议焦点而对法庭的管辖权存在异议时,法庭主要从以下两个方面分析船旗国身份的认定问题。

1. 船旗国身份的时间认定

《海洋法公约》并未明确规定迅速释放案件中申请主体何时具有船旗国身份的具体时间,但是在国际海洋法法庭审判实践中,一般认为只要申请主体在提起申请时为船旗国身份即可,并不需要其一直是船旗国身份。例如,法庭在"卡莫科号"案和"蒙特·卡夫卡号"案中要求申请主体应在有关事件发生时与提起迅速释放申请时均具有船旗国身份。而在"大王子号"案中,法庭认为,认定伯利兹为船旗国应当是申请主体提交申请时船只进行了船舶登记。法庭在"伏尔加河号"案中的要求也是如此,即申请主体在提起迅速释放申请时具有船旗国身份即可。其中图利奥·特维斯(Tullio Treves)法官在"大王子号"案中提出,迅速释放程序在一定意义上相当于外交保护,在外交保护中,国籍要求至少应当在提起申请时与实施不法行为时被满足,在迅速释放案件中也应如此。[1] 可见,申请主体在迅速释放申请提交的当时对于认定被扣船只的船旗国身份至关重要。

在认定船只国籍时需要考虑的因素包括船旗国是否实际授予国籍、船只是否依法经过登记,以及船只在航行时是否正确悬挂船旗国国旗。大多数国家法律均要求船只取得船舶登记,这是最普遍的国籍要素。如果船只仅仅取得船旗国的临时登记或者临时国籍证书,那么在有效期届满而未申请延期,或者在提起迅速释放申请时船舶登记已经过期的情形下,法庭不会完全将船舶登记与船只国籍画等号,而是先区分有国籍和有证明国籍的证据这两种状态,进一步认为表明船只国籍的证据可以代替登记,最终在没有充分证据证明国籍的情况下,还是以船舶登记为准。[2] "塞加号"案和"大王子号"案即是如此。

"塞加号"是一艘悬挂圣文森特和格林纳丁斯国旗的油轮。1997年在几内亚专属经济区内向当地渔船供应汽油涉嫌走私行为,被几内亚海关巡逻船逮捕,该船及其船员被拘留。当时"塞加号"的临时登记证在扣船日之前已经到期,直到被扣留一个月后才获得永久登记证。[3] 但是法庭基于已经收到圣文森特和格林纳丁斯当局签发的授权证明的核证副本,以此驳回了几内亚的反对意见。[4] 即证明船只国籍的证据表明"塞加号"当时仍然具有圣文森特和格林纳丁斯国籍。同样,在2000年"大王子

---

[1] See The Grand Prince Case (*Belize v. France*), Prompt Release, Separate Opinion of Judge Treves, para. 1.

[2] Tullio Treves, "Flags of Convenience before the Law of the Sea Tribunal," *San Diego International Law Journal* (2004): 186.

[3] See The M/V SAIGA Case (*Saint Vincent and the Grenadines v. Guinea*), Prompt Release, Judgement, para 57.

[4] See The M/V SAIGA Case (*Saint Vincent and the Grenadines v. Guinea*), Prompt Release, Judgement, para 67.

号"案中,悬挂着伯利兹国旗的"大王子号"渔船在法国专属经济区内涉嫌非法捕鱼被法国护卫舰扣押。在"大王子号"被扣留3日后临时航行许可证即到期,伯利兹的代理人3个月后提交迅速释放请求时该船尚未获得新的登记证。① 但法庭并没有因为船只的临时航行许可证失效而直接否定船旗国的地位,而是因为伯利兹当局作出的撤销行为会导致船只国籍的丧失进而认定伯利兹不具有船旗国身份。可见,在实践中法庭对于提交申请时船舶登记失效的船只,并不会因为登记失效而直接否定其船旗国身份,而是会根据涉案双方所提交的其他证据进行综合判断。

2. 认定船旗国身份的证据规则

在法庭实践中,迅速释放案件的证明标准通常采用初步举证责任的证明标准,即首先由申请方承担初步举证责任,一旦其提供初步证据,举证责任则转移给被申请方,若其不能适当举证则应承担举证不能的后果。在"塞加号"案中,由于申请方(圣文森特和格林纳丁斯)已经履行了初步举证责任,而对方几内亚未能合理举证,故而法庭认定圣文森特和格林纳丁斯为"塞加号"的船旗国。

在"大王子号"案中,申请人伯利兹依据其国内1989年《商船登记法案》"悬挂伯利兹国旗的权利源于登记行为本身"的规定,提供了初步证据——存在临时航行许可证。但是由于伯利兹向"大王子号"颁发的唯一文件是临时航行许可证,并且其有效期即将届满,故法庭认为申请方必须有充分的证据证明船只已经在伯利兹登记,从而才有权在一定期限内悬挂伯利兹的国旗,因此伯利兹又出示了国际商船登记处出具的登记证明。同时,被申请方法国提交了伯利兹出具的撤销该船舶登记的照会。根据证据效力规则,法庭认为照会的证明效力高于伯利兹提供的行政文书——国际商船登记处出具的登记证明。法庭的结论是,涉案双方提交的证明材料足以对提出申请时的船只身份状态产生合理怀疑,并且不能充分证明伯利兹是《海洋法公约》第292条第4款所规定的有权提出申请的船旗国,故而法庭认定伯利兹不具有船旗国身份。

---

① See The Grand Prince Case (*Belize v. France*), Prompt Release, Judgement, para 76.

二、迅速释放程序中的专属经济区所属国

在国际海洋法法庭的迅速释放案件中,与申请方船旗国相对应的一般是专属经济区所属国。《海洋法公约》第 55 条确立了专属经济区制度①,第 73 条第 1 款明确了沿海国在其专属经济区内享有极大的管辖权②,即专属经济区所属国有权登临、检查、逮捕在其管辖海域内违法捕鱼的船舶。在法庭已受理的迅速释放案件中,专属经济区所属国行使的均是这项权利,并且法庭并未否认该项权利的行使。法庭之所以能够接受专属经济区所属国扣押违法渔船,并作出要求其迅速释放船旗国船只及其船员的裁决,主要是基于《海洋法公约》第 73 条有关人道主义的保护以及第 292 条关于迅速释放的要求,这不仅有利于维护船旗国船只的经济利益及其船员的人身权益,而且促使专属经济区所属国与船旗国的利益得以均衡。

《海洋法公约》第 73 条第 2 款与第 292 条第 4 款出于人道主义的保护,均要求扣押国(即专属经济区所属国)在存在合理的保证金或其他财政担保的情况下迅速释放被扣留的船只及其船员。③ 也就是说,专属经济区所属国迅速释放被扣船只及其船员的前提是船旗国能够提供适当的保证金或其他财政担保。这表明,《海洋法公约》第 73 条第 2 款和第 292 条第 4 款的目的均是确保两个利益之间的平衡,一个是专属经济区所属国有权采取必要措施以确保其所通过的法律法规得以遵守的利益,另一个是船旗国在确保其船只与船员获得迅速释放方面的利益④,即《海洋法公

---

① 1982 年《联合国海洋法公约》第 55 条规定:"专属经济区是领海以外并邻接领海的一个区域,受本部分规定的特定法律制度的限制,在这个制度下,沿海国的权利和管辖权以及其他国家的权利和自由均受本公约有关规定的支配。"

② 1982 年《联合国海洋法公约》第 73 条第 1 款规定:"沿海国行使其勘探、开发、养护和管理在专属经济区内的生物资源的主权权利时,可采取为确保其依本公约制定的法律和规章得到遵守所必要的措施,包括登临、检查、逮捕和进行司法程序。"

③ 1982 年《联合国海洋法公约》第 73 条第 2 款规定:"被逮捕的船只及其船员,在提出适当的保证书或其他担保后,应迅速获得释放。"
第 292 条第 4 款规定:"在法院或法庭裁定的保证书或其他财政担保经提供后,扣留国当局应迅速遵守法院或法庭关于释放船只或其船员的裁定。"

④ See The Monte Confurco Case (*Seychelles v. France*), Prompt Release, Judgement, para 70.

约》不仅保护船旗国船只的财产利益和船员的人道主义权利,而且还保护沿海国在专属经济区内有效执行其法律法规的能力。①

　　《海洋法公约》平等地保护专属经济区所属国与船旗国的利益,二者没有先后顺序之分。这就要求法庭应当充分考虑专属经济区所属国的利益主张,在其裁定过程中确保船旗国应当提供的保证金或其他财政担保适当且合理,既不能使沿海国在其专属经济区内的渔业资源利益受损,也要确保船旗国船只及其船员的利益。从实践来看,专属经济区所属国为维护自身的海洋权益,通常会依据国内法律法规提出相应的保证金或其他财政担保的主张,有时也会依法先行扣留船旗国船只并启动国内诉讼程序对外国船只作出没收的判决。法庭无法阻止专属经济区所属国的国内诉讼程序,但是在评估其主张的保证金或其他财政担保是否合理时有着自己的判断标准,同时也会将专属经济区所属国国内法律及其法院的判决视为有关事实。② 最终,基于双方利益平衡的考量,法庭以往判例的裁定均是降低了专属经济区所属国主张的数额。这表明,法庭对于迅速释放案件的立场是平衡专属经济区所属国与船旗国之间的利益,既要维护沿海国在其专属经济区域内对渔业资源及环境保护的主权权利,又要排除专属经济区所属国长期扣押违法船只及其船员的情形,防止损害船旗国利益以及船员的人身权益。

　　事实上,争端当事国在《海洋法公约》第 292 条所规定的保证金或其他财政担保问题上也经常存在争议,尽管《海洋法公约》和《法庭规则》均未明确保证金的量化标准,但法庭在解决争议的过程中已经逐渐形成较为成熟的保证金标准。在"卡莫科号"案中,法庭认为评价保证金或其他财政担保的合理性的考虑因素应包括所称违法行为的严重性、被扣船只和货物的价值、扣留国要求的保证金数额和形式等。③ 另外,在"蒙特·卡夫卡号"案中,法庭进一步指出这些因素并不是全部考虑因素,法庭也

---

① See Jillaine Seymour, "The International Tribunal for the Law of the Sea: A Great Mistake," *Indiana Journal of Global Legal Studies* (2006):16.
② See The Monte Confurco Case (*Seychelles v. France*), Prompt Release, Judgement, para 72.
③ See The Camouco Case (*Panama v. France*), Prompt Release, Judgement, para 67.

无意规定每项因素所占的确切权重。① 在之后的案件中,法庭基本上按此标准并对个案进行细化,最终确定相对合理的保证金和其他财政担保。

1. 所称违法行为的严重性

《海洋法公约》第73条第1款规定了沿海国采取的为确保其行使勘探、开发、养护和管理专属经济区内的生物资源的主权权利所制定的法律和规章得到遵守所必要的措施。在法庭目前已受理的迅速释放案件中,除"塞加号"案是油轮涉嫌走私行为以外,其余案件均被沿海国指控在其专属经济区内非法捕鱼。这些非法捕鱼行为,即"非法、不报告和不受管制的"捕捞行为大多数被《南极海洋生物资源保护公约》所规制。例如,在"卡莫科号"案中,法国将法庭的注意力吸引到与在南部海洋非法捕捞巴塔哥尼亚齿鱼有关的经济和生态问题上②;在"蒙特·卡夫卡号"案中,法国主张关于非法捕鱼造成的威胁及根据《南极海洋生物资源保护公约》的规定为养护齿鱼采取的措施③;同样,在"伏尔加河号"案中,扣留国澳大利亚提出,"伏尔加河号"渔船在赫德岛和麦克唐纳群岛的非法捕鱼活动造成了巴塔哥尼亚齿鱼种群的严重减损,这一所属海域(南印度洋)受《南极海洋生物资源保护公约》保护。④ 法庭承认了对该区域内的渔业养护存在的威胁的国际关切的程度,并承认维持环境的生态平衡允许严厉的处罚。因此,法庭不应仅依据判例来判断保证金的合理性,而应充分考虑海洋资源的变化、个案的特殊情况,以及国际社会在保护海洋生物资源中所做出的努力,将这些因素纳入判断和理性的考虑因素之中。⑤

2. 被扣船只和货物的价值

《法庭规则》第111条2款要求在适当的情况下,释放船只及其船员

---

① See The Monte Confurco Case (*Seychelles v. France*), Prompt Release, Judgement, para 76.
② See The Camouco Case (*Panama v. France*), Prompt Release, Judgement, para 68.
③ See The Monte Confurco Case (*Seychelles v. France*), Prompt Release, Judgement, para 79.
④ See The Volga Case (*Russian Federation v. Australia*), Prompt Release, Australian Response, para 42-47.
⑤ 参见任虎、姚妍鞾:《国际海洋法法庭迅速释放问题研究》,载《太平洋学报》2015年第1期。

的申请中需要包含与确定船只价值相关的资料。① 即法庭只要在争端当事国提交的证据的基础上即可确定被扣船只和货物的价值,但这并不是确定保证金或其他财政担保数额的决定性因素。一方面,当扣留国在确定保证金数额可能考虑船只的价值时,法庭就会将其作为考虑因素。例如在"丰进丸号"案中,俄罗斯认为"丰进丸号"的违法行为在性质上十分严重以至于可能导致船只被征收以及被处以最高罚金,因此将船只的价值计算在保证金数额内。② 另一方面,船上的货物或者设备的价值能够抵消一部分保证金。在"蒙特·卡夫卡号"案中,法庭认为船上的渔获物和渔具都应当被作为认定保证金合理性的相关标准。③ 法庭确定保证金为 1800 万法郎,船上 158 吨被强制拍卖的齿鱼的等值货币 900 万法郎应当被认为是担保的一部分,剩余部分除双方另有协议外,应以银行担保的形式支付给法国。④ 但在"伏尔加河号"案中,法庭认为保证金必须以船只及其设备的价值为基础,只有与释放船只及其船员有关的担保才构成《海洋法公约》第 292 条意义上的保证金。⑤ 在之后的"朱诺商人号"案和"丰进丸号"案中,法庭不仅没有将扣押渔获物的价值作为保证金的一部分,而且还命令扣留国几内亚和俄罗斯将其返还给船只所有人。⑥ 这表明货物的价值在法庭确定担保金时所起的作用较小。

3. 扣留国要求的保证金数额和形式

《法庭规则》第 113 条第 2 款规定,如果法庭判定指控是有根据的,它应决定释放船只和船员应交保证金和财政担保的数额、性质和形式。法庭不受扣留国设定或要求的保证金条件拘束,也不受申请国认为合理数

---

① 《国际海洋法法庭规则》第 111 条第 2 款规定:"……(b)包含有关船舶和船员的有关信息,包括该船舶的名称,船旗和注册港口或地点及其吨位,载重量以及与确定其价值有关的数据,名称和地址船东和经营人以及有关船员的资料;……"
② See The Hoshinmaru Case (*Japan v. Russian Federation*), Prompt Release, Judgement, para 92.
③ See The Monte Confurco Case (*Seychelles v. France*), Prompt Release, Judgement, para 86.
④ Ibid, para 93。
⑤ See The Volga Case (*Russian Federation v. Australia*), Prompt Release, Australian Response, para 48-50.
⑥ See The Hoshinmaru Case (*Japan v. Russian Federation*), Prompt Release, Judgement, para 104.

额的拘束。在到目前为止法庭判决的 6 起迅速释放案件中,最终裁定的保证金数额都低于扣留国要求的保证金数额,如表 2 所示。

表 2 争端当事国主张的保证金数额和法庭判决数额

案件	扣留国要求数额	船旗国主张数额	法庭判决数额
"塞加号"案 (The M/V SAIGA Case)	未要求	未主张	40 万美元
"卡莫科号"案 (The Camouco Case)	2000 万法郎	95 万法郎	800 万法郎
"蒙特·卡夫卡号"案 (The Monte Confurco Case)	5640 万法郎	220 万法郎	900 万法郎
"伏尔加河号"案 (The Volga Case)	357.75 万澳元	50 万澳元	192 万澳元
"朱诺商人号"案 (The Juno Trader Case)	未要求	5 万欧元	30.877 万欧元
"丰进丸号"案 (The Hoshinmaru Case)	2500 万卢布	800 万卢布	1000 万卢布

由于法庭考虑释放问题的出发点是平衡沿海国与船旗国的利益,而沿海国可能更多地从打击非法捕鱼的效果方面考虑,导致法庭与当事国国内法院在确定合理保证金因素的内容上有所不同,最终造成二者确定的保证金数额差别较大。例如,在"丰进丸号"案中,俄罗斯法院根据可能对船长和船主处以的罚款、被指控非法捕捞红大马哈鱼的数量可能被处以的罚金、船只的价值以及俄罗斯联邦主管机关进行调查所花费的行政费用确定了最高处罚。① 而法庭则仅将"丰进丸号"的行为定性为在一个大体令人满意的合作框架内的不当行为,并不应遭受俄罗斯法上的最高处罚。② 最终,法庭根据比例性标准和船只的价值,减少了扣留国要求的保证金数额,从 2000 万卢布降到 1000 万卢布。为了缩小法庭与当事国国内法院在确定合理保证金数额的差距,图利奥·特维斯法官在"卡莫科

---

① See The Hoshinmaru Case (*Japan v. Russian Federation*), Prompt Release, Judgement, para 90.

② Ibid, para 99.

号"案中提出了确定合理保证金的国际标准,该国际标准要求平等地反映沿海国执行其法律和规章的利益以及船旗国保护航行自由的利益。① 这种国际标准既保护船旗国的利益,也保护沿海国的利益,可以使得对被扣船只和船员的处理更具有可预见性,减少释放争端的发生。

另外,法庭依据《海洋法公约》第73条第2款的规定,在以往审判实践中判决释放船只的担保必须是财政性质的担保,且除争端当事国另有协议外,保证金应为银行担保的形式。例如,在"伏尔加河号"案中,法庭认为澳大利亚主张的非财政性质的条件不能被认为是所指的保证金或其他财政担保的组成部分,并且施加非财政性质的条件违反《海洋法公约》第73条第2款的目的和宗旨。② 在"蒙特·卡夫卡号"案中,虽然法国国内法院提出以保付支票或银行汇票的现金形式作担保,但法庭认为应以银行担保的形式。③

三、迅速释放案件对我国的启示

随着远洋捕捞事业的发展,各国更加重视与维护本国的海洋权益。作为海洋大国,我国船只与船员被其他国家扣留的情形时常发生。例如,2018年1月14日韩国扣押5艘中国渔船④;同年1月28日我国一渔船在韩国专属经济区内因涉嫌"故意不记载捕鱼量"而被韩国渔业管理团扣押;2020年10月马来西亚海警在该国柔佛州附近水域扣留了6艘中国渔船和船上的60名渔民,原因是未能提供在马来西亚水域捕捞的许可文件。同时,对于进入我国专属经济区非法捕鱼的外国船只,我国作为专属经济区所属国也依法扣留过。据2014年统计,30年来中国海事法院扣押

---

① See The Camouco Case (*Panama v. France*), Prompt Release, Dissenting Opinion Of Judge Treves, para 7.
② See The Volga Case (*Russian Federation v. Australia*), Prompt Release, Judgment, para 78-80.
③ See The Monte Confurco Case (*Seychelles v. France*), Prompt Release, Judgement, para 93.
④ 其中4艘拖网渔船在韩国西海域因非法捕捞鳀鱼、鹤尾鱼约40多吨被扣押。另外一艘温岭拖网渔船在韩国专属经济区内涉嫌配置与韩国政府发出的作业许可证不同的船证进行作业而被扣押送至济州港。

外国轮船1660艘次。① 2016年5月,"鲁荣渔号"在东海沉没,中国扣留了涉事船只——马耳他籍散货船"卡塔丽娜号"进行调查取证。虽然我国在加入《海洋法公约》时对国际海洋法法庭的管辖权作出了保留,但是法庭对于迅速释放案件的处理办法却值得我国借鉴,以避免在专属经济区扣押船舶后,与被扣船只的涉事国家之间发生摩擦与争端,也为了更好地维护我国船员的合法权益和船只的财产安全。

(一)作为船旗国:应加强监督与规制

根据《海洋法公约》规定,迅速释放程序的申请要求船旗国或以船旗国名义提出,可见船旗国在迅速释放案件中扮演着重要角色。因此,我国作为船旗国应当遵守《海洋法公约》的规定,履行好自身的责任和义务。

1. 规范船舶登记手续,严格落实捕捞许可证制度

船舶登记是船舶具有一国国籍的重要标志,发放船舶法定证书是船旗国主管机关的法定职责。我国《渔业船舶登记办法》第4条和第16条规定了渔船进行登记取得我国国籍后才能悬挂我国国旗航行②,第21条规定渔业船舶国籍证书的有效期为5年。我国2014年《船舶登记条例》第18条规定,临时船舶国籍证书的有效期一般不超过1年。在有效期届满前3个月内所有人未申请换发新的国籍证书的,船舶登记机关有权直接注销该渔船的国籍。③ 因此作为船旗国,首先应当明确船舶登记统一标准,使船舶登记流程规范具体,以便对于悬挂我国国旗的船舶实行有效的管理。

另外,要严格落实好捕捞许可证制度。根据我国《渔业法》第23条和第24条的规定,国家对捕捞业实行捕捞许可证制度,只有具备发放条件

---

① 参见《最高法:30年来中国海事法院扣押外国轮船1660艘次》,载新浪网(http://news.sina.com.cn/c/2014-09-02/143830782982.shtml),访问日期:2021年11月24日。

② 2019年《渔业船舶登记办法》第4条规定:"渔业船舶依照本办法进行登记,取得中华人民共和国国籍,方可悬挂中华人民共和国国旗航行。"
第16条规定:"渔业船舶应当依照本办法进行渔业船舶国籍登记,方可取得航行权。"

③ 2019年《渔业船舶登记办法》第39条规定:"有下列情形之一的,登记机关可直接注销该渔业船舶国籍:(一)国籍证书有效期满未延续的;(二)渔业船舶检验证书有效期满未依法延续的;……"
第45条规定:"渔业船舶所有人应当在渔业船舶国籍证书有效期届满三个月前,持渔业船舶国籍证书和渔船舶检验证书到登记机关申请换发国籍证书。"

的,才可向其发放捕捞许可证①,即从事远洋捕捞船舶的捕捞许可证应由国务院渔业行政主管部门批准发放,且捕捞许可证不得随意买卖、转让。而且,应当对许可的捕捞活动进行严格监管,保证我国渔船按照许可证的规定从事远洋捕捞活动。

2. 保证船只具有"真正联系",加强对船只的管理

为方便船旗国对本国船只实行有效的管辖和控制,1986 年《联合国船舶登记条件公约》第 1 条明确其宗旨就是要加强一国与悬挂其国旗的船舶之间的真正联系。我国《船舶登记条例》也对此作出了规定,比如第 9 条规定船舶登记港由船舶所有人依据其住所或者主要营业所在地就近选择;第 13 条规定了船舶所有人申请船舶所有权登记时应当提交足以证明其合法身份的文件;第 15 条规定了船舶所有人申请船舶国籍时应提交的证明文件;等等。② 尽管《船舶登记条例》第 49 条明确禁止中国籍船舶假冒外国国籍以及外国船舶假冒中国国籍③,但是也不乏方便旗船的情况。鉴于方便旗船的境外登记地的船舶登记条件较为宽松且税收优惠,我国有许多船舶属于在外登记的方便旗船,例如巴拿马、利比里亚、塞浦路斯、马来西亚等方便旗国。自 2016 年起,我国交通运输部发布《关于实施有关中资"方便旗"船回国登记进口税收政策的公告》,对于报关进口、办理船舶登记的中资船舶免征关税,鼓励"方便旗"船登记成为"五星红旗"船。④ 但是涉及范围

---

① 2013 年《渔业法》第 23 条规定:"国家对捕捞业实行捕捞许可证制度。到中华人民共和国与有关国家缔结的协定确定的共同管理的渔区或者公海从事捕捞作业的捕捞许可证,由国务院渔业行政主管部门批准发放……"

第 24 条规定:"具备下列条件的,方可发给捕捞许可证:(1)有渔业船舶检验证书;(2)有渔业船舶登记证书;(3)符合国务院渔业行政主管部门规定的其他条件。"

② 2014 年《船舶登记条例》第 9 条规定:"船舶登记港为船籍港。船舶登记港由船舶所有人依据其住所或者主要营业所在地就近选择……"

第 13 条规定:"船舶所有人申请船舶所有权登记,应当向船籍港船舶登记机关交验足以证明其合法身份的文件,并提供有关船舶技术资料和船舶所有权取得的证明文件的正本、副本。"

第 15 条规定:"船舶所有人申请船舶国籍,除应当交验依照本条例取得的船舶所有权登记证书外,还应当按照船舶航区相应交验文件。"

③ 2014 年《船舶登记条例》第 49 条规定:"假冒中华人民共和国国籍,悬挂中华人民共和国国旗航行的,由船舶登记机关依法没收该船舶。中国籍船舶假冒外国国籍,悬挂外国国旗航行的,适用前款规定。"

④ 2016 年至今,财政部、海关总署、税务总局联合批准了四批享受进口税收优惠政策的中资"方便旗"船舶,共计 80 艘中资"方便旗"船舶。

大部分是国有大型航运企业的船舶,船舶类型主要为货船,尚未涉及渔船。因此,为促使远洋捕捞业的发展,对我国的"方便旗"渔船也可以实施相应的优惠政策,使其成为"五星红旗"船,便于渔业管理部门和海上交通安全部门加强管理。

3. 制定合理的保证金标准,建立渔业担保机制

作为船旗国,当我国国籍的渔船远洋捕捞被沿海国扣押时,除应当依据《远洋渔业管理规定》第 37 条联系农业农村部同外交部协商及时与沿海国交涉外[1],还应当有明确的保证金标准,以便与沿海国提出的保证金加以比照和谈判。此时,可以借鉴国际海洋法法庭在审理迅速释放案件中有关保证金合理性的做法,综合所称违法行为的严重性、被扣船只和货物的价值,以及扣留国要求的保证金数额和形式等因素,尽可能与沿海国协商出合理的保证金,保障好船员的合法权益。

另外,当渔船远洋捕鱼被扣押时,扣押国往往会索要高额的保证金。截至 2015 年底,被韩国海警扣留的中国渔船共计 378 艘,需要向韩国政府缴纳 238.6 亿韩元保证金。[2] 如果被扣渔船未能缴纳保证金,则在扣押期间无法从事捕捞活动,甚至面临被韩方没收的风险。这表明我国远洋捕捞业缺乏担保机制,需要船长或者船东个人承担巨额保证金,对走出去到公海捕鱼产生畏惧心理。1981 年中国人民保险公司公布了《国内渔船保险条款》,其中第 3 条和第 8 条规定了保险责任范围[3],但只承保渔船本身的毁损灭失,对于渔船被扣押的情况尚未提及,因渔船被扣押而产生的

---

[1] 2020年《远洋渔业管理规定》第37条规定:"远洋渔业企业、渔船和船员在国外发生涉外事件时,应当立即如实向农业农村部、企业所在地省级人民政府渔业行政主管部门和有关驻外使(领)馆报告,省级人民政府渔业行政主管部门接到报告后,应当立即核实情况,并提出处理意见报农业农村部和省级人民政府,由农业农村部协调提出处理意见通知驻外使(领)馆。发生重大涉外事件需要对外交涉的,由农业农村部商外交部提出处理意见,进行交涉。"

[2] 参见《中国渔船睡梦中遭韩国渔民"拖走"索要天价保证金》,载环球网(https://m.huanqiu.com/article/9CaKrnJVNPj.),访问日期:2021年11月24日。

[3] 1981年《国内渔船保险条款》第3条规定:"保险渔船由于下列原因造成完全灭失或推定完全灭失,以及部分损失,保险人(即保险公司)负赔偿责任。(一)火灾、雷击、爆炸、搁浅、触礁、碰撞、倾覆、沉没、暴风、海啸;(二)全船失踪在6个月以上;(三)保险渔船入坞修理及停泊、停放……"

第8条规定:"保险渔船由于下列原因造成的损失,保险人不负赔偿责任:(一)战争或军事行动;(二)不具备适航或作业条件;(三)渔船所有人及其代表的故意行为或船上人员的违法行为。……(八)其他不属于保险责任范围内的损失。"

保证金不属于保险责任范围内的损失。因此,对于我国渔船及其船员被其他沿海国扣留的问题,我国可以构建渔业担保机制,通过渔船的船只性能、航程,以及捕捞不同鱼类等方面综合量化保险金,避免船主或船东因较高担保金而承受巨大的经济压力,使其能够有机会继续远洋捕捞,有利于促使我国海洋渔业资源休养生息。

(二)作为专属经济区所属国:应加强对外籍船舶的监督

《海洋法公约》强调公海自由,包括捕鱼自由,并且允许其他国家在沿海国的专属经济区内从事渔业活动。① 我国《专属经济区和大陆架法》第5条规定,只要外国船舶经过我国主管机关批准,即可在我国专属经济区内合法捕鱼。② 依据该法第12条的规定,当外国船舶违反我国相关法律法规而非法捕鱼时,我国主管机关有权依法扣留渔船。③ 此时,鉴于我国不承认法庭对迅速释放案件的管辖权,而我国法院作为沿海国法院对领海以外其他海域具有司法管辖权④,因此,可以立即启动国内诉讼程序,借鉴俄罗斯在"富丸号"案中的经验,以减少我国所属海域内生物资源的损失,维护我国的海洋经济权益。

2006年10月31日,日本籍渔船"富丸号"在俄罗斯专属经济区违规捕鱼被俄方扣押。同年11月14日,俄罗斯当局立即根据国内法律对"富丸号"船东提起行政诉讼,12月28日,堪察加彼得罗巴甫洛夫斯克(Petropavolvsk-Kamchatskii)市法院作出判决,判定没收渔船"富丸号",并指出可在10天之内向堪察加地区法院提出上诉。船东于2007年1月6日向堪察加地区法院提出上诉,地区法院在1月24日的判决中维持原判,该

---

① 1982年《联合国海洋法公约》第62条第4款规定:"在专属经济区内捕鱼的其他国家的国民应遵守沿海国的法律和规章中所制定的养护措施和其他条款和条件。"
② 1998年《专属经济区和大陆架法》第5条规定:"任何国际组织、外国的组织或者个人进入中华人民共和国的专属经济区从事渔业活动,必须经中华人民共和国主管机关批准,并遵守中华人民共和国的法律、法规及中华人民共和国与有关国家签订的条约、协定。"
③ 1998年《专属经济区和大陆架法》第12条规定:"中华人民共和国在行使勘查、开发、养护和管理专属经济区的生物资源的主权权利时,为确保中华人民共和国的法律、法规得到遵守,可以采取登临、检查、逮捕、扣留和进行司法程序等必要的措施。中华人民共和国对在专属经济区和大陆架违反中华人民共和国法律、法规的行为,有权采取必要措施,依法追究法律责任,并可以行使紧追权。"
④ 参见黄西武、周海洋、阎巍:《〈关于审理发生在我国管辖海域相关案件若干问题的规定〉的理解与适用》,载《人民司法(应用)》2016年第31期。

判决在其交付后立即生效。于是,负责管理堪察加地区联邦财产的联邦机构通过实施2007年4月9日第158-p号法案,根据法院的判决将该渔船没收为俄罗斯联邦财产,并在联邦财产登记处登记注册。之后,船东又根据监督审查程序对地区法院作出的判决提出再审申请。当日本于2007年7月6日向国际海洋法法庭提出迅速释放申请时,俄罗斯联邦最高法院尚未审理该案件。在法庭听证会结束后,俄罗斯联邦最高法院于2007年7月26日驳回了再审申请并通知法庭。由于俄罗斯联邦最高法院的判决已经终结了涉及该渔船的国内司法程序,且为终局判决,因此法庭认定日本的申请缺乏标的,俄罗斯的司法程序尚未违背国际司法正当程序,故不予判决。①

《海洋法公约》第292条第3款规定,当审查释放申请时,国际海洋法法庭应仅处理释放问题,而不影响、不干涉、不评价主管的国内法庭对该船只、其船主或船员的任何案件的是非曲直。可见,法庭对沿海国已经作出没收决定的迅速释放案件管辖权问题的考虑,在某种程度上就意味着承认了没收的合法性。② 实际上,许多国家的国内法都规定将没收渔船作为对于非法捕鱼采取的处罚措施,我国《渔业法》第46条也对此作出了规定。③ 因此,面对外籍船舶损害我国海洋资源的情形,在我国依法将其扣押之后,有关部门可以立即通过国内司法程序对渔船处以罚款和没收,应当就船员和船只的迅速释放问题及时与船旗国协商,提出合理的财产性担保要求,使案件得以迅速有效地解决。

结　　论

《海洋法公约》第292条明确规定了国际海洋法法庭对迅速释放案

---

① See The Tomimaru Case (*Japan v. Russian Federation*), Prompt Release, Judgement, para 78.
② 参见朱振华:《国际海洋法法庭迅速释放程序中的征收问题研究》,载《研究生法学》2008年第2期。
③ 2013年《渔业法》第46条规定:"外国人、外国渔船违反本法规定,擅自进入中华人民共和国管辖水域从事渔业生产和渔业资源调查活动的,责令其离开或者将其驱逐,可以没收渔获物、渔具,并处五十万元以下的罚款;情节严重的,可以没收渔船;构成犯罪的,依法追究刑事责任。"

件具有管辖权,在以往法庭实践中,许多国家倾向于将迅速释放案件提交于法庭处理,但是当争端当事国对法庭的管辖权存在异议时,法庭就会首先审查这些国家的申请是否符合管辖迅速释放案件的各项条件,其中申请主体和认定船旗国的身份尤为关键。而随着远洋捕捞渔业的发展,迅速释放案件争端不断增多,国际海洋法法庭的既往判例为我国处理相关案件提供了宝贵经验。因此笔者从法庭对迅速释放案件的管辖权出发,介绍了有权向法庭提出迅速释放案件的申请主体,着重分析了法庭在审理过程中对船旗国身份的认定,包括船旗国身份认定的时间及认定船旗国身份的证据规则。这对我国在面对本国船只或外籍船舶非法捕鱼时如何处理所涉及的迅速释放案件具有重要启示和借鉴意义:首先,作为船旗国,一是要规范船舶登记手续,落实好捕捞许可证制度;二是应保证船只的"真正联系",加强对船只的管理;三是需制定合理的保证金标准,建立渔业担保机制。其次,作为专属经济区所属国,在面对外籍船舶非法捕鱼时应当通过国内程序依法没收和处以罚款,以维护好我国的海洋权益。

另外,随着21世纪海上丝绸之路建设的深入推进,我国在提升经济实力与增强综合国力的过程中,应当秉持"海洋命运共同体"的理念,推动构建双边或者多边的区域性海洋合作机制,加强与周边沿海国之间的协商与合作,特别是南海沿岸诸国,以便船旗国在专属经济区所属国海域内的迅速释放案件的处理高效便捷,使争端当事国实现共赢。综上,我国应结合实际情况,汲取国际海洋法法庭审判经验,全方位、多角度地提升我国对迅速释放案件的处理能力,为我国向海洋强国的发展提供有利条件。

完善司法支持监督仲裁机制 促进中国仲裁事业高质量发展*

胡 方** 马 玲***

摘要：人民法院高度重视仲裁在纠纷解决机制中的重要作用，在依法对仲裁活动予以支持的同时，对仲裁活动进行相应的监督，积极推动仲裁制度的发展和完善，持续促进我国仲裁制度公信力与国际竞争力的提升，为中国仲裁事业的高质量发展提供了有力的司法服务和保障。

关键词：仲裁司法审查；多元化纠纷解决；仲裁友好型司法环境

仲裁作为国际通行的纠纷解决方式，是我国社会治理体系中多元化纠纷解决机制建设的重要组成部分，对于高效便捷解决商事海事纠纷，营造市场化、法治化、国际化营商环境，推动国家重大战略实施具有重要意义。随着"一带一路"倡议的深入推进，中国与世界各国在政治、经贸、人文等各领域的合作更为密切，国际国内各界对仲裁服务的需求日益增加，为我国仲裁事业的蓬勃发展提供了机遇。长期以来，人民法院高度重视仲裁在纠纷解决机制中的重要作用，在依法对仲裁活动予以支持的同时，对仲裁活动进行相应的监督，积极推动仲裁制度的发展和完善，持续促进我国仲裁制度公信力与国际竞争力的提升，为中国仲裁事业的高质量发展提供了有力的司法服务和保障。

---

* 本文完成于2022年1月。
** 最高人民法院民四庭副庭长。
*** 最高人民法院民四庭法官助理。

一、依法履行司法审查职能,引导仲裁行业健康发展

根据我国《仲裁法》《民事诉讼法》等法律的规定,人民法院目前受理的仲裁司法审查案件主要包括以下五类:(1)申请确认仲裁协议效力案件;(2)申请执行我国内地仲裁机构的仲裁裁决案件;(3)申请撤销我国内地仲裁机构的仲裁裁决案件;(4)申请认可和执行香港特别行政区、澳门特别行政区、台湾地区仲裁裁决案件;(5)申请承认和执行外国仲裁裁决案件。此外,《最高人民法院关于审理仲裁司法审查案件若干问题的规定》还规定了"其他仲裁司法审查案件"作为兜底条款,为将来可能出现的一些新类型案件(如《最高人民法院关于为自由贸易试验区建设提供司法保障的意见》规定的临时仲裁案件)留有余地。人民法院在对上述案件进行司法审查的过程中一直立足现实国情,以引导仲裁健康发展作为司法审查的出发点,界分程序事项与实体事项的边界,平衡仲裁瑕疵与司法过度审查的关系,着力提高仲裁公信力和司法保障力,提升中国仲裁的国际化水平与竞争力。就近年来的仲裁司法审查案件的趋势看,全国法院审结的撤裁类案件一直保持着较低的撤裁率,同时仲裁保全案件一直保持着较高的保全率,这一方面体现了我国仲裁质量呈逐步提升趋势,另一方面也体现了我国司法支持和促进仲裁发展的坚定立场。

(一)尊重当事人仲裁意愿,对仲裁协议从宽解释

相较英美国家,我国《仲裁法》对仲裁协议的内容要件和形式要件作了相对严格的规定,要求必须同时具备请求仲裁的意思表示、仲裁事项和选定的仲裁委员会三个要件。在过去的司法实践中,也曾经严格将"选定的仲裁委员会"作为仲裁协议的必备要素。随着仲裁司法审查实践的不断丰富,现在法院更加注重充分尊重当事人订约时的仲裁意愿,在法律规定的范围内,对仲裁协议的有效要件作尽量宽泛的解读。如对于实践中经常出现的当事人约定仲裁机构名称不准确、不规范的情形,法院会按照有利于仲裁协议有效的原则进行解释,只要可以确定仲裁机构的唯一性,就认可仲裁协议的效力。又如仲裁协议约定争议适用某仲裁机构的仲裁规则解决,除非仲裁规则有相反规定,现在的司法实践也不再会将此

归为没有"选定的仲裁委员会",而会视为约定该仲裁机构仲裁。再如当事人约定争议发生后"先仲裁后诉讼",在过去的司法实践中可能因未将仲裁约定为唯一的纠纷解决方式而导致仲裁协议无效,但现在一般认为这种情况不属于"或裁或诉"情形,而视为关于诉讼的约定无效,不影响约定仲裁的效力。同样的情况还有约定"Arbitration, if any, in Hong Kong and English law to be applied"(如果提起仲裁,在香港特区适用英国法)此类的条款。以往的司法实践认为,该约定因未排除诉讼管辖而不构成双方之间唯一的纠纷解决方式,但现在的司法实践逐渐倾向于认为,此类条款应当依据约定的仲裁地法律判断其效力。《最高人民法院关于审理仲裁司法审查案件若干问题的规定》还明确规定,当事人没有选择仲裁协议准据法的,适用仲裁机构所在地法律与仲裁地法律中有利于认定仲裁协议有效的法律。总之,不断完善、成熟的司法实践对待仲裁协议的效力呈现了趋向宽松的审查态度。只要双方当事人具有将争议提交仲裁的明确意思表示,法院通常会按照尽量使仲裁协议有效的原则,灵活宽容地解释存在表述缺陷的仲裁条款,充分体现了中国司法对仲裁的大力支持。

(二)依照法定事由,审慎审查仲裁裁决

人民法院严格依据法定事由,审慎审查当事人提出的撤销和不予执行仲裁裁决的申请,尊重仲裁一裁终局性,尽量维持已经完结的仲裁程序和裁决效力。如当事人约定了多层次争议解决条款,将一定期限内的协商、和解、调解等作为提起仲裁的前置程序,其后以协商程序未满足为由申请撤销或者不予执行仲裁裁决。现在的司法实践认为,法律规定应予审查的"仲裁程序"仅指进入仲裁程序后仲裁过程中的程序性事项,而不包括仲裁之前的协商解决争议程序,是否进行协商不能成为撤销或者不予执行仲裁裁决的理由,对此类申请均予以驳回。又如对当事人选择仲裁员、参与仲裁程序等程序性事项的审查,只有程序错误达到可能影响公正裁决的情形下,才能被认定为撤裁理由。再如法院对能否以违反社会公共利益为由撤销或不予执行仲裁裁决一直从严把握,避免该事由因解释空间较大而被滥用。从这两年最高人民法院办理的报核案件来看,裁决违反法律强制性规定、违反当地法院或其他法院类似案件的裁判规则、涉及地方政府或相关行政机关财政收支、涉及国有资产或特定社会公益项目的,都没有被认为违反社会公共利益。上述司法实践均体现了在强调监督的同时,法院对仲裁裁决总体上秉持的支持态度。司法支持与促进仲裁发展的理念已经确立。

(三)采取仲裁保全措施,保障仲裁裁决执行

仲裁是民间解决纠纷的方式,仲裁机构无权对当事人的财产、行为及案件有关证据采取强制措施。这些问题需要通过司法的协助与支持得到解决。仲裁保全是仲裁制度与诉讼程序衔接中的重要一环,对保障仲裁程序的顺利进行及保证仲裁裁决最终执行具有重要作用。据统计,我国法院受理的仲裁保全类案件数量甚至超过确认仲裁协议类案件或申请不予执行类案件数量。2019年,全国法院审结的仲裁保全类案件中87%的保全申请得到了法院的支持;2020年,上述保全率进一步提升至97%。相对于民事诉讼法的规定,海事诉讼特别程序法及其司法解释已经建立了更为全面的海事保全制度。无论是国内仲裁还是外国仲裁,无论是在提起仲裁前还是在仲裁程序中,海事请求人都可以向海事法院申请,对被请求人所有的在我国国内的船舶、船载货物、船用燃油及物料进行海事请求保全,该保全申请不受当事人之间关于该海事请求的诉讼管辖协议或者仲裁协议的约束。海事法院依法受理并高效执行海事保全,必然提高仲裁自身的效率,提升解决纠纷的吸引力,亦是司法支持仲裁的一个重要体现。

(四)准确适用国际条约,依法承认和执行外国仲裁裁决

最高人民法院陶凯元副院长在"2021中国仲裁高峰论坛暨第二届'一带一路'仲裁机构高端论坛"主旨演讲中提到:"外国仲裁裁决的承认和执行是检验一国司法水平的重要窗口。"我国法院一直以来恪守国际条约义务,遵循条约善意履行原则,秉持"有利于裁决执行"的司法立场,在承认和执行外国仲裁裁决案件中,严格依照《承认及执行外国仲裁裁决公约》(又称《纽约公约》)第5条规定的法定事由进行司法审查,凡以《纽约公约》第5条规定情形以外的事由请求人民法院拒绝承认和执行外国仲裁裁决的,人民法院不予审查;且对于第5条第1款规定的拒绝事由,亦坚持当事人举证证明的原则,法院不主动审查。据统计,2020年全国法院

审结的申请承认和执行外国仲裁裁决的案件中,裁定驳回申请的仅占20%。绝大多数的申请承认和执行外国仲裁裁决的案件得到了法院的承认与执行。人民法院对外国仲裁裁决在我国的承认与执行尽可能地持支持态度,体现了越来越成熟的司法审查理念和裁判思路。对少数驳回申请案件的原因均予以详细释明,体现了我国法院对仲裁领域国际司法协助机制的友好支持态度。

二、发布司法解释和规范性文件,营造支持仲裁友善监督的司法环境

最高人民法院先后发布了三十余项与仲裁相关的司法解释和规范性文件,不断创新保障仲裁发展的体制机制,致力于创建仲裁友好型司法环境。尤其是党的十八大以来,最高人民法院围绕服务保障"一带一路"倡议和自由贸易试验区建设等国家重大战略,建立仲裁司法审查归口办理机制,规范仲裁司法审查案件报核制度,细化仲裁司法审查案件程序规则,明确仲裁裁决执行审查标准,持续促进我国仲裁制度公信力与国际竞争力的提升,为营造市场化、法治化、国际化营商环境提供了有力的司法服务和保障。

(一)完善报核规定,建设更加高效的仲裁司法审查制度

1995年,《最高人民法院关于人民法院处理与涉外仲裁和外国仲裁事项有关问题的通知》发布,建立了涉外涉港澳台仲裁司法审查案件的内部报核制度,对人民法院正确审理涉外、涉港澳台司法审查案件,提升我国内地司法国际公信力、促进仲裁发展,发挥了积极作用。2017年,为平等保护各方当事人合法权益,根据审判实践需要,《最高人民法院关于仲裁司法审查案件报核问题的有关规定》发布,增加了对非涉外涉港澳台仲裁司法审查案件,根据不同情况分别由各地高级人民法院和最高人民法院审核的规定。该规定实施以来,最高人民法院共办理各类仲裁司法审查报核案件900多件,有力推动了仲裁司法审查案件的整体规范和裁判尺度的统一,提升了仲裁司法审查的透明度,保障了仲裁事业的蓬勃发展。2021年,为了更加合理地划分最高人民法院与高级人民法院之间关

于仲裁司法审查案件的审核权限,提高审查效率,缩短案件审查周期,《最高人民法院关于修改〈最高人民法院关于仲裁司法审查案件报核问题的有关规定〉的决定》发布,自 2022 年 1 月 1 日起,将当事人住所地跨省级行政区域的非涉外涉港澳台仲裁司法审查案件的最终审核权由最高人民法院下放至高级人民法院。同时,为总体掌握仲裁司法审查案件情况,加强指导监督,增加了报备制度,要求高级人民法院对其行使最终审核权的案件在作出审核意见之日起 15 日内,将复函向最高人民法院报备。为了配合新规定的实施,更好地指导下级法院正确办理仲裁司法审查案件,最高人民法院民四庭于 2021 年 12 月 31 日出台《全国法院涉外商事海事审判工作座谈会会议纪要》,对仲裁司法审查案件涉及的 21 个问题进行了归纳总结,统一了裁判尺度,充分体现了支持仲裁的司法宗旨和理念。自《仲裁法》实施近 30 年以来,最高人民法院通过陆续出台司法解释和规范性文件不断完善仲裁司法审查案件报核制度,更加切合各级人民法院的职能定位,更加符合当事人公正高效解决争议的司法需求,更加符合支持和监督这一报核制度设立的初心。

(二)强化区际司法协助,便利仲裁裁决的区际执行

近年来,最高人民法院先后制定实施了多个司法解释,以推进我国港澳地区仲裁裁决在内地的认可与执行。香港特区回归祖国以来,在两地的共同努力下,先后签署了八项民商事司法协助安排,基本实现了两地民商事司法协助全面覆盖。其中 1999 年签署的《最高人民法院关于内地与香港特别行政区相互执行仲裁裁决的安排》(以下简称《安排》)在解决两地跨境纠纷、支持香港特区仲裁发展、增进两地民生福祉方面发挥了重要作用。2019 年《最高人民法院关于内地与香港特别行政区法院就仲裁程序相互协助保全的安排》公布,对两地相互协助保全的途径、可申请保全的范围、申请保全的程序以及保全申请审查处理等问题作出了明确规定。这是自香港特区回归祖国以来,内地与其他法域签署的第一份有关仲裁保全协助的文件。该安排生效后两年内,内地法院受理的此类仲裁保全申请中,大约92%的申请得到了法院支持。2020 年,最高人民法院与香港特别行政区政府律政司签署《关于内地与香港特别行政区相互执行仲裁裁决的补充安排》(以下简称《补充安排》),对 1999 年《安排》作了重要

修改和补充。《补充安排》明确了认可仲裁裁决的程序,扩大了相互认可和执行仲裁裁决的范围,规定了申请人可同时向两地法院申请执行,增加了诉前保全和诉中保全的规定。上述文件的签署增进了两地百姓的民生福祉,促进了香港特区融入大湾区发展大局,是司法领域丰富完善"一国两制"方针的重大举措,是以法治方式保持香港特区长期繁荣稳定的具体体现,也是构建共商、共建、共享多元化纠纷解决机制的有益探索。如今两地之间的司法协助已经实现了一国之内更紧密的合作和更广泛的互信,充分证明了"一国两制"的制度优势。

(三)发布《最高人民法院商事仲裁司法审查年度报告》,总结仲裁司法审查经验

为全面展现近年来人民法院仲裁司法审查工作取得的成绩,及时总结仲裁司法审查经验,统一裁判尺度,最高人民法院首次发布了中英双语版《最高人民法院商事仲裁司法审查年度报告(2019年)》(以下简称"报告"),为国际社会了解中国仲裁司法审查提供了全景视角。报告对中国仲裁司法审查制度的发展历史进行了宏观概括梳理,总结了仲裁司法审查工作历经探索、完善、创新的三个阶段,同时介绍了全国法院2019年仲裁司法审查案件基本数据,分析了各类仲裁司法审查案件的基本情况、特点与趋势,并且根据最高人民法院办理的仲裁司法审查报核案件,结合全国高级人民法院选报的典型案例,对仲裁司法审查思路与裁判标准进行了归纳总结。报告体现了人民法院为深入落实党的十八届四中全会和中共中央办公厅、国务院办公厅《关于完善仲裁制度 提高仲裁公信力的若干意见》的整体部署;展示了人民法院为此付出的不懈努力和取得的积极成果;加深了社会各界对仲裁司法审查制度的认识和了解;显示了仲裁及其司法审查对保障中国经济发展、促进营商环境建设和深化多元化纠纷解决机制改革的重要意义。2020年度《最高人民法院商事仲裁司法审查年度报告》的发布持续进行,进一步提升中国司法、中国仲裁的透明度,增强中国司法和仲裁的公信力、影响力和国际竞争力。

三、参与仲裁法修订,积极推动仲裁法律制度完善

2020年,为贯彻落实中共中央办公厅、国务院办公厅印发的《关于完善仲裁制度 提高仲裁公信力的若干意见》,根据第十三届全国人民代表大会常务委员会立法规划和国务院立法工作计划,司法部启动组织《仲裁法》的修订工作,最高人民法院是修法最重要的协同参与部门。鉴于仲裁司法审查工作可以集中反映仲裁法律制度实施中的问题,能动反映仲裁实践需求和政策文件实施效果,最高人民法院自始至终对《仲裁法》修订工作高度重视,在广泛征求地方各级法院意见的基础上组织专班进行详细研究。最高人民法院由民四庭牵头,就可仲裁性、仲裁协议效力、仲裁裁决撤销制度与执行制度等热点难点问题,多次与司法部修法专班进行充分沟通,提出的很多建设性修改意见均被草案吸收和采纳,为《仲裁法》的修改以及改革完善中国仲裁法律制度提供了更多司法实践的支持。

四、建设国际商事纠纷多元化解决机制,支持中国仲裁国际化发展

党的十八届四中全会提出,"健全社会矛盾纠纷预防化解机制,完善调解、仲裁、行政裁决、行政复议、诉讼等有机衔接、相互协调的多元化纠纷解决机制"。最高人民法院近年来发布了《关于人民法院进一步深化多元化纠纷解决机制改革的意见》《关于建设一站式多元解纷机制 一站式诉讼服务中心的意见》,多次强调合理配置纠纷解决的社会资源,要求各级法院加强与仲裁机构的对接,积极支持仲裁制度改革,推动建立诉讼、调解和仲裁相衔接的"一站式"争议解决服务。最高人民法院于2018年相继设立了国际商事法庭和国际商事专家委员会。建立"一站式"国际商事纠纷多元化解决机制,既是法院与仲裁、调解机构紧密合作的又一尝试,也是实现诉讼与仲裁、调解良性互动、优势互补的制度创新。目前,已有中国国际经济贸易仲裁委员会、中国海事仲裁委员会等5家仲裁机构首批进入最高人民法院"一站式"国际商事纠纷多元化解决机制,为国际商事案件当事人提供"一站式"便利、快捷、低成本的纠纷解决服务。2020

年 7 月 21 日,最高人民法院"一站式"国际商事纠纷多元化解决平台在国际商事法庭网站上线启动试运行,为中外当事人提供立案、调解、证据交换、开庭等纠纷解决全流程线上办理,实现了国际商事法庭诉讼机制与调解、仲裁机制的在线对接和信息共享,将形成协同效应,有力推动国际商事纠纷多元化解决机制的落地见效。此外,上海、宁波、武汉等海事法院与中国海事仲裁委员会建立的委托调解机制亦在不断扩展应用范围、完善程序流程。很多案情复杂,涉外性、专业性强的海事海商纠纷经委托调解得到了及时、妥善的解决,受到当事人的高度认可。国际商事纠纷多元化解决机制的不断完善,切实提高了解决纠纷的效率,满足中外当事人纠纷解决的多元需求,为打造具有国际影响力的中国商事海事仲裁品牌提供了实践平台。

在深入推进"一带一路"建设过程中,中国的商事海事仲裁将会面临更加激烈的竞争,提升我国的商事海事仲裁机构的公信力刻不容缓。在新的历史时期,人民法院作为商事海事仲裁的支持者和监督者,将继续秉承开放、包容的精神,始终坚持支持仲裁发展的理念,立足我国仲裁和司法实践,一如既往地支持和监督仲裁,为完善中国仲裁制度、提升中国仲裁公信力提供有力的司法服务和保障。

国际仲裁中心是形成的*

司玉琢** 王 伟***

摘要:打造国际仲裁中心或者区域国际仲裁中心,已成为诸多国家与地区的追求目标与前行方向。我国的仲裁界也一直在探索内地形成国际仲裁中心的可能性。国务院发布的《关于促进海运业健康发展的若干意见》和《进一步深化中国(上海)自由贸易试验区改革开放方案》,将发展包括海事仲裁在内的现代航运服务业作为重点任务加以部署,并进一步提出"探索建立全国性的自贸试验区仲裁法律服务联盟和亚太仲裁机构交流合作机制,加快打造面向全球的亚太仲裁中心"的目标。在此背景下,我国《仲裁法》进入修订程序,国内涉外仲裁机构为提升仲裁服务水平投入巨大的成本进行路径探索。本文回顾和借鉴当前世界仲裁服务业处于领先地位的几个国家、地区或机构的发展历程,提出国际仲裁中心是形成的,而非建成的观点,在此基础上,进一步探讨中国进军国际仲裁中心的时代机遇及策略方向。

关键词:国际仲裁中心;形成;建成

伦敦大学玛丽皇后学院联合其合作伙伴发布的《2021年国际仲裁调查报告》(2021 International Arbitration Survey: Adapting Arbitration to a Changing World)[①],是其发布的第十二版年度报告,一经发布,便迅速引发

---

* 本文完成于2022年2月。
** 司玉琢,大连海事大学原校长,法学院教授。
*** 王伟,大连海事大学法学院博士研究生,上海汉盛律师事务所合伙人。
① See 2021 International Arbitration Survey: Adapting Arbitration to a Changing World, accessed December 13, 2021, http://www.arbitration.qmul.ac.uk/research/2021-international-arbitration-survey/.

业内高度关注与热议,成为业内人士判断国际仲裁市场发展水平与竞争力的重要依据。调查报告显示,通过国际仲裁方式解决跨境经济纠纷的受访者支持度,从2006年度的73%增长至2021年度的90%,可以看出近十余年国际仲裁服务的迅速发展,尤其是2018年度,优选国际仲裁解决跨境争议的支持度更是达到了97%。伴随国际仲裁服务行业的繁荣与发展,其所能起到的助力外贸航运经济建设、提升国际影响力、创造商业价值等叠加效应引人注目。大力发展国际仲裁服务,打造国际仲裁中心或区域国际仲裁中心,成为包括中国在内的诸多国家与地区的追求目标与前行方向。

影响国际仲裁中心地位的优势因素中,除硬件条件外,其决定性因素是仲裁软实力。硬件可以建成,而软实力则需要依靠培育、发展和积累,经过漫长的积淀过程,逐步形成。所以,打造国际仲裁中心或区域国际仲裁中心,必定是一个仲裁软实力的形成过程,是国际社会认可的过程,这一过程是被动的、无形的,没有明确的时间节点。即使广义的"建设"①可以包括硬件建设和软实力建设,也只是实现中心地位的措施手段,并不改变仲裁中心是形成的特质。

一、国际仲裁中心是仲裁服务软实力动态竞争后形成的市场格局

国际仲裁中心,从其表面字义理解,可以指向某一个仲裁机构,也可以指向某一个提供优质仲裁服务的区域,可以是一个国家,也可以是一个城市或地区。从政策指引层面所谈论的国际仲裁中心,自然是以其宏观含义为研究对象,即提供优质仲裁服务的区域。根据中国社科院国际法研究所的研究,以一定区域为基础,以仲裁机构为引擎,聚合其他上下游法律服务机构或组织,为境内外市场主体预防和解决纠纷提供仲裁及相关法律服务的具有国际公信力的优质生态圈,是国际仲裁中心的核心要义。具体而言,国际仲裁中心的软实力应具备完善的仲裁法律制度,良好的仲裁环境,专业的仲裁从业人才,谙熟仲裁制度的法官、律师群体,高效

---

① 本文其他部分内容中所出现的"建设"应理解为广义的"建设"。

的办事效率以及成熟的仲裁员培训体系。①

"国际仲裁",顾名思义,一方面,意味着打开大门,面向国际市场提供仲裁服务;另一方面,也意味着所提供的仲裁服务应该是具有国际性格局与视野的,符合国际市场公共预期的一种产品,而非镌刻某一个国家或地区的法律规则与规范烙印。

不同于依托一国司法权的法院管辖,仲裁市场具有自愿性、开放性与可供选择性的特点,不仅存在诸多仲裁服务提供主体,也存在差异化的仲裁制度、仲裁程序与仲裁方式等,故必然存在竞争。与我国国内仲裁服务市场几乎处于地区分割的不竞争状态②不同,国际仲裁中心的打造自然需要面向国际市场,以海事仲裁为例,海事纠纷往往具有很强的国际性,海事仲裁服务在全球范围内面临的竞争更为激烈。

所以,国际仲裁中心的核心要义是在国际同行业软实力竞争中,具有话语权和主导地位,广受当事人选择与认可。因而,"中心"地位的确立既不是金钱的堆积,更不是自诩自封,实则是一系列仲裁服务市场动态竞争后形成的市场格局,它需要时间的沉淀与市场的检验,是在国际范围内逐渐被认可的过程。

二、现代国际商事仲裁发源于专业人士的自发性创造

作为与诉讼并行的解决民商事纠纷的争端解决方式,仲裁发端于古希腊和古罗马时代,发展于欧洲的中世纪,而且早于诉讼的诞生,具有非常悠久的历史。③ 仲裁不是国家公权力或者法学家的发明创造,而是源自人们解决生活中的争议需求而自发形成的一种定分止争的方式。所

---

① 新加坡国际仲裁专家黄锡义(Miachel Huang)提出国际仲裁中心应具备的七项条件标准:完善的仲裁法律制度、谙熟仲裁制度的法官群体、优秀的仲裁机构、强大的仲裁从业者队伍、成熟的仲裁员培训体系、友好的仲裁环境,以及便利的地理区位。转引自赵健在"第六届东湖国际法律论坛"的发言"加快国际仲裁中心建设,推动构建公正、合理、透明的国际贸易规则体系"。

② 参见 张圣翠:《我国仲裁市场竞争法律制度的困境与突破》,载《政治与法律》2015年第7期。

③ 参见陈忠谦:《仲裁的起源、发展及展望》,载广州仲裁委员会主办:《仲裁研究》(第九辑),法律出版社2006年版。

以,最初的仲裁形式是临时仲裁,在中世纪的欧洲非常盛行。现代国际商事仲裁制度起源于英国,英国在1698年颁布了世界上第一部《仲裁法》,这部仲裁法案因为由约翰·洛克(John Locke)先生独立起草,故也被称为"洛克法"(Locke Act)。[1] 而且,国际商事仲裁在很长的一段时间里主要甚至只是用来解决海商贸易或海事领域的纠纷。[2] 英国伦敦是目前国际社会公认的国际海事仲裁中心,海事仲裁服务在伦敦的形成与发展也体现了民间专业人士的自发性创造与形成,而非政府或专业机构刻意建设的特征。

作为世界航运业和航运服务业的早期开拓者,英国抢占先机掌握了相关领域规则的制定权和话语权,这在较大程度上成就了今天英国在诸多海运相关领域的领先地位,包括海事仲裁服务领域。谈及伦敦海事仲裁的历史一定绕不开成立于18世纪中叶,至今其发布的航运指数仍在世界航运市场占据重要地位的波罗的海交易所(Baltic Exchange)。波罗的海交易所成立后,非常迅速地发展成为租船订舱市场的世界中心,至少到20世纪末期,世界上绝大多数的租约基本上都在波罗的海交易所完成[3],伦敦由此出现了一大批经验丰富、业务能力优秀的船舶经纪人,他们将公正作为船舶经纪业务的核心品质进行经营。大量租约订立之后,难免会出现履约争议,起初一般都是由双方当事人的船舶经纪人进行协商,然后达成一致的解决意见,如果两位经纪人不能达成合意,则他们会共同寻找更有经验的经纪人定夺,从而解决纠纷,这便是海事临时仲裁的雏形。后来,波罗的海交易所便把愿意从事仲裁员工作的经纪人名单张贴于布告栏中,供有争议的当事方选择,便形成了著名的波罗的海名单(Baltic List)。1960年2月12日,波罗的海名单上的仲裁员决定自主成立伦敦海事仲裁员协会(London Maritime Arbitration Association, LMAA),专业

---

[1] See Brekoulakis, *The 2019 Roebuck Lecture: The Unwavering Policy Favouring Arbitration Under English Law*, 86 Arb. 97, 99–100 (2020) (1698 English Arbitration Act was "first Arbitrations statute in the world"; Act was drafted "single-handedly" by John Locke).

[2] 参见杨良宜先生于2021年在"2021海上丝绸之路国际法律服务论坛"上的发言"国际商事仲裁/调解发展下的挑战与应对"。

[3] See Bruce Harris, "London Maritime Arbitration, an address to an International Maritime Arbitration Seminar organized by the Shanghai Sub-Commission of the China Maritime Arbitration Commission in Shanghai," June 23, 2010.

从事海事仲裁纠纷解决工作。自此,伦敦海事仲裁中心的形成完成了从无意识地自发形成,到有意识、有计划地推动中心发展的角色转变;从随机提供解决纠纷的基础仲裁服务,逐渐发展成为真正的国际海事仲裁中心。其走过的逾 300 年的仲裁发展历史①,深刻地影响和引导了后续其他国际仲裁中心的形成和发展。

三、现代国际商事仲裁中心地位的确立是仲裁软实力培育发展的结果

当今,国际社会公认的国际仲裁中心主要有伦敦、斯德哥尔摩、新加坡和我国香港特别行政区(以下简称香港特区)等。衡量国际仲裁服务竞争力水平的直观判断标准,首先是仲裁案件的受理数量,其次是受理案件总量与涉外案件的案源比例。

从各地具有代表性的仲裁机构或委员会所公布的 2020 年仲裁年报和数据上看,伦敦作为国际海事仲裁中心,LMAA 的仲裁员接受海事仲裁指认 3010 次,出具裁决书 523 份②;而且,LMAA 全年受案量的统计数据,仅包括人数相对较少的全职仲裁员(full member)③和准全职仲裁员(aspiring full member)④以及部分大律师(barristers)⑤,并不包括 LMAA 协会中数量庞大的支持仲裁员(supporting member)的海事仲裁受理情况,支持仲裁员同样为 LMAA 在全球贡献庞大的案件受理量和卓越的仲裁影响力;同时,LMAA 还有一个显著特点,即仅处理海事仲裁案件且涉外的国际性案件占比非常高,超过 90%;伦敦国际仲裁院(London Court of International Arbitration,LCIA)的全年受案量为 440 件,其中运输贸易方面的

---

① 参见 https://lmaa.london/history/,访问日期:2021 年 11 月 24 日。
② 参见 https://lmaa.london/wp-content/uploads/2021/02/Statistics-2020-For-Website.pdf,访问日期:2021 年 11 月 24 日。
③ 伦敦海事仲裁员协会现有全职仲裁员 36 人,参见 https://lmaa.london/arbitrators-full-members/,访问日期:2021 年 11 月 24 日。
④ 伦敦海事仲裁员协会现有准全职仲裁员 28 人,参见 https://lmaa.london/arbitrators-aspiring-full-members/,访问日期:2021 年 11 月 24 日。
⑤ 参见 https://lmaa.london/statistics-of-appointments-awards/,访问日期:2021 年 11 月 24 日。

案件大约占了22%,约100件,涉外案件占比86%。① 传统的斯德哥尔摩商事仲裁业务使得瑞典可称得上是欧洲的商事仲裁中心。根据斯德哥尔摩商会(Stockholm Chamber of Commerce,SCC)仲裁院所公布的受案数据统计,其2019年受理新案件175件,国际案件数量占比50%(88件),关涉44个国家和地区的当事人;2020年新登记案件213件,国际案件105件,占比接近50%,当事人分布于42个国家和地区②。这无疑体现了瑞典作为倍受国际商界青睐的投资争议解决地的优势地位。同时期的新加坡国际仲裁中心(Singapore International Arbitration Centre,SIAC)的全年受案量为1080件,国际案件占比达到了94%③,首次超过了国际商会(International Chamber of Commerce,ICC)仲裁院的受案量946起,这也是ICC仲裁院2016年度以来的受案新高④。我国香港国际仲裁中心(Hong Kong International Arbitration Centre,HKIAC)处理了483件新登记案件,约18.6%涉及海事纠纷,涉外案件占比72.3%。⑤

(一)伦敦国际海事仲裁中心

从船舶经纪人自发地协助客户定分止争,到伦敦发展成为国际公认的海事仲裁中心,其所具备的软实力优势因素非常典型,总结来看,主要包括以下几点:

第一,海事仲裁带动伦敦发展成为国际仲裁中心。英国作为一个历史悠久、曾拥有世界最庞大的殖民体系和海上运输舰队的海运强国,借助其历史及地理的优势,在几百年间逐步形成了一套成熟、完备、具有广泛国际影响力的海事仲裁制度。同时,英国的商法也是在海运和贸易实践基础上发展起来的,作为判例法国家,组成英国商法的重要判例大约有25%以上是源自航运或者与航运领域有关的案件纠纷,海事仲裁是推动

---

① 参见https://www.lcia.org/News/lcia-news-annual-casework-report-2020-and-changes-to-the-lcia-c.aspx,访问日期:2021年11月24日。
② 参见https://sccinstitute.com/statistics/,访问日期:2021年12月19日。
③ 参见https://siac.org.sg/2013-09-18-01-57-20/2013-09-22-00-27-02/annual-reports,访问日期:2021年11月24日。
④ 参见https://iccwbo.org/publication/icc-dispute-resolution-statistics-2020/,访问日期:2021年12月14日。
⑤ 参见https://www.hkiac.org/about-us/statistics,访问日期:2021年11月24日。

英国海商法发展的重要力量。① 伦敦每年基本上有 3000 次案件的仲裁裁决,占世界海事仲裁案件数量的 70%以上,其中 90%以上的案件属于国际性案件,具有涉外因素。② 2019 年,伦敦签发了全球 90%以上的海事仲裁裁决,在该领域的优势地位一骑绝尘。

第二,英国政府从法律和政策双层面大力支持发展国际仲裁服务。从法律层面,英国政府对仲裁的态度也经历了从抑制到支持的发展历程。英国作为世界上第一个颁布仲裁法的国家,早期对仲裁的发展带有敌意,认为仲裁侵占了国家的管辖权③,这在"Kill v. Hollister 案"④中得到了集中的体现。法院在保险单中存在有效仲裁协议的情况下支持了原告启动诉讼程序的请求,理由是"当事人的协议不能排除法院管辖"。直至 19 世纪中期的"Scott v. Avery 案"⑤,法院为仲裁正名,改变了"Kill v. Hollister 案"的先例地位,认为采用仲裁替代法院诉讼,并不违反公共政策(public policy)。此后的 1889 年、1950 年以及 1979 年《仲裁法》,呈现出逐步减少法院干涉仲裁程序的变化,直至 1996 年《仲裁法》,更是通过立法,赋予仲裁员作出中间措施(interim measures)的权利,同时确立了仲裁当事人意思自治、兼顾效益与公正,以及有限的法院干预几项一般原则(general principles),为伦敦海事仲裁的发展提供了有利的法律环境和良好的保障。

在政策方面,英国政府也一直重视和支持在国际航运领域内推广海事仲裁。例如,英国政府代表团经常派出庞大的阵容参加联合国贸易和发展委员会、国际海商法协会、国际海事组织、联合国国际贸易和法律委员会等的会议,维护伦敦海事仲裁中心的利益;在波罗的海国际航运公会(The Baltic and International Maritime Council, BIMCO)、国际航运公会(International Chamber of Shipping, ICS)、船舶经纪人和代理商国家协会联盟

---

① 参见杨良宜先生在 2021 年"第四届广州海法论坛"上的录播发言"国际海事仲裁实务问题"。
② See Petros N. Tassios, "Choosing the Appropriate Venue: Maritime Arbitration in London or New York?", Journal of International Arbitration, pp. 355-365.
③ See Gary B. Born, International Commercial Arbitration (Third Edition) (Kluwer Law International 2021) pp. 7-250.
④ See Kill v. Hollister [1746] 95 ER 532, 532 (English K. B.).
⑤ See Scott v. Avery [1856] 5 HL Cas 811, 853 (House of Lords).

(The Federation of National Associations of Ship Brokers and Agents, FONASBA)等国际航运组织起草标准文件时大力推荐伦敦仲裁条款。① 近年来,为捍卫伦敦的国际仲裁中心地位,英国也频繁采取排他性措施来维护其仲裁管辖权,包括英国法院针对域外诉讼程序签发禁诉令等,呈现出支持仲裁发展的新特点。

第三,航运产业链为伦敦海事仲裁带来了巨大的案源市场。从爱德华·劳埃德先生于1688年开始经营的咖啡馆,到归航船长的海外见闻沙龙每隔两周一次的有关国际贸易和航运的"劳埃德新闻",再到引领世界的第一部海上保险法——1906年《英国保险法》,以及今日的劳氏日报(Lloyd's List)②、劳氏船级社(Lloyd's Register)③、劳氏保险社(Lloyd's)、船东互保协会(the P&I Clubs)等,经过百余年的实践与积淀,铸就了英国伦敦海上保险中心、航运中心的地位。这些高端航运产业所呈现的规模化、体系化使得英国航运产业和参与者之间紧密联系,成为一个整体。悠久的航运历史所积累的产业优势,一方面使得英国海事仲裁坐拥大量的市场和客户资源,为英国海事仲裁业提供了巨大的市场源动力;另一方面,也使得英国对航运规则的制定与解释具有强大的话语权,航运市场上采用国际组织所制定的标准合同条款已成为常态。而基于百年仲裁实务所占得的先机以及对英国航运商法的信任,当事人一般将默认选择伦敦作为仲裁地的标准条款视为惯例或常规操作,为伦敦形成国际海事仲裁中心起到了关键性的助推作用。

第四,临时仲裁的灵活性和高水平专业人才,是伦敦海事仲裁保持领先优势的核心要素。当事人选择诉诸仲裁解决争端,并不仅是考虑依据固定的程序完成一个争端解决流程,更为需要的是在程序中运用各种法律和商业策略来达到维护其权益最大化的目标。临时仲裁所具有的程序灵活性和对当事人意思自治的保护,是伦敦海事仲裁维持中心地位的重要原因。多年来,LMAA的仲裁规则不断地根据市场的实际需求进行修正,并推出新的程序创新,如先后推出的调解规则、小额索赔程序规则等

---

① 参见蔡鸿达:《中国海事仲裁发展有关问题的探讨》,载《中国仲裁咨询》2005年第1期。
② 最早的海运相关出版物,于1734年在伦敦刊行,早期每周一期,现在每天一期。
③ 劳氏船级社,成立于1760年,世界第一家船舶入级及检验机构。

都对促进争议的快捷、经济解决起到了良好的效果,在航运市场中很受欢迎。同时,临时仲裁从仲裁开始、程序推进、费用收取等各个方面均体现了当事人的意思自治,而这种意思自治也使得当事人对于仲裁程序有力掌控,便于富有经验的当事人在仲裁中制定和实施灵活的策略以达到目标诉求。这也是在仲裁机构遍布全球的情况下,临时仲裁依然为国际仲裁领域所继承和发展的主要原因。从人才储备而言,伦敦的优势在于产业人才生态化。伦敦主要处理海事仲裁的仲裁员早已不局限于波罗的海交易所的经纪人,而是包括了来自各个航运相关产业的专业人士,仲裁员来源的多样性使得各种类型的纠纷都可以得到很好的解决,为伦敦海事仲裁赢得了良好的声誉,而且丰富的海事仲裁案例进一步为伦敦培养了更多高水平的专业人才,形成人才聚集效应,进一步支撑了伦敦的海事仲裁中心地位。LMAA 对专职会员(full member)的严格要求与管理,一方面使协会赢得了国际社会的信任,另一方面也在一定程度上限制了 LMAA 仲裁员的规模发展,毕竟拥有至少 15 年从事商事或法律工作实践经验,且是英国公民等硬性限制较难满足;但 LMAA 创新设置的准全职仲裁员(aspiring full member)①和"支持会员"(supporting member)机制,满足了 LMAA 对专职会员的梯队化培育需求,同时,因其不限制支持会员的所在地,吸引了世界各地诸多优秀的专业人士申请加入 LMAA,也反向吸引了更多的非英语类国家纠纷当事人选择伦敦仲裁,对扩大 LMAA 的全球影响力具有重要作用。

  第五,完备的海事仲裁配套服务提升了英国海事仲裁的服务品质。应仲裁当事方需求,位于伦敦的国际争议解决中心(the International Dispute Resolution Centre Limited, IDRC)可以为当事人提供优质的仲裁配套服务,包括高效便利的开庭场地、设备以及翻译、速录服务等,临时仲裁的灵活性和实用性在配套服务中也得到了很好的体现。"海事仲裁的配套服务是造就伦敦国际海事仲裁中心的一个重要因素"②。然而,随着互联

---

① 伦敦海事仲裁员协会现有准全职仲裁员 28 人,参见 https://lmaa.london/arbitrators-aspiring-full-members/,访问日期:2021 年 11 月 24 日。
② 参见 Kenneth Rokison QC 在 2008 年"航运、保险、贸易和海上安全论坛"的发言 "What makes a good arbitration",载 http://www.shippinglbc.com/content/uploads/members_documents/what%20makes%20a%20good%20arbitration_16_01-2008_full.pdf.,访问日期:2015 年 11 月 28 日。

网、大数据、人工智能等科学技术的发展,尤其是受新冠肺炎疫情影响,仲裁开庭的需求和必要性越来越小,开庭场所等硬件配套服务的功能也极大地弱化,以 LMAA 为例,2020 年所受理的 3010 起案件中,经由开庭作出最终裁决的数据是零。① 远程开庭、电子送达等拥抱现代化科技的替代方案更能满足当事方的经济与快捷需求,根据《2021 年国际仲裁调查报告》,在现场开庭与个人的时间安排出现冲突的情况下,80%的被调查方表示更愿意接受以远程开庭的方式替换现场开庭。②

(二)斯德哥尔摩国际商事仲裁中心

瑞典是继英国之后,世界上第二个制定仲裁法的国家。③ 不同于伦敦以海事仲裁为主,瑞典仲裁的特点是处理国际投资争端更为见长,其繁荣和发展更为倚重国家层面的支持。成立于1917年的SCC 仲裁院在20世纪70年代为美国和苏联所承认,成为中立的东西方贸易争端解决中心,我国也于同一时期承认 SCC 仲裁院为解决国际争端的机构。此后,SCC 仲裁院不断扩展其在国际商事仲裁领域的服务,从而成为国际上最重要的、经常被选用的仲裁院之一。据统计,目前至少有 120 份双边投资协定(Bilateral Investment Treaty,BIT)选择瑞典或 SCC 仲裁院作为解决投资者与东道国间争议的机构,SCC 仲裁院已经成长为全球第二大投资争议解决机构。④

同时,斯德哥尔摩发展成为商事仲裁中心也具有其独特的软实力优势。首先,瑞典政府对外奉行的永久中立原则以及对内秉承的有限政府施政原则,为瑞典营造了清廉、稳定、健康的政治环境和国家氛围,同时也为瑞典仲裁的中立和公正形象进行了强有力的背书,是国外当事人放心将争议交于其仲裁解决的首要因素。其次,瑞典拥有完善的培训交流机制以保证仲裁服务业良性发展。瑞典除定期举办大型论坛活动之外,还以学位教育、集中授课与小范围业余学习活动相结合的方式,形成低成

---

① 参见 https://lmaa.london/wp-content/uploads/2021/02/Statistics-2020-For-Website.pdf,访问日期:2021 年 11 月 24 日。
② 参见 http://www.arbitration.qmul.ac.uk/research/2021-international-arbitration-survey/,访问日期:2022 年 1 月 23 日。
③ 瑞典仲裁法颁布于1887年,参见陈忠谦:《仲裁的起源、发展及展望》,载广州仲裁委员会主办:《仲裁研究》(第 9 辑),法律出版社 2006 年版,第 45 页。
④ 参见 https://sccinstitute.com/about-the-scc/,访问日期:2021 年 12 月 19 日。

本、多维度、个性化的仲裁员长效交流培训体制。这既有利于仲裁员不断提高自身业务水平,也为仲裁员之间的交流提供了良好的平台,更对提高仲裁员和仲裁服务业的社会声望起到了良好的宣传效果。最后,实用至上的立法理念是仲裁服务业得以推广的内因。瑞典法律以分散的成文法和判例相结合,其内在的法律基本原则兼容两大法系,有法学家评价瑞典法律足以担当起"联结英美法与大陆法的桥梁"的重任。[①] 瑞典的法律条文均倾向于简洁直接,对不同法系、不同文化背景的外国当事人高效率领会瑞典法律的基本精神和价值取向非常有利,提高了国际仲裁市场对瑞典仲裁的信任度和接受度。

(三)中国香港特区及新加坡——立足亚洲的国际仲裁中心

除了欧洲的伦敦和斯德哥尔摩,同为后起之秀的中国香港特区和新加坡,在亚洲商事海事仲裁领域的仲裁中心地位同样不可忽视。二者从历史和现实的视角,同样符合从专业人士自发组建到政府支持发展的中心形成路径,而且促使二者发展成为仲裁中心的软实力优势因素有诸多相似之处:

首先,在政府支持上,两地政府均一直给予包括海事仲裁在内的仲裁行业提供多方面的支持。就中国香港特区而言,香港特区律政司一直将加强和推广香港特区作为亚太区国际法律和争议解决服务中心作为一项首要工作,我国中央政府也大力支持香港特区仲裁服务事业,前有《最高人民法院关于内地与香港特别行政区法院就仲裁程序相互协助保全的安排》(以下简称《两地保全安排》),通过协助保全支持两地仲裁发展;今有《中华人民共和国国民经济和社会发展第十四个五年规划和 2035 年远景目标纲要》,将支持香港特区建设亚太区国际法律及解决争议服务中心列入规划与目标。而且,中国将同亚非法律协商组织(Asian-African Legal Consultative Organization, AALCO)在香港特区设立区域仲裁中心,坚持"一国两制",维护香港特区稳定,为亚非国家提供更加便捷高效的争端解

[①] 参见[瑞典]斯梯克·斯特罗霍姆:《瑞典的法律制度》,董立坤译,载《国外法学》1987 年第 3 期。

决服务①。新加坡政府给新加坡仲裁服务业的支持同样可圈可点。纵观新加坡主要的仲裁组织发展的历史,从麦士威法事厅(Maxwell Chambers)到SIAC,再从新加坡海事基金会(Singapore Maritime Foundation,SMF)到新加坡海事仲裁院(Singapore Chamber of Maritime Arbitration,SCMA),所有的这些支持和促进仲裁发展的组织机构在成立之初均得到了新加坡政府的大力支持。新加坡政府意识到了法律服务业可能为社会创造的巨大经济和社会价值,不仅为这些机构的成立提供必要的种子基金,同时,也在政策上大力扶持仲裁服务业的发展,不断提升"法律服务业"作为产业集群的优势地位。例如,自2012年起对在新加坡开展的仲裁服务减免高达50%的税费,同时为在新加坡国内从事国际仲裁的法律职业者的法律收入提供税收免除政策,这些举措极大地提升了新加坡法律服务业的国际竞争优势。

其次,中国香港特区和新加坡都为仲裁的发展提供了宽松和鼓励性的司法环境。中国香港特区一直采用普通法体系,由中立、专业、高效的法官组成独立的司法系统。中国香港特区法院高度支持仲裁,对仲裁采取"不干预"的态度。新加坡法院在对待仲裁程序以及仲裁裁决也长期秉持司法谦抑主义(judicial deference)和尊重当事人意思自治(party autonomy)的原则,赋予仲裁庭较为广泛的权限。

再次,中国香港特区有着深厚的仲裁文化,成就了大量的国际化律师。国际化律师懂得国际习惯,知晓中国国情,有能力和水平为当事人提供符合其需求的法律服务,这是中国香港特区持续保持国际仲裁中心地位的重要优势。新加坡在2012年后也实施了更大力度的人才引进开放措施,促进本土律师事务所与外资律师事务所密切合作,同时启动了外国职业律师考试(Foreign Practitioner Examination,FPE),以满足新加坡蓬勃发展的商业和经济对涉外法律人才的需求。②

最后,中国香港特区和新加坡得天独厚的地理位置造就了两地繁荣的航运产业和国际性文化,为仲裁中心建设提供了有利的自然条件。同

---

① 参见http://www.takungpao.com/news/232109/2021/1130/660278.html,访问日期:2022年1月24日。

② 参见https://www.contactsingapore.sg/cn/job-seekers/key-industries/legal-services/,访问日期:2015年12月3日。

为世界航运中心,发达的航运经济为商事与海事仲裁在中国香港特区和新加坡的蓬勃发展创造了行业基础。多元文化使得两地更加开放,面对各国或地区人士时展示了更加包容和开放的态度,国际性让世界不同国家或地区的当事人对两地作为国际仲裁中心保有信心。

比较分析以上样本可知,国际仲裁中心的形成,是仲裁软实力竞争的结果,它受制于经济、政治、文化、法律成熟度等综合因素。商事仲裁始于专业人士的自发性创造,地区的经济发展水平、地域便利条件、国际性文化属性以及开放程度、专业人才储备、仲裁机构的治理结构等因素是提升仲裁服务国际竞争软实力的内驱力,同时,仲裁市场的持久发展也离不开政府的政策倾向与法律制度的保护支持,这种支持应平衡好外力和内力的关系,旨在从根本上建设和培养仲裁可持续发展所应该具备的优势因素。

四、中国特色国际仲裁中心形成之时代机遇

对我国而言,当前是提升国际仲裁服务竞争力、建设有中国特色的国际仲裁中心的最好时机:

第一,在经济上,在推进"一带一路"建设,实施海洋强国的战略部署过程中,我国的航运和对外贸易经济取得了长足发展。《2021 新华·波罗的海国际航运中心发展指数报告》显示,全球航运中心城市综合实力前十强中有一半位于亚洲,我国占了三席:上海依旧保持全球第三的优势,香港特区紧随其后,尤其值得关注的是,连续 12 年保持着全球货物吞吐量之最的宁波舟山,首次跻身前十,成为中国港航的另一股"硬核"力量。① 广州、青岛同样不容忽视,二者分别位于第二梯队的第 13 位和第 15 位②,发展态势良好。世界经济重心和国际航运中心"东移"的趋势日益清晰,为我国建设国际仲裁中心创造了经济依托。

第二,在法治环境与政策层面上,国务院推出多项鼓励政策与举措将

---

① 参见 https://www.cs.com.cn/xwzx/hg/202107/t20210712_6182913.html,访问日期:2022 年 2 月 3 日。

② 参见 https://baijiahao.baidu.com/s?id=1672003476206344617&wfr=spider&for=pc,访问日期:2021 年 12 月 14 日。

发展海事仲裁等现代航运服务业作为重点任务部署①,号召"完善仲裁制度,提高仲裁公信力"②。习近平总书记在2019年2月25日召开的中央全面依法治国委员会第二次会议上,深刻阐述了"法治是最好的营商环境"这一重要论断,推进法治化、国际化营商环境,是提升中国仲裁的国际竞争力,助推国际商事海事仲裁中心形成的重要举措。

第三,在立法上,我国已启动修改完善《仲裁法》,为中国仲裁高质量发展提供法律支持。当前也是对中国仲裁立法进行全面审核与思考的良好机遇,从目前公布的征求意见稿看,我国的仲裁修法已经迈出了坚实步伐,从根本上抛弃旧制度,与国际先进经验接轨。此外,最高人民法院先后发布了30余项与仲裁相关的司法解释和规范性文件,指导和监督全国法院依法履行仲裁司法审查职能,支持仲裁的健康有序发展。

第四,在行业意识上,随着中国司法改革步伐的推进和国际仲裁市场的繁荣发展,发展仲裁助力中国司法改革、服务国家参与全球治理的发展战略,已成为政府和行业的共识。北京、上海、深圳的主要仲裁机构与行业主体,秉承开放包容、兼收并蓄的精神,积极探索与推进区域国际仲裁中心建设;同时,上海、大连、厦门、南昌等地的仲裁委员会已启动仲裁机构体制机制改革,推动仲裁机构建适应法治化、市场化要求的体制机制。全国各地呈现出以多元、互鉴的思维探索交流,为中国仲裁的发展与建设献言献策的喜人形势。同时,中国的仲裁发展也得到了国际社会的关注,《2021年国际仲裁调查报告》指出,除了中国香港特区和新加坡,更多的受调查者,超过以往任何一次调查,反馈曾指定北京、上海、深圳作为仲裁地。

第五,在人才培养上,随着国际航运和贸易经济的繁荣发展,中国内地的市场参与主体实际参与国际仲裁的经历越来越多,中国内地企业是伦敦、新加坡和香港特区仲裁机构的主要客户群体。一方面,增强了中国内地企业的法律意识,树立了中国内地企业积极解决经济纠纷的依法守法形象;另一方面,也锻炼培养了一批参与国际仲裁业务的仲裁员、律师等专业人才,为中国国际仲裁中心建设提供了基础人才储备力量。

---

① 参见2014年8月发布的《国务院关于促进海运业健康发展的若干意见》。
② 参见 https://baijiahao.baidu.com/s? id = 1630964476519404639&wfr = spider&for = pc,访问日期2021年12月13日。

五、中国特色国际仲裁中心形成之策略方向

在我国建设面向世界的国际仲裁中心的进程中,除了硬件建设,更重要的是推进影响仲裁服务可持续性发展的软实力建设,包括法律制度先进化、仲裁程序国际化、法律人才专业化、仲裁服务便捷化。当然,最核心的当属仲裁结果的公正与科学性,这是仲裁服务的根本价值之所在。据此,提升我国仲裁服务国际竞争力应重视以下几个方面:

(一)以发展海事仲裁为龙头,牵引推动国际仲裁中心的形成

国际性是国际仲裁中心的突出特征之一,也是建设国际仲裁中心的内在需求。因此,以国际化程度较高的产业做牵引对国际仲裁中心的形成有促进作用。海事领域的跨境性特点使得海事仲裁服务具有明显的国际性,海事仲裁在服务主体、消费群体、争议事实等方面具有广泛的国际性;虽然在国际竞争的视角下,我国海事仲裁的竞争力尚难适应我国作为航运大国的需要,但是,我国海事仲裁的国际竞争力,目前展现了良好的发展势头。除了香港特区,北京、上海也是我国海事仲裁服务的主要市场,中国海事仲裁委员 2020 年度受案量为 111 件,涉外案件占比 35%[①],上海受理的海事仲裁案件数量为 342 件,总争议标的达 27.79 亿元[②]。同时,我国的海商立法和司法也具有国际性和先进性水平,而且我国的《海商法》正在修改,进一步与国际接轨。这不仅能够更好地促进航运经济发展,助力我国的航运强国建设,而且为进一步提升我国海事仲裁服务的发展提供了先进的法律制度保证。因此,中国建设国际仲裁中心,应该以海事仲裁为龙头,提升我国海事仲裁服务的发展水平和竞争力是关系我国海运业健康发展和国际仲裁中心建设的重要命题。

(二)"引进来""走出去",为国际仲裁服务提供更多中国方案

基于目前我国海事仲裁服务的竞争力现状和发展需求,比较研究当

---

① 参见 http://www.cmac.org.cn/index.php?id=75,访问日期:2021 年 11 月 24 日。
② 参见 https://finance.eastmoney.com/a/202201102241737069.html,访问日期:2022 年 1 月 12 日。

前世界及亚太地区海事仲裁竞争力领先国家(地区或机构)的经验,进而总结有助于增强我国海事仲裁竞争力的要素和措施,是促进我国海事仲裁发展的捷径。在学习借鉴的同时,更应该注意完善并推广具有中国特色的仲裁制度或程序机制,例如,我国的司法调解制度积极影响和推动了国际社会替代性纠纷解决机制中的调解制度的形成等。采取引进来和走出去相结合,积极参与国际经贸规则和标准的制定,提升话语权,增强影响力,力争为国际仲裁服务注入更多中国智慧,提供更多中国方案。

(三)《仲裁法》修改中应思考革新立法理念

《仲裁法》修改内容的重点应该是解决在没有仲裁规则规定或缺乏当事人约定的情况下,仲裁程序如何进行的问题。可以由当事人约定或仲裁规则规定或者授权仲裁庭决定的情况,则不宜细致地写入法律规范,且仲裁程序方面的问题,除了临时仲裁,立法应该以规定原则性问题为主。所以,中国《仲裁法》的修改重点应该是仲裁协议效力的审查、仲裁庭组成以及组成前的程序问题、仲裁和司法的关系等。从立法表现上看,《仲裁法》的修订条款内容过于微观的话,必然无法穷尽,反而会显得法律条文或浅尝辄止,或顾此失彼。比如,《仲裁法(修订)(征求意见稿)》中,规定仲裁庭可由一名或三名仲裁员组成,但是没有说明在仲裁协议中没有约定的情形下由几名仲裁员组成,而需要法律调整的重点恰恰是后者。关于这个问题,英国仲裁法和我国香港特区的仲裁条例均有明确规定,前者设定默示仲裁庭为独任仲裁员,后者指定仲裁机构,即HKIAC,根据当事人的申请决定仲裁庭组成人数。否则,在启动仲裁程序之时,会因为仲裁庭组成问题缺乏明确的法律依据而导致当事人花费大量时间和费用予以解决,不利于仲裁便捷效益价值的实现。

(四)将培养仲裁业国际性专业化人才作为根本,徐徐图之

一方面,联合高校,建立专门化仲裁人才培养模式,全方位培养掌握普通法思维和国际商业游戏规则的国际化、专业化仲裁产业从业人员,不仅包括具有国际视野、专业学识的仲裁员、律师或法律顾问,也包括仲裁服务的必要参与方,如仲裁秘书、庭审速录员等人员。2022年8月,教育部、司法部联合印发《关于实施法律硕士专业学位(国际仲裁)研究生培

养项目的通知》,明确在全国范围内选取20所高校①会同仲裁委员会、律师事务所等涉外仲裁实务单位,实施法律硕士专业学位(国际仲裁)研究生培养项目。教育部、司法部实施法律硕士专业学位(国际仲裁)研究生培养项目,旨在支持有关高校和法律实务部门积极探索和创新涉外法治高层次人才培养模式,完善涉外仲裁人才培养体系,力争培养一批法学功底扎实、具有国际视野、通晓国际仲裁法律制度的高层次应用型涉外仲裁人才。本项目2023年至2025年招生计划,合计招收培养不少于1000人。专门化培养模式不仅可以注重提高学生的专业知识储备,而且可以更注重开拓学生以国际性视野和思维看待和思考问题,从文化层面更深地融入国际市场。

另一方面,就当前国际仲裁中心人才建设而言,应采取开放仲裁服务市场、吸纳世界各国或地区各专业的顶级仲裁员的方式承上启下。仲裁员作为仲裁活动最为核心的要素之一,对于仲裁的竞争力影响至关重要,无论从案件的解决质量还是对发展仲裁的宣传力度看,仲裁员数量的多寡和分布是否广泛对特定国家(地区或机构)仲裁服务的竞争力都有显著影响。LMAA通过设置支持会员的方式吸引世界各地优秀的专业人士担任仲裁员;ICC国际仲裁院不设仲裁员名册,也不限制当事人选择仲裁员的范围。当需要由仲裁院指定仲裁员时,则会由分布在全球70多个国家和地区的国际商会国家委员会(ICC National Committee)推荐仲裁人选。文化背景多元化的仲裁员队伍赋予了当事人更多选任仲裁员的自由,增强了其对仲裁的信心,同时也扩大了仲裁在相应国家和地区的影响力,更有利于开拓市场业务。

(五)加强内地与香港特区仲裁的协同合作,共建"亚太国际法律及争议服务中心"

目前世界上主要的国际仲裁中心皆为普通法法域,而香港特区有150年的普通法经验和传统,也有相当数量的普通法人才,而且,香港特区在

---

① 20所院校是:北京大学、清华大学、中国人民大学、中国政法大学、对外经济贸易大学、复旦大学、华东政法大学、上海政法学院、武汉大学、中南财经政法大学、西南政法大学、中山大学、广东外语外贸大学、深圳大学、厦门大学、西安交通大学、西北政法大学、大连海事大学、吉林大学、黑龙江大学。

国际仲裁领域所取得的成绩有目共睹,位列全球最受欢迎仲裁地第三位,也是继伦敦、纽约、新加坡后第四个被 BIMCO 指定的仲裁地。① 作为亚洲长期以来的航运中心之一,香港特区的海事仲裁服务业在国际上亦具有广泛的影响。内地与香港特区联手,可以进行资源共享和优势互补,打造中国特色的区域国际仲裁中心,兼具大陆法和普通法的优势。可以引进香港特区人才资源,助力内地培育熟悉普通法和国际仲裁规则的人才,加强仲裁机构、仲裁员、律师等专业人才的交流与合作,协同合作共建"亚太国际法律及争议服务中心"。

结　　语

伦敦等国际仲裁中心的发展历程启示我们,任何纠纷解决中心都不是建成的,而是形成的。硬件可以建成,增加资金投入即可,软件则不然。仲裁服务的价值本质是高效公正地解决纠纷,这一价值的实现靠的是人才、法律、环境等一系列的软件的综合影响,这些软件需要靠长期的文化底蕴滋养,司法实务积淀,靠优良的法制环境和营商环境保障;服务、效率、观念、意识等软实力是无法靠金钱实现的。而想要成为人们心目中的国际仲裁中心,硬件不是核心,硬件不硬,软件硬,可以成为中心;硬件再硬,软件不硬,亦难成中心,只是徒留视觉辉煌,乏了基业传承。

建设国际仲裁中心,需要几代人的艰苦努力,需要携手潜心做好软实力建设的基础工作,"咬定青山,矢志不渝"地坚持,相信定能实现国际仲裁中心的战略目标。

---

① 参见 https://www.sohu.com/a/423040992_173888,访问日期:2021 年 12 月 14 日。

CHINA REVIEW OF MARITIME AND COMMERCIAL ARBITRATION (2021)

The Innovative Development
of China Maritime and Commercial Arbitration in the New Era

The Practice and Legal Issues of Concurrent Arbitration and Consolidated Arbitration from a London Arbitration

SONG Bin[*]　YANG Yuntao[**]

Abstract: This article takes a London arbitration the writer witnessed before as an example. Firstly, introduces the application of concurrent arbitration rules in practice, and analyses differences between concurrent arbitration and consolidated arbitration on the basis of their respective characteristics, various arbitration rules and laws, then studies basic position on these two arbitral proceedings under common law and their potential challenges in practice, and lastly provides some suggestions for the improvements of these two mechanisms in Chinese maritime arbitration rules.

Key words: concurrent arbitration; consolidated arbitration; multi-party dispute

It is well-known that arbitration, as a dispute resolution method, has conspicuous advantages such as privacy and enforceability. Compared with litigation, arbitration is more acceptable to the parties in international commercial field, either in concluding contracts beforehand or solving disputes afterwards.

---

[*] Deputy General Manager of Commercial Depe, Hong Kong Ming Wan Shipping Co., LtD.
[**] General Manager, Risk Management Dept, Legal Compliance Dept and Audit Dept, China Merchants Group Limited.

For a long time due to historical reasons, London Maritime Arbitrators Association (LMAA) has always been widely recognized in the shipping industry as the first choice to resolve maritime disputes. As indicated by the statistics of LMAA in 2020, despite the negative effect of COVID-19 pandemic, LMAA still accepted 3010 appointments in total to settle disputes throughout the year, it is reported that LMAA registered 1775 new cases and delivered 523 awards in total. LMAA took a leading position among arbitration associations all over the world in 2020 and the number of cases it handled that year has also been its highest since 2015.

In China, since the establishment in 1959, China Maritime Arbitration Commission (CMAC) has heard and awarded thousands of cases, of which foreign arbitrations accounted for up to 60%, involving 40 countries and regions such as China, the United Kingdom, Denmark, the United States, Singapore, Panama. The arbitrations cover numerous areas including freight forwarding, bill of lading, charter parties, ship collision, shipbuilding, crew service, ship repair, insurance, etc. The international credibility and influence of CMAC are growing day by day.

Under the current global background of information technology innovation, international commercial transactions are gradually expanding, which is accompanied by many changes in transaction patterns. Many commercial contracts have gradually broken through the traditional bilateral contract transactions, and multi-party contracts have become more and more frequent, especially in international trade, shipping and construction fields. As a result, the number of chain disputes and parallel disputes is increasing, leading to a rise in concurrent arbitration and consolidated arbitration in practice.

This article takes one London arbitration as an example and discusses the practice and legal issues in concurrent arbitrations and consolidated arbitrations.

The Practice and Legal Issues of Concurrent Arbitration and Consolidated··· 201

I . Brief Introduction of the Case

In 2007, shipowner Company A chartered a capesize vessel to Company B who then relet her to Company C, both under time charterparties. Later Company D chartered the vessel from Company C by a voyage charterparty, then relet to Company E mostly on back to back terms except for the applicable law and jurisdiction clauses, to carry 150000 tons of iron ores from Brazil to China. There were five parties in total in the charterparty chain. At the same time, Company E was the buyer and Company X was the seller under the contract of sale, whereas Company Y was a terminal subsidiary to Company X. (See Figure 1)

The vessel collided with the terminal in the process of berthing at Brazilian loading port Itaguai, causing the Terminal Y to claim for damages against Shipowner A for about 30 million dollars. Shipowner A provided security in Brazil, then it started to claim against Company B for compensation on the ground of unsafe berth based on time charterparty. A series of claims were then passed down along the charterparty chain, basically with the same issues of fact and law. This is a very typical and common scenario in charter party practice.

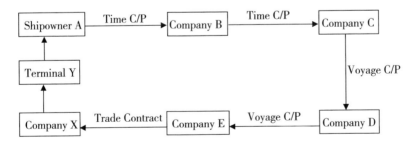

Figure 1 The Diagrammatic Sketch

The writer was representing Company D facing a claim from Company C at that time. In order to obtain security from D, Company C not only applied for Rule B attachment in USA, but also arrested one of D's self-owned ships, which seriously affected the normal operation of Company D.

It should have been a relatively simple back-to-back dispute for Company D, but owing to several factors, this case turned to be a complicated one. Due to jurisdiction and governing law clauses' non-back to back position, i.e. disputes with C was submitted to London arbitration and English law applied while disputes with E was to be resolved by Beijing arbitration under Chinese law. The inconsistency in jurisdiction and governing law created huge uncertainty in both arbitrations. In addition, Company E was also a strategic partner for Company D, in light of commercial relationship between parties, aggressive steps against E seemed to be impractical, so the burden of proof and defence mostly rested on Company D.

II. Handling of the Case

In this case, Company C entered into one time charter trip and one voyage charterparty up and down the chain. Considering Company C's contractual obligations under the charterparties may not be fully back-to-back, and Company D was also under great financial stresses arising from large amount of bank guarantee, in order to force Company C to join with D to defend the claim together, and relieve D's bank guarantee stress, we objected Company C's concurrent hearing application by reason of privacy. This refusal put C under great pressure and forced it to cooperate with us against shipowner's claims.

Afterwards by coincidence in another judgment handed down by English High Court it was held that the same berth in port Itaguai was unsafe, which obviously made huge adverse impact on Company D's position, in order that evidence and submissions can be directly used in other arbitrations up the charterparty chain, the parties eventually agreed that the arbitrations could be held concurrently.

In 2012, a mediation was held in London among all the parties. In the end, a settlement was reached successfully, under which every party shared the loss of the terminal together.

III. Concurrent Arbitration and Consolidated Arbitration

In above case, concurrent arbitration was discussed and argued adequately by parties, however, in practice, many people mistakenly regard concurrent arbitration as consolidated arbitration. Although these two arbitration models probably both involve multiple relevant contracts or parties, deal with common facts or legal issues, have claims arising out of the same transaction or series of transactions, there are still major differences between them. Under Chinese and English arbitration acts, there are few express provisions on the legal definitions of these two arbitrations models. They are more of common expressions used in academic and practical fields, to describe arbitrations which involve multi-contracts or multi-parties.

In accordance with common understanding, consolidated arbitration means to consolidate multiple arbitrations with relevant issues of fact or law into one single arbitration. It may result in the arbitral tribunal having right to issue a single award determining all the issues which have arisen between the different parties involved. Concurrent arbitration means the holding of concurrent hearings involves hearing the evidence and legal submissions arising in one arbitration at the same time as hearing the evidence and legal submissions in a different arbitration, one arbitral tribunal handles multiple arbitrations with relevant issues of fact or law concurrently, and deliver respective arbitral awards to each arbitration accordingly.[①] Such differences can be reflected from the words "consolidate" and "concurrent".

By reference to Oxford Dictionary, "consolidate" usually means "to join things together into one" while "concurrent" usually means "existing or happening at the same time". Although "concurrent" has meanings of "combine" and "consolidate" to some extent, it places more emphasis on "simultane-

---

① Chartered Institute of Arbitrators Practice Guideline 15: Guidelines for Arbitrators on how to approach issues relating to Multi-Party Arbitrations, 27 March 2019, pora. 2.2.

ous". In some Chinese articles, "concurrent arbitration" or "concurrent hearing" are translated directly into "consolidated arbitration" or "consolidated hearing", which is not accurate, strictly speaking.

The writer summarises down below the differences of global major arbitration associations or institutions describing and regulating these two arbitrations.

Taking several versions of LMAA Terms as examples, they do not have definitions of "consolidation" or "consolidated arbitration", but do mention some procedures of "concurrent arbitration".① For example:

Article 17 of LMAA Terms 2021: Powers of the Tribunal

(b) Where two or more arbitrations appear to raise common issues of fact or law, the tribunals may direct that they shall be conducted and, where an oral hearing is directed, heard **concurrently**. Where such an order is made, the tribunals may give such directions as the interests of fairness, economy and expedition require including:

(i) that time limits for service of submissions may be abbreviated or modified in the interests of saving costs or minimizing delay, or otherwise enhancing efficiency;

(ii) that the documents disclosed by the parties in one arbitration shall be made available to the parties to the other arbitration upon such conditions as the tribunals may determine;

(iii) that the evidence given in one arbitration shall be received and admitted in the other arbitration, subject to all parties being given a reasonable opportunity to comment upon it and subject to such other conditions as the tribunals may determine.

Obviously, concurrent hearing or concurrent arbitration refers to a situation where two or more arbitrations proceed at the same time, instead of consolidating them into one arbitration. A typical example of concurrent arbitration is the abovementioned charterparty chain dispute which is very common in ship

---

① The London Maritime Arbitrators Association (LMAA) Terms 2002, 2006, 2012 Article 14; The LMAA Terms 2017 Article 16; The LMAA Terms 2021 Article 17.

chartering business.

However, Singapore International Arbitration Centre (SIAC) formulates completely different arbitration rules. Taking its 2016 version as an example, it does not mention concurrent arbitration but set down procedural rules on "Multiple Contracts" and "Consolidation".

Rule 6 of SIAC Rules 2016: Multiple Contracts

6.1 Where there are disputes arising out of or in connection with more than one contract, the Claimant may:

a. file a Notice of Arbitration in respect of each arbitration agreement invoked and concurrently submit an application to consolidate the arbitrations pursuant to Rule 8.1; or

b. file a single Notice of Arbitration in respect of all the arbitration agreements invoked which shall include a statement identifying each contract and arbitration agreement invoked and a description of how the applicable criteria under Rule 8.1 are satisfied. The Claimant shall be deemed to have commenced multiple arbitrations, one in respect of each arbitration agreement invoked, and the Notice of Arbitration under this Rule 6.1(b) shall be deemed to be an application to consolidate all such arbitrations pursuant to Rule 8.1.

Rule 8 of SIAC Rules 2016: Consolidation

8.1 Prior to the constitution of any Tribunal in the arbitrations sought to be consolidated, a party may file an application with the Registrar to consolidate two or more arbitrations pending under these Rules into a single arbitration, provided that any of the following criteria is satisfied in respect of the arbitrations to be consolidated:

a. all parties have agreed to the consolidation;

b. all the claims in the arbitrations are made under the same arbitration agreement; or

c. the arbitration agreements are compatible, and: (i) the disputes arise out of the same legal relationship(s); (ii) the disputes arise out of contracts consisting of a principal contract and its ancillary contract(s); or (iii) the disputes arise out of the same transaction or series of transactions.

Referring to Hong Kong International Arbitration Centre (HKIAC) Administered Arbitration Rules 2018, it is rather different from the abovementioned LMAA Terms and SIAC Rules. HKIAC Rules specifically regulate the procedures of both consolidated arbitration and concurrent arbitration. For example:

Article 28 of HKIAC Rules 2018: Consolidation of Arbitrations

28.1 HKIAC shall have the power, at the request of a party and after consulting with the parties and any confirmed or appointed arbitrators, to consolidate two or more arbitrations pending under these Rules where:

(a) the parties agree to consolidate; or

(b) all of the claims in the arbitrations are made under the same arbitration agreement; or

(c) the claims are made under more than one arbitration agreement, a common question of law or fact arises in all of the arbitrations, the rights to relief claimed are in respect of, or arise out of, the same transaction or a series of related transactions and the arbitration agreements are compatible.

Article 30 of HKIAC Rules 2018: Concurrent Proceedings

30.1 The arbitral tribunal may, after consulting with the parties, conduct two or more arbitrations under the Rules at the same time, or one immediately after another, or suspend any of those arbitrations until after the determination of any other of them, where:

(a) the same arbitral tribunal is constituted in each arbitration; and

(b) a common question of law or fact arises in all the arbitrations.

Therefore, it is obvious that consolidated arbitration and concurrent arbitration are stipulated respectively under HKIAC Rules. The former is to consolidate multiple arbitrations into one while the latter is to hold multiple arbitrations simultaneously.

Go back to English Arbitration Act 1996 which does not mix "consolidated arbitration" with "concurrent arbitration" neither. Section 35 describes their procedures as follows:

Section 35: Consolidation of proceedings and concurrent hearings

(1)The parties are free to agree——

(a)that the arbitral proceedings shall be **consolidated** with other arbitral proceedings, or

(b)that **concurrent hearings** shall be held, on such terms as may be agreed.

(2) Unless the parties agree to confer such power on the tribunal, the tribunal has no power to order **consolidation of proceedings** or **concurrent hearings**.

It can be reflected from the wording that under English Arbitration Act 1996, "consolidation" and "concurrent" are two distinct concepts and shall apply different procedures.

With further and deeper development of China's foreign trade and commerce, arbitration commissions in China, such as China International Economic and Trade Arbitration Commission (CIETAC) and China Maritime Arbitration Commission (CMAC), are also keeping pace with time in terms of consolidated arbitration and concurrent hearing. Article 14 of CIETAC Arbitration Rules 2015 is "Multiple Contracts"[1] and Article 19 is "Consolidation of Arbi-

---

[1] China International Economic and Trade Arbitration Commission (CIETAC) Arbitration Rules 2015, Article 14 The Claimant may initiate a single arbitration concerning disputes arising out of or in connection with multiple contracts, provided that:
  (a) such contracts consist of a principal contract and its ancillary contract(s), or such contracts involve the same parties as well as legal relationships of the same nature;
  (b) the disputes arise out of the same transaction or the same series of transactions; and
  (c) the arbitration agreements in such contracts are identical or compatible.

trations"①. The exact content of these two articles can also be found in CMAC Arbitration Rules 2021. Compared with CIETAC Rules, CMAC Rules has one more provision concerning "Consolidation of Hearings" which is in Article 53.

Article 53 of CMAC Arbitration Rules: Consolidation of Hearings

To progress fair, economic and efficient arbitration, if two or more cases on arbitration involve the same issues of facts or of law, after consulting with all the parties, the arbitral tribunal shall have consultation with the Arbitration Court and may decide to consolidate two or more cases in the oral hearing, and may also decide:

(a) that documents submitted by the parties in one case may be forwarded to the parties in another case;

(b) that evidence produced in one case may be accepted and admitted in another case, provided that all parties have been offered opportunities to comment on such evidence.

Although the title of Article 53 is "Consolidation of Hearings", it is substantially more like "concurrent arbitration" and "concurrent hearing" under the LMAA Terms or HKIAC Rules. Taking preciseness of legal language into account, and in order to be consistent with international general terms, the writer suggests that CMAC should consider changing the title from "Consolidation of Hearings" to "Concurrent Arbitration" or "Concurrent Hearing". This would be more accurate and more in line with practice, and can avoid confusion with consolidated arbitration as well.

---

① Article 19.1 At the request of a party, CIETAC may consolidate two or more arbitrations pending under these Rules into a single arbitration if:

(a) all of the claims in the arbitrations are made under the same arbitration agreement;

(b) the claims in the arbitrations are made under multiple arbitration agreements that are identical or compatible and the arbitrations involve the same parties as well as legal relationships of the same nature;

(c) the claims in the arbitrations are made under multiple arbitration agreements that are identical or compatible and the multiple contracts involved consist of a principle contract and its ancillary contract(s); or

(d) all the parties to the arbitrations have agreed to consolidation.

IV. Consolidated/Concurrent Arbitration Under Common Law

Under English law, the basic principle of consolidated or concurrent arbitration is respecting autonomy of will of both parties. It can be shown clearly from the explicit provisions of English Arbitration Act that consolidated or concurrent arbitration can only be conducted if both parties unanimously agree so. According to Section 35 of English Arbitration Act, only when the parties agree or agree to confer such power on the tribunal, can it order consolidation of proceedings or concurrent hearings.

English courts have made their positions clear on this issue in the case of the Eastern Saga[①] in 1984. In this case, the shipowner chartered the ship to the charterer who then relet her to the sub-charterer on a back-to-back basis. After the disputes arose, two arbitral tribunals were constituted with the same arbitrators appointed. Afterwards, the tribunal decided to order concurrent hearings since the issues of facts and law between these two arbitrations are the same. The shipowner raised an objection on the ground that the tribunal had no power to determine concurrent hearings of two separate arbitrations.

After trial, the tribunal held that "the arbitrators enjoyed no power to order concurrent hearings or anything of that nature without the consent of the parties. Neither the tribunal nor any of the parties could insist that the dispute should be heard or determined concurrently with or even in consonance with another dispute however convenient that course might be and however closely connected the dispute in question might be. The only powers which an arbitrator enjoyed related to the reference in which he had been appointed and they could not be extended merely because a similar dispute existed which was capable of being and was referred separately to arbitration under a different agree-

---

① Oxford Shipping Co. LTD. v. Nippon Yusen Kaisha(The Eastern Saga), 2 *Lloyd's Law Report* 373(1984).

ment." This shows that without contractual authorization or legal authorization, English courts are reluctant to support compulsory concurrent or consolidated arbitration.

In the case of United Kingdom v. Boeing Co.[①] in 1993, the US court also affirmed that unless both parties unanimously agree to consolidate arbitrations, the court has no right to order consolidation. In this case, the British government incurred loss in a test flight. The helicopter under test was constructed by Boeing and Textron, who had both signed construction contracts with the British government. After the accident occurred, the British government initiated arbitration proceedings against these two companies in New York. The parties disagreed on whether the arbitrations can be consolidated. Eventually, Supreme Court of the US held that under the Federal Arbitration Act, arbitration agreement shall be regarded as the contract concluded between two parties. Thus, if they do not agree on consolidated arbitration in the agreement, the court is not entitled to order so.

In conclusion, under common law, consolidated or concurrent arbitration is more likely to be recognized if parties have reached a clear agreement.

V. Potential Problems of Consolidated/Concurrent Arbitration

Consolidated or concurrent arbitration is a new way to handle multi-party arbitration. Although it may meet the practical requirements for arbitration, attributable to ambiguity in this issue in many national laws and international conventions, it will potentially face very complicated problems of recognition and enforcement in the future.

The purpose of choosing arbitration as a dispute resolution method is to obtain an enforceable arbitral award. As one of the most important treaties in international trade area, New York Convention has had 168 state parties up to

---

[①] Government of United Kingdom v. Boeing Co., 998F, 2nd 68(1993).

July 2021. Article 5 of the Convention explicitly lists the situations under which courts of the contracting states can refuse to recognize and enforce the arbitral award, being:

(c) The award deals with a difference not contemplated by or not falling within the terms of the submission to arbitration, or it contains decisions on matters beyond the scope of the submission to arbitration… or

(d) The composition of the arbitral authority or the arbitral procedure was not in accordance with the agreement of the parties, or, failing such agreement, was not in accordance with the law of the country where the arbitration took place…

Consequently, for consolidated arbitration, if the arbitral tribunal delivers only one arbitral award in the end, it could potentially violate Article 5(c); and if the consolidation is ordered by tribunal compulsorily, the resulting arbitral award could potentially violate Article 5(d) leading to be denied recognition and enforceability.

In view of the current attitudes towards consolidated or concurrent arbitration under common law, if the arbitral tribunal arbitrarily orders such proceedings without explicit consensus of both parties, it is very likely that the losing party would take violation of New York Convention as an excuse to refuse recognition and enforceability of the arbitral award.

For China, the latest Arbitration Rules of CIETAC and CMAC also contain several forward-looking provisions on consolidated or concurrent arbitration (regarding "Consolidation of Hearings" under CMAC Rules as Concurrent Arbitration in essence), some of which even empower the arbitral tribunal or commission to determine consolidation. However, as to the current legislations on arbitration, neither Arbitration Law nor Civil Procedure Law of PRC has provisions on consolidated or concurrent arbitration, which means they may not be applicable in practice. Article 4 of Arbitration Law clearly states that "In setting disputes through arbitration, an agreement to engage in arbitration should first of all be reached by parties concerned upon free will. Without such an agreement, the arbitration commission shall refuse to accept the application for arbitration by any one single party." According to this provision, an arbitration agreement reached by both parties is the precondition of initiating an arbitration.

Nevertheless, in practice, once a dispute arose, each party would focus more on its own interests. It is unlikely for them to reach a consolidated or concurrent arbitration agreement. If the arbitral tribunal or commission determine consolidated or concurrent arbitration procedures by themselves, domestic arbitrations would probably violate Article 4 of Arbitration Law, while international arbitrations would go against New York Convention resulting in foreign courts' refusal of recognizing and enforcing the arbitral awards. For this reason, the writer suggests that in future revision of Arbitration Law, the practical necessity of consolidated or concurrent arbitration can be taken into account. Relevant provisions on these two arbitrations shall be included, to confirm their legality and provide legal basis for their application.

Consolidated and concurrent arbitrations are two different but correlated patterns of arbitral proceedings. In addition to legislation, it is necessary for each arbitration commission to set down more comprehensive and precise rules on their respective premises, procedures, scope of application and so on. Through distinguishing and specific regulations, consolidated and concurrent arbitrations can operate their functions properly. If we only generalize these two models of arbitration indiscriminately under the definition of "consolidation", it would certainly lead to more chaos in legal practice.

Conclusion

From the development of current international commercial arbitration trend, the number of multi-party disputes is increasing remarkably, the necessity and advantages of consolidated or concurrent arbitration in solving such disputes are also becoming more significant and conspicuous. Although it may be facing challenges from principle of privacy and autonomy of will, and contracting states to New York Convention may even refuse to recognize and enforce the arbitral awards delivered under such arbitration proceedings, consolidated or concurrent arbitration can effectively avoid conflicting arbitral awards, promote fairness and justice, and improve arbitration efficiency as well. Therefore, when dealing with problems on consolidated and concurrent arbitrations, whether by amending laws or revising arbitration rules, it is crucial to find a balance between procedural and substantive justice, between autonomy of will, efficiency and fairness.

Consolidated and concurrent arbitrations do exert a great impact on traditional principles of arbitration, but keeping up with the trend of international commercial arbitration, establishing and continuously improving China's own consolidated and concurrent arbitration system will not only help to effectively solve disputes between multiple parties, but also play an important role in promoting the progress of China's arbitration cause, especially the internationalization of China's maritime arbitration.

（郑秋钰、莫之颖　审校）

Focuses in Arbitration of Disputes in the Standard Ground Handling Agreement

NIE Ying[*]　　GAO Feng[**]

Abstract: Ground handling agreement refers to the contract or agreement executed by and between a handling company and an air carrier in respect of the provision of various professional services (including check-in, cargo transportation, passenger transportation, aircraft line maintenance, tractor and trailer, passenger boarding bridge, shuttle bus, etc.) for the operation of the carriers within the airport area. The authors intend to take the Standard Ground Handling Agreement of the International Air Transport Association as an example to analyze the main focuses of this type of agreement dispute cases, including the nature of the agreement, the right of rescission, exemption clause and arbitration clause, and factual determination of service fees and disbursement fees. Aviation disputes are highly professional, international and very suitable for resolution with arbitration. The arbitration commissions in Chinese mainland are also basically qualified to provide high-quality and international aviation arbitration services. While providing professional and efficient dispute resolution services for civil aviation industry in China, the arbitration commissions will also further promote the establishment and improvement of the existing rules of the aviation industry, and further enhance China's international dis-

---

　　[*]　Director of Beijing Hengli Management Consulting Co., LTD; arbitrator of China Maritime Arbitration Commission.
　　[**]　Partner of Grandall Law Firm; arbitrator of China Maritime Arbitration Commission.

course power in the civil aviation industry.

Key words: civil aviation; Standard Ground Handling Agreement; international air transport association; arbitration; dispute resolution

On December 16, 2017, the Aviation Dispute Arbitration Center of China Maritime Arbitration Commission (CMAC) was formally established in Beijing. CMAC is committed to providing a more professional and efficient way for arbitration of disputes in China's civil aviation industry. As stipulated in Article 3 of CMAC Rules, which came into effect on October 1, 2018, that: Jurisdiction:

1. CMAC accepts cases based on the agreement of parties, including:
...
(b) related disputes arising from aviation, railways, highways etc.;
...

2. The preceding cases include:
(a) international or foreign-related disputes;
(b) disputes related to the Hong Kong Special Administrative Region, the Macao Special Administrative Region and the Taiwan region; and
(c) domestic disputes.

It can be seen that CMAC has also clearly included aviation-related dispute cases in the main scope of acceptance. Based on the authors' years of work experience in the civil aviation industry, aviation disputes are highly professional and international, and dispute cases are very suitable for resolution with arbitration. The authors intend to take the Standard Ground Handling Agreement (SGHA) of the International Air Transport Association (IATA) as an example to analyze the main focuses of this type of contract dispute cases.

Ground handling agreement is a contract or agreement executed by and between a handling company with a carrier in respect of various professional services (including check-in, cargo transportation, passenger transportation, aircraft line maintenance, tractor and trailer, passenger boarding bridge, shuttle bus and other services), and it provides for the normal operation of the carrier in the airport area. Carriers generally execute a comprehensive ground handling agreement with the handling company, or may separately execute different agreements with relevant handling company and professional ground handling companies for different services. With the development of the aviation industry and the popularization of the SGHA, other professional companies related to the operation of carriers are also increasingly using the SGHA or executing relevant service contracts with carriers by referring to the terms of the SGHA, such as the Air Catering Contract executed between air catering or food companies and carriers, the Fueling Service Contract or the Aviation Fuel Supply Agreement executed between aviation oil companies and carriers, the Aircraft Maintenance Contract executed between aircraft maintenance companies and carriers, and the Information System Service Contract executed between aviation information service companies and carriers. Although the contents of aviation services are different, the rights and obligations of the parties thereto, especially the Liability and Indemnity clause, are basically the same. Therefore, the discussion on SGHA herein also includes the above relevant air service contracts.

In order to improve the efficiency of aviation operations, clarify the division of responsibilities and facilitate insurance arrangements, the IATA has formulated a SGHA that is updated from time to time. According to the update time, there have been SGHAs of 1998 edition, 2004 edition, 2008 edition, 2013 edition, and 2018 edition, etc. Up to now, the above editions are all valid documents available to all parties. Because the SGHA of 1998 edition is still widely used in China, the authors' analysis below will also be based on this edition. An SGHA is generally composed of a main agreement and two annexes. The main agreement mainly sets out the main rights and obligations of both parties; Annex A is the ground handling service items, generally setting out the contents of various ground handling services (such as check-in, cargo transportation, passenger transportation, aircraft line maintenance, tractor and trailer, passenger boarding bridge, catering, fueling and so on available to the parties); Annex B is the location, service items and charging standards, generally setting out the location of ground handling services, the service items agreed by both parties, the charging standards, and other matters that need to be agreed upon by both parties (e. g. , supplementing or modifying the terms in the main agreement on the limit of liability, court of jurisdiction, or dispute resolution methods).

I . Is SGHA a Commission Contract and Whether the Parties Have the Statutory Right to Unilaterally and Arbitrarily Rescind the Agreement

Article 919 of the Civil Code of the People's Republic of China (hereinafter referred to as "Civil Code") stipulates that: "An entrustment contract is a contract under which a principal and an agent agree that the agent shall handle the matters for the principal. " Article 920 stipulates that: "A principal may specially entrust an agent to handle one or several matters, and may also generally entrust the agent to handle all matters of his. " Article 933 stipulates that: "A principal or an agent may rescind the entrustment contract at any time. Where rescission of the contract by a party causes losses to the other party, the party rescinding a gratuitous entrustment contract shall compensate for the direct losses caused by the rescission, and the party rescinding a non-gratuitous entrustment contract shall compensate for the direct loss caused and the expected profit obtainable if the contract has been performed, unless the coss is caused by a reason not attributable to the rescinding party. According to Article 410 of the expired Contract Law of the People's Republic of China (hereinafter referred to as "Contract Law"), the principal or the agent may rescind the commission contract at any time. Where the termination of the contract causes losses to the other party, the losses shall be indemnified by the terminating party except for reasons not attributable to the terminating party.

As the service content of the SGHA generally involves that the handling company or other professional service company is commissioned by the carrier to provide ground handling services, which basically conforms to the characteristics of a commission contract. However, by searching the relevant decided cases of courts, the authors found that the SGHA is generally recognized as a service contract rather than a commission contract, while the aircraft operation management agreements or aircraft management contracts similar to the SGHA are generally recognized as commission contracts. For instant, in the case of the appellant, First Mandarin Business Aviation Co., Ltd. (hereinafter referred to as "First Mandarin") and the appellee, Beijing Yidu Investment Co., Ltd. (hereinafter referred to as "Yidu") on the commission contract dispute[①], the court held that the Aircraft Commissioned Operation Agreement executed by and between Yidu and First Mandarin according to the Regulations on the Operation and Management of Business Jets represented the true intentions of both parties and shall be legitimate and valid. The Agreement was a paid commission contract. The commissioned affairs prescribed in the Agreement included the services during the business jet introduction phase and the operational management services after the introduction of business jets. The case only involved the aircraft commissioned introduction service disputes. In the case of service contract dispute between Siam Air Transport Co., Ltd. (hereinafter referred to as "Siam Air") and Guangzhou Baiyun International Airport Co., Ltd. (hereinafter referred to as "Baiyun Airport")[②], the court held that the Ground Handling Agreement of Guangzhou Baiyun International Airport and the Comprehensive Support Service Agreement of Guangzhou Baiyun International Airport executed by and between Siam Air and Baiyun Airport represented the true intentions of both parties, and the contents did not violate the mandatory provisions of People's Republic of China (PRC) laws and administrative regulations and should be legitimate and valid. The same ruling was also made in the case of service contract dispute between Baiyun

---

① Civil Judgment (2017) L. 01 M. Z. No. 4433 of Shenyang Intermediate People's Court of Liaoning Province.

② Civil Judgment (2018) Y. M. Z. No. 765 of the High People's Court of Guangdong Province.

Airport and VIM Airlines of Russia[①]. Among the SGHA disputes decided by the Beijing Arbitration Commission/Beijing International Arbitration Center (BAC), including the case of dispute on the Aviation Fuel Supply Agreement between an aviation oil company and a carrier, the case of dispute on the System Service Agreement between an aeronautical information service company in Hong Kong and a carrier in Thailand, and the case of dispute on the Ground Handling Agreement for Business Jets between an aviation service company in Beijing and a business jet company, the arbitration tribunals' decisions on the cases were generally that the aforementioned agreements represented the true intentions of both parties, and were general service contracts; given the fact that their contents did not violate the mandatory provisions of PRC laws and administrative regulations then in effect, and no other circumstance that might cause the agreements to be invalid was found, the arbitration tribunals recognized their validity. The arbitration tribunals did not recognize the aforementioned agreements as commission contracts, mainly because the arbitration tribunals focused on the special circumstances and relevant regulations of the civil aviation industry in addition to taking the contents of the agreements into account. For example, Article 21 of the Regulation on the Administration of Civil Airports stipulates that airport administration agency shall open and operate the transportation airport in accordance with the scope of the transportation airport use license, and shall not close it without authorization … If the airport administration agency intends to close the transportation airport, it shall report to the authority that issued the transportation airport use license 45 days in advance to get approval for closure, and shall make an announcement to the public. Article 45 stipulates that: if the aviation fuel supply enterprise of a transportation airport intends to cease its supply of aviation fuel to the transportation airport, it shall notify the civil aviation administration authority, the airport administration agency and the relevant air transportation enterprises in the area

---

[①] Civil Judgment (2017) Y. 0111 M. C. No. 14470 of the Primary People's Court of Baiyun District of Guangzhou City, Guangdong Province.

where the transportation airport is located 90 days in advance. On this basis, the authors believe that the SGHA shall not be directly recognized as a commission contract, and the parties thereto shall not have the statutory unilateral right to rescind the agreement. Instead, the rights and obligations of both parties shall be determined according to the specific terms and conditions of the agreement. The authors believe that the service standards of the carrier and the industry standards should also be taken into consideration. If the airport's services fail to meet the relevant service standards, the carrier should have the right to unilaterally rescind the agreement.

II. How to Interpret the Exemption Clause in the SGHA

The Liability and Indemnity clause in the SGHA (take the agreement between the carrier and the handling company as an example) generally provides that: Except as stated in this Agreement, the carrier shall not make any claim against the handling company and shall indemnify it against any legal liability for claims or suits, including costs and expenses incidental thereto, in respect of: (a) delay, injury or death of persons carried or to be carried by the carrier; (b) injury or death of any employee of the carrier; (c) damage to or delay or loss of baggage, cargo or mail carried or to be carried by the carrier, and (d) damage to or loss of property owned or operated by, or on behalf of, the carrier and any consequential loss or damage; arising from an act or omission of the handling company in the performance of this Agreement unless done with intent to cause damage, death, delay, injury or loss or recklessly and with the knowledge that damage, death, delay, injury or loss would probably result. In addition, the agreement also stipulates that: the aforementioned "the carrier" or "the handling company" shall include their employees, servants, agents and sub-contractors; and "act or omission" shall include negligence.

According to the above provisions of the SGHA, as far as the ground handling service is concerned, unless the legal liability for the claim or lawsuit is caused by the handling company's intentional or reckless act or omission knowing that loss may be caused, the carrier shall have no right to claim the handling company's liability for compensation and shall give the handling company full exemption. The authors believe that due to the high risk, high investment and high volatility of the aviation industry, its statutory liabilities need to be transferred through purchase of high level of insurance, while accordingly, to ensure the normal operation of air transportation, professional aviation service companies in terms of airport, aviation fuel, maintenance and other services do not need to repeatedly purchase relevant insurance for the same purpose. They just need to charge relatively low service handling fees and require the carrier to offer corresponding exemptions. All the compensation liabilities of the carrier are indemnified by its statutory liability insurance. This is the inherent operation logic of the aviation industry, and also the commercial basis and reason for the aforementioned exemption clause of the SGHA. That is, under normal circumstances, the carrier should unconditionally exempt the handling company from liabilities unless there is an exclusion clause in the agreement, i.e. act or omission of the handling company, either intentionally or recklessly knowing that loss may be caused. So what is "knowing"? What is "reckless"? The authors believe that the interpretation should be based on the law applicable to the agreement. Different countries and different jurisdictions have different understandings and legal regulations on this issue, and the international community does not have a uniform applicable standard for this. The authors now intend to interpret it in light of PRC laws. Article 132 of the Civil Aviation Law of the People's Republic of China stipulates that: The carrier shall not be entitled to avail himself of the provisions of Articles 128 and 129 of this Law concerning the limit of liability if it is proved that the damage in the air transport resulted from an act or omission of the carrier or its servants or agents, done with intent to cause damage or recklessly and with knowledge that damage would probably be resulted. Article 118 of the Maritime Law stipulates that: If it has been proved that the personal injury or death of the passenger or the loss or damage to the passenger's luggage resulted from an act or omission of the carrier done with the intent to cause such loss or damage or recklessly and with knowledge that such death or personal injury or such loss or damage would probably result, the carrier shall have no right to invoke Article 116 and Article 117 of this Law concerning the limitation of liability for compensation. As seen from the judicial practices in China, there are also corresponding understandings or judgments. For example, the case (MAO Xuebo v. CHEN Wei and Shengsi County Jiangshan Marine Shipping Co., Ltd. [1]) in the Gazette of Supreme People's Court stated that: To determine whether the right of limitation of liability for maritime claims is lost, it is necessary to comprehensively consider whether the ship owner or other person in charge has intentionally caused the damage, or has reckless act or omission knowing that loss may be caused. However, the collection and long-term, multiple or repeated implementation of many serious illegal navigation behaviors (such as unlicensed navigation, navigation beyond the navigation zone, navigation without visa, leaving the scene without authorization after the accident, etc.) may be sufficient to presume that the ship owner and other person in charge have significant subjective fault. Therefore, for serious illegal navigation, the content and nature of the act and the severity of the violation should be integrated to determine whether the person in charge has the right of limitation of liability for maritime claims. Thus it can be seen that the court has clarified what is meant by "reckless act or omission knowing that loss may be caused" by recognizing "significant subjective fault". For another example, in the case of dispute on the ground handling agreement between a carrier and a handling company[2], the court held that: the handling company neglected safety precautions and did not immediately stop using the platform vehicle when its repeated faults were not completely solved and the operation safety and normal use could not be guaranteed, which violated Article 24 of the Provisions on the Administration of Special Equipment for Civil Airports and Article 5 of the Provisions on the Admin-

---

[1] Civil Judgment (2016) Z. G. F. M. S. No. 1487 of the Supreme People's Court of P. R. C..
[2] Civil judgments of the second instance and the final instance (2019) Q. 01 M. Z. No. 2507 of the Intermediate People's Court of Haikou City of Hainan Province.

istration of Civil Airports Operation Safety, and it is sufficient to determine that the handling company was in serious negligence in this accident. Thus it can be seen that, the serious negligence recognized by the court falls into the "reckless act or omission knowing that loss may be caused". For another example, the Supreme People's Court held that in the final judgment of a ground handling agreement dispute between an aircraft engineering company and a cargo air transport company: Based on the above statement, the aircraft maintenance engineer was aware that the landing gear handles were in the retracted position, the ground safety latch was pulled out, the hydraulic button was activated and the aircraft might touch the ground. However, because he did not notice that the landing gear handles were in the retracted position during operation, and recklessly ordered to remove the ground safety latch and activate the hydraulic button, causing the aircraft to touch the ground. His behavioral characteristics were consistent with the second exception stipulated in the main agreement (the authors' note: that is, the main agreement of the SGHA), that is, reckless act knowing that his behavior may cause damage. Because he was an engineer appointed by the aircraft engineering company to perform maintenance on the aircraft involved, the aircraft engineering company should be held liable for his acts of duty. Therefore, the aircraft engineering company shall not be entitled to the right of exemption. Of course, the reality is always complicated and requires specific analysis of specific issues. For example, at 08:03 on December 10, 2015, the Operational Command Center of Fuzhou Airport received a call from the Fujian Air Traffic Control Tower that the right engine of flight CA1822 of Air China at the end of runway 03 was on fire. At 08:07, when the 8 fire trucks of the airport's fire department arrived at the scene, they found two Boeing 737-800 planes were near the end of runway 03, including an aircraft of Air China which was shut down and was not in any abnormal situation. On the aircraft of Fuzhou Airlines with the same engine model next to it, exhaust gas coming out of the engine's tail nozzle. The incident was urgent. In the case of emergency rescue at the time, in order to avoid accident, the on-site fire commander decided to cool down the aircraft of

Fuzhou Airlines. At 08:09, the Operational Command Center notified to correct the situation immediately after it found the situation. After receiving the instruction, the fire brigade turned to Air China's flight CA1822 for rescue. At 08:15, the scene was under control①, but the incident caused significant losses to both Air China and Fuzhou Airlines. In the authors' opinion, this incident is a typical ground handling agreement dispute involving multiple parties. Whether the losses of Air China and Fuzhou Airlines should be borne by Fuzhou Airport, or whether Fuzhou Airport can be exempted from liability should be determined after analyzing and judging whether Fuzhou Airport had "reckless act or omission knowing that loss may be caused" according to the relevant facts. As seen from the several SGHA dispute cases, according to PRC laws, "intentional or reckless act or omission knowing that loss may be caused" is close to the expression of "intentional act or gross negligence" stipulated in the Civil Code or the Contract Law.

In the aforementioned arbitration cases heard by the BAC, the ground handling agreements involved still had some different provisions on the above exemption clauses, such as the provision that "all losses caused by the handling company providing services under this Agreement shall be borne by the handling company". However, upon closer examination, Article 506 of the Civil Code stipulates that: "An exculpatory clause in a contract exempting the liability on the following acts are void: (1) causing physical injury to the other party; or (2) causing losses to the other party's property intentionally or due to gross negligence." Therefore, according to the authors' understanding, the aforementioned provision with one-sided compensation liability may be partially invalidated due to violation of the mandatory provisions of the law. For another example, the provision that "all losses caused by the intentional or gross negligence of the handling company shall be borne by the handling company; all losses caused by the intentional or gross negligence of the carrier shall be borne

---

① http://news.carnoc.com/list/331/331044.html About the Explanation on Handling of the Right Engine Fire Incident of Flight CA1822 on "10/12".

by the carrier" or the provision that "all losses shall be borne by the carrier unless caused by the handling company's intentional or gross negligence; all losses shall be borne by the handling company unless caused by the carrier's intentional or gross negligence". According to the above provisions, the authors believe that for the losses not caused by the intentional act or gross negligence of one party (i. e. the carrier or the handling company), the party (or parties) causing the losses or the damage shall not be exempted from liability, and it shall be deemed that there is no agreementon this issue between the carrier and the handling company.

The liability assumption between the carrier and the handling company depends on the insurance contract arrangement with the insurance company. Under normal circumstances, the carrier's insurance policy covers the aviation service industry chain, and the handling company can be exempted from liability to some extent. The carrier and the insurance company must have a clear scope and boundary of exemption, and the carrier and the handling company shall also have clear scope of liability.

III. Factual Determination of Service Fees and Disbursement Fees in SGHA Disputes

The same issue was encountered in the case of dispute on the System Service Agreement between an aeronautical information service company in Hong Kong SAR(China) and a carrier in Thailand, and the case of dispute on the Ground Handling Agreement for Business Jets between an aviation service company in Beijing and a business jet company, that is, in the process of air service, the service provider often regularly sends bills of service fees and disbursement fees (including the service fees paid on behalf of the carrier to other third-party professional service companies) to the carrier at the time agreed in the agreement (usually monthly or quarterly). The bills are sometimes sent by mail, sometimes by courier. The agreement generally stipulates that the carrier has the right to raise an objection within a few working days from the date of receipt of the bill. If the service provider does not receive the objection from the carrier, it will issue an invoice to the carrier to charge the relevant fees. Subsequently, the two parties had disputes during the performance of the agreement, which included objections to the amount of the aforementioned fees. During the trial, the arbitration tribunal found that there were many reasons for the aforementioned problem: e. g. , the handling company did not send bills to the designated mailbox or designated address of the contact person (the designated contact person as agreed in the agreement) on schedule by method (such as email) as agreed in the agreement; the failure of the handling company to obtain the carrier's prior consent for the disbursement expenses exceeding the scope or standard agreed in the agreement, causing the carrier's subsequent rejection and refusal to pay; the carrier did not raise an objection to the handling company on the amount or standard of the relevant fees in time during the objection period agreed in the agreement, and did not raise the objection until at court in the arbitration process, and refused to pay on the ground that it had not been confirmed by both parties. For example, in the aforementioned case of dispute on the Ground Handling Agreement for Business Jets, Article 7. 1 of the agreement stipulates that the two parties shall settle the accounts on a monthly basis. Before the 15th of each month, the handling company shall send the bill to the business jet company, which shall make a reply within 5 working days after the receipt of bill, and no reply shall be deemed as a confirmation of the bill amount. The business jet company recognizes the settlement method between the handling company and the third party. For the part of the bill that the business jet company raises objections, the handling company shall provide the business jet company with the bills, receipts, invoices or other charging records of the third-party for supporting, and the business jet company shall not unreasonably refuse to give confirmation. After the two parties confirm the amount, the handling company shall issue an invoice to the business jet company, which shall pay the money to the handling company by transfer. Article 7. 6 stipulates that: The business jet company shall indemnify the handling company for other expenses that should be paid by the business jet company, including but not limited to government charges, taxes and dues, aircraft and cabin cleaning fees, aircraft satellite communication fees, data link fees… and the disbursement fees other than the service fee as specified in this agreement and its annexes. The handling company shall provide relevant vouchers or other supporting documents to prove the actual expenditures of the bill. According to the aforementioned provisions, during the trial process, the handling company, as the claimant, submitted evidence to the arbitration tribunal to prove that it had sent the bills and notes of disbursement fees and the reminder letter to the respondent (i. e. , the business jet company) in accordance with the agreement. The business jet company did not raise any objections to the delivery of the bills, nor did it submit any relevant evidence to the arbitration tribunal showing that it had raised objections to the bills. According to the agreement, the business jet company shall reply within 5 working days after receiving the bill from the handling company, and no reply shall be deemed as confirmation of the bill amount. In the end, the arbitration tribunal held that the business jet company failed to provide evidence to prove that it had raised objections to the handling company's bills and charging standards during the performance of the agreement, so the arbitration tribunal supported the handling company's claim for relief. In view of the fact that many charging standards of the civil aviation industry are government-guided, such as the charging standards for professional services such as aviation fuel, passenger bridge fees, passenger service fees, and security inspection fees, if there are regulatory documents issued by the civil aviation authority from time to time (such as the Civil Airport Charging Standard Adjustment Plan, etc.), the arbitration tribunal will also take it into consideration.

  The settlement system in the aviation industry is not yet sound, and some settlements between customers and handling companies are still manually processed. The IATA has the Billing and Settlement Plan, and we hope that the China Air Transport Association will develop a commercial settlement system for Chinese aviation industry as soon as possible.

Ⅳ. The Arbitration Clause of the SGHA

It is well known that arbitration is advantaged in many ways such as professionalism, confidentiality, certainty of jurisdiction, flexible procedures, final and binding award, extraterritorial enforcement, allowing both parties to select arbitrators, etc., but the premise is that the parties to the agreement must select the arbitration method according to the dispute resolution clause in the arbitration agreement or contract, and the arbitration provision must be valid. Many civil aviation companies don't know enough about commercial arbitration and the benefits of arbitration. Some don't even know what arbitration is.

In an arbitration case of an SGHA dispute, Article 9.1 of the agreement stipulates that: if the two parties have disagreements or disputes on the content, expression, or performance of the Agreement, the two parties shall try their best to take all reasonable actions to resolve them internally. If a solution cannot be reached, the parties to the Agreement can resolve the problem through arbitration (the parties can choose an arbitrator or an arbitration tribunal). If the parties do not agree to adopt arbitration, they shall resolve the dispute through litigation procedures in accordance with the laws and scope of jurisdiction of the country specified in Annex B. Annex B executed by the two parties stipulates that: According to Article 9.1 of the main agreement, this Agreement shall be governed by the PRC laws, and the court of jurisdiction for the dispute is blank and was not agreed upon by the parties. The carrier, as the respondent in the case, filed an objection to the jurisdiction of the arbitration commission that accepted the case, arguing that the arbitration clause agreed in the SGHA is an "arbitration or trial" clause and shall be invalid. Finally, the arbitration commission authorized the arbitration tribunal to make a decision on this. The arbitration tribunal reviewed the aforementioned provision and concluded that: Article 16 of the Arbitration Law of the People's Republic of China stipulates that "an agreement for arbitration shall include the arbitration clauses in the contracts or other written agreements for arbitration reached before or after the dispute occurs. An arbitration agreement shall contain the following: (1) The expression of application for arbitration; (2) Matters for arbitration; (3) The arbitration commission chosen. " Article 18 stipulates that: "Whereas an agreement for arbitration fails to specify or specify clearly matters concerning arbitration or the choice of arbitration commission, parties concerned may conclude a supplementary agreement. If a supplementary agreement cannot be reached, the agreement for arbitration is invalid. " Article 20 stipulates that: "Whereas parties concerned have doubt on the validity of an agreement for arbitration, a request can be made to the arbitration commission for a decision or to the people's court for a ruling. If one party requests the arbitration commission for a decision while the other party requests the people's court for a ruling, the people's court shall pass a ruling. A doubt to the effectiveness of an arbitration agreement, should be raised before the first hearing at the arbitration tribunal. " According to the aforementioned laws and regulations, a valid arbitration agreement or arbitration clause shall have content in three respects: an expression of intent to request arbitration, arbitration matters, and the clearly selected arbitration commission. If there is no provision on a definite arbitration commission , or if the provision is not clear, and the parties do not have a supplementary agreement, the arbitration agreement or arbitration clause shall be invalid. In this case, the arbitration clause in the SGHA (i. e., the main agreement) did not specify the arbitration commission, and the parties did not reach a supplementary agreement on this in Annex B, so the arbitration clause was invalid. In addition, because the SGHA involved in this case had the same legal effect as Annex B, and the arbitration clause contained the provision of "arbitration or trial", the arbitration provision was also invalid. In the end, the arbitration tribunal held that the arbitration commission that accepted the case had no jurisdiction over the case.

In addition, in an arbitration case of an SGHA dispute , the agreement stipulates that: this Agreement shall be governed by French laws, and the agreed arbitration shall be ad hoc arbitration. Each party shall elect one arbitrator, and the presiding arbitrator shall be jointly chosen by the arbitrators chosen by both parties. The Arbitration Rules of the Arbitration Commission of IATA shall apply. The Chinese carrier represented by the authors was the respondent, while a French freight forwarding company was the claimant. At the early stage of the trial, because the claimant failed to pay all the arbitration fees (mainly the estimated fees for the three arbitrators) in advance, the respondent raised objection, and the arbitration tribunal finally dismissed the case on the basis that the claimant was deemed to have withdrawn the arbitration claim. In accordance with the Arbitration Rules of the Arbitration Commission of IATA, the arbitration fee shall be paid in advance by the claimant and the respondent in half respectively. If the respondent refuses to pay in advance, the claimant shall pay in full, otherwise the arbitration claim shall be deemed to have been withdrawn. The purpose of taking this example is to show that the ad hoc arbitration agreed in the SGHA is valid under French laws. If the agreement was governed by PRC laws, it should be invalid at present. According to Article 18 of the Law of the People's Republic of China on Choice of Law for Foreign-related Civil Relations, "The parties concerned may choose the laws applicable to arbitral agreement by agreement. If the parties do not choose, the laws at the locality of the arbirtral authority or of the arbitration shall apply", that is, the arbitration clause shall have a selected arbitration commission. If there is no provision on the arbitration commission (such as ad hoc arbitration), the arbitration clause shall be invalid.

Through the arbitration settlement of the aforementioned SGHA disputes, the arbitration commissions in China's mainland are basically qualified to provide high-quality international aviation arbitration services. While providing professional and efficient dispute resolution services for civil aviation in China, the arbitration commissions will also further influence and promote the establishment and improvement of existing rules of the aviation industry, and further enhance China's international discourse power in the civil aviation industry, so as to build a powerful country with civil aviation, and assist aviation industry with advanced arbitration.

(郑秋钰、张傲霜　审校)

Research on Ad Hoc Arbitration Regime and Its Judicial Review*

LIU Jingdong** LIU Yan***

Abstract: Ad hoc arbitration is an important method to solve modern international commercial disputes, and also a significant part of the arbitration law system of various countries.

Although the Supreme People's Court has provided in the relevant judicial opinions a tentative mechanism that allows ad hoc to be conducted in the FTZ with "three spefic conditions" satisfied, the current Arbitration Law of the People's Republic of China (hereinafter referred to as "Arbitration Law") does not provide for an ad hoc arbitration regime. Ad hoc arbitration is thus left with insufficient statutory basis in China, as well as many problems in terms of its legal relief and its judicial review which does not have a definite presence in the existing judicial review system. The amendment to the Arbitration Law will incorporate the ad hoc arbitration into China's arbitration system, which will not only have a positive and far-reaching impact on the existing arbitration system, but also become an important symbol that China's commercial arbitration system is in line with the world and becoming more and more mature.

---

* Translated by CHEN Xun, HONG Huimin.
** Office Director of the International Economic Law Department of the Institute of International Law, Chinese Academy of Sciences, and researcher and supervisor of doctoral students, Vice President of China Academy of Arbitration Law, Arbitrator of China Maritime Arbitration Commission.
*** Postgraduate student in International Law of Chinese Academy of Science.

Based on this, this paper analyzes the necessity and feasibility of bringing the ad hoc arbitration into Arbitration Law. In addition, based upon the analysis of the characteristics of ad hoc arbitration, this paper studies and discusses the construction of the judicial review system related to ad hoc arbitration, and puts forward countermeasures and suggestions on how to modify the Arbitration Law to incorporate the judicial review system of ad hoc arbitration into it.

Key words: ad hoc arbitration; judicial review; amendment of Arbitration Law

Foreword

According to Article 16 and 18 of the Arbitration Law, when the parties conclude an arbitration agreement, they must have a selected arbitration commission. If no arbitration commission is selected or no supplementary agreement can be reached, the arbitration agreement shall be null and void.① It can be seen that the Arbitration Law only recognizes institutional arbitration at the legislative level and does not provide for the application of ad hoc arbitration in our jurisdiction.

The Legislative Affairs Commission of the Standing Committee of the National People's Congress has made the following explanations on the reasons why the ad hoc arbitration regime is not established in the Arbitration Law:

There are mainly two reasons. Firstly, ad hoc arbitration was adopted

---

① The Arbitration Law of the People's Republic of China, Article 16: An agreement for arbitration shall include the arbitration clauses stipulated in the contracts or other written agreements for arbitration reached before or after a dispute occurs.
An arbitration agreement shall contain the following:
1. The expression of application for arbitration.
2. Matters for arbitration.
3. The arbitration commission chosen.
Article 18: Whereas an agreement for arbitration fails to specify or specify clearly matters concerning arbitration or the choice of arbitration commission, parties concerned may conclude a supplementary agreement. If a supplementary agreement cannot be reached, the agreement for arbitration is invalid.

before the institutional arbitration came into existence in history. In view of the future development of modern arbitration, ad hoc arbitration has been decling. Secondly, arbitration in China has a relatively short history with only institutional arbitration available but no ad hoc arbitration.①

Some scholars har voiced their opposition to the above explanations since the very beginning of the legislation. In their opinion, the fact that ad hoc arbitration predates institutional arbitration does not necessarily indicate the decling of the former. Nor can we assume that ad hoc arbitration would not grow out from nothing in the future.② Some scholars believe that the Arbitration Law did not include the ad hoc arbitration because the objective conditions in China were not in place at the time. This, coupled with the arbitrary and private nature of ad hoc arbitration, leaves us with no concrete data to examine in studying ad hoc arbitration, and its hasty introduction would make the system uncontrollable in dispute resolution, which would most likely affect the credibility of the judiciary.③ It has also been argued that China has experienced a long-period planned economy where economic activities are strictly controlled by the government and that ad hoc arbitration based on party autonomy is incompatible with a planned economy. If the parties were allowed to choose one or more individuals to perform quasi-judicial functions and make a decision which should be enforced by the court, it would be contrary to the economic and social norms at that time.④

The author believes that these considerations are signs of the times. At a time when China's commercial arbitration market was still immature and the social integrity system had not yet been established, the introduction of ad hoc arbitration does not contribute to the regulation of arbitration market and the development of the commercial arbitration system. But with the continuous im-

---

① Jiang Wei, Xiao Jianguo and Xie Wenzhe, *Arbitration Law*, China Renmin University Press, 2016, p. 22.
② Ibid.
③ Gao Fei and Xu Jianguo, *Guide for China Ad Hoc Arbitration Practice*, Law Press China, 2017, p. 1.
④ Judy Li Zhu, "Time to Losson Up on Ad Hoc Arbitration in China," 15 *Asian Intornational Arbitration JournalL* 44(2019).

provement of China's arbitration market and the increasing demand of the parties for arbitration, especially with the great achievements in the construction of the rule of law society and the improvement of the social integrity system, the introduction of ad hoc arbitration, an internationally popular arbitration system, is of particular importance to the development of commercial arbitration in China. It is therefore important to move away from the wholly conservative attitude of the past and actively promote the integration and convergence of the ad hoc arbitration with our existing arbitration legal system.

I. Recent Exploration and Practice of China's Ad Hoc Arbitration Regime

Article 9 of the Supreme People's Court Opinion on Provision of Judicial Safeguards for the Construction of the Pilot Free Trade Zones (hereinafter referred to as the "Opinions") in 2017 provides for an ad hoc arbitration under certain conditions (hereinafter referred to as "three specific conditions"). ①

---

① Supreme People's Court Opinion on Provision of Judicial Safeguards for the Construction of the Pilot Free Trade Zones, Article 9: Correctly determine the validity of arbitration agreements, and regulate the judicial review of arbitration cases. Where a foreign enterprise registered in the FTZ is bound to submit cross-border arbitration for commercial disputes, the relevant arbitration agreement shall not be invalidated on the ground that the dispute does not involve foreign factors.

Where one party or both parties concerned which are foreign-funded enterprises registered in the FTZ have agreed to submit cross-border arbitration for commercial disputes, after the occurrence of a dispute, the parties concerned submit the dispute for arbitration abroad but then claim to not acknowledge, recognize or execute the award on the ground of invalidity of the arbitration agreement after the relevant award is made, the people's court shall not uphold such request; where the other party concerned did not raised an objection to the validity of the arbitration agreement in the arbitration procedure, but claims that the arbitration agreement is invalid and refuses to acknowledge, recognize or execute the award therefor on the ground that the relevant dispute does not involve any foreign factor after the award is made, the people's court shall not support the request.

In case companies registered within the Pilot Free-Trade Zones agree to arbitration in certain locations in the Mainland of China, with certain arbitration rules, and by certain persons, such arbitration agreement may be recognized as valid. In case a people's court finds such arbitration agreement to be invalid, it shall report the matter to a higher court for review. In case the higher court agrees with the lower court, it shall further report the matter to the SPC and shall only decide on the matter upon the Supreme People's Court's reply.

This is a beneficial attempt to introduce the ad hoc arbitration and this important attempt by the Supreme Court undoubtedly embodies the Central Government's principle of "try first" in the Pilot Free Trade Zone.

Following the publication of the said Opinions, according to the information available to the author, up to now, Shanghai Banking and Insurance Dispute Mediation Centre completed the first ad hoc arbitration case in the Free Trade Zone(FTZ) in September 2017 and accepts the first cross-FTZ ad hoc arbitration case on April 3, 2018. A number of other arbitration institutions have also made relevant explorations. However, in practice, some arbitration institutions still have considerable concerns as to whether arbitration rules made under the Opinions in respect of ad hoc arbitration would be confirmed by the People's Court and whether ad hoc arbitral awards made pursuant to the arbitration rules will be enforced by the courts. All of this needs to be dispelled by specific cases and judicial decisions accepted by the courts in the future.

On March 23, 2017, the Hengqin New Area Administrative Committee and the Zhuhai Arbitration Commission held a launch event in the Hengqin Pilot Free Trade Zone to officially release the Ad Hoc Arbitration Rules of Hengqin Pilot Free Trade Zone (hereinafter referred to as the "Hengqin Rules"). This is the first specific ad hoc arbitration rule in China, an important innovation to the existing commercial arbitration rules and a milestone in the history of China's arbitral system development. [1]

In terms of structure and content, the Hengqin Rules adopts a dual-track model of institutional and ad hoc arbitration, emphasizing on the one hand. On the one hand, it emphasizes the service function of institutions for ad hoc arbitration. On the other hand, it provides on the ad hoc arbitration within the framwork of the Opinions, and carefully applies the ad hoc arbitration

---

[1] "Hengqin Free Trade Zone issues and implements China's first ad hoc arbitration rules" (cngold, 23 March 2017) accessed April 30, 2020, http://kuaixun.cngold.org/c/2017-03-23/c530706.html.

regime.① Moreover, in order to apply for ad hoc arbitration, there must be an unequivocal representation to opt for ad hoc arbitration according to Article 3 (4), and if the arbitration agreement agrees to apply the Zhuhai Arbitration Commission Arbitration Rules, it is still deemed to be an selection of institutional arbitration,② which is a major feature of the Hengqin Rules.

On August 19, 2017, the China Internet Arbitration Alliance (CIAA) released the CIAA Rule for Bridging Ad Hoc Arbitration and Institutional Arbitration (hereinafter referred to as the "Internet Bridging Rules") at the 7th Greater China Arbitration Forum held in Guangzhou.③

CIAA operates a web-based cloud platform for briding institutional and ad hoc arbitrations (also known as "yijian.com").④ The establishment of this

---

① Yangjun, "The Path of Ad Hoc Arbitration and Institutional Arbitration in the Era of 'Internet Plus' – Taking the Hengqin Free Trade Zone Ad Hoc Arbitration Rules as an Entry Point," 5 *Journal of Heilongjiang Administrative Cadre College of Politics and Law* 115(2018).

② Hengqin Rules, Article 3(4): Any representation that the parties have agreed to select the Zhuhai Ad Hoc Arbitration Rules, the Hengqin New Area Ad Hoc Arbitration Rules, the Zhuhai Arbitration Commission Ad Hoc Arbitration Rules, or any other representation that can be inferred as the sole selection of the Ad Hoc Arbitration Rules, shall be deemed to be a valid selection of the Rules. Where the parties agree that the Zhuhai Arbitration Commission Arbitration Rules or the Zhuhai Court of International Arbitration Arbitration Rules shall apply, the arbitration shall not be ad hoc and the case shall be governed by the Zhuhai Arbitration Commission or the Zhuhai Court of International Arbitration.

③ Cai Mingjie, "China Internet Arbitration Alliance issues ad hoc arbitration rules," *China News* (Guangzhou, 20 September 2017), http://www.chinanews.com/gn/2017/09 – 20/8335406.shtml, accessed April 30, 2020.

④ China Internet Arbitration Alliance Rule for Bridging Ad Hoc Arbitration and Institutional Arbitration, Article 3: The China Internet Arbitration Alliance (hereinafter referred to as "the Alliance") is an non-governmental organizations formed by arbitral institutions, universities, bar associations, arbitrators' associations and Internet technology enterprises, with the aim of promoting innovation and development of arbitration through exchange and cooperation, interconnection and sharing among arbitration institutions and related sectors. The Alliance has a general coordinator. The Internet Arbitration Cloud Platform (also known as "yijian.com") is operated by the Alliance and is an online platform for ad hoc arbitration and institutional arbitration, with services and technical support provided by Guangzhou Yijian Online Dispute Legal Services Co. An arbitral institution refers to an arbitral institution in Mainland of China established by the municipal people's government in accordance with the provisions of the Arbitration Law of the People's Republic of China or by the China Chamber of International Commerce, or an arbitral institution in another country or region in accordance with local laws.

platform is the distinguishing feature of the Internet Bridging Rules, which covers more arbitrators than an ordinary arbitration institution, including not only arbitrators of CIAA, but also arbitrators of non-CIAA arbitration institutions and persons eligible to become arbitrators under the *lex arbitri*. ①

In addition, the Internet Bridging Rules looked at the longer run, as it did not ignore the need of non-FTZ registered enterprises to apply for ad choc arbitration and the possibility of such enterprises applying for ad choc arbitration abroad, and was keenly aware of the need for ad hoc arbitration to be allowed in China, in order to facilitate the recognition and enforcement of arbitral awards, facilitating the recognition and enforcement of arbitral awards in the future. It is widely accepted in the industry that the rule is a strong impetus to the development of arbitration rules in the high-tech era, but it will no longer be necessary in the future if ad hoc arbitration can be conducted independently in China. It could be drawn upon by legislators if we still have to interface with and obtain confirmation from arbitral institutions when enforcing ad hoc arbitral awards. ②

Although the Supreme People's Court has made beneficial attempts at ad hoc arbitration, in the long run, an ad hoc arbitration regime stipulated in the Arbitration Law is still needed to ensure that ad hoc arbitration can really be widely used in commercial dispute resolution. This is the fundamental way to i-

---

① Bridging Rules, Article 7: Yijian has an open and convenient pool of arbitrators for parties to select, which consists of
 (ⅰ) Arbitrators on the panel of arbitrators of all arbitration institutions of the Alliance.
 (ⅱ) Arbitrators on the panel of arbitrators of non-Alliance arbitration institutions
 (ⅲ) other persons who have the qualifications of arbitrators as provided for in the Arbitration Law or the *lex arbitr*.
② Bridging Rules, Article 21: The parties to an ad hoc arbitration proceeding or the arbitral tribunal may choose to interface their proceedings or award with institutional arbitration in accordance with the Rules, depending on the needs of the dispute resolution. Ad hoc arbitrations between enterprises registered in the FTZ that are agreed to be conducted under specific rules, at specific locations and by specific personnel may choose to be interfaced with institutional arbitration or not. Ad hoc arbitrations between non-FTZ registered enterprises may be interfaced with institutional arbitrations through the Alliance. Awards made abroad under ad hoc arbitration procedures may be interfaced with domestic institutional arbitration through the Alliance in order to facilitate recognition and enforcement.

dentify the proper status of ad hoc arbitration in China.

II. The Importance of Incorporating the Ad Hoc Arbitration Regime into the PRC Arbitration Law

The long-standing absence of ad hoc arbitration in China's arbitration legislation has had a negative impact on commercial arbitration and even on the construction of a foreign commercial dispute resolution system, mainly shown as follows.

2.1 Resulting in *De Facto* Supranational Treatment for Foreign Applicants

Obligations under the Convention on the Recognition and Enforcement of Foreign Arbitral Awards (also known as the "New York Convention") include the recognition and enforcement of both institutional and ad hoc arbitral awards.① China is a contracting party to the New York Convention and the courts are obliged to recognize and enforce arbitral awards made by foreign ad hoc arbitral tribunals. And indeed, we do fulfil this obligation, for example, when Singapore's Amarante Shipping Pte Ltd. applied to the Tianjin Maritime Court for recognition and enforcement of an ad hoc award made in London by arbitrator David Farrington②, and when Sweden's Svensk Honungsforadling AB applied to the Nanjing Intermediate People's Court for recognition and enforcement of an ad hoc award made in Stockholm, Sweden, by arbitra-

---

① The Covention on the Recognition and Enforencement of Foreign Arbitral Awards, Article I(2): The term "arbitral awards" shall include not only awards made by arbitrators appointed for each case but also those made by permanent arbitral bodies to which the parties have submitted.

② On 23 March 2019, Singapore's Amarante Shipping Pte Ltd. applied to the Tianjin Maritime Court for recognition and enforcement of the award made by arbitrator David Farrington in an ad hoc arbitration in London. After hearing the application, the Tianjin Maritime Court made a ruling (2019) Jin 72 Xie Wai Recognition No. 1, deciding to recognise and enforce the arbitral award.

tors Peter Thorp, Sture Larsson and Nils Eliasson①. For both ad hoc arbitral awards, the courts after judicial review, upheld the applicants' applications for recognizing and enforcing their awards in accordance with Article 5 of the New York Convention and the relevant provisions of the Civil Procedure Law of the People's Republic of China and judicial interpretations. ②

But in reality, ad hoc awards made in China have not been recognized by the law for a long time, and are even less likely to be enforced. This has resulted in the *de facto* "super-national treatment" for ad hoc arbitral awards made outside China and a mismatch between the treaty rights and obligations China has.

2.2 A Significant Impediment to the Right of Contracting Parties Access to Remedies

Ad hoc arbitration in China at present is not established by law, but provided in the Opinions and in the arbitration rules issued by several arbitral institutions, which, moreover, only provide for the right of the parties to choose ad hoc arbitration to settle their disputes under certain conditions, without specifying rules on proceeding matters including how to deal with uncertainty

---

① On 22 November 2018, Sweden's Svensk Honungsforadling AB applied to the Nanjing Intermediate People's Court of Jiangsu Province for recognition and enforcement of an ad hoc arbitral award made in Stockholm, Sweden by arbitrators Peter Thorp, StureLarsson and Nils Eliasson. After hearing the application, the Nanjing Intermediate People's Court of Jiangsu Province made a decision (2018) Su 01 Xie Wai Recognition No. 8, deciding to recognize and enforce the foreign arbitral award.

② Interpretation of the Supreme People's Court concerning the Civil Procedure Law of the People's Republic of China, Article 545: Where a party to an arbitration award that is rendered by a temporary arbitration tribunal outside the territory of the People's Republic of China applies to a people's court for recognition and enforcement of the same, the people's court shall handle the application in accordance with Article 283 of the Civil Procedure Law. See also the Civil Procedure Law of the People's Republic of China, Article 283: If an award made by a foreign arbitration institution must be recognized and executed by a people's court of the People's Republic of China, the party concerned shall directly apply to the intermediate people's court of the place where the party subject to execution is domiciled or where his property is located. The people's court shall handle the matter pursuant to international treaties concluded or acceded to by the People's Republic of China or in accordance with the principle of reciprocity.

on validity of the arbitration agreement, whether and how interim measures can be taken, and how to enforce the awards made by a ad hoc arbitration tribunal. This could lead to great difficulties in ad hoc arbitration conducted under the Opinions and the governing arbitration rules. For instance, there may also be a double dilemma——with a valid ad hoc arbitration agreement, the arbitral tribunal having a jurisdiction over the case find itself unable to move forward the proceeding while the parties cannot submit the disputes to the court instead, resulting in the interests of the right holder not being remedied. ① This implicitly reduces the dispute resolution options available to parties and increases the cost for parties requiring ad hoc arbitration – forcing them to resort to litigation or to go abroad for ad hoc arbitration②, which is not conducive to the development of arbitration in China.

2.3 Impact on the Facilitation of a Complete Belt and Road Commercial Dispute Resolution Mechanism

In order to promote the construction of a rule of law system for the Belt and Road, China should promote the establishment of a comprehensive commercial dispute resolution mechanism. Ad hoc arbitration, as a very essential method of dispute resolution, is an important option for commercial entities and is an indispensable component of the Belt and Road commercial dispute resolution mechanism. A look at the main partner countries along the Belt and Road will reveal that China is now surrounded by countries whose arbitration laws are legislated based upon the Model Law. The influential arbitration hub such as Singapore have a tendency to build its arbitration law on the Model Law and go beyond it, as evidenced by the fact that their legislation is constantly touching areas not covered by the Model Law. In contrast, Arbitration Law in China has

---

① Sun Wei, "Recent Development of Ad Hoc Arbitration in China and Suggestions for Institutional Improvement – Interpretation of the Opinion on Providing Judicial Protection for the Development of the Pilot Free Trade Zones and Hengqin Pilot Free Trade Zone Ad Hoc Arbitration Rules," *Beijing Arbitration Quarterly* 88(2017).

② Li Guanghui and Wang Ha, *Arbitration Law*, UIBEP Press, 2011, p. 19.

lagged behind, and there is still much to be "upgraded". ① The absence of the ad hoc arbitration regime is an important factor in the relative backwardness of our arbitration law.

If ad hoc arbitration is not legislated for a long time to come, China will lose the market for legal services related to ad hoc arbitration and an important way to safeguard the legal rights of Chinese citizens and enterprises, which is clearly detrimental to the construction of the Belt and Road commercial dispute resolution mechanism. In order to create a global arbitration centre in Asia Pacific and to safeguard the legitimate interests of Chinese parties, "upgrading" the Arbitration Law and including ad hoc arbitration are a very important first step.

In view of the above considerations, China's Arbitration Law, which is currently being revised, should include the ad hoc arbitration regime as a form of arbitration parallel to institutional arbitration, providing commercial subjects with more solutions for commercial disputes. Moreover, the incorporation of such a system is of great significance to the internationalization and modernization of China's arbitration and the enhancement of China's voice in the field of international arbitration, mainly reflected in the following points:

Firstly, it is conducive to promoting the implementation of the Opinions of the Two Offices and the "2022 Plan for China Arbitration". On 10 September 2018, the amendment of the Arbitration Law of China has been included in the second category of the legislative plan of the 13th NPC Standing Committee. ② Taking the opportunity of this Arbitration Law revision to incorporate the ad hoc arbitration regime into China's arbitration legal system, it contributes to promoting

---

① Wang Hui, "Model Law on International Commercial Arbitration: Creation, Influence and Inspiration," 3 *Wuhan University International Law Review* 104(2019).

② The second category of projects in the legislative plan of the 13th NPC Standing Committee refers to draft laws that need to be worked on urgently and submitted for consideration when conditions are ripe. The amendment of the Arbitration Law is ranked 46th in this list and is led by the State Council. Source: NPC, Legislative Plan of the 13th NPC Standing Committee (10 September, 2018), accessed March 27, 2020, http://www. npc. gov. cn/npc/c30834/201809/ f9bff485a57f498e8d5e22e0b56740f6. shtml.

the implementation of the Opinions of the Two Offices[①] and the "2022 Plan for China Arbitration". It also helps to improve the arbitration mechanism and enrich the arbitration service methods, accelerating the construction of an arbitration center with regional and even global influence.

Secondly, incorporation of ad hoc arbitration into China's arbitration law system is conducive to promoting China's commercial dispute resolution system in line with international standards and making China's voice better heard during the construction of the "Belt and Road"[②], thereby accelerating the establishment of a global Asia-Pacific arbitration centre and helping to attract more foreign investors and capital to the Chinese market.[③]

Thirdly, it is conducive to better fulfilling international treaty obligations, demonstrating China's active role in fulfilling its obligations under international law and fully safeguarding the legitimate rights and interests of our commercial subjects. Since ad hoc arbitration is an important part in the New York Convention, incorporation of the ad hoc arbitration will be an important embodiment of China's full implementation of the New York Convention. At the same time, it would also eliminate the supranational treatment of foreign citizens and enterprises in the ad hoc arbitration in China, better protect the legitimate rights and interests of China's parties, and completely change the current embarrassing situation that China's courts can only recognize and enforce for-

---

[①] On 31 December 2018, the General Office of the CPC Central Committee and the General Office of the State Council issued a notice on "Several Opinions on Improving the Arbitration System and Enhancing the Credibility of Arbitration", in which it was proposed that the judicial support and supervision mechanism should be improved. The people's courts should actively support the development of arbitration, establish a mechanism for coordinating work with arbitration committees, communicate in a timely manner about the situation and improve the efficiency of hearing cases related to judicial review of arbitration. Reform and improve the judicial supervision mechanism, improve the judicial interpretation of the Arbitration Law, regulate the determination of the validity of arbitration agreements, arbitration preservation, award cancellation and non-enforcement procedures, and support and supervise arbitration in accordance with the law.

[②] See Wang Hui, "Model Law on International Comnercial Arbitration: Creation, Influence and Inspiration," 3 *Wuhan Universing International Law Review* 3(2019).

[③] Song Lianbin, Zhao Jian and Li Hong, "Approaches to the Revision of the 1994 Arbitration Act of the People's Republic of China," 20 *Journal of International Arbitration* 186(2003).

eign ad hoc arbitral awards but not domestic ad hoc arbitration awards, from a legal basis.

Fourthly, it is conducive to improving the existing civil and commercial judicial system in China. By resolving disputes in a timely manner, it could relieve the enormous pressure of caseload the people's courts which are faced with. For the domestic judicial environment, incorporating ad hoc arbitration into China's dispute resolution legal system is, on the one hand, conducive to alleviating the pressure of limited judicial resources, broadening the offering of methods of dispute resolution and expediting the construction of a sound civil and commercial dispute resolution system, and on the other hand, conducive to encouraging domestic parties to resolve disputes by way of ad hoc arbitration, saving their own time and valuable judicial resources.

III. Some Suggestions on Establishing the Judicial Review System of Ad Hoc Arbitration

Arbitration as an effective alternative to litigation is featured by the enforceability of arbitral awards, which is guaranteed by the coercive power of the country. It is very necessary to build a judicial review system for ad hoc arbitration.[1] Judicial review is the supervision (mainly reflected in the legitimacy review) and guarantee of arbitration (mainly reflected in the judicial assistance to the arbitration process and the remedy for the rights of the parties). This principle also applies to the ad hoc arbitration.

In order to realize the integration of ad hoc arbitration and institutional arbitration, and to practice the concept of "friendly arbitration", this paper studies several important issues related to the judicial review system in the ad hoc arbitration and puts forward relevant suggestions.

---

[1] Zhang Weiping, "The Basic Structure and Jurisprudence of Judicial Supervision over Arbitration Enforcement: On the System of Non-enforcement of Arbitral Awards," 42 *Modern Law Science* (2020).

3.1 Review of the Validity of the Ad Hoc Arbitration Agreement

The validity of the arbitration agreement is a prerequisite for the legality of arbitration, which is all the more important and salient for the ad hoc arbitration. According to the theory and practice of the Arbitration Law in force and the characteristics of ad hoc arbitration, the author believes that the following efforts should be made to improve the review of the validity of the ad hoc arbitration agreement:

Firstly, disscontinue taking the physical location of the arbitration institution as the jurisdictional connecting factor.

China's Arbitration Law in force takes the seat of the arbitration institution as the jurisdictional connecting factor. Specifically, Article 12 of the 2006 Interpretation of the Supreme People's Court on Certain Issues Concerning the Application of the "Arbitration Law of the People's Republic of China" makes a distinction between the jurisdiction in cases of determining the validity of domestic and foreign related arbitration agreements,[①] that is, for domestic arbitral awards, the People's Court at the location of the arbitration institution has priority, and only if the arbitration institution is unclear does it choose the jurisdiction of the intermediate People's Court at the place where the arbitration agreement was signed or where the respondent is domiciled, and for foreign arbitral awards, one of the above three connecting points is sufficient.[②] After that, in 2017, Article 2 of Provisions of the Supreme People's Court on Several

---

[①] Interpretation of the Supreme People's Court on Certain Issues Concerning the Application of the "Arbitration Law of the People's Republic of China", Article 12: A case filed with a people's court by a party seeking to determine the validity of an arbitration agreement shall be subject to the jurisdiction of the intermediate people's court of the place where the agreed arbitration institution is located. If the arbitration institution is not explicitly provided for in the arbitration agreement, the case shall be subject to the jurisdiction of the intermediate people's court of the place where the respondent is domiciled. Cases related to application for ascertainment of the validity of arbitration agreements involving foreign elements shall be under the jurisdiction of an intermediate people's court at the place where the agreed arbitration institution is located, or where the arbitration agreement is concluded, or where the applicant or respondent is domiciled.

[②] Zhu Huafang and others, "2019 Annual Report on Judicial Review of Arbitration in Practice – Theme 1: Observations on the System for Confirming the Validity of Arbitration Agreements in Practice," WeChat Public No. tiantongsusong (March 23, 2020) accessed May 7, 2020.

Issues concerning Deciding Cases of Arbitration-Related Judicial Review adopted a unified criterion to determine the courts that have jurisdiction in cases over the validity of domestic and foreign related arbitration agreements, but still used the location of the arbitration institution as a connecting point. ①

The author holds that the taking the location of an arbitration institution as the connecting point was set up specifically for institutional arbitration in a special period. After we have established the ad hoc arbitration system, the connecting point of both the institutional and ad hoc arbitration should be the seat of arbitration, which will help to reduce the cost of defending the rights of the parties and also help to speed up the process of China's international integration.

Secondly, the arbitral tribunal shall be given full jurisdiction to make awards.

China has adopted a positive attitude towards the principle of competence-competence in international law, which is mainly reflected in the international treaties to which China is a contracting party. ② For example, when acceding to the Convention on the Settlement of Investment Disputes Between States and Nationals of Other States, China did not make a reservation to the Convention's competence-competence articles. ③ However, according to Article 20 of the Chinese Arbitration Law, it is the Arbitration Commission and the People's Court that are eligible to determine the validity of an arbitration agreement, i.

---

① 2017 Provisions of the Supreme People's Court on Several Issues concerning Deciding Cases of Arbitration-Related Judicial Review, Article 2: For a case for an application for recognition of the effect of an arbitration agreement, an intermediate people's court, or a special people's court, in the place where the arbitral institution as stipulated in the arbitration agreement is located, or where the arbitration agreement is entered into, or in the place of domicile of the applicant or the respondent, shall have jurisdiction.

② Convention on the Settlement of Investment Disputes Between States and Nationals of Other States, Article 41(2): Any objection by a party to the dispute that that dispute is not within the jurisdiction of the Centre, or for other reasons is not within the competence of the Tribunal, shall be considered by the Tribunal which shall determine whether to deal with it as a preliminary question or to join it to the merits of the dispute.

③ Huo Wei, "On the Principle of Competence-Competence in Arbitration," in *Proceedings of China Academy of Arbitration Law* 2010 *Annual Conference & China Arbitration and Justice Forum* 2010, P. 191.

e. the Arbitration Law does not entitle the arbitral tribunal to adjudicate on the above procedural matter itself. Although in practice the Arbitration Committee often delegates that authority to the arbitral tribunal according to arbitration rules, there is still no direct legal basis for the arbitral tribunal to determine the validity of the arbitration agreement.① From a practical point of view, if there are still many concerns about empowering the tribunal to decide its jurisdiction directly, it is suggested that the court could be granted certain power of judical review afterwards.

Some countries have taken a similar route.

For example, Singapore law provides an additional opportunity to bring an action for arbitral awards. That is, if a party is not satisfied with the arbitral tribunal's ruling on its jurisdiction, he or she may first bring an action in the High Court of Singapore. If the party is not satisfied with the High Court's decision, the party may also bring a second instance to the Singapore Court of Appeal.② Besides, Article 16, Paragraph (3), of the UNCITRAL Model Law says:

> …If the arbitral tribunal rules as a preliminary question that it has jurisdiction, any party may request, within thirty days after having received notice of that ruling, the court specified in article 6 to decide the matter, which decision shall be subject to no appeal; while such a request is pending, the arbitral tribunal may continue the arbitral proceedings and make an award.

In accordance with the actual needs of the development of arbitration in China, we can refer to the successful experience of the above-mentioned countries or regions, take into account the qualification of arbitrators and the efficiency of arbitration, and ensure in the law that the arbitral tribunal has full power to decide, while enacting legal provisions for the corresponding judicial supervision procedures.

Thirdly, clarify the requirements for a valid ad hoc arbitration agreement.

---

① Wang Hui n21, 120.
② Ibid, 111.

The arbitration agreement includes the arbitration clause in the contract and the arbitration agreement reached in other written forms before or after the dispute. Articles 16, 17 and 18 of China's Arbitration Law stipulate the constituent elements and exclusion requirements of a valid arbitration agreement from both sides, which is also an important basis for the institutional arbitration in the Arbitration Law. In order to introduce ad hoc arbitration into the current legal framwork of arbitration , it would also be possible to start with these articles by deleting the mandatory provision in the law that requires a selected an arbitral institution, by no longer making a strict distinction between institutional and ad hoc arbitration and by making the regime currently applicable to institutional arbitration directly applicable to ad hoc arbitration.

In fact, documents such as the Singapore International Arbitration Act, the 2001 Taiwan (China) Arbitration Act, the 1923 Protocol on Arbitration Clauses and the UNCITRAL Model Law all have the same requirements for the validity of institutional arbitration and ad hoc arbitration agreements, except that the 2001 Taiwan (China) Arbitration Act requires a written arbitration agreement and the appointment of an arbitrator or arbitral tribunal, whereas the Singapore International Arbitration Act emphasizes that an arbitration agreement can be determined as valid as long as one party claims to have an arbitration agreement and the other party does not express its intention to the contrary, and the arbitration agreement is not required to be in a fixed document. [1]

The UNCITRAL Model Law has more liberal requirements for arbitration agreements, and there is a chance to be recognized even if it is concluded orally. According to international practice, the agreement is valid if the parties

---

[1] Singapore International Arbitration Act, 2. Interpretation of Part II (3): Where in any arbitral or legal proceedings, a party asserts the existence of an arbitration agreement in a pleading, statement of case or any other document in circumstances in which the assertion calls for a reply and the assertion is not denied, there shall be deemed to be an effective arbitration agreement as between the parties to the proceedings.

show their willingness to arbitrate.[①] Moreover, the arbitration agreement between the parties should be respected as long as it does not violate the mandatory provisions of the relevant law and does not harm the third party or public policy.[②]

In order to further create an arbitration-friendly judicial environment, the Arbitration Law could be amended by removing the strict distinction between institutional and ad hoc arbitration, and arbitration agreements between the parties, in whatever form they exist, should be judicially recognized as long as they do not violate the mandatory provisions of the relevant law and do not harm the interest of the third parties or go against the public policy.

3.2 Review of Revoked and Unenforced Ad Hoc Arbitral Awards

At present, the remedies could be sought under the domestic arbitration legal system are revocation or non-enforcement of the arbitral award. According to Article 9 of the Arbitration Law, setting aside an arbitral award would lead to the same result as the non-enforcement, i.e. the parties can either go to the court or re-enter into an arbitration agreement to apply for arbitration.

In the light of the internationally prevailing view, a revoked arbitral award means that the arbitral award is null and void *ab initio*. There is no possibility of revoked award being enforced, either domestically or abroad, unless the court in the seat of enforcement considers that the revoked arbitral award is still enforceable. There is, of course, a difference in the legal consequences between a revoked arbitral award and an unenforceable arbitral award. Generally speaking, an unenforceable arbitral award is only not enforced in the courts of the place where enforcement is sought, whereas if enforcement is sought in the courts of another country or region, it will be enforced as long as there is prop-

---

① UNCITRAL Model Law Article 7(2): The arbitration agreement shall be in writing. And Article 7(3): An arbitration agreement is in writing if its content is recorded in any form, whether or not the arbitration agreement or contract has been concluded orally, by conduct, or by other means.

② Song LIANBIN, Zhao JIAN and Li HONG n25, 174.

erty available for enforcement and the courts of the place where the property is located agree to enforce it. The court decision that the arbitral award shall be revoked is binding in its own territory and in a country that does not recognize the validity of the revoked arbitral award.

It is clear that in China there is no fundamental difference in effect between the two remdies. Both revoked and unenforceable arbitral awards are void *ab initio*, and the parties can be applied for re-arbitration or go to the court. Some scholars believe that the non-enforcement system is only meaningful in that China can refuse to enforce the foreign arbitral award which violates China's laws or public interests. But for domestic arbitral awards, the non enforcement system is unnecessary. The system of setting aside arbitral awards is sufficient to prevent the existence of unlawful arbitral awards and to achieve the purpose of the remedy for which the system of non-enforcement was intended. ① From this perspective, revocation and non-enforcement should be distinguished as two different regimes, with a regime of revocation only for domestic arbitral awards and two regimes of recognition and non-enforcement for foreign awards and foreign-related awards.

However, the legal framework of arbitration in China has given an outsider the right to apply for the remedy of non-enforcement of an arbitral award under Article 18 of the Provisions of the Supreme People's Court on Several Issues concerning the Handling of Cases regarding Enforcement regarding Arbitral Awards by the People's Courts, and Article 58 of the Arbitration Law denies an outsider's right to apply for setting aside an arbitral award by way of an "exhaustive" enumeration. If the right of an outsider to apply for non-enforcement is abolished in the enforcement procedure, it will inevitably lead to a number of outsiders being deprived of a remedy mechanism to safeguard their legitimate

---

① Zhang Weiping n26 ,120.

rights and interests.① The possibility of replacing the non-enforcement of a domestic arbitral award with a mere revocation therefore remains to be considered.

Article 21 of the IntInterpretation of the Supreme People's Court concerning Some Issues on Application of the Arbitration Law of the People's Republic of China provides that the court are entitled to decide whether to allow the arbitration institution to re-arbitrate in the case of the parties falsifying evidence or concealing important evidence, which is a judicial protection over the parties' arbitration right to some extent.② However, for an ad hoc arbitral award, it is open to question whether the court can require the arbitrators or the tribunal to re-arbitrate on such grounds. There is no arbitral institution involved in the ad hoc arbitration, the appointment of arbitrators may be relatively random and short-term, and the arbitral tribunal is dissolved once the arbitral award has been rendered. If the court decides to re-arbitrate on the grounds that the parties have falsified evidence or concealed important evidence, it will increase the cost of the parties on the one hand, and on the other hand, it will run against the parties' original intention of choosing ad hoc arbitration.

---

① Provisions on Several Issues Concerning the Handling of Cases of Enforcement of Arbitral Awards by the People's Courts, art 18: The People's Court shall support an application for non-enforcement of an arbitral award or an arbitral conciliation letter by an outsider under Article 9 of the Provisions if the following conditions are met: (a) the outsider is the subject of the rights or interests; (b) the rights or interests claimed by the outsider are lawful and genuine; (c) there is a fictitious legal relationship between the parties to the arbitration case and the facts of the case are fabricated; (d) the main text of the arbitral award or the arbitral conciliation dealing with the civil rights and obligations of the parties is partly or wholly wrong, to the detriment of the lawful rights and interests of the outsider. Cited in Kong Deyue, 'An empirical study on the cancellation or non-enforcement of arbitration awards: A sample of 103 civil rulings' (2021) 2 Commercial Arbitration & Mediation 118.

② Interpretation of the Supreme People's Court concerning Some Issues on Application of the Arbitration Law of the People's Republic of China, Article 21: Where a case regarding which a party concerned applies for revoking the domestic arbitral award is under any of the following circumstances, the people's court may, in accordance with Article 61 of the Arbitration Law, notify the arbitral tribunal to arbitrate the case for a second time within a time limit:

(1) The evidence on which the arbitral award is based is forged; or

(2) The other party concealed any evidence, which is enough to impact the impartial award.

The people's court shall state in the notice the specific ground for requiring re-arbitration.

Therefore, it is questionable whether the above-mentioned provision on "re-arbitration" can be applied to ad hoc arbitration.

In terms of judicial review, the standard set by the Arbitration Law should be the same for ad hoc and institutional arbitrations. There are precedents, for example, the grounds for ruling not to enforce arbitral awards involving Hong Kong SAR, Macao SAR and Taiwan Region are stipulated separately in Article 7 of the 2000 Arrangements of the Supreme People's Court on the Mutual Enforcement of Arbitral Awards between the Mainland and the Hong Kong Special Administrative Region①, Article 7 of the 2007 Arrangement between the Mainland and the Macao SAR on Reciprocal and Enforcement of Arbitration Awards and Article 14 of the 2015 Provisions of the Supreme People's Court on Recognition and Enforcement of Arbitral Awards of the Taiwan Region, all of which are essentially paraphrases of the UNCITRAL Model Law and do not strictly distinguish between institutional and ad hoc arbitrations.

---

① 2000 Arrangement of the Supreme People's Court on the Mutual Enforcement of Arbitral Awards between the Mainland and the Hong Kong Special Administrative Region, Article 7: Where an arbitral award applied for enforcement in the Mainland or the HKSAR is notified to the respondent and the respondent submits evidence proving any of the following circumstances, the court concerned may, after examination and verification, rule that the enforcement shall not be enforced: (i) The parties to the arbitration agreement are under some form of incapacity according to the law applicable to them; or the arbitration agreement is invalid according to the agreed governing law; or the law of the place where the arbitral award is made is not specified as being punctual and is invalid according to the law of that place; (ii) The respondent has not been duly notified of the appointment of an arbitrator, or has for any other reason failed to be heard; (iii) Where the award deals with a dispute that is not the subject of a reference to arbitration or is not within the terms of the arbitration agreement, or where the award contains a decision on a matter outside the scope of the reference to arbitration; provided that, where the decision on a matter referred to arbitration is separable from a matter not referred to arbitration, the part of the award deciding on the matter referred to arbitration shall be enforced; (iv) Where the composition of the arbitral tribunal or the procedure of the arbitral tribunal is inconsistent with the agreement between the parties or, in the absence of such agreement by the parties concerned, with the law of the place of arbitration; and (v) The award is not yet binding on the parties or has been set aside or suspended by the court of the place of arbitration or under the law of the place of arbitration. If the court concerned finds that the matter in dispute cannot be settled by arbitration under the law of the place of enforcement, it may refuse to enforce the award. An arbitral award may not be enforced if a mainland court determines that enforcement of the award in the mainland is contrary to the public interest, or if a court of the HKSAR decides that enforcement of the award in the HKSAR is contrary to the public policy of the HKSAR.

For foreign ad hoc arbitral awards, China has fulfilled its obligations under the New York Convention, and Article 543 of Interpretation of the Supreme People's Court on the Application of the Civil Procedure Law of the People's Republic of China① stipulates that foreign ad hoc arbitral awards shall be treated in accordance with Article 290 of the Civil Procedure Law of the People's Republic of China, i. e. , both foreign ad hoc arbitral awards and arbitral awards made by foreign institutions shall be treated in accordance with international treaties or the principle of reciprocity, which is in line with the prevailing international practice, and shall continue to be retained.②

3.3 Interim Measures in Ad Hoc Arbitration

The term "interim measures" has not been introduced into our legal system, but the provisions on preservation measures similar to "interim measures" are stipulated scatteredly in the Arbitration Law, the Civil Procedure Law and other laws and relevant judicial interpretations. At present, a unified term for this have not been adopted among the legislations of other countries. It is called an intermediate award, an interim measure of protection, an interim award, a mandatory order, etc.③ Regardless of the name, the purpose and nature of an interim measure is the same – for the interests of the parties to the interim relief.

---

① Interpretation of the Supreme People's Court on the Application of the Civil Procedure Law of the People's Republic of China, Article 543: Where an arbitration award rendered by a temporary arbitration tribunal outside the territory of the People's Republic of China applies to a people's court for recognition and enforcement of the same, the people's court shall deal with the application in accordance with Article 290 of the Civil Procedure Law.

② Civil Procedure Law of the People's Republic of China, Article 290: Where an arbitration award of a foreign arbitral institution requires recognition and enforcement by a people's court of the People's Republic of China, a party shall apply directly to the intermediate people's court at the place of domicile of the party against whom enforcement is sought or at the place where the property thereof is located, and the people's court shall process the application in accordance with an international treaty concluded or acceded to by the People's Republic of China or under the principle of reciprocity.

③ Lin Yuqiong and Lin Fuchen, "Legislation and Improvement of the System of Interim Measures in International Commercial Arbitration in China in the Context of the Belt and Road," 39 *Journal of Southwest Minzu University (Humanities and Social Science)* 94(2018).

The interim measures under Article 26 of the 1976 UNCITRAL Arbitration Rules relate only to the protection of the subject-matter.① 1985 UNCITRAL Model Law made interim measures more specifically and comprehensively. Procedural provisions include the power of the arbitral tribunal to order interim measures, the conditions for granting interim measures, the application for preliminary orders and the conditions for the issuance of preliminary orders, securities, disclosure, costs and damages, recognition and enforcement of interim measures, grounds for refusing to recognize or enforce interim measures, interim measures ordered by the court, etc.② In terms of content, it includes property preservation, conduct preservation and evidence preservation③. The Hong Kong Arbitration Ordinance largely adopts the UNCITRAL Model Law, but excludes the application of section 17I (Grounds for refusing recognition or enforcement) and section 17J (Court-ordered interim measures).

If the division is based on the subjects entitled to decide interim measures, the countries or regions that implement interim measures can be divided into three categories, those where only the court has the power to decide

---

① 1976 UNCITRAL Arbitration Rules, Article 26.1: At the request of either party, the arbitral tribunal may take any interim measures it deems necessary in respect of the subject-matter of the dispute, including measures for the conservation of the goods forming the subject-matter in dispute, such as ordering their deposit with a third person or the sale of perishable goods.

② UNCITRAL Model Law, Article 17J: A court shall have the same power of issuing an interim measure in relation to arbitration proceedings, irrespective of whether their place is in the territory of this State, as it has in relation to proceedings in courts. The court shall exercise such power in accordance with its own procedures in consideration of the specific features of international arbitration.

③ UNCITRAL Model Law, Article 17: (1) Unless otherwise agreed by the parties, the arbitral tribunal may, at the request of a party, grant interim measures.

(2) An interim measure is any temporary measure, whether in the form of an award or in another form, by which, at any time prior to the issuance of the award by which the dispute is finally decided, the arbitral tribunal orders a party to:

(a) Maintain or restore the status quo pending determination of the dispute;

(b) Take action that would prevent, or refrain from taking action that is likely to cause, current or imminent harm or prejudice to the arbitral process itself;

(c) Provide a means of preserving assets out of which a subsequent award may be satisfied; or

(d) Preserve evidence that may be relevant and material to the resolution of the dispute.

on interim measures, those where both the court and the arbitral tribunal can decide, and those where only the arbitral tribunal has the power to take interim measures, which can be supplemented by court review if necessary. According to the Arbitration Law, the only subject entitled to decide on such measures in China is the People's Court.

First, revise provisions on the commencment of property preservarton in ad hoc arbitration .

According to the Chinese law, it is not necessary to apply to the court through the arbitration institution for property preservation before arbitration; if property preservation is applied for in arbitration proceedings, it is necessary to apply to the court through the arbitration institution①. But for ad hoc arbitration there is no arbitral body, only an arbitral tribunal or arbitrator, meaning that there is currently no legal basis for applying for the preserving property in ad hoc arbitration in our courts. ②

Article 3 of the Provisions of the Supreme People's Court on Several Issues concerning the Handling of Property Preservation Cases by the People's Courts (hereinafter referred to as the Provisions on Property Preservation) says that parties to an arbitration cannot submit an application for property preservation directly to the People's Court, but must submit the application to the People's Court through the arbitral institution, and the arbitration committee shall submit the parties' application to the People's Court in accordance with the relevant provisions of the Civil Procedure Law. The Arbitration Commission acts as a transmitter of application materials between the parties and the People's Court, and has no power of substantive review, let alone the power to decide

---

① Chen Tongtong, "How to Apply for the Preservation of Property in Arbitration," *WeChat Public No. Chaolvqingshengshuo* (15 July 2019) accessed July 15, 2019.

② Sun Wei, "Recent Development of Ad Hoc Arbitration in China and Suggestions for Institutional Improvement-Interpretation of the Opinion on Providing Judicial Protection for the Development of the Pilot Free Trade Zones and Hengqin Pilot Free Trade Zone Ad Hoc Arbitration Rules," *Beijing Arbitration Quarterly* 83-94(2017).

whether to grant.①

If the Arbitration Law incorporates the ad hoc arbitration regime, consideration must be given to changing the role of arbitration institutions as data transmitters, stipulating that the People's Court should rule on enforcement whenever the arbitral tribunal makes a decision, or by turning such information transmitters into arbitral property preservation service providers. For example, Article 13 of the Hengqin Rules says:

> Parties may apply for preservation to the court having jurisdiction, either directly or through the arbitral tribunal. Where the parties' application for preservation requires the cooperation of an arbitral institution, they may make a request to the appointing authority for arbitrators, and if the appointing authority is not an arbitral institution or does not perform its duties, the Zhuhai Arbitration Commission shall assume that duty.

Under the above rules, the arbitration institution becomes the service provider for property preservation.

Secondly, clarify the submission requirements for property preservation in ad hoc arbitration.

While the Civil Procedure Law and the Judicial Interpretation of the Civil Procedure Law provide for parties to apply for property preservation, they do not specify what documents parties need to submit. The same applies to the Arbitration Law. A more specific provision could be found in Article 1 of the Provisions of the Supreme People's Court on Several Issues concerning the Handling of Property Preservation Cases by the People's Courts:

> Parties and interested parties applying for property preservation shall submit an application to the People's Court and provide relevant evidential materials. The application shall contain the following matters:
> (a) the identity, address for service and contact information of the ap-

---

① Zhao Qi, Yan Hui and Wang Ruihua, "Improvement of the Property Preservation Mechanism for Commercial Arbitration," 1 *Beijing Arbitration Quarterly* 37(2019).

plicant and the person to be preserved;

(b) the subject matter of the request and the facts and reasons on which it is based;

(c) the amount requested to be preserved or the subject matter of the dispute;

(d) clear information on the property to be preserved or specific clues to the property to be preserved;

(e) information on the property or proof of creditworthiness to provide security for the preservation of property, or the reasons for not requiring creditworthiness; and

(f) other matters that need to be set out.

This provision adopts a non-exhaustive approach to the listing of the materials to be submitted for property preservation, which in practice gives the People's Courts a lot of space for discretion. Therefore, in practice, the requirements for the relevant materials vary from one court to another, the examination standards are not uniform, and the examination standards of the courts are not available through public channels, which makes it difficult for parties to meet the requirements at one time. Returning the materials and not filing the case happens from time to time, which seriously affects the efficiency of this dispute resolution method[①]. More importantly, this provision is not specific to the preservation of property in arbitration. Taking the opportunity of the revision of the Arbitration Law, we could clarify the content of the documents to be submitted for the preservation of property in arbitration (including interim preservation) so as to reduce the difficulty of practical operation.

In recent years, the arbitration rules of some arbitral institutions have set out the materials to be submitted, for example, Article 19 and 20 of the China (Shanghai) Pilot Free Trade Zone Arbitration Rules set out the materials to be submitted by the applicant for ad hoc arbitration when applying for assistance

---

[①] Zhao Qi, "The process, problems and improvements of property preservation in commercial arbitration," *People's Court Daily*, 10 October 2019.

from that arbitration commission as:

(1) the arbitration agreement; and

(2) the application for interim measures in accordance with the provisions of Article 20(1) of the Rules. If, after examination, the Arbitration Committee considers that it can assist, it shall, within three days from the date of receipt of the aforementioned documents, transmit the documents to the court having jurisdiction and notify the applicant for interim measures.

And the application should include:

(1) the name and domicile of the party;

(2) the reasons for applying for the provisional measure;

(3) the specific provisional measure applied for;

(4) the place where the provisional measure is to be enforced and the court with jurisdiction; and

(5) the relevant legal provisions of the place where the interim measure is to be enforced.

This provision on application materials can be used as a reference for us in future legislation.

Thirdly, grant the arbitral tribunal the power to decide on the preservation of property.

Article 17 H (1) of the UNCITRAL Model Law stipulates:

An interim measure issued by an arbitral tribunal shall be recognized as binding and, unless otherwise provided by the arbitral tribunal, enforced upon application to the competent court, irrespective of the country in which it was issued, subject to the provisions of article 17I.

Our law provides that the decision to preserve can only be made by the People's Court and enforced accordingly, while the arbitral tribunal has no such right.

Although the Model Law is not enforceable compulsorily, the arbitration laws of many countries have been adapted from it, which has resulted in a conflict between our domestic law and the prevailing international rules, making it an urgent legal challenge as to how a decision by a foreign arbitral tribunal to take interim measures should be enforced in our courts.

If the decisions of foreign arbitral tribunals on interim measures are wholly rejected and not recognized and enforced, it will not be conducive to the construction of an arbitration-friendly environment and will increase the cost of defending the rights of the parties. However, if the decisions of foreign arbitral tribunals on interim measures are recognized and enforced but not those made domestically, a certain market for arbitration services will inevitably be lost. It is therefore necessary to give the arbitral tribunal a certain degree of power to decide on the preservation of property.

In addition, transfering the power to decide on the preservation of the arbitral proceedings in whole or in part to the arbitral tribunal may add to the accuracy of the decision as to whether the preservation measure is necessary, and can also reduce the cost of transferring the parties' applications for preservation from the arbitral institution and to the court, reduce the pressure on the court to review preservation and divert the court's enforcement work.① On the other hand, it can also better meet the parties' demands for confidentiality and efficiency, and provide a more neutral perspective in making decisions in international commercial arbitration.②

In recent practice, the arbitration rules of some arbitration institutions have partially allocated this power to "emergency arbitral tribunals" in order to be in line with international practice, such as the interim measures provided for in Chapter Ⅲ of the China (Shanghai) Pilot Free Trade Zone Arbitration Rules, including the scope of interim measures, interim measures before arbitration, interim measures during arbitration proceedings, emergency arbitral tribunals, the making of decisions on interim measures, changes to decisions

---

① Zhao Qi, Yan Hui and Wang Ruihua n50, 46
② Sang Yuan, "Research on Emergency Arbitrator Procedure in International Arbitration," 10 *CUFE Law Review* 125(2018).

on interim measures and compliance with decisions on interim measures. Arbitration Rules of the China Maritime Arbitration Commission (CMAC) also include similar provisions, giving the arbitral tribunal or the arbitrators the right to decide on interim measures, but this emergency arbitrators system is only for exceptional conditions occurring prior to the constitution of the arbitral tribunal, and in the event of exceptional conditions occurring during the arbitral proceedings, whether the arbitral tribunal or the arbitrators have the right to decide is not provided for in the aforementioned rules.

Fourthly, specify rules on preservation of evidence and conduct in commercial arbitration.

For evidence preservation and conduct preservation in commercial arbitration, Arbitration Law, Civil Procedure Law and their relevant judicial interpretations provide for few provisions, except that Article 68 of the Arbitration Law provides for the jurisdictional court for its power to conduct evidence preservation in foreign-related arbitration①, Article 81 of the Civil Procedure Law provides for the circumstances in which the preservation of evidence prior to arbitration may be applied for, Article 103 of the Civil Procedure Law provides for the circumstances and conditions under which a party may apply for the preservation of conduct②, and Article 50 of the Copyright Law provides for the cir-

---

① Arbitration Law, Article 68: Whereas the parties involved in a foreign arbitration case apply for the custody of evidences, the foreign arbitration commission shall submit the application to the intermediate people's court at places where the evidences are produced.

② Civil Procedure Law, Article 100: In the event that the judgment on the case may become impossible to enforce or such judgment may cause damage to a party because of the conduct of the other party to the case or because of any other reason, the people's court may, upon the request of the said party, order the preservation of the property of the other party, specific performance or injunction; in the absence of such request, the people's court may, where it deems necessary, may also order property preservation measures.

When a people's court adopts any preservation measure, it may order the applicant to provide security; where the party refuses to provide such security, the court shall reject the application.

When a people's court receives an application for preservation in an emergency, it shall decide within 48 hours after the receipt of the application; if the court accepts the application, such measures shall come into force immediately.

cumstances in which an application for the preservation of conduct may be made[①]. But whether the conduct preservation provided for in the Civil Procedure Law and the Copyright Law can be applied to conduct preservation in the field of arbitration is not clear.

In view of this, it is imperative to consolidate the existing provisions and concretize the relevant procedural rules relating to the preservation of evidence and conduct in commercial arbitration. The Arbitration Law could include a special section on interim measures, such as the documents to be submitted for the application of interim measures, the specific content of the procedure related to the initiation of interim measures, the competent decision authority and the enforcement authority, and the review criteria, etc. On the basis of facilitating arbitration applicants to take interim measures, the effective integration of institutional arbitration and interim arbitration in the regime of interim measures could be achieved.

Apart from the above procedural provisions on the preservation of evidence in commercial arbitration, we can also include specific provisions on court assistance in taking evidence so as to solve the problem of difficulties in obtaining evidence for parties in China under special circumstances, and to assist parties in completing the arbitration process and efficiently resolving disputes. The Hong Kong Arbitration Ordinance applies the provisions of Article 27 of the Model Law on "court assistance in taking evidence" and makes more specific provisions in accordance with the actual situation in Hong Kong. The Mainland of China could also make efforts in this regard by providing for court assistance in the taking of evidence by parties to commercial arbitrations, in order to support the development of an arbitration-friendly environment.

[①] Li Jin, "The New Development of Interim Measures in International Commercial Arbitration in China: From the Perspective of the Revised Civil Procedure Law and Amendments of Arbitration Rules," 44 *Journal of Northwest University (Philosophy and Social Sciences Edition)* 22 (2014).

Conclusion

The ad hoc arbitration regime is one of the most important type of modern international commercial dispute resolution and is an important part of the legal system in various countries. Although the Supreme People's Court has provided in the relevant judicial opinions of the "three specific" arbitration rules in the FTZ, the current Arbitration Law is silent on the ad hoc arbitration regime. Ad hoc arbitration is thus left with insufficient statutory basislegal protection in China, as well as many problems in terms of its legal relief and its judicial review which does not have a definite presence in the existing judicial review system.

At the beginning of the enactment of Arbitration Law, when China's commercial arbitration market was still immature and the system of social integrity had not yet been established, the hasty introduction of ad hoc arbitration was indeed not conducive to the regulation of China's arbitration market and the development of the commercial arbitration system. However, with the continuous improvement of China's arbitration market, the increasing demand for arbitration from the parties, especially today when China has made great achievements in building a society under the rule of law and the system of social integrity is becoming more and more comprehensive, the introduction of ad hoc arbitration, which is an internationally popular arbitration system, is of special importance to the development of China's commercial arbitration.

Therefore, it is important to abandon the conservative attitude of the past and actively promote the integration of the ad hoc arbitration system with the existing arbitration legal system in China. This amendment to the Arbitration Law will have a positive and far-reaching impact on the existing arbitration system in China, and will be an important indicator of the maturity of China's commercial arbitration system in line with the world.

The construction of a judicial review system of arbitration is necessary for ad hoc arbitration. Judicial review is the supervision (mainly reflected in the legitimacy review) and protection (mainly reflected in the judicial assistance to the arbitration process and the remedy for the rights of the parties) of arbitration by the judiciary. This principle also applies to the ad hoc arbitration.

Therefore, an in-depth study should be conducted on the validity of ad hoc arbitration agreements, the judicial review system for the revocation and non-enforcement of ad hoc arbitral awards, and interim measures in ad hoc arbitration by taking into account China's own characteristics, and incorporating the Model Law and the successful experience of developed countries or regions in ad hoc arbitration, so as to develop a judicial review system for ad hoc arbitration that is both in line with international practices and with Chinese characteristics, and ensure that ad hoc arbitration takes root and grows up in China.

(莫之颖、肖鹏　审校)

Consolidation Provision in Arbitration Rules: Interpretation and Application of Article 19 (Consolidation of Arbitrations) of the CMAC Arbitration Rules and Proposal for Amendments[*]

LIU Kaixiang[**]

Abstract: Rules on consolidation of arbitration play an important role in effectively resolving complex commercial disputes. This article addresses the definition of consolidation, roles and functions of consolidation as a procedural mechanism, as well as general advantages and perceived weakness that consolidation may have. It goes on to compare various consolidation provisions of different arbitral institutions together with applicable laws, and examines the core elements to ensure consolidation, in particular compulsory consolidation. The article further investigates to what extent CMAC's consolidation provision (Article 19) shall be interpretated and implemented, and provides proposals for its future amendment.

Key words: Consolidation of Arbitrations; Compulsory Consolidation; Consolidation with Implicit Consent; Scope of Application and Interpretation

---

[*] Translated by MO Zhiying, HONG Huimin.
[**] Faculty of Law, Beijing University, full professor, Doctoral Supervisor, CIETAC panel arbitrator, CMAC panel arbitrator. Hereby thanks my post-graduate Ms. LU Jiazhen for her contribution in conducting research, data collection and discussion to complete this article.

I. Background and Values of Consolidation of Arbitration

1.1 Origin and Development of Consolidation of Arbitration

To realize certain goals of business, a large number of interrelated agreements[1] have been concluded in the performance of many major projects, particularly engineering and construction contracts, carriage of goods by sea, and contracts signed in related transactions[2]. This fact is becoming a cause for concern. The interrelated agreements, while lay out a parallel or interdependent structure of deal, often lead to complex multi-party and multi-contract arbitrations in recent years. In such arbitrations, an arbitral award made upon one of these agreements may have a ripple effect on other parties which were ushered into the same project by another agreement.[3] According to the findings of the research abroad, only 20% of the arbitrations administered by the International Chamber of Commerce (ICC) involved three or more parties[4] thirty years ago, while it has risen to about 30%[5] recently. In this regard, many leading arbitral institutions have introduced consolidation provisions in their arbitration rules, providing a more efficient and fair mechanism for dispute resolution.

For the purpose of this article, consolidation of arbitrations is used to referred to the merging of two or more separate but connected arbitrations admin-

---

[1] Richard Bamforth and Katerina Maidment, "'All Join In' or Not? How Well Does International Arbitration Cater for Disputes Involving Multiple Parties or Related Claims?," 3 ASA Bulletin (2009).

[2] Vladimir Filipovic, "Multiparty Arbitration and Consolidation of Arbitral Proceedings," 39 ZBORNIK PFZ 506 (1989).

[3] Sandeep Bhalothia, "Joinder and Consolidation of Parties in Arbitration," 5 CT. UNCOURT2 (2018).

[4] Martin Platte, "When Should an Arbitrator Join Cases?," 67 Arbitration International (2002).

[5] Ioannis Giakoumelos, "The Need for Implementation of a Consolidation Provision in Institutional Arbitration Rules," 17 PEPP. Disp. Resol. L. J. 23 (2017).

istered by the same arbitration institution. ① There are several types of consolidation. These include consolidation with parties' consent and compulsory consolidation. The first type requires the consent of all parties, while compulsory consolidation can apply absent consent of a party or parties, even if the parties haven't agreed to consolidate. ② There is also consolidation of arbitrations between the same parties and consolidation of arbitrations involving different parties. The latter however requires a higher threshold for consolidation. In terms of decision-making, consolidation can be ordered by an arbitration institution, an arbitral tribunal or a court, which varies with the approaches adopted in different jurisdictions. Moreover, arbitrations can be consolidated before and/or after the arbitral tribunal is formed.

1.2 Values of Consolidated Arbitration

There is a wide spectrum of opinions on the roles and functions of the consolidation. Advocates assert that consolidation could save time and cost③. For instance, if two related arbitrations are consolidated, the presentation of evidence and witness/expert testimony supporting the same or related facts can be made once rather than duplicated. For intermediaries, consolidation will also have an impact on decreasing expenses on collection of evidence and avoiding expiration of the limitation period. ④ Another advantage of consolidation is that it allows to avoid inconsistent and/or conflicting decisions. Conversely opponents argue that since arbitration is a creature of contract, consolidation could

---

① Mauro Rubino-Sammartano, "International Arbitration Law and Practice," 297 CITIC Press Group (2013).

② T. Evan Schaeffer, "Compulsory Consolidation of Commercial Arbitration Disputes," 33 St. Louis U. L. J. 495 (1989).

③ YI Yang, "Consolidation of Arbitration and Modern International Commercial Arbitration," Legal Review, Vol6(1996)

④ In series transactions, an intermediary may be at risk of the expiration of the limitation period that he/she could only request for an arbitration against the prior party after the awarding of the previous arbitration.

be challenged owning to party autonomy, which is the hallmark attribute of arbitration①. Another issue concerns the maintenance of confidentiality/privacy since consolidation allows parties to one arbitration to join another, particularly in the case of compulsory consolidation. ② Furthermore, consolidation may violate due process. It should be noted that both the United Nations Convention on the Recognition and Enforcement of Foreign Arbitral Awards (New York Convention) and Chinese domestic laws remain silent on consolidation of arbitrations, international commercial arbitration thus may lose its advantage as an alternative dispute resolution whenever the arbitral awards cannot be recognized and enforced abroad. ③ Besides, difficulties regarding the constitution of the arbitral tribunal, choice of law to foreign-related disputes, application of expedited procedure and calculation of time limits are also posed therein. ④

Notwithstanding the advantages and disadvantages of consolidating arbitral proceedings, this article suggests it is of necessity and importance that consolidation as a procedural device promotes procedural justice and substantive fairness, as international business transactions become more complex in today's globalized economy. Negative impact of consolidation could be avoided by amending respective provisions, nevertheless.

1.3 Distinction Between Consolidation and Other Similar Arbitration Procedures

1.3.1 Consolidation of Arbitrations *vis-à-vis* Multi-contract Arbitration

Multi-contract arbitration permits the parties to consolidate claims arising out of more than one contract in a single arbitration, provided pre-conditions

---

① CHEN Zhidong, "International Commercial Arbitration Law," 6-9 Law Press China (1998).
② MA Xiaoxiao, "A Comparative Study on Consolidation of Arbitrations," Beijing Arbitration Quarterly.
③ FAN Rui, "Some Thoughts on Consolidation of Arbitration: Analysis of Consolidated Proceedings," Beijing Arbitration Quarterly Vol102.
④ Zhangjian, "Transplantion and Dilemma of Consolidated Arbitration Mechanism: Feasibility Analysis of the BAC Consolidation Provision (Article 29)," Beijing Arbitration Quarterly Vol 91.

are met. In similar cases, both multi-contract arbitration and consolidation require that the provisions of the arrbitration agreements are identical or compatible, or the disputes arise out of the same or a series of related transaction (s) or the legal relations involved are the same. However, the term multi-contract arbitration should not be confused with consolidation. The former only involves two parties between whom there is only one arbitration. ① In contrast, consolidation is the merging of separate but related arbitrations, often where the arbitrations involves more than two parties.

1.3.2 Consolidation of Arbitrations *vis-à-vis* Consolidation of Hearings

Consolidation of hearings refers to the arbitral proceeding that the competent authority may, after consulting with the parties, consolidate or combine two cases or matters into one hearing due to the fact that they have related to the same set of facts or question of law. Much as consolidated arbitration, consolidated hearing promotes efficiency on that any evidence and material common to all arbitrations pending could be 'shared'. However, consolidation of hearings may only be conducted for hearings, whilst the arbitrations are still independent of each other in that other arbitral proceedings including arbitral awards remain separate.

1.3.3 Consolidation of Arbitrations *vis-à-vis* Concurrent Hearings

Concurrent hearings (also 'concurrent proceedings' under the 2018 HKIAC Administered Arbitration Rules) are designed for two or more arbitrations pending, in which the competent authority may, after consulting with the parties, conduct two or more arbitrations at the same time, or one immediately after another, or suspend any of those arbitrations until the determination of any other of them, upon meeting certain specified conditions. ② Both procedural devices are promising way to handle complex arbitrations but in different manners. Distinguished from consolidation, the concurrent hearings are condcuted

---

① Martin Platte, "When Should an Arbitrator Join Cases?," 67 Arbitration International (2002).

② Hong Kong International Arbitration Centre Administered Arbitration Rules, § 30 (2018).

without impacting the separablity of each arbitration. This mechanism is intended to avoid conflicting awards or difficulties in fact-finding by arranging concurrent hearings.

1.3.4 Consolidation of Arbitrations vis-à-vis Joinder of Third Parties

Joinder of third parties refers to the proceeding that allows an additional party to actively or passively join an existing arbitration.[1] Consolidation also allows more than two parties involved in a single arbitration, yet requires the mergering of at least two arbitrations in existence. Moreover, in the arbitrations to be consolidated, the parties must have agreed to solve the disputes by arbitration, while joinder may be challenged as the third party may not necessarily agree.

II. A Comparative Perspective: Consolidation of Arbitrations in the United States

In the United States, consolidation of related arbitrations are largely ordered by court. Modern arbitration statutes in the United States include the Federal Arbitration Act (FAA) enacted by the parliament in 1925, Uniform Arbitration Act (UAA) and Revised Uniform Arbitration Act (RUAA) promulgated by the National Conference of Commissioners on Uniform State Laws (NCCUSL) respectively in 1955 and 2000, Commercial Arbitration Rules of American Arbitration Association (AAA)[2]. Additionally, some courts may order the consolidation of arbitrations according to the Federal Rules of Civil Procedure[3].[4] Un-

---

[1] LIN Yifei, "Arbitration and Third Parties," Law Review Vol1 (2000).

[2] The consolidation procedure is provided in the Chapter titled Preliminary Hearing Procedure in the Commercial Arbitration Rules of American Arbitration Association.

[3] Federal Rules of Civil Procedure, Article 42 (a) Consolidation. If actions before the court involve a common question of law or fact, the court may: (1) join for hearing or trial any or all matters at issue in actions; (2) consolidate the actions; or (3) issue any other orders to avoid unnecessary cost or delay.

[4] Andrew A. Davenport, "Consolidation of Separate Arbitration Proceedings: The Effect of the United States Arbitration Act on the District Court's Power under Federal Rules of Civil Procedure 42(a) and 81(a)(3)," 42 MERCER L. REV. 1675 (1991).

like arbitration laws in some other countries, neither the FAA nor the UAA contains regulations on such a procedure. Section 10 of the RUAA stipulates the court may order consolidation of separate arbitration proceedings if: (1) the claims subject to the agreements to arbitrate arise in substantial part from the same transaction or series of related transactions; (2) the existence of a common issue of law or fact creates the possibility of conflicting decisions in the separate arbitration proceedings; and (3) prejudice resulting from a failure to consolidate is not outweighed by the risk of undue delay or prejudice to the rights of or hardship to parties opposing consolidation. Since the RUAA has not yet been adopted by most states①, judicial decisions concerning the consolidation in the United States have been largely made by following the precedent.

The frameworks under which Circuit Courts of Appeals deal with consolidation of arbitrations are varied. Upon judicial precedents, a general rule adopted by the majority of circuits is that a court has no authority to order consolidation unless it has been explicitly stipulated in the arbitration agreement.② To be specific, three approaches are adopted by different Federal Circuits, namely compulsory consolidation, consolidation with explicit consent and consolidation with implicit consent.

The adoption of compulsory consolidation by the Second Circuit is illustrated in *Compania Espanola de Petroleos, S. A. v. Nereus Shipping, S. A.* (Cepsa v. Nereus). The consolidation is ordered according to the Rules of Federal Civil Procedure and the court points out that ' the two arbitrations had common questions of law and fact, and because the extensive and complicated issues were so intertwined and overlapping that it could have caused great and irreparable injustice... ③ Cepsa as the guarantor is actually bound to the same contract between the shipowner's agent and the charterer. In signing the same ad-

---

① Jonathan R. Waldron, "Resolving a Split: May Courts Order Consolidation of Arbitration Proceedings Absent Express Agreement by the Parties," 2005 J. Disp. Resol. 177 (2005).

② Okuma Kazutake, "Party Autonomy in International Commercial Arbitration: Consolidation of Multiparty and Classwide Arbitration," 9 ANN. Surv. INT'l & COMP. L. 189 (2003).

③ Compania Espanola de Petroleos, S. A. v. Nereus Shipping, 527 F. 2d 966 (2d Cir. 1975), cert. denied, 426 U. S. 936 (1976).

dendum and invoking the same arbitration clause, the shipowner, charterer, and guarantor were deemed to reach an agreement to a single arbitration. ① The *Nereus* test was followed by *Elmarina, Inc. v. Comexas, N. V.*. In *Elmarina* case, the United States District Court for the Southern District of New York holds that a consolidation provision, whether explicit or implicit, shall not be a necessary condition to order consolidation. ② In other words, the court can order to consolidate separate arbitral proceedings even absent the parties' agreement, provided the requirements for consolidation are met. In the *Nereus* case, the Second Circuit takes into account below factors, *inter alia* (a) whether common questions of fact and law exist; (b) the possibility of conflicting awards; (c) whether substantive right would be prejudiced under separate arbitral proceedings; and (d) whether substantive right would be prejudiced under consolidated arbitral proceeding.

The Fifth and Ninth Circuits permitted the consolidation only on the basis of finding of explicit constent by the parties. *Weyerhaeuser v. US Fish and Wildlife Service* involves two related arbitrations, one between the shipowner and charterer, the other between the charterer and the sub-charter. Faced with two separate arbitration proceedings, the charterer petitions the court for an order of consolidation. Despite identical arbitration clauses contained in both charterparties, the court rejects charterer's request to order consolidation as it finds no explicit consent of all of the parties. The court concludes that it lacks authority to order consolidation since the arbitrations are governed by the FAA which does not provide for such a procedure. As a creature of contract, arbitration cannot be compelled absent explicit consent of all parties. Furthermore, the FAA only empowers the court to confirm and enforce a valid

---

① QIAO Xin, ZHAO Ling, "Analysis on Compulsory Consolidation," Beijing Arbitration Quarterly, Vol 1 (2008).

② T. Evan Schaeffer, "Compulsory Consolidation of Commercial Arbitration Disputes," 33 St. Louis U. L. J. 495 (1989).

arbitration agreement①, but not to create an arbitration agreement for the parties.

The Fourth Circuit holds that the parties' consent to consolidation can be determined through interpretation under FAA. The test is called "consolidation with implicit consent". It is illustrated in *Maxum Foundations, Inc, Appellants v. Salus Corporation and United Pacific Insurance Company, Appellants*, a case governed by the FAA and interpreted to empower courts to consolidate separate arbitration proceedings upon finding of implicit consent. The *Maxum* case involves two arbitrations, one between the owner and the contractor, the other between the contractor and the subcontractor. The court finds that implicit consent to consolidation can be interpreted from the structure and the terms in both

---

① FAA Section 4 Failure to arbitrate under agreement; petition to United States court having jurisdiction for order to compel arbitration; notice and service thereof; hearing and determination. A party aggrieved by the alleged failure, neglect, or refusal of another to arbitrate under a written agreement for arbitration may petition any United States district court which, save for such agreement, would have jurisdiction under title 28, in a civil action or in admiralty f the subject matter of a suit arising out of the controversy between the parties, for an order directing that such arbitration proceed in the manner provided for in such agreement. Five days' notice in writing of such application shall be served upon the party in default. Service thereof shall be made in the manner provided by the Federal Rules of Civil Procedure. The court shall hear the parties, and upon being satisfied that the making of the agreement for arbitration or the failure to comply therewith is not in issue, the court shall make an order directing the parties to proceed to arbitration in accordance with the terms of the agreement. The hearing and proceedings, under such agreement, shall be within the district in which the petition for ab order directing such arbitration is filed. If the making of the arbitration agreement for the failure, neglect, or refusal to perform the same be in issue, the court shall proceed summarily to the trial thereof. If no jury trial be demanded by the party alleged to be in default, or if the matter in dispute is within admiralty jurisdiction, the court shall bear and determine such issue. Where such an issue is raid=sed, the party alleged to be in default may, except in cases of admiralty, on or before the return day of the notice of application, demand a jury trial of such issue, and such demand the court shall make an order referring the issue or issues to a jury in the manner provided by the Federal Rules of Civil Procedure, or may specially call a jury for that purpose. If the jury find that no agreement in writing for arbitration was made or that there is no default in proceeding thereunder, the proceeding shall be dismissed. If the jury find that an agreement for arbitration was made in writing and that there is default in proceeding thereunder, the court shall make an order summarily directing the parties to proceed with the arbitration in accordance with the terms thereof.

contracts. ① Thus the Fourth Circuit, instead of explaining whether the FAA has empowered the court to order consolidation of arbitration, adopted an alternative approach.

With regard to the non-consolidation clause clearly stated in the arbitration agreement, the Fourth Circuit, the Fifth Circuit and the Ninth Circuit adopt a strict approach on consolidation subject to party autonomy.

In short, different approaches adopted by the Circuit Courts rely on whether a court interprets the FAA under doctrine of freedom of contract or upon judicial discretion. ②

III. The Logic Behind Compulsory Consolidation: Interpretation of Implicit Consent

As mentioned above, the "consolidation with implicit consent" test adopted by the Fourth Circuit lies on that the consolidation clause is an essential part of an arbitration agreement. However, not all arbitration agreements include the consolidation clause, the courts therefore are empowered to determine whether there exists an implicit consent to consolidation by means of supplementary interpretation, a step taken to fix the omission of the contract. The courts usually take into account the following factors for interpretation: (a) wording of the arbitration agreements; (b) structure and inter-relations of related contracts in the same transaction or a series of transactions; (c) purpose of such agreements.

To specify, the more specific that arbitral proceedings are stipulated in an

---

① The court holds that the Salus-Maxum subcontract incorporates a duty to submit to arbitration comports with the decisions of numerous other courts construing similar contractual language. The general conditions make the arbitration duty of the general and subcontractor coextensive with the obligation to the owner and prime contractor, therefore the dispute between Salus and Maxum must be resolved in the contractual forum.

② Michael L. DeCamp, "Consolidation of Separate Arbitration Proceedings: Liberal Construction versus Contractarian Approaches – United Kingdom of Great Britain v. Boeing Co.," 1994 J. Disp. Resol. 113 (1994).

agreement, the more likely that the parties are against consolidation. In contrast, it might be implied from a sketchily. drafted arbitration agreement that the parties mutually agree to consolidation. The same or the alike arbitration clauses in different contracts can also be deemed as consent for consolidation. Moreover, the intention of the parties can also be implied from the structure of contracts and their interrelations. For instance, it could be implied from the arbitration clause of a general agreement with ancillary agreement(s) attached that the parties intend to resolve disputes arising from the ancillary agreement(s) at court on the lump-sum basis. ① Furthermore, the primary purpose of consolidated arbitration is to effectively resolve disputes and avoid conflicting awards. In this regard, if the parties choose arbitration for the sake of efficiency, it could be interpreted that the parties mutually agree to consolidation.

Based on the above, one of the biggest challenges for the courts when they determine whether implicit consent to consolidation exists by means of interpretation is that they do not have a uniform diagnostic criteria so that the interpretations may vary among different interpreters. In order to clarify the criteria and to some extent, limit the decision-making power of the competent authority, it is necessary to specify the requirements for consolidation.

IV. Criteria for Consolidation of Arbitrations: Consolidation Provisions in Major Institutional Arbitration Rules

The requirements for consolidated arbitration can be divided into procedural and substantive elements. Procedural elements include, *inter alia* commencement of consolidation, the initiating applicant and the decision-making body. Substantive elements refer to factors such as question of law and facts. It should be noted that different procedural and substantive elements are required by different types of consolidated arbitration. In the case of consolidation with

---

① Ioannis Giakoumelos, "The Need for Implementation of a Consolidation Provision in Institutional Arbitration Rules," 17 PEPP. Disp. Resol. L. J. 23 (2017).

explicit consent, for instance, procedurally it requires application by one or more parties, and substantively it requires mutual agreement for consolidation. The substantive requirements for compulsory consolidation are higher, including disputes arising from the same or a series of related transactions, upon the same question of law or facts, or upon the identical, the identical or compatible arbitration agreements. Requirements for consolidation between different parties are stricter on the legal relations and connections between the transactions than that between the same parties. Furthermore, requirements for consolidation after constitution of arbitral tribunal is higher than that before the arbitral tribunal is formed.

It is worth to mention that the criteria of consolidated arbitration are not absolute. In other words, even if both of the procedural and substantive requirements for consolidation are met, it does not mean that the arbitrations will be consolidated. Whether or not the arbitral proceedings can be consolidated fundamentally depends on the decision by the competent authority. Reviewing the consolidation mechanisms under different arbitration rules, it is not difficult to conclude that whether consolidation of arbitrations can be granted relies on the appropriateness of the criteria and the justification of the decision-making.

Before comparing and analyzing the consolidation mechanisms in different jurisdictions, this article selects consolidation provisions from the rules of ten major institutional arbitration home and abroad. Special attentions will be drawn on seven aspects[①], including commence of consolidation, procedural requirements for consolidation, requirements for parties, requirements for arbitration agreement(s), substantive legal relations, competent authority and relevant circumstances concerned to determine consolidation, as is shown in Table 1:

---

① Constitution of tribunal after consolidation will be further discussed in this article thus hereby incorporated in Table 1.

Consolidation Provision in Arbitration Rules: Interpretation and... 275

Table 1 Comparison of Rules and Systems of Major Arbitration Institutions in the World[①]

	Arbitration Rules	Commence of consolidation	Procedural requirements for consolidation	Requirements for parties	Requirements for arbitration agreement	Substantive legal relations	Competent authority	Relevant circumstances concerned for deciding consolidation	Constitution of tribunal after consolidation
1	ICC Rules[②]	At the request of a party	Two or more arbitrations pending	Between the same parties	under the same arbitration agreement or compatible arbitration agreements	Disputes arise in connection with the same legal relationship	the ICC Court	confirmation or appointment of arbitrators	——
2	HKIAC Rules[③]	At the request of a party	Two or more arbitrations pending	——	Under the same arbitration agreement or compatible arbitration agreements	a common question of law or fact arises in all of the arbitrations, or arise out of the same transaction or a series of related transactions	HKIAC	comments of the non-requesting parties or any confirmed or appointed arbitrators	HKIAC shall appoint the arbitral tribunal in respect of the consolidated proceedings with or without regard to any party's designation

① Table 1 mainly focuses on provisions of compulsory consolidation, since consolidation with consent is commonly accepted. 32 ICC Arbitration Rule, §10 (2021).
② International Chamber of Commerce (ICC) Arbitration Rules, §10(2021).
③ Hong Kong International Arbitration Centre (HKIAC) Administered Arbitration Rules, §28(2018).

(Continued)

	Arbitration Rules	Commence of consolidation	Procedural requirements for consolidation	Requirements for parties	Requirements for arbitration agreement	Substantive legal relations	Competent authority	Relevant circumstances concerned for deciding consolidation	Constitution of tribunal after consolidation
3	SIAC Rules[①]	At the request of a party	prior to the constitution of any tribunal, or after the constitution of any tribunal	—	Under the same arbitration agreement or compatible arbitration agreements	Disputes arise out of the same legal relationship(s), or arise out of contracts consisting of a principal contract and its ancillary contract(s), or arise out of the same transaction or of series of transactions	the SIAC Court (prior to the constitution of any Tribunal) or the Tribunal (after the constitution of any Tribunal)	the same Tribunal has been constituted in each of the arbitrations or no Tribunal has been constituted in the other arbitration(s)	the Court may revoke the appointment of any arbitrators appointed prior to the decision on consolidation
4	LCIA Rules[②]	Order of the LCIA Court, or order of the Arbitral Tribunal, with the approval of the LCIA Court and upon the application of any party	prior to the constitution of any tribunal, or after the constitution of the same tribunals	Between the same disputing parties	Under the same arbitration agreement or compatible arbitration agreements	Claims arise out of the same transaction or series of related transactions	the LCIA Court the Arbitral Tribunal (with the approval of the LCIA Court)	views of the parties	—

---

① Arbitration Rules of the Singapore International Arbitration Center (SIAC), §8 (2016).
② Arbitration Rules of the London Court of International Arbitration (LCIA), §22 (2020).

(Continued)

	Arbitration Rules	Commence of consolidation	Procedural requirements for consolidation	Requirements for parties	Requirements for arbitration agreement	Substantive legal relations	Competent authority	Relevant circumstances concerned for deciding consolidation	Constitution of tribunal after consolidation
5	CEPANI Rules①	At the request of a party or decision of arbitral tribunal	Two or more arbitrations pending	—	Under the same arbitration agreement or compatible arbitration agreements	concern disputes arise from the same legal relationship or arise out of the same series of connected legal relationships	The Appointments Committee or the President	whether the parties have not excluded consolidation in the arbitration agreement; the progress made in each of the arbitrations and whether one or more arbitrators have been appointed or confirmed in more than one of the arbitrations and whether the persons appointed or confirmed are the same; the place of arbitration provided for in the arbitration agreements; Except if agreed otherwise by the parties with regard to consolidation and the manner in which it shall occur, the Appointments Committee or the President may not order consolidation of arbitrations in which a preliminary decision, a decision on admissibility or as to the merits of a claim has already been rendered.	The Appointments Committee or the President appoints the sole arbitrator or each of the members of the Arbitral Tribunal and designates one of them as chair; The parties can by agreement designate the sole arbitrator or the members of the Arbitral Tribunal for confirmation by the Appointments Committee or the President

---

① Arbitration RULES of the Belgian Center for Arbitration and Mediation (CEPANI), § 13 & § 15.8(2020).

(Continued)

	Arbitration Rules	Commence of consolidation	Procedural requirements for consolidation	Requirements for parties	Requirements for arbitration agreement	Substantive legal relations	Competent authority	Relevant circumstances concerned for deciding consolidation	Constitution of tribunal after consolidation
6	JCAA Rules①	at the written request of a Party	no arbitral tribunal has been constituted	between the same Parties or the parties to the other claim(s) to be consolidated have agreed in writing when the party has not been a Party to the pending claim(s)	under the same arbitration agreement	the same or a similar question of fact or law arises from the claims	The arbitral tribunal	the dispute is referred by the arbitration agreement to arbitration under the Rules or at the JCAA; the arbitral proceedings are capable of being conducted in a single proceeding with regard to the place of arbitration, the number of arbitrators, language(s) of the arbitration, and other issues governed by the arbitration agreements under which the claims arise	—
7	SCC Rules②	At the request of a party	newly commenced arbitrations and/or pending arbitrations	—	Identical or compatible arbitration agreements	Same transaction or series of transactions	the SCC Board	Opinions of the parties and the Arbitral Tribunal; the stage of the pending arbitration; the efficiency and expeditiousness of the proceedings	the Board may release any arbitrator already appointed

① Commercial Arbitration Rules of the Japan Commercial Arbitration Association (JACC), § 53 (2015).
② Arbitration Rules of the Arbitration Institute of Stockholm Chamber of Commerce (SCC), § 15 (2017).

(Continued)

	Arbitration Rules	Commence of consolidation	Procedural requirements for consolidation	Requirements for parties	Requirements for arbitration agreement	Substantive legal relations	Competent authority	Relevant circumstances concerned for deciding consolidation	Constitution of tribunal after consolidation
8	BAC Rules[1]	With the agreement of all parties, or decision of the BAC upon the application of a party	two or more arbitrations pending	—	—	—	BAC	arbitration agreements on which the relevant arbitrations are based, the nexus between those arbitrations, the stage that each set of arbitration proceedings has reached, the arbitrators already nominated or appointed in the relevant arbitrations	—
9	CIETAC Rules[2]	At the request of a party	Two or more arbitrations Pending	—	under multiple arbitration agreements that are identical or compatible	the arbitrations involve the legal relationships of the same nature; the multiple contracts involved consist of a principle contract and its ancillary contract(s)	CIETAC	opinions of all parties; the correlation between the arbitrations concerned; the nomination and appointment of arbitrators in the separate arbitrations	—
10	SCIA Rules[3]	With the written consent by all parties	Two or more pending arbitrations	—	—	—	SIAC	written consent by all parties	—

[1] Beijing Arbitration Commission (BAC) Arbitration Rules, § 30 (2019).
[2] China International Economic and Trade Arbitration Commission (CIETAC) Arbitration Rules, § 19 (2015).
[3] Shenzhen Court of International Arbitration (SCIA) Arbitration Rules, § 18 (2020).

The selected consolidation provisions bear below features in common: First, consolidation generally is initiated by the parties, orally or in written, while arbitration institution and the arbitral tribunal are in a passive position. Second, most provisions allow consolidation at any stage of the arbitration before the award is issued, despite a few prior to the constitution of the tribunal. Third, most provisions allow consolidation of arbitrations between different parties. Fourth, the same, identical or compatible arbitration agreement(s) existed is(are) a common requirement for compulsory consolidation. Fifth, the logic behind the requirements for the substantive legal relations is how to interpret the implicit consent of the parties. Last, the competent authorities before decision-making usually take into account the opinions of the parties and the ongoing arbitral proceedings.

The function and efficiency of a consolidation mechanism are largely relied on its criteria. Therefore balance between procedural efficiency and party autonomy is of great significance when such criteria are drafted. In other words, focusing on efficiency but disregarding the true intention of the parties may undermine the pillar of commercial arbitration; likewise interpretation of underlying intention of the parties should not merely build upon the *prima facie* evidence without probing into the interconnections between a series of transactions, between legal relations and between different arbitrations. In sum, a sound decision to consolidate arbitrations should not only demonstrate the respect for the right and interest of the parties but also promote efficiency for complex arbitrations. [1]

V. Latest Practice for Judicial Review of Consolidated Arbitration in China

As China's Arbitration Law remains silent on the consolidation of arbitra-

---

[1] Ioannis Giakoumelos, "The Need for Implementation of a Consolidation Provision in Institutional Arbitration Rules," 17 PEPP. Disp. Resol. L. J. 23 (2017).

tions, the consolidation provisions of domestic institutional arbitration rules virtually lack an explicit statutory basis and their legitimacy needs further examination. However, the judicial approaches towards consolidation of arbitrations can be inferred from the judicial reviews launched by the People's Court, the body empowered to review the validity and enforcement of arbitration awards in China.

Upon preliminary search, the top two causes of cases requesting judicial review are revocation of arbitration awards and non-enforcement of arbitration awards, with a total of 94 cases. Ten cases selected and analyzed in this article share the following three characteristics: (a) consolidation is launched in the arbitrations; (b) setting aside or non-enforcement of arbitration awards is initiated on the ground of consolidated arbitration; (c) the judicial review is launched at the issue of the legitimacy of consolidation. Special attention will be drawn on aspects such as the grounds for judicial review, the verdict, type of consolidation (consolidation with consent or compulsory consolidation), grounds for consolidation of arbitrations, manner of judicial review (procedural matters or substance matters)① and the administered arbitration institution, as is shown in Table 2.

One may note that six out of nine arbitrations in Table 2 are administrated by the China International Economic and Trade Arbitration Commission (CIETAC), revealing that consolidation as a procedural device is more frequently used in CIETAC. Besides, such consolidated arbitrations are governed by parties' consent, which reveals that consolidation with consent is more common than compulsory consolidation. In addition, application for setting aside the arbitral awards is generally on the ground of illegalityof arbitral

---

① Substantive review hereby refers to the judicial review on substantive legal relations, transactions and/or arbitration agreement, etc..

Table 2 Summary of Related Cases[①]:

	Verdict Reference Number	Court	Cause of the Case	Verdict	Type of Consolidation	Grounds for Upholding the Consolidation of Arbitrations	Manner of Judicial Review	Arbitration Institution
1	(2018) JING04 MINTE172	the Beijing Fourth Intermediate People's Court	Illegality in arbitral proceedings	Case dismissed	Consolidation with consent	Arbitrations were consolidated at the request of applicant subject to procedural fairness	Substantive	CIETAC
2	(2018) JING04 MINTE 461	the Beijing Fourth Intermediate People's Court	Illegality in arbitral proceedings	Case dismissed	Consolidation with consent	Arbitrations were consolidated at the request of applicant subject to procedural fairness	Substantive	CIETAC
3	(2020) JING04 MINTE 662	the Beijing Fourth Intermediate People's Court	Illegality in arbitral proceedings	Case dismissed	Consolidation with consent	Arbitrations were consolidated with the agreement of all parties, and the arbitrations involve the same parties as well as legal relationships of the same nature	Substantive	CIETAC
4	(2019) JING04 MINTE2	the Beijing Fourth Intermediate People's Court	Illegality in arbitral proceedings	Case dismissed	consolidation with consent	Arbitrations were consolidated with the agreement of all parties, and all of the claims in the arbitrations are made under the same arbitration agreement	Substantive	CIETAC
5	(2021) JING04 MINTE37	the Beijing Fourth Intermediate People's Court	Illegality in arbitral proceedings	Case dismissed	Consolidation with consent	Arbitrations were consolidated with the agreement of all parties.	Substantive	CIETAC

① CIETAC in Table 2 is short for China International Economic and Trade Arbitration Commission.

(Continued)

	Verdict Reference Number	Court	Cause of the Case	Verdict	Type of Consolidation	Grounds for Upholding the Consolidation of Arbitrations	Manner of Judicial Review	Arbitration Institution
6	(2017) YUE06 MINTE31	the Foshan Intermediate People's Court of Guangdong Province	Illegality in arbitral proceedings	Case dismissed	Compulsory consolidation	The guarantee contract and the contract of supervision over the mortgage involved in the arbitrations are ancillary to the contract of loan invoveld in other arbitration. The consolidation would help the tribunal to figure out the rights and obligations of each party and avoid duplicate payment. b) All parties to arbitrations shall have rights to know all the claims and defenses involved and have obligations to assist the tribunal to find out the facts.	Substantive	Foshan Arbitration Commission
7	(2019) XIANG04 MINTE17	The Hengyang Intermediate People's Court of Hunan Province	Illegality in arbitral proceedings	Case dismissed	Compulsory consolidation	a) The disputes involved arise out of the same legal relationship; b) Since the PRC Arbitration Law remains silent on whether the consent to consolidation by the party is required, such consolidation does not violate the law but is more cost-effective; c) Consolidation is without prejudice to finding of facts.	Substantive	Hengyang Arbitration Commission

(Continued)

	Verdict Reference Number	Court	Cause of the Case	Verdict	Type of Consolidation	Grounds for Upholding the Consolidation of Arbitrations	Manner of Judicial Review	Arbitration Institution
8	(2017) QIAN01 MINTE130	The Guiyang Intermediate People's Court of Guizhou Province	Illegality in arbitral proceedings	Case dismissed	Consolidation with consent	The arbitrations involve the same parties as well as claims arising of the same question of fact, and the tribunal decided to consolidate the arbitrations upon agreement of all parties, subject to the PRC Arbitration Law and Guiyang Arbitration Commission Arbitration Rules	Substantive	Guiyang Arbitration Commission
9	(2016) WAN01 ZHIYI60	The Hefei Intermediate People's Court of Anhui Province	Illegality in arbitral proceedings	Application dismissed	Compulsory consolidation	Claims in the arbitrations are the same kind; b) The arbitrations were consolidated by the tribunal in its discretion, at the request of the applicant, for the purpose of efficiency and cost-effectiveness subject to procedural fairness	Substantive	Huaibei Arbitration Commission

proceedings. ①Illegality of arbitral proceedings means the arbitral proceedings is against the Arbitration Law or the arbitration rules governing the arbitral proceedings may seriously impede the parties from exercising their procedural rights so as to substantially preclude a right award. ② One may also note that all of the selected cases are dismissed, which proves that consolidation *per se* does not constitute the ground of illegality of arbitral procedure. Furthermore, whether the matters of substance will be reviewed is highly related to the type of consolidation, namely whether it is consensual or compulsory.

---

① Arbitration Law of the People's Republic of China (2017) Article 58: If parties concerned have evidences to substantiate one of the following, they may apply for the cancellation of arbitral award with the intermediate people's court at the place where the arbitration commission resides. 1. There is no agreement for arbitration. 2. The matters ruled are out the scope of the agreement for arbitration or the limits of authority of an arbitration commission. 3. The composition of the arbitration tribunal or the arbitration proceedings violate the legal proceedings. 4. The evidences on which the ruling is based are forged. 5. Things that have an impact on the impartiality of ruling have been discovered concealed by the opposite party. 6. Arbitrators have accepted bribes, resorted to deception for personal gains or perverted the law in the ruling. The people's court shall form a collegial bench to verify the case. Whereas one of the aforesaid cases should be found, arbitral award should be ordered to be cancelled by the court. Whereas the people's court establishes that an arbitral award goes against the public interests, the award should be cancelled by the court. Also see Civil Procedure Law of the People's Republic of China (Revised in 2017), Article 237: Where a party fails to perform an award of an arbitration institution established according to law, the other party may apply for execution to the people's court with jurisdiction. The people's court to which an application is made shall execute the award. Where the party against whom the application is made presents evidence that the arbitral award falls under any of the following circumstances, the people's court shall, after examination and verification by a collegiate bench formed by the people's court, rule to deny execution: 1. the parties have neither included an arbitration clause in their contract, nor subsequently reached a written arbitration agreement; 2. the matters decided in the award exceed the scope of the arbitration agreement or are beyond the arbitral authority of the arbitration institution; 3. the composition of the arbitral tribunal or the arbitration procedure did not conform to statutory procedure; 4. the evidence used as a basis for rendering an award is fabricated; 5. the other party to the case conceals important evidence, which is substantial enough to affect the impartial ruling by the arbitration institution; or 6. one or several arbitrators acts corruptly, accepts bribes or engages in malpractice for personal benefits or made an award that perverted the law. Where the people's court determines that the execution of the award would be against the public interest, it shall rule to deny execution. The written ruling shall be served on both parties and on the arbitration institution. Where a people's court rules to deny execution of an arbitral award, a party may, in accordance with the written arbitration agreement between the two parties, re-apply to the arbitration institution for arbitration or institute an action in a people's court.

② Yinlong Energy Co., Ltd vs CITIC Securities Co., Ltd., (2018)JING04MINTE172, the Beijing Fourth Intermediate People's Court.

If the parties reach an agreement on consolidation, the court generally will not focus on the substance, otherwise the court will review the arbitration agreement and the connections between the arbitrations. Last, some local courts towards a more open approach to compulsory consolidation on the ground that it is left to the discretion of the court under the law. ①

Conclusion thus could be drawn as follows: (a) consolidation *per se* does not constitute a ground for illegality of arbitral procedure; (b) consolidation of arbitrations is not a common practice in China and in current regime the majority is consolidation with consent; (c) the Chinese courts generally adopt an open and dynamic approach towards consolidated arbitration; (d) consolidation as an emerging procedural device in arbitration has huge potential for future development in China.

VI. CMAC's Consolidation Provision (Article 19): Scope of Application and Interpretation

China Maritime Arbitration Commission (CMAC) is one of the leading arbitral institutions in China that has introduced and applied consolidation of arbitrations. In 1996, two CMAC arbitrations invovling demurrage disputes were consolidated. ② Despite the consolidation was agreed by the parties, the Tian-

---

① Hengyang Construction Co., Ltd. vs FU Xiaonian, FU Qiaoyun and LI Xiaozha, (2019)XIANG04MINTE17, the Beijing Fourth Intermediate People's Court.

② See CAI Hongda, Analysis of Re-arbitration, Arbitration and Law Vol 2 (2000). Company K (the shipowner) and company D (the charter) signed a voyage charter party to delivered pallets from Port of Zhangjiagang PRC to the Port of Vancouver USA, upon which another voyage charter party was concluded later between company D (the charterer) and company I (the subcharterer). The contents of the two charterparties are very similar. Later company D requested an arbitration against company I before China Maritime Arbitration Commission(CMAC) and claimed that the shipping and demurrage rates should be calculated upon bulk volume. Company K also applied for an arbitration before the CMAC at the same day and requested company D to compensate shipping and demurrage rates. The CMAC consolidated hearings of two arbitrations upon the consent of all parties and suggestions of both arbitral tribunals. Afterwards two arbitral awards were issued at the same day and both held that company D shall bear the primary obligation. Company D thus appealed for cancelation of the arbitral awards at Tianjin Maritime Court.

jin Maritime Court remanded re-arbitration on the grounds that there was no consolidation provisions in the CMAC Arbitration Rules. The same awards were issued after re-arbitration and voluntarily performed by the parties. The CMAC afterwards added the consolidation provision into the 2000 CMAC Arbitration Rules and the provision has been retained in the 2015, 2018 and the latest 2020 editions.

Article 19 of the latest amended China Maritime Arbitration Commission Arbitration Rules (hereinafter as the CMAC Arbitration Rules) [1] stipulates the consolidation of arbitrations including both consensual and compulsory consolidation between the same or multiple parties. Additionally the provision stipulates the substantive and procedural requirements for consolidation, as well as other factors concerned for decision-making; Moreover, it clarifies that arbitral institution is the competent authority for consolidation and stipulates the types of consolidation as well as the proceedings after the consolidation. Like stated above, a complete consolidation provision should include: (1) competent authority that determines the consolidation; (2) the commencement of consolidation; (3) the statutory requirement for consolidation and additional factors concerned; (4) the time limit for consolidation. In this regard, Article 19 of the CMAC Arbitration Rules is relatively comprehensive as a consolidation provi-

---

[1] CMAC Arbitration Rules, 19 (2018), Consolidation of Arbitrations: 1. At the request of a party, CMAC may consolidate two or more arbitrations pending under these Rules into a single arbitration if: (a) all of the claims in the arbitrations are made under the same arbitration agreement; or (b) the claims in the arbitrations are made under multiple arbitration agreements that are identical or compatible and the arbitrations involve the same parties as well as legal relationships of the same nature; (c) the claims in the arbitrations are made under multiple arbitration agreements that are identical or compatible and the multiple contracts involved consist of the principal contract and the CMAC Arbitration Rules ancillary contract(s); or (d) all the parties to the arbitrations have agreed to consolidation. 2. In deciding whether to consolidate the arbitrations in accordance with the preceding Paragraph 1, CMAC shall take into account the opinions of all parties and other relevant factors such as the correlation between the arbitrations concerned, including the nomination and appointment of arbitrators in the separate arbitrations. 3. Unless otherwise agreed by all the parties, the arbitrations shall be consolidated into the arbitration that was first commenced. 4. After the consolidation of arbitrations, the conduct of the arbitral proceedings shall be decided by the Arbitration Court if the arbitral tribunal is not formed, or shall be decided by the arbitral tribunal if it has been formed.

sion.

Special attention should be drawn on the following questions: First, how to understand the four requirements under Article 19.1 and their relations in between; Second, how to define 'compatible arbitration agreements'; Third, how to determine the principal - ancillary contractual relationship; Fourth, what are the 'relevant factors' stipulated in Article 19.2; Fifth, what is the inter-relation between Article 19.2 and Article 19.3; Last, how to understand Article 19.3 and Article 19.4.

First of all, Article 19.1 essentially provides requirements for consolidated arbitration, besides the definition, initiation and competent authority of consolidated arbitration. In particular, Article 19.1(a) to (c) stipulate compulsory consolidation, while Article 19.1(d) refers to consolidation with the consent of the parties. It is widely acknowledged that consolidation with consent requires unanimous consent of all parties, Article 19.1(d) thus could be deemed as a friendly reminder. Like most consolidation provisions in comparative law, the parties' agreement on consolidation could be reached in oral or written forms. [①] In terms of compulsory consolidation, Articles 19.1(a) to (c) are integral and independent. On one hand that compulsory consolidation could be requested Article 19.1(a), 19.1(b) or 19.1(c), on the other hand they are overlapped providing various circumstances of compulsory consolidation. Regarding the arbitration agreement that the consolidation based on, Article 19.1(a) refers to the same arbitration agreement, while Articles 19.1(b) and 19.1(c) refer to identical or compatible arbitration agreements. As for the parties involved, Article 19.1(b) provides for compulsory consolidation between the same parties, Article 19.1(c) refers to multi-party consolidation, while Article 19.1(a) remains silent on this aspect.

It is important to analyze the such requirements on the purpose of this pro-

---

[①] Among the arbitration rules selected in Table 1, JCAA Rules requires consolidation shall be applied at the written request of a party and SCIA Rules requires that consolidation shall be applied at the written consent of parties.

vision. Given the consensual nature of arbitration, there are almost no disputes in consolidation with parties' consent. In terms of compulsory consolidation, however, interpretation should be conducted upon party autonomy. The Articles 19.1 (a) to (c) literally stipulate three requirements for compulsory consolidation, in nature however interpret criteria for consolidation with implicit consent①. In other words, Article 19.1 does not provide requirements for compulsory consolidation but for consolidation with implicit consent. ②

Secondly, 19.1(b) stipulates that the claims should be under identical or compatible arbitration agreement when the arbitrations involve the same parties. Regarding the term 'compatible', the same is adopted in the arbitration rules of the HKIAC, ICC and LCIA. The correspondent Chinese term (相容) used in the CMAC Arbitration Rules (Chinese version) however is slightly different from that (兼容) in the HKLAC Administered Arbitration Rules (Chinese version), problems thus may arise from the interpretation of the arbitration agreements. As consolidated arbitration mechanism is an example of legal transplantation, it is important to examine its original meaning in English. On one hand, meaning of the term 'compatible' in Oxford Dictionary is defined as: (a) (of a computer, piece of software, etc.) able to be used with a specified piece of equipment or software without special adaptation or modification; (b) (of one thing) consistent with another; and (c) (of two people) able to have a harmonious relationship. Among them, the third meaning is ap-

---

① The consolidation with implicit consent could be implied upon meeting any of the following requirements: (a) all of the claims in the arbitrations are made under the same arbitration agreement; or (b) the claims in the arbitrations are made under multiple arbitration agreements that are identical or compatible and the arbitrations involve the same parties as well as legal relationships of the same nature; (c) the claims in the arbitrations are made under multiple arbitration agreements that are identical or compatible and the multiple contracts involved consist of the principal contract and the CMAC Arbitration Rules ancillary contract(s); or (d) all the parties to the arbitrations have agreed to consolidation.
② In scenario of the non-consolidation clause, the difference between compulsory consolidation and consolidation with implicit consent lies on that consolidation of arbitrations would be allowed based on the former while refused upon the latter.

plicable to interpersonal relations only. In addition, meaning of the term 'compatibility' ① in the Chinese-English Dictionary of Anglo-American Law② is defined as (a) harmonious relationship between a couple; and (b) consistent and harmonious relations among different things. In short, we suggest that the term 'compatible' should be interpreted as: (b) (of one thing) consistent with another; and (c) (of two people) able to have a harmonious relationship, thus the Chinese term adopted by HKIAC Administered Arbitration Rules (Chinese version) is more appropriate than that used in the CMAC Arbitration Rules (Chinese version). On the other hand, the term 'compatible' under consolidated arbitration mechanism should be interpreted on a case by case basis in the scenario of multiple arbitration agreements. With reference to Article 16 of the PRC Arbitration Law, CMAC Model Clause③, HKIAC Model Clause④ and SCC Model Clause⑤, we suggest that an arbitration agreement should include following factors: (a) intent to arbitrate; (b) claims; (c) arbitral institution; (d) applicable arbitration rules; (e) applicable law;

---

① Compatibility is the noun of compatible.
② 268 Chinese-English Dictionary of Anglo-American Law (2003).
③ China Maritime Arbitration Commission (CMAC) Model Arbitration Clause: Any dispute arising from or in connection with this Contract shall be submitted to China Maritime Arbitration Commission (CMAC) for arbitration which shall be conducted in accordance with the CMAC's arbitration rules in effect at the time of applying for arbitration. The arbitral award is final and binding upon both parties.
④ HKIAC Arbitration Model Clause: Any dispute, controversy, difference or claim arising out of or relating to this contract, including the existence, validity, interpretation, performance, breach or termination thereof or any dispute regarding non- contractual obligations arising out of or relating to it shall be referred to and finally resolved by arbitration administered by the Hong Kong International Arbitration Centre (HKIAC) under the HKIAC Administered Arbitration Rules in force when the Notice of Arbitration is submitted. The law of this arbitration clause shall be … (Hong Kong law). The seat of arbitration shall be … (Hong Kong). The number of arbitrators shall be … (one or three). The arbitration proceedings shall be conducted in … (insert language).
⑤ Arbitration Institute of the Stockholm Chamber of Commerce (SCC) Model Arbitration Clause: Any dispute, controversy or claim arising out of or in connection with this contract, or the breach, termination or invalidity thereof, shall be finally settled by arbitration in accordance with the Arbitration Rules of the Arbitration Institute of the Stockholm Chamber of Commerce. *Recommended additions*: The arbitral tribunal shall be composed of three arbitrators/a sole arbitrator. The seat of arbitration shall be […]. The language of the arbitration shall be […]. This contract shall be governed by the substantive law of […].

(f) seat of arbitration; (g) number of arbitrators; (h) language of arbitration. Among them, (a)(b)(c) are core elements of a valid arbitration agreement.

Thus conclusions can be drawn that: first, an express intent to arbitrate in all arbitration agreements involved; second, the claims, though different, should not be contradictory①, and merely overlapped claims shall be consolidated; third, the arbitral institution shall be the same; fourth, the selected arbitration rules shall be the same; fifth, the number of arbitrators shall be identical; sixth, the language of arbitration shall be the same. Moreover, whether or not the applicable law and the seat of arbitration should be identical, it needs to be examined on a case by case basis. For instance, in the *Elmarina* case②, the court takes into account the seat of arbitration as one in London and the other in New York.

Thirdly, the literal and purposive approach of interpretation should as well be adopted when analyzing the interrelation between the principal contract and ancillary contracts. In the 2015 CMAC Arbitration Rules (Chinese version), the consolidation provision stipulated for the first time that multiple contracts involved shall consist of the principal contract and ancillary contract (s). In the context of Chinese law, an ancillary contract is subordinated to the principal contract in terms of the establishment, change, termination, terms and clauses, validity and the scope. If the principal contract is null and void, the ancillary contract should be null and void. The contract of guarantee, for instance, is a typical ancillary contract to principal contract that contemplates the principal debtor, the creditor and the surety. Should literal approach be used to interpret the principal-ancillary contractual relationship, the

---

① For instance, conflicts may occur in case some contracts agree to arbitration yet others do not or remain silent.

② See T. Evan Schaeffer, "Compulsory Consolidation of Commercial Arbitration Disputes," 33 St. Louis U. L. J. 495 (1989). In the *Elmarina* case, the charterparty between the shipowner and the charter agrees to arbitrate in London, while the agreement between the charter and the cargo owner requests to arbitrate in New York. The court ordered consolidation of the two arbitrations by citing Nereus case as preceding.

scope of application would be rather narrow. If the surety agrees to provide guarantee for the principal debtor in the principal contract, the ancillary contract might reference the principal arbitration clause. In a situation of consolidated arbitration, Article 19. 1 could be applied, thereby frustrating the purpose of Article 19. 3.

Likewise, in respect of consolidation of arbitrations, the terms 'principal contract' and 'ancillary contract(s)' ① are adopted by Article 8. 1(c) of the SIAC Rules providing that the disputed contracts shall consist of a principal contract and its ancillary contract(s) in a situation of multiple arbitration agreements. ②

---

① The terms principal contract and the ancillary contract(s) are both adopted by the 2016 SCIA Arbitration Rules and the 2018 CMAC Arbitration Rules.

② SIAC Arbitration Rules (2016) Article 8 consolidation, 8. 1 Prior to the constitution of any Tribunal in the arbitrations sought to be consolidated, a party may file an application with the Registrar to consolidate two or more arbitrations pending under these Rules into a single arbitration, provided that any of the following criteria is satisfied in respect of the arbitrations to be consolidated: a. all parties have agreed to the consolidation; b. all the claims in the arbitrations are made under the same arbitration agreement; or c. the arbitration agreements are compatible, and: (ⅰ) the disputes arise out of the same legal relationship(s); (ⅱ) the disputes arise out of contracts consisting of a principal contract and its ancillary contract(s); or (ⅲ) the disputes arise out of the same transaction or series of transactions. 8. 2 An application for consolidation under Rule 8. 1 shall include: a. the case reference numbers of the arbitrations sought to be consolidated; b. the names, addresses, telephone numbers, facsimile numbers and electronic mail addresses, if known, of all parties and their representatives, if any, and any arbitrators who have been nominated or appointed in the arbitrations sought to be consolidated; c. the information specified in Rule 3. 1 (c) and Rule 3. 1(d); d. if the application is being made under Rule 8. 1(a), identification of the relevant agreement and, where possible, a copy of such agreement; and e. a brief statement of the facts and legal basis supporting the application. 8. 3 The party applying for consolidation under Rule 8. 1 shall, at the same time as it files an application for consolidation with the Registrar, send a copy of the application to all parties and shall notify the Registrar that it has done so, specifying the mode of service employed and the date of service. 8. 4 The Court shall, after considering the views of all parties, and having regard to the circumstances of the case, decide whether to grant, in whole or in part, any application for consolidation under Rule 8. 1. The Court's decision to grant an application for consolidation under this Rule 8. 4 is without prejudice to the Tribunal's power to subsequently decide any question as to its jurisdiction arising from such decision. The Court's decision to reject an application for consolidation under this Rule 8. 4, in whole or in part, is without prejudice to any party's right to apply to the Tribunal for consolidation pursuant to Rule 8. 7. Any arbitrations that are not consolidated shall continue as separate arbitrations under these Rules. 8. 5 Where the Court decides to consolidate two or more arbitrations under Rule 8. 4, the arbitrations shall be consolidated into the arbitration that is deemed by the Registrar to have commenced first, unless otherwise agreed by all parties or the Court decides otherwise having regard to the (转下页)

In the language of common law,[1] the relationship between principal contract and ancillary contracts not only refers to that between the contract of guarantee and the principal contract, but also the controlling-subordinate status of contracts in series of transactions, such as the general contract and sub-contracts in engineering procurement construction.

Therefore, combined with the parties' position in the transaction and the purpose of the consolidated arbitration, this article suggests it is proper adop-

---

(接上页) circumstances of the case. 8.6 Where an application for consolidation is granted under Rule 8.4, the Court may revoke the appointment of any arbitrators appointed prior to the decision on consolidation. Unless otherwise agreed by all parties, Rule 9 to Rule 12 shall apply as appropriate, and the respective timelines thereunder shall run from the date of receipt of the Court's decision under Rule 8.4. 8.7 After the constitution of any Tribunal in the arbitrations sought to be consolidated, a party may apply to the Tribunal to consolidate two or more arbitrations pending under these Rules into a single arbitration, provided that any of the following criteria is satisfied in respect of the arbitrations to be consolidated: a. all parties have agreed to the consolidation; b. all the claims in the arbitrations are made under the same arbitration agreement, and the same Tribunal has been constituted in each of the arbitrations or no Tribunal has been constituted in the other arbitration (s); or c. the arbitration agreements are compatible, the same Tribunal has been constituted in each of the arbitrations or no Tribunal has been constituted in the other arbitration (s), and: (i) the disputes arise out of the same legal relationship(s); (ii) the disputes arise out of contracts consisting of a principal contract and its ancillary contract(s); or (iii) the disputes arise out of the same transaction or series of transactions. 8.8 Subject to any specific directions of the Tribunal, the provisions of Rule 8.2 shall apply, *mutatis mutandis*, to an application for consolidation under Rule 8.7. 8.9 The Tribunal shall, after giving all parties the opportunity to be heard, and having regard to the circumstances of the case, decide whether to grant, in whole or in part, any application for consolidation under Rule 8.7. The Tribunal's decision to grant an application for consolidation under this Rule 8.9 is without prejudice to its power to subsequently decide any question as to its jurisdiction arising from such decision. Any arbitrations that are not consolidated shall continue as separate arbitrations under these Rules. 8.10 Where an application for consolidation is granted under Rule 8.9, the Court may revoke the appointment of any arbitrators appointed prior to the decision on consolidation. 8.11 The Court's decision to revoke the appointment of any arbitrator under Rule 8.6 or Rule 8.10 is without prejudice to the validity of any act done or order or Award made by the arbitrator before his appointment was revoked. 8.12 Where an application for consolidation is granted under Rule 8.4 or Rule 8.9, any party who has not nominated an arbitrator or otherwise participated in the constitution of the Tribunal shall be deemed to have waived its right to nominate an arbitrator or otherwise participate in the constitution of the Tribunal, without prejudice to the right of such party to challenge an arbitrator pursuant to Rule 14.

① See Bryan A. Garner, The Black's Law Dictionary (9th Edition). A principal contract is one which stands by itself, justifies its own existence, and is not subordinate or auxiliary to any other. Ancillary means aiding, auxiliary, attendant upon, subordinate, a proceeding attendant upon or which aids another proceeding considered as principal.

ting a broad approach on the scope of Article 19.1(c) of the CMAC Arbitration Rules. That is to say, the term 'the multiple contracts involved consist of the principal contract and the ancillary contract(s)' could be interpreted as that multiple contracts involved are from the same transaction or a number of related transactions.

Fourthly, Article 19.2 provides an unlimited list of factors concerned when the arbitral institution exercises its decision-making power. For one, Article 19.2 clarifies that CMAC should take into account the opinions of the parties and other relevant factors such as the correlation between the arbitrations concerned, including the nomination and appointment of arbitrators in the separate arbitrations; For another, CMAC should also take into account additional factors that are not specified in this provision, such as the opinions of the appointed arbitrators. As for the nomination and appointment of arbitrators in the different arbitrations, the arbitral institution should examine whether or not the arbitral tribunals are constituted, whether or not the number and personnel of the arbitral tribunals are identical. On the assumption that the arbitral tribunal has not yet been constituted, or the number and personnel of the arbitral tribunals constituted are identical, and in the absence of non-consolidation clause, it is likely that the arbitral institution would consolidate the arbitrations.

Fifthly, Article 19.1 stipulates the requirements for consolidated arbitration, while Article 19.2 provides for the competent authority for consolidation and factors concerned with decision-making. Regarding the interrelation between Article 19.1 and Article 19.2, logically Article 19.1 is the premise for Article 19.2. However, pragmatically the competent authority is entitled to reject the consolidation even if the requirements are met. In SESDERMA, S.L. case, the Beijing Fourth Intermediate People's Court dismissed the applicant's claim for cancelling an arbitral award on the grounds that arbitral institution has the power to consolidate arbitrations pending. ①

---

① SESDERMA, S. L. vs GOLONGCO., LIMITED, (2021) JING04MINTE114, Beijing Fourth Intermediate People's Court.

Finally, Article 19.3 and Article 19.4 respectively stipulates the manner and proceeding of consolidation. In terms of the manners, arbitrations shall be consolidated into the earliest arbitration for the purpose of efficiency, as stipulated by most consolidation provisions. As for procedural requirement, Article 19.4 provides that before the constitution of the arbitral tribunal the CMAC shall be the competent authority for consolidation, while the arbitral tribunal shall be the competent authority after the constitution.

Ⅶ. Amendment Proposals for Article 19 (Consolidation of Arbitrations) of the CMAC Arbitration Rules

Based on the above, the consolidation provisions (Article 19 of CMAC Rules) can be amended on the following aspects: first, respect the validity of the non-consolidation clause between the parties since party autonomy is the baseline of arbitration; second, in the case of compulsory consolidation, the parties should be given the right of defense; third, requirement for compulsory consolidation arising from the same transaction or related transactions should be added; fourth, the constitution of arbitral tribunal after consolidation should be clearly stipulated; fifth, charges of consolidated arbitration cases need to be amended appropriately.

First, compulsory consolidation is not unlimited, nor is an absolute decision made by the competent authority. Indeed it is the interpretation of implicit consent of the parties. If the parties clearly reject the consolidation in advance, there is no possibility to imply the consent of consolidation. In this regard, the competent authority cannot determine the consolidation. Article 19 however does not provide for the limitation, and there are possibilities that the Arbitration Commission may decide to consolidate arbitrations regardless of the non-consolidation clause. Meanwhile, a more clarified provision could be a guidance for parties to make reasonable arrangements in advance on whether or not accept the consolidated arbitration, thereby reduce the conflicts and challenges when apply the compulsory consolidation provision.

Second, in the case of compulsory consolidation, it should endow the parties right to defense. On one hand, compulsory consolidation essentially deprives the right from the party against consolidation, while they are entitled for defense upon the principle of private rights. On the other hand, the evidence submitted by the defendant may help the arbitral institution to examine whether the criteria for consolidation are satisfied. Finally, right to defense is the requirement of procedural legality. Despite Article 19.2 stipulates that CMAC shall take into account the opinions of all parties, the provision merely allows the arbitral institution discretion in given scope yet fails addressing the rights of the parties and the responsibilities of the arbitral institution.

Third, the principal-ancillary contractual relationship prescribed in Article 19.1(c) takes a narrow approach regarding the scope and application. As a multi-party arbitration mechanism, consolidated arbitration should apply to disputes arose from same transaction or a number of related transactions. Current provision fails to contain all purposes and the institutional functions of consolidated arbitration. Therefore, we suggest that the dispute arises from the same transaction or a number of related transactions should be added into the current provision.

Fourth, if arbitral tribunal has not yet been constituted in each and every arbitration, or the same arbitral tribunal has been constituted in all arbitrations before the consolidation, consolidation will not be a challenge for constitution of the arbitral tribunal. If different arbitral tribunals have been constituted in all arbitrations or the arbitral tribunal has not yet constituted in some arbitrations before the consolidation, it is necessary to clarify the requirements for constitution of the arbitral tribunal in the scenario of consolidation. For example, in the *Nereus* case, the arbitral tribunal consists of five members, including three arbitrators respectively selected by three parties, and two arbitrators selected by those three selected arbitrators, [1] despite this article cannot agree

---

[1] Okuma Kazutake, "Party Autonomy in International Commercial Arbitration: Consolidation of Multiparty and Classwide Arbitration," 9 ANN. Surv. INT'l & COMP. L. 189 (2003).

with the manner of constitution of the arbitral tribunal. In practice, constitution of arbitral tribunal after consolidation is generally empowered to a third party or its functional department. Examples could be found in the rules of HKIAC, SCC, SIAC and CEPANI. In this regard, some scholars believe that if there are different arbitral tribunals before consolidation, and the parties intent for consolidation, the parties should be given the opportunity to replace the unmatched arbitrator within a reasonable period; if the parties fail to reach a consensus, the appointment should be made by the competent authority of the arbitral institution. ① This approach is taken by this article as it not only ensure the parties' right to participate in the arbitration, but also address the efficiency of the arbitration procedure. Furthermore, the time limit for re-negotiation on the replacement of arbitrators needs to be reasonably amended.

Fifth, regarding the arbitration fees for consolidation, consolidation of arbitrations is cost-effective in that evidence about disputes arising from a common question of facts can be examined in a single arbitration. ② The costs will be reduced on two aspects: one is the charge of arbitral institution and arbitral tribunal, for instance less working hours of arbitrators; the other is costs of the parties, for instance in the collection of evidence. However, consolidation does not necessarily lower the costs of both sides nor equally. The benefit has to be analyzed on a case by case basis, yet the parties may also benefit from the lower costs charged by the arbitral institution and arbitral tribunal. As previously stated, consolidated arbitration is not yet prevalent in China, such benefit may encourage the parties to reach a consensus on consolidated arbitration. ③ Furthermore, arbitral institution should be empowered to lower the arbitration fees in an appropriate manner depends on the situation, as that prescribed in the

---

① K. S. Stepanova, "Consolidation of Cases in International Commercial Arbitration," 2016 HERALD CIV. PROC. 210 (2016).

② YI Yang, "Constitution of Arbitrations and Contemporary International Commercial Arbitration," Law Review Vol 6 (1996).

③ QIAO Xin, ZHAO Ling, "Analysis on Compulsory Consolidation," Vol 1 Beijing Arbitration Quarterly (2008).

HKIAC Rules[①].

Based on the above, proposals on amendment of Article 19 are as follows:

(1) Except as otherwise agreed by the parties in arbitration agreement against consolidation, at the request of a party, CMAC may consolidate two or more arbitrations pending under these Rules into a single arbitration if:

(a) all of the claims in the arbitrations are made under the same arbitration agreement; or

(b) the claims in the arbitrations are made under multiple arbitration agreements that are identical or compatible and arbitrations involve the same parties as well as legal relationship of the same nature; or

(c) the claims in the arbitrations are made under multiple arbitration agreements that are identical or compatible and multiple contracts involved consist of principal contract and the ancillary contract(s), or the disputes arise out of the same transaction or series of transactions; or

(d) all the parties to the arbitration have agreed to consolidation.

(2) In deciding whether to consolidate the arbitrations in accordance with the preceding Paragraph 1, CMAC shall take into account the opinions of all parties, the opinions of arbitral tribunal constituted, and other relevant factors such as the correlation between the arbitrations concerned, including the nomination and appointment of arbitrators in the separate arbitrations.

(3) Unless otherwise agreed by the parties, the arbitrations shall be consolidated into the arbitration that was first commenced.

(4) Provided that no arbitral tribunal has yet been constituted for the arbitration(s) sought to be consolidated, the appointment of arbitral tribunal shall be conducted in accordance with the preceding Paragraph 3; Provided that arbitral tribunal(s) has(have) already constituted for all the arbitration(s) sought to be consolidated, that such arbitral tribunal(s) is (are) com-

---

① HKIAC Administered Rules (2018), Article 28.10, HKIAC may adjust its Administrative Fees and the arbitral tribunal's fees (where appropriate) after a Request for Consolidation has been submitted.

posed of the same arbitrators, no arbitral tribunal shall be constituted after such consolidation; Provided that arbitral tribunal (s) has (have) constituted for some arbitration (s) sought to be consolidated, or if already constituted for all, that such arbitral tribunal (s) is (are) composed of the different arbitrators, the parties, following discussion, shall jointly nominate or jointly entrust Chairman of CMAC to appoint the arbitral tribunal pursuant to Article 33 of these Rules[①], where the parties fail to make such appointment within fifteen (15) days from the date of receipt of the Notice of Consolidation, the CMAC chairman shall appoint all three members of the arbitral tribunal and designate one of them as the presiding arbitrator.

(5) Prior to the constitution of any tribunal in the arbitrations sought to be consolidated, CMAC shall determine the arbitral proceedings; After the constitution of any tribunal in the arbitrations sought to be consolidated, the arbitral tribunal shall determine the arbitral proceedings.

(6) CMAC may adjust its Administrative Fees and the arbitral tribunal's fees (where appropriate) after a Request for Consolidation has been submitted.

Conclusion

In general there are two types of consolidated arbitration, namely consolidation with consent and compulsory consolidation. Distinguished from consolidation with consent, compulsory consolidation is more controversial in theory and in prac-

---

[①] See 2018 CMAC Arbitration Rules, Article 33, 1. Where there are two or more Claimants and/or Respondents in an arbitration case, the Claimant side and/or the Respondent side, following discussion, shall each jointly nominate or jointly entrust the Chairman of CMAC to appoint one arbitrator. 2. The presiding arbitrator or the sole arbitrator shall be nominated in accordance with the procedures stipulated in Paragraphs 2, 3 and 4 of Article 31 of these Rules. When making such nomination pursuant to Paragraph 3 of Article 31 of these Rules, the Claimant side and/or the Respondent side, following discussion, shall each submit a list of their jointly agreed candidates. 3. Where either the Claimant side or the Respondent side fails to jointly nominate or jointly entrust the Chairman of CMAC to appoint one arbitrator within fifteen (15) days from the date of its receipt of the Notice of Arbitration, the Chairman of CMAC shall appoint all three members of the arbitral tribunal and designate one of them to act as the presiding arbitrator.

tice. The advantages of consolidation are that it not only promotes efficiency of arbitral proceedings, but also avoids conflicting awards. Substantive justice can also be achieved upon consolidating two or more arbitrations pending. However, consolidation, in particular compulsory consolidation, may be challenged owning to party autonomy.

To overcome the drawbacks of consolidation, this article suggests that the compulsory consolidation should be prohibited by shifting regime from compulsory consolidation to consolidation with implicit consent. By reviewing consolidated arbitration in the United States and the institutional consolidation provisions, this article suggests that uniform diagnostic requirements should be drafted, and the effectiveness of non-consolidation clause should be affirmed. Furthermore, this article proposes that the parties to consolidation should be given the right of defense for the purpose of the legitimacy of consolidation.

As for the interpretation and application of the consolidation provision (Article 19) of the CMAC Arbitration Rules, this article has drawn special attention on six aspects. Among which this article suggests that (a) the compatibility of the arbitration agreements should be interpreted on a case by case basis; (b) to better realize the purpose of consolidation, a less strict test should be adopted in determining whether there are 'multiple contracts consisting of principal contract and ancillary contracts'; (c) for the purpose of consolidation, balance between the justification of the criteria and the rationality of the decision-making should be reached; (d) in deciding whether to consolidate the arbitrations, CMAC shall take into account other relevant factors such as the opinions of the arbitral tribunal constituted prior to consolidation. Above all, this article proposes an amendment to the CMAC consolidation provision on five aspects.

It could be concluded from China's judicial review that even if consolidation of arbitration is not a common practice in China, the courts adopt an open and dynamic approach towards consolidation of arbitrations. Therefore, consolidation as an emerging procedural device in arbitration has huge potential for future development in China.

（陈迅、肖鹏　审校）

Intellectual Property Risk Management in Digital Trade

XUE Hong[*]

Abstract: Digital trade, although empowers international transactions, brings new intellectual property risks to traders. On one hand, business operators can utilize the rules and facilities of digital platforms to manage the risks of intellectual property; on the other, intellectual property warranty system has been revitalized in international trade and reshaped the allocation of risks and benefits between the importers and exporters. In the new environment of digital trade, traders' capacity of intellectual property risk management should be renewed and upgraded to avoid or mitigate losses and protect legitimate trade interests.

Key words: digital trade; risk management; digital platforms; dispute resolution; intellectual property warranty

International trade has been profoundly changed by digital technology and Internet. The globalized market has grown into an effective information system. The unprecedented growth of international trade of goods, services and intellectual property rights signalizes the new level of globalization. Digital trade supported by digital technology has become the mainstream of trade.

---

[*] Professor of Beijing Normal University, Member of State Expert Council on Trade Digitization.

The World Trade Organization (WTO) is holding the negotiations on market access and competition of digital trade. The Asia Pacific Economic Cooperation (APEC) initiates the project on cross-border data flow. The international negotiations and legislation on paperless trade, electronic signatures, and electronic identities (e-IDs) are going on at the United Nations Commission on International Trade Law (UNCITRAL) and United Nations Economic and Social Commission for Asia and the Pacific (UNESCAP). The United Nations Conference on Trade and Development (UNCTAD) launched the projects to assist the development countries and bridge the digital divide. Although all these initiatives are, from different aspects, building up the international legal system for digital trade, the international trade rules meeting the needs of digital trade are still under development.

The Outline for Building on Intellectual Property Powerhouse (2021 – 2035), issued by the CPC Central Committee and the Council on September 22, 2021, emphasize the importance of building the chain of intellectual property creation, implementation, protection, management, and services and strengthening international cooperation for intellectual property protection. Since digital trade amplifies the intellectual property risks, it is essential for the business operators to reassess the relevant risks and establish the effective means, measures and strategies for risk control and management.

I. Digital Trade: Scope and Characteristics

Although well known in the world, the term "digital trade" is yet to acquire a commonly-recognized definition. Its scope is subject to many different interpretations. What's clear, though, is that digital trade cannot be equal to international trade supported by digital network technologies. Otherwise, it would embrace the whole international trade nowadays.

Digital trade is viewed by many people as cross-border e-commerce. However, cross-border e-commerce is the international sales of goods or services via digital network, in which the trade must be concluded online. The digital trade not concluded online but performed online is therefore excluded from cross-border e-commerce. For example, international e-banking service agreements cannot be concluded online because the overseas customers are normally required to physically approach to banks for identity authentication and other information verification. But the e-banking service agreements, after conclusion, are primarily performed online. In fact, most important B2B contracts (especially on software services or product designs) are still concluded offline for security and other legal compliance requirements but can be entirely or partially performed on the network, particularly in the times of COVID pandemic. Therefore, digital trade should not be limited to cross-border e-commerce.

Neither should digital trade be limited to the trade performed or delivered online. Otherwise, the trade of goods or services concluded online but performed offline, such as online car rental or ride hail service, would be excluded from digital trade.

Therefore, digital trade should cover the international trade concluded and/or performed online.

Digital trade includes the trade of goods, services as well as intellectual property rights (such as digital goods). Enterprises, individuals, consumers, governmental agencies, and other public institutions can all participate in digital trade in the form of B2B, B2C or C2C.

Digital platforms are vital for digital trade. They are the businesses generating value by enabling multiple sellers and buyers to interact directly on specific medias supported by network technologies. Digital platforms do not own the goods or services on the platforms, neither do they directly take part in the transactions on the platforms. Instead, they provide the so-called 3rd-party or intermediary services to the sellers and buyers on the platforms. Some platforms like Amazon offer their own B2C services in addition to platform services. Digital platforms are in different business models. For example, Apple's App Store charges the commission fees (Apple tax) to users, but Alibaba's Taobao primarily profits from advertisements and technical service fees offered to users.

Irrespective of the business models, digital platforms that carry tens of millions of business operators and consumers, provide the automated information system for conclusion and/or performance of trade, and make the rules to maintain the transactional order have become the critical infrastructure of digital trade and deeply changed the landscape of international trade.

Supported by digital platforms, many Micro-Small and Medium Enterprises (MSMEs) enter the market of international trade and directly trade with foreign parties. Compared with the traditional B2B international trade, B2C and C2C in digital trade is as important as B2B trade, thanks to the numerous MSMEs that newly join the international market. Digital goods, contents and services take much bigger share in digital trade than in traditional trade. The definition of international trade may also be refreshed by digital trade because many enterprises have globalized their supply and value chain and synchronized the domestic and overseas market. The penetration of international trade has been substantively enhanced by digital trade.

II. Analysis of Intellectual Property Risks in Digital Trade

Intellectual property risks in digital trade should not be undermined. Digital trade operators, unless involved in illegal counterfeit or piracy activities, are in acute need of intellectual property risk management strategies and measures to predict, identify and assess the potential intellectual property risks in business operations for the purpose of mitigation or prevention of the losses. The intellectual property risks can be assessed from the dimensions of frequency and severity. Some risks occur in low frequency but may result in serious losses, while others occur frequently but in relatively low costs. Business operators, therefore, should consider the correlation of both dimensions and take robust measures to serve the goals of control of costs, mitigation and prevention of the losses, and safeguard of operation.

Although international intellectual property legal system consisting of conventions, treaties and agreements largely harmonizes the intellectual property laws of major countries and regions, differences among jurisdictions are becoming bigger than ever. Compared with the globalized trade at the beginning of 21st century, digital trade faces to much more complicated intellectual property system, harsher and more comprehensive intellectual property enforcement measures, and unprecedented new legal issues. Meanwhile, many unexperienced MSMEs and individuals join the market of digital trade and are more likely to be exposed to intellectual property risks and suffer from serious losses than traditional multinational enterprises operating decades in the international trade.

Given than the market dominance of digital platforms, many operators of digital trade mistake the notice-and-takedown measures taken on the platforms for primary intellectual property risks. However, intellectual property risks in digital trade are much broader than that and cover the whole business process from promotion, transaction, payment to delivery or other performance. There exist the risks not on the platforms and not limited to takedown measures. Newcomers of digital trade may miss the opportunities of risk management for lack of knowledge of intellectual property legal system.

In the new intellectual property environment, business operators generally must manage bigger risks in the conflicts of laws from different jurisdictions. The paper analyzes the most typical scenarios of intellectual property risks in digital trade and presents the corresponding risk management strategies and measures for the business operators.

III. Intellectual Property Risk Management for Businesses Operating on Digital Platforms

Digital platforms like cross-border e-commerce, social media, app stores govern the platforms through establishing and implementing their rules (or polices). The governance serves the interests of digital platforms and especially aims to avoid the risks of platform liabilities. Based on contractual relationship with the businesses operating on the platform, a digital platform sets up the rules on intellectual property protection and takes actions, if necessary, to prevent or stop the business operators from conducting infringing activities. Digital platforms' intellectual property governance has been legalized and supervised under the laws. On one hand, the legal liability systems stimulate digital platforms to govern intellectual property issues, on the other, the justification and appropriation of platform governance are being supervised and monitored in laws. Without the deep understanding of the platform governance, businesses operating on platform can hardly be able to establish sufficient and effective strategies and measures to manage intellectual property risks.

3.1 Rules of Digital Platforms

The intellectual property risks that the businesses operating on platform primarily come from the platform's measures to restrict or discontinue the businesses' capacity of conclusion or performance of transactions. Although having no public powers, digital platforms can bind the businesses with the rules/polices that are incorporated into the service agreements. The intellectual property rules of digital platforms have developed into complexity and may be categorized into two clusters, i.e. prevention of intellectual property risks and punitive measures taken against intellectual property infringements.

3.1.1 Legitimacy of Platform Rules

Although the platform preventive rules purport to help the businesses to manage their intellectual property risks, they can be burdensome and costly to businesses. For example, Amazon Brand Registry provides automated brand protections information to proactively remove suspected infringing or inaccurate content and the search tools to find and report suspected violations with a simple and guided process. Previously, any business owning trademark registration from any country is eligible for the scheme. From 2019, Amazon revised the rules and only the businesses owing the trademark registrations in the countries to which the goods are sold are eligible for the scheme. As a result, Chinese sellers exporting to the United States must register the trademarks or service marks through the United States Patent and Trademark Office (USPTO), which will take at least a year and considerable costs of American trademark agents.

The businesses that are punished for violation of platform rules suffer from severe consequence. Up to September 2021, Amazon permanently banned over 600 Chinese brands across 3000 different seller accounts in its global crackdown against "knowingly, repeatedly, and significantly violating Amazon's policies, especially the ones around review abuse". Amazon stated that "Customers rely on the accuracy and authenticity of product reviews to make informed purchasing decisions and we have clear policies for both reviewers and selling partners that prohibit abuse of our community features. We suspend, ban, and take legal action against those who violate these policies, wherever they are in the world."

Digital platforms, though in contractual relationship, are more powerful than the businesses operating on platforms in respect of bargaining status and capacity. The large platforms (especially those very large ones) act as the critical digital gatekeepers and the businesses are largely relying on the platforms to operate. It should be vigilant that digital platforms not turn against the public good. The major economies in the world are experimenting the regulatory measures to monitor the growing platform power and governance. If a digital platform illegally or unjustifiably hurts the rights or legitimate interests of the businesses, the businesses operating on platforms should be entitled to legal remedies.

In May 2021, Epic Games, the maker of popular games of Fortnite, sued Apple Inc. against the Appstore polices of taking a 30% slice of the payment as commission. In September 2021, the legal battle between Epic Games and Apple Inc. completed the first episode. The district court ruled that Apple violated the law by forcing people to pay for apps and in-app items through the App Store and were ordered to ease up and let in other payment options, within 90 days. The Judge, however, did not rule that Apple had an illegal monopoly over how developers can process payments for mobile games. Apple contended that these changes would have created new privacy and security risks, and appealed to the Ninth Circuit Court for a stay of the injunction order of the district court. In December 2021, the appeals court granted the stay. In the widely-reported case, despite that App Store has long been Apple's walled garden, the legitimacy and reasonableness of its policies and governance of are subject to legal supervision and examination.

The case is not only a milestone of antitrust jurisdiction but provides a legal means to supervise the platform rules and governance. Businesses on platforms can sue to invalidate the platform rules and terminate the implementation of the rules. Digital platforms along with their rules must comply with the laws of the countries where the platforms reside. In some countries, digital platforms have been fined by the competition authorities for hampering market competition. Business operators may also sue the platforms or petition to the competent authorities to invalidate or terminate the platforms' intellectual property rules/polies that are against competition. In the case of Amazon taking down Chinese operators' listings from the platform, the operators may bring the antitrust litigation if Amazon's platform rules/policies are proved harming legitimate competition.

3.1.2 Business Operators in Platform Governance

Businesses operating on platforms rarely take the extremely costly and risky measures to invalidate the platform rules. Instead, they prefer to engaging with the platform to influence the formation and implementation of the platform rules/polices.

Compared with the other big economies, Chinese laws on digital economy develop quickly. 2019 E-Commerce Law of the Peoples's Republic of China has revealed the platforms' governance through rules and service agreements. Platform rules/polices, after being incorporated into the service agreements, become binding to all the operators and consumers on the platforms. The E-Commerce Law recognizes the platforms' governance responsibilities as well as governing power.

The E-Commerce Law sets out a series of regulatory requirements on formation and implementation of platform rules. Platform operators shall continuously post their platform service agreements and transaction rules at prominently visible places in their website homepages to ensure that business operators on their platforms and consumers may read and download the aforesaid information completely and conveniently. Platform operators, in accordance with the platform service agreements and transaction rules, take actions, such as warning, suspension, or termination of services, against the acts of violations of laws or regulations by business operators on their platforms, and they shall make a public announcement of the actions in a timely manner.

Most prominently, the E-Commerce Law establishes the principle of multistakeholder governance. Platform operators shall, on the principles of openness, fairness, and impartiality, develop a platform service agreement and transaction rules, and specify the rights and obligations in respect of joining and leaving their platforms, assurance of the quality of goods and services, protection of consumer rights and interests, and protection of personal information. Platform operators, before modifying their platform service agreements or transaction rules shall solicit public comments at prominently visible places in their homepages and take reasonable measures to ensure that the parties involved are able to express opinions in a timely manner.

Under the E-Commerce Law, businesses operating on platforms are no longer passively governed by the platform rules but enjoy the legal rights to take part in governance process. Apart from complaining or reporting against the platforms, they can engage in modification of the platform rules and express their views. The modified contents shall be publicly released at least seven days prior to the implementation.

Under the E-Commerce Law, a platform operator like Amazon intends to modify its intellectual property policies, such as brand registry, must listen to the businesses. This legal mechanism enables the businesses to manage their intellectual property risks more effectively. The other countries are also intensifying regulations on digital platforms.

Although the Chinese legal approach may not be adopted by the other countries, it's become clear that those very large platforms would not sustain their market success without improving the governance system and acquiring the support of businesses on platforms, which provides a good opportunity for the businesses to manage their intellectual property risks. With the growth of digital economy, all the stakeholders on digital platforms need to work together in orchestra, rather than playing solo, in effective corporative system.

3.2 Copyright Notices

The United States Digital Millennium Copyright Act (DMCA), passed in 1998 and signed by President Clinton, introduced the so-called safe harbors through which the specific online service providers can enjoy limitations on copyright liability under certain conditions, while right holders can get an expeditious and extra-judicial method for addressing infringement of their works. Despite the variations among legal frameworks (e.g. Chinese E-Commerce Law adopts the notice-and-takedown for all types of intellectual property rights, not just copyright), the influence of the notice-and-takedown method is worldwide.

United States government pushes for the inclusion of the provisions modeling on the DMCA's safe harbors in the intellectual property rights chapters of many free trade agreements concluded with the trade partner countries. The most recent example is in the intellectual property rights chapters of the Comprehensive and Progressive Agreement for Trans-Pacific Partnership (CPTPP) signed by 11 countries in 2018.

3.2.1 Evolution of copyright notices

Under American law, a provider shall perform the following actions in a notice-and-takedown method: receiving a takedown notice from a right holder; expeditiously disabling access to the notified material; undertaking reasonable steps promptly to notify the subscriber (user) regarding the removal of the material; receiving and forwarding to the right holder any counter-notice filed by the subscriber, and restoring access to the material that is the subject of a counter-notice within 10-14 days of receipt of the counter notice unless the rightsholder takes a court action against the subscriber.

Clearly, the service providers, in the notice-and-takedown method, are only required to duly act upon the notices (and the counter-notices), rather than to take on the role of adjudicating the infringement claims (or defenses) contained in the notices (or counter notices). However, the service providers cannot rely on the safe harbors to shield their liability unless having no knowledge of infringement on its system. The knowledge requirements have dramatically reshaped the availability of the safe harbors for hosting and information location tool service providers, because knowledge could be established irrespective of whether the providers have acted upon the notices.

After developing into large digital platforms, service providers are no longer in sync with the responsive role in the notice-and-takedown method. Instead, they play a more active role in evaluating the sufficiency of such notice. Large digital platforms that offer comprehensive online services and facilitate large-number interactions among users (like Facebook, Amazon, or Apple's App Store) have established their intellectual property rules in governance system and incorporated the legal requirements into their copyright notice method.

Digital platform governance stimulates the copyright notice to evolve from version 1.0 to 2.0. 2019 Directive on Copyright in the Digital Single Market (hereinafter as "the DSM Directive") provides the updated copyright notice method, in which online content-sharing service providers shall act expeditiously to disable access to, or to remove from their websites, the notified materials upon receiving the sufficiently substantiated notices from the right holders and made best efforts to prevent their future uploads. The right holders, when requesting to have access to their specific works or other subject matter disabled or to have those works or other subject matter removed, shall duly justify the reasons for their requests. the DSM Directive requires that the online content-sharing service providers, in cooperation with the right holders, not result in the prevention of the availability of non-infringing works or other subject matter uploaded by users.

Compared with the original notice-and-takedown method, the service providers in the reformed method have got the discretion power to adjudicate the substance of the notices and consider the possible exceptions or limitations available to the users and the potential of counterbalance against the right holders' excessive enforcement requests. The method reinforces the platforms' adjudicator position with respect to the right holders' notices.

Compared with the original method, the users in the reformed notice-and-takedown method are more capable of defending the businesses' legitimate rights and interests through presenting proofs to rebut the notices. The businesses may also complain to suspend or terminate the measures taken by the service providers upon the notices.

3.2.2 Expansion of the Scope of Application

In digital trade, copyright notices inevitably involve international legal issues. For example, if a Chinese copyright owner notifies to a digital platform in European Union, the platform shall verify the copyright notices and relevant measures according to the laws of residence. Since most large digital platforms locate in world major economies, copyright works that have been published in any major country of the world are legally protected on the platforms in accordance with the international copyright laws. Businesses operating on digital platforms shall, therefore, be sufficiently aware of the legal defenses under the relevant laws of the countries where the platforms reside, such as international transfer of copyright works for visually impaired people to access under the Marrakesh Treaty.

Under the DSM Directive, the copyright notice method only applies to large-scale and commercial online content-sharing service providers. 2020 EU Proposal for the Digital Service Act extends the application of notices to all the providers of hosting services. They should put in place the user-friendly notice and action mechanisms, through which the notices should be sufficiently precise and adequately substantiated to allow a diligent economic operator to reasonably identify, assess and where appropriate act against the allegedly illegal content including sale of counterfeit goods and use of pirate materials against copyright. Under the proposal, where a hosting service provider decides to remove or disable information provided by a recipient of the service, upon a notice, the provider should inform the recipient of its decision, the reasons for its decision and the available redress to contest the decision. It shows that digital platforms that implement the removal or deletion measure upon notices are legally accountable and subject to the supervision of dispute resolution proceedings in European Union.

In digital trade, right notices, if extending to apply to industrial property rights such as patents or plant varieties, would unavoidably involve legal conflict and choice of different countries. Some platforms merely recognize the rights under the laws of the resident countries. For example, the notices based on the trademark registrations or patents acquired in Europe but not approved in China are not recognized by Chinese platforms. There are also platforms recognized the rights from the global market. For example, Amazon recognizes the notices that can prove subsistence of rights in the countries where the rights are alleged infringed. Therefore, businesses operating on platforms, upon receiving the notices, shall verify the territorial legal basis in the first place and present the relevant reasons of defense.

3.3 Dispute Resolution

A few large platforms, after receiving the right holders' notices, resort to dispute resolution mechanisms to resolve the disputes that involve the factual or legal issues too complicated to be judged by the platforms. The platform Alternative Dispute Resolution (ADR) should be based on the right holders' expressed consent. The adjudications of the ADR proceedings should be recognized and/or implemented by the platforms.

3.3.1 Characteristics of Platform ADR

Digital platform dispute resolution should be legitimate, professional, network-based, and highly efficient. Under the Chinese E-commerce Law, e-commerce platform operators may establish online dispute settlement mechanisms, by developing and publishing the dispute settlement rules, and fairly and equitably settling the disputes between parties based on the principle of voluntariness. Businesses operating on platforms are bound by the dispute settlement mechanisms incorporated into the platform rules and service agreements. Once intellectual property right holders choose to file the complains through the platform dispute settlement mechanism, they are bound by the platform rules as well. Like the domain name dispute resolution policies, platform rules lay out the foundation of platform dispute settlement mechanisms.

Uniform Domain Name Dispute Resolution Policy (UDRP) is developed and published by the Internet Corporation for Assigned Names and Numbers (ICANN), the global steward of domain name system, and operated by the professional dispute-resolution organizations to independently resolve the disputes between the trademark rights and domain name registrants.

EU Regulation on Online Dispute Resolution present another example. The Regulation provides a European Online Dispute Resolution (ODR) platform facilitating the independent, impartial, transparent, effective, fast, and fair out-of-court resolution of disputes between consumers and traders online. The ODR platform shall be a single point of entry for consumers and traders seeking the out-of-court resolution of disputes covered by this Regulation. It shall be an interactive website which can be accessed electronically and free of charge in all the official languages of the institutions of the European Union. In order to submit a complaint to the ODR platform the complainant party shall fill in the electronic complaint form. The complaint form shall be user-friendly and easily accessible on the ODR platform. Upon receipt of a fully completed complaint form, the ODR platform shall, in an easily understandable way and without delay, transmit to the respondent party, in one of the official languages of the institutions of the European Union chosen by that party. The platform then forwards the parties' disputes to the accredited professional and independently-operating ADR entities for resolution.

Therefore, digital platforms may establish online dispute resolution mechanisms, delegate third-party intellectual property or other professional organizations to operate according to the platform rules, and resolve the disputes through mediation, expert adjudications, or other forms. Independently-operating organizations may guarantee the procedural justice of the platform dispute resolution mechanism and avoid the actual or potential conflict of interests with the platforms themselves.

The dispute resolution mechanisms on digital platforms utilize digital and network technology and ensure the proceedings to conduct quickly, such as completing the whole proceeding within 60 days. Online case management and procedural operation can significantly improve the efficiency and reduce the costs. Many digital platforms have deployed the automated system to receive the complains and activate the dispute resolution mechanisms. For example, since Alibaba launched the public review mechanism from 2012, more than 100 million disputes between the sellers and buyers have been resolved by the volunteer advisors of the mechanism.

3.3.2 Intellectual Property Dispute Resolution on Digital Platforms

In 2019, Amazon launched its Patent Neutral Evaluation process to resolve patent infringement disputes in simple and effective way. Firstly, a patent holder initiates the process by sending an email to Amazon identifying its utility patent and the products infringing one specific claim of that patent. Secondly, Amazon sends an email to the accused businesses letting them know about the patent infringement complaint filed against them and urging them to reach out to the patent owner to amicably resolve the issue. If the accused ignores Amazon's warning, the patent owner may send a follow-up email to Amazon requesting to move forward with the Neutral Patent Evaluation Process. Thirdly, Amazon sends its Neutral Patent Evaluation agreement to both the patent owner and the accused infringers. Both parties have 21 days to agree to participate in the process by signing the agreement and sending $4000 to Amazon. If the businesses do not cooperate, Amazon will simply shut down the listing. If both parties agree to participate in Amazon's Neutral Patent Evaluation Process and deposit the required $4000 respectively, the process moves into the actual patent evaluation stage. After both parties present their case, a patent attorney Amazon selected to be a neutral patent evaluator decides whether the patent owner has established that the accused product infringes its patent. If the patent owner prevails, Amazon refunds the $4000 to the patent owner and takes down the infringing listing. Also, the loser forfeits its $4000.

Digital platform dispute resolution is not exclusive to the judicial proceedings. Any party unsatisfied with the result of dispute resolution may still resort to litigation at court. But as far as intellectual property disputes may be resolved efficiently and fairly by the alternative mechanisms on platform, parties are not likely to sue to the courts, as proved by the domain name dispute resolution.

Digital platform mechanisms are especially valuable for resolving cross-border disputes and helps both intellectual property holders and businesses on platforms to avoid the complicated foreign jurisdiction issues. Platform dispute resolution mechanisms generally enable businesses to negotiate with intellectual property holders to settle the disputes amicably in the first place. Only if the disputes cannot be settled, they are adjudicated by neutral experts. Platform dispute resolution provides the important opportunity for businesses to manage their intellectual property risks.

Ⅳ. Intellectual Property Warranty in Digital Trade

In digital trade, although intellectual property holders would not frequently bring costly legal actions in foreign courts, businesses shall never undermine the importance of intellectual property risk management.

Digital trade may be in the forms of B2C, C2C as well as B2B. In B2B trade, sellers export goods or services and buyers import them for resale or other commercial use. According to laws or contractual terms, sellers/exporters shall provide the buyers/importers intellectual property warranty. If intellectual property holders sue for infringement after the goods or services are imported into their countries, the sellers/exporters shall shield the buyers/importers of the infringement liabilities. Given that intellectual property warranty may "reflect" the risks of infringement liabilities in digital trade, businesses operators should have the management strategy to avoid the substantive losses.

Intellectual property warranty of digital trade operators covers both legitimacy and validity of rights and indemnification of buyers from third‐party claims of infringement. Business operators are obliged of intellectual property warranty either under the laws or by the parties' agreements.

Many SMSEs in digital trade wrongly believe that they won't be accountable for intellectual property warranty unless agreed in trade contracts. However, even without agreed warranty, sellers/exporters are obliged of warranty under the laws of application.

4.1 Intellectual Property Warranty in Chinese Laws

The scope of intellectual property warranty is different in laws. If Chinese laws are the law of the contract agreed by the parties or chosen under the conflict law, the relevant provisions of the Chinese Civil Code shall be applied. Although the Civil Code contains no specific provision on intellectual property warranty, it stipulates the sellers of sale contracts are obliged to deliver the goods free of any third-party rights, unless the laws stipulate otherwise. Intellectual property rights should be included in the rights of third parties under the Civil Code. In respect of technology transfer or licensing contracts provided by the Civil Code, only those who legally own the technologies are eligible to conclude the contracts. It means that the assignors or licensors of technologies must warrant that the intellectual property rights involved are legitimate and valid to the other parties of the contracts.

Under the Civil Code, sellers/exporters in digital trade must provide intellectual property warranty to buyers/importers. Buyers that can sufficiently prove that there are third‐party intellectual property rights in the goods of trade, may stop paying to the sellers unless the sellers offer the appropriate guarantees. Therefore, sellers shall assume the obligation of intellectual property warranty irrespective of whether the sellers know the rights or whether the third parties claim the rights.

To balance the interests of both buyers and sellers, the Civil Code provides the safeguards for sellers, i.e. sellers may be exempted from the obligation of intellectual property warranty provided that the buyers have known or should have known the third-party rights in the goods when concluding the contracts. The legal design, to some extent, alleviate the sellers' burden of liabilities. The intellectual property information of the buyers' affiliated companies, shareholders, and transaction records may be used to prove the buyers' actual or constructive knowledge of the third-party rights. Regarding the intellectual property rights that are legally published, such as patents, registered trademarks, enterprise (trade) names, plant varieties or layout designs of integrated circuits, theoretically buyers should have known the third-party rights by conducting due diligence before concluding the contracts. However, if trade secret or other undisclosed rights are involved, buyers can hardly be presumed to have known of the third-party rights. With respect to copyright, performers' rights or rights of phonogram producers, buyers are only presumed to have known the third-party rights that are legally registered with competent authorities. Unlike the US or other countries that require copyright registration for enforcement purpose, Chinese Copyright Law only provides voluntary copyright registration system that affects neither subsistence nor enforcement of the rights. Therefore, sellers generally cannot presume the buyers have known the third-party copyright when concluding the contracts.

In sum, under the Civil Code, where the buyers can prove the third-party intellectual property rights in the goods but the sellers cannot prove that the buyers knew or should have known the rights, the sellers shall be liable for breach of intellectual property warranty duties. The buyers are immune from paying the relevant prices of the goods and eligible to claim the losses for concluding the contracts. In addition, when the Civil Code is adopted as the law of digital trade contracts, sellers, although shall provide intellectual property warranty to buyers irrespective of whether they know or should have known the third-party rights in the goods, are only liable for compensation of the buyers' losses that are foreseeable to the sellers when concluding the contracts. Therefore, the sellers are exempted from intellectual property warranty where the buyers knew or should have known the third-party rights when concluding the contracts.

4.2 Intellectual Property Warranty under the United Nations Convention on Contracts for the International Sale of Goods

The purpose of the 1980 United Nations Convention on Contracts for the International Sale of Goods (CISG) is to provide a modern, uniform, and fair regime for contracts for the international sale of goods. The CISG contributes significantly to contract law reform of many countries. China and other 94 countries are the member states of the CISG.

4.2.1 Scope of Application

The CISG applies to the contracts for the sale of goods concluded between parties with a place of business in Contracting States. It may also apply to the contracts for international sale of goods when the rules of private international law point at the law of a Contracting State as the applicable one, or by virtue of the choice of the contractual parties, regardless of whether their places of businesses locate in a Contracting State.

The CISG does not apply to the contracts of service trade. Regarding the contracts of intellectual property trade, the CISG has the potential to be applied. In a case concerning an online software license agreement between a Canadian software company (seller) and a Dutch buyer (buyer), the court considered that the CISG should be interpreted by considering its international character, the need to promote uniformity in its application and the observance of good faith in international trade, and the general principles on which it is based. The Court noted that "sale of goods" is not defined in Article 1 (1) CISG and a broad definition of goods must be assumed to include intangible property. Thus, the Court found that the CISG applies to computer software even if it is not recorded on a physical medium such as a DVD, CD or USB stick. Therefore, at least in case law, the CISG can be applied to intellectual property licensing or transfer contracts.

Recently, the trade of digital goods such as computer software (including APPs on mobile network), online games, music and videos developing quickly. Although the new trading forms in metaverse or non-fungible tokens

(NFTs) are emerging, the relevant international trade rules are largely missing. The businesses therefore face considerable uncertainty and intellectual property risks in trade. The intellectual property warranty provided by the CISG, however, can offer the new risk management channels as well as the essential legal support for trade.

4.2.2 Intellectual Property Warranty under the CISG

B2B sales contracts in digital trade commonly apply the CISG, including its intellectual property warranty provision. Under Article 42 of the CISG,

(1) The seller must deliver goods which are free from any right or claim of a third party based on industrial property or other intellectual property, of which at the time of the conclusion of the contract the seller knew or could not have been unaware, provided that the right or claim is based on industrial property or other intellectual property;

(a) under the law of the State where the goods will be resold or otherwise used, if it was contemplated by the parties at the time of the conclusion of the contract that the goods would be resold or otherwise used in that State; or

(b) in any other case, under the law of the State where the buyer has his place of business.

(2) The obligation of the seller under the preceding paragraph does not extend to cases where:

(a) at the time of the conclusion of the contract the buyer knew or could not have been unaware of the right or claim; or

(b) the right or claim results from the seller's compliance with technical drawings, designs, formulate or other such specifications furnished by the buyer.

The provision of the CISG, despite its complicated structure and ambiguous wording, is impactful to international trade. The UNCITRAL case law system includes the leading cases applying Article 42 of the CISG by the courts of the member states, which reveals the practical issues of this legal system.

Under Article 42 of the CISG, a seller's intellectual property warranty is subject to the seller's knowledge, timing, and territory, which are examined in the case law.

In a case decided by Austrian Supreme Court, a German Private Limited Company (the seller) sold blank CDs to an Austrian company (the buyer). The seller had bought the CDs from its Chinese parent company which had the license to produce the blank CDs and sell them in Germany. However, the license was silent on whether the products are entitled to sell in Austria. Furthermore, the license contract had been dissolved by the licensor due to the license fee disputes between the Chinese parent company and the licensor, and court proceedings had been filed. When the buyer learned about the proceedings, it asked the seller for clarifications but did not receive any further information. Therefore, the buyer decided to exercise their right of retention of payment of those seller's invoices relating to the goods sold and delivered after the license contract had been dissolved. The seller argued that there was no risk that the buyer could be held liable for the license fees, because there had been no breach of contract by the parent company. Furthermore, the CDs delivered to the buyer had been produced before the license contract had been dissolved and the delivered goods were free from any third-party claim. Finally, the buyer had not given notice of the alleged defects of the goods within a reasonable time.

The court of first instance dismissed the seller's claim. According to Article 42 of the CISG, the court agreed that the buyer should not be liable for any license fees because the buyer was not obliged to investigate whether the license contract was still valid or whether its dissolution was lawful. After the buyer informed the seller of its intention within reasonable time, the buyer had the right to avoid the contract. In appeal, the Court of Appeal recognized the right of the buyer to avoid the contract and to claim for damages, but not to retain the payment.

The Supreme Court, on the contrary opined that the buyer had a right of retention in the case of breach of contract by the seller and until the seller fulfilled its contractual obligations. The court of first instance, however, had failed to determine the State in which the goods would be resold or used as contemplated by the parties at the time of the conclusion of the contract. The case was remanded to the court of first instance in order to clarify the facts in this regard.

In the opinion of the Supreme Court, the seller's obligation to provide licensed goods was to be interpreted in the way that the goods had to be licensed in the State where they were resold, if at the time of the conclusion of the contract the parties had contemplated that the goods would be resold or otherwise used in the State. Under Article 42 of the CISG, the buyer, therefore, must prove the specific "State" in which the seller is obliged.

In a case tried by Seoul High Court, Korea, the plaintiff (buyer), an American corporation established under Californian law, and the defendant (seller), a Korean company manufacturing and selling LED illuminators for automobiles, concluded three contracts under which the defendant would manufacture and supply illuminators to the plaintiff, and the plaintiff would have exclusive right of sales in US. However, during the contract's performance, a non-party American corporation demanded that the plaintiff cease and desist the infringement on its patent in US. The demand was made on the ground that the illuminator supplied to the plaintiff by the defendant infringed on its patent. The plaintiff argued that the defendant supplied illuminators likely to infringe on the non-party company's patent, and therefore, the defendant is liable for damages arising from the breach.

The court confirmed that this case might fall under Article 42(1) of the CISG as the goods were claimed to have infringed the US patent by a third party. Nevertheless, the court eventually rejected the plaintiff's damages claim on the following grounds: for the defendant to be liable under Article 42(1) of the CISG, it had to have known or not have been unaware about the claim of the company owner of the patent, who was a third party at the conclusion time of each of the sales contracts. As the patent was only registered after the formation of each of the three sales contracts, under which the goods were supplied, it is difficult to conclude that the seller already knew or should not have been unaware of the application for the patent before the buyer notified the seller of the patent infringement claim. Therefore, the court concluded that the defendant could not be deemed to have breached its obligation under the sales contract.

The case shows that under Article 42(1) of the CISG, the seller must deliver goods which are free from any right or claim of a third party based on industrial property or other intellectual property rights, of which, at the time of the conclusion of the contract, the seller knew of or could not have been unaware of. According to the Court's interpretation of Article 42(1) of the CISG regardless of whether the intellectual property is rightfully claimed, this falls within the seller's sphere of risk.

According to Article 42 (2) of the CISG, the seller is immune not only from intellectual property warranty to the right or claim results from the seller's compliance with technical drawings, designs, formulate or other such specifications furnished by the buyer but from the right or claim that the buyer knew or could not have been unaware of when concluding the contract, as confirmed in the case law.

In a case decided in France, the French company (buyer) owned six clothing shops and acquired a batch of shirts from the German company (seller). The shirts were made of a fabric that reproduced the features of two types of fabric to which the third-party company had exclusive rights. Sued by the third-party company for infringement, the French company brought warranty proceedings against its German supplier.

In its judgement, the Colmar District Court found the French company of infringement and ordered the seller to indemnify the buyer for the awards made against the buyer. The Court of Appeal upheld that ruling insofar as the ruling accepted that there had been an infringement of which the buyer was guilty of infringement, but it reduced the damages of infringement. The Court of Appeal further ordered that the warranty proceedings should be reopened. Since both parties took the view that CISG was applicable to the dispute, the Court of Appeal applied Article 42 of the CISG and ruled that the buyer could not, in its professional capacity, have been unaware of this infringement. It therefore acted with knowledge of the intellectual property right that has been invoked and the seller was no longer required to provide goods free of all intellectual property rights. The Court of Appeal accordingly set aside the District Court's ruling and dismissed the warranty proceedings brought by the buyer.

In another case decided in France, the seller, a Spanish company, delivered to the buyer, a French company, shoes with counterfeit ribbons. The holder of the intellectual property right received compensation from the buyer. The buyer brought an action against the Spanish company for reimbursement of the damages paid to the victim of the counterfeit and for payment of damages. The buyer's claim was dismissed by the Court of Appeal of Rouen. The Court of Cassation rejected the appeal lodged against the decision of the Court of Appeal and found that the buyer could not, as a professional, have been unaware of the counterfeit; therefore, the buyer acted with knowledge of the property right invoked. The Court of Cassation found that the Court of Appeal correctly applied article 42(2)(a) of the CISG and had properly concluded that the obligation of the seller did not extend to delivering goods free from any intellectual property right.

Both French cases shows that buyers, as professional companies, should not be unaware of the third-party intellectual property rights invoked when concluding the contracts. The sellers should not be responsible for warranty duty where the buyers intentionally or negligently ignore the third-party rights. By assessing both parties' duty of care, intellectual property warranty ensures the fair and effective risk management.

In sum, Article 42 of the CISG, despite its complexity, generally protects both parties in balance. In practice, this system is not proved to be unfairly burdensome to sellers. However, thanks to Article 42's complicated structure, ambiguous wording, and inaccurate Chinese translation, many MSMEs misunderstand the warranty duty under the CISG and give up the opportunities to defend themselves in disputes. In fact, if MSMEs in digital trade can enhance their intellectual property management capacity, they should be able to protect their legitimate rights and interests in trade.

4.3 Agreed Intellectual Property Warranty

Intellectual property risks largely derive from uncertainty and unpredictability in trade. Compared with the risks of applying the warranty in laws, business operators in digital trade would better negotiate and settle the scope, condition, and form of warranty as well as both parties' rights and duties in contractual agreements. Parties' agreed warranty can specify and clarify the legal stipulation and avoid ambiguity and multiple interpretations in laws. Agreed warranty may also be more extensive than warranty in laws, provided that the sellers' higher-level duties are corresponding to their more gains from the contracts (such as higher prices of the goods). Nonetheless, agreed warranty shall neither exclude nor mitigate the warranty in laws. Otherwise, the sellers may be suspected of selling/exporting counterfeit or pirate goods to the buyers and the contracts may be void in laws.

Thanks to digital networks, the globalized market is more active than ever. If business operators' warranty duties cover all types of intellectual property rights, they would face to unprecedented risks. The agreed warranty, on the other hand, can limit and specify the types and scope of the intellectual property rights covered by the warranty and effectively low the risks of business. The Agreement on Trade-Related Aspects of Intellectual Property Rights (TRIPS) is an international legal agreement between all the WTO member nations. It establishes the common principles and rules for the regulation by national governments of different forms of intellectual property as applied to nationals of other WTO member nations. However, over the past 30 years, trade-related intellectual property laws in different countries have evolved to different directions and become more complicated with many new rights and obligations introduced. Some countries have established the sui generis intellectual property legal systems on traditional knowledge, genetic resources, etc. Although these new legal rules are yet to be incorporated into the TRIPS, they are impactful to businesses in digital trade. For example, the goods of wood crafts exported from Bulgaria to New Zealand were seized by import customs because New Zealand indigenous community protested the wood crafts containing the indigenous ornamentations without permission.

The agreed warranty may limit the scope of warranty to copyright, trademarks, patents, designs, geographical identifications, and other intellectual property rights commonly recognized by international laws. The parties may also specify the conditions that the warranty is invoked.

The agreed warranty can also specify the term of warranty. Under legal stipulations, the buyers must notify the sellers to invoke the warranty (such as retention or reduce of payment) in the reasonable term. To avoid the disputes regarding the interpretation of reasonable terms, the parties may agree upon the term of the sellers' warranty or the term of buyers' notification. The parties' agreements can ensure the fair treatment of both parties.

Under legal stipulations, the parties frequently dispute over the territory in which the sellers' warranty may be invoked. The parties' agreements that specify the country (or countries) in which the warranty can be invoked resolves this problem. Compared with Article 42 of the CISG under which only one country may be invoked for warranty, the parties' agreements can specify multiple countries, which is valuable for digital trade. Compared with the TRIPS, many free trade agreements of 21st century have expanded the enforcement of intellectual property. For example, under the TRIPS, Members shall, adopt procedures to enable a right holder, who has valid grounds for suspecting that the importation of counterfeit trademark or pirated copyright goods may take place, to lodge an application in writing with custom authorities for the suspension of the release into free circulation of such goods; and Members may also provide for corresponding procedures concerning the suspension by the customs authorities of the release of infringing goods destined for exportation from their territories. However, EU laws permit the trademark right holders to apply custom authorities for the suspension of the release the goods in transit, although the goods are neither imported into or exported from EU. In the new enforcement environment, it is important for the warranty to cover not only the country in which the buyers reside or the goods are resold but the countries in transit. Surely, the sellers' more warranty duties can be compensated with more gains through mutual agreements.

The agreed warranty is helpful to resolve the complicated question of parallel import. Parallel import (or exhaustion or gray market) refers to intellectual property goods that are imported into a market and sold there without the right holders' consent in that market. Although parallel-imported goods are not counterfeit goods, the intellectual property issues involved are complicated. If the sellers export the goods with the knowledge that they have no permission to sell in the import country, they shall be responsible for warranty duties. However, it is normally difficult to prove if the sellers knew or could not have been unaware of the issue of parallel import when concluding the contracts. In addition, there is no uniform international rules on right exhaustion or parallel import. Therefore, the parties' agreement may clarify whether the buyers may invoke the warranty in case of parallel import and if so, on what conditions.

In digital trade, it is common for business operators to adopt the automated information system for conclusion and performance of transactions, which brings new intellectual property risk and management solution. If the automated system operates according to the fixed parameters, rather than adjusts to specific circumstances, the business operators would face to considerable risks of intellectual property disputes. Fortunately, most automated systems have introduced the element of artificial intelligence to adjust the scope, condition, and form of intellectual property warranty according to the applicable laws, which can effectively manage the intellectual property risks.

Conclusion

The characteristics of digital trade, on one hand, amplify intellectual property risks, on the other, provide the new channel, model, and opportunity for risk management. Business operators on digital platforms may establish risk management measures and strategies to avoid or mitigate the losses of intellectual property infringements. The traditional legal system like intellectual property warranty has become robust and resilient in digital trade. Effective use of risk management is essential for businesses to reduce losses and protect legitimate interests.

(唐嘉玮、王辰、陈末末　审校)

Review of Maritime Arbitration in Post-Covid-19 Era

Abstract: When the Covid-19 turns a "new normal", maritime arbitration practices on a global scale have accordingly progressed with many new characteristics. Virtual hearings, electronic delivery and other new practices facilitated by technologies add to the convenience of arbitration services, further digitalize the arbitration proceedings and enable arbitration to be conducted despite the distance and time difference. A number of maritime arbitration institutions or arbitrator associations have revised their arbitration rules with a heightened focused upon efficiency and impartiality of the arbitration. The arbitration legislation and legal framework of judicial review have been updated, better ensuring the legality of maritime arbitration proceedings and awards and creating a "arbitration-friendly" environment. To offer a review of maritime arbitration in post-covid-19 era, we have invited senior maritime lawyers and arbitrator from China, Singapore and U.K to contribute to this article, sharing with readers their observations on revisions of arbitration rules, legislation, judicial review and other aspects concerning the maritime arbitration.

Key words: revisons of arbitration rules; legislation; judicial review

Report on Development of Maritime Arbitration in China's Mainland (2020-2021) *

Since the COVID-19 outbreak in early 2020, all legal industry, including maritime arbitration, have undergone many new developments and changes. This article reports on the development of maritime arbitration in China during this period as follows.

Ⅰ. Developments in the Law and Legislation Relating to Maritime Arbitration

1.1 Legislative Progress Related to Maritime Arbitration

As a country with unity of civil and commercial law (that does not have separation of commercial law with civil law legislation), China does not have a specific law on maritime arbitration, but applies the relevant civil and commercial laws. From the perspective of legislation, China's civil and commercial legislation is in rapid change in recent years, and new laws have been introduced frequently. However, the admiralty and maritime legislation is relatively stable, and not many new admiralty and maritime legislation has been introduced recently. In terms of those related to arbitration, the following are noteworthy:

(1) In January 2020, the Ministry of Transport of the People's Republic of China submitted the Maritime Law (revised draft for examination) to the State

---

* The author is PENG Xianwei (Philip PENG), PhD candidate of Dalian Maritime University Law School, arbitrator of China Maritime Arbitration Commission (CMAC), partner of Beijing De-Heng Law Offices; Mr. Peng is also Legal Expert for Civil and Administrative Cases Advisory of the Supreme People's Procuratorate of China, Pool Lawyer of "Talent Pool of One Thousand International Lawyers" of PRC Ministry of Justice, Legal Expert of ICC Commission of Commercial Law and Practice, vice-chair of Maritime Law Committee of Beijing Lawyers'Association, vice-chair of International Transportation Committee of ABA Section of International Law; Mr. Peng is in the panel of arbitrators of Shanghai, Nanjing, Hainan, Baotou and other 22 domestic arbitration commissions in China.

Council for deliberation. The revision of the current Maritime Law has attracted widespread attention from all sectors, including the sector of maritime arbitration. Moreover, according to news reports, the Special Maritime Procedure Law of the People's Republic of China is also undergoing preliminary research for revision. ①

(2) In April 2021, the Twenty-eighth Session of the 13th of National People's Congress Standing Committee amended and adopted the new Maritime Traffic Safety Law of the People's Republic of China, which comes into effect on September 1, 2021. Article 115 of this Law provides that in case of civil disputes arising from maritime traffic accidents, the parties concerned may apply for arbitration or file a lawsuit in a people's court in accordance with the law.

In practice, when civil disputes arise from maritime traffic accidents, the parties often consider the government-led administrative model or litigation as the channel of relief, and rarely go to arbitration. However, the administrative or litigation model has its shortcomings. For example, after the oil spill accident at Conoco Phillips' "Penglai 19-3" oilfield in Bohai Bay on June 4, 2011, a government-led compensation model was formed after negotiation. Some people believe that under the government-led compensation model, it is difficult to implement unified compensation rules and standards in practice because of the uneven professional quality of administrative personnel, which may easily lead to consequence that some oil spill victims are not compensated, or different compensation for the same kind of damage, causing dissatisfaction of victims and new conflicts and disputes. In response to the inadequacy of the claim model led by government agencies, some arbitration institutions studied the possibility of resolving the "Penglai 19-3" oil spill claim dispute through mediation and arbitration. ②

In contrast, Article 46 of the Maritime Traffic Safety Law (1983) provides that "A civil dispute arising from a maritime traffic accident may be set-

---

① "Teachers of International Law School joining the modification and researching activities of Maritime Procedure Law of PRC," (18 oct 2019), accessed January 12, 2022, https://gjf.ecupl.edu.cn/2020/0102/c8985a153195/page.htm.

② Hongsong Wang, "Advantages of Third-party Dominated Claims in the View of Oil Spill Cases," (29,8,2012), accessed January 12, 2022, https://www.bjac.org.cn/news/view?id=2109.

tled through mediation by the competent authority. If the parties are unwilling to have the case mediated or if the mediation is unsuccessful, the parties may bring a suit in the people's court. Parties to a case involving foreign interests may also submit the case to an arbitration agency for mediation, in accordance with the written agreement concluded between them. " Article 46 of the Maritime Traffic Safety Law (2016) also provides as so. Literally, since the previous wording is that parties to foreign-related cases can submit civil disputes arising from maritime traffic accidents to arbitration, it seems that non-foreign parties does not enjoy this right. This amendment makes it possible for civil disputes arising from maritime traffic accidents, such as personal injury and environmental pollution caused by maritime traffic accidents, to be resolved by arbitration in non-foreign cases. For maritime arbitration institutions, in case of large maritime accidents (e. g. ship oil pollution accidents), they can liaise with government agencies to promote arbitration for disputes resolution. For example, a special compensation fund could be set up by the polluter, and the government agency could compensate the pollution victims from the fund based on the arbitration award or mediation decision issued by the maritime arbitration institution. If this model is adopted, the governmental authorities should be able to avoid such disputes to a large extent by relying on the arbitration or mediation results of the third party to compensate to maritime accident victims.

1.2 Developments in Judicial Interpretation Related to Maritime Arbitration

With the Supreme People's Court releasing judicial interpretations on marine insurance, limitation of maritime liability and ship oil pollution damage etc one after another, the pace of the Supreme People's issuance of maritime related judicial interpretations has gradually slowed down in recent years. Since 2020, the only maritime judicial interpretation issued by the Supreme People's Court is the Provisions of the Supreme People's Court on Several Issues Concerning the Trial of Cases Involving Seaman-related Disputes (hereinafter referred to as Judicial Interpretation of Crew Members Labor Disputes), which was adopted by the 1803rd meeting of the Judicial Committee of the Supreme People's Court on June 8, 2020 and came into effect on September 29, 2020.

In drafting this judicial interpretation, its draft version provided that: Article 1 [based on whether the matters involved in the litigation request is related to the period on board, different ways to determine the method of dispute resolution] regarding dispute between crew and the ship owner for the confirmation of labor relations, or the conclusion, performance, change and termination of the employment contract or labor contract disputes, based on whether the litigation request is related to the period of crew's on board the vessel, in the following different circumstances: (a) If the litigation request is related to the period of crew's working on board, the parties may file a lawsuit directly to the maritime court, except where there is an arbitration agreement between the parties.

However, this draft provision has been questioned by some people, for example, the Hubei Provincial Crew Service Association thinks that it is doubtful whether the "arbitration agreement" in this article is a valid agreement, because the Labor Dispute Arbitration Commission is the only legal arbitration body for labor disputes resolution. ①

At present, the Judicial Interpretation of Crew Members Labor Disputes has deleted the provision of "arbitration agreement between the parties" in Article 1 of the draft. In some sense, there may still be some controversy as to whether a crew labor dispute can be resolved by ordinary commercial arbitration. ② However, judging from the recent judicial practice, Chinese courts have adopted a supportive attitude towards this issue. For example, in the case

---

① "Comments on 'Several Regulations on Adjudicating Cases Relevant to Crewman Disputes (I) Issued by the the Supreme People's Court (Draft for Comments)'," accessed January 12, 2022, http://www.hbcsa.org/show.aspx? id=1570.

② Shumei Wang, Zaiyu Guo, "Comprehension and Application of 'Some Rules of the Supreme People's Court on the Scope for Maritime Courts to Accept Cases'": Traditionally, labor contract and labor dispatching contracts distinguishes in the field of civil law adjudication and Notice of the Supreme People's Court on Printing and Distributing the "Provisions on Cause of Action for Civil Cases" also specified the difference. In the field of maritime law, Maritime Procedure Law of PRC only used the description of crew labor dispute to cover both crewing labor contract and crewman labor contract, accessed January 12, 2022, https://m.thepaper.cn/baijiahao_11720287.

of Zheng Xiangshe vs Shenzhen Kairuite Ship Management Ltd. and Shenzhen Lianda Tugboat Co., Ltd., there was also a view within the court that the arbitration clause of the crew service agreement agreeing to be arbitrated by China Maritime Arbitration Commission was invalid, for reason that only the relevant Labor Dispute Arbitration Committee was entitled to accept the case for crew labor disputes. Ultimately, Guangzhou Maritime Court issued (2020) Y 72 MC565 civil ruling, deciding that the arbitration clause was valid, for reason that it should uphold the attitude of supporting maritime arbitration and judging whether the parties had the intention to submit to arbitration according to the Arbitration Law and other legal provisions.① In the case between a Mr. Lin and a shipping company, the two parties signed a "Crew on board Agreement", agreeing to arbitrate their disputes by China Maritime Arbitration Commission. The plaintiff was injured in work and was dissatisfied with the labor arbitration award, and sued the defendant to Quanzhou Quangang District People's Court. Subsequently, Quanzhou City Intermediate People's Court decided that the case was under the exclusive jurisdiction of the maritime court, and made (2020) M 05 MZ no. 848 civil ruling to transfer the case to Xiamen Maritime Court for trial. During hearing of the case by Xiamen Maritime Court, the defendant raised jurisdictional objection, arguing that the case should be submitted to China Maritime Arbitration Commission for arbitration. The plaintiff argued that the parties had labor contract relationship, and the arbitration clause of the agreement violated the mandatory legal provisions that the labor contract dispute should be resolved by Labor Dispute Arbitration Committees and should not be arbitrated by other arbitration institutions. Finally, Xiamen Maritime Court heldthat China's law does not expressly exclude maritime arbitration in crew labor disputes, and the arbitration clause in the "Crew on board Agreement" shall be valid.②

---

① "Disputes over Labor Contract between Xiangshe Zheng and Qingdao Kairuite Ship Management Company, Shenzhen Lianda Tugboat Company," accessed January 12, 2022, https://www.gzhsfy.gov.cn/hsmh/web/content?gid=92739.

② "Comments on the Validity of Arbitration Clauses in Crewman Labor Contracts," accessed January 12, 2022, https://www.163.com/dy/article/FKQ2SB5J0518JG8L.html.

In addition, in August 2020, Nanjing Maritime Court issued the "Nanjing Maritime Court Guide for Judicial Review of Maritime Arbitration Cases". There are noteworthy provisions that[1]: if the parties reach a separate repayment agreement on the original contractual arrears, the repayment agreement is still subject to the arbitration clause of the original contract; in the case of concurrent claims for breach of contract and tort, if the parties file a tort suit, the dispute is still subject to the arbitration clause of the contract. If the parties agree to *ad hoc* arbitration within China, the arbitration agreement shall be invalid; for maritime disputes with no foreign element, if the parties agree to arbitration by a foreign arbitral institution or to arbitration in a foreign country, the arbitration agreement shall be deemed invalid.

In December 2020, Xiamen Maritime Court adopted the "Xiamen Maritime Court Guide for Arbitration Judicial Review".[2] It is worth noting that this Guide specifically provides that: if an arbitral award is to be set aside after review, the opinion of the arbitration institution may be heard before it is reported to the Fujian High People's Court for approval; a copy of the ruling shall be served to the relevant arbitration institution after conclusion of the judicial review of arbitration case.

II. The Development of Maritime Arbitration in China's Mainland

During 2020–2021, there are some important developments of the maritime arbitration in China. On November 6, 2020, with the support of the Ministry of Justice, the Shanghai Branch of the China Maritime Arbitration Commission (CMAC) was upgraded and renamed as "China Maritime Arbitration

---

[1] "Nanjing Maritime Court Ajudication Guidances on Judicial Reviews of Maritime Arbitration," accessed January 12, 2022, http://njhsfy.gov.cn/zh/service/detail/id/1418.html.

[2] "Xiamen Maritime Court Ajudication Guidances on Judicial Reviews of Maritime Arbitration," accessed January 12, 2022, http://www.xmhsfy.gov.cn/swxx/gfxwj/202102/t20210218_175377.html.

Commission Shanghai Headquarter", per the decision of the CCPIT (China Council for the Promotion of International Trade) and the Shanghai Municipal People's Government and the approval of the Shanghai Judicial Bureau, and a formal inauguration ceremony was held for "China Maritime Arbitration Commission Shanghai Headquarter". [1] On May 1, 2021, after careful preparation, the new roster of arbitrators of CMAC was inaugurated for a five-year term. The new roster of arbitrators is composed of 826 arbitrators from 36 countries and regions. Among them, 704 arbitrators are from China's Mainland, covering 35 cities, with a more reasonable geographical distribution; 122 arbitrators are from Hong Kong SAR, Macao SAR, Taiwai Region and foreign countries, with a wider distribution; the current roster of arbitrators is more complete in professional fields and more scientific in composition, which can better meet the needs of CMAC business development. [2]

On October 9, 2021, CMAC held a press conference in Beijing to release the "CMAC Arbitration Rules (2021 Edition)" (hereinafter reffered to as the "2021 Arbitration Rules"), which will come into effect on October 1, 2021. Compared with the previous version of the Arbitration Rules, the 2021 Arbitration Rules systematically provide for electronic service of process, video hearings, video testimony, electronic signatures, as well as cybersecurity and privacy and data protection, whilst taking into account the problems caused by the new Covid epidemic. The 2021 Arbitration Rules also contain a number of noteworthy innovations, such as

(1) Regarding the secretary of the arbitration tribunal. Due to the growing complexity of international arbitration and the increasing caseload and workload, secretaries have gradually emerged to support the arbitral tribunal. The use of tribunal secretaries has become a common phenomenon in practice.

---

[1] "China Maritime Arbitration Commission announces renaming CMAC Shanghai Sub-Commission as CMAC Shanghai Headquarters," accessed January 12, 2022, http://www.cmac.org.cn/index.php? id=105.

[2] "CMAC issued new panel of arbitrators," accessed January 12, 2022, http://cmac.org.cn/index.php? id=77.

However, due to the lack of necessary transparency, the identity, background and role of the secretary of the arbitral tribunal are not disclosed to the parties and conflicts of interest are not reviewed, and some secretaries even participate in the analysis of evidence and law application in the discussion and preparation of drafting of the arbitral award, essentially turning into a fourth arbitrator.[①] Therefore, in the context of due process, it is necessary to regulate the secretaries of arbitral tribunals. In this regard, Article 40 of the 2021 Arbitration Rules specifically provides for issues related to the secretary of the arbitral tribunal, in which a distinction is made for the first time between an institutional case manager and the secretary of the arbitral tribunal, providing that a staff member of the Arbitration Court of CMAC may act as the secretary of the arbitral tribunal, but may not act as the case manager of the same arbitration case. Article 40 also provides that the secretary of the arbitral tribunal shall sign a declaration disclosing any facts or circumstances that may give rise to reasonable doubts as to his or her impartiality and independence before accepting the appointment, and that the parties may also request the recusal of the secretary of the arbitral tribunal. These provisions of Article 40 will be helpful to safeguard the parties' right to know and prevent conflicts of interest.

(2) Regarding the expert consultation system. In arbitration practice, in order to deal with major and difficult cases, many arbitration institutions have a system related to expert consultation. On December 31, 2018, the General Office of the CPC Central Committee and the General Office of the State Council (hereinafter referred to as the "Two Offices") jointly issued "Several Opinions on Improving the Arbitration System and Enhancing the Credibility of Arbitration" (hereinafter referred to as the "Two Offices' Opinions"). Article 6 of the "Two Offices' Opinions" also specifically proposes to establish an expert consultation mechanism for major and difficult cases. In order to further implement the system of expert advisory committees, which has worked well in prac-

---

① Yuanke Sang, "Researches on Tribunal Secretaries in International Arbitration," *Beijing Arbitration Quarterly*, 2017 Vol. 4. Also see reference of Ole Jensen, Tribunal Secretaries in International Arbitration, Oxford University Press, 2019.

tice and is confirmed by the "Two Offices' Opinions", Article 61 of the 2021 Arbitration Rules specifically provides that the arbitral tribunal or CMAC may request the arbitration committee's expert advisory committee to study and provide advice on major and difficult issues concerning the procedure and substance of the arbitration case. The arbitral tribunal shall decide whether to accept the expert advisory opinion.

Dr. Li Hu, Vice Chairman of CMAC, in an interview with the news reporter, pointed out in particular that the system of secretary and the system of expert advisory committee are the most important in this revision.① The case manager is different with the secretary of the arbitral tribunal. The case manager provides management services for the arbitration institution and the secretary of the tribunal provides secretarial services for the tribunal; the secretary of the tribunal may not participate in the voting on the case or in writing the substance of the award. This can further clarify the scope of responsibilities between the institution and the arbitral tribunal, prevent conflicts of interest and effectively improve the transparency of arbitration.

(3) Regarding publication of the award. Traditionally, one of the important reasons why parties choose arbitration is its ability to maintain confidentiality, in order to protect their privacy, trade secrets, etc. However, the confidential nature of commercial arbitration requires that the case documents not be disclosed to the public, which in turn makes it difficult for outsiders to understand the arbitration techniques, the arbitral tribunal's view on the application of the law of the cases, etc., and in turn this confidentiality mechanism makes the parties doubt the predictability of commercial arbitration. For this reason, many foreign arbitral institutions provide for the publication of awards after declassification measures have been taken. For example, in June 2021 the International Chamber of Commerce (ICC) announced that it would collaborate with Jus Mundi, the world's most extensive international law and arbitra-

---

① Rules of Arbitration of the China Maritime Arbitration Commission (CMAC) (2021) Formally Implemented, Achieving 8 First Breakthroughs, accessed January 12, 2022, https://www.sohu.com/a/494149063_362042.

tion search engine, to make all available ICC arbitral awards and related documents available to the public as of January 1, 2019.① On December 22, 2021, the Ministry of Justice of China declassified and released three "Arbitration Guidance Cases", focusing on three areas: tourism contract disputes, construction contract disputes and investment contract disputes.② Therefore, there is a consensus that arbitration requires a certain degree of disclosure of awards. The 2021 Arbitration Rules draw on the practices of the American Arbitration Association and the ICC, and provide in Article 58 that, with the consent of the parties, CMAC may publicly release an award after declassifying it, so as to enhance the transparency of the arbitration.

(4) Regarding service of the arbitration documents. Article 8 of the Arbitration Rules 2021 provides that service may be made on the master of the ship in question in the arbitration. With regard to the service of court's judicial documents on the master, Article 8 of Special Maritime Procedure Law of the Peoples's Republic of China provides that "legal documents relating to the arrest of a ship may also be served on the master of the ship in question". Article 8 of the Arbitration Rules 2021 draws on the provisions of Article 8 of the Special Maritime Litigation Procedure Law, which provides for the first time that the arbitral documents may be served on the master of the ship in question. This is a very innovative provision, which is also in line with the characteristics of maritime arbitration and the tradition of maritime dispute resolution.

(5) Regarding the issue of conflicts of interest arising from change of party's representation in an arbitration. Generally, before the arbitration panel is constituted, the arbitrator will consider the situation of the parties to the case and the attorneys representing them in order to decide whether the appointment can be accepted. However, if a party changes counsel after the arbitration tri-

---

① "ICC's Coorperation With Jus Mundi Providing Free and Open Arbitration Awards," accessed January 12, 2022, http://www.sdad.org.cn/cms/cms_ContentPage.do?ARTICLE_ID=c0e97f29-ab01-4952-87c3-df39418a7975.

② "Guidance Cases on Arbitration Issued by Ministery of Justice of the People's Republic of China," accessed January 12, 2022, http://www.moj.gov.cn/pub/sfbgw/gwxw/xwyw/202112/t20211222_444268.html.

bunal has been constituted, this may result in a threat to the fairness of the arbitration process if the party's newly appointed counsel has a conflict of interest with the already constituted tribunal. To address this issue, Article 5 of the IBA Guidelines on Party Representation issued by the International Bar Association (IBA) provides that once the Arbitral Tribunal has been constituted, a person should not accept representation of a Party in the arbitration when a relationship exists between the person and an Arbitrator that would create a conflict of interest, unless none of the Parties objects after proper disclosure. Article 6, on the other hand, provides that the Arbitral Tribunal may, in case of breach of Guideline 5, take measures appropriate to safeguard the integrity of the proceedings, including the exclusion of the new Party Representative from participating in all or part of the arbitral proceedings. In judicial practice, in both the Hrvatska Elektroprivreda d. d. vs. Slovenia and Rompetrol vs. Romania investment arbitration cases[1], the parties requested change of representative for reason of conflict of interest between the parties' arbitration representative and the arbitrator. In Hrvatska Elektroprivreda case, the arbitral tribunal relied on the principle of "immutability of properly-constituted tribunals", decided that the tribunal was presumed to have the right to decide on challenges to the arbitral representative and to require the parties to replace the challenged representative. The 2021 Arbitration Rules draw on the IBA Guidelines on Party Representation in International Arbitration (2013) to provide, for the first time, that an arbitral tribunal may take necessary measures to avoid conflicts of interest arising from changes in the parties' representation.

(6) Regarding the civil liability of arbitrators and the limitation of liability. Like soccer referees, arbitrators are also human beings and may make mistakes due to intent or negligence, resulting in the parties being victimized. Article 38 of China's Arbitration Law stipulates that an arbitrator who has made a mistake under the circumstances specified in Article 34(4) of this Law, or under the circum-

---

[1] "Cultivation in Professional Ethics of Agents in International Arbitration: Still a Long Way To Go," accessed January 12, 2022, https://www.sohu.com/na/496142915_120677543.

stances specified in Article 58(6) of this Law, shall bear legal liability in accordance with the law. However, whether the legal liability here includes civil liability is highly controversial. As early as in the annual meeting of the National Conference on Private International Law in October 2008, the Secretary-General of China International Economic and Trade Arbitration Commission (CIETAC) revealed that there have been several civil litigation cases against arbitrators or arbitration institutions in China, but the details of the cases have not publicly reported. [1]

The recent relevant public report is the case of a Mr. Li's claims against an arbitration committee in a dispute over unjust enrichment. In that case, Mr. Li requested the court to order an arbitration committee to return RMB224998 yuan in arbitration fees for reason that the award made by the arbitration committee had been set aside by the court. Ultimately, Shiyan Intermediate People's Court issued (2017) E03 MZ No. 2210 civil ruling and upheld the ruling of dismissing the lawsuit by the first instance court. Shiyan Intermediate People's Court's reason is that civil law adjusts personal and property relations among natural persons, legal persons and unincorporated organizations of equal footing. However, during the arbitration process, the arbitration commission and the parties are not civil legal subjects with equal footing; the arbitration commission handles civil disputes in accordance with the arbitration agreement between the arbitration parties, and there is no property and personal relations between the arbitration parties and the arbitration commission. During arbitration, the arbitration committee charged arbitration fees in accordance with the relevant provisions of law; whether its fees charged is reasonable is not actionable, and is not within the scope of civil cases acceptable by the people's court (lack of Justiciability, i.e., Justiciability refers to the types of matters that a court can adjudicate. If a case is "nonjusticiable," then the court cannot hear it). After this case came out, the civil liability of arbitrators and arbitration institutions became a hot topic for a while.

There have been similar cases abroad recently, such as in the case of Tex-

---

[1] Shengcui Zhang, "Analysis on Civil Liabilities of Arbitration," *Journal of Shanghai University of Finance and Economics*, Vol. 1(2019).

as Brine Co. v. Am. Arbitration Assc., No. 18 - CV - 31184①, on July 6, 2018 Texas Brine filed a lawsuit against the American Arbitration Association and two arbitrators, by alleging that the three defendants engaged in intentional fraud in the arbitration proceedings and requested $12 million in damages and equitable relief. In response, the 2021 Arbitration Rules also introduced a limitation of liability clause for the first time, by drawing on the rules of the London Court of International Arbitration (LCIA) and the Hong Kong International Arbitration Centre (HKIAC).

(7) In addition, other important changes include: the 2021 Arbitration Rules also add a schedule of arbitration fees consisting of the institution's administrative fee and the arbitrator's remuneration, allowing the parties to choose to apply them by special agreement, in order to better meet the needs of the parties and to stimulate the dynamics of arbitration. The 2021 Arbitration Rules also provide that the parties may select arbitrators from outside the arbitrator roster of the CMAC, while providing that the presiding arbitrator and the sole arbitrator shall be from the arbitrator roster; and that if the parties are unable to jointly appoint the presiding arbitrator, the two arbitrators chosen by the parties shall jointly appoint the presiding arbitrator; and if they are unable to do so within the time limit, the Director of CMAC shall make the appointment. ②

In terms of case load, according to CCPIT's President Gao Yan, who presented at the 2021 China Maritime Commercial Arbitration High Level Seminar③ on July 16, 2021, the number of maritime commercial cases decided by China Maritime Arbitration Commission in 2020 was among the highest in the world, with foreign-related cases accounting for 35% of all cases received, with

---

① "The court rejected the parties' claim that the arbitrators and the arbitrators involved should compensate for the arbitration fees based on the arbitrators' failure to disclose potential conflicts of interest," accessed January 12, 2022, https://zhuanlan.zhihu.com/p/345170820.

② "Rules of Arbitration of the China Maritime Arbitration Commission (CMAC) (2021)," accessed January 12, 2022, http://www.cmac.org.cn/index.php?id=542.

③ Yan gao, "Anchor the direction and move forward vigorously: promote the steady and long-term development of China's maritime arbitration industry," accessed January 12, 2022, http://www.ccpit.org/Contents/Channel_3434/2021/0804/1358085/content_1358085.html.

parties coming from 22 countries and regions, and the degree of internationalization of arbitration increasing. As far as arbitration-mediation is concerned, on November 11, 2021 Shanghai Maritime Court issued White Book regarding Entrusted Mediation Between China Maritime Arbitration Commission and Shanghai Maritime Court (《上海海事法院与中国海事仲裁委员会海事案件委托调解白皮书(2011—2021)》)[1] and it is reported that: (1) from 2011 to 2020, the entrusted mediation mechanism has maintained a stable operation, and Shanghai Maritime Court entrusted more than 200 cases to be handled by the Shanghai Headquarter of China Maritime Arbitration Commission for mediation, with the number of cases showing a steady upward trend year by year; (2) the cases involved parties from forty-two countries and regions, with the total amount of the subject matter exceeding RMB500 million, and 141 of all cases had foreign-related factors; (3) the total amount of monetary claims involved in all cases reached RMB 568 million, and the average amount of cases reached RMB 2692200. Among them, the highest amount was RMB 56718200; (4) Among all the cases, 102 cases were successfully mediated, with a success rate of 48.34%. Moreover, the mediation success rate has improved significantly in recent years. In particular, in year 2020, the success rate of entrusted mediation went to the highest value in ten years, at 75%.

III. Development of Judicial Practice Relating to Maritime Arbitration in China

Regarding the development of judicial review of maritime arbitration in year 2020-2021, according to the Guidance on Commercial and Maritime Trials in Foreign-related Matters (36th Volume) published by the People's Court Press in November 2020, the Annual Report on Judicial Review of Commercial Arbitration by the Supreme People's Court (2019) published by the People's

---

[1] "White Paper of Entrusted Mediation of Maritime Cases between Shanghai Maritime Court and China Maritime Arbitration Commission (2011-2021)," p43-44, accessed January 12, 2022, http://shhsfy.gov.cn/hsfyytwx/hsfyytwx/spdy1358/hsspbps1434/web/viewer.html?file=2011-2021.pdf.

Court Press in September 2021, the white papers on maritime trials issued by various maritime courts, and the online research of the adjudication documents, it will be summarized in this paper as follows.

3.1 Regarding the Validity of the Arbitration Agreement

(1) In the case of voyage charter contract dispute case between Sinotrans Limited Engineering Equipment Transportation Branch and Shanghai China Merchants Minghua Shipping Company Limited, the fixture note of both parties provided that "G/A arbitration if any to be settled in Beijing with China Maritime Arbitration Commission, Chinese law to apply". Shanghai Maritime Court issued (2020) H 72 MC No. 1588 civil ruling and held that this clause was invalid for reason that it was a special agreement between the parties as to the place of arbitration and the applicable law in the event of arbitration of the dispute in question, which did not constitute the sole/only means of dispute resolution between the parties and did not exclude court's jurisdiction. ①

---

① In (2009) People's Supreme Court Minsita No. 36 Reseponse Letter, People's Supreme Court Minsita No. 3 Response Letter, it was agreed in the relevant arbitration clause that Arbitration if any to be settled in hongkong with english law tp apply. The People's Supreme Court did not confirm it invalid, but only held that arbitration clause did not constitute the sole means of dispute resolution, in other words, the clause did not exclude the jurisdiction of court litigation. Reversely, in (2015) People's Supreme Court Minsita No. 21 Response Letter, it was agreed in the arbitration clause that: Arbitratiog if any in benxi and chinese law to be applied. In face of this clause, the Supreme People's Court held the opinion that it not only didn't constitute the solely means of dispute resolution which did not exclude the jurisdiction of court litigation, but the clause should be certainly invalid in the accordance of article16 paragraph2(1) of Arbitration Law. Moreover, similar problem exists in the validity of arbitration clause using words like "may" "can" other than "if any". In (2003) People's Supreme Court Minsita No. 7 Response Letter, the People's Supreme Court held that, in English arbitration clauses, "may" primarily acts as the subject clause meaning that any party may bring up the arbitration request instead of both party may bring up the arbitration request or litigation, so this dispute should be resolved through arbitration. In (2011) Minminzhongzi No. 819, it was agreed in article 25 of the subcontract that, "In face of any disputes related to the performance of this contract, parties may re-conciliate according to their own accord or require relevant institutions to mediate, if unwillingness of any party to re-conciliate or mediate or failure of reconciliation or mediation appears, the case may be submitted to Qingdao Arbitration Commission." The Higher People's Court held that, this clause only stipulated that disputes "may" resolve through arbitration instead of "must" resolve through arbitration and now that the party chose the means of court litigation which means he abandoned the intend to arbitrate and this should be granted.

(2) In the case between Zurich Property and Casualty Insurance (China) Company Limited (Zurich Insurance) and Tokio Marine & Nichido Fire Insurance (China) Company Limited (Tokio Marine Insurance), Zurich Insurance requested to confirm there was no arbitration clause in the "REINSURANCE SLIP" signed between Zurich Insurance and Tokio Marine & Nichido Fire Insurance (China) Company Limited, Shanghai Branch (hereinafter referred to as Tokio Marine Shanghai Branch). Ultimately, Shanghai Financial Court issued (2019) H 74 MC No. 27 civil ruling to reject Zurich Insurance's application for reason that the reinsurance contract agreed that other matters, including jurisdiction etc, should refer to the original policy. This is the incorporation of the contractual terms. The reinsurance contract lists jurisdiction separately from matters such as insurance benefits and insurance term, and expressly agrees that these matters should refer to the original insurance policy. Zurich Insurance argued that jurisdiction only refers to court jurisdiction, and since the original policy only agreed an arbitration clause without any court jurisdictional agreement, the reinsurance contract had no way of reference to arbitration and could not be applied. Shanghai Financial Court held that both parties to the case were foreign insurance companies, and the contracts in question were drafted and signed in English. In the event of a dispute between the parties over the meaning of "jurisdiction", this term should be defined/interpreted in accordance with its usual meaning. In English, "jurisdiction" does not refer specifically to court jurisdiction only, and it can also be applied by referring to litigation, arbitration and other dispute resolution methods. In this case, there is no jurisdictional agreement in the original policy, and the parties agreed to refer to the arbitration clause of the original policy (arbitration with China Maritime Arbitration Commission Shanghai Branch) and this should be a valid arbitration clause.

3.2 Regarding the Issue of the Incorporation of the Charter Party Arbitration Clause into Bills of Lading

In the (2018) ZGFMT no. 52 Reply Letter to the Request for Instruction of the Hubei Provincial High People's Court on the Validity of the Arbitration Clause in the Case of Xiamen International Trade Group Co. v. King Navigation Co. in the Dispute over the Contract of Carriage of Goods by Sea, the Supreme People's Court pointed out that: in the contents of the bill of lading, it does not specify the name of the parties to the charter party, the charter party number, etc. and other exact information of the charter party, so it can not be determined which specific charter party is incorporated into the bill of lading. As such, the charter party arbitration clause is not binding on the bill of lading holder or consignee. Moreover, the Supreme People's Court specifically pointed out that the UK court's determination of the validity of the arbitration clause and the issuance of the injunction order, also does not affect that the consignee can file a lawsuit in China.[①] In the (2020) LMXZ No. 201 civil ruling, Shandong High People's Court also held that the bill of lading in question only contained a record on the front that "freight payable as per the charter party dated May 24, 2019", with no specific information on the names of the parties to the charter party and no information on the incorporation of the particularized charter party. Accordingly its arbitration clause was not incorporated into the bill of lading and could not bind the bill of lading holder.

3.3 Regarding the Relationship Between Insurance Subrogation and Arbitration Clause

In the case between Zhuhai JieTeng Shipbuilding Co., Ltd. and Yingda Taihe Property Insurance Co., Ltd. Zhuhai Central Branch, the (2020) YMXZ No. 258 civil ruling of Guangdong High People's Court held that the arbitration clause agreed in the shipbuilding contract provided arbitration by the Singapore Chamber of Maritime Arbitration, but this arbitration clause did not bind the insurer when the insurer files subrogated claims. In the case between PICC Nanchang Branch and Jiangxi COSCO Shipping Container Transportation Co., Ltd., the (2020) G 01 MZ 1950 civil ruing of Nanchang Intermediate People's Court held that the arbitration clause (by China Maritime Arbitration

---

① Compiled by the Fourth Trial Division of the Supreme People's Court, "Adjudication Guidance on Foreign-related Maritime Cases" (vol. 36), the People's Court Press(2020), p32.

Commission) agreed in the contract of carriage could bind the insurer who filed the subrogation claim. In this regard, it should be noted that Article 98 of the Minutes of the National Conference on Civil and Commercial Judicial Work of the Courts (the 9th Civil and Commercial Judicial Work Minutes) distinguishes between domestic and foreign cases, i. e., in non-foreign cases, the arbitration agreement reached between the insured and the third party before occurrence of the insurance accident is binding on the insurer. In the case of foreign related cases, the 9th Civil and Commercial Judicial Work Minutes is silent on this matter, but the prevailing view is basically that such arbitration agreement does not bind the insurer who initiates subrogation claims.

3. 4 Regarding the Question of Whether the Arbitration Clause is Applicable When the Parties Sue for Liability in Tort or Culpa in Contrahendo

(1) In a refund guarantee dispute case heard by Shanghai Maritime Court, Hengshun Shipping Company filed arbitration in London, demanding the payment of USD 14. 22 million and the corresponding interest from Pudong Development Bank. After the arbitral tribunal ruled against Hengshun Shipping Company, it filed a lawsuit against Pudong Development Bank in Shanghai Maritime Court for reason that Pudong Development Bank was negligent in issuing the guarantee. Finally, Shanghai Maritime Court held that Hengshun Shipping Company applied for arbitration based on the arbitration clause in the letter of guarantee, and after its request for arbitration was rejected, it claimed that Pudong Development Bank was at fault in issuing the letter of guarantee (liability of *culpa in contrahendo*), which belonged to the dispute related to the letter of guarantee. The dispute had already been settled by arbitration in London, and the court had no jurisdiction over it. [1]

(2) In the case of China Garment Group Co., Ltd (China Garment) v.

---

[1] See "White Paper of Entrusted Mediation of Maritime Cases between Shanghai Maritime Court and China Maritime Arbitration Commission(2011-2021)," p43-44.

Yangzhou Yuan Yang International Terminal Co. , Ltd and Yangzhou Yuan Yang International Terminal Co. , the court ruled to reject the application of Yuan Yang for setting aside of an arbitral award. Subsequently, Yuan Yang filed a maritime tort lawsuit against China Garment and filed an application for property preservation against China Garment. China Garment won the lawsuit and demanded compensation from Yuan Yang for the wrongful property preservation. In this regard, Tianjin Maritime Court held that the infringement lawsuit filed by Yuan Yang was still in essence an objection to the arbitral award, and that it was subjectively at fault for filing infringement lawsuits and taking property preservation measures again after the arbitration been completed. As such, Yuan Yang should bear the corresponding losses resulting from the wrongful application for preservation. ①

3.5 Regarding Issue of Preservation of Property outside Mainland of China Related Maritime Arbitration

(1) In the case of application of Skyline International Corp. for the arrest of the M/V NERISSA, the applicant applied to Qingdao Maritime Court for the arrest of the approximately 300000-ton Marshall Islands registered tanker M/V NERISSA prior to arbitration in London. Qingdao Maritime Court granted the application. Moreover, considering that the vessel was scheduled to unload more than 130000 tons of crude oil at Qingdao port and then continue to Tianjin to unload the remaining 150000 tons, and if it could not go to Tianjin to unload the cargo as scheduled, it would incur demurrage of USD 30000/day and would lead to delay in delivery, plant shutdown and other losses, Qingdao Maritime Court made (2019) L 72 CB no. 108-1 civil ruling, granting that the vessel M/V NERISSA was allowed to continue its operation and complete the voyage from Qingdao Port to Qinhuangdao Port via Tianjin Port. Finally, the case was successfully mediated by the parties organized by Qingdao Maritime

---

① This case is classified as a classic case published in "White Paper of 2020 Ajudication of Tianjin Maritime Court," accessed January 12, 2022, https://tjhsfy.chinacourt.gov.cn/article/detail/2021/03/id/5927724.shtml.

Court. This case was highly praised by the Supreme People's Court and was selected as one of the "2019 National Maritime Trial Typical Cases" issued by the Supreme People's Court in September 2020. ①

(2) In the voyage charter dispute case of China Capital Chartering Co., Ltd. v. Fuqing Tianyi Building Materials Co., Ltd., the applicant, China Capital Chartering Co., Ltd. initiated arbitration proceedings in Hong Kong against the charterer, a Malaysian company and the guarantor, Fuqing Tianyi, and then applied to Xiamen Maritime Court to preserve the bank deposits or other property of the respondent, Fuqing Tianyi. Xiamen Maritime Court issued (2020) M72 CB no. 17 civil ruling to approve the property preservation application. It is worth noting there is a view that: there is some breakthrough in the Special Maritime Litigation Procedure Law as to whether parties to overseas arbitration can apply to Chinese courts for property preservation. ② However, the scope of the breakthrough is limited to maritime claims preservation, and cannot be extended to other non-maritime claims preservation. Regardless of pre-arbitration or in-arbitration, the object of preservation is limited to the ship, its cargo, bunker and marine materials, and cannot be extended to other property. Therefore, whether the respondent's bank account can be preserved before or during an offshore arbitration may still be in dispute.

(3) According to the Trial Briefing regarding Services to Protect the Development of the Ship Industry (《上海海事法院服务保障船舶产业发展审判情况通报》) issued by Shanghai Maritime Court on May 25, 2021, the Shanghai Maritime Court reviewed the first case of granting an application for property preservation in arbitration proceedings in Hong Kong in 2020 in accordance with the Arrangement of the Supreme People's Court on Mutual Assistance in Preservation between the Courts of the Mainland and the Hong Kong Special Administrative Region in relation to Arbitration Proceedings. ③

---

① See *People's Court Daily*, 8 September 2020, Page 4.
② Shengshun Wu, "On the Limitation of Non-maritime Claim Preservation in Overseas Arbitration," Chinese Journal of Maritime Law, 2015 vol. 3
③ See "Shanghai Maritime Court Report on Trials Involving Shipbuilding Industry," p25.

3.6 Regarding the Recognition and Enforcement outside Mainland of China Arbitral Awards

(1) In the matter of the application of CHINALAND CHARTERING LIMITED for recognition and enforcement of a Hong Kong arbitral award, Shanghai Maritime Court issued (2019) H 72 RG No. 1 civil ruling to recognize and enforce five arbitral awards rendered by Mok Sai Kit and Philip Yang in relation to the dispute over the chartering contract of the vessel "SILVIA GLORY".

(2) In the case between the claimant COSCO SHIPPING Specialized Carriers Co. Ltd and the respondent Henguan Shipping Ltd, Xiamen Maritime Court issue (2020) M 72 RG no. 1 civil ruling to recognize and enforce an arbitration award of HKIAC. Moreover, on February 18, 2020, Xiamen Maritime Court also recognized Singapore International Arbitration Center's Partial Final Arbitration Award No. 023 of 2019 and the Final Arbitration Award No. 059 of 2019. It is reported that this is the first case of Xiamen Maritime Court's recognizing a Singaporean arbitral award. [1]

(3) In the case of application for the recognition and enforcement of a foreign arbitral award between Shanghai Jia Ship Machinery Equipment Import & Export Co. and Mekers Offshore Company Limited, Jiaxing Intermediate People's Court issue (2019) Z 04 XWR No. 1 civil ruling deciding that the arbitral award (relating to a ship construction contract dispute) made by Clive Aston, the sole arbitrator of the London Maritime Arbitrators Association (LMAA), was recognized.

(4) In the case of application for the recognition and enforcement of a foreign arbitral award between Anfur Free Trade Zone Company (hereinafter reffered to as "Anfur") and Guangdong Yuexin Offshore Engineering Equipment Company Limited (hereinafter reffered to as "Yuexin"), Guangzhou Maritime Court issue (2020) Y 72 XWR No. 1 civil ruling that the arbitral award made

---

[1] See "Xiamen Maritime Court's first Acknowledgement on Singapore Maritime Arbitration Award," accessed January 12, 2022, http://www.xmhsfy.gov.cn/xwzx/fydt/202002/t20200220_166987.html.

by Jaya Prakash, the sole arbitrator of the Singapore Chamber of Maritime Arbitration is recognized. It is worth noting that in this case, the respondent Yuexin argued that Anfur only requested Yuexin to pay $7262 for the inspection cost of Zhongshan Shipyard, but the Arbitration Tribunal also ordered Yuexin to pay interest on the cost at 6% per annum, which exceeded the scope of the arbitration request and constituted an over-arbitration. In this regard, Guangzhou Maritime Court did not support this argument, for reason that according to Article 37.2 of the Third Edition of the Arbitration Rules of the Singapore Chamber of Maritime Arbitration, the arbitral tribunal may award simple or compound interest on any amount of the award at such rate as it deems just; Article 8.1 of the arbitral award in this case also provides that the arbitral tribunal has great discretion in awarding interest. Therefore, the arbitral tribunal's award of interest on Zhongshan Shipyard's inspection costs is not excessive.

(5) In a case of ship chartering dispute, VERTEX SHIPPING CO., LTD. applied to enforce arbitral award issued by Timothy Marshall and Ian Guant, arbitrators of the LMAA, in relation to the dispute over the chartering of the vessel IZUMI. Shanghai Maritime Court issued (2019) H 72 XWR No. 3 civil ruling to recognize and enforce it. It is noteworthy that in this case, Shanghai Maritime Court did not support the respondent's defense that it had filed a lawsuit against the final award in the English court, for reason that the filing of the lawsuit (against the arbitral award) did not mean that the arbitral award rendered by the arbitral tribunal had lost its binding effect. ①

(6) In a case of dispute between Hailong Yacht Ltd and Qingdao Shipyard over a yacht construction contract, after the LMAA arbitrator made the award, Hailong applied for recognition and enforcement. Qingdao Maritime Court, after examining the case, found that there was a discrepancy between the arbitration procedure and the agreement of the parties, and intended to re-

---

① See "Judicial Review on the Binding Force of Foreign Arbitration Award," accessed January 12, 2022, http://m.shhsfy.gov.cn/hsfyytwx/hsfyytwx/spdy1358/jpal1435/2020/09/10/09b080ba744e77de017476c4671d3387.html.

fuse to recognize the enforcement application and reported it to the Shandong Provincial High People's Court for decision. The majority opinion of Shandong High People's Court agreed with the Qingdao Maritime Court's opinion, mainly for the following reasons: Article 13 of the shipbuilding contract signed by both parties agreed that the notice of award should be sent to both parties by fax or email; Article 17 "Notice" section also agreed that emails sent with return receipt are deemed to be delivered upon return of the read receipt. On January 9, 2014 and January 21, 2014, the arbitrator sent emails notifying the parties that the award had been made and sent the unsigned award to them. However, Hailong did not have evidence to prove that the arbitrator received the reading receipts after sending the aforementioned two emails. Therefore, the arbitrator's sending of the above emails did not have the effect of notifying Qingdao Shipyard of the award. Since it could not be confirmed that the above emails were opened by the recipients, the arbitrator could have notified Qingdao Shipyard by fax as soon as possible in accordance with Article 13 of the shipbuilding contract, but the arbitrator did not send the notice of the award by fax. Because the arbitrator did not send the notice of the award to Qingdao Shipyard by the method as agreed by the parties, the arbitration procedure was not in compliance with the parties' agreement. Ultimately, the Supreme People's Court did not endorse the majority opinion of the Shandong High People's Court for reason that Article 17 of the yacht construction contract was an agreement between the parties regarding sending notices, not an agreement on the arbitration procedure; and that the agreement on notice in that article did not apply to the sending of notice of the award in the arbitration procedure. ①

(7) In the case between Amarante Shipping Pte Ltd and Intermarine Shipping Co. Ltd., Tianjin Maritime Court issue (2019) J72 XWR no. 1-1 civil ruling for recognition and enforcement of an arbitral award made by LMAA ar-

---

① Compiled by the Fourth Trial Division of the Supreme People's Court, *Ajudication Guidances on Foreign-related Maritime Cases*(*vol.* 36), the People's Court Press(2020), p52-56.

bitrator David Farrington on October 26, 2017 in relation to a dispute over a time charter contract, and an award made on the arbitration costs on August 23, 2018.

3.7 Regarding Chinese Courts' Refusal to Recognize and Enforce outside Mainland of China's Arbitral Awards

On the whole, Chinese courts have adopted a rather supportive attitude towards foreign, Hong Kong, Macao and Taiwan maritime arbitral awards. However, it is noteworthy that there are some awards that have been refused to be recognized for enforcement, or partially refused to be recognized for enforcement.

(1) In the Reply of the Supreme People's Court to the Request of the Tianjin High People's Court on the Application for Recognition and Enforcement of Foreign Arbitral Award in the case between the Claimant Palmer Shipping Company and the Respondent Zhongmu Industrial Co. Ltd.[1], the Supreme People's Court refused to enforce a London arbitral award for reason that: Zhongmu filed a lawsuit against Palmer Marine to Guangzhou Maritime Court to bear the responsibility of cargo damage, and Palmer Marine filed a jurisdictional objection of Guangzhou Maritime Court for reason of the existence of an arbitration agreement between the parties. The Supreme People's Court issued (2017) ZGFMTZ no. 83 Letter of Reply to Guangdong Provincial High People's Court, holding that the arbitration clause in the charter party was not incorporated into the bill of lading and the arbitration clause on the back of the bill of lading was invalid. Since Chinese courts have made negative judgment on the existence and validity of the arbitration clause between the parties, the recognition and enforcement of the arbitral award based on the above-mentioned arbitration clause results in a diametrically opposing judicial judgment on the same facts of the same jurisdiction, which contradicts the unity and con-

---

[1] Compiled by the Fourth Trial Division of the Supreme People's Court, *Ajudication Guidances on Foreign-related Maritime Cases*(vol. 36), the People's Court Press, 2020, p74-75.

sistency of national legal values of China. Regardless of howsoever restrictive interpretation of the "public policy" in the New York Convention, the consistency and unity of the national legal concept and the conclusive effect of Chinese court's judicial judgment should not be excluded from the scope of "public policy".

In practice, the Supreme People's Court has not often refused to recognize and enforce outside mainland of China's arbitration awards for reason of public policy, but it has generally refused to recognize and enforce arbitral awards that result in conflicts with the jurisdiction of Chinese courts. For example, in the Yongning Company case and the Haopu Company case, the Supreme People's Court issued (2008) MSTZ no. 11 Letter of Reply and (2016) ZGFMTZ no. 8 Letter of Reply, both refused to recognize the enforcement of foreign awards for this reason.

However, it is worth noting that the Supreme Court, in its (2013) MSTZ no. 46 Letter of Reply stated that: "the arbitral awards in question were made on December 23, 2010 and January 27, 2011, while the decision of our country's court on the invalidity of the arbitration clause was made on December 20, 2011; the arbitral awards were clearly made earlier than the time of Chinese court's decision;... Although there is a conflict between the foreign arbitral award and the decision of Chinese court regarding the validity of the same arbitration clause, it is not enough to constitute a violation of our country's public policy." Therefore, if the foreign arbitral tribunal's determination on the validity of the arbitration clause predates Chinese courts' decision, its arbitral award may still be possible to be recognized for enforcement.

(2) In an application for recognition of an ICDR (International Centre for Dispute Resolution) arbitration award by Triton International Containers Limited hereinafter referred to as Triton, six container leasing agreements were entered into between 2010 and 2011 between Hainan PO Shipping Company Limited (hereinafter referred to as PO), Hainan PO Shipping Company Limited (Hong Kong) (hereinafter referred to as PO Hong Kong) and Triton International Containers Limited (registered in Bermuda). Yangpu Economic Devel-

opment Zone Construction Investment and Development Company Limited (hereinafter referred to as Yangpu) signed one of the agreements, i. e., agreement No. HPO42, as a co-lessee and authorized PO, PO Hong Kong to exercise its rights in relation to this Agreement on its behalf and undertake to pay for the costs and damages associated with this (No. HPO42) Agreement. However, for other agreements, Yangpu had not signed or made similar commitments. Triton submitted an arbitration application to ICDR based on the aforementioned six agreements due to the default of paying rental fee by PO and PO Hong Kong. In the course of the arbitration, PO, PO Hong Kong and Triton signed a Letter of Agreement on Default Handling, which made a consolidated handling of the six Agreements. PO signed the Letter of Agreement on behalf of Yangpu. Based on the Letter of Agreement on Default Handling, ICDR awarded PO and Yangpu to pay Triton $65817973.41 for the six leasing agreements in question. Ultimately, Haikou Maritime Court held that PO had no authority to sign the Letter of Agreement on Default Handling for all six leasing agreements on behalf of Yangpu; Yangpu was only a party to Leasing Agreement No. HPO42, but not to the other five agreements, so the arbitration clauses in the other five agreements other than Agreement No. HPO42 were not binding on Yangpu. Eventually, after reporting to the Supreme People's Court for review, the ICDR arbitration award was partially recognized and enforced by the Haikou Maritime Court. [1]

3.8 Regarding the Jurisdictional Issues Involved in the Enforcement outside the Mainland of China's Awards

In shipping practice, many Persons subject to Enforcement may be offshore companies, but their actual place of business is in the mainland. Under such situation, whether courts in mainland have jurisdiction over them may be

---

[1] (2015) Qionghaita No. 1 ruling paper of Haikou Maritime Court, see *Annual Report on The Supreme People's Court's Judicial Review of Commercial Arbitration* (2019), compiled by The Fourth Civil Trial Division of the Supreme People's Court, The People's Court Press, 2021, p. 373-381.

controversial. From the following cases, it can be seen that the courts may have jurisdiction over the enforcement of an arbitral award in respect of an offshore company if its actual place of business is in the meinland.

(1) In the Case (2020) H 72 XWR No. 1 of Shanghai Maritime Court, the arbitrator of LMAA made a final decision on the dispute of chartering contract between the applicant ORIENTAL PRIME SHIPPING CO. Ltd. and the respondent HONG GLORY INTERNATIONAL SHIPPING CO., and the applicant applied to Shanghai Maritime Court for recognition and enforcement of the arbitral award. The respondent (Person subject to Enforcement) objected to the court's jurisdiction for reason that it was registered in the Marshall Islands, its place of main business office was not in China, and did not have any property in China. Ultimately, Shanghai Maritime Court rejected this objection for reason that the charter confirmation (fixture note) signed between the claimant and the respondent stated that the respondent's address was in Shanghai, China. The arbitration award stated that the respondent's place of business was in Shanghai, China, and the content of the relevant business correspondence during the performance of the voyage in question showed that the respondent confirmed that it and HONG GLORY SHIPPING CO., LIMITED are the same company and that the office address of HONG GLORY SHIPPING CO., LIMITED is the same as the respondent's address as stated in the charter confirmation. Accordingly, the court concluded that the respondent's principal office was located in Shanghai, China. It is worth pointing out that Shanghai Maritime Court particularly emphasizes[①] that the respondent in question was an offshore company registered outside of China, and in judicial practice, the standard for determining the location of the main business office of such companies can be appropriately lowered, as long as there is evidence that the respondent had a certain degree of contact with the court.

(2) Similarly, in the case of (2019) J 72 XWR No. 1 heard by Tianjin

---

① "Confirmation of jurisdiction of disputes relevant to offshore company under the New York Convention," accessed January 19, 2022, http://shhsfy.gov.cn/hsfyytwx/hsfyytwx/spdy1358/jpal1435/2021/12/10/09b080ba7d9ee309017da314737a06d5.html.

Maritime Court, the applicant applied for the enforcement of an LMAA award and the respondent raised similar defenses of jurisdiction objection. Ultimately, Tianjin Maritime Court and Tianjin High Court held that based on factors such as the issuance of a cargo release bond and the use of an email address consistent with the corporate email address of a company in Beijing for communication, the use of an address consistent with the corporate correspondence address of the company for rental payment, and the consistency of the sole shareholder and director of the Person subject to Enforcement with the legal representative of the (Beijing) company, the BVI company's main business office should be determined to be located in Beijing and Tianjin Maritime Court had jurisdiction. This case was selected as one of the top ten cases of Tianjin Maritime Court in 2020, and Tianjin Maritime Court particularly emphasizedthat for the review of the domicile of a legal person or other organization, the court should first determine the location of its main business office. Especially for foreign registered offshore companies, it should be determined by identifying the location of its main business activities, office place, etc. to determine its domicile, so as to prevent these offshore companies operating in China through its foreign company status, to evade responsibility, circumvent legal supervision, and damage the market environment of fair trade. ①

3.9 On the Recognition and Enforcement of Domestic Maritime Arbitration Awards

(1) In March 2020, Nanjing Maritime Court recognized an arbitral award made by China Maritime Arbitration Commission in relation to a ship repair contract dispute. It is noteworthy that this is the first case in which Nanjing Maritime Court enforced the arbitral award of China Maritime Arbitration Commission. ②

---

① See "White Paper of 2020 Ajudication of Tianjin Maritime Court," accessed January 19, 2022, https://tjhsfy.chinacourt.gov.cn/article/detail/2021/03/id/5927724.shtml.

② See "Over 2 million RMB on account! The first arbitration award executed by Nanjing Maritime Court," acessed January 19, 2022, http://news.ynet.com/2020/06/16/2666344t70.html.

(2) According to Xiamen Maritime Court's "2019 Xiamen Maritime Court Trial Work White Paper" released in July 2020, Xiamen Maritime Court enforced an award of China Maritime Arbitration Commission Shanghai Branch. It is noteworthy that in this case, the Person subject to Enforcement argued that the arbitration award did not require it to pay interest for delayed performance and that the claimant's request for enforcement of this element (paying interest) lacked legal basis.① Xiamen Maritime Court did not accept this argument, for reason that the calculation and collection of interest on delayed performance is based on Article 253 of the Civil Procedure Law, not on the arbitral award.

(3) In the case of Zhang Xin vs. Zhang Kefu, Zhang Kefu's bulk carrier MV "Haina 5188" sank due to negligent navigation. After the sunken cargo was salvaged from the water, Zhang Kefu and his ship's insurer, Sunshine Property Insurance Company Limited, Chongqing Wanzhou Central Branch (Sunshine Property Insurance), approached Zhang Xin and negotiated a sale and purchase contract for the sunken cargo, and agreed in the sale and purchase contract to arbitrate disputes by China Maritime Arbitration Commission Shanghai Branch. Subsequently, the sunken cargo owner's insurer compensated the cargo owner and then filed a recovery action against Zhang Kefu and Sunshine Property Insurance, and the case was settled by mediation. As Zhang Xin failed to make payment in accordance with the sales contract, Zhang Kefu and Sunshine Property Insurance signed a "Claims Assignment Agreement" to assign the right of claims under the sale and purchase contract to Sunshine Property Insurance, and issued a "Notice Letter" to Zhang Xin for the assignment of right of claims. Thereafter, Zhang Kefu and Sunshine Property Insurance filed arbitration against Zhang Xin with China Maritime Arbitration Commission Shanghai Branch, and the arbitral tribunal ordered Zhang Xin to pay the purchase price of RMB 480938 yuan and interest to Sunshine Property In-

---

① See "White Paper of Xiamen Maritime Court 2019 Ajudication," acessed January 19, 2022, http://www.xmhsfy.gov.cn/sjbg/bps/202007/t20200716_168900.html.

surance. In the arbitral award enforcement procedure, Zhang Xin objected that: the "Claims Assignment Agreement" did not have the basis of assignment, and the agreement and the notice of debt assignment did not have legal effect; there was no arbitration agreement between Zhang Xin and Sunshine Property Insurance, and Sunshine Property Insurance was not entitled to apply for arbitration directly through the act of debt assignment. In this regard, Wuhan Maritime Court issued (2020) E72 ZY no. 44 civil ruling to reject this defence of Zhang Xin for reasons that: as the assignee of part of the claims involved in the case, Sunshine Property Insurance accepted the dispute resolution clause in the sale and purchase contract, voluntarily accepted to be bound by it. Sunshine Property Insurance filed arbitration against Zhang Xin with Zhang Kefu together, without harming Zhang Xin's legitimate rights and interests. From this case, it can be seen that insurance companies can also obtain the insured's right to claim compensation against third party through the assignment of right of claims.

(4) In the case between China Power Construction Co., Ltd. and Sinotrans Ltd., Tianjin Maritime Court issued (2021) J 72 MT no. 6 civil ruling and dismissed the applicant's application for setting aside the (2020) ZGHZJCZ No. 0010 award (hereinafter referred to as Award No. 20-10) of China Maritime Arbitration Commission. It is noteworthy that in this case, the applicant argued that the arbitration violated the statutory procedures, because the content of the award 20-10 and the content of the award (2017) ZGHZJCZ No. 0015 of China Maritime Arbitration Commission (hereinafter referred to as award Award No. 17-15) are contradictory, and the adjudication standards in the two awards were obviously not uniform, which violated the statutory procedures of "Search for Similar Cases to Unify the Application of Law". In the end, Tianjin Maritime Court did not approve the application for annulment for reason that "violation of statutory procedures" as stipulated in Article 58 of the Arbitration Law refers to the violation of the arbitration procedures as stipulated in the Arbitration Law and the arbitration rules chosen by the parties, which may affect the correct awarding of the case. The applicant's reason for violation

of statutory procedures was that the standard of interpretation of the contract terms in the Award No. 20-10 and the Award No. 17-15 was not uniform and did not comply with the Opinions of the Supreme People's Court on Implementing the Judicial Responsibility System and Improving the Trial Supervision and Management Mechanism (for Trial Implementation). However, this document is the requirement issued by the Supreme People's Court on improving the trial supervision and management mechanism of the people's courts for the relevant trial work of the people's courts at all levels, but does not belong to the arbitration procedures under the Arbitration Law or the arbitration rules chosen by the parties. Moreover, the Award No. 20-10 and the Award No. 17-15 were determined separately for different request matters and contract terms, and there was no substantial conflict.

(5) In the case of Zheng Xianzhong's application for setting aside the award (2019) ZGHZHCZ No. 042 of China Maritime Arbitration Commission Shanghai Branch, the applicant argued that China Maritime Arbitration Commission had no authority to determine the validity of the parties' contract and had no authority to make arbitration decision thereon. Shanghai Maritime Court issued (2020) H 72 MT No. 27 civil ruling to reject the applicant's application for revocation and pointed out that the interpretation or determination of the validity of the contract by the arbitration tribunal actually belonged to interpretation of the contract, and the interpretation of the contract and the determination of the validity of the contract are prerequisites for determining the performance of the contract and its legal consequences. In this case, the claimant requested the respondent to pay the ship sale price of RMB390000 yuan and interest, and the tribunal made a ruling on this, which is an issue of performance of the contract. The above matters are not beyond the scope of the arbitration agreement between the parties to the contract, and the applicant's reasons for setting aside of the award are not valid.

(6) In a case between Shanghai CSIC Wanbang Shipping Company Limited (CSIC) and Nanjing Zhonggang Shipping Company Limited (hereinafter referred to as Zhonggang), China Maritime Arbitration Commission issued the

(2019) ZGHZHCZ No. 002 award, and Zhonggang applied for enforcement. CSIC was not satisfied with the court's enforcement action for reason that the involved arbitration case is relating to an optional right in ship purchase. According to the award, in case that Zhonggang chose to purchase the ship, the two parties should need to negotiate the terms of sale and purchase of the ship and sign the ship sale and purchase contract before the ship change registration procedure. Zhonggang had no right to directly request CSIC to cooperate with the ship registration procedure without fulfilling the payment obligation of the ship sale and purchase contract first. In this regard, Nanjing Maritime Court made civil ruling (2021) S 71 ZY No. 10 to reject the same for reason that: the first item of the arbitration award ruled that the fourth part of the option clause of MV "Double Dragon Sea" bareboat charter contract is valid, and CSIC should cooperate with Zhonggang to handle matters related to ship sale and purchase and change of ship registration procedures. According to the content of the award, CSIC had two obligations at the same time, one was to cooperate with the sale and purchase of the vessel and the other was to cooperate with the change of vessel registration; if any one of the obligations was not fulfilled by CSIC, Zhonggang could apply to the court for enforcement. After the arbitration award was made, as the two parties failed to reach a ship sale and purchase contract by themselves after negotiation, and failed to cooperate in the change of ship registration, Zhonggang applied to the court for compulsory execution, and delivered all the final payment of RMB17.8 million yuan for the purchase of the ship as agreed in the "Double Dragon Sea" bareboat charter contract to the account of the court. Under this circumstance, the Court made an enforcement ruling (2021) S 71 Z No. 139-1, requiring the transfer of shipowner of MV "Double Dragon Sea" from CSIC to Zhonggang, which has good legal basis.

Concluding Remarks

Overally speaking, despite the impact of the Covid epidemic, the law and judicial practice relating to maritime arbitration in China is continuing to develop steadily during 2020 and 2021, and the international influence of Chinese maritime arbitration is continuing to expand. As demonstrated by Qingdao Maritime Court in the case of the MV Nerissa case, Chinese courts have consistently supported the preservation of property (including arrest of ships) for support of foreign maritime arbitration. As far as judicial review of arbitration is concerned, Chinese courts have recognized and enforced arbitral awards from Singapore, London, etc., and only a few application for recognition and enforcement is dismissed or partially dismissed. Moreover, many awards of CMAC have also been recognized and enforced, which shows the consistent support and friendly attitude of courts in China's mainland towards maritime arbitration.

In addition, it is worth mentioning that in the case between BOA BARGES AS and Nanjing Yichun Shipbuilding Co., the parties agreed in the contract to settle dispute by arbitration at the London Court of International Arbitration and application of English law. Later on, the parties signed a Supplementary Agreement on May 16, 2020, changing the dispute resolution clause to the jurisdiction of the Nanjing Maritime Court with Chinese law to apply. Afterwards, Nanjing Maritime Court organized mediation via internet and facilitated the parties to reach a mediation agreement in only 27 days. This case is successfully selected as a national maritime trial typical case in 2020, and the Supreme People's Court specially praised that: foreign parties in the dispute voluntarily changed the English law and arbitration clause to jurisdiction of Nanjing Maritime Court and the application of Chinese law, which is both based on China's endeavors in the construction of international maritime justice hub, and the professional judicial capacity of the Chinese maritime courts.① From this case, the author of this article also believes that, with China's maritime justice and arbitration continue to be recognized by domestic and foreign parties, China's maritime justice and arbitration will have greater development in the future.

---

① "National Classic Litigation Cases over Maritime Disputes," accessed January 19, 2022, http://www.court.gov.cn/zixun-xiangqing-317811.html.

Maritime Arbitration in Hong Kong *

Introduction

Being a free port, Hong Kong Special Administrative Region of the People's Republic of China (hereinafter referred to as Hong Kong) has developed and evolved from a small fishing village into today's prosperous metropolitan city. Shipping and trading have traditionally been ingrained in Hong Kong. The business is heavily influenced by geopolitics and the global economy and therefore has a propensity to generate a lot of disputes. Given its international nature, disputes are usually resolved by arbitration.

Hong Kong, being one of the world's leading financial and business centres which enjoys an excellent reputation for its independent and impartial legal system, is a natural venue for international arbitration of all kinds. Since the mid or late 1990s, commercial men have increasingly agreed on Hong Kong as an arbitration venue for maritime contracts. This was largely a result of the rapid growth of the Asian economies and the rise of China as a major locomotive in the global shipping and commodity trade.

I. Expertise

Hong Kong has expertise in all aspects of the maritime and trade industry. Being a traditional shipping centre, Hong Kong is now the hub for shipping and maritime services such as ship management, shipbroking, ship finance, marine insurance and ship classification. Major P&I Clubs have offices in Hong Kong to serve the needs of their members from all over the world. A strong pool of

---

* The author is Danny Mok (莫世杰), independent commercial and maritime arbitrator. The opinions expressed in this article are the author's views only.

experienced shipping and international trade lawyers here provides competent legal advice to their clients. Experts with commercial and technical knowledge can assist at short notice and give expert evidence in arbitration hearings.

The Hong Kong Maritime Arbitration Group (HKMAG) is a homegrown arbitral body providing specialised arbitration services in maritime disputes. It was set up in 2000 by a group of maritime professionals with diverse backgrounds, expertise and industry experience. Originally a division of the Hong Kong International Arbitration Centre (HKIAC), it aimed to promote the use of maritime arbitration and mediation in Hong Kong. In order to cope with the needs of the rapidly changing market, the HKMAG established itself as an independent organisation in March 2019. The business of the HKMAG is now conducted through the HKMAG Committee. The members of the HKMAG Committee are Full Members of the HKMAG, who have proven records of appointments as maritime arbitrators in Hong Kong. Other membership categories include Members and Supporting Members. The Full Members and Members are residents in and of Hong Kong.

The emphasis on "the connection with the shipping industry" is a peculiar and vital feature of the HKMAG. The multi-national members of HKMAG are interested in maritime dispute resolution, enjoying commercial or legal experience in shipping and related disciplines and with extensive knowledge of and experience in international arbitral processes. Given our diverse background and ethnic origins, we are more conscious of the cultural differences between East and West. The effect of cultural differences is generally accepted as a valid concern in international arbitration.

Some of the HKMAG's members can read and write Chinese and English. While bilingual proficiency may not be crucial in the context of maritime arbitration, the use of Chinese in documentary and oral evidence is not uncommon. The translation expenses can be huge and there is a chance that the evidence, especially oral evidence, can be lost in translation. With bilingual arbitrators sitting in the tribunal, such expenses and risks can be reduced or even avoided.

II. An Independent and Impartial Legal System

The law of Hong Kong is based on the rule of law and judicial independence. Under the "One Country, Two Systems" regime, Hong Kong retains the English common law system after China resumed its sovereignty over Hong Kong in 1997. It is the only common law jurisdiction within China and its law is the only bilingual common law in the world.

Every seat of arbitration invariably emphasises the importance of the principles of natural justice to arbitration. In Hong Kong, these principles are embodied in the Hong Kong Arbitration Ordinance (Cap. 609) (hereinafter referred to as the "Arbitration Ordinance"), which is the procedural law applicable to arbitration.①

Section 46 (2) of the Arbitration Ordinance imposes a duty on the arbitral tribunal to treat the parties equally. Section 46 (3) of the Arbitration Ordinance further requires the arbitral tribunal to be independent, act fairly and impartially as between the parties and adopt fair and suitable procedures to help the parties resolve their disputes efficiently and costs effectively. These statutory requirements lay down the foundation of how arbitration is conducted in Hong Kong. This foundation is supported by a trustworthy legal system, the integrity of Hong Kong professionals and the low rate of corruption② here.

In a recent English High Court judgment, Shagang South Asia (Hong Kong) Trading Co. Ltd. v. Daewoo Logistics (The Nikolaos A) [2015] EWHC 194 (Comm), Lord Justice Hamblen③ described Hong Kong as

a well-known and respected arbitration forum with a reputation for

---

① See https://www.elegislation.gov.hk/hk/cap609.

② Corruption is detrimental to the development of dispute resolution services. See, for example, "Michael Cherney and Oleg Vladimirovich Deripaska [2008] EWHC 1530 (Comm)," accessed January 19, 2022, http://www.bailii.org/ew/cases/EWHC/Comm/2008/1530.html.

③ Lord Justice Hamblen was a former shipping counsel and is now a Justice of the Supreme Court of the United Kingdom.

neutrality, not least because of its supervising courts.①

Neutrality, impartiality and independence are peculiar features in Hong Kong arbitration. These features are widely recognised by the users and arbitration practitioners.② According to the 2021 International Arbitration Survey,③ Hong Kong is ranked the third most preferred seat of arbitration worldwide.

III. The Arbitration Ordinance (Cap. 609)

The procedural law applicable to Hong Kong seated arbitrations is the Arbitration Ordinance (Cap. 609). It is mainly based on the UNCITRAL Model Law and supplemented by provisions similar to the English Arbitration Act 1996. It respects the parties' autonomy in arbitration and serves the purpose of maximising the authorities of the arbitrators and minimising court interventions. It is modern, comprehensive, well-structured and user-friendly and is amended as and when appropriate to keep abreast of international arbitration developments.④ Below are some features of the Arbitration Ordinance:

3.1 The HKIAC as the Authority

The HKIAC⑤ is a non-profit making organisation incorporated in Hong Kong. It serves several roles and functions, one of which is to act as the authority to exercise certain statutory powers as per the Arbitration Ordinance.⑥

---

① Accessed January 19, 2022, http://www.bailii.org/cgi-bin/format.cgi?doc=/ew/cases/EWHC/Comm/2015/194.html.

② See the 2015 International Arbitration Survey conducted by White & Case in conjunction with Queen Mary University, accessed January 19, 2022, http://www.arbitration.qmul.ac.uk/media/arbitration/docs/2015_International_Arbitration_Survey.pdf.

③ Accessed January 19, 2022, http://www.arbitration.qmul.ac.uk/media/arbitration/docs/LON0320037-QMUL-International-Arbitration-Survey-2021_19_WEB.pdf.

④ The Arbitration Ordinance has recently been amended. It provides that disputes over intellectual property rights may now be resolved by arbitration. It also provides for the use of third-party funding in arbitration.

⑤ Accessed January 19, 2022, www.hkiac.org.

⑥ See Section 13 of the Arbitration Ordinance.

Section 23 of the Arbitration Ordinance confers power on the HKIAC to determine the number of arbitrators if the parties fail to agree. The HKIAC is also empowered under section 24 of the Arbitration Ordinance to appoint a sole arbitrator, co-arbitrator or third arbitrator in the case of default or in a situation where no agreement has been reached.

3.2 The Arbitral Tribunal May Rule on Its Own Jurisdiction

Under section 34 of the Arbitration Ordinance, an arbitral tribunal may rule on its own jurisdiction, including any objections concerning the existence or validity of the arbitration agreement. Parties can apply to the arbitral tribunal at the outset (but no later than the submission of the statement of defence) to establish whether the arbitral tribunal has the jurisdiction to hear the disputes. The arbitral tribunal may rule on the challenge either as a preliminary question or in an award on the merits. If the arbitral tribunal rules as a preliminary question that it has jurisdiction, any party may request the Hong Kong court to decide the challenge within 30 days of the notification of the arbitral tribunal's decision that it has jurisdiction.

3.3 Interim Measures

An arbitral tribunal is empowered by section 35 of the Arbitration Ordinance to grant interim measures in the form of an award. This section provides useful means to the parties:

(1) to maintain or restore the status quo – for example, to restrain a party from withdrawing its specially built vessel from a pool operation by way of an award[1]

(2) to obtain an anti-suit injunction from the arbitral tribunal to restrain proceedings brought in a foreign jurisdiction in breach of the arbitration

---

[1] See Lauritzen Cool AB v. Lady Navigation Inc. (2004) EWHC 2607 (Comm), accessed January 19, 2022, https://www.bailii.org/ew/cases/EWHC/Comm/2004/2607.html.

clause;①

(3) to preserve assets for the purpose of satisfying subsequent awards. This interim measure could be in the form of a freezing order. A freezing order is used to prohibit a party, usually a respondent to an arbitration, from removing, dissipating or disposing of its assets so that the claimant's claim would not become nugatory if it later succeeds in the arbitration;② and

(4) to preserve evidence. The serve the purpose of promoting fair resolution of the issues in dispute.

The Arbitration Ordinance recognises the parties' needs for interim measures, particularly when the arbitration is yet to commence or the arbitral tribunal is yet to be properly constituted. Section 45 of the Arbitration Ordinance provides that the court may grant interim measures in relation to arbitral proceedings "which have been or are to be commenced in or outside Hong Kong".

3.4 General Powers of the Tribunal and Power to Order Security for Costs

In addition to the power of granting interim measures, the arbitral tribunal also has the powers under section 56 of the Arbitration Ordinance to make various orders in the course of arbitration proceedings. The powers are mainly related to evidence. For instance, the arbitral tribunal can order discovery of documents, direct evidence to be given by affidavit and make an order of sample taking, inspection or preservation of the relevant property.

Section 56(1)(d)(i) allows the arbitral tribunal to give an order to sell the relevant property. This power is useful, for example, in dealing with perish-

---

① See Ever Judger Holding Co Ltd v Kroman Celik Sanayii Anonim Sirketi [2015] 3 HKC 246, accessed January 19, 2022, http://www.hklii.org/eng/hk/cases/hkcfi/2015/602.html.

② It is noted, however, that an arbitral tribunal cannot make an order which binds a party other than the parties to the arbitration agreement. Application should then be made to the Hong Kong court as per section 45 of the Arbitration Ordinance. See, for example, Top Gains Mineral Macao Commercial Offshore Limited and TL Resources Pte Ltd [2015] HKCFI 2101, accessed January 19, 2022, https://www.hklii.org/cgi-bin/sinodisp/eng/hk/cases/hkcfi/2015/2101.html.

able goods under lien by a shipowner for unpaid hire. ①In that case, the Owners applied to the English High Court under section 44(2)(d) of the Arbitration Act 1996 for an order for sale of cargo which was subject to a contractual lien being exercised by the Owners for unpaid time charter hire. It is worth noting that the power is only available to the English court. Whereas, under the Arbitration Ordinance, both the Hong Kong seated arbitral tribunal [section 56(1)(d)(i)] and the Hong Kong court [section 60(1)(a)] can make such order.

Section 56(1)(a) of the Arbitration Ordinance allows the arbitral tribunal to require a party bringing a claim or a counterclaim to provide security for the costs of another party in case the claim or counterclaim fails and the claiming party does not pay the costs awarded against it. The arbitral tribunal will make an order if there is a real risk that the claiming party will not pay the costs of the other party who has successfully defended the claim or counterclaim.

The consequence of the failure to furnish a satisfactory form of security for costs as ordered will be that the claim (or counterclaim) will be stayed or dismissed: see section 56(4) of the Arbitration Ordinance.

3.5 Extension of Time Limit

Section 58 of the Arbitration Ordinance provides that the arbitral tribunal may make an order to extend time where the arbitration agreement stipulates that a claim is to be barred after the elapsing of a certain period of time: see, for example, Korbetis v. Transgrain Shipping BV [2005] EWHC 1345 (QB).② In the English authority Perca Shipping Ltd v Cargill Inc [2012] 3759 (QD) 12D,③ the English High Court considered the application under

---

① See Dainford Navigation Inc v PDVSA Petroleo SA (The "Moscow Star") [2017] EWHC 2150, accessed January 19, 2022, http://www.bailii.org/ew/cases/EWHC/Comm/2017/2150.html.

② Accessed January 19, 2022, https://www.bailii.org/cgi-bin/format.cgi?doc=/ew/cases/EWHC/QB/2005/1345.html.

③ See also Haven Insurance Company Limited v. Eui Limited (T/A Elephant Insurance) [2018] EWCA Civ 294, accessed January 19, 2022, https://www.bailii.org/ew/cases/EWCA/Civ/2018/2494.html.

section 12 of the Arbitration Act 1996, the wording of which resembles section 58 of the Arbitration Ordinance, and refused to extend the time bar for commencing arbitration proceedings.

3.6 Striking out for Want of Prosecution

Section 59 of the Arbitration Ordinance allows the arbitral tribunal to make an award dismissing a party's claim and an order prohibiting the party from commencing further arbitral proceedings in respect of the claim if it is satisfied that the party has unreasonably delayed in pursuing the claim in the arbitral proceedings: see, for example, Dera Commercial Estate v Derya Inc [2018] EWHC 1673 (Comm).①

3.7 Finality of the Award

Under section 73 of the Arbitration Ordinance, an award issued by an arbitral tribunal is final and binding on the parties and is not subject to a review of its merits. It can be set aside only in certain specified circumstances② but the issues of facts and law in dispute are irrelevant to the consideration.③

If parties want to have a limited right of appeal against an award on a question of law similar to that as provided in the English Arbitration Act 1996, they can agree to the opt-in provisions in Schedule 2 of the Arbitration Ordinance to form part of the arbitration agreement which allows them to appeal on a question of law: see, for example, Maeda Kensetsu Kogyo Kabushiki Kaisha and others v Bauer Hong Kong Limited [2017] HKCFI 1582; HCMP 1342/2017.④

---

① The case concerned a strike out application awarded by the tribunal as per section 41(3) of the English Arbitration Act 1996. Under section 41(3), an arbitral tribunal can dismiss the claim if there has been first "inordinate and inexcusable" delay on the part of the claimant. Section 59 of the Arbitration Ordinance is different. It requires the delay to be "unreasonable". Accessed January 19, 2022, https://www.bailii.org/ew/cases/EWHC/Comm/2018/1673.html.
② See Section 81 of the Arbitration Ordinance.
③ See Section 81(3) of the Arbitration Ordinance.
④ Accessed January 19, 2022, http://www.hklii.org/eng/hk/cases/hkcfi/2017/1582.html.

Schedule 2 also contains opt-in provisions similar to that provided in the Arbitration Act 1996 and allows an award to be challenged on grounds of serious irregularity.

IV. Arrangement Concerning Mutual Assistance in Court-ordered Interim Measures in Aid of Arbitral Proceedings by the Courts of the Mainland and of the HKSAR

Section 61 of the Arbitration Ordinance provides that an interim measure order issued by an arbitral tribunal, whether in or outside Hong Kong, will be enforceable in the same manner as an order of the court that has the same effect. It is worth noting that other jurisdictions may not have similar provisions in their arbitration law.

Parties may want to seek interim measures from national courts, especially when the issue of enforcement is in consideration or when the required interim measures involve a third party. However, the availability of interim measures in aid of arbitration proceedings outside mainland of China depends on the procedural law of the particular national court.

In China's Mainland, the courts have been unwilling to grant interim measures in aid of arbitration proceedings outside mainland of China. They will not enforce an interim measure order issued by foreign arbitral tribunals. Although maritime claims receive special treatment in China as the Chinese maritime courts used to grant interim measures in aid of arbitration proceedings under the Special Maritime Procedure law[1] and the Interpretation of the Supreme People's Court on the Application of the Special Maritime Procedure Law,[2] the scope of application is limited to "the ship, the cargo carried by the ship and

---

[1] Article 14 of the Special Maritime Procedure Law.
[2] Article 21 of the Interpretation of the Supreme People's Court on the Application of the Special Maritime Procedure Law.

the ship's fuel and supplies"①.

In 2019, the Supreme People's Court of the People's Republic of China and the Department of Justice of the Hong Kong SAR signed the "Arrangement Concerning Mutual Assistance in Court-ordered Interim Measures in Aid of Arbitral Proceedings by the Courts of the Mainland and of the Hong Kong Special Administrative Region". Under the Arrangement, parties to arbitral proceedings seated in Hong Kong and administered by the eligible arbitral institutions which have been designated would be able to apply to the Chinese courts for interim measures.② The types of interim measures available from the Chinese courts include "property preservation, evidence preservation and conduct preservation" measures. The HKMAG is one of the qualifying institutions under the Arrangement.

V. Enforcement of the Award

Arbitration is a civilised and consensual method of resolving commercial disputes. However, if enforcement of the rights as allowed in the award turns out to be difficult if not impossible, it serves little purpose for the parties to invest time and money to go through the arbitration process. This is particularly the case since many companies involved in maritime and sale of goods contracts are located in different jurisdictions.

The Convention on the Recognition and Enforcement of Foreign Arbitral Awards③ (hereinafter referred to as the "Convention") has alleviated much of this concern. The Convention provides a convenient means to recognise and enforce foreign arbitral awards within the contracting states. More than 160 states around the world have adopted the Convention.

---

① Article 18 of the Interpretation of the Supreme People's Court on the Application of the Special Maritime Procedure Law.
② Parties to ad hoc arbitration, unfortunately, cannot take advantage of the Arrangement.
③ Accessed January 19, 2022, http://www.uncitral.org/uncitral/zh/uncitral_texts/arbitration/NYConvention.html.

Hong Kong is a member of the Convention and the awards issued in Hong Kong can be enforced in all states to the Convention.

There is an arrangement between the mainland and Hong Kong to facilitate the enforcement of Hong Kong arbitral awards in the mainland. With effect from May 19, 2021, parties can commence simultaneous enforcement proceedings in both the mainland and Hong Kong, provided that the total amount to be recovered from enforcing the award in the courts of the two places does not exceed the amount of the award.

A similar reciprocal enforcement arrangement has also been made between Hong Kong and Macau SAR.

So far as the enforcement of an arbitration award in Hong Kong is concerned, the judgment of KB v S and Others [HCCT 13/2015][1] emphasises, among other things, that enforcement should be "almost a matter of administrative procedure" and the courts should be "as mechanistic as possible". This case is one of the many examples that demonstrates the pro-arbitration and pro-enforcement approach of the Hong Kong courts.

VI. Substantive Law

The substantive law of maritime contracts refers to the choice of law by the parties in their contract to govern the substantive disputes under their contract. English law is usually chosen as the governing law in maritime contracts for its transparency, predictability, pro-business approach and wealth of legal precedents.

As already mentioned above, the English common law system applies in Hong Kong. English commercial law is closely followed here to resolve commercial disputes. Commercial men who used to regulate their business in accordance with English law should feel comfortable arbitrating their disputes in Hong Kong and under Hong Kong law.

---

[1] Accessed January 19, 2022, http://www.hklii.org/eng/hk/cases/hkcfi/2015/1787.html.

VII. The Practice of Hong Kong Maritime Arbitration, the HKMAG Terms and the Procedures for the Administration of Arbitration

7.1 The Practice

A vast majority of maritime arbitrations in Hong Kong are conducted on an ad-hoc basis. The practice of ad-hoc maritime arbitrations in Hong Kong is similar to that conducted in London. The arbitration procedures, which are governed by the Arbitration Ordinance, are flexible and less formal. The arbitral tribunal can tailor-make a set of agreed procedures with the parties that will streamline the particular arbitration process. The maritime arbitrations will usually be held before a sole arbitrator or two arbitrators appointed by the parties without the need to appoint a third arbitrator. The majority of them are conducted on a "documents-only" basis.

7.2 The HKMAG Terms and Small Claims Procedures

With the permission of the London Maritime Arbitrators Association (LMAA), the HKMAG has adopted the LMAA Terms and the LMAA SCP and made them the HKMAG Terms (2021) and the HKMAG Small Claims Procedure (2021) with changes made to incorporate references to Hong Kong procedural law. They are intended to be used in maritime arbitration in Hong Kong. This brings Hong Kong maritime arbitration in line with international practices.

The HKMAG Terms are essentially the same as the LMAA Terms. Apart from the general provisions concerning the conduct of the arbitration, the HKMAG Terms allows an arbitral tribunal to decide whether the dispute is to be determined by documents and whether two or more arbitrations are to be conducted concurrently. In response to the Covid-19 situation, the HKMAG Terms make it clear that hearings include virtual or hybrid hearings through the use of technology and provide guidelines for virtual hearings. The HKMAG Terms embrace the idea of digitalisation and provide for electronic signature of the award. No wet-ink hard copy will be issued unless advice is received prior to the production of the award. This expedites the publication of the award, saves the arbitrators' time and costs and reduces the carbon footprints.

There are two points which are worth mentioning in more detail.

First, it is the problem caused by using a sloppily drafted arbitration clause where the number of arbitrators is not specified. According to the Arbitration Ordinance, a party who wishes to refer a dispute to arbitration may require to make an application to the HKIAC to decide whether a sole arbitrator or three arbitrators should hear the dispute. ① This will bring delays and incur costs unnecessarily. Paragraph 9 (a) of the HKMAG Terms deals with the problem by making it clear that the default number of arbitrators is three. Paragraph 9 (b) (i) provides an appointment mechanism (i.e. a 14-day default procedure) to ensure a speedy establishment of an arbitral tribunal. Under the default procedure, if a party fails to appoint its arbitrator within 14 calendar days of receipt of a notice from the other party requesting it to do so, the arbitrator already appointed can be appointed as sole arbitrator. Paragraph 9 (b) (ii) provides that the two arbitrators thus appointed can dispense with the need to appoint a third arbitrator until a substantive hearing or if they cannot agree on any matter in relation to the arbitration.

Second, paragraph 26 of the HKMAG Terms allows the parties to challenge an award on grounds of serious irregularity and appeal against an award on a question of law by opting in the provisions of sections 4, 5, 6 and 7 of Schedule 2 of the Arbitration Ordinance. The challenge and appeal may provide additional safeguards for the quality and standard of the maritime arbitrators and allow the Hong Kong courts to develop and explain the law.

Parties who wish to have the option to appeal against an award on a question of law under the HKMAG Terms should ensure that Hong Kong law is chosen as the governing law of their maritime contracts. The reason is that foreign

---

① In case of three arbitrators, Section 24 (3) (a) of the Arbitration Ordinance provides that a party will have 30 days of receipt of a request from the other party to appoint its arbitrator and the two arbitrators will have another 30 days of their appointment to agree on the third arbitrator.

law is a question of fact in the Hong Kong Courts. Any legal issue arising from English law as the substantive law of a contract would therefore be considered as an issue of fact rather than law: see, for example, Reliance Industries Ltd. v. Enron Oil and Gas India Ltd. and Oil & National Gas Corporation (2002) 1 Lloyd's Rep 645. In other words, if English law is chosen as the governing law, the parties may be viewed as opting out of sections 5 and 6 of Schedule 2 of the Arbitration Ordinance.

7.3 Procedures for the Administration of Arbitration Under the HKMAG Terms

The HKMAG has produced Procedures for the Administration of Arbitration under the HKMAG Terms to enable parties to take advantage of the benefits of the "Arrangement Concerning Mutual Assistance in Court-ordered Interim Measures in Aid of Arbitral Proceedings by the Courts of the Mainland and of the HKSAR". The Procedures adopt a very light touch administered approach for arbitration to be supervised by the HKMAG. The HKMAG will charge registration and administration fees under the Procedures. The fees are subject to review by the HKMAG Committee. Currently, no registration fee is charged and the administration fee is fixed at HKD 5000 only.

Whether it is an ad-hoc or administered arbitration, the use of the HKMAG Terms ensures that the arbitration proceedings are conducted in an efficient, expeditious, and cost-conscious manner.

VIII. Recommended Arbitration Clauses

Arbitration is a consensual process based on the parties' agreement. Usually, a simple arbitration clause such as the one below will suffice for parties to refer their disputes to arbitration in Hong Kong:

Arbitration in Hong Kong. English law to apply.

This kind of arbitration clause is commonly found in charterparties / fixture notes and sale of goods contracts agreed by parties in Asia. Its simplicity, however, may lead to delay, hinder the process of the arbitration and even bring unwanted satellite litigation. See paragraph 43 above and Shagang South Asia (Hong Kong) Trading Co. Ltd. v. Daewoo Logistics (The Nikolaos A) [2015] EWHC 194 (Comm). ①

The HKMAG has produced two arbitration clauses for use in maritime contracts. They are drafted with the specific aims of tackling the known problems and ensuring that maritime arbitration proceedings are conducted smoothly and efficiently. One is the ad-hoc arbitration clause which has long and short forms. The other is the administered arbitration clause which is recommended to be used by parties who want to have the means to obtain interim measures in aid of a Hong Kong seated arbitration in the mainland.

In 2020, the Baltic and International Maritime Council (BIMCO) designated Hong Kong as one of the four arbitration venues in the BIMCO Law and Arbitration Clause 2020. The unified wording of the clause has been agreed by all four venues. The designation reflects the long-standing market recognition of Hong Kong as a reputable maritime dispute resolution centre.

The recommended HKMAG arbitration clauses and the BIMCO Law and Arbitration Clause 2020, Hong Kong can be found on the HKMAG's website (www. hkmag.org.hk). All of them provided for the use of the HKMAG Terms.

Singapore Maritime Industry Users in a New Era the SCMA Arbitration Rules (4th Edition) *

The maritime trade has been the lifeblood of Singapore's economy from the

---

① Accessed 19 January, 2022, http://www.bailii.org/cgi-bin/format.cgi?doc=/ew/cases/EWHC/Comm/2015/194.html.

* The author is Nicholas Lum, a Partner of Clyde & Co Shanghai and a Director of Clasis LLC (a Singapore law firm associated with Clyde & Co). He is also a member of the SCMA Procedure Committee and Promotion Committee and was actively involved in the drafting and formulation of the SCMA Rules 2022 (4th Edition). Jennifer Li of Clyde & Co Singapore was actively involved in contributing to this article.

time of its founding in 1819 and continues to be so. It is today a global port connected to 600 ports in over 120 countries and regions and is widely regarded as one of the world's busiest and most important ports. The statistics speak for themselves[①]:

(1) The Port of Singapore handled a total of 590.3 million tonnes of cargo in 2020;

(2) The vessel arrival tonnage totalled 2.9 billion Gross Tonnage (GT) in 2020;

(3) Singapore was the world's top bunkering port with sales amounting to 49.8 million tonnes in 2020;

(4) The Singapore Registry of Ships is amongst the 10 largest ship registries in the world, reflecting Singapore's reputation as a quality flag of choice for international ship owners.

Closely linked to the seaborne trade is Singapore's position as one of the largest trading hubs in the world. It is a leader in all major commodity sectors, ranging from the metals sector to oil trading, and is a jurisdiction where many key international traders have set up base.

Given the importance of the maritime and trading sectors to Singapore, it is paramount to have a framework in place to ensure that disputes are effectively and timeously resolved.

The Singapore Chamber of Maritime Arbitration (SCMA) was originally established in 2004 and was reconstituted in 2009, acting on industry feedback and to cater to the demand for maritime and trade related disputes in the region.

Despite the challenges of COVID, the SCMA saw a rise in the number of cases handled in the year 2020, wherein there were 43 case references involving a total claim amount of more than USD 49 million, with more than half of the disputants coming from Asia.

---

① Press release from the Maritime Port Authority of Singapore (MPA)," January 13 2021, accessed January 19, 2022, https://www.sgpc.gov.sg/media_releases/mpa/press_release/P-20210113-1.

With its commercially focussed and cost-effective ad-hoc framework for arbitration, the SCMA has no doubt given parties flexibility over the arbitration process. At the same time, parties have access to a diverse panel of arbitrators hailing from both common and civil law jurisdictions. At hand is also a dedicated Secretariat which assists parties as necessary.

Having said that, the maritime arbitration scene is constantly evolving. In order to remain relevant, the SCMA, in mid-2020, had launched a public consultation exercise on the revision of the 3rd Edition of its Rules. Some of the proposed amendments concern the appointment procedure for the members of the tribunal, the default number of arbitrators to be appointed, time for delivery of case statements and the need for hearings. Following more than a year of consultations and deliberations, the SCMA has now published the 4th Edition of the SCMA Rules, which came into effect on January 1, 2022 and will apply to any SCMA arbitrations commenced after this date. With this update, the SCMA Rules have been further streamlined to reflect modern arbitration practice and aim to promote a user-friendly, cost-effective and efficient approach to the resolution of maritime and trading disputes, particularly in Asia.

This article does not seek to address all the updates to the SCMA Rules in entirety but focusses instead on a number of key amendments. As a snapshot, it may be said that the SCMA Rules 2022 focus on three key areas:

(1) Cost efficiency;

(2) Promoting the use of technology, particularly in the post-Covid era; and

(3) Enhanced sharing of information.

It is common knowledge that post-Covid, arbitration proceedings and hearings are conducted virtually or in a hybrid manner (part virtually / part in-person). The SCMA Rules 2022 provide greater clarity as to the use of technology in conducting arbitration proceedings which, in turn, brings about significant cost savings and promotes, overall, a more efficient arbitration process.

Ⅰ. The Use of Technology

1.1 Service by Way of Email

Under the SCMA Rules 2015, while written communication could be effected by email, the service of any substantive notice was only deemed received once physically delivered. ①. Rule 3.1 of the SCMA Rules 2022 now makes it clear that any notice and / or communication may be served electronically via email, in addition to the conventional methods. Rule 3.2 of the SCMA Rules 2022 suggests that a delivery receipt via email would constitute proof of effective service. On this note, parties are recommended to avail themselves to the "delivery receipt" function when serving notices and / or sending communications in the arbitration proceedings.

1.2 Modernising Arbitration via Electronic Means

The SCMA Rules 2022, by way of Rule 34.4, now allow for arbitral awards to be signed electronically.

In addition, the updated Rules have, by way of Rules 17.3 and 25.3, now made it explicit that hearings and case management conferences, if held, may be conducted virtually.

1.3 Enhanced Information Sharing

Rule 6 of the SCMA Rules 2022 (previously Rule 4 under the SCMA Rules 2015) now deals with the issue of commencement of arbitration. The new addition of Rule 6.1 imposes more requirements on the contents of the Notice of Arbitration (NOA). Claimants are now required to include a description of the nature of the claim where this was non-mandatory in the 2015 Rules. It also requires the claimant to identify a choice of law clause and a claim

---

① Rule 3 of the SCMA Rules 2015 (3rd Edition).

value, were possible.

The objective of Rule 6 is to promote advanced sharing of information between the parties and the tribunal. This means that the parties will have greater clarity from the outset as to what the claimant's case is, and the respondent will, in turn, know in detail the case it is required to meet and the response to be prepared. The tribunal will certainly benefit, from a case management perspective, as it now has an idea at an early stage of what *exactly* the issues are.

In this connection, we must remind a claimant that these requirements for the contents of the NOA should be strictly complied with as non-compliance may potentially result in arguments being raised by the respondent on validity of the NOA and hence validity of the commencement of the arbitration proper.

It is submitted that the increased requirements in relation to the NOA are to be welcomed because it will result in parties becoming more efficient, reduce persistent delays from an uncooperative respondent, and lead to greater cost savings in turn.

It is interesting to note that Rule 6.2 of the SCMA Rules 2022 invites the claimant to send a copy of the NOA to the SCMA Secretariat at the same time it has been delivered to the respondent. This is no doubt an effort by the SCMA to ensure that it is adequately informed of the arbitrations proceeding under its Rules. Given the ad-hoc nature of SCMA arbitration, there may have been many arbitrations which had proceeded under the SCMA Rules but which were never notified to the SCMA. This amendment would allow the SCMA to better take note of the actual number of SCMA arbitrations being conducted and provide more accurate statistics in due course. However, it must be highlighted that the NOA will **not** be invalidated for a claimant's late or non-compliance with this rule.

Ⅱ. Constitution of the Tribunal

The default position in the number of arbitrators constituting a tribunal remains unchanged from the 2015 Rules, i.e. three arbitrators.

However, there is now an important development from the SCMA Rules 2015, which provide that if three arbitrators are to be appointed, then the two appointed arbitrators are to appoint a third①. Under the SCMA Rules 2022, by way of Rule 8.4, the two appointed arbitrators shall constitute the tribunal and the arbitration can proceed without a third appointment, as long as this is done before any substantive hearing or if they do not agree on any matter. While Rule 8.4(c) does require a third arbitrator to be appointed before any substantive hearing, if the arbitration proceedings do not result in a substantive hearing, the two arbitrators have the power to make decisions, orders and awards.② This has the result of streamlining the process and reflects the changes in the maritime arbitration scene.

Ⅲ. Oral Hearings-optional

Under the SCMA Rules 2015, an oral hearing had to be held unless the parties agreed otherwise.③ Rule 25.1 of the SCMA Rules 2022 allows, instead, for the tribunal to decide whether the arbitration should proceed with an oral hearing or on a document only basis. If however, a party requests for an oral hearing, then a hearing must be held.

Ⅳ. Time Frame for Issuance of an Arbitral Award

Unless parties agree or a tribunal directs otherwise, proceedings shall be deemed closed after 3 months from the date of any final written submission or hearing (see Rule 27.1). This rule is complemented by Rule 34.1 which imposes a deadline of 3 months from the close of the proceedings for the tribunal to publish its final award.

Of course, the parties may agree to an extended period by which the tribu-

---

① Rule 6 of the SCMA Rules 2015 (3rd Edition).
② Rule 33.2 of the SCMA Rules 2022 (4th Edition).
③ Rule 28 of the SCMA Rules 2015 (3rd Edition).

nal may make its final award. Please note, however, that the tribunal will be entitled to refuse the delivery of the final award if its fees remained outstanding (see Rule 34.5).

V. Increased Claim Threshold for Expedited Proceedings

Under the SCMA Rules 2015, the Small Claims Procedure would apply to claims in which the aggregate amount of the claim and / or counterclaim was less than USD 150,000①. The Small Claims Procedure provided for a sole arbitrator②, abridged timelines for serving case statements③ and the default position was that there would be no oral hearing unless the tribunal so requires④.

The SCMA Rules 2022 now provides for an Expedited Procedure with a threshold of $ 300000. This replaces the previous Small Claims Procedure (as mentioned above). Where no oral hearing is required, the Expedited Procedure provides for an arbitral award to be issued within 21 days from the date of receipt of the parties' case statements.

VI. Standard Terms of Appointment

Rule 40.2 of the SCMA Rules 2022 now provides for a set of Standard Terms of Appointment to apply if the parties and their respective arbitrator (s) have not agreed on the terms of arbitrator's appointment. The purpose behind these standard terms is to ensure greater certainty and transparency in the appointment of arbitrators, which will apply by default unless otherwise agreed.

---

① Rule 46.1 of the SCMA Rules 2015 (3rd Edition).
② Rule 46.11 of the SCMA Rules 2015 (3rd Edition).
③ Rule 46.4 of the SCMA Rules 2015 (3rd Edition).
④ Rule 46.6 of the SCMA Rules 2015 (3rd Edition).

VII. Power to Prevent Change of Counsel

There is a growing consensus that a reluctant party to an arbitration proceeding will often subject its opponent to delay tactics, for example, a change of legal representatives late in the day. Rule 4.4 of the SCMA Rules 2022 now accords the tribunal the power to withhold approval of a change in counsel where it is satisfied that there is a substantial risk that such change may prejudice the conduct of the proceedings or the enforceability of any award.

Conclusion

The newly-minted SCMA Rules 2022 are to be welcomed in the constantly evolving and fast paced maritime industry. The SCMA has heard the industry's calls for a better, more enhanced version of the rules, and it answered. The amendments made to the SCMA Rules 2015 reflect a conscious and careful effort by the SCMA to modernise its rules with the ultimate goal of benefiting end users by increasing efficiency and reducing costs. It is anticipated that these updated SCMA Rules will go a long way in providing SCMA as an attractive choice for users to resolve their maritime and trading disputes.

Maritime Arbitration in the UK [*]

Introduction

Whilst the UK and more specifically London, was once heralded as the centre of the shipping industry, global freight trends and the increasing dominance of China in world trade has resulted in the industry shifting eastward – with 7 out of 10 of the world's busiest ports by container throughput in China's

---

[*] The author is Nicholas Poynder, Partner of Holman Fenwick Willan (HFW).

mainland alone. However, London to this day still remains the centre of maritime arbitration. London is the seat for around 90% of international shipping arbitrations held in London, Hong Kong SAR of China or Singapore.

London maritime arbitration is often understood to be distinct from "international commercial arbitration" seated in London. However, while there are some differences, particularly in the strength of connection between some institutions and London as a seat of arbitration, these differences should not be overstated. Both types of arbitration share common characteristics. They both relate to international commercial disputes and are subject to the English Arbitration Act 1996. There is also a significant overlap between those involved in both types of arbitrations, from the arbitrators and practitioners themselves, to the parties as the users of arbitration. The vast majority of arbitrations in London are commenced under London Maritime Arbitrators Association (LMAA) Terms each year, more than are referred to institutional arbitration, and many of the appeals to the Commercial Court on points of law arise from shipping cases.

This article will look at the recent updates to the Arbitration Act 1996, key developments in various LMAA Terms, Lloyd's Salvage Arbitration Branch Rules and the London Court of International Arbitration Rules. It will end with a brief consideration of two recent English judgments which highlight interesting arbitration developments.

I. The Arbitration Process Under English Law

Any arbitration, maritime or otherwise, which is seated in London will be subject to the English Arbitration Act 1996 (AA 1996). In general, the process of appealing from London arbitration or challenging London arbitration awards is governed by the AA 1996 under sections 67, 68 and 69 pursuant to the principles under section 1 set out here.

1. General Principles.

The provisions of this Part are founded on the following principles, and shall be construed accordingly——

(a)the object of arbitration is to obtain the fair resolution of disputes by an impartial tribunal without unnecessary delay or expense;

(b)the parties should be free to agree how their disputes are resolved, subject only to such safeguards as are necessary in the public interest;

(c)in matters governed by this Part the court should not intervene except as provided by this Part.

The AA 1996 weighs up two considerations: the first is finality. Many court systems face the prospect of endless appeals. The second is the need for a right of judicial review to recognise that the law is not final, and continues to evolve. Appeals from arbitration in shipping matters have provided many of the important cases at the heart of English common law.

Under the AA 1996, there are only 3 grounds for appeal/challenge: (1) section 67, that the tribunal has no substantive jurisdiction; (2) section 68, that there has been serious irregularity affecting the tribunal, the proceedings or the award; and (3) section 69, an appeal on point of law. Sections 67 and 68 are mandatory provisions and, unlike section 69, cannot be excluded.

The other significant difference is that an appeal under section 69 requires the permission of the court before it may be brought, whereas that is not required for challenges under sections 67 or 68. A jurisdiction challenge under section 67 even results in a mandatory full re-hearing with evidence before the court.

This year, despite the business interruptions caused by the COVID-19 pandemic, the arbitration statistics released suggest that challenges had a similarly low success rate as previous years. The English Commercial Court announced that in 2020-2021, 25 applications to challenge arbitral awards were made citing section 68, although at the time of writing as is normal at this point in the Court's reporting year, this figure has not been finalised yet, due to a number of cases awaiting a hearing owning to service out and lead time to the longer hearings. ① This is only a slight decrease from 28 as of 2019-2020.

Court statistics show that in an average year, permission to appeal as required under section 69 is only granted to an estimated 30 % of applications②. Further to this, at substantive hearings, applicants must overcome the more challenging hurdle of establishing that the arbitral tribunal erred on a point of law. In recent statistics for the previous legal year (2019-2020), a total of 4 out of 37 challenges were successful, which equates to around 11%. ③

Despite a recent flurry of successful challenges to arbitration awards, the English courts generally do not take an interventionist approach and the chances of successfully challenging a final arbitration award are low.

Section 67 challenges are generally viewed as a last resort as the challenge can only be made once a final award on jurisdiction has been issued since the arbitrator is entitled to first rule on his or her on jurisdiction. Recent cases④ have further clarified the application of section 67, confirming, for example, that a failure to comply with a pre-condition (such as a requirement to engage in negotiation prior to the commencement of arbitration via a so-called waterfall clause) goes to the admissibility to arbitration and is not an issue of substantive jurisdiction.

In respect of section 68 the House of Lords, held that the section "is really designed as a long stop, only available in extreme cases, where the tribunal has gone wrong in its conduct ... and justice calls out for the tribunal's conduct to he corrected". ⑤

Section 69 requires amongst other factors in order for a party to be given

---

① Accessed January 19, 2022, https://www.judiciary.uk/wp-content/uploads/2021/12/Commercial-Court-User-Committee-Meeting-Minutes-24Nov21.pdf.

② Accessed January 19, 2022, https://www.judiciary.uk/wp-content/uploads/2020/12/CCUG-Minutes-November-2020-0112.pdf.

③ Accessed January 19, 2022, https://www.judiciary.uk/wp-content/uploads/2021/12/Commercial-Court-User-Committee-Meeting-Minutes-24Nov21.pdf.

④ Accessed January 19, 2022, https://www.judiciary.uk/wp-content/uploads/2021/12/Commercial-Court-User-Committee-Meeting-Minutes-24Nov21.pdf.

⑤ Accessed January 19, 2022, https://publications.parliament.uk/pa/ld200506/ldjudgmt/jd050630/leso-1.html.

permission that the decision of the tribunal is "obviously wrong" or that the decision is "one of public importance" and "at least open to serious doubt". For an example of a successful section 69 challenge, please see the below section on Recent Case Law.

II. Important Update

On November 30, 2021, the Law Commission of England and Wales announced that a review of the AA 1996 would be included in its 14th programme of law reform. The Law Commission recognised the Act's 25th anniversary as a good opportunity to ensure that it remains effective, especially as a number of other jurisdictions have recently enacted reforms.

The overarching aim of the review is said to be to "maintain the attractiveness of England and Wales as a" destination "for dispute resolution and the pre-eminence of English Law as a choice of law". The review is yet set to be launched in the first quarter of 2022, with an aim to be publish a consultation paper in late 2022. The scope of the review will be determined in the coming months and possible issues to be considered include:

(1) the power to summarily dismiss unmeritorious claims or defences in arbitration proceedings;

(2) the courts' powers exercisable in support of arbitration proceedings;

(3) the procedure for challenging a jurisdiction award;

(4) the availability of appeals on points of law;

(5) the law concerning confidentiality and privacy in arbitration proceedings; and

(6) electronic service of documents, electronic arbitration awards, and virtual hearings.

The review will also look at introducing trust law arbitration along with wider work on modernising trust law.

III. London Maritime Arbitration Rules and Developments

In the UK, there are a number of different arbitration rules which can be adopted by parties. A large majority of London maritime arbitrations are governed by terms and procedures set out by LMAA. LMAA arbitration tends to be used for commercial disputes, such as claims under bills of lading and contracts of affreightment, charterparty disputes, ship sale and shipbuilding cases, maritime insurance disputes and for the offshore, oil and gas industries. Salvage matters and collisions are dealt with by specialist rules. For example, the Salvage Arbitration Branch of the Council of Lloyd's has established a two-tier process of arbitration known as the London Salvage Arbitration. Some maritime disputes are also referred to arbitration under the rules of the London Court of International Arbitration (LCIA). These disputes tend to be shipbuilding, ship finance and energy-related contracts.

The following paragraphs highlight the key updates to commonly used arbitration rules which have been introduced in 2021.

3.1 LMAA Terms 2021

There are a number of maritime arbitration rules which can be chosen, and which are applicable in the UK. The most popular terms are the LMAA Terms. These were originally drafted in 1997, with revisions over the years since, and have been recently updated. The current LMAA Terms 2021 apply to all appointments which take place on or after May 1, 2021. In 2020, the LMAA received an around 1775 references, members received 3010 new arbitration appointments and 523 awards were issued.

The committee which revises the LMAA Terms states that they take a "light touch" when updating the Terms, and keep in mind the constant need to improve time and costs efficiency. The committee has described their approach for the LMAA Terms 2021 as "pragmatic and practical". It is clear from the new Terms, that the updates were made to reflect the changing times and specific issues which had developed since 2017. For example, due to the increased use of virtual hearings, the LMAA Guidelines for the Conduct of Virtual and Semi-Virtual Hearings are included as a new Sixth Schedule to the revised terms. More detailed commentary on the new terms is available on the LMAA website and summarised below.

LMAA Terms 2021 Key Updates:

(1) Paragraph 10: The appointment procedure for a sole arbitrator now adopts the procedure in the LMAA Arbitration Clause which is simpler and speedier than the procedure set out in the Arbitration Act 1996.

(2) Paragraph 12: The President now has the power to appoint a substitute arbitrator where it becomes apparent that the original arbitrator is incapable of conducting the proceedings or attending the hearing. This is to address the concerns expressed by users surrounding issues with arbitrators and appointing a substitute.

(3) Paragraph 15(c) and (d): the Terms now expressly recognise that hearings may take place virtually.

(4) Paragraph 24: The Terms now expressly provide that awards may be signed electronically, and in counterparts, and may be notified to parties by electronic means. This gives greater flexibility as to the preparation and publication of awards, particularly in circumstances in which it may be difficult to obtain handwritten signatures from arbitrators. ①

3.2 LMAA Small Claims Procedure

The LMAA Small Claims Procedure (SCP) has a fixed fee and is used for simple claims. The 2012 Terms suggested the SCP should be used where any claims or the total amount of any counterclaims does not exceed $50000. This was increased to $100000 under the 2017 and 2021 Terms.

LMAA SCP Key Updates:

---

① Accessed January 19, 2022, https://lmaa.london/wp-content/uploads/2021/05/COMMENTARY-ON-THE-LMAA-TERMS-2021.pdf.

(1) Paragraph 7: Introduces an express requirement that arbitrators should produce a reasoned award unless parties agree otherwise, which replicates the position under the AA 1996.

(2) Paragraph 8: Wherever possible, there should be one award under the Procedure, which deals with any relevant rulings as to costs, rather than a separate, second costs award. ①

3.3 LMAA Intermediate Claims Procedure

The LMAA Intermediate Claims Procedure (ICP) was introduced in 2009 and updated in 2021. The ICP was brought in for claims of between $100000 and $400000 with an aim of limiting the cost of arbitrating. Thus, a key characteristic of the ICP is the introduction of costs caps on the costs of the parties and tribunal.

LMAA ICP Key Updates:

(1) Paragraph 5: Similar to paragraph 10 LMAA Terms 2021, the procedure for the appointment of a sole arbitrator has been adopted from the LMAA Arbitration Clause as it is simpler and quicker than the procedure set out in the Arbitration Act 1996.

(2) Paragraph 13: The wording has been clarified to indicate that, in a situation where the tribunal is proceeding following a default by one of the parties, the tribunal has a discretion to permit or require the party not in default to provide further material to the tribunal.

(3) Paragraph 16: The wording is now clear on the fact that the applicable cap to the parties' recoverable costs (usually 30% of the claimant's monetary claim) should be calculated excluding claims for interest and costs. ②

---

① Acessed January 19, 2022, https://lmaa.london/wp-content/uploads/2021/05/COMMENTARY-ON-THE-LMAA-SMALL-CLAIMS-PROCEDURE.pdf.

② Accessed January 19, 2022, COMMENTARY-ON-THE-LMAA-INTERMEDIATE-CLAIMS-PROCEDURE-2021.pdf.

3.4 Lloyd's Salvage Arbitration Branch

In mid 2021, Lloyd's announced that it was deciding whether to close its Salvage Arbitration Branch (LSAB). This would have had a profound impact on the future administration of the Lloyd's Standard Form Salvage Agreement and the continued use of the Lloyd's Open Form (LOF). However, in July 2021, Lloyd's announced that after an outcry from the international maritime community and following a review of its agency services, Lloyd's will continue to operate the LSAB and LOF. A key update has been the amended charging structure for use of LOF which came into effect on October 1, 2021 with further developments being considered.

3.5 LCIA Rules

As previously mentioned, the LCIA Rules are sometimes used to govern maritime arbitrations in London. These Rules were updated by the past President Judith Gill QC, and are effective from October 1, 2020. The update was intended to make the arbitral and mediation processes more streamlined and clearer for arbitrators, mediators and the parties. Due to the timing of the COVID-19 pandemic, the update has taken into account the new ways of conducting business, including the use of virtual hearings and the use of electronic communication.

Key Updates:

Significant amendments highlighted by the LCIA commentary to the Rules are as follows:

(1) additional tools allowing arbitrators to expedite proceedings, with an explicit reference to the possibility of early dismissal determination;

(2) refinement and expansion of the provisions accommodating the use of virtual hearings, also supporting arbitrations taking place in the new normal;

(3) confirming the primacy of electronic communication with the LCIA and in the arbitration, as well as confirming the facilitation of electronically signed awards;

(4) inclusion of explicit provisions addressing the role of tribunal secretaries;

(5) broadening of LCIA Court and Tribunal power to order consolidation and concurrent conduct of arbitrations; and

(6) explicit consideration of data protection and regulatory issues. ①

The maximum hourly rate for arbitrators and mediators was discussed and increased from £ 450 to £ 500 in order to reflect the demands of complex disputes. The updated rules can be found here.

IV. Recent Case Law

In 2021 there have been a number of important maritime arbitration cases held in London. This section explores two of the most important decisions of the year: the case of K Line PTE Ltd v Priminds Shipping (HK) Co. Ltd [2021] EWCA Civ 1712 and the case of CVLC Three Carrier Corp v Arab Maritime Petroleum Transport Company [2021] EWHC 551 (Comm).

4.1 K Line PTE Ltd v Priminds Shipping (HK) Co. Ltd (The Eternal Bliss) [2021] EWCA Civ 1712

This case clarified that a party in an on-going arbitration may also apply to the court to determine a preliminary point of law under section 45 AA 1996. It should be noted that this procedure is rarely used in practice. The Court had to determine a preliminary point of law concerning the nature of demurrage payable under a voyage charter when the charterer had failed to load or discharge the ship within the agreed upon laytime. The Court applauded the parties for their decision and joint agreement to bring the case to the Court under section 45 AA 1996 in order to provide legal clarification for future matters. The legal issue related to whether demurrage is liquidated damages for all the consequences of a charterer's failure to load or unload within the designated

---

① Acessed January 19, 2022, https://lcia.org/lcia-rules-update-2020.aspx.

laytime, or only some of them. The Court accepted that this question of law substantially affected the rights of the parties so as to bring it within section 45. The first instance judgment on this issue was reversed by the Court of Appeal.① Where Males L. J. , giving the Court of Appeal's decision, determined that demurrage (in the absence of agreement by the parties to the contrary) liquidates all the ship owner's losses arising from a charterer's breach in failing to complete cargo operations within laytime and not just the loss of earnings resulting from the delay as had been held to be the position at first instance. A separate breach would need to be shown for the shipowner to recover damages in addition to demurrage arising from delay.②

4. 2 CVLC Three Carrier Corp v Arab Maritime Petroleum Transport Company [2021] EWHC 551 (Comm)

As mentioned above, successful section 69 AA 1996 challenges are extremely rare. Section 69 allows for challenges to made to the English courts on a question of law which arises from an arbitral award. This right to challenge is not mandatory and so can be excluded. Arbitration institutions such as the LCIA and the International Chamber of Commerce (ICC) exclude section 69 of the AA 1996 from their Rules. The case provides a detailed discussion of what exactly makes a successful section 69 application and underlines the high standards by which the Court will review applications.

By way of brief background, the case stems from an arbitration which arose out of two almost identical charterparties between CVLC Three Carrier Corp and CVLC Four Carrier Corp (the Owners) and Al-Iraqia Shipping Services and Oil Trading (the Charterer). The Owners were given letters of guarantee (the Letters) from Arab Maritime Petroleum Transport Company

---

① See" K Line Pte Ltd. v Priminds Shipping (Hk) Co. , Ltd. ," accessed January 19, 2022, https://www. bailii. org/cgi - bin/format. cgi? doc =/ew/cases/EWCA/Civ/2021/1712. html&query = (K) +AND+(Line) +AND+(Pte) +AND+(Ltd).

② See "HFW, 'Bliss for charterers – Court of Appeal rules in next round of Eternal Bliss,'" accessed January 19, 2022, https://www. hfw. com/Bliss - for - charterers - Court - of - Appeal - rules-in-next-round-of-The-Eternal-Bliss-Nov-2021.

(AMPTC) which guaranteed the punctual performance of the Charterer's payment obligations as the primary obligor. The Owners alleged that the Charterer had breached the charterparties and as a result they commenced arbitration proceedings against AMPTC. The Owners also sought to arrest a vessel owned by AMPTC in order to have security for their claims under the Letters. AMPTC proceeded to file an urgent application to the sole arbitrator. AMPTC requested a declaration that the Letters included an implied term that the Owners would not seek "additional security" when it came to the matters covered by the Letters. AMPTC argued that the implied term thus, prevented the Owners from arresting AMPTC's vessel under the Letters. The arbitrator found in the Charterer's favour. The Owners applied to the English Commercial Court for permission to appeal the award under section 69 of the AA 1996. [1]

An interesting outcome of the judgment is that Cockerill J clarified that applications under section 69 do not have to be limited to pure questions of law. It is possible for questions of contractual interpretation to also be appealed, despite being closely linked to the factual matrix. Cockerill J went on to add that "the recasting of questions of law is by no means unheard of by judges considering applications for permission". This highlights the Court's power to reformulate the question at the permission stage to pare back the matter to the real issue of law to be decided by the tribunal. Cockerill J discussed the consequences of a successful section 69 application, suggesting that in some cases it is possible for the Court not remit the matter back to the arbitrator if the circumstances allow and for the Court to overturn an arbitral award fully without further consideration from the tribunal. [2]

---

[1] Accessed January 19, 2022, https://www. bailii. org/ew/cases/EWHC/Comm/2021/551. html.

[2] Accessed January 19, 2022, https://www. bailii. org/ew/cases/EWHC/Comm/2021/551. html.

Summary

Looking ahead, London Maritime arbitration is alive to the challenges and global developments in arbitration practice. As it stands, London clearly remains a "go-to" destination for maritime arbitration. The English Courts continue to support the arbitration process and take a measured approach to challenges to arbitration awards which are not often successful. It is also likely that London will further capitalise on its position as a leading hub for maritime arbitration with the long-term move to virtual and hybrid hearings removing any pressing need for many arbitration practitioners, lawyers and clients to travel to benefit from London maritime arbitration services.

(陈迅、王辰、唐嘉玮　审校)

Characteristics of Applicants in Prompt Release Cases of the ITLOS and Enlightenment for China

CHEN Heng[*] BAI Yan[**]

Abstract: In recent years, the International Tribunal for the Law of the Sea (ITLOS) has dealt with several disputes concerning prompt release cases between the coastal States. In such cases, the investigation and identification of the flag State status, the confirmation of the rights of coastal States with exclusive economic zones by the Tribunal are the key to the progress of cases. During marine fishing, China, as a marine power, on one hand, will request the prompt release of ships and the crew as a flag State, on the other hand, will detain foreign illegal ships and the crew as a coastal State with the exclusive economic zone. The practice relating to prompt release cases by the ITLOS is worth studying by giving the inspiration to explore the corresponding solutions involving China's disputes under different status as a flag State, convenient flag State, or coastal State with exclusive economic zone, to optimize the protection of China's maritime rights and interests.

Key words: prompt release; flag State; jurisdiction

---

[*] Juris master in Northwest University of Political Science and Law, juris master in Northwest University of Political Science and Law.

[**] Associate professor in Northwest University of Political Science and Law, associate professor in Northwest University of Political Science and Law.

Introduction

Since 1996, the International Tribunal for the Law of the Sea (hereinafter referred to as the "Tribunal") has heard 29 cases, and 10 cases among them are prompt release cases as follows, the M/V SAIGA Case in 1997, the M/V SAIGA (No. 2) Case in 1999, the Camouco Case and the Monte Confurco Case in 2000, the Grand Prince Case and the Chaisiri Reefer 2 Case in 2001, the Volga Case in 2002, the Juno Trader Case in 2004, the Hoshinmaru Case and the Tomimaru Case in 2007.

Except for the withdrawal of the No. 9 case, namely the Chaisiri Reefer 2 Case, six cases have been ruled by the Tribunal asking the detaining State to release the detained ships and crew promptly, and they are the M/V SAIGA Case, the Camouco Case, the Monte Confurco Case, the Volga Case, the Juno Trader Case and the Hoshinmaru Case. ①

According to the United Nations Convention on the Law of the Sea (UNCLOS), the Statute of the International Tribunal for the Law of the Sea (hereinafter referred to as the "Statute of the Tribunal"), and the Rules of the International Tribunal for the Law of the Sea (hereinafter referred to as the "Rules of the Tribunal"), the Tribunal effectively resolved the matter about the release of ships and crew among maritime disputes, which shows its important international position in handling such cases, and gives full play to its role in the peaceful settlement of international disputes over maritime rights and interests. The two parties in the prompt release case are the flag State and the coastal State with the exclusive economic zone. Generally, the flag State ap-

---

① Three other cases:
(a) The 1999 M/V SAIGA (No. 2) Case: Guinea, the detaining State, immediately released the ship and crew, but violated the provisions of the UNCLOS on the right of hot pursuit.
(b) The 2001 Grand Prince Case: Belize had no evidence to prove that it was the flag State, and the Tribunal has no jurisdiction over this case.
(c) The 2007 Tomimaru Case: Russia, the detaining State, firstly filed a domestic lawsuit and confiscated the ship.

plies to the Tribunal for prompt release as an applicant, while the coastal State with the exclusive economic zone as the respondent shall take corresponding measures to safeguard their maritime rights and interests.

I. The Flag State in the Prompt Release Procedure

The UNCLOS gives the Tribunal compulsory jurisdiction in the prompt release case, but the applicant who has the right to file an application for the Tribunal over the prompt release case could only be the flag State or an agent authorized on behalf of the flag State of the vessel. Therefore, the parties in disputes have some objections whether the Tribunal could have jurisdiction over the prompt release case, the Tribunal shall first investigate and identify the status of the flag State.

According to the provisions of Article 287 and Article 292 of the UNCLOS, the International Court of Justice, the international arbitral tribunal, the international special arbitral tribunal, and the ITLOS have jurisdiction over the prompt release case. ① If both of the parties, the flag State and coastal State, are the State party to the UNCLOS, each party could be free to choose one or more of the first three means for the settlement of disputes concerning the prompt release. If the application of release from detention fails to be submitted to any court or tribunal agreed upon by the parties within 10 days

---

① Article 287(1) of the 1982 United Nations Convention on the Law of the Sea:

When signing, ratifying or acceding to this Convention or at any time thereafter, a State shall be free to choose, by means of a written declaration, one or more of the following means for the settlement of disputes concerning the interpretation or application of this Convention: (a) the International Tribunal for the Law of the Sea established in accordance with Annex Ⅵ; (b) the International Court of Justice; (c) an arbitral tribunal constituted in accordance with Annex Ⅶ; (d) a special arbitral tribunal constituted in accordance with Annex Ⅷ for one or more of the categories of disputes specified therein.

Article 292(1) of the 1982 United Nations Convention on the Law of the Sea: …the question of release from detention may be submitted to any court or tribunal agreed upon by the parties or, failing such agreement within10 days from the time of detention, to a court or tribunal accepted by the detaining State under article 287 or to the International Tribunal for the Law of the Sea, unless the parties otherwise agree.

from the time of detention, the two parties to the dispute could agree to apply for the ITLOS, then the ITLOS has jurisdiction over such case. Specifically, when the parties, through a declaration, accept the Tribunal as a means for the settlement of disputes, the Tribunal has compulsory jurisdiction over all disputes concerning the interpretation and application of the UNCLOS. Even if no declaration is made under Article 287 of the UNCLOS, and there is no agreement on submitting the dispute to another court or tribunal within a certain period, the Tribunal still has compulsory jurisdiction over the prompt release case in the light of the provisions of Article 292 of the UNCLOS. [①] Since the Tribunal began to operate in 1996, most of the submitted cases have initiated prompt release proceedings under these two provisions of the UNCLOS, and these cases could be filed for investigation by any State party.

Among the prompt release cases that have occurred so far, the disputed States choose to apply for the Tribunal to make a judgment. As soon as the case is accepted and heard, the Tribunal will investigate and identify the qualification of the applicant in the case.

1.1 The Applicant

The detention of a ship by a coastal state will not only affect the property interests of the ship owner, but also endanger the personal rights and interests of the captain and crew. Most of the time, the nationality of the detained vessel is different from that of the crew so that there are many applicants to request prompt release. However, Article 292(2) of the UNCLOS provides that the application for release may be made only by or on behalf of the flag State of the vessel. This indicates that there are only two applicants, one is the flag State that is the State to which the vessel flying the flag belongs, not that of the nationality of the crew. Another is the agent authorized on behalf of the flag State, that is, the agent must be authorized by the competent department of the

---

[①] See Guidelines for Trial Procedures of the International Tribunal for the Law of the Sea, Compulsory Jurisdiction, page 6.

flag State before applying, and the certificate of authorization should be issued by the competent state agency, such as the foreign minister, minister of justice or the attorney general of the State. ①

1.1.1 By the flag State

As mentioned above, the flag State of the detained vessel is the subject of an application for prompt release as specified by Article 292 of the UNCLOS, so the nationality of the vessel shall be the only consideration during the investigation by the Tribunal. The provision concerning the nationality of ships in Article 91 of the UNCLOS provides that ships shall be registered in its territory of one State, and there must exist a genuine link between the State and the ship, otherwise, the flag State has no right to apply for prompt release. ② Article 1 of the United Nations Convention on Ship Registration Conditions in 1986 clarifies the purpose of the Convention, stating that there must be a genuine relationship between the State and the ships. ③ This indicates that as long as the ship has one State nationality, even if the ship owner or crew does not have the nationality of the flag State, the flag State still can apply for the Tribunal to initiate the prompt release proceedings. After the competent department of the flag State has registered and issued the certificate according to law, the flag State shall exercise effective management and control over the vessels flying the flag of the State. Therefore, when the ship and its crew are detained, the flag State, on behalf of the disadvantaged, is the most qualified ap-

---

① See Guidelines for Trial Procedures of the International Tribunal for the Law of the Sea, Procedures, page 23.

② Article 91 of the 1982 United Nations Convention on the Law of the Sea: 1. Every State shall fix the conditions for the grant of its nationality to ships, for the registration of ships in its territory, and for the right to fly its flag. Ships have the nationality of the State whose flag they are entitled to fly. There must exist a genuine link between the State and the ship. 2. Every State shall issue to ships to which it has granted the right to fly its flag documents to that effect.

③ Article 1 of the 1986 United Nations Convention on Conditions for Registration of Ships: For the purpose of ensuring or, as the case may be, strengthening the genuine link between a State and ships flying its flag, and in order to exercise effectively its jurisdiction and control over such ships with regard to identification and accountability of ship owners and operators as well as with regard to administrative, technical, economic and social matter, a flag State shall apply the provisions contained in this Convention.

plicant for the prompt release case.

The Tribunal has heard ten prompt release cases so far, three of which were filed directly by the authority of the flag State. For example, Russia, as the flag State, filed the Volga Case in 2002 under the provision of Article 292 of the UNCLOS. In this case, the vessel "Volga" flying the Russian flag was detained by Australia for illegal fishing in the southern waters of Australia. Russia and Australia didn't agree to submit an application of release from detention to other courts or tribunals within ten days from the time of detention. Therefore, the flag State Russia directly applied to the Tribunal for the prompt release of the vessel "Volga" and its crew. Another example is the Hoshinmaru Case and Tomimaru Case in 2007, the factual backgrounds of the two cases were roughly the same: two vessels flying the Japanese flag, "Hoshinmaru" and "Tomimaru", were detained by the Russian Coast Guard for illegal fishing in the waters of Russia's exclusive economic zone. The Japanese government filed two applications to the Tribunal under Article 292 of the UNCLOS, requesting Russia to release the two detained vessels and crew. The above cases were directly filed by the government of the flag State, and the government officials participated in the case as agents. But there are few similar cases in practice comparatively, in which the flag State will be the applicant.

1.1.2 On behalf of the flag State

Most of the ships involved in the prompt release case are the ships flying the flag of convenience so that there is no genuine link between the State and the ship.[①] That is, the actual ship owners are barely nationals of the flag State, neither are the crew from labor export. Individuals, not the subjects of international law, have no right to apply to the Tribunal for prompt release procedures in this condition.

For humanitarian protection of individual rights to life and safety in the international community, Article 292 of the UNCLOS provides that the question

---

① Note: A flag of convenience means that the ships are not registered in their own countries but in other countries with loose ship registration, thereby flying the national flag of the registered country.

of release from detention may be submitted on behalf of the flag State to help ships and crews to get timely relief. That is, individuals such as the captain or owner can employ some agents to apply to the Tribunal for prompt release. ① To prevent the agent from abusing the legal procedures for the release from detention and the agent's application from being too personal, Article 292 of the UNCLOS requires the agent's application on behalf of the flag State should be made in the name of the State. In other words, the agent must be authorized by the authority of the flag State before applying, otherwise, the Tribunal will not accept and hear the application. Article 110(2) of the Rules of the Tribunal provides that a flag State may at any time notify the Tribunal of some matters, including the State authorities competent to authorize persons to make applications on its behalf, and the name and address of the authorized agent. This means that the State authority shall make the notification of authorization, and an application on behalf of a flag State shall be accompanied by all supporting documents, including the authorization and certification that a copy of the application under Article 110(3) of the Rules of the Tribunal. ②

When the authorized agents have the right to apply on behalf of the flag State, most of them are lawyers employed by the ship owner to protect the interests of the ship owner in practice. And the flag State only participates in the litigation nominally, so the result of the case directly acts on the ship owner. At this time, the agent authorized by the State will actively take part in the hearing, and the detained ship and crew will obtain timely relief. Most countries provisionally designate authorized agencies after disputes, and the designation varies from country to country based on the domestic laws, as shown in Table 1.

---

① Article 292(2) of the 1982 United Nations Convention on the Law of the Sea: The application for release may be made only by or on behalf of the flag State of the vessel.

② Article 110(3) of the Rules of the Tribunal: An application on behalf of a flag State shall be accompanied by an authorization under paragraph 2, if such authorization has not been previously submitted to the Tribunal, as well as by documents stating that the person submitting the application is the person named in the authorization. It shall also contain a certification that a copy of the application and all supporting documentation has been delivered to the flag State.

Table 1　The Applicant of the Prompt Release Case and Other Information

Case	The Flag State	Agent	Authority	Nationality of Captain and Crew
The M/V SAIGA Case	Saint Vincent and the Grenadines	British lawyer	Ministry of Justice	Ukrainian
	Facts: The oil tanker M/V Saiga was arrested by Guinean Customs, allegedly for smuggling gasoline to the local fishing vessels in the exclusive economic zone of Guinea.			
The Camouco Case	Panama	Belgian lawyer	Ministry of Foreign Affairs	Spanish
	Facts: French authorities seized the fishing vessel "Camouco", allegedly for unlawful fishing into the exclusive economic zone of Crozet Islands, and the Captain was charged under court supervision.			
The Monte Confurco Case	Seychelles	Belgian lawyer	Ministry of Agriculture and Marine Resources	The captain is Spanish; The crews are Spanish, Peruvian, Chilean, and others.
	Facts: The fishing vessel "Monte Confurco" was seized by a French frigate in the exclusive economic zone of the Kerguelen Islands in the French Southern and Antarctic Territories, allegedly for unlawful fishing, and the Captain was charged under court supervision.			
The Grand Prince Case	Belize	Spanish lawyer	Ministry of Justice	The Captain is Spanish; The crews are Spanish and Chilean.
	Facts: The fishing vessel "Grand Prince" was arrested by the French authorities, allegedly for unlawful fishing and failure to notify its entry in the exclusive economic zone of Kerguelen Islands, and French authorities leveled charges against the Captain.			

(Continued)

Case	The Flag State	Agent	Authority	Nationality of Captain and Crew
The Juno Trader Case	Saint Vincent and the Grenadines	French lawyer	Ministry of Justice	All are Russians except for one Ukrainian crew.
	Facts: The refrigerated cargo vessel "Juno Trader" was arrested by the Guinea-Bissau authorities, allegedly for illegally fishing in the exclusive economic zone of Guinea-Bissau. And the authorities of Guinea-Bissau adopted a decision to impose a fine on its captain and declared the catch found on board was reverted to the State.			

It can be seen that there are foreign lawyers, as the agent, from another State rather than the flag State in these five cases, being authorized by the designated State authority to protect and relieve the rights and interests of the ship and crew. These authorized agencies can be divided into two types, one of which is the agency in charge of judicial or foreign affairs. And it's the litigation between countries for the flag State in this circumstance, in which the agent, the non-interested person on behalf of the flag State, is granted by the ministry of justice or ministry of foreign affairs. The other is the fishery authority, which is the most closely linked to the prompt release case owing to the detention from illegal fishing in the waters under the jurisdiction of the coastal State. Then this type of authorization may facilitate the communication and cooperation between the flag State and the convenient flag State.

1.2 Identification of the Flag State Status

The application for the prompt release can only be filed by or on behalf of the flag State of the vessel, and the Tribunal must always be convinced that it has jurisdiction over the case that has been filed in previous cases. After the Tribunal accepts the case, if the parties have different opinions with the identification of the flag State querying the jurisdiction of the Tribunal, the Tribunal will investigate the flag State status in the following two aspects.

1.2.1 The Time of the Identification of the Flag State

The UNCLOS does not stipulate the specific time when the applicant becomes the flag state in the prompt release case. However, in court trial practice, it is generally believed that as long as the applicant is the flag state at the time of filing the application, it does not need to be the flag state all the time. For example, the Tribunal requested the applicant shall be the flag state when the detention occurred and the application was submitted in the Camouco Case and the Monte Confurco Case. But the Tribunal is convinced that the applicant may be qualified, that is the ship has been registered only when applying to the Grand Prince Case. Similarly, the applicant only needs to be authorized by the flag State when applying prompt release in the Volga Case. And Judge Treves proposed that the prompt release procedure is in a sense equivalent to diplomatic protection in the Grand Prince Case because the requirements of nationality should be at least satisfied in the filing of the application and the implementation of wrongdoing in diplomatic protection.[①] It can be seen that the moment of submitting an application for release from detention is crucial to the identification of the flag State.

The following factors shall be considered when identifying the nationality of a vessel, for instance, whether the vessel actually has been granted by the flag State, registered by the law, and properly flying the flag during sailing. The laws in many countries generally stipulate that the vessel shall be registered, which is the most common factor of nationality. If the vessel simply has the provisional registration or the nationality certificate of the flag State, the Tribunal will not be convinced that the registration is exactly equivalent to the nationality of the vessel in the condition that the certification of registration expired and was overdue. What the Tribunal does is to make a distinction between definite nationality and abundant evidence showing the nationality, and further believe that evidence can replace registration to prove the nationality of

---

① See The Grand Prince Case (Belize v. France), Prompt Release, Separate Opinion of Judge Treves, para. 1.

vessels. Finally, the ship registration shall prevail when there is short of abundant evidence,[1] as shown in the M/V SAIGA Case and the Grand Prince Case.

The vessel "M/A Saiga" is an oil tanker flying the flag of Saint Vincent and the Grenadines, detained by Guinea for smuggling gasoline to a local fishing vessel in the exclusive economic zone of Guinea in 1997. At that time, the provisional registration certificate for "M/A Saiga" had expired before the day of detention, and the vessel obtained a permanent registration certificate until after a month of detention.[2] The Tribunal, having received a certified copy from the authorities of Saint Vincent and the Grenadines, overruled Guinea's objection.[3] That means that the evidence showing flying the nationality of the vessel indicates that the vessel "M/A Saiga" was still the flag of Saint Vincent and the Grenadines. Similarly, the "Grand Prince" Case is that the fishing vessel "Grand Prince" flying the flag of Belize was detained by the French frigate for illegal fishing within the French exclusive economic zone in 2000. The temporary navigation license expired three days after the vessel "Grand Prince" was detained, and the vessel had not obtained a new registration certificate when the agent on behalf of Belize applied for prompt release three months later.[4] The Tribunal did not directly deny the status of the flag State due to the invalidity of the vessel's temporary navigation license in this case, but the cancellation of the Belize authorities resulting in the deprivation of the vessel's nationality made the Tribunal determine that Belize was not the flag State. It can be seen that, if the ship registration has been invalid when applying for the prompt release, the Tribunal will make a comprehensive judgment based on other evidence submitted by both State parties in the case instead of denying

---

[1] Tullio Treves, "Flags of Convenience before the Law of the Sea Tribunal," *San Diego International Law Journal*, Fall (2004): 186.

[2] See The M/V SAIGA Case (Saint Vincent and the Grenadines v. Guinea), Prompt Release, Judgement, para 57.

[3] See The M/V SAIGA Case (Saint Vincent and the Grenadines v. Guinea), Prompt Release, Judgement, para 67.

[4] See The "Grand Prince" Case (Belize v. France), Prompt Release, Judgement, para 76.

the flag State status directly.

1.2.2 The Rules of Evidence on the Identification of the Flag State

The standard of proof in prompt release cases usually adopts the standard of the preliminary burden of proof in juridical practice, which asks the applicant to afford proof firstly. Once the preliminary evidence is provided by the applicant, the burden of proof will be transferred to the respondent who may bear the responsibility for failing to offer evidence properly. For example, the applicant, Saint Vincent and the Grenadines, has fulfilled the preliminary burden of proof in the M/V SAIGA Case, while the respondent Guinea failed to provide abundant proof, so the Tribunal was convinced that Saint Vincent and the Grenadines was the flag State of the vessel "M/A Saiga".

In the Grand Prince Case, the applicant Belize provided preliminary evidence of the temporary navigation license under the domestic law, the Merchant Ship Registration Act of 1989, which stipulated that the right to fly the Belize flag originates from the act of registration. However, the temporary navigation license that was about to expire was the only document issued by Belize to the vessel "Grand Prince". Then the Tribunal held that the applicant must have abundant evidence to prove that the vessel had been registered in Belize, entitled to fly the flag of Belize within a certain period. Hence, Belize presented a registration certificate issued by the International Merchant Shipping Registry. At the same time, the respondent France submitted the note that was issued by Belize to cancel the ship registration. According to the rules of the effect of evidence, the Tribunal considered that the effect of the note may precede that of the administrative document, the registration certificate issued by the International Merchant Shipping Registry. The Tribunal concluded that there was no abundant proof showing that Belize was the flag State of the vessel under Article 292(2) of the UNCLOS when the documentary evidence submitted by both State parties were sufficient to raise reasonable doubts about the identity of the vessel at the time of filing the application.

II. The Coastal State with the Exclusive Economic Zone in Prompt Release Procedure

The country that corresponds to the flag State is generally the coastal State with the exclusive economic zone in the prompt release cases. Article 55 of the UNCLOS provides the special legal regime of exclusive economic zone,[1] Article 73(1) stipulates that coastal States enjoy great jurisdiction in exclusive economic zones, including boarding, inspecting, arresting the ships for violations of fisheries laws and regulations in the waters under their jurisdiction.[2] The coastal State has almost exercised this right in these heard cases, and the Tribunal did not refuse to accept the application based on this right. According to the humanitarian protection in the provision of Article 73 of the UNCLOS and prompt release in Article 292, the Tribunal makes a ruling that the coastal State with exclusive economic zones shall release the detained vessels and crew of the flag State promptly. This is not only conducive to safeguarding the economic interests of vessels and the personal rights of the crew of the flag State, but also keeping a balance between the interests of the coastal State with the exclusive economic zone and the flag State.

Article 73(2) and Article 292(4) of the UNCLOS, for the humanitarian protection, provide that arrested vessels and their crews shall be promptly released by the detaining State upon the posting of a reasonable bond or other se-

---

[1] Article 55 of the 1982 United Nations Convention on the Law of the Sea: The exclusive economic zone is an area beyond and adjacent to the territorial sea, subject to the specific legal regime established in this Part, under which the rights and jurisdiction of the coastal State and the rights and freedoms of other States are governed by the relevant provisions of this Convention.

[2] Article 73(1) of the 1982 United Nations Convention on the Law of the Sea: The coastal State may, in the exercise of its sovereign rights to explore, exploit, conserve and manage the living resources in the exclusive economic zone, take such measures, including boarding, inspection, arrest and judicial proceedings, as may be necessary to ensure compliance with the laws and regulations adopted by it in conformity with this Convention.

curity.① And the prerequisite of release from detention is that the flag State could post a reasonable bond or other security. This shows that the purpose of Article 73(2) and Article 292 of the UNCLOS is to make a balance between the interests of the two parties, one is that the coastal State has the right to take the necessary measures to ensure conformity of domestic laws and regulations, another is that the flag State could protect the detained vessels and crew in the prompt release case.② That is, the UNCLOS not only protects the property interests of vessels and the humanitarian rights of their crew from the flag State, but also the ability of coastal States to effectively enforce their laws and regulations in the exclusive economic zone.③

There is no prioritized distinction between the interests of the coastal States with exclusive economic zone and those of the flag States under the UNCLOS. Therefore, the Tribunal shall fully consider the proposal on marine interests of the coastal State, which ensure the bond or other security posted by the flag State be appropriate and reasonable. Importantly, the benefit from fishery resources of the coastal State in the exclusive economic zone shall not be impaired, meanwhile, the detained vessel and crew of the flag State shall be protected. Judging from juridical practice, the coastal State usually proposes a certain amount of bonds or other security to ensure its maritime rights and interests under domestic laws and regulations, and sometimes will arrest the vessel for illegal fishing and initiate domestic proceedings to make a judgment of confiscating the detained vessel. The Tribunal cannot prevent the domestic litiga-

---

① Article 73(2) of the 1982 United Nations Convention on the Law of the Sea: Arrested vessels and their crews shall be promptly released upon the posting of reasonable bond or other security.

Article 292(4) of the 1982 United Nations Convention on the Law of the Sea: Upon the posting of the bond or other financial security determined by the court or tribunal, the authorities of the detaining State shall comply promptly with the decision of the court or tribunal concerning the release of the vessel or its crew.

② See The Monte Confurco Case (Seychelles v. France), Prompt Release, Judgement, para 70.

③ Jillaine Seymour, "The International Tribunal for the Law of the Sea: A Great Mistake," *Indiana Journal of Global Legal Studies*, Winter 2006, p. 16.

tion of the coastal State, but it has its standard of judgment when assessing whether the bond or other security proposed by the coastal State is reasonable. At the same time, the Tribunal will also consider the domestic laws and the judgments of the courts as relevant facts to appraise the amount of bond. ① In the end, the Tribunal may cut down the amount claimed by the coastal State based on the balance of both benefits in previous judgments of prompt cases. This shows that the standpoint of the Tribunal is to balance the interests between the two State parties. On the one hand, the sovereign rights of the coastal State over fishery resources and environmental protection in its exclusive economic zone need to be safeguarded. On the other hand, the detention of vessels and crew for a long time by the coastal State shall be excluded in case the interests of the flag State and the personal rights of crews are impaired.

The State parties often have disputes on the bond or other security as stipulated in Article 292 of the UNCLOS. ② Although neither the UNCLOS nor the Rules of Tribunal clearly quantify the standards of bond, the Tribunal has gradually formed a preferable standard of financial security in the process of resolving disputes. For example, the Tribunal held what makes the bond or other security reasonable may be considered from the following factors, including the seriousness of the alleged illegal act, the value of the detained vessel and cargo, the amount and form of the bond claimed by the detaining State in the Camouco Case. ③ Besides, the Tribunal further pointed out that these factors are not all considerations, and it will not prescribe the exact weight of each factor in the Monte Confurco Case. ④ In the subsequent cases, the Tribunal followed this standard basically and refined the standard in different cases, and

---

① See The Monte Confurco Case (Seychelles v. France), Prompt Release, Judgement, para 72.
② Article 292(4) of the 1982 United Nations Convention on the Law of the Sea: Upon the posting of the bond or other financial security determined by the court or tribunal, the authorities of the detaining State shall comply promptly with the decision of the court or tribunal concerning the release of the vessel or its crew.
③ See The Camouco Case (Panama v. France), Prompt Release, Judgement, para 67.
④ See The "Monte Confurco" Case (Seychelles v. France), Prompt Release, Judgement, para 76.

finally ascertained a relatively reasonable bond and other financial security.

2.1 The Seriousness of the Alleged Illegal Act

The Provision of Article 73(1) of the UNCLOS provides that the coastal State may, in the exercise of its sovereign rights to explore, exploit, conserve and manage the living resources in the exclusive economic zone, take such measures as may be necessary to ensure compliance with the laws and regulations adopted by it in conformity with this Convention.① Among the prompt release cases that have been filed by the Tribunal so far, nearly all the cases have been accused by the coastal State for illegal fishing in its exclusive economic zone except for the M/V SAIGA Case, which was suspected of smuggling gasoline. These illegal fishing activities, namely illegal, unreported and unregulated fishing practices, mostly are regulated by the Convention for the Conservation of Antarctic Marine Living Resources (CCAMLR). For example, France drew the Tribunal's attention to economic and ecological issues related to the illegal fishing of Patagonian toothfish in the southern ocean in the Camouco Case.② France claimed that the sea may be damaged by illegal fishing and the measures will be taken to protect fishery resources under the provisions of the CCAMLR in the Monte Confurco Case.③ Similarly, the detaining State Australia in the "Volga" Case, proposed that the illegal fishing activities of the fishing vessel "Volga" in Heard Island and McDonald Islands caused severe loss of Patagonia toothfish, while this sea area, the South Indian Ocean, is protected under the CCAMLR.④ The Tribunal realized that there is

---

① Article 73(1) of the 1982 United Nations Convention on the Law of the Sea: The coastal State may, in the exercise of its sovereign rights to explore, exploit, conserve and manage the living resources in the exclusive economic zone, take such measures, including boarding, inspection, arrest and judicial proceedings, as may be necessary to ensure compliance with the laws and regulations adopted by it in conformity with this Convention.
② See The Camouco Case (Panama v. France), Prompt Release, Judgement, para 68.
③ See The Monte Confurco Case (Seychelles v. France), Prompt Release, Judgement, para 79.
④ See The Volga Case (Russian Federation v. Australia), Prompt Release, Australian Response, para 42-47.

international concern about the threats to fishery conservation in the region, and the tough penalty is allowed to maintain the ecological balance of the environment. Therefore, the Tribunal should not only judge the reasonableness of the security based on precedents, but should fully consider many factors as the standard of judgments, including the changes in marine resources, the special circumstances of indifferent cases, and the efforts made by the international community in protecting marine resources. ①

2.2 The Value of the Detained Vessel and Cargo

Article 111(2) of the Rules of Court stipulates that applications for release from detention should properly contain data relevant to the determination of its value. ② That is, the value of the detained vessel and cargoes will be determined simply based on the evidence presented by the State parties, which is not the decisive factor in making sure the amount of the bond or other financial security. On the one hand, the Tribunal takes the value of the detained vessel as a consideration as long as the detaining State may consider it in ascertaining the amount of the bond. Taking the Hoshinmaru Case as an example, Russia believed that the violation was so serious that the vessel would be confiscated and punished by the maximum fine, thus reckoning the value of the vessel. ③ On the other hand, the value of the cargo or equipment on board can offset part of the bond. For instance, the Tribunal held that the catches and fishing gears on board could be used as relevant standards for determining the

---

① Ren Hu, Yao Yanwei, "Research on Prompt Release of the International Tribunal for the Law of the Sea," *Pacific Journal*, Vol. 23, No. 1, 2015, p18.

② Article 111(2) of the Rules of the Tribunal:

(b) contain relevant information concerning the vessel and crew including, where appropriate, the name, flag and the port or place of registration of the vessel and its tonnage, cargo capacity and data relevant to the determination of its value, the name and address of the vessel owner and operator and particulars regarding its crew;...

③ See The Hoshinmaru Case (Japan v. Russian Federation), Prompt Release, Judgement, para 92.

reasonable security in the Monte Confurco Case.① Especially, the Tribunal ensured that the bond was up to 18 million francs, and the equivalent of 9 million francs, this is the value of the 158 tons of fish on board which should be considered as part of the guarantee. In addition, the remaining part should be paid in the form of a bank guarantee to France unless the two parties have agreed otherwise.② However, in the Volga Case, the Tribunal held that the bond must be based on the value of the vessel and its equipment, and the bond of Article 292 of the UNCLOS refers to the guarantee only related to the release of the vessel and its crew.③ In the subsequent Juno Trader Case and Hoshinmaru Case, the Tribunal didn't make the value of the seized catches as part of the financial security and ordered the detaining State Guinea and Russia to return them to the ship owners.④ This shows that the value of the cargoes is less useful in determining the security by the Tribunal.

2.3 The Amount and Form of the Security Claimed by the Detaining State

The provision of Article 113(2) of the Rules of the Tribunal provides that if the Tribunal decides that the allegation is well-founded, it shall determine the amount, nature, and form of the bond or financial security to be posted for the release of the vessel or the crew. The Tribunal is not restricted by the conditions of the bond claimed by the detaining State, or the reasonable amount considered by the applicant. Among the six prompt release cases to date, the amount of the bond ultimately decided by the Tribunal is lower than that claimed by the detaining State, as shown in Table 2.

---

① See The Monte Confurco Case (Seychelles v. France), Prompt Release, Judgement, para 86.
② See The Monte Confurco Case (Seychelles v. France), Prompt Release, Judgement, para 93.
③ See The Volga Case (Russian Federation v. Australia), Prompt Release, Australian Response, para 48-50.
④ See The Hoshinmaru Case (*Japan v. Russian Federation*), Prompt Release, Judgement, para 104.

Table 2 The amount claimed by the State Parties and bond decided by the Tribunal

Cases	Amount claimed by the detaining State	Amount proposed by the flag State	Amount decided by the Tribunal
The M/V SAIGA Case	No claim	No propose	0.4 million dollars
The Camouco Case	20 million francs	0.95 million francs	8 million francs
The Monte Confurco Case	56.4 million francs	2.2 million francs	9 million francs
The Volga Case	3.5775 million Australian dollars	0.5 million Australian dollars	1.92 million Australian dollars
The Juno Trader Case	No claim	50000 euros	308700 euros
The Hoshinmaru Case	25 million rubles	8 million rubles	10 million rubles

The Tribunal usually balances the interests between the coastal State and the flag State, while the coastal State mostly considers the amount of bond for combating illegal fishing, so that there is a large difference in the amount of bond presented by the two parties due to the distinct considering factors. For example, the Russian court in the Hoshinmaru Case, calculated the bond based on the potential fines imposable upon the captain and the owner of the vessel, a penalty on the basis of the amount of sockeye salmon allegedly taken illegally, the value of the vessel and administrative expenses incurred by the Russian authorities for carrying out the investigation. ① Nevertheless, the Tribunal held that the offence considered of the vessel "Hoshinmaru" may be seen as transgressions within a broadly satisfactory cooperative framework, so the vessel shall not suffer the maximum penalties based on Russian law. ② Finally, the Tribunal reduced the amount of bond required by the detaining State from 20 million rubles to 10 million rubles based on the standard with

---

① See The Hoshinmaru Case (Japan v. Russian Federation), Prompt Release, Judgement, para 90.

② See The Hoshinmaru Case (Japan v. Russian Federation), Prompt Release, Judgement, para 99.

proper proportion and the value of the vessel. To narrow the gap between the domestic court and the Tribunal in determining the amount of reasonable bond, Judge Treves proposed an international standard for determining reasonable bond in the Camouco Case. The international standard should equally reflect the interests of enforcing domestic laws and regulations of coastal States and the freedom of navigation of the flag State.① That is, the standard should protect both the interests of flag States and coastal States, which can make the release from detention more predictable and reduce the occurrence of release disputes to some extent.

In addition, the Tribunal usually judges that the bond of the release from detention must be one of financial security in the form of bank guarantee under the provision of Article 73 (2) of the UNCLOS in previous juridical practice.② For example, the Tribunal held that the non-financial guarantee proposed by Australia could not be considered as the bond or other financial security, which infringed the purpose of this provision in the Volga Case.③ In the Monte Confurco Case, although the French domestic court offered security in the form of a certified check or bank draft, the Tribunal decided that the security shall be in the form of a bank guarantee.④

III. The Enlightenment for China in Prompt Release Cases

With the development of the pelagic fishing industry, many countries pay more attention to safeguarding their maritime rights and interests. As a mari-

---

① See The Camouco Case (Panama v. France), Prompt Release, Dissenting Opinion Of Judge Treves, para 7.
② Article 73(2) of the 1982 United Nations Convention on the Law of the Sea: Arrested vessels and their crews shall be promptly released upon the posting of reasonable bond or other security.
③ See The Volga Case (Russian Federation v. Australia), Prompt Release, Judgment, para 78-80.
④ See The Monte Confurco Case (Seychelles v. France), Prompt Release, Judgement, para 93.

time power, Chinese ships and crews are often detained by other countries. For example, South Korea arrested five Chinese fishing vessels on January 14, 2018. ① On January 28, a Chinese fishing vessel was detained by the South Korean Fisheries Management Corps on suspicion of deliberately failing to record catches in its exclusive economic zone. And in October 2020, the Malaysian Coast Guard detained six Chinese fishing boats and 60 fishermen in the waters near Johor, because they failed to provide a license for fishing in Malaysian waters. At the same time, as a coastal State with the exclusive economic zone, China has also detained foreign vessels for illegal fishing in the exclusive economic zone. According to statistics of 2014, the Chinese maritime court has detained 1660 foreign ships in 30 years. ② In May 2016, due to the vessel "Lu Rong" sunk in the East China Sea, China detained Malta bulk carrier "Catalina" for investigation and evidence collection. Although China made reservations on the jurisdiction of the Tribunal when it joined the UNCLOS, the practice of the Tribunal on prompt release cases is worthy of reference, which is to avoid friction and disputes between the State parties after the detention in the exclusive economic zone but also to better maintain the legitimate rights and interests of Chinese vessels and crew.

3.1 As a Flag State: to Strengthen Supervision and Regulation

According to the Convention on the Law of the Sea, the application for release may be made only by or on behalf of the flag State of the vessel, which shows that the flag State plays an important role in prompt release cases. Therefore, China, as a flag State, should abide by the provisions of the UNCLOS and fulfill its responsibilities and obligations.

---

① Among them, four trawlers were detained for illegal fishing with more than 40 tons of anchovy and crane tail fish in the western waters of South Korea. Another trawler "Wenling" was taken under escort to Jeju Port for fishing in South Korea's exclusive economic zone with a ship license different from the one issued by the South Korean government.

② See "The Supreme Court: The Chinese Maritime Court has seized 1660 foreign ships over the past 30 years," accessed November 24, 2021, http://news.sina.com.cn/c/2014-09-02/143830782982.shtml.

3.1.1 To Standardize Ship Registration Procedures and Strictly Implement the Fishing License System

Ship registration is a symbol that a ship is provided with one nationality, and it is the statutory duty for the competent authority of the flag State to issue the legal certificate for a ship. Article 4 and Article 16 of Measures of the People's Republic of China on the Registration of Fishing Vessels (hereinafter referred to as "these Measures") stipulate that fishing vessels are allowed to sail under the national flag of China only after being registered under these Measures and granted the nationality of China.① Article 21 provides that a fishing vessel nationality certificate shall be valid for five years. The provision of Article 18 of the Regulations of the People's Republic of China Governing the Registration of Ships (hereinafter referred to as "these Regulations") of 2014 provides that the validity period of a provisional certificate of ship's nationality shall generally not exceed 1 year. The registration organ may directly cancel the nationality of a fishing vessel if the fishing vessel owner fails to apply to the registration organ for renewing the Nationality Certificate three months before the expiration of the valid period.② Therefore, as a flag State, China should first make clear the unified standard of vessel registration, and enable the vessel registration process can be standardized and specif-

---

① 2019 Measures of the People's Republic of China on the Registration of Fishing Vessels:
Article 4 Fishing vessels are allowed to sail under the national flag of the People's Republic of China only after being registered in accordance with these Measures and granted the nationality of the People's Republic of China.
Article 16 A fishing vessel may obtain the right of navigation only after it has undergone the formalities for fishing vessel nationality registration in accordance with these Measures.

② 2019 Measures of the People's Republic of China on the Registration of Fishing Vessels:
Article 39 Under any of the following circumstances, a registration organ may directly cancel the nationality of a fishing vessel:
(1) The Nationality Certificate fails to be renewed upon its expiration.
(2) The Fishing Vessel Inspection Certificate fails to be renewed upon its expiration in accordance with the law. ...
Article 45 A fishing vessel owner shall, three months before the expiration of the valid period of the Fishing Vessel Nationality Certificate, apply to the registration organ for renewing the Nationality Certificate by holding the Fishing Vessel Nationality Certificate and the Fishing Vessel Inspection Certificate.

ic, to implement effective management of vessels flying the Chinese national flag.

In addition, the fishing license system shall be carried out strictly. According to Article 23 and Article 24 of the Fisheries Law of the People's Republic of China (hereinafter referred to as the "Fisheries Law"), the State implements a fishing license system on fishery industry, and a fishing license may be issued to the applicant only if he fulfills some conditions. ① That is, fishing licenses for pelagic fishing shall be granted by the fishery administrative department of the State Council, and fishing licenses may not be sold, leased, or transferred by other illegal means. Besides, the granted fishing activities should be strictly supervised to ensure that the fishing vessels flying the Chinese flag engage in ocean-going fishing under the provisions of the licenses.

3.1.2 To Ensure the Genuine Link of the Vessel and Strengthen the Management of Ships

To exercise effectively its jurisdiction and control over vessels of the flag State, the United Nations Convention on Condition for Registration of Ships of 1986 makes it clear that the purpose is to strengthen the genuine link between a State and ships flying its flag. ② This is also stipulated in these Regulations. For example, Article 9 of these Regulations provides that the owner of a ship may choose a port closer to his residence or his principal place of business as

---

① 2013 The Fisheries Law of the People's Republic of China: Article 23 The State implements fishing license system on fishery industry. Fishing licenses for fishing operations in the jointly managed fishery zones defined in the agreements concluded between the People's Republic of China and the relevant countries or on the high seas shall be granted by the fishery administrative department of the State Council.

Article 24 A fishing license may be issued to the applicant only if he fulfills the following conditions: (1) he has the fishing vessel inspection certificate; (2) he has the fishing vessel registration certificate; (3) he fulfills other conditions stipulated by the department in charge of fishery administration of the State Council.

② Article 1 of the 1986 United Nations Convention on Condition for Registration of Ships For the purpose of ensuring or, as the case may be, strengthening the genuine link between a State and ships flying its flag, and in order to exercise effectively its jurisdiction and control over such ships with regard to identification and accountability of ship owners and operators as well as with regard to administrative, technical, economic and social matters, a flag State shall apply the provisions contained in this Convention.

the port of registry, Article 13 provides that a ship owner applying for registration of the ownership of a ship shall produce the documents adequately evidencing his legitimate identification, and Article 15 provides a ship owner shall submit the documentary evidence when applying for the nationality of a ship, etc.① Although Article 49 of these Regulations do not permit a foreign ship to forge the nationality of the People's Republic of China or a Chinese ship to forge a foreign nationality,② there are lots of vessels under the flag of convenience. Given the loose registration conditions and preferential taxation for the overseas registration of flag-of-convenience ships, many of the ships are also the flag-of-convenience ships registered abroad, such as Panama, Liberia, Cyprus, Malaysia, and other flag-of-convenience States. Since 2016, the Chinese Ministry of Transport has begun to issue Announcement of the Import Tax Policies Relating to the Registration in China of Chinese-funded Vessels Sailing under a "Flag of Convenience" (hereinafter referred to as "the Announcement"), the Announcement makes any Chinese-funded ship for which import declaration is made, and which is registered exempt from tariffs and import value-added tax, and encourages the vessels under the "Flag of

---

① 2014 Regulations of the People's Republic of China Governing the Registration of Ships
Article 9 The port where a ship is registered shall be the port of registry of the ship.
The owner of a ship may choose a port closer to his residence or his principal place of business as the port of registry, but not allowed to choose two or more ports as the port of registry.
Article 13 A ship owner applying for registration of the ownership of a ship shall produce to the ship registration authority at the port of registry the documents adequately evidencing his legitimate identification, and submit the originals and copies of the documents evidencing the procurement of his ownership over the ship and the technical information thereof.
Article 15 A ship owner applying for the nationality of a ship shall, in addition to the certificate of registration of ship's ownership, submit the following documents according to the ship's navigation Zone.
② 2014 Regulations of the People's Republic of China Governing the Registration of Ships
Article 49 A ship that forges the nationality of the People's Republic of China and illegally sails under the national flag of the People's Republic of China shall be confiscated by the ship registration authority according to the law.
The provisions of the preceding paragraph shall be applicable to a Chinese ship that forges a foreign nationality and illegally sails under the national flag of a foreign country.

Convenience" to become Chinese vessels through legal registration.① However, most of the vessels mentioned in the Announcement are the ships of large state-owned shipping companies, types of which are mainly cargo ships, not involving fishing vessels that have not yet been involved. Therefore, in order to promote the development of the pelagic fishery, some preferential policies can also be implemented for fishing vessels under the "flag of convenience" in China, making them become vessels flying Chinese flag through registration, which will be more convenient for the department in charge of fishery administration and maritime traffic safety departments to strengthen management.

3.1.3 To Formulate Reasonable Standards of Security and Establish a Fishing Guarantee Mechanism

As a flag State, when a fishing vessel of Chinese nationality is caught by coastal States, apart from contacting the Ministry of Agriculture and Rural Affairs with the Ministry of Foreign Affairs to negotiate with the coastal State under Article 37 of the Provisions for the Administration of Pelagic Fishery,② there also shall be a clear standard of the bond to negotiate with the coastal State. At this time, the practice of the Tribunal on financial security in prompt release cases is worth learning from, that is to bring together lots of

---

① Note: Since 2016, the Ministry of Finance, the General Administration of Customs, and the State Administration of Taxation have jointly approved four batches of Chinese-funded flag of convenience ships enjoying import tax preferential policies, which is a total of 80 Chinese-funded flag of convenience ships.

② Article 37 of the 2020 Provisions for the Administration of Pelagic Fishery When pelagic fishery enterprises, fishing vessels and crews have accidents in the sea areas under the jurisdiction of any other country, the interested parties shall immediately and truthfully report to the Ministry of Agriculture and Rural Affairs, the fishery administrative department of the provincial people's government where the enterprise is located, and relevant embassies or consulates abroad. After receiving the report, the fishery administrative department of the provincial people's government will immediately verify the situation and submit its handling opinions to the Ministry of Agriculture and Rural Affairs and the provincial people's government. The Ministry of Agriculture and Rural Affairs shall take measures and notify the embassies or consulates abroad. In the major foreign event that requires foreign negotiation, the Ministry of Agriculture and Rural Affairs shall put forward handling suggestion and negotiate with the Ministry of Foreign Affairs.

considerations, including the seriousness of the illegal behavior, the value of detained ships and cargoes, and the amount and form of security, in order to negotiate reasonable bond with coastal States as far as possible and protect the legitimate rights and interests of the crew.

In addition, when fishing vessels are caught in pelagic fishing, the detaining States usually tend to ask for heavy security. By the end of 2015, there are 378 Chinese fishing vessels detained by the South Korean Coast Guard, which are required to pay 23.86 billion won to the South Korean government.① If the detained fishing vessels fail to pay the bond, they cannot engage in fishing activities during the seizure period, and even face the risk of confiscation by South Korea. This shows that China's pelagic fishing industry lacks a guarantee mechanism. And the Captain or ship owner is afraid of going out to fish on the high seas because of a huge bond. In 1981, the People's Insurance Company of China promulgated and implemented the Insurance Clauses of Domestic Fishing Vessels, in which Articles 3 and Article 8 stipulated the scope of insurance liability.② However, these provisions only covered the damage of the fishing vessel itself, not to mention the detention of the fishing vessel, which means that the security from the detention is not part of the scope of insurance liability. Therefore, when Chinese fishing vessels and crew are detained by other coastal States, China shall establish a fishery guarantee mechanism to comprehensively quantify insurance premiums through the per-

---

① See "Chinese fishing ships were towed away by South Korean fishermen, asking for a sky-high security," accessed November 24, 2021, https://m.huanqiu.com/article/9CaKrnJVNPj.

② 1981 Insurance clauses of domestic fishing vessels Article 3 The insurer, namely the insurance company, shall be liable for the complete loss or presumed complete loss of an insured fishing vessel, as well as part of the loss due to the following reasons: (1) Fire, lightning strike, explosion, stranding, rocking, collision, overturning, sinking, storm, tsunami. (2) The whole vessel has been missing for more than 6 months. (3) Dock repair, berthing and parking of insured fishing vessels …

Article 8 The insurer shall not be liable for compensation for losses caused by the insured fishing vessel due to the following reasons: (1) War or military operation; (2) Not having airworthiness or operating conditions; (3) The deliberate act of the ship owner and his agent or the illegal act of the persons on board… (8) Other losses that are not within the scope of insurance liability.

formance and voyage of the fishing boats, as well as the different types of catches, to avoid the high risk of the ship owner under tremendous economic pressure, which allows them to continue pelagic fishing and is conducive to the recuperation of China's marine fishery resources.

3.2 As a Coastal State with the Exclusive Economic Zone: to Strengthen the Supervision of Foreign Ships

The UNCLOS emphasizes freedom in the open sea, including fishing freedom, and allows nationals of other States to fish in the exclusive economic zone of the coastal State. ① Article 5 of Law on the Exclusive Economic Zone and the Continental Shelf of the People's Republic of China (hereinafter referred to as "the Law") stipulates that the foreign vessels entering the exclusive economic zone of China for fishing shall be subject to the approval of the Chinese competent authorities. ② According to Article 12 of the Law, Chinese competent authorities have the right to detain foreign vessels for illegal fishing by violating Chinese laws and regulations. ③ Besides, China does not recognize the Tribunal's jurisdiction over prompt release cases, so Chinese courts, belonging to the coastal State, have jurisdiction over other waters outside the territorial

---

① Article 62(4) of the 1982 United Nations Convention on the Law of the Sea Nationals of other States fishing in the exclusive economic zone shall comply with the conservation measures and with the other terms and conditions established in the laws and regulations of the coastal State...

② Article 5 of the 1988 Law on the Exclusive Economic Zone and the Continental Shelf of the People's Republic of China All international organizations, foreign organizations or individuals that wish to enter the exclusive economic zone of the People's Republic of China for fishing shall be subject to approval of the competent authorities of the People's Republic of China and shall comply with its laws and regulations as well as the accords and agreements it has signed with the states concerned.

③ Article 12 of the 1988 Law on the Exclusive Economic Zone and the Continental Shelf of the People's Republic of China The People's Republic of China may, in the exercise of its sovereign rights to explore its exclusive economic zone and to exploit, conserve and manage the living resources there, take such necessary measures as visit, inspection, arrest, detention and judicial proceedings in order to ensure that the laws and regulations of the People's Republic of China are complied with. The People's Republic of China has the right to take necessary measures against violations of its laws and regulations in its exclusive economic zone and on its continental shelf and to investigate for legal responsibility according to law, and may exercise the right of hot pursuit.

waters.① Therefore, courts in China could immediately start domestic proceedings, learning from Russia's experience in the "Tomimaru" Case, to reduce the loss of biological resources in the China's sea waters, and safeguard China's marine economic rights and interests.

On October 31, 2006, the Japanese fishing vessel "Tomimaru" was detained for illegal fishing in the Russian exclusive economic zone. On November 14, the Russian authorities filed an administrative lawsuit against the ship owner of vessel "Tomimaru" based on domestic law, and on December 28, Petropavolvsk-Kamchatskii City Court made a judgment that the fishing vessel "Tomimaru" would be confiscated, indicating that an appeal could be filed to the Kamchatka District Court within 10 days. The ship owner appealed to the Kamchatka District Court on January 6, 2007, but the District Court maintained the original verdict on January 24, which came into force immediately after its delivery. Thereupon, the federal agency in charge of managing the federal property in the Kamchatka area confiscated the fishing vessel by implementing Act 158-p of the 9 April 2007 under the judgment and made it registered again in the Federal Property Registry. After that, the ship owner filed an application for retrial by trial supervision procedure against the judgment made by the District Court. When Japan applied to the Tribunal for prompt release on July 6, 2007, the Supreme Court of the Russian Federation had not yet heard the case. After the Tribunal hearing, the Supreme Court rejected the application of retrial on July 26, 2007, and notified the Tribunal. Since the Supreme Court's decision, the final decision had ended the domestic judicial procedures involving the fishing vessel, the Tribunal didn't make a judgment, holding that Japan's application lacked the subject matter, and Russia's judicial procedures had not violated international judicial due process.②

---

① Huang Xiwu, Zhou Haiyang, Yan Wei, "Understanding and Application of the Provisions of the Supreme People's Court on Several Issues concerning the Trial of the Relevant Cases Occurring in Sea Areas under the Jurisdiction of China," *People's Judicature* (*Application*), No. 31(2016).

② See The Tomimaru Case (Japan v. Russian Federation), Prompt Release, Judgement, para 78.

Article 292(3) of the UNCLOS provides that the Tribunal shall deal only with the question of release, without prejudice to the merits of any case before the appropriate domestic forum against the vessel, its owner, or its crew. The Tribunal to some extent recognizes the legality of the forfeiture if the coastal State has made a judgment of confiscation. ① The domestic laws of many countries stipulate that confiscating fishing vessels is one of the punitive measures for illegal fishing, as well as stipulated in Article 46 of the Fisheries Law of the People's Republic of China. ② Therefore, in the event of impairing China's marine resources by foreign vessels, China shall impose the fine and confiscate the fishing vessel through domestic judicial procedures in good time, and negotiate with the flag State on question of release to require reasonable financial security, so that the case will be solved quickly and effectively.

Conclusion

Article 292 of the Convention on the Law of the Sea stipulates that the International Tribunal for the Law of the Sea has jurisdiction over prompt release cases. In the previous practice, many countries tend to submit the question of release to the Tribunal. When there is an objection to the jurisdiction between the State parties, the Tribunal will first examine whether the applications of these States meet the conditions of the jurisdiction. Among them, the status of the applicant and the identification of the flag State are particularly critical. With the development of pelagic fisheries, disputes in the release from detention have continued to increase, and the Tribunal's practice has provided valua-

---

① Zhu Zhenhua, "Research on the Expropriation in the Prompt Release Procedure of the ITLOS," *Graduate Law Review* 23, No. 2(2008).

② Article 46 of 2013 Fisheries Law of the People's Republic of China: Where a foreigner or a foreign fishing vessel violates the provisions in this Law by entering the jurisdictional water areas of the People's Republic of China to be engaged in fishery production or activities for investigation of fishery resources, he/it shall be ordered to leave or be banished, the fishing gains and fishing facilities may be confiscated, and a fine of 500000 yuan or less may also be imposed; if the case is serious, the fishing vessel may be confiscated; if such acts constitute an offence, criminal liabilities shall be investigated in accordance with the law.

ble experience for China to handle relevant cases. Therefore, starting from the Tribunal's jurisdiction over prompt release cases, this article introduces the applicant that has the right to apply for release from detention to the Tribunal and particularly analyzes the status of the flag State, including the time and rules of evidence for determining the identity of the flag State. This is of important enlightenment and reference for China to deal with the prompt release cases when vessels flying Chinese flags or foreign vessels illegally fish in jurisdictional water areas. Firstly, as a flag State, the first thing is to standardize ship registration procedures and implement the fishing license system. The second is to ensure the genuine link of the vessel and strengthen the management of ships. The third one is to formulate reasonable standards of security and establish a fishing guarantee mechanism. Secondly, as a coastal State with the exclusive economic zone, China may confiscate the foreign vessels for illegal fishing and impose fines through domestic procedures by operation of law so as to safeguard China's maritime rights and interests.

Moreover, as the construction of the 21st Century Maritime Silk Road advances, China should uphold the concept of a maritime community with a shared future and promote the establishment of bilateral or multilateral regional maritime cooperation mechanisms in the process of enhancing economic strength and strengthening overall national strength. China will also strengthen consultation and cooperation with neighboring coastal countries, especially the countries along the coast of the South China Sea so that the prompt release of flag States in the exclusive economic zone of the coastal State can be dealt with efficiently and conveniently, which will make the two State parties be in a win-win situation. To sum up, we should combine the actual conditions and learn from the experience of the Tribunal for studying, for the sake of improving China's ability to handle the question of release from all angles and providing favorable conditions for China's development into a maritime power.

(贾云鹏、周昕　审校)

Improve Judicial Supervision and Support for Arbitration and Promote the High-quality Development of Arbitration in China[*]

HU Fang[**] MA Ling[***]

Abstract: The people's courts have attached great importance to the significant role of arbitration in the dispute resolution mechanism, supporting and supervising arbitration in a manner consistent with the rule of law. The people's courts actively promote the development and improvement of arbitration mechanism, and continuously enhance the credibility and international competitiveness of China's arbitration so as to ensure strong judicial services and guarantees for the high-quality development of arbitration in China.

Key words: judicial review of arbitration; ADR; arbitration-friendly judicial environment

As an internationally accepted dispute resolution mechanism, arbitration is an important part of the construction of diversified dispute resolution mechanisms in China's social governance system, which is of great significance for efficient and convenient settlement of maritime and commercial disputes, creating a market-oriented, internationalized business environment based on rule of

---

[*] Translated by MO Zhiying, CHEN Xun, HONG Huimin.
[**] Deputy Chief Judge of the Civil Adjudication Tribunal No. 4 of Supreme People's Court, Senior Judge of the Second Rank.
[***] Judge Assistant of the Civil Adjudication Tribunal No. 4 of Supreme People's Court.

law, and promoting the implementation of major national development strategies. In in-depth advancing the Belt and Road initiative, the cooperation between China and other countries in the fields of politics, trade and economy and culture has become closer. The rising demand for arbitration services at home and abroad provides great opportunities for the vigorous development of arbitration in China. For a long time, the people's courts have attached great importance to the significant role of arbitration in the dispute resolution mechanism, supporting and supervising arbitration in a manner consistent with the rule of law. The people's courts actively promote the development and improvement of arbitration mechanism, and continuously enhance the credibility and international competitiveness of China's arbitration so as to ensure strong judicial services and guarantees for the high-quality development of arbitration in China.

Ⅰ. The People's Courts Conduct Judicial Review in a Manner Consistent with the Rule of Law and Provide Guidance on the Healthy Development of Arbitration

According to the Arbitration Law, the Civil Procedure Law and relevant laws and regulations, the arbitration-related judicial review cases currently accepted by the people's courts mainly include the following categories: (1) A case of an application for recognition of the effect of an arbitration agreement; (2) A case of an application for enforcement of an arbitral award made by a Chinese mainland-based arbitral institution; (3) A case of an application for revocation of an arbitral award made by a Chinese mainland-based arbitral institution; (4) A case of an application for recognition and enforcement of an arbitral award made in the Hong Kong Special Administrative Region, the Macao Special Administrative Region, or Taiwan region; and (5) A case of an application for recognition and enforcement of a foreign arbitral award. In addition, Article 1.6 of Provisions of the Supreme People's Court on Several Issues concerning Deciding Cases of Arbitration-Related Judicial Review stipulates a general category termed as 'other arbitration-related judicial review cases', opening a door for the emerging arbitration-related cases (such as ad-hoc arbitrations provided for in Opinions of the Supreme People's Court on Providing Judicial Guarantee for the Building of Pilot Free Trade Zones). With an intention to guide the healthy development of arbitration, the people's courts conduct judicial review of the above-mentioned cases based on China's realities, defining the scope of procedural and substantive matters, well-balancing the relationship between the flaws of arbitration and excess of discretion, putting emphasis on improving the credibility and judicial guarantee of arbitration, as well as enhancing the internationalization and competitiveness of Arbitration in China. Among the trends as seen in recent years, the adjudication cases concluded by the people's courts have maintained a low rate of revocation, while cases involving preservation measures in arbitration have maintained a high preservation rate, which not only showcases the improvement of arbitration services in China, but also the strong judicial support in promoting the development of arbitration in China.

1.1 The People's Courts Respect the Parties' Willingness to Submit Their Dispute to Arbitration and Apply Wide Interpretation of the Arbitration Agreement

Compared with common law countries, there are more legal requirements for a valid arbitration agreement under the PRC Arbitration Law, including an expression of intention to apply for arbitration; matters that should be referred to arbitration; and a designated arbitration commission. In previous judicial practice, the people's courts had a rigorous attitude towards "a chosen arbitration commission" as an essential element of the arbitration agreement. In contrast, the courts now address more attention to fully respecting the parties' willingness to arbitrate, and interpreting the requirements for arbitration agreements as broadly as possible pursuant to the law. In practice, the full name of an arbitration institution prescribed in the arbitration agreement is often inaccurate or ambiguous, for instance, the court shall incline to recognize the validity of the arbitration agreement, as long as a specific arbitration institution could be identified. In addition, in case where the arbitration agreement stipulates that disputes shall be resolved under the specific arbitration rules of an arbitration institution, unless the arbitration rules provide otherwise, such shall be interpreted by the court as the parties agree to submit their disputes under the above arbitration institution, rather than absent of "a selected arbitration commission". Moreover, in case where the parties agree to resolve the dispute by arbitration as a condition precedent to bringing further litigation, such arbitration agreement could be deemed invalid in previous judicial practice as arbitration was not agreed upon as the only dispute resolution method. However, the courts today would no longer hold the same opinion. In other words, although the agreement on litigation is void, it will not affect the validity of the agreement on arbitration. Likewise, arbitration clause such as "Arbitration, if any, in Hong Kong (SAR) and English law to be applied" could be deemed invalid in previous judicial practice since it fails to exclude litigation jurisdiction from the dispute resolutions, yet nowadays the courts have gradually switched to consider that the validity of such clauses should be reviewed in accordance with lex arbitri. Provisions of the Supreme People's Court on Several Issues concerning Deciding Cases of Arbitration-Related Judicial Review also stipulates that where neither party chooses an applicable law, between the *lex arbitri* and the law in the place of the arbitral institution, the court should choose the applicable law under which the arbitration agreement is much likely to be recognized as valid. With the development and improvement of judicial practice, people's court has shown a more favorable attitude towards the recognition of the validity of arbitration agreements. As long as the parties make an expression to submit the dispute to arbitration, the court shall interpret the defective arbitration clauses in a more flexible and tolerant manner upon the pro arbitration principle, demonstrating the strong judicial support for arbitration in China.

1.2 The People's Courts Exercise Judicial Review of Arbitral Awards in Due Diligence upon the Statutory Grounds

The people's courts shall, in strict accordance with the statutory grounds, review the application to revoke or set aside an arbitral award with due diligence, respect the finality of and maintain the validity of the arbitral awards. For example, in case where the parties agree on a multi-level dispute resolution clause that requires the parties to go through negotiation, conciliation or mediation within a certain period of time prior to arbitration, and a party often later applies to the court for revoking or setting aside the arbitral award on the grounds that such preliminary procedure has not been satisfied. Such application shall be rejected by the court on the ground that the 'arbitration procedure' that shall be reviewed under the current arbitration law only refers to the procedural matters throughout the arbitral proceeding, rather than the dispute resolution conducted before arbitration, therefore whether or not such preliminary procedure has been satisfied shall not be deemed as a justified ground for revocation or set aside of an arbitral award. For another example, in judicial review of procedural matters, such as the selection of arbitrators and parties' participation in arbitral proceedings, the arbitral awards might be dismissed only if the flaws in arbitral proceeding may affect the independence and impartiality of the arbitral awards. Furthermore, in order to avoid the abuse of right due to a wide scope of interpretation of 'public policies', the court always have a rigorous attitude towards revocation or set aside of arbitral awards on this ground. In view of the cases reported to the Supreme People's Court in the past two years, situations such as violation of mandatory legal provisions, violation of the adjudication rules of local or other courts, arbitral awards involving financial revenue and expenditure of local governments or relevant administrations, state-owned assets or specific social welfare programs were not deemed as in violation of the public interest. The above-mentioned judicial practices showcase the generally supportive attitude of courts towards arbitral awards over judicial supervision, and the establishment of judicial support and promotion of arbitration.

1.3 The People's Courts Adopt Arbitration Preservation Measures to Ensure the Enforcement of Arbitral Awards

Since arbitration is a civil dispute resolution mechanism, arbitration institutions have no power to take compulsory measures against the property, conduct and evidence of the case. Therefore, these issues have to be settled through judicial assistance and support. As a key sector in connection between arbitration and litigation procedures, arbitration preservation plays an important role in ensuring the conduction of arbitration procedures and the enforcement of arbitral awards. According to the statistics, the number of arbitration preservation cases accepted by the people's courts even exceeds the number of cases confirming the validity of arbitration agreements or applying for non-enforcement of arbitral awards. In 2019, 87% of the applications for interim measures were supported by the courts in arbitration preservation cases concluded by courts at all levels; in 2020, the above-mentioned preservation rate was increased to 97%. Compared with the Civil Procedure Law, the Special Maritime Procedures Law of the People's Republic of China and its judicial interpretations have established a more comprehensive system of preservation for maritime claims. A maritime claimant may apply to the maritime court for the preservation of a maritime claim against the vessels, cargos on board, bunker oil and possessions owned by the respondent in China, before initiating the arbitration or during the arbitral proceedings, in both domestic and international arbitration. Such application for preservation shall not subject to litigation jurisdiction agreement or arbitration agreement on maritime claim between the parties. With the acceptance and efficient enforcement of the preservation for maritime claims by the maritime court in accordance with law, the efficiency and popularity of arbitration as an alternative dispute resolution has been highly improved, which also reflects the judicial support for arbitration.

1.4 The People's Courts Correctly Apply International Treaties, Recognize and Enforce Arbitral Awards According to Law

Dr Tao Kaiyuan, Vice President of the Supreme People's Court, addressed in her keynote speech at the 2021 China Arbitration Summit Forum and the Second Belt and Road Arbitration Institutions High-end Forum that "recognition and enforcement of foreign arbitral awards is a mirror that reflects a country's judicial efficiency". The people's courts in China have always abided by the treaty obligations, performed the treaty obligations upon the principle of good faith, and adhered to the judicial position of preference for the enforcement of the arbitral award. In cases of recognition and enforcement of foreign arbitral awards, the courts conduct judicial review in strict accordance within the statutory grounds provided for in Article V of the Convention on the Recognition and Enforcement of Foreign Arbitral Awards (the New York Convention). In case a party requests for refusal of recognition and enforcement of a foreign arbitral award beyond grounds set out in Article V of the New York Convention, the people's court shall refuse to conduct the judicial review. In addition, the grounds set forth in paragraph 1, Article V of the New York Convention have to be established by the party resisting enforcement, which will not be invoked the court on its own initiative According to the statistics, in 2020, only 20% of the cases applying for recognition and enforcement of foreign arbitral awards were rejected by the courts. The vast majority of cases applying for recognition and enforcement of foreign arbitral awards are recognized and enforced by the courts. The highly supportive attitude of people's court towards the recognition and enforcement of foreign arbitral awards in China showcases the progressive judicial thinking wherein the court involves in conducting judicial review. As for a small number of cases applying for recognition and enforcement of foreign arbitral awards, the grounds for refusal have been clarified in detail, which also reflects that the people's courts keep a positive attitude towards the international judicial assistance in the field of arbitration.

II. The Supreme People's Court Publishes Judicial Interpretations and Normative Documents and Create an Arbitration-friendly Environment with Judicial Support and Supervision

The Supreme People's Court has issued more than 30 judicial interpretations and normative documents related to arbitration, and has continuously innovated institutional mechanisms to ensure the development of arbitration, committed to creating an arbitration-friendly judicial environment. In particular, since the 18th National Congress of the Communist Party of China, the Supreme People's Court, engaging in major national strategies including the Belt and Road Initiative and the construction of pilot free trade zone, has established a centralized handling mechanism of judicial review of arbitration cases, standardized the approval and reporting system for arbitration-related judicial review cases, refined the procedural rules for arbitration-related judicial review cases, clarified the judicial review standards for the enforcement of arbitral awards, continuously enhancing the credibility and international competitiveness of China's arbitration system, providing strong judicial services and guarantees for building a market-oriented, internationalized business environment based on rule of law.

2.1 The Supreme People's Court Further Improves Rules on Working Mechanism Handling Arbitration-related Cases Reported to SPC and Building a More Efficient Judicial Review System for Arbitration

In 1995, the Supreme People's Court issued the Notice of the Supreme People's Court on the Handling by People's Courts of Issues Concerning Foreign-related Arbitration and Foreign Arbitration, establishing an internal reporting system for judicial review cases involving foreign-related, Hong Kong, Macau and Taiwan-related arbitrations, which has played a positive role in the people's courts'handling of the above cases, enhancing the international credibility of the Mainland of China's judiciary and promoting the development of arbitration.

In 2017, in order to protect the legitimate rights and interests of the parties equally, the Supreme People's Court, in accordance with the needs of trial practice, formulated the Relevant Provisions of the Supreme People's Court on Issues concerning Applications for Verification of Arbitration Cases under Judicial Review, adding the provision that the review of non-foreign-related or non-Hong Kong, Macao, or Taiwan-related arbitration judicial cases shall be conducted by the Higher People's Court of each place and the Supreme People's Court respectively according to different circumstances. Since the implementation of the Provisions, the Supreme People's Court has handled more than 900 arbitration-related judicial review cases seeking judicial review reported to the Supreme People's Court, which has given a strong impetus to the overall standardization of judicial review of arbitration cases and the uniformity of adjudication standards, enhanced the transparency of judicial review of arbitration, and safeguarded the prosperous development of arbitration industry.

In 2021, in order to more reasonably define the scope of power the Supreme People's Court and the High People's Court respectively exercises in reviewing the arbitration-related cases to improve the review efficiency and shorten the case review duration, the Supreme People's Court promulgated the Decision on Amending the "Relevant Provisions of the Supreme People's Court on Issues concerning Applications for Verification of Arbitration Cases under Judicial Review". From January 1, 2022, for judicial review cases regarding arbitrations without connections to either foreign countries or regions or Hong Kong, Macao or Taiwan, if the parties'domicile are located in dofferent provinces, the ultimate decision-making power shall be exercised by the High People's Court instead of the Supreme People's Court.

At the same time, in order to have an overall picture of the judicial review of arbitration cases and to strengthen guidance and supervision, a reporting system has been added, requiring the High People's Court to report its reply letter to the Supreme People's Court within fifteen days from the date of making its review opinion on the cases in which it exercises final review power. In order to complement the implementation of the new regulations and better guide the lower courts in the proper handling of arbitration judicial review cases, the Fourth Civil Division of the Supreme People's Court issued on December 31, 2021 the Minutes of the Symposium on Foreign Commercial Maritime Judicial Work of National Courts, which summarized 21 issues involved in judicial review of arbitration and unified the scale of adjudication, fully reflecting the judicial purpose and philosophy of supporting arbitration.

Since the implementation of the Arbitration Law nearly 30 years ago, the Supreme People's Court has continuously improved the system of judicial review of arbitration cases through the issuance of judicial interpretations and normative documents, which is more in line with the functions and positioning of the people's courts at all levels, the judicial needs of the parties to resolve disputes in a fair and efficient manner, and the original intention of supporting and supervising arbitration as a reporting system.

2.2 The Supreme People's Court Strengthens Inter-district Judicial Assistance and Facilitating Inter-district Enforcement of Arbitral Awards

In recent years, the Supreme People's Court has formulated and implemented a number of judicial interpretations to promote the recognition and enforcement of arbitral awards from Hong Kong and Macao in the mainland of China. Since Hong Kong's return to China, eight arrangements for judicial assistance in civil and commercial matters have been signed through the joint efforts of Hong Kong and mainland of China, basically realizing full coverage of judicial assistance in civil and commercial matters between the two places. In particular, the Arrangement of the Supreme People's Court on the Mutual Enforcement of Arbitral Awards between the Mainland and the Hong Kong Special Administrative Region (hereinafter referred to as the 1999 Arrangement) signed in 1999 has played an important role in resolving cross-border disputes concerning the two places, supporting the development of arbitration in Hong Kong and enhancing the well-being of the people of the two places.

In 2019, the Supreme People's Court issued the Arrangement Concerning Mutual Assistance in Court-ordered Interim Measures in Aid of Arbitral Proceedings by the Courts of the Mainland and of the Hong Kong Special Administrative Region , which sets out clear provisions on the means of mutual assistance in preservation between the two places, the scope of preservation that may be applied for, the procedures for applying for preservation and the examination and processing of preservation applications. This is the first document on arbitration preservation assistance signed between the Mainland and other jurisdictions since Hong Kong's return to China. Within two years after this document came into effect, about 92% of such arbitration preservation applications received by the Mainland courts were upheld.

In 2020, the Supreme People's Court and the Department of Justice of the Government of the Hong Kong Special Administrative Region signed again the Supplementary Arrangement of the Supreme People's Court for the Mutual Enforcement of Arbitral Awards between the Mainland and the Hong Kong Special Administrative Region (hereinafter referred to as the Supplementary Arrangement), which made important amendments and supplements to the 1999 Arrangement. The Supplementary Arrangement clarified the procedures for the recognition of arbitral awards, expanded the scope of mutual recognition and enforcement of arbitral awards, provided that an applicant may apply to the courts of both places for enforcement at the same time, and added provisions for preservation before litigation and during the litigation.

The signing of the above documents has added to the well-being of the people of the two places and facilitated Hong Kong's integration into the development of the Greater Bay Area. It is a major initiative to enrich and improve the judicial measures realizing the principle of " One country, Two systems" , a concrete manifestation of maintaining Hong Kong's long-term prosperity and stability by means of the rule of law, and a constructive exploration of building a diversified dispute resolution mechanism for mutual consultation, construction and sharing. Today, judicial assistance between the two places has led to closer cooperation and broader mutual trust within a country, which fully proves the institutional advantages of "One country, Two systems".

2.3 The Supreme People's Court Publishes the *Annual Report on Judicial Review of Arbitration in China* to Summarize the Experience of Judicial Review of Arbitration

In order to comprehensively present the achievements of the People's Court's judicial review of arbitration in recent years, summarize the experience of judicial review of arbitration in a timely manner and unify the scale of adjudication, the Supreme People's Court has released for the first time a bilingual version of the Annual Report on Judicial Review of Arbitration in China (2019), providing a panoramic perspective for the international community to understand the judicial review of arbitration in China.

The report provides a macro overview of the history of the development of China's working system handling judicial review of arbitration, summarising the exploration, improvement and innovation the Chinese courts have gone through in conducting judicial review of arbitration as well as introducing the basic statistics of arbitration judicial review cases accepted by the Chinese courts in 2019, analysing the characteristics and trends of various types of arbitration judicial review cases, and summarising the thinking and adjudication standards of arbitration judicial review based on the arbitration judicial review cases reported and approved by the Supreme People's Court and the typical cases selected and reported by the National High People's Court.

The report reflects the overall plan of the people's courts to further implement the Opinions of the Fourth Plenary Session of the 18th CPC Central Committee and the Opinions on improving arbitration system and the credibility of arbitration issued by the General Office of the Central Committee of the Communist Party of China and the General Office of the State Council, demonstrates the unremitting efforts of the people's courts and the positive results achieved, deepens the awareness and understanding of the judicial review system of arbitration by all sectors of society and shows the importance of arbitration and its judicial review in safeguarding China's economic development, promoting the construction of a business environment and deepening the reform of the diversified dispute resolution mechanism. The publication of the 2020 Annual Report on Judicial Review of Chinese Arbitration will be ongoing and will certainly further increase the transparency of Chinese justice and Chinese arbitration, and strengthen their credibility, influence and international competitiveness.

III. The Supreme People's Court Participates in the Revision of the Arbitration Law and Actively Promoting the Improvement of the Arbitration Legal System

In 2020, in order to implement the Opinions on Improving the Arbitration System and Enhancing the Credibility of Arbitration issued by the General Office of the Central Committee of the Communist Party of China and the General Office of the State Council, the Ministry of Justice initiated the revision of the Arbitration Law of the People's Republic of China in accordance with the legislative plan of the Standing Committee of the 13th National People's Congress and the legislative work plan of the State Council, with the Supreme People's Court being the most important collaborative department participating in it.

Given that problems in the implementation of the arbitration law, the practical needs and the effects of the implementation of policy documents are most often discovered in the judicial review of arbitration. The Supreme People's Court has attached great importance to the revision of the Arbitration Law from the very beginning and organised a special team to conduct a detailed study on the basis of extensive consultation with local courts at all levels.

The working group of the Supreme People's Court, led by the Fourth Chamber of the Civil Court, has communicated fully with the Ministry of Justice on a number of occasions on hot issues such as arbitrability, the validity of arbitration agreements, the system of setting aside and enforcement of arbitral awards, and has proposed many constructive amendments that have been absorbed and adopted in the draft, providing more support based upon the judicial practice for the amendment of the Arbitration Law and the reform and improvement of China's arbitration legal system.

IV. The Supreme People's Court Builds a Diversified Mechanism for the Settlement of International Commercial Disputes and Supporting the International Development of Chinese Arbitration

The Fourth Plenary Session of the 18th CPC Central Committee proposed to "improve the mechanism for preventing and resolving social contradictions and disputes, and refine a diversified dispute resolution mechanism that is organically linked and coordinated with mediation, arbitration, administrative adjudication, administrative reconsideration and litigation". In recent years, the Supreme People's Court has issued the Opinions of the Supreme People's Court on People's Courts on Further Deepening the Reform of Diversified Dispute Resolution Mechanism of the People's Courts and the Opinions on Building a One-Stop Litigation Service Centre for the Diversified Dispute Resolution Mechanism, which have repeatedly emphasized the reasonable allocation of social resources for dispute resolution, requiring courts at all levels to strengthen the interface with arbitration institutions, actively support the reform of the arbitration system, and promote the establishment of a "one-stop" dispute resolution service that integrates litigation, mediation and arbitration.

In 2018, the Supreme People's Court set up the China International Commercial Court (CICC) and the International Commercial Expert Committee of CICC to establish a "one-stop" mechanism for the diversified settlement of international commercial disputes, which is another attempt to achieve close cooperation between courts and arbitration and mediation institutions, as well as an institutional innovation to realize the positive interaction and complementary advantages of litigation, arbitration and mediation.

At present, five arbitration institutions, including the China International Economic and Trade Arbitration Commission (CIETAC) and the China Maritime Arbitration Commission (CMAC), have been the first to be included in the Supreme People's Court's "one-stop" mechanism for the diversified settlement of international commercial disputes, providing parties to international commercial cases with convenient, fast and low-cost "one-stop" services. On 21 July 2020, the Supreme People's Court's "one-stop" platform for the diversified settlement of international commercial disputes was launched on the CICC website for trial operation, providing domestic and foreign parties with online access to the entire dispute resolution process, including filing, mediation, evidence exchange and hearing, realising online docking and information sharing in CICC between the litigation mechanism and the mediation and arbitration mechanisms, which will create a synergistic effect and strongly promote the implementation of the diversified settlement of international commercial disputes.

In addition, the entrusted mediation mechanism established by the maritime courts in Shanghai, Ningbo and Wuhan with the CMAC is expanding its application scope and improving its procedural flow. Many complex, foreign-related and professional maritime disputes have been resolved in a timely and appropriate manner through the entrusted mediation, which is highly recognized by the parties. The continuous perfection of the diversified international commercial dispute resolution mechanism has improved the efficiency of dispute resolution, fulfilled the diversified needs of domestic and foreign parties in it, and provided a practical platform for building a Chinese brand of commercial maritime arbitration with international influence.

In the process of further promoting the Belt and Road construction, China's commercial and maritime arbitration will face even fiercer competition, and it is urgent to enhance the credibility of China's commercial and maritime arbitration institutions. In this new historical period, the People's Court, as a supporter and supervisor of commercial maritime arbitration, will continue to uphold the spirit of openness and inclusiveness, always adhere to the concept of supporting the development of arbitration, and, based on China's arbitration and judicial practice, continue to support and supervise arbitration, providing strong judicial services and protection to improve China's arbitration system and enhance the credibility of China's arbitration.

(周雨琳、黄智含、陈末末　审校)

A Review on the Formation of International Arbitration Hub

SI Yuzhuo[*]　WANG Wei[**]

Abstract: It has become the goals and directions pursued by many countries and regions to develop the international arbitration services vigorously so as to establish an international arbitration hub or regional international arbitration hub. China's arbitration community has been exploring the possibility of China forming an international arbitration hub as well. The State Council of P. R. China issued the "Several Opinions on Promoting the Healthy Development of the Maritime Industry" and the "Plan for Further Deepening the Reform and Opening-up of the China (Shanghai) Pilot Free Trade Zone", which take the development of modern shipping services including maritime arbitration as a key task. It further proposes the goal of "exploring the establishment of a national pilot free trade zone arbitration legal service alliance and an exchange and cooperation mechanism for Asia-Pacific arbitration institutions, and accelerating the creation of a global-oriented Asia-Pacific Arbitration Hub". In this context, China's Arbitration Law has entered the revision process, and domestic and foreign arbitration institutions are also constantly exploring feasible paths to improve the level of arbitration services and facilitate the formation of

---

[*] Prof. SI Yuzhuo, the former president of Dalian Maritime University, professor of the Law School of Dalian Maritime University.

[**] Ms. WANG Wei, Doctoral Candidate of the Law School of Dalian Maritime University, Partner of Shanghai Hansheng Law offices.

Arbitration Hubs by investing huge costs. In view of this, this paper reviews by comparison and draws lessons from the advantageous factors of forming an international arbitration hub of several major countries, regions or institutions that are currently in the leading position in the arbitration service industry in the world, and puts forward the view that the international arbitration hub is formed, not constructed. Based on which, it further discusses the opportunities and strategic directions for China to establish international arbitration hubs.

Key words: international arbitration hub; formation; construction

Queen Mary University of London, in collaboration with its partners, published an international arbitration survey in 2021 ("2021 International Arbitration Survey: Adapting arbitration to a changing world")[①], which is their twelfth edition of its annual report. It quickly aroused great attention and heated discussions in the industry upon its released and became an important basis for industry insiders to judge the development level and competitiveness of the international arbitration market. According to the Survey, the support of respondents to resolve cross-border economic disputes through international arbitration has increased from 73% in 2006 to 90% in 2021, indicating the rapid development of international arbitration services in the past decade. Especially in 2018, the support for settling cross-border disputes through international arbitration reached 97%. Along with the prosperity and development of the international arbitration service industry, its superimposed effects are eye-catching including helping the construction of international trade and shipping economy, enhancing international influence, and creating commercial value, etc. It therefore has become the goals and directions of many countries and regions, including China, to vigorously develop the international arbitration services so as to establish an international arbitration hub or regional international arbitration hub.

---

① Accessed December 13, 2021, http://www.arbitration.qmul.ac.uk/research/2021-international-arbitration-survey/.

Apart from the hardware condition, the decisive factor of influencing the status of international arbitration hubs is the soft power of arbitration. Hardware can be constructed, while soft power needs to be gradually formed relying on cultivation, development and accumulation, which is a long process of accumulation. Therefore, the establishment of an international arbitration hub or regional international arbitration hub must be a process of forming arbitration soft power and a process of being recognized by the international arbitration community. This process is passive and invisible, and there is no clear time node for forming such a hub. Even if the broad sense of "construction" ①can include the construction of both hardware and soft power, it is only a measure to achieve the central status, and does not change the characteristics of the arbitration hub is formed.

I. The International Arbitration Hub is a Market Pattern Formed by Dynamic Competition in the Soft Power of Arbitration Services

"International Arbitration Hub", from its literal meaning, can point to a certain arbitration institution, or a certain area that provides high-quality arbitration services, which can be a country, a city or a region. The International Arbitration Hub discussed from the perspective of policy guidance shall be its macroscopic meaning, that is, an area that provides high-quality arbitration services. According to the research report of the Institute of International Law of the Chinese Academy of Social Sciences, the essence of the International Arbitration Hub shall be a high-quality ecosystem with international credibility, which is, based on a certain region, to provide arbitration and related legal services for domestic and foreign market players to prevent and resolve disputes by the arbitration institutions as the engine in collaboration with

---

① "Construction" as it appears elsewhere in this article should be understood as "construction" in the broad sense.

other upstream and downstream legal service institutions or organizations. is. Specifically, the soft power of an International Arbitration Hub should be composed of a sound arbitration legal system, a friendly arbitration environment, a professional team of arbitration practitioners, a group of judges and lawyers familiar with the arbitration system, a good work habit of high efficiency and a mature arbitrator training system. [1]

"International Arbitration", as the name implies, means to open the door to the international market to provide arbitration services; also, it means the arbitration service provided should be a product with international pattern and vision, in line with the public expectations of the international market, rather than engraved with the legal rules and norms of a certain country.

Different from the jurisdiction of the court relying on the jurisdiction of one country, the arbitration market is characterized by voluntariness, openness and selectivity. There are not only numerous arbitration service providers, but also different arbitration systems, arbitration procedures and arbitration methods, so there is inevitably competition. Unlike China's domestic arbitration service market, which is almost in a state of regional division and non-competitiveness[2], the establishment of an International Arbitration Hub naturally needs to face the international market. Taking maritime arbitration as example, maritime disputes are often of a strong international nature, maritime arbitration services therefore face more fierce competition in the global scope.

Therefore, the essence of an International Arbitration Hub is to have a right of speech and a dominant position in the competition of soft power in the international industry, and to be widely chosen and recognized by the parties. Therefore, the establishment of "central" status is neither accumulation of money, nor self-proclaimed. It is a market pattern formed after a series of dy-

---

[1] Miachel Huang, a Singapore-based international arbitration expert, proposed 7 criteria for an international arbitration center, quoted from Zhao Jian's speech at "the 6th East Lake International Legal Forum", "Accelerate the formation of an International Arbitration Hub, and promote the construction of a fair, reasonable and transparent system of international trade rules".

[2] Zhang Shengcui. The Dilemma and Breakthrough of China's Arbitration Market Competition Legal System. Politics and Law, 2015(7): 95-97.

namic competition in the arbitration service market, which needs time to settle and market testing. The establishment of an International Arbitration Hub is a process of being gradually recognized in the world.

II. Modern International Commercial Arbitration Originated from the Spontaneous Creation of Professionals

Arbitration, as a widely influential non-judicial dispute resolution mechanism, could be traced back to the Ancient Greek and Rome Times, and developed in the Middle Ages in Europe. It has a longer history than litigations.① Arbitration is not a creation made by neither national public power nor jurisconsults, but merely a dispute resolution originated from the spontaneous creation of people in their life to settle their civil disputes. Consequently, the initial form of arbitration is *ad hoc* arbitration, which is very popular in Medieval Europe. The modern international commercial arbitration is originated from Britain, who published the first extant arbitration statute in the world in 1698, namely, "Arbitration Act 1698". It is also called the "Locke Act" since it was drafted "single-handedly" by John Locke.② International commercial arbitration is mainly used to resolve shipping and trading disputes or the disputes in connection with maritime disputes for a long time.③ London is the world recognized international maritime arbitration hub. The arbitration service of London reflected as well the feature of the arbitration that it was formed and created by professionals spontaneously, rather than created by public power or institutes deliberately.

---

① Zhongqian Chen, 'Arbitration: Origin, Development and Outlook', Arbitration Study, 2006(9): 44-49.
② Brekoulakis, *The 2019 Roebuck Lecture: The Unwavering Policy Favouring Arbitration Under English Law*, 86 Arb. 97, 99-100 (2020).
③ Mr. Yang Liangyi delivered a speech on "Challenge and Answer to the Development of International Commercial Arbitration and Mediation" at the "21st-Century Maritime Silk Road International Legal Service Forum" in 2021.

As an early pioneer of the world's shipping industry and shipping service industry, Britain took the opportunity to master the formulation and discourse power of rules in relevant fields, which to a large extent achieved today's leading position in many maritime related fields, including maritime arbitration services. When it comes to the history of London Maritime Arbitrators Association, it must be inseparable from the Baltic Exchange, which was established in the mid-18th century and whose shipping index still occupies an important position in the world shipping market nowadays. After the establishment of the Baltic Exchange, it has developed very rapidly into the world center of the chartering and booking market. At least by the end of the 20th century, most of the charterparties in the world were basically completed in the Baltic Exchange.① A large number of experienced and excellent ship brokers appeared in London, who took justice as the core quality of ship brokerage business. After a lot of leases were made, it is inevitable that disputes arise from the performance of charterparties. At first, the ship brokers of both parties generally negotiate and reach an agreed solution. If the two brokers cannot reach an agreement, they will jointly find a more experienced broker to settle the dispute, which is the prototype of maritime *ad hoc* arbitration. Later, the Baltic Exchange posted the list of brokers willing to work as arbitrators on the bulletin board for the parties in dispute to choose, that is the famous Baltic List. On 12 February 1960, the arbitrators on the Baltic List decided to independently establish the London Maritime Arbitrators Association (LMAA), specializing in Maritime Arbitration dispute resolution. Since then, London maritime arbitration has completed the role transformation from spontaneous and unconscious formation state to the conscious and planned development. From the original arbitration service of random dispute settlement, it has gradually developed into a real international maritime arbitration hub. Its development history of more

---

① Bruce Harris. London Maritime Arbitration, an address to an International Maritime Arbitration Seminar organized by the Shanghai Sub-Commission of the China Maritime Arbitration Commission in Shanghai, June 23, 2010.

than 300 years① has profoundly influenced and guided the formation and development of other international arbitration hubs.

III. Cultivation of Soft Power is the Core Factor Affecting the Formation of International Commercial Arbitration Hubs

London, Stockholm, Singapore and Hong Kong, inter alia, are the main international arbitration hubs recognized by the international community currently. The core criterion to measure the competitiveness of international arbitration services is firstly the number of arbitration cases accepted, and then the ratio of the total number of international cases accepted.

Judging from the number of arbitration cases in 2020 announced by the representative arbitration institutions of each place, London, as the international maritime arbitration hub, LMAA's arbitrators accepted 3010 maritime arbitration appointments and issued 523 awards. ② Moreover, it is worth noting that the statistical data of LMAA's annual caseload only includes relatively small number of full members③, aspiring full members④ and some barristers⑤. It does not include the cases dealt with by the supporting members in LMAA, who in fact contribute a large number of cases and excellent arbitration influences in the world. At the same time, LMAA also has a remarkable feature that it only resolves maritime arbitration cases, and the proportion of international cases is more than 90%. LCIA received 440 cases in the whole year, including approximately 22% cases in transportation and trade, running

---

① Accessed November 24, 2021, https://lmaa.london/history/.

② Accessed November 24, 2021, https://lmaa.london/wp-content/uploads/2021/02/Statistics-2020-For-Website.pdf.

③ The London Maritime Arbitrators Association currently has 36 full-time arbitrators, Accessed November 24, 2021, https://lmaa.london/arbitrators-full-members/.

④ The London Maritime Arbitrators Association currently has 28 quasi full-time arbitrators, Accessed November 24, 2021, https://lmaa.london/arbitrators-aspiring-full-members/.

⑤ Accessed November 24, 2021, https://lmaa.london/statistics-of-appointments-awards/.

to 100 cases, and 86% of international cases. ①The traditional Stockholm commercial arbitration makes Sweden a commercial arbitration hub in Europe. According to the statistics of cases accepted by the Arbitration Institute of Stockholm Chamber of Commerce (SCC), the core representative arbitration institution of Sweden, it accepted 175 new cases in 2019, accounting for 50% of international cases, involving parties from 44 countries. In 2020, 213 new cases were registered, including 105 international cases, accounting for nearly 50%, involving parties from 42 countries,② which undoubtedly reflects Sweden's dominant position as a dispute settlement center favored by the international business community. At the same time, SIAC received 1080 cases in the whole year, accounting for 94% of international cases. ③ This is the first time for SIAC having more cases than ICC arbitration court of 946 cases, which is also the highest number of cases received by ICC arbitration court since 2016. ④ HKIAC handled 483 new arbitration cases, about 18.6% of which involved maritime disputes, and international cases accounted for 72.3%. ⑤

3.1 International Maritime Arbitration Hub: London

From the ship broker's spontaneous assistance to customers to settle disputes, to London's development into an internationally recognized maritime arbitration hub, its characteristics and advantages of soft power are very typical, which mainly includes the following points:

Firstly, maritime arbitration drives London to become an International Arbitration Hub. Britain, as a major maritime nation with a long shipping history and the largest colonial system in the world, has gradually formed a set of ma-

---

① Accessed November 24, 2021, https://www.lcia.org/News/lcia-news-annual-casework-report-2020-and-changes-to-the-lcia-c.aspx.
② Accessed November 19, 2021, https://sccinstitute.com/statistics/.
③ Accessed November 24, 2021, https://siac.org.sg/2013-09-18-01-57-20/2013-09-22-00-27-02/annual-reports.
④ Accessed November 24, 2021, https://iccwbo.org/publication/icc-dispute-resolution-statistics-2020/.
⑤ Accessed November 24, 2021, https://www.hkiac.org/about-us/statistics.

ture, complete maritime arbitration systems with extensive international influence over hundreds of years. At the same time, English commercial law is also developed based on shipping and trade cases. As a case law country, more than 25% of the important cases that make up British commercial law originate from shipping disputes or disputes related to shipping. Maritime arbitration has played an important role in promoting the development of English commercial law.① There are basically 3,000 arbitration cases in London every year, accounting for more than 70% of the world maritime arbitration cases. And more than 90% of the cases are international ones with foreign-related factors.② In particular, London issued more than 90% of the world's maritime arbitration awards in 2019, evidencing that its dominant position in this field is impressive and unique.

Secondly, the British government supports strongly the development of international arbitration in both law and policy respects. From the perspective of law, the British government's attitude towards arbitration has also experienced the development process from inhibition to support. As the first country in the world to promulgate arbitration statute, Britain was hostile to arbitration in the early stage and thought that arbitration encroached on the national jurisdiction,③ which was epitomized in the case of Kill v. Hollister④. In which, the court supported the plaintiff to start the proceedings under the circumstance where there was a valid arbitration agreement in the insurance policy, on the grounds that "the agreement of the parties cannot exclude the jurisdiction of the court". Until the Scott v. Avery case⑤ in the mid-19th century, the court vindicated the arbitration, which changed the precedent status

---

① Mr. Yang Liangyi's speech delivered in 2021 at the 4th Guangzhou Haifa Forum "Practical Issues of International Maritime Arbitration".
② Petros N. Tassios. "Choosing the Appropriate Venue: Maritime Arbitration in London or New York?", Journal of International Arbitration, pp. 355-365.
③ Gary B. Born, International Commercial Arbitration (Third Edition) (Kluwer Law International; Kluwer Law International 2021) pp. 7 -250.
④ Kill v. Hollister [1746] 95 ER 532, 532 (English K. B.).
⑤ Scott v. Avery [1856] 5 HL Cas 811, 853 (House of Lords).

of Kill v. Hollister case, and considered that the use of arbitration instead of court litigation did not violate public policy. Since then, the arbitration acts of 1889, 1950, and 1979 have gradually reduced the court's interference in the arbitration procedure. In 1996, the arbitration act even grants arbitrators with the right to make interim measures, at the same time, several general principles have been established, such as autonomy of the parties to arbitration, consideration of benefits and justice, and limited court intervention, which provide a favorable legal environment for the development of London maritime arbitration.

From the perspective of policy, the British government has always supported the promotion of maritime arbitration in the field of international shipping. For example, the British government delegation often sends a large team to attend the meetings of the United Nations Trade and Development Committee, the International Maritime Law Association, the International Maritime Organization, the United Nations International Trade and Law Commission, etc., to safeguard the interests of the London Maritime Arbitration Hub. Further, it strongly recommended the London arbitration clause when international shipping organizations such as BIMCO, ICS, and FONASBA draft standard documents.[1] In recent years, in order to defend London's position as an International Arbitration Hub, the British has frequently taken exclusive measures to protect its arbitration jurisdiction, including issuing anti-suit injunction, showing new features of supporting the development of arbitration.

Third, the shipping industry chain has nourished a huge market of case for London maritime arbitration. There are many high-end shipping industries in London, including Lloyd's List[2], Lloyd's Register[3], Lloyd's Insurance

---

[1] CAI Hongda. Discussion on the development of Maritime arbitration in China. China Arbitration Consulting, 2005(1).

[2] The first shipping publication, published in London in 1734, appeared weekly in its early days and now daily.

[3] Lloyd's Register of Shipping, founded in 1760, is the world's first classification and survey institution.

Market, the P&I Clubs and so on. Based on more than 100 years of practice and accumulation of the shipping industries, London has become the maritime insurance center and shipping center. The scale and systematization of these high-end shipping industries make the British shipping industry closely linked with the participants and become a whole. The industrial advantages accumulated by the long history of shipping, on the one hand, provide British maritime arbitration with a large market and customer resources. On the other hand, it also gives the UK the discourse power in the formulation and interpretation of shipping rules. It has become the norm to adopt the standard contract terms provided by international organizations in the shipping market, in which, the arbitration clause usually goes that in case you make no specific choice the London arbitration shall apply. It plays a key role in expanding London's development as a center for international maritime arbitration since parties rarely make a different "specific choice" in most cases.

Fourth, the flexibility and high level of *ad hoc* arbitration are the core elements of London maritime arbitration to maintain a leading advantage. When the parties choose to arbitrate their disputes, they are not only considering to settle the dispute by a fixed procedure, the utilize of various legal and business strategies are also what they need to maximize their rights and interests during the process. The procedural flexibility of *ad hoc* arbitration and the protection of party autonomy are the core reasons for London Maritime Arbitration to maintain its dominant position. Over the years, the LMAA rules have been constantly revised in compliance with the actual needs of the market. The unceasing procedural innovations, such as mediation rules and small claims procedure rules, are very significant to create more efficient and economic dispute resolution services. Meanwhile, party autonomy embodies in *ad hoc* arbitration in almost all respects, such as the commencement of arbitration, the process of procedures and the collection of fees, etc. Party autonomy also brings the parties a strong control over the arbitration procedures, which is more convenient for experienced parties to formulate and implement flexible strategies to achieve their goals in arbitration. This is also the main reason why *ad hoc* arbitration continues to be inherited and developed in the international arbitration, despite of the global spread of arbitration institutions. In terms of talent reserves, London's advantage lies in the ecological development of industrial talents. The arbitrators who mainly deal with maritime arbitration in London are not limited to the brokers of the Baltic Exchange, but include professionals from various shipping related industries. The diversity of sources of arbitrators makes all kinds of disputes well solved, which earns a good reputation for London Maritime Arbitration. On the other hand, more high-level professionals are trained further for London, which forms a talent aggregation effect supporting London's position as a maritime arbitration hub. The strict requirements and management of LMAA on its full member have assisted LMAA in earning the trust of the international arbitration community. But it also has limited the scale development of LMAA arbitrators to a certain extent. After all, it is difficult to meet the prerequisites of having at least 15 years of practical experience in commercial or legal work and being a British citizen, etc. However, LMAA's innovative mechanism of aspiring full member[①] and supporting members satisfy its demand for training echelons of full members. At the same time, no restriction on the location of the supporting Members has attracted many excellent professionals from all over the world to join LMAA, and it has also attracted more parties from non-English speaking countries to choose arbitration in London. Apparently, the innovative mechanism plays an important role in expanding the global influence of LMAA.

Fifth, the complete supporting services of maritime arbitration have improved the service quality of London Maritime Arbitration. In response to the needs of the arbitration parties, the International Dispute Resolution Centre Limited (IDRC) in London provides high-quality arbitration supporting services for the parties, including efficient and convenient hearing venues, equipment, translation, shorthand, etc. The flexibility and practicality of *ad hoc* ar-

---

① There are now 28 Aspiring Full Members in LMAA. Access November 24, 2021, https://lmaa.london/arbitrators-aspiring-full-members/.

bitration has also been well reflected in the supporting services. "The supporting service of maritime arbitration is an important factor in the formation of London International Maritime Arbitration Hub" ① However, with the development of science and technology of the internet, big data and artificial intelligence, especially affected by the blocking of COVID-19, the demand and necessity of on-site hearing has been reduced tremendously, and the functions of hardware services such as hearing venues are also greatly weakened. Take LMAA as an example as well, no arbitration award is published after on-site hearing among the 3010 cases accepted in 2020. ② Alternatives embracing modern technology, such as virtual hearing and electronic delivery, can better meet the parties' needs of economy and efficiency. According to the survey report, if there is a conflict between the on-site hearing and the parties' personal schedule, 80% of the respondents said they were more willing to accept the way of virtual hearing to replace the on-site hearing. ③

3.2 International Commercial Arbitration Hub: Stockholm

Sweden is the second country in the world to enact arbitration statute after Britain. ④ Different from maritime arbitration in London, Swedish arbitration is characterized by being better at dealing with international investment disputes, and its prosperity and development rely more on the support of the national level. Founded in 1917, SCC was recognized by the United States and the former Soviet Union in the 1970s, and became a neutral center for settling trade disputes between East and West. At the same time, China also recognized SCC as an international dispute settlement institution. Since then, SCC

---

① Kenneth Rokison QC, "What makes a good arbitration, London Shipping Law Centre", a speech delivered at the "Shipping, Insurance, Trading and Maritime Security Forum" in 2008.

② Statistics of 2020, LMAA London, Accessed November 24, 2021, https://lmaa.london/wp-content/uploads/2021/02/Statistics-2020-For-Website.pdf.

③ Dr Maria Fanou, 2021 International Arbitration Survey: Adapting Arbitration to a Changing World, Queen Mary University of London, Accessed January 23, 2022, http://www.arbitration.qmul.ac.uk/research/2021-international-arbitration-survey/.

④ The Swedish arbitration law was promulgated in 1887, See Zhongqian Chen, 'Arbitration: Origin, Development and Outlook', Arbitration Study, 2006(9): p.45.

has continuously expanded its services in the field of international commercial arbitration, thus becoming one of the most important and frequently used arbitration institutes in the world. According to its statistics, at present, at least 120 bilateral investment agreements (BITs) choose Sweden or SCC as the institution to settle disputes between investors and host countries, and SCC has grown into the second largest investment dispute settlement institution in the world. [1]

Apart from the above, Stockholm's development into a commercial arbitration hub also has its unique advantages of soft power. Firstly, the principle of permanent neutrality pursued by the Swedish government and the principle of limited government governance to the inside world have created a clean, stable and healthy political environment and national atmosphere for Sweden, and have strongly endorsed the neutral and fair image of Swedish arbitration, which is the primary factor for foreign parties to refer disputes to their arbitration for settlement. Secondly, Sweden has a perfect training and exchange mechanism to ensure the sound development of arbitration service. In addition to holding regular large-scale forum activities, Sweden also forms a low-cost, multi-dimensional and personalized long-term exchange training system for arbitrators by combining degree education, centralized teaching and small-scale amateur learning activities. This not only helps arbitrators to continuously improve their business level, but also provides a good platform for communication between arbitrators. Further, it also has a good publicity effect to improve the social prestige of arbitrators and arbitration service industry. Thirdly, the legislative idea of practicality is the internal cause for the promotion of arbitration service industry in Sweden. Swedish law is a combination of scattered statutory law and case law, and its inherent basic legal principles are compatible with the two legal systems. Some jurists have commented that Swedish law is enough to take on the important task of "connecting Common law and Civil law". [2] Swedish

---

[1] Access November 19, 2021, https://sccinstitute.com/about-the-scc/.
[2] Tick Stroholm & Dong Likun, *Swedish legal system*, Peking University Law Journal, 1987 (3):19.

laws tend to be concise and direct, and they are so friendly to foreign parties with different legal systems and different cultural backgrounds that the latter can efficiently understand and apply Swedish law easily. That leads more trust and acceptance to Swedish arbitration in the international arbitration market.

3.3 International Arbitration Hubs in Asia: Hong Kong Special Administrative Region and Singapore

In addition to London and Stockholm in Europe, Hong Kong Special Administrative Region (HKSAR) and Singapore are rising stars as International Arbitration Hub in the field of commercial and maritime arbitration in Asia who can't be ignored. They both follow the similar path of formation, from spontaneous creation by professionals to development consciously supported by government. There are also many similarities in the advantageous soft power as follows that have contributed to the development of both as International Arbitration Hubs.

Firstly, in terms of government support, both governments have always provided various support to the arbitration industry, including maritime arbitration. The Department of Justice of HKSAR always considers it a priority to promote HKSAR as the Asia-Pacific International Law and Dispute Resolution Service Center. China's Government support HKSAR strongly to develop arbitration services. Arrangement Concerning *Mutual Assistance in Court-ordered Interim Measures in Aid of Arbitral Proceedings by the Courts of the Mainland and of the Hong Kong Special Administrative Region* has supported the development of arbitration in both places through mutual assistance in interim measures. Besides what, there is *Outline of the People's Republic of China 14th Five-Year Plan for National Economic and Social Development and Long-Range Objectives for* 2035, which includes to provide support to promote HKSAR as the Asia-Pacific International Law and Dispute Resolution Service Center. Furthermore, a decision was made by China and Asian-African Legal Consultative Organization (AALCO) jointly to establish the AALCO Hong Kong Regional Arbitration Hub. It will be of great significance to help to build

HKSAR into a center for international legal and dispute resolution in the Asia-Pacific region. The support from Singapore Government to Singapore's arbitration service is also commendable. In the development history of Singaporean major arbitration organizations, including SIAC, SCMA etc., Singapore Government provided them not only with great financial support for their establishment, but also a series of strong policy support for the development of the arbitration services industry, and continued to enhance the advantages of the "legal services industry" as an industry cluster. For example, Singapore offered a 50% tax credit for the arbitration service conducted in Singapore since 2012, and provided tax exemption policy for the legal income of legal professionals engaged in international arbitration in Singapore. These measures greatly enhance the international competitiveness of Singaporean arbitration services.

Secondly, both HKSAR and Singapore have provided a liberal and encouraging judicial environment for the development of arbitration. HKSAR practices common law with an independent judicial system composed of neutral, professional and efficient local and foreign judges. The courts in HKSAR have all along been supportive of the use of arbitration, playing both a supervisory and enforcement role. Singapore courts have also accepted the principles of Judicial deference and Party autonomy in the treatment of arbitral procedures and arbitration awards, giving the arbitral tribunal a wide range of powers.

Thirdly, HKSAR has a profound arbitration culture, which has trained a large number of international lawyers, who can assist their clients better since they know both international customs and Chinese situation very well. These talents are the important advantages for HKSAR to maintain leading position as an international arbitration hub. Singapore has implemented more open talent introduction policy since 2012, promoted close cooperation between local and foreign law firms, and launched the Foreign Practitioner Examination ("FPE") to attract and cultivate more international legal talents to meet the needs of rapid economic growth.

Fourthly, the unique geographical advantages of HKSAR and Singapore has created the prosperous shipping industry and international culture. The developed shipping economy has created the industry foundation for the vigorous development of commercial and maritime arbitration in HKSAR and Singapore. Multi-culture makes the two places more open. Their internationalism has given parties from different countries around the world more faith in both places as International Arbitration Hub.

The comparative analysis of the above samples shows that the formation of international arbitration hubs is the result of the competition of advantageous soft power of arbitration, which is subject to comprehensive factors such as economy, politics, culture, legal maturity and so on. Commercial arbitration originated from the spontaneous creation of professionals, while the core factors composed of the economic development level, geographical advantages, international cultural attributes and openness, professional talent reserves, and the governance structure of arbitration institutions are the internal driving force to enhance the soft power of arbitration service in international competition. The sustainable development of the arbitration market is also inseparable from the government's support in policy and laws. This kind of support should balance the relationship between external force and internal force for the purpose of cultivating the advantageous factors in favor of the sustainable development of arbitration services.

IV. Opportunities for Establishing an International Arbitration Hub with Chinese Characteristics

As far as China is concerned, it is the best opportunity to promote the competitiveness of international arbitration service to establish an international arbitration hub with Chinese characteristics.

First, economically, along with the process of B&R Initiative and implementation of the strategy of building China into a strong maritime nation, China's shipping and trading industry has made a great progress. According to the Xinhua–Baltic International Shipping Center Development Index Report (2021), five of the top 10 cities where international shipping in terms of comprehensive strength are located in Asia, with China occupying three seats: Shanghai still ranks third worldwide, immediately followed by Hong Kong, and it is particularly noteworthy that Ningbo Zhoushan, which has maintained the highest cargo throughput in the world for 12 consecutive years, ranks among the top 10 for the first time, becoming another "hardcore" power of China's port and shipping;① Guangzhou and Qingdao also perform well, both entering the second echelon.② The trend of the "eastward move" of the world's economic centers and international shipping centers has become increasingly clear, creating a good economic support for China to establish an international arbitration hub.

Second, in terms of legal environment and policy, the State Council has launched several policies and measures to encourage the development of maritime arbitration and other modern shipping services,③ calling for "improving the arbitration system and enhancing the credibility of arbitration"④ On February 25, 2019, President Xi Jinping profoundly expounded that "the rule of law is the best business environment" in the second meeting of the Commission for Law-based Governance under the CPC Central Committee. To promote a law-based and international business environment is an important measure to enhance the international competitiveness of China's arbitration service, which will also promote the formation of an international commercial and maritime arbitration hub.

Third, legally, China has started to revise Arbitration Law to provide legal

---

① https://www.cs.com.cn/xwzx/hg/202107/t20210712_6182913.html, last access date: 3rd February, 2022.

② https://baijiahao.baidu.com/s?id=1672003476206344617&wfr=spider&for=pc, last access date: 14th December, 2021.

③ Several Opinions of the State Council on Promoting the Sound Development of the Maritime Industry (2014) No. 32., accessed November 22, 2021, http://www.gov.cn/zhengce/content/2014-09/03/content_9062.htm.

④ Decision of the CPC Central Committee on Major Issues Pertaining to Comprehensively Promoting the Rule of Law, accessed November 22, 2021, http://www.gov.cn/xinwen/2014-10/28/content_2771714.htm.

support for the high-quality development of arbitration. It is a good opportunity to review and consider China's arbitration legislation comprehensively. According to the Draft Amendments to the Arbitration Law released for public consultation, a wide range of ground-breaking changes has been promulgated to the existing arbitration system and would likely bring China's Mainland in line with international best practices. Additionally, the Supreme People's Court of the PRC has successively issued more than 30 judicial interpretations and normative documents related to arbitration, instructing and supervising the courts across China to perform the judicial review function of arbitration by law, and supporting the healthy and orderly development of arbitration.

Fourth, in terms of industry ideologies, along with the advancement of the judicial reform in China and the proposition of the B&R Initiative, arbitration, as a widely influential non-judicial dispute resolution mechanism, has drawn more and more attention from the Chinese government, related authorities and legal professionals. It has become a consensus that the promotion of arbitration will assist the judicial reform and serve the national development strategy. The main arbitration commissions in Beijing, Shanghai and Shenzhen and relevant industries have actively explored and proceeded with the establishment of the regional international arbitration hubs. Meanwhile, the arbitration commissions in Shanghai, Dalian, Xiamen, and Nanchang have initiated and accelerated the institutional reforms to adapt to the requirements of legalization and marketization. Chinese arbitration services industry has shown a promising sign of exploring and communicating with the diversified and mutual learning thinking so as to offer advice and suggestions for the development of Chinese arbitration services as well as the establishment of international arbitration hub. At the same time, the development of arbitration in China has also attracted the attention of the international community. According to *the 2021 International Arbitration Survey*[①], "Besides Hong Kong and Singapore, much more respondents (than

---

① Access March 19, 2022, http://www.arbitration.qmul.ac.uk/research/2021-international-arbitration-survey/, "2021 International Arbitration Survey: Adapting Arbitration to a Changing World", published by Queen Mary University of London, in junction with its partners.

those in any previous survey) reported that they have ever designated Beijing, Shanghai or Shenzhen as the seat of arbitration."

Fifth, in terms of talent cultivation, more and more Chinese entities have been involved in or choose international arbitration as a dispute resolution. It is reported that Chinese enterprises are the main users of London, Singapore, and HKSAR arbitration. It not only strengthens the Chinese enterprises' legal awareness, but also establishes their good images of law-abiding to resolve commercial disputes positively and legally. In the meantime, the prosper international arbitration practice also trains a number of arbitrators, lawyers and other professionals etc. who knows international arbitration well, providing a talent reserve for establishing an international arbitration hub in China.

V. Strategic Directions for Forming an International Arbitration Hub with Chinese Characteristics

In the process of formation of an international arbitration hub facing the world, apart from the construction of hardware, it is more important to cultivate the soft power that affects the sustainability of arbitration services, including the advanced legal system, modern and international arbitral procedures, specialized law talents, the convenient and efficient arbitration services, in particular, the impartial and acceptable arbitration awards, which is core value of arbitration services. Accordingly, the following aspects should be emphasized to enhance the international competitiveness of Chinese arbitration services for purpose of forming a China's International Arbitration Hub.

5.1 Promoting the Formation of International Arbitration Hub by Developing Maritime Arbitration as the Leading Role

Internationality is the notable feature but also the inherent demand for establishing an international arbitration hub. Hence, it will help the formation of international arbitration hub to choose an industry with high degree of internationalization as the leading role. Maritime arbitration is typically international resulting from the nature of cross-border shipping activities. The foreign-related elements might be found in its service providers, users or the facts of disputes, etc. Although, from the perspective of international competition, Chinese maritime arbitration service industry has not been in the top list, there is a great potential in its prosper growth. Apart from HKSAR, Beijing and Shanghai are also the main maritime arbitration market in China. CMAC received 111 cases in 2020, accounting for 35% of foreign-related cases.① Shanghai accepted 342 cases with a total amount of 2.779 billion yuan.② As a great power country in shipping, Chinese maritime legislation and maritime justice is of an international and advanced level. Further, China's Maritime Law is also in the process of revision, which will provide a better legal support for the development of shipping industry and the maritime arbitration services in China. To sum up, maritime arbitration shall take the lead in establishing an international arbitration hub in China, and it shall be a key point to develop our maritime arbitration services so as to enhance its international competitiveness.

5.2 Bringing in and Going out to Inject More Chinese Characteristics into International Arbitration Services

Based on the current situation of competitiveness of Chinese maritime arbitration services and the needs of development, it is essential for starting a comparative study on the experience of the leading countries (regions or institutions) in the world to summarize the advantages and effective measures enhancing the competitiveness of Chinese maritime arbitration services. Nevertheless, while learning and drawing lessons from others are certainly beneficial to internationalization and also a convenient path to convergence, more attention should be paid to upholding, improving, and carrying forward the arbitration system or procedural mechanism with Chinese characteristics. Take judicial mediation in our country as example, the judicial mediation system of Chi-

---

① Accessed November 24, 2021, http://www.cmac.org.cn/index.php?id=75.
② Accessed January 12, 2022, https://finance.eastmoney.com/a/202201102241737069.html.

na positively influences and promotes the formation of mediation system in the international community of alternative dispute resolution mechanism, etc. We will take an active part in the formulation of international economic and trade rules and standards through a combination of bringing in and going global, so as to enhance our voice and influence. We shall cultivate new advantages with Chinese characteristics to participating in and leading the international economic and trade rule-making, and strive to inject more Chinese wisdom and offer more Chinese solutions to international arbitration services.

5.3 Reflecting on the Concept of Legislation in the Revision of Arbitration Law

The key point of the amendment to the Arbitration Law should be focused on addressing the issue of how the arbitration procedure shall be conducted in the absence of provisions in the arbitration rules or agreement of the parties. It is inappropriate to include detailed regulations that can be agreed upon by the parties or regulated in the arbitration rules or authorized to be decided by the arbitral tribunal. In addition, the legislation should focus on the principles of arbitral procedures, except for *ad hoc* arbitration. Otherwise, the stability of Arbitration law will be affected badly in case there is too much detailed regulations in respect of arbitral procedures. Therefore, it is significant that the amendment of the China's Arbitration Law should focus on the review of the validity of the arbitration agreement, the composition of the arbitral tribunal, the procedural issues before its composition, and the relationship between arbitration and justice. For example, the Draft Amendments provide that the arbitral tribunal may consist of one or three arbitrators, however, it does not specify the number of arbitrators in case there is no such agreement. In fact, it is precisely the latter that needs to be legally adjusted. On this issue, English Arbitration Act sets the implied arbitral tribunal as a sole arbitrator, and HKSAR Arbitration Ordinance designates HKIAC to make its decision on the number of arbitrators based on the parties' application. Otherwise, no specific provisions related to the composition of the arbitral tribunal will result in a tremendous difficulty of commencement of arbitration proceedings, so it will take parties to costs significant amount of time and expense to resolve the issue, undoubtedly, it will not meet the arbitration's advantages of convenience and efficiency.

5.4 Taking the Cultivation of International Professional Talents in the Arbitration Industry as the Foundation Which Shall be Pursued Gradually

The first thing to do is to cooperate with colleges and universities to establish a specialized arbitration talent training mode, comprehensively cultivating international and professional arbitration practitioners who master common law thinking and international business rules, including not only arbitrators, lawyers or legal advisors with international vision and professional knowledge, but also necessary participants in arbitration services, such as arbitration secretaries, court stenographers and other service managers. In August 2022, the Ministry of Education and the Ministry of Justice jointly published "Notice on the Implementation of Postgraduate Training Program for Master of Law Professional Degree (International Arbitration)" (the "Notice"). The Notice makes clear that 20 universities[①] in conjunction with the arbitration commission, law firms and other foreign-related arbitration units nationwide will be selected for the implementation of postgraduate training program for master of law professional degree (International Arbitration), the aim of which is to support relevant universities and legal practice departments to actively explore and innovate the training mode of high-level talents in relation to foreign-related law and

---

① The 20 universities include Peking University, Tsinghua University; Renmin University of China; China University of Political Science and Law; University of International Business and Economics; Fudan University; East China University of Political Science and Law; Shanghai University of Political Science and Law; Wuhan University; Zhongnan University of Economics and Law; Southwest University of Political Science & Law; Sun Yat-sen University; Guangdong University of Foreign Studies; Shenzhen University; Xiamen University; Xi'an Jiaotong University; Northwest University of Political Science and Law; Dalian Maritime University; Jilin University and Heilongjiang University.

improve the personnel training system for foreign-related arbitration. This program will strive to cultivate a group of high-level application-oriented foreign-related arbitration talents with solid legal foundation, international vision and a good understanding of the international arbitration legal system. This program will recruit students from 2023 to 2025, with a total enrollment of no less than 1000 students. the specialized training mode can not only focus on improving students' professional knowledge reserves, but also pay more attention to developing students to view and think about issues with an international perspective and thinking, for the purpose of achieving deeper integration into the international market from the cultural level.

As far as talent construction of International Arbitration Hub is concerned, the way of opening up the arbitration service market and attracting top-level arbitrators from all over the world should be the link between the past and the next. As one of the most core elements of arbitration activities, arbitrators are crucial to the competitiveness of arbitration. Therefore, whether in terms of the arbitration capacity of the case or the strength of publicity, the number and distribution of arbitrators for a particular country (region or institutions) have a significant impact on the competitiveness of maritime arbitration services. LMAA's mechanism of supporting members gives outstanding professionals from all over the world the opportunity to serve as arbitrators in LMAA. The ICC International Court of Arbitration does not set the roster of arbitrators nor does it limit the scope of arbitrators selected by the parties. When it requires the appointment of an arbitrator by the Court of Arbitration, the ICC National Committee in more than 70 countries or regions around the world are invited to recommend arbitrators. Diversified arbitrators give the parties more freedom to select arbitrators and enhance their confidence in arbitration. Meanwhile, it also expands the influence of arbitration in the corresponding countries and regions and is more conducive to developing market business.

5.5 Strengthening Coordination and Cooperation in Arbitration Service Between China's Mainland and HKSAR and Working Together for the Goal to be the Asia-Pacific International Law and Dispute Resolution Service Center

At present, the major International Arbitration Hubs in the world are common law jurisdictions, and HKSAR has 150 years of common law experience and tradition, as well as a considerable number of common law talents. Moreover, HKSAR's achievements in the field of international arbitration are obvious to all, ranking among the world's third place of the most popular seat of arbitration, and the fourth seat of arbitration appointed by BIMCO after London, New York and Singapore.[①] As one of the long-standing shipping centers in Asia, HKSAR's maritime arbitration service industry also has extensive international influence. The mainland and HKSAR can join forces to share resources and complement each other's advantages, creating a regional International Arbitration Hub with Chinese characteristics, which has the advantages of both civil law and common law. It can introduce human resources from HKSAR, help the mainland to cultivate talents familiar with common law and international arbitration rules, strengthen the exchange and cooperation of professional talents such as arbitration institutions, arbitrators, and legal professions and work together for the goal to be the "Asia-Pacific International Law and Dispute Resolution Service Center".

Epilogue

The development of International Arbitration Hubs such as London has revealed that any dispute resolution center is not to be built, but to be formed. Hardware can be built by increasing investment, while software does not. The essence of the value of arbitration service is to solve disputes efficiently and

---

① Accessed December 14, 202,1 https://www.sohu.com/a/423040992_173888.

fairly. The realization of this value depends on the superposition of a series of software such as talents, laws, and environment, etc. This software should be nurtured by long-term cultural heritage, judicial practice accumulation, and guaranteed by excellent legal environment and business environment. Soft power such as service, efficiency, concept and awareness cannot be achieved with money. To have the status of an arbitration hub, hardware is not the core. If the software is well - developed, even with the incomplete hardware facilities, the international arbitration hub can still be formed; however, the formation of the International Arbitration Hub will be a ticklish problem in the opposing situation, only left brilliant vision and lack of inheritance.

The formation of an International Arbitration Hub requires arduous efforts of several generations of people, and the basic work of promoting the development of soft power needs to be done hand in hand. It is believed that the strategic goal of an International Arbitration Hub can be realized by adhering to the spirit of "firm determination and unswerving determination".

（周雨琳、黄智舍　审校）